Contemporary
Theories and Systems
in Psychology

SECOND EDITION, Expanded and Revised

Contemporary Theories and Systems in Psychology

SECOND EDITION, Expanded and Revised

Benjamin B. Wolman

Professor Emeritus
Long Island University
Brooklyn, New York

IN COLLABORATION WITH

Susan Knapp

Postgraduate Center for Mental Health
New York, New York

PLENUM PRESS · NEW YORK AND LONDON

Library of Congress Cataloging in Publication Data

Wolman, Benjamin B
  Contemporary theories and systems in psychology.

  Bibliography: p.
  Includes indexes.
  1. Psychology—Philosophy. I. Knapp, Susan, joint author. II. Title. [DNLM: 1.
Psychological theory. BF38 C761]
BF38.W78 1980   150.'1   80-21058
  ISBN 0-306-40530-X (pbk)

© 1981 Plenum Press, New York
A Division of Plenum Publishing Corporation
227 West 17th Street, New York, N.Y. 10011

Printed in the United States of America

KH
4-18-83

Preface to the Second Edition

Twenty years is a long time in the life of a science. While the historical roots of psychology have not changed since the first edition of this book, some of the offshoots of the various theories and systems discussed have been critically reexamined and have undergone far-reaching modifications. New and bold research has led to a broadening of perspectives, and recent developments in several areas required a considerable amount of rewriting.

I have been fortunate in the last fifteen years to have worked with about 2,000 psychologists and other behavioral scientists who contributed to several collected volumes I have edited. As the editor-in-chief of the *International Encyclopedia of Psychiatry, Psychology, Psychoanalysis and Neurology*, I have had the privilege of reading, scrutinizing, and editing the work of 1,500 experts in psychology and related disciplines. In addition, I have written several books and monographs and over one hundred scientific papers.

Armed with all that experience, I have carefully examined the pages of the first edition. Chapter 8 required substantial rewriting and several new sections have been added to other chapters: "Current Soviet Psychology" (Chapter 2, Section 7); "New Ideas on Purposivism" (Chapter 5, Section 4); "Recent Developments in the Sociological School of Psychoanalysis" (Chapter 9, Section 4); and "Present Status of Gestalt Psychology" (Chapter 12, Section 4). Chapter 15 was omitted, and two new chapters were added: Chapter 14 ("Humanistic Psychology") and Chapter 16 ("Selected Research Areas").

I was fortunate in securing the help of Dr. Susan Knapp in this extensive rewriting. Dr. Knapp is my former student and research assistant in the Doctoral Program in Clinical Psychology at Long Island University. At the present time she teaches at the Postgraduate Center for Mental Health in New York City.

I would also like to take this opportunity to express my profound gratitude to all my colleagues who have used the first edition of this text in their classes in hundreds of colleges and universities.

BENJAMIN B. WOLMAN

New York
May, 1980

Preface to the First Edition

The objective of the present volume is to give a comprehensive picture of contemporary psychological theory. The emphasis is on a general psychological theory, and this is why the contributions of Piaget, Rorschach, Terman, and many other great psychologists have been omitted. Moreover, Thorndike's contribution to educational psychology and Freud's studies in psychotherapeutic techniques had to be left out also. Priority was given to methodological problems such as concept formation, relationship to other sciences, methods of research, and interpretation of empirical data.

The entire volume is divided into four parts. The first three deal with the theories, grouped in accordance with the principle of "common roots." The first part includes all theories that started with the orientation toward natural sciences. Pavlov and Watson are the leading exponents of this trend. The second part deals with psychoanalytic theories. The third part discusses all the theories that have been influenced by Kant, Windelband, Husserl, Dilthey, and the cultural sciences.

The last part, Part IV, devoted to the scientific method, is the exposé of my own "philosophy" of psychology. It is divided into a discussion of methodological problems (Chapter 14) and into a series of theoretical proposals (Chapter 15).

The various theories are presented, whenever possible, in a chronological order of their appearance, but the logical order of presentation has been given priority over the chronological one. Since this volume is written primarily for American universities, special attention has been given to American psychology.

It would have been rather easy to present all the theories in the same logical order, for example, what each of them has to say on a series of questions prepared by the author of the book; this would result in a greater uniformity of presentation but it would not do justice to the respective theorists. Each theorist developed his theory on certain assumptions and in a certain logical order, and there could be no justification for forcing all theories into a uniform frame of reference, foreign to the philosophy of the men who developed them.

Each of the four parts of this book is followed by a summary which

highlights the main problems discussed in the respective parts. Each summary gives a bird's-eye view on the issues under consideration and may
serve as an introductory statement of these issues.

In a book of this type some repetitions have been inevitable. They have
been kept at a reasonable minimum dictated by pedagogic considerations.

In presenting the ideas and theories of the various psychological
theorists, I tried to be as objective as possible. Hence extensive quotations
were introduced in support of the descriptive parts and sometimes even instead of them. Thus the reader has first-hand contact with the creative work
of the theorists. New and deviant theories received more attention than
faithful elaborations of the works of the masters. For example, the rebellious Rank received several pages whereas the scholarly and orthodox psychoanalyst Fenichel did not.

A mere presentation would, however, not do justice to the purpose of
this book. Critical comments and evaluations were part of the thinking and
working through the ideas of others. Moreover, the selection of authors, the
assignment of space, the order, the emphasis on some of their works—all
this was inevitably influenced by my preferences. An absolute impartiality
could be accomplished only at the price of lack of analytic understanding.
The way out was to be as impartial as possible while presenting the views
of the various authors and then to make my own opinions explicit, which I
did in my remarks at the end of each presentation.

For the idea of this book and the initiative to write it, for the friendly
encouragement and competent advice during the work, I am immensely indebted to the editor of their series, Gardner Murphy. It took six years to
implement the idea. Hundreds of volumes and thousands of journal articles
in seven languages have been read, scrutinized, abstracted, and elaborated.
Quotations have been made, whenever available, from existing English
sources or translations. An extensive bibliography, covering almost the entire relevant literature, has been prepared for each chapter or even for a part
of it. Letters have been written to several authors for the sake of clarifying
their ideas, but the presentation of their theories is my own responsibility.
I am grateful for the advice of my distinguished colleagues, among them K.
Goldstein, O. Klineberg, G. Razran, B. F. Skinner, and R. L. Thorndike,
some of whom read parts of this book.

BENJAMIN B. WOLMAN

New York
February, 1960

Contents

PART I CONDITIONING, BEHAVIORISM, AND PURPOSIVISM 1

CHAPTER 1 *THE GREAT BEGINNINGS* 3

1. Psychophysical Parallelism and Introspectionism 3
2. Functionalism 20
3. Edward L. Thorndike: Connectionism 31

CHAPTER 2 *CONDITIONED REFLEXES* 41

1. The Objective Study of the Higher Nervous Processes 41
2. Conditioning 47
3. Theory of Personality 55
4. Concluding Remarks on Pavlov 60
5. Vladimir M. Bekhterev: Reflexology 62
6. Under the Banner of Marx and Pavlov 65
7. Current Soviet Psychology 73

CHAPTER 3 *BEHAVIORISM AND REDUCTIONISM* 76

1. John B. Watson: Psychology as the Science of Behavior 76
2. The Early Behaviorists 84
3. Karl S. Lashley: Brain Mechanisms 88
4. Donald O. Hebb: Organization of Behavior 92

CHAPTER 4 *NEO-BEHAVIORISM AND LEARNING THEORY* 97

1. Edwin R. Guthrie: Learning by Contiguity 97
2. Clark L. Hull: Deductive Behaviorism 103
3. B. F. Skinner: Inductive Behaviorism 124
4. Edward C. Tolman: Purposive Behaviorism 138
5. Gregory Razran: Evolutionary Levels of Learning 154
6. Learning Theory Influenced by Psychoanalysis 163
7. Some Problems in the Theory of Learning 170
8. The Current Status of Learning Theory 173

CHAPTER 5   *HORMIC AND HOLISTIC THEORIES*   180

   1. William McDougall: Hormic Psychology   180
   2. Kurt Goldstein: Holistic System   187
   3. Jacob R. Kantor: Organismic Psychology   193
   4. Some New Ideas on Purposivism   195

Summary of Part 1   197

PART II   PSYCHOANALYSIS AND RELATED SYSTEMS   201

CHAPTER 6   *PSYCHOANALYSIS*   203

   1. Methodology   203
   2. Postulates   208
   3. The Unconscious   216
   4. Theory of Instincts: Eros and Thanatos   225
   5. Developmental Stages   232
   6. Theory of Personality   243
   7. Society and Culture   267
   8. Psychoanalysis as a Philosophy of Life   273
   9. Concluding Remarks on Psychoanalysis   277

CHAPTER 7   *INDIVIDUAL AND ANALYTIC PSYCHOLOGIES*   283

   1. Alfred Adler: Individual Psychology   283
   2. Carl Gustav Jung: Analytic Psychology   297

CHAPTER 8   *NEW THEORIES IN PSYCHOANALYSIS*   316

   1. Psychoanalysis Modified by Clinical Experience: Orthodox and Unorthodox   316
   2. Early Modifications in Psychoanalytic Theory   317
   3. Ego Psychology   324
   4. Psychoanalysis and Studies of Culture   331
   5. Interactional Psychoanalysis   341
   6. Psychoanalysis and Experimental Psychology   351
   7. Critical Analyses of Psychoanalytic Concepts   359

CHAPTER 9   *AWAY FROM FREUD: THE SOCIOLOGICAL SCHOOL*   362

   1. New Ways in Psychoanalysis   362
   2. Karen Horney: Psychoanalysis without Libido   364
   3. Erich Fromm: Historical and Ethical Psychoanalysis   373

4. Harry S. Sullivan: A Theory of Interpersonal Relations   385
5. Recent Developments in Horney's Theory   400

Summary of Part II   403

PART III   UNDERSTANDING, GESTALT, AND FIELD PSYCHOLOGIES   407

CHAPTER 10   *UNDERSTANDING PSYCHOLOGY*   409

1. Kant's Heritage   409
2. Wilhelm Dilthey: The Understanding Psychology   414

CHAPTER 11   *PERSONALISTIC PSYCHOLOGY*   423

1. Edward Spranger: Psychology of Personality   423
2. William Stern: Persons versus Things   426
3. Gordon W. Allport: Personality Traits   433

CHAPTER 12   *GESTALT PSYCHOLOGY*   438

1. Opposition to Associationism   438
2. Gestalt: Theoretical Foundations   444
3. Gestalt: Perception, Learning, and Thinking   450
4. Present Status of Gestalt Psychology   457

CHAPTER 13   *FIELD THEORY*   460

1. Field Theory versus Class Theory   460
2. Lewin's Mathematical Concepts   467
3. Lewin's Logical Constructs   473
4. Locomotion: Theory of Behavior   479
5. Theory of Personality   487
6. Group Dynamics   491
7. Field Theory as an Experiment in Theory Construction   496

CHAPTER 14   *HUMANISTIC PSYCHOLOGY*   507

1. The Humanistic Movement   507
2. Andras Angyl   509
3. Abraham Maslow   510
4. Henry A. Murray   511
5. J. F. T. Bugental   512
6. Gardner Murphy   512
7. Carl Rogers   514

Summary of Part III   516

PART IV   PSYCHOLOGY AND THE SCIENTIFIC METHOD   519

CHAPTER 15   *THE SCIENTIFIC METHOD*   521

1. First Principles   521
2. Collection of Data   526
3. Interpretation of Data and Theory Construction   539
4. The Language of Sciences   549
5. Some Current Methodological Problems   552

CHAPTER 16   *SELECTED ISSUES*   557

1. The Mind–Body Dichotomy   557
2. Beyond Pleasure and Pain   567
3. Perception   572
4. Personality   579

Summary of Part IV   586

BIBLIOGRAPHY   589

AUTHOR INDEX   627

SUBJECT INDEX   633

Part I

Conditioning, Behaviorism, and Purposivism

1

The Great Beginnings

1. Psychophysical Parallelism and Introspectionism

The Common Roots

Contemporary psychological theory is far from uniform. Psychologists are divided to a greater extent than are physicists or biologists. Psychological systems differ in methods of research, in the selection of problems to be studied, and in conclusions arrived at. When psychologists, like all other scientists, form theories or general and comprehensive systems of interpretation of their empirical findings, the differences among them are quite apparent.

In the second and third decade of our century these differences reached a climax. Psychological theory looked like a huge field covered by several independent groups, some fighting one another, some oblivious of the existence of others. It seemed that there was no room for a psychology; instead, several psychologies, independently pursuing their own causes, working their way through with minimum or no cooperation with each other, occupied the stage.[1]

Contemporary psychology witnesses the encourgaging phenomenon of *rapprochement* between the respective schools. We are still miles away from a generally accepted psychological theory and still divided into groups of disciples of Adler, Freud, Goldstein, Jung, Hull, Köhler, Lewin, Pavlov, Skinner, Tolman, and others. However, an ever growing desire to learn from one another is predominant today, especially in American psychology. There is a rapidly growing body of empirical evidence, both experimental and clinical, and an increasing desire to stick to it. Men belonging to various schools of thought have learned to respect the contributions made by their adversaries. There is an eager exchange of information concerning

---

[1] Cf. Edna Heidbreder, *Seven Psychologies*, Century, 1933; G. Murchison (Ed.), *Psychologies of 1925*, Clark University, 1925; C. Murchison (Ed.), *Psychologies of 1930*, Clark University, 1930; Robert S. Woodworth, *Contemporary Schools of Psychology*, Ronald, 1931.

the empirical data and their theoretical interpretation. Psychologists today show more willingness to test hypotheses developed independently by the various theorists and a growing inclination to borrow concepts from one another.

In such an atmosphere, the study of similarities and differences between the various systems seems to be both timely and useful. Before one introduces new hypotheses or proposes new syntheses, one should take a good look at what has been made available by scores of workers. A thorough examination of the contemporary psychological systems, which do not yet form a unified psychological theory, may be of great help to all interested in the future research and theory formation in psychology.

Presentation of the existing differences and the potential similarities may proceed in either of two directions. One may start from the *common roots;* we do not have as yet a common root for all the interpretations of empirical data in psychology, but there are, probably, several common roots or similarities in the results independently obtained by research workers. Needless to say, there are still deep differences between the various systems. The last part of this book is devoted to a discussion of some of these potential common roots or similar solutions of a given problem, but it would be rather precocious to present contemporary psychological theory in a continuum of uniformities or similarities.

Thus, the present status of psychological theory seems to warrant grouping the respective systems according to their *common roots,* or similarities in the problems posed by the various theorists. Even when the suggested solutions are different (consider Hull and Skinner, Horney and Sullivan, Stern and Lewin), the respective groups of systems represent communities of problems, similarities in areas under consideration, and proximities in methodology. Apparently, these communities depend on their historical background and the intellectual heritage presented to them by their respective father systems.

Accordingly, some consideration must be given to the fact that at the crossroads of the centuries the foundations were laid for contemporary psychological theory. Thorndike published *Animal Intelligence* in 1898; Pavlov's theory of conditioning came four years later; McDougall's theory was published first in 1908; Wertheimer's famous experiment was conducted in 1912; Freud's *Interpretation of Dreams* appeared in 1900.

The present volume does not deal with the history of psychology, and we shall not describe in detail the events leading to the origin of the great systems.[2] We shall sketch them briefly, just to "set the stage" for the twentieth-century psychological theory, which is the subject matter of this book.

---

[2] The reader is referred to the following excellent studies in the history of psychology: Edwin G. Boring. *A History of Experimental Psychology* (2nd ed.), Appleton, 1950; J. G. Flugel, *A Hundred Years of Psychology* (2nd ed.), Duckworth, 1951; Gardner Murphy, *An Historical Introduction to Modern Psychology* (rev. ed.), Harcourt, Brace, 1950.

Away from Metaphysics

The second part of the nineteenth century brought spectacular achievements in the natural sciences. Great empirical discoveries were followed by daring theories and were supported by an unprecedented development of precise tools and methods of research. Chemistry and physics, biology, and especially its two branches, physiology and neurology, far outdistanced everything that men had known previously. The glorious march of science enhanced the general belief in the ultimate and not too distant solution of the eternal problems of man and universe.

The sweeping victories of the empirical sciences considerably influenced the thoughts of those research workers who unsuccessfully tried to unveil the mysteries of the human soul. Psychology was generally considered a branch of philosophy. For centuries philosophers strove to understand human deeds and thoughts and to disentangle the body–soul dichotomy.

In the early decades of the nineteenth century, these efforts came to a deadlock. Psychologists felt that nothing new could be added without a radical change in the frame of reference. Psychology was a branch of philosophy, and a part in that division of philosophy called *metaphysics*. Logic dealt with the rules of reasoning, epistemology with problems of cognition, and metaphysics analyzed the existing universe. Problems of matter and spirit were in the realm of metaphysics. Psychology, often called *mental philosophy*, was a legitimate province of metaphysical speculations.

Yet metaphysics could not offer a solution to the psychological problems. The only tool applied by metaphysics was speculation, and the only proof offered was either a superficial observation of some selected phenomena or reasoning not supported by empirical data. No wonder psychological theories were produced in considerable numbers and differed from each other as much as their underlying metaphysical systems did. There was no way to prove which of these theories were true, nor was there any method available that could disprove them.

Thus, the history of psychology until the latter part of the nineteenth century was rather a history of intuition, reflections, some arbitrary decisions, and just plain guesswork. Even great philosophers were unprepared to deal with psychological problems scientifically, and they often made arbitrary statements concerning the nature of soul, emotions, and reasoning. The leading mental philosophy was the theory of "mental faculties," which distinguished the respective "powers" or "faculties," such as willpower, reason, memory, and emotion. Actually nothing was explained or predicted by the mere conversion of a verb into a noun. The classification of functions by forces that supposedly perform them failed to explain the discussed processes and did not help to predict them.

Some philosophers tried to relate psychology to what was known about the physical world. These materialistic interpretations followed, as a rule, in the footsteps of their contemporary science in the belief that the universe is built of little indivisible parts—atoms.

Atoms can be combined to form larger bodies. By analogy, mental processes could be interpreted by combinations or *associations* of ideas. The British philosophers John Locke and David Hume emphasized the importance of sensory perceptions and associations. David Hartley in 1749, in his *Observations of Man, His Frame, His Duty, and His Expectations*, which was a fundamental work in associationism, developed a psychological theory largely influenced by Newton's system. Hartley believed that physical and mental processes are united in the functions of the sensory apparatus. The muscular motions, sensations, and ideas can become associated in such a manner that the repetition of one of them will evoke the repetition of the other. James Mill in 1829 elaborated further the theory of associationism by temporal contiguity. Ideas of objects are reproduced the way the objects have been perceived. The later British associationists A. Bain and J. S. Mill introduced, besides contiguity in time, association by similarity, difference, etc.

Johann Friedrich Herbart: Metaphysics and Associations

The last great system of metaphysical psychology was produced by Johann Friedrich Herbart. Herbart maintained that his system was based on "metaphysics, empiricism and mathematics."[3] Herbart stood at the crossroads between the British and French philosophy of empiricism and the German philosophy at idealism. His empiricism was a sort of armchair strategy striving toward empiricism rather than a truly empirical research system. Actually no empirical studies were conducted by Herbart, and his entire system was based on sheer speculation.[4]

Herbart's metaphysics was materialistic. He considered the soul one of the indivisible units of the physical world (*das Reale*, "the real"). This unit, like all other physical bodies, acted somehow in accordance with the laws of Newton's physics. Action called for reaction, and nature resisted destruction. The soul responded to external stimuli by defensive responses which, "for the lack of better terminology," Herbart called *perceptions*. These perceptory responses of the *Reale* (or soul) to external stimuli are the self-preservatory defenses of the soul (*Selbsterhaltungen*).

The quality of the responses depends on stimuli as well as on the nature of the human soul. All responses, that is, perceptions, are forces. These forces can be measured, and Herbart developed a mathematical system for their measurement.

The soul is a unit of matter and its activities are units of force, said

[3] Johann F. Herbert, *Psychologie als Wissenschaft*, Unger, 1824–25.
[4] Benjamin B. Wolman, 'The Historical Role of Johann Friedrich Herbart." In B. B. Wolman (Ed.) *Historical Roots of Contemporary Psychology;* Harper & Row, 1968, pp. 29–46.

Herbart. His psychology closely corresponded to physics and dealt with matter and energy. Forces can be combined and divided, directed in the same or opposite directions, mutually related, or mutually excluded. These forces are *perceptions,* and Herbart's dynamics dealt with the struggle of perceptions for a place in human consciousness. The repressed forces are drowned in the unconscious; they strive toward the surface and sometimes attain it.

This mechanistic-associationistic system of forces was developed independently of any physiological consideration. If Herbart's system was reductionistic, it was a reductionism to physics. Organic sensations, such as hunger and thirst, are represented by the *Gemeingefühl,* which is the general feeling or self-perception of the organism. Moods are the product of these organic sensations.

Herbart's theory of learning combined the concept of physical forces with associationism. Herbart believed in the "apperceptive mass" or some superfactor in the soul that accepted new perceptions and assimilated and combined them with the old ones. The apperceptive mass is the totality of conscious perceptions that controls the activity of the soul.

Herbart's system of metaphysical psychology was the last great one. Any new metaphysics could have produced a corresponding new system in psychology, but no proof could have been offered by Herbart or by anyone else. Psychologists had to make a crucial decision: either to detach psychology from metaphysics and follow in the footsteps of the rapidly progressing empirical sciences or to doom their own efforts to eternal sterility.

The choice was readily made.

The Impact of Physiology

Some scientific discoveries may not have a permanent value and may not be able to survive criticism, but they are to be considered from a historical point of view as necessary stages in the development of human thought. Actually, each step forward is a product both of the ingenuity of an individual mind and of the state of minds in a given culture at a given time. One may dare to say that Einstein's theory of relativity is a product of this genius's insight and of all the research that had been done by his predecessors and made available to him. Research workers live at a certain time and within a certain space and they create something out of something else. Even creative minds need knowledge and stimulation, and both are offered to them by past and contemporary generations.

The new era in psychology started with influences that came from without. Physics and biology were the sciences that stimulated the shift from speculative to empirical and scientific psychology.

The great discoveries in physiology and Darwin's theory of evolution broke ground for a new scientific psychology. Physiology studied human and animal organisms and analyzed the functions of the nervous system.

These studies were empirical par excellence and dealt with problems of sensation and perception. Both the method and the problem were challenges to psychology.

In 1830, Charles Bell published a book on the *Nervous System of the Human Body*. Bell had proved in 1811 that the ventral roots of the spinal cord are composed of motor nerves only, whereas the sensory nerve fibers composed the dorsal roots and the spinal ganglia. Actually, the distinction between motor and sensory functions had been made much earlier, but Bell (and simultaneously and independently François Magendie) discovered that these functions are performed by different nerve fibers. This discovery later enabled psychologists to present mental life as a stimulus–response relationship. Moreover, Bell and Magendie showed that conduction in a nerve fiber goes only one way, the stimulus always being conducted from the sensory organ to the center of the nervous system and never in the opposite direction. The response continues from the center to the muscle, never from the muscle to the center. This Bell-Magendie "law of forward conduction" paved the way for the later concept of the *reflex* as a one-way action of the organism.

Bell's theory was taken up and developed by Johannes Müller and Ernst Heinrich Weber. Müller conducted a series of experiments on frogs that permitted the division of neural activity of a reflex into three stages: (1) centripetal conduction, (2) connections within the center, and (3) response going from the center to the proper muscles.

Johannes Müller followed in the footsteps of Bell and concluded, logically, that, since perception depends on sensory nerves, the content of perception cannot depend only on stimulus but is colored by the nature of the sensory nerve and its ending (the sensory organ). This led to the law of "specific energies of sensory nerves," which states that "external agencies give rise to no kind of sensation which cannot also be produced by internal causes exciting changes in the condition of our nerves." For example, sensations of vision are "perceived independently of all external exciting causes. . . . The excited condition of the nerve is manifested even while the eyes are closed, by the appearance of light or luminous flashes which are merely sensations of the nerve, and not owing to the presence of any matter of light, and consequently are not capable of illuminating any surrounding objects." The same external stimulus may give rise to different sensations in the various senses. "The mechanical influence of a blow, concussion, or pressure excites, for example, in the eye, the sensation of light and colours."[5]

A sensory nerve may fail to respond to certain kinds of stimuli, either because the nerve is irresponsive to them (such as ear to light), or because of insufficient stimulation. Whenever a sensory nerve responds to a stimulus, it is always the same sort of response. Eyes can never hear; they always see.

[5]Johannes Müller, *Handbook of Physiology* (W. Baly, Trans.), 1838–42.

Müller was much concerned with measurement of the speed of nerve conduction; this problem gave rise later to the study of reaction time. Müller believed that nerve conduction was very rapid and could not see how such velocity could be measured in living organisms.

While Müller in Germany was concentrating on the sensory nerves, Pierre Flourens in France was doing experimental work on the brain. He extirpated various parts of the brains of pigeons and carefully observed the psychological impact of the extirpation. Flourens's studies led to later discoveries of localization of brain functions. On the other hand, Flourens's work encouraged a reductionist type of psychology. Flourens found that cerebral lobes perform the functions of perceiving, understanding, memorizing, and willing and that the cerebellum coordinates movements. Psychologists could feel now that the relationship between memory, understanding, etc., and the functions of the nervous system was firmly established. The next step was to conclude that psychology and physiology were mutually related and complementary disciplines, and that psychology might become a truly scientific branch of human knowledge.

Psychophysical Parallelism

Weber's findings have proved that the discrimination of weight is finer when weight is perceived by several senses. The old division into five senses was to be replaced by a newer concept of a larger number of senses. In Weber's experiments the problem was whether differences in weight could be determined better by the subjects if they were instructed to lift the weights instead of just holding them. Obviously in lifting the weights the muscular sense was added to the senses that perceive weight.

The result was affirmative: the more senses used, the more precise sensation. Besides this main result, a highly significant discovery was made in the experiment, namely, that the discrimination of change in weight was not simply related to the increase in weight. Weber found that the ability to discriminate small differences in a stimulus depends not on the intensity of the stimulus alone but on a certain ratio between the difference and the standard weight used in the experiment.[6]

This important discovery led to the formulation by Fechner of the so-called *Weber's law*. Weber's study was a milestone in the experimental research on sensation and it encouraged more general concepts regarding the nature of perception.

In 1860, Gustav Theodor Fechner published a volume entitled *Elements of Psychophysics*.[7] Fechner believed that he had found the bridge connecting physical and mental phenomena. All stimuli belong to the physical world; all sensations belong to the mental. A definite relation between

[6] Ernst Heinrich Weber, *De Tactu: Annotationes Anatomicae and Physiologicae*, 1834.
[7] Gustav Theodor Fechner, *Elemente der Psychophysik*, 1860.

mental and physical was discovered by Fechner and presented in a mathematical formula. Thus, the process of sensation became the cornerstone of
the new scientific approach.

Fechner's method was experimental; his data were quantitative; the
mathematical relations between physical stimuli and mental sensations
were clearly stated. As stimuli increase in geometrical progression, sensations increase in arithmetical progression. This was the generalization of
Weber's findings which became known as Weber's law.

Fechner also elaborated on the concept of threshold. The *initial threshold*
was the minimal intensity of a stimulus necessary for the stimulus to be
perceived. The *differential threshold* was the minimum of increase or decrease in intensity of the stimulus necessary for the perception of these
decreases or increases.

Besides his careful studies concerning thresholds, which are an important contribution to physiology and psychology, Fechner developed three
psychophysical methods: (1) the method of *limits,* in which the stimuli in an
experiment are ordered either in increasing or in decreasing intensity; (2)
the method of *production,* in which the subject controls the stimuli according to the experimenter's instructions; (3) the *constant* method, in which
stimuli act on the subject in an irregular order.

The impact of Fechner's work was tremendous. His study of the sensory processes became the generally accepted frame of reference in psychology for at least half a century. Even Fechner's critics, says William James,
"should always feel bound, after smiting his theories hip and thigh and
leaving not a stick of them standing, to wind up by saying that nevertheless
to him belongs the imperishable glory, of first formulating them and
thereby turning psychology into an *exact science.*" [8]

James felt that Fechner's method was arid and futile, but one should
not forget that Fechner introduced a quantitative method into the study of
sensation and developed a system of experimentation in psychology.

Another outstanding scientist, Hermann von Helmholtz, studied the
speed of neural conduction in both motor and sensory nerves. He found
that the speed of conduction in the motor nerve was thirty meters per second. Although his estimate was much below today's estimate, his experiments gave impetus to the very popular studies of "reaction time." Of even
greater importance for the growing psychological science was his monumental work in vision and hearing. Helmholtz applied Müller's law of specific energies and developed a thoroughly experimental method for the
study of sensory reactions. [9]

All the aforementioned studies had been done by physiologists. It was
quite natural that, since these studies dealt with sensation and perception,
they attracted psychologists. Psychologists were seeking a way to escape
from metaphysics, speculation, and philosophy and hopefully looked to-

---

[8] William James, *Principles of Psychology,* Holt, 1890, Vol. I, p. 549.
[9] Hermann von Helmholtz, *Handbuch der Physiologischen Optik,* 1856–66.

ward physiology to provide the very much needed guidance in a scientific method of inquiry.

Wilhelm Wundt: "Scientific Psychology"

Ground was broken for an experimental psychology, but many were still doubtful whether the old "mental philosophy" could be converted into a "pure science." Obviously, physiologists did a good job with sensation and nerves; apparently, these issues were on the border of psychology. Yet many problems, such as soul–body dichotomy, mental faculties, and introspection, were unresolved. The road leading from a scientific and an experimental physiology toward the promising scientific and experimental psychology was blocked by too many barriers.

It took a great deal of courage to establish in Leipzig in 1879 the first psychological laboratory. A man was needed who was well versed in contemporary psychology, philosophy, and physiology and capable of combining all three. Wundt was the man. "The new discipline," he stated in his preface to the first edition of *Principles of Physiological Psychology* in 1873, "rests upon anatomical and physiological foundations." Psychology was to become an experimental science that dealt with measurable stimuli and responses.

Could psychology become an experimental science? This was just what Wundt undertook to establish. But first he had to get rid of the nonscientific past and sever the relationship between the young and growing "scientific psychology" and the metaphysical "mental philosophy." The problems, inherited from the past, that confronted him, were soul, mental faculties, and introspection. The first two had to be discarded. The last had to be manipulated somehow so as to make it acceptable to the scientific psychology.

Wundt took a new road. He postulated that the subject matter of psychology was experience, and psychology was an *Erfahrungswissenschaft* ("science based on experience"). This, indeed, was a great decision, which enabled him to evade the never-ending discussions of the nature of the immortal soul and its relationship to the perishable body. Psychology simply does not deal with this issue, said Wundt.

According to Wundt, the subject matter of psychology is the experience itself, the immediate experience. This experience has two sides. On the one hand, it is the immediate experience of the experiencing person.[10] On the other hand, the experiencing person is a living organism that responds to external stimuli. Sensations are the elements of immediate experience. But sensations are aroused when a sensory organ is stimulated and sensory neurons conduct the excitations to the centers of the nervous system. Excitations of neurons and sensations are parallel phenomena.

The method appropriate for psychological study must combine (1)

[10] Brentano took up the matter and suggested a sharp distinction between the "act" and the "content" of experience.

physiological type of experimentation, (2) self-observation of the experiencing subject, and (3) analysis of cultural products of human minds.

Self-observation or introspection, as it was applied by earlier psychologists, could hardly yield any scientific data. Wundt was convinced that "the endeavor to observe oneself must inevitably introduce changes into the course of mental events—changes which could not have occurred without it, and whose usual consequence is that the very process which was to have been observed disappears from consciousness." Therefore, he suggested combining introspection with experimentation, because psychological experiment "creates external conditions that look towards the production of a determinate mental process at a given moment. In the second place, it makes the observer so far master of the general situation, that the state of consciousness accompanying this process remains approximately unchanged. The great importance of the experimental method, therefore, lies . . . also and essentially in the further fact that it makes observation itself possible for us."[11]

Wundt recognized the limits of the experimental method. In his day, experimentation could be applied to certain processes but not to all of them. Thus, he cautioned (1892) that in every department of investigation the experimental method takes on a special character, according to the nature of the fact investigated. In psychology, only those mental phenomena which are directly accessible to physical influences, not the totality of psychological phenomena, can be made the subject matter of experiment.

This remark clearly indicates that scientific and experimental psychology had to be limited to a fraction of the total area. The higher mental processes, said Wundt, cannot be studied by the experimental method. They can be studied indirectly by investigation of their products. These products are language, customs, beliefs, tradition, social institutions—that is, the totality of human culture. Wundt suggested three research methods in psychology: introspection, experiment, and interpretation of historical achievements. By combining all three methods, psychology could achieve its objectives and cover the entire area of research.

Mind, said Wundt, is not an object (like soul); it is a process; it is something that goes on and of which we are aware. Mind is the conscious process that takes place in accordance with laws of causation.

The elements of this conscious process are ideas, feelings, and impulses. The first elements come from outside, the second and third from the organism itself. Ideas are composed of sensations. Sensations can be distinguished according to their quality and intensity. They are conducted by *afferent* nerves. Each sensation is followed by a muscular movement controlled by an *efferent* nerve. Association is a connection between sensation and movement and not, as in the old associationism, a connection between ideas.

[11]Wilhelm Wundt, *Principles of Physiological Psychology* (5th ed., translated), Macmillan, 1910, author's preface.

Feelings do not come from any sense organ. They can be divided into pleasant or unpleasant, tense or relaxed, excited or depressed. Feeling is the "mark of reaction of apperception upon sensory content; feeling is active."

Volition can hardly be distinguished from feeling. Will is some sort of feeling, namely, a decision or a resolution feeling, that leads to overt action. Volition is the very essence of life; it represents the needs of the organism and its tendency to purposive behavior.

Wundt maintained that psychology studies the processes of sensation, volition, and feeling. The unity of all these processes is called *consciousness*. The processes take place, change, and pass away in one's consciousness. What one can observe is the momentary state of consciousness or the "actuality" of it.

The unifying factor in mental processes is *apperception*. Apperception means assimilation, inclusion of new sensations, and their synthesis in the totality of consciousness. Feeling is the reaction of apperception to new sensory content. Volition is the active response. Apperception is the focal point of consciousness.

Obviously, the content of Wundt's findings could not match his scientific strivings. Wundt's psychology was a combination of quite a few scientific data based on physiology with some general impressions gained from daily observations. His system leaned heavily on the metaphysics of Kant, Herbart, and Schopenhauer. Despite Wundt's endeavor to be thoroughly empirical, neither the introspectionist method nor the amount of empirical data permitted fruitful generalizations at this stage of the development of psychological research.

Edward Bradford Titchener: Structuralism

The man who developed and systematized the "scientific" psychology established by Wundt was his pupil Titchener at Cornell University. Titchener was perhaps more Wundtian than Wundt himself. He felt that psychology, like any other science, dealt with experience. The subject matter of psychology was a certain kind of experience: experience in relation to the organism, in contradistinction to the biological experience of the organism in relation to the environment.

Psychology is "experience dependent on an experiencing person" in contradistinction to other sciences, which are independent of experiencing persons. The temperature in this room is 85° whether one experiences heat or not. If one feels uncomfortable, this feeling is experienced by and is dependent on the experiencing individual, Titchener said.

The method of psychology, as of any other natural science, is observation. But in psychology observation is directed by the experiencing subject to his own experiences—it is *introspection*. Yet no interpretation of psychological experience is possible without physiology. The nervous system offers the final answers to the puzzles of introspection, but the nervous system is not a part of psychology; it is physiology. Physiology is the science to which psychological data have to be related for causal explanation. Thus, Titchener made clear his stand on the issue of psychophysical parallelism.

Psychology deals with mind as the total sum "of mental processes occurring in the lifetime of the individual," and consciousness is defined by Titchener as the sum of mental processes occurring "at any given present time." The basic units of consciousness are sensations, images, and affections. Sensations are the elements of perception, images are the elements of ideas, and affections are the elements of emotions. The first two elements can be classified according to four attributes: quality, intensity, duration, and clearness. Affections can be classified on the basis of the first three attributes only because they have no clearness. Titchener did not like Wundt's concept of apperception. It seemed to him unempirical to assume the existence of an interpreting function such as apperception. Instead he emphasized the "attention" which adds clarity to functions.

Titchener distinguished between description and explanation in psychology. Description is given by answering the questions What? and How? The first question deals with facts and the second with combinations of facts and their interrelationships.

The explanation of psychological processes (the question Why?) requires investigation into the functions of the nervous system. Titchener can be considered a radical reductionist. Psychological phenomena can be described in mentalistic terms derived from self-observation, but ultimately they have to be related to physiological factors.

According to Titchener, "The primary aim of the experimental psychologist has been to analyze the structure of mind to ravel out the elemental processes from the tangle of consciousness. . . ." Psychology is morphological in its character. "I do not think that anyone who has followed the course of the experimental method, in its application to the higher processes and states of mind, can doubt that the main interest throughout has lain in morphological analysis, rather than in ascertainment of function. . . . The experimental psychology arose by way of reaction against the faculty psychology of the last century. This was a metaphysical, not a scientific, psychology. There is in reality, a great difference between, say, memory regarded as a function of the psycho-physical organism and memory regarded as a faculty of the substantial mind." [12] Titchener did not exclude the study of functions; he only stressed that structure is prior to function, and unless the structure of mind is revealed, none of its functions can be understood.

Titchener was a rigorous research worker and adhered strictly to the rules of scientific inquiry within the area determined by Wundt and by himself. Since psychology is the science of consciousness, the main method of study is rigorous introspection conducted by especially trained subjects.

[12] Edward Bradford Titchener, "The Postulates of a Structural Psychology," *Philosophical Review*, 1898, 7, 449–465.

Concluding Remarks on Wundt and Titchener

Despite all criticisms, Wundt's and Titchener's work must be regarded as important scientific systems in psychology. The subject matter was well defined; it was the human consciousness. The research methods were empirical, namely, observation, experiment, and measurement. Since consciousness was best perceived by someone whose consciousness was observed, obviously the best method was self-observation or introspection. Surely this was, at that time, the best solution for psychology. Neither speculative philosophy nor objective physiology could have offered a better solution. Because of introspection, psychology could have joined the respectable family of sciences and yet retained its specific characteristics resulting from the subject matter—mind or consciousness. Never does the topic of a scientific inquiry determine whether the inquiry is scientific or not. In any case, why should science withdraw from dealing with a certain topic? The *method* of study, not the area, determines whether a given inquiry is scientific or not.

To Wundt and Titchener the subject matter of psychology was the experience of the experiencing person. This was, for all purposes, as legitimate a topic for study as any other. This issue, said the introspectionists, eluded external observation, and the best research method was that of self-observation. In order to make this observation more dependable, special types of well-trained subjects were used in the Leipzig and Cornell psychological laboratories.

Here some objections can be raised. Is introspection the best research method available? Does introspection provide for scientific study of this experience, called "inner" by Sully, "immediate" by Wundt, or "dependent on the experiencing person" by Titchener? Does consciousness cover the entire field of interest to psychologists, and if so, does introspection fully cover this field?

Animal psychologists covered their field without introspection. Child psychologists criticized introspection on several counts. First, it had definite limitations, imposed by the selection of subjects, who had to be well trained and carefully chosen. At best, introspective psychology was the psychology of certain types of individuals and of only those aspects of their mentality that were open to introspection. Finally, there was practically no way to prove the validity and reliability of introspective findings.

Moreover, introspectionist psychology tended to strengthen a dualistic approach to human problems. Muscles, bones, blood, circulation, perspiration, and digestion belonged to the physical world; memory, learning, emotions, and reasoning belonged to the mental world. No one could actually build a bridge between these two worlds. Descartes assumed that animals were machines, automats, with no mentality whatsoever. Human bodies, to be sure, do not differ from animal bodies; the only difficulty was that it was impossible to reduce human emotions and reasoning to some sort of physiology. Descartes arbitrarily assigned the seat of the human soul to the pineal gland.

Introspectionism was not in a position to offer any better solution to the body–soul dichotomy. Of course, consciousness was a better term than soul; it contained a promise for an empirical approach. Titchener presented the issue clearly and forcefully; the Why? question in psychology had to be related to physiology. Unfortunately, it was not easy to find the way from consciousness to the nervous system. Physiology did not know the answer at that time, nor does it today.

The Challenge to Introspectionism

Several factors prepared the ground for new psychological systems, which have expanded the area of psychological inquiry far beyond the limits of "what is being given in the inner experience." The most outstanding factors were mental tests, animal psychology, and psychiatry.

Binet's and Simon's tests have been a major development in the method of psychological research. Binet and Simon dealt with highly complicated processes of reasoning, comparing, and problem solving, brought together under the name of intelligence. The idea of mental tests, originally published in 1905 in Paris, was accepted, modified, restructured, and developed by several outstanding psychologists, such as Spearman and Burt in Great Britain, Stern and Meumann in Germany, Kuhlman, Thorndike, Terman, and Yerkes in the United States.

In the United States the mental measurement movement gained momentum in army testing in 1917, in the Stanford Revision of Binet's tests in 1916 and again in 1937, and in several widely used mental scales.

Mental measurements do not require introspection, yet the higher mental functions are being measured in a manner that enables one to predict future behavior and achievements. Although the theoretical discussion concerning the nature of intelligence still goes on, there can be little doubt of the diagnostic and prognostic value of mental tests in educational, clinical, and industrial psychology. Moreover, intelligence tests served as ample evidence that highly important mental processes evade introspection, and the best way of getting some insight into their nature is to put them to test. The "atmosphere" of mental tests was entirely different from the one prevailing in the laboratories of Wundt and Titchener. While Binet dealt with a problem of a school system which had to be solved, while Yerkes faced a huge "human engineering" problem for the armed forces of the United States, Wundt's and Titchener's experiments were remote from life, and as arid as they were scientifically rigorous.

The second challenge to the introspectionist psychology came from animal psychology. Charles Darwin's study on the *Expression of the Emotions in Man and Animals* (1872) contained many truthful although not too precise observations. Darwin ascribed to animals emotional reactions similar to human feelings, and often used anthropomorphic expressions in talking about animals. Despite their shortcomings, Darwin's observations suggest in an irresistible way that there is quite a similarity between animal and human behavior, and human psychology can gain much by the study of animal behavior.

The introspectionists imposed on themselves the limitations of self-observed phenomena. The vigorous pursuit of animal studies broke down the artificial barriers between laboratory subjects capable of introspection and other men and animals. The "new" psychology was sometimes careless about detail and eager to apply unproved analogy; it often oversimplified the issues under consideration. For instance, Loeb's concept of tropism was eagerly introduced into psychology, although it still remains doubtful whether a scientific law derived from the study of the lower biological species can be applied to the interpretation of life processes in the higher organisms. Lloyd Morgan's *principle of parsimony* enchanted psychologists. It reads: "In no case may we interpret an action as the outcome of a higher psychical faculty, if it can be interpreted as the outcome of the exercise of one which stands lower in the psychological scale." [13] This principle, far from being proved, strongly influenced the thoughts of psychologists in the direction of a nonintrospectionistic and reductionistic psychology.

Another challenge to introspectionism came from psychiatric sources. Charcot, Liebault, Janet, and others (Chapter 6) have proved beyond doubt that people can love and hate, remember and desire, without being aware of what is going on in their minds. A psychology which deals only with conscious phenomena fails to encompass the totality of mental processes. Moreover, a psychology limited to conscious processes is doomed to fail even in its limited area, because unconscious factors seem to determine the conscious ones. The studies of suggestion and hypnosis, the analysis of what is going on below the conscious surface, and later on the Breuer-Freud studies (see Chapter 6) of unconscious motivation have shown that a psychology limited to the study of "what is being given in the inner experience" is hardly capable of interpretation and prediction of human behavior.

The accusation of aridity and futility in psychological inquiry, despite its scientific strictness, came from several sources. Some psychologists sadly admitted that psychology will never be able to interpret problems of human life. Obviously the highly scientific laboratory in the style of Wundt or Titchener could hardly be of any help in the understanding of human interaction, of social relations and institutions, of cultural problems, and of historical events. No wonder the philosopher–psychologist Wundt had to make a compromise and to find room for a nonlaboratory psychology. The founder of the first psychological laboratory openly admitted that the great problems of social psychology and culture could not be dealt with by his introspecto-experimental method.

The introspectionist psychology was forced by its own limitations to

[13] C. Lloyd Morgan, *An Introduction to Comparative Psychology*, W. Scott, 1894, p. 53.

give way to an entirely different conception of what psychology was and
how it should go about its business. The introspectionists used to view the
surface of the human volcano and avoid the study of the hidden forces.
They observed carefully the smoke of a fire, described and measured its direction and size, but avoided the fire itself.

First Solution: Conditioning, Behaviorism, and Purposivism

There were three ways out of the impasse. The first, initiated by functionalism, opened new vistas for psychology by the study of totality of actions. Instead of the small fraction of phenomena observed by introspection, the theories of conditioning and behaviorism encompassed the entire
behavior. In their effort to be rigorously scientific they had to expel introspection and introduce objective observation as practiced in physics and
chemistry. Once psychologists embarked on a policy of radical empiricism,
no room was left for the concept of consciousness. The introspectionists'
slogan "What is being given in the *inner* experience" was translated into
the behavioristic slogan "What is being given in the *outer* experience."
Outer experience, overt behavior, stimulus and response, action and reaction—these were the new areas of psychology. Strangely enough, this new
psychology did not include the old area but denied its existence. The continuity of psychological research was seriously impeded, and many interesting and insightful ideas of the past were lost in the rapidly growing research into overt behavior, patterned on the models applied in the natural
sciences.

The new research was directed toward physiology of motor and glandular processes. It was highly reductionist and biologically minded.

Of the several possibilities that opened up, one was functionalism,
which considered psychological phenomena as biological tools in adjustment processes. Another was a physiological reductionism suggested by
Pavlov and related systems. Another was a highly mechanistic interpretation of human life based on conditioning and physiology suggested by
Watson. Still another was the purposive, biologically oriented behaviorism
of McDougall. Then came Guthrie, Hull, Skinner, Tolman, and many others in a series of efforts to select or to combine various interpretations of
conditioning. All these diverse systems started from the rejection of structuralism on the grounds of opposition to consciousness and introspection.
All of them applied some sort of reductionism and all went far from the narrow path of introspection toward the study of total human behavior.

Second Solution: Psychoanalysis and Related Systems

The second solution was offered by Freud and his associates. While the
behavioristic school broadened the horizon by including the totality of
overt behavior and the *Kultur* school included social and cultural factors,

psychoanalysis attacked the problem from the point of view of causation. Freud posed the questions: What is going on below the surface? Why do people act the way they act? Behaviorism introduced a precise method of observation of overt behavior. The "understanding" psychology introduced historical and culture background and made it possible to see human behavior in perspective. Freud introduced the dynamic point of view inasmuch as "dynamics" indicates causation.

Psychoanalysis broke away from both organic psychiatry and reductionistic experimental psychology. It was a daring enterprise that violated the principles of academic psychology and psychiatry. Psychoanalysis started from the irrational elements in human behavior, such as dreams and psychopathological symptoms, and developed into an all-embracing theory of human nature. It penetrated into the unknown, into what is not given in introspection, into the unconscious, deep-lying forces. Self-observation became an outdated and inefficient method in view of the discovered mechanisms of rationalization, denial, reaction formation, and projection.

In interpreting human behavior, psychoanalysis went further than the two other schools. As in any other theory, controversies and schism were unavoidable. Jung and Adler were the early deviants from Freudianism, and scores of psychoanalysts interpreted human nature in a manner quite different from the one proposed by Freud. Gradually, more emphasis has been put on environmental factors, and the great students of the social and cultural issues, Kardiner, Horney, and Sullivan, developed their own frame of reference based on the Freudian concepts of unconscious motivation.

Third Solution: Understanding, Gestalt, and Topological Psychologies

The third way out was indicated by followers of Immanuel Kant. W. Windelband, E. Husserl, and especially Wilhelm Dilthey attacked the Wundt-Titchener type of psychology from a standpoint diametrically opposed to that of behaviorism. What was going on in the psychological laboratory was merely a "description" of certain phenomena, but never an "understanding" of them (see Chapter 10). Dilthey distinguished between humanities (*Geisteswissenschaften*) and natural sciences (*Naturwissenschaften*); the latter applies mathematics, the first applies psychology. At that time, Windelband emphasized that the natural sciences were *nomothetic* or law-seeking, whereas the cultural sciences dealt with individual and unrepeatable *idiophenomena*. Dilthey went further and emphasized that psychology cares for the individual; its main objective is not to describe or analyze but to "understand" (*verstehen*) him.

Actually, Dilthey took up the problem as it was posed by Wundt. Wundt did not believe that involved mental processes could be studied by the experimental method. The lower mental processes, according to Wundt, can be studied by experiments that follow strictly the pattern set by physiological experiments; but no higher mental processes can be studied in the same way; Wundt called Külpe's experiments in thinking "mock experiments." History of civilization or of social institutions, law, religion, and the arts are areas in which a study of the higher mental processes can be successful.

Dilthey felt that psychology should be the method of cultural sciences, as mathematics is the method of natural sciences. It was a challenging idea, but at that time psychology was not ready to play this distinguished role. History, anthropology, and sociology did not wait. E. Spranger reversed the order and developed psychological concepts derived from social and cultural sciences. His psychological types are some sort of "reductionism" to the study of social institutions.

The dichotomy between natural and cultural sciences continued to perplex psychologists. W. Stern tried to resolve it in his treatise on person versus object, *Person und Sache* (Chapter 11). The gestalt psychologists tried to solve the problem by ascribing *Gestalt* to the physical world (Chapter 12). Lewin's field theory was a "working through" of Windelband's theory of idiophenomena (Chapter 13).

The three main sources of contemporary psychology are Pavlovianism, Freudianism, and neo-Kantianism. In planning this book we grouped the various systems around their common roots in one of the three great "father" systems of contemporary psychology. It may be rather difficult to find substantial similarities in conclusions reached by the respective systems grouped together. But the problems dealt with by them are rooted in one of the three father systems, and the present book was divided accordingly.

We shall start with the first group of systems. The functionalists and E. L. Thorndike are the forerunners of this group.

2. FUNCTIONALISM

Under the Aegis of Biology

Under the impact of Charles Darwin, some psychologists turned to biology. Biology seemed to be better prepared than any other science to resolve psychological problems. Biologists had regarded humans as living organisms that struggle for survival, adjust to environment, and crave satisfaction. Hardly any other idea could lead to more fruitful studies in psychology. Psychology followed in the footsteps of biology and grasped the significance of mental functions as related to the totality of the functions of life.

The biologically oriented workers introduced the problems of heredity and environment, of adjustment to life and fight for survival. Living organisms display certain flexibility; they change, develop, and learn. How do they learn? Are the acquired changes inherited, as Lamarck suggested? Biologists were split on this issue. Should these changes be interpreted as a purely mechanistic causation and the "survival of the fittest," as Darwin and Huxley saw it? Or is there perhaps some general aim and purpose in life, as Driesch explained?

Whether psychologists sided with Lamarck or Darwin, Spencer or Weismann, Driesch or Huxley, whether they accepted a mechanistic or a vitalistic point of view, these were relevant problems that led to the development of the respective psychological systems. Almost all psychologists became increasingly aware of the vitality of this research area. Human psychology became an indispensable area in the study of the human species. Anatomy and physiology analyzed the human organism in its details. Psychology dealt with human life in its totality; it became par excellence a molar and functionalistic science.

The shift to general biology represents the second great revolution in the short history of psychology. With the first revolution, psychology broke away from philosophy and, owing to the support received from physiology and neurology, became a respectable, though a bit arid, empirical science. Now, the great ideas of evolution, adjustment, learning, instincts, fight for survival, recapitulation, heredity, etc., opened new horizons for psychology.

The Forerunners of Fuctionalism

Darwin, Spencer, and Galton introduced the biological principles of evolution and adjustment into psychology. In 1855, Spencer published his *Principles of Psychology*. Evolution is a change "from indefinite, coherent homogeneity to a definite, coherent heterogeneity through continuous integrations and differentiations," said Spencer. These changes are functions of a continuous process of *adjustment* to external conditions. Each animal responds in a certain way to his environment; the higher the place of a species in the ladder of evolution, the more complex and differentiated are its responses. The simplest reactions are inflexible and represent a gross adjustment to environment. These are the *reflexes*. Higher animals have *instincts*, which are "compound reflex actions."

The higher the species, the more complex and more flexible is its behavior. The higher functions evolve from the lower ones in the process of adjustment. Mental activities are part of this process and thus are biologically useful. Spencer said that the more useful a function is, the more pleasant it is. The useful functions, even if acquired in one's life span, are transmitted by heredity to later generations.

Spencer's theory is *associationism*. "The persistence of the connection between states of consciousness is proportionate to the persistence of the connection between the agencies to which they answer." It is, however, an associationism rooted in biology and the laws of heredity.

In his emphasis on pleasure in adjustment, Spencer is, in a way, a forerunner of Sigmund Freud.

Charles Darwin's *Origin of Species* was published in 1859 and his *Expressions of the Emotions in Man and Animals* in 1872. Darwin maintained that life is a struggle for existence. Better-equipped individuals have more chance for survival and for reproduction. Human behavior is *goal directed*. Those who adjust better to outer conditions have better chances for survival. Psychology has to study the ways of human adjustment. Emotions are biologically useful functions, and their overt expression serves a definite purpose. For example, the showing of teeth in anger indicates the power of the teeth and readiness to fight; crying is calling for help; etc. All mental activities should be interpreted as adjustive functions of the organism.

Francis Galton studied differences in men and related them to hereditary factors. His studies on *Hereditary Genius* appeared in 1869. Galton applied statistical method to genetics, and his studies of individual differences led to the development of *mental tests* and methods of *correlation* between mental traits. Galton was interested in the improvement of the human race. His utilitarian point of view in scientific inquiry has had considerable influence on psychologists in pointing to the applicability of psychological inquiry to the betterment of human life.

William James: Functionalism and Pragmatism

The man who grasped the significance of the biological-utilitarian approach to psychology and posed to psychology the question: What for? was William James.

James was a psychologist, biologist, expert in anatomy and physiology, and, above all, a philosopher. His psychological theory cannot be properly understood unless it is viewed in the larger context of his philosophical system. His credo was: "My thinking is first and last and always for the sake of my doing." [14]

One aspect of James's philosophy was of notable importance for psychological theory. Virtually all contemporary psychologists strive toward a monistic interpretation of the human organism and behavior and face the difficult problem of reductionism. James was par excellence a nonreductionist. He was a *radical empiricist* and recognized the multiplicity and diversity of the universe. He saw no way to reconcile the empirically perceived diversity; to him reality was both unity and diversity. Therefore, although "no mental modification ever occurs which is not accompanied or followed by bodily damage," [15] mental and somatic processes are both sides of life.

Life is a process of adjustment. All we do, we do in the direction of better adjustment. It should be clear that "the distribution of consciousness shows it to be exactly such as we might expect in an organ added for the

[14] James *Principles of Psychology*, Holt, 1890, Vol. II, p. 333.
[15] James, *op. cit.*, Vol. I, p. 5.

sake of steering a nervous system grown too complex to regulate itself," said James. Consciousness represents the experiences, or the "phenomena" of mental life, whereas the organism and particularly the nervous system are the "conditions" of mental life.

Consciousness is a product of evolution. It has "been evolved, like all other functions, for a use—it is to the highest degree improbable *a priori* that it should have no use." This use can be seen in various ways.

As a radical empiricist James challenged the unity of personality. He believed that each individual has more than one "self." The *material self* is the totality of all material possessions, including one's own body, property, money, etc. Elation and depression are the emotional responses to the respective increase or decrease of possessions. The *social self* depends on identification with various social groups such as family, occupation companions, etc. Rise and decline in social status causes the same shift in emotions as rise and decline of the material self. The *spiritual self* includes all mental dispositions together; it is a sort of continuity of the various activities performed by an individual. The spiritual self is the center of action and adjustment.

No one is a homogeneous personality. "With most objects of desire," said James, "physical nature restricts our choice to but one of many represented goods, and even so it is here. I am often confronted by the necessity of standing by one of my empirical selves and relinquishing the next. . . . To make any of them actual, the rest must more or less be suppressed. So the seeker of his truest, strongest, deepest self must review the list carefully, and pick out the one on which to stake his salvation. All other selves thereupon become unreal, but the fortunes of this self are real." [16]

James was fully aware of the complexity of the problem. He knew the problems of abnormal psychology and was well acquainted with the research work of French psychiatry. There are unconscious states, split consciousness, amnesias, and morbid changes in personality. Thus, James could not agree with Wundt's or Titchener's concepts; consciousness is, James said, a stream of thought, a changing continuum, a unity in diversity, and nothing else.

Irrational elements pervade our life. Even reasoning serves action, and actions are determined by needs, ends, and purposes. The way in which concepts are formed depends upon the conceiving person, and the "whole function of conceiving, of fixing, of holding fast to meanings has no significance apart from the fact that the conceiver is a creature with partial purposes and private ends." [17]

It is quite understandable that James was much concerned with learning, emotions, and motivation and paid considerable attention to the acquisition of habits. Habits are acquired by association. Contiguity is the basic law of association, which James defined as follows: "When two elementary

[16] *Ibid.*, p. 309.
[17] *Ibid.*, p. 482.

brain-processes have been active together or in immediate succession, one of them, on reoccurring, tends to propagate its excitement into the other." [18] James' theory of learning did not deviate from the pattern established by the associationists. His associationism was mechanistic and non-introspectionistic and led to behaviorism.

James's theory of memory rejected the "faculty psychology" notion that memory is a mental faculty or power. He proved by experiments that memory cannot be improved by practice; practice can only improve the retention of the practiced material. The implication was that the idea of a memorizing power could not be accepted.

James introduced a systematic and classified list of instincts. He strove to find in the biological theory of evolution the answer to the dynamics of human nature. Instincts are inherited, common to a given species, usually useful and pleasant patterns of behavior. They are the ways of behavior. "Every creature likes its own ways, and takes to following them as a matter of course. . . . It is not for the sake of their utility that they are followed, but because at the moment of following them we feel that that is the only appropriate and natural thing to do." [19] Again, James emphasized usefulness and pleasure as motives of behavior.

James's theory of emotions was a logical outcome of his evolutionistic-biological approach. It is the well-known James–Lange conception of emotions as a function of bodily changes, mainly physiological changes in muscles and viscera. "We feel sorry because we cry, angry because we strike, afraid because we tremble, and not that we cry, strike, or tremble because we are sorry, angry, or fearful, as the case may be. Without the bodily states following on the perception, the latter would be purely cognitive in form, pale, colorless, destitute of emotional warmth." [20]

It is hard to say whether James developed a new psychological theory. His original contribution, the theory of emotions, aroused much controversy and has been largely disproved by later studies. The greatness of James does not lie in this or any other particular research. He influenced psychology by his new and fresh approach to the problem, by his philosophical idea of pragmatism and his perception of psychological function as a part of the process of adjustment. What for? was the question he asked. And even if he himself could not furnish the answer, he guided psychologists in posing this fruitful question.

John Dewey: Functionalism and Instrumentalism

It is often said that functionalism came to life with the publication of John Dewey's paper on the "Reflex Arc Concept" in 1896. In this paper,

[18] *Ibid.*, p. 566.
[19] James, *op. cit.*, Vol. II, p. 386.
[20] *Ibid.*, p. 450.

Dewey said: "The older dualism between sensation and idea is repeated in the current dualism of peripheral and central structures and functions; the older dualism of body and soul finds a distinct echo in the current dualism of stimulus and response." Dewey complained about the "rigid distinctions" between sensations, thoughts, and acts and continued as follows: The reflex arc idea "leaves us with a disjointed psychology," which deals with sensation or peripheral stimulus, idea or central process, and motor response or act, as "three disconnected existences, having to be somehow adjusted to each other, whether through the intervention of an extra-experimental soul, or by mechanical push and pull."[21]

According to Dewey, one may distinguish between stimulus and response, but the distinction must be functional, not existential. This distinction is made for the convenience of research and should not lead to a misconception of reality. There is but one *process of adjustment* of the organism to the environment, and in this purposeful process, stimuli and responses are a chain of deeds and not separate entities.

It would be rather difficult to understand Dewey's contribution to psychological theory without paying due attention to his philosophical inquiries. In fact, Dewey's philosophical studies reached greater prominence and had more influence than his psychological studies.

Dewey was one of the leading American pragmatists; he could agree with Peirce and James that action precedes knowledge. Life is action. And what is the role of thinking?

Dewey answers with his concept of *instrumentalism*. People think in order to live. Thinking is an instrumentality which is used by man "in adjusting himself to the practical situations of life." Knowledge results from human effort to survive. Knowledge is a weapon in the fight for survival or a tool in the effort for adjustment. The business of knowledge is to help men to clarify their ideas in regard to nature, society, and ethics. "The prime function of philosophy is that of rationalizing the possibilities of experience, especially collective human experience."[22]

Dewey was mainly a social philosopher concerned with the well-being of men and their physical, social, and moral adjustment. Man was the center of Dewey's philosophy. Man and his adjustment to life, or "man's traffic with nature," was the main problem in his philosophy and psychology.

Life is learning, Dewey said, and this idea influenced the studies of Thorndike, Watson, and all the neo-behaviorists. The problem of learning was considered by Dewey to be the focal issue in psychology. "The child learns," he wrote, "to avoid the shock of unpleasant disagreement, to find the easy way out, to appear to conform to customs which are wholly myste-

[21] John Dewey, "The Reflex Arc Concept in Psychology," *Psychological Review*, 1896, 3, 357–370.
[22] John Dewey, *Reconstruction in Philosophy*, Holt, 1922, p. 122.

rious to him in order to get his own way, that is to display some natural impulse without exciting the unfavorable notice of those in authority."[23]

What is innate is impulse. Dewey rejected the theory of specific and schematized instincts. He suggested instead that "impulses are highly flexible starting points for activities which are diversified according to the ways in which they are used. Any impulse may become organized into almost any disposition according to the way it interacts with surroundings. Fear may become abject cowardice, prudent caution, reverence for superiors or respect for equals. . . . The actual outcome depends upon how the impulse of fear is interwoven with other impulses. This depends in turn upon the outlets and inhibitions supplied by the social environment."[24]

Impulses may find direct, blind, unintelligent, and infantile outlets. They may be modified by learning, that is, changed by interaction with environment. These modified impulses are called by Dewey "sublimated," which corresponds, although not too closely, to what was called "sublimation" by Freud (cf. Chapters 4 and 6). In Dewey's terminology, sublimation means something like social adjustment through learning. For example, anger may be converted into "an abiding conviction of social injustice to be remedied, and furnish the dynamic to carry the conviction into execution."

The mechanisms that control the interaction between organism and environment are habits. Habits, Dewey said, "assimilate objective energies, and eventuate in command of environment."[25] The impulses carry the energy or "dynamic" and, when they are incorporated in dispositions, they "furnish the dynamic."

Habits are complex and flexible mechanisms of behavior. Dewey distinguished between "routine" habits and "intelligent" habits. Routine habits offer satisfactory adjustment to more or less static environment. When environment is changing, a more flexible adjustment is necessary. Intelligence is the flexible habit that guides the organism in a better adjustment to a changing situation.

The most important function of intelligence is "reflective thought." "The function of reflective thought is to transform a situation in which there is experienced obscurity, doubt, conflict, disturbance of some sort, into a situation that is clear, coherent, settled, harmonious. . . . When a situation arises containing a difficulty or perplexity, the person who finds himself in it may take one of a number of courses. . . . He may face the situation. In this case, he begins to reflect."[26]

Dewey distinguished several stages in the process of thinking as follows:

1. Suggestions in which the mind leaps forward to a possible solution
2. Intellectualization of the difficulty into a problem

[23] John Dewey, *Human Nature and Conduct,* Holt, 1922, p. 98.
[24] *Ibid.,* p. 95.
[25] *Ibid.,* p. 15.
[26] John Dewey, *How We Think,* Heath, 1933, p. 100.

3. Hypothesis, the use of one idea after another as a leading idea
4. Reasoning, the mental elaboration of the idea or supposition
5. Verification or experimental corroboration obtained by testing the hypothesis

As said before, Dewey's influence in psychology is related more to his broadly conceived philosophy than to his specific contributions to psychological research. First, his concept of instrumentalism paved the road for the functionalist approach to and purposivistic conception of psychology. Then, the emphasis on adjustment and learning led to a series of fruitful investigations in several laboratories. Dewey was opposed to the structuralists' "anatomy of mind" and introduced the molar point of view. And last, Dewey's theory of scientific inquiry stimulated the minds of Hull, Tolman, and scores of other research workers in psychology. It is worth while to mention that Dewey was in favor of operationism (Chapter 4) and, in a way, prepared the ground for his method of investigation.

Angell, Carr, and Robinson

The most outspoken exponent of functionalism was James Rowland Angell. Angell forcefully emphasized the evolutionary aspects in psychology. The human mind, he said, grows and develops, as centuries go by, in the continuous effort of better adjustment to environment. Angell regarded sensations, emotions, and acts of will as expressions of adaptation of the organism to its environment. To him functionalism was a turning point in interests rather than in methods: He believed that the fundamental psychological method is introspection, but that we are able to supplement introspection by immediate objective observation of other individuals.[27]

This shift in interests had a tremendous impact on the future development of psychological theory. Instead of dealing with mental structures, functionalism considered human life an integral part of the biological processes of change and adjustment. Angell wrote: "We shall adopt the biological point of view. . . . We shall regard all the operations of consciousness—all our sensations, all our emotions, and all our acts of will—as so many expressions of organic adaptations to our environment, an environment which we must remember is social as well as physical. . . ."[28]

Angell said that the structuralists dealt with the "what" psychology, while the functionalists dealt with the "how" and "why" psychology. Psychological functions are "accommodary" or adjustment services. Very little can be gained by the study of mental elements; in order to understand human life one has to consider the totality of the organism. A molar and not a molecular approach is needed in psychology. It is not the elements of con-

[27] James R. Angell, *Psychology, An Introductory Study of the Structure and Function of Human Consciousness,* Holt, 1904, p. 4.
[28] *Ibid.,* p. 7.

sciousness that should serve as the topic for psychological inquiry but the functions of the mind as a mediator between organism and environment.

Since adjustment is the main problem of functionalism, Angell and the other functionalists have attached great importance to the process of modification of behavior. This led to an increased interest in habit formation and learning theory, which became the main concern of Carr, Robinson, Melton, McGeoch, and all other functionalists.

Harvey A. Carr believed that functionalism is a continuation and modification of associationism and that adaptation to the environment is the main idea of functionalism. In the adaptive process, motives act upon the organism; there is always a sensory situation and a response to the stimulus. Response is the activity that leads to a change in the entire situation in the direction of satisfaction of the motive. Once the motive is satisfied, the organism does not react to it any longer. The object by which the motive is satisfied, for example, food in experiments with hungry animals, is called an incentive. A motive represents a genuine need; satisfaction of a motive is necessary for the survival and well-being of the organism. When the adaptive act is completed, the action of the motivating stimulus is terminated and the goal of the response accomplished.

Together with Edward S. Robinson, Carr introduced a series of new laws of association. Carr believed that his functionalism represented a new, quantitative, and experimental development of the associationist psychology. In his textbook, Carr emphasized the adaptive nature of human behavior.[29] Every organism needs food, but food is not always easily available and the organism must actively seek it. Some organisms—infants, for example—are unable to satisfy their own needs. Sometimes conflicting needs arise and a solution to the conflict has to be found. The process of adjustment is a problem-solving process in which the organism must find its way in accordance with its own needs, its responsive equipment, and the environment.

Carr's ideas have been continued by Edward S. Robinson. Instead of stimulus and response, Robinson suggested the terms "instigating" and "instigated" actions. Among the instigating actions are sensory processes and sensations, perceptions, and ideational processes. The instigated actions include glandular secretion, perceptions, ideas, feelings, and muscular movements.

Robinson distinguished between laws of learning, called laws of "associative formation," and laws of recall and recognition, called laws of "associative revival." He believed that the strength "of any associative connection is a function of the conditions of contiguity, frequency, vividness, and so on, obtaining at the time the association was formed."[30]

Robinson introduced several new laws of association. He believed that association takes place in accordance with the laws of contiguity, assimilat-

[29] Harvey A. Carr, *Psychology, A Study of Mental Activity*, Longmans, Green, 1925.
[30] Edward S. Robinson, *Association Theory Today*, Appleton-Century, 1932, p. 66.

ion, frequency, intensity, duration, context, acquaintance, composition, and individual differences. "It is my conviction that the facility of associative fixation is a function of all the factors enumerated. Probably several specific relationships are involved for each named factor and almost certainly there are other factors that have not been included in this list. But, if the assumption that these factors are important determiners of association be correct, then there are 'laws' of these factors whether our knowledge of them is definite or not." [31]

Robinson's associationism is not associationism in the traditional connotation of this term. For a functionalist, the functions of motivation, adaptation to the environment, and motor activities are the main vehicles of human behavior, but associations are the main method by which the human mind learns and adapts.

Robert Sessions Woodworth: Dynamic Psychology

A. A. Roback, in his biography of James [32] and later in his *History of American Psychology*,[33] has said that in 1908 James wrote with a pencil on page 58 of Titchener's *Lectures on the Elementary Psychology of Feeling and Attention:* "shows how different the dynamic point of view is from the structural." Roback remarks that although Dewey used the word "dynamic" as early as 1884, this term was not much in use in 1908.

James's and Dewey's theories invited the term "dynamic." If "dynamic" is related to change and interprets the causal factors in change, functionalism is undoubtedly a theory of dynamics. If structuralism could be compared to mental anatomy or histology, which dealt with the "elements" of mind and consciousness, functionalism could be compared to physiology.

Woodworth's dynamic psychology was, in a way, an outcome and continuation of the teachings of James and Dewey. The main question to be resolved by psychology was not what humans and animals feel and do, but *why* they feel and act in a certain way. Why, the physicist would ask, do trains move? And his answer points to the *dynamic* factor, the electricity. Analogously, psychology cannot be confined to the observation of behavior but must deal with the dynamics or causation of behavior. The stimulus-response chain does not answer the question. A very important link is missing, and Woodworth undertook to consider it. It was the living organism that had to be interpolated between the stimulus and the response. The stimulus stimulates the organism, which responds to the stimulus in accordance with its inner drives. Food stimulates the organism, provided the organism is hungry. Each organism has native capacities to do things in

[31] *Ibid.,* p. 124.
[32] A. A. Roback, *William James: His Marginalia, Personality and Contribution,* Science and Art, 1942, p. 55.
[33] A. A. Roback, *History of American Psychology,* Library Publishers, 1953, p. 146.

a certain way. The stimulus–response relation is the *mechanism* of behavior, but the driving power behind it is the *drive* that activates the mechanism.

Woodworth preferred the idea of general motivation as opposed to the idea of special instincts proposed by McDougall. Even more was Woodworth opposed to McDougall's conception of teleological motivation (Chapter 5). "The question is, whether the mechanisms for the thousand and one things which the human individual has the capacity to do are themselves wholly passive, requiring the drive of these few instincts, or whether each such mechanism can be directly aroused and continue in action without assistance from hunger, sex, self-assertion, curiosity."[34]

A mechanism can act as a drive if it facilitates and reinforces another mechanism. Acquired habits can act as driving forces or drives which can lead to new actions.

Woodworth was opposed both to Titchener's conception that psychology has to study mainly sensations and perceptions and to Watson's denunciation of introspection and his limiting of psychology to the study of motor and glandular behavior. Woodworth felt, as did all other functionalists, that psychology should embrace both behavior and consciousness in "an unbroken series of events." The S-R chain was modified by Woodworth into an S-O-R chain, O standing for the structures and functions of the organism. Psychology and physiology do not study two parallel processes, but one and the same "real process," and the motivating drives can be organic, such as hunger or fatigue, or not organic, such as self-assertion or curiosity.

Woodworth's dynamic psychology introduced an important emphasis on motivation and came quite close to the Würzburg school (Chapter 12) in its efforts to find the driving forces behind human actions.

In a way, Woodworth's motivation theory was a forerunner of Tolman's "intervening variable" (Chapter 4). To the observable stimulus and response factors, Woodworth added the drives that act as motivating forces within the organism and that together with the stimuli represent the totality of factors that cause action.

Concluding Remarks on Functionalism

Titchener said that structural psychology dealt with facts "as they are" while functional psychology dealt with "what it is for." The purposivism of the functionalists was considered by Titchener a serious deviation from the scientific method. He believed that the business of science was to investigate things as they were without asking questions of aim or purpose. Titchener's criticism is probably only partially justified because some facts cannot be understood without the "what for" question. To this category belong all facts or activities which are goal directed. If a child raises a hand

[34] Robert S. Woodworth, *Dynamic Psychology*, Columbia University, 1917, p. 67.

to pick up a piece of candy or to hit a playmate, a purely factual description of hand movements will miss the most relevant issue in this purposeful act.

Moreover, structuralism did not deal with all facts but mainly with those which could be perceived through introspection. Structuralism confined itself to a very precise study of a fraction of what should be regarded as the legitimate area of psychological research.

Functionalism prepared the ground for behaviorism and conditioning. Although the early functionalists preferred introspective methods, all of them admitted that the processes of adjustment could be observed from without and not necessarily by introspection. Learning and habit formed the main issue in adjustment, and this is precisely why Angell and all other functionalists attached so much importance to these processes.

On the other hand, functionalism led to purposivism; both the behavioristic-mechanistic system of Watson and the purposive-hormic psychology of McDougall originate in functionalism. The "what for" question posed by the functionalists was taken up and answered by McDougall.[35]

3. EDWARD L. THORNDIKE: CONNECTIONISM

Historical Roots

Associationism has a long history, starting with the Aristotelian laws of association, the laws of similarity, difference, contiguity in time, and contiguity in space. The English associationists in modern times based their theory mainly on contiguity in time.

David Hartley in *Observations on Man*, published in 1749, regarded simple sensations as elements of mental life closely interrelated with the sensory apparatus and therefore dependent on somatic processes. Alexander Bain further developed the neurological theory of associations. He said: "As the brain advances in size and in complication, there is an advance not merely in those lower functions called Reflex and Automatic, but of the higher functions named intelligence, emotion and will. . . . With development of the brain proceeds, *pari passu*, development of the mind."[36]

Bain did not deal with associations in mentalistic terms. Being Dawin's and Spencer's contemporary and follower, he applied the mechanistic theory of evolution to psychology. He believed that the evolution of mind is a result of the development of the nervous tissues and their connections: the more complex these connections, the more complex the mental processes.

Associationism was the leading idea in the psychology of the nineteenth century. Herbart's metaphysico-mathematical system of psychology

[35] Cf. F. V. Smith, *Explanation of Human Behavior*, Constable, 1951, Chapter 6.
[36] Alexander Bain, *The Emotions and the Will* (4th ed.), Longmans, Green, 1899, p. 47.

was permeated with associationism. The first truly experimental study of memory by Ebbinghaus in 1885 was based on associationism. Even Freud's theory is based on assumptions rooted in associationism (cf. Chapter 6).

Associationism took a new turn in this century. It was taken up by two great investigators, Thorndike in the United States and Pavlov in Russia and elevated into a series of theoretical concepts by scores of research workers.

Neurons

Edward Lee Thorndike accepted Bain's ideas as a starting point for his own research. Thorndike put these ideas to a test and developed a full-fledged psychological theory which combines functionalism with associationism.

The foundations of this theory were physiological and reductionist. Thorndike firmly believed, at least at the earlier stage of his studies, that psychological findings should and could be related to the nervous system. The nervous cells, the neurons, offer the solution to the enigma of human behavior. Sensory processes depend on *afferent* neurons, which carry the impulses received by the sensory organs to the spinal cord or brain, and on *efferent* neurons, which work from the nervous centers to muscles, glands, etc. The neurons have extensions—dendrites—which contact the axons of other cells. Through the connections, or *synapses*, between the neurons, a neural current is conducted. "The essence of my account of the physiological mechanism of learning," said Thorndike, "may be stated as follows. . . . The connections formed between situation and response are represented by connections between neurones and neurones whereby the disturbance, or neural current, arising in the former is conducted to the latter across the synapses. The strength or weakness of the connection means the greater or less likelihood that the same current will be conducted from the former to the latter rather than to some other place. The strength or weakness of the connection is a condition of the synapse."[37]

Thorndike's multivolumed work was based on the assumption that the connections between nerves determine the flow of neural current, which controls all psychological functions. Thus far, Thorndike was an associationist. But he was also James's pupil. To Thorndike life meant adjustment, and adjustment takes place through learning. He believed, with all other functionalists, that learning was the main issue in psychology, and this belief was shared by others who were influenced by James's pragmatism and Dewey's instrumentalism, including Watson, Hull, Tolman, and Skinner.

[37] Edward L. Thorndike, *Educational Psychology*, Teachers College, Columbia University, 1913–14, Vol. I, p. 227.

Learning

Years ahead of Pavlov and Watson, Thorndike developed a theory of behavior based upon studies of learning. He considered learning a trial-and-error process, and later he called it a *selecting* and *connecting* process.

One of Thorndike's best-known experiments was with a cat confined in a puzzle box. The cat was hungry, and food was outside. The box or cage was closed, and a concealed mechanism operated by a latch could open the door. The hungry cat bit, clawed, jumped, pushed, and dashed till the door opened. On succeeding trials the number of unsuccessful efforts declined slowly and irregularly. Finally the cat had "learned" how to operate the latch and get the food outside the box.

Careful analysis of this and similar experiments disclosed the nature of the learning process. A satiated cat would not try to gain access to the food outside and apparently would not learn. Hunger or some other motive was necessary for learning.

The theoretical explanation of learning was based on neural connections between stimulus and response. Some connections were strengthened, some weakened. After a great number of trials to get out of confinement, and after some successful efforts, all the nonsuccessful impulses will be *stamped out* and the particular impulse leading to the successful act will be *stamped in* by the resulting satisfaction. After many trials, the cat will, when put into the box, immediately claw the button or loop in a definite way, said Thorndike.

At this point Thorndike departed from a purely physiological interpretation of associations. His insistence on pleasure as the determinant in learning opened a discussion which is still very much alive among the various psychological schools. The radical behaviorist-type theories, such as Watson's, Guthrie's, and others, reject the terms of "satisfaction" and "annoyance" and stick to contiguity of stimulus and response," while Hull and others accept Thorndike's theory of reward.

Thorndike followed in the footsteps of James, who wrote: "If pleasure and pain have no efficacy, one does not see why the most noxious acts, such as burking might not give thrills of delight, and the most necessary ones, such as breathing cause agony."[38]

This principle of *usefulness of pleasure* was common to the entire group of biologically minded thinkers such as Spencer, James, Dewey, McDougall, and others. On the other hand, Thorndike's neoassociationism was influenced by the earlier associationists, especially by Bain's pleasure-and-pain theory of association. Watson hoped to develop a psychological theory without recourse to subjectively perceived emotions. Thorndike felt that this was impossible, and that even in the most "objective" studies of animal psychology, the postulate of pleasure is an indispensable one.

[38]James, *op. cit.*, Vol. II, p. 143.

Thorndike emphasized this postulate over and over again. "Of several responses made to the same situation, those which are accompanied or closely followed by satisfaction to the animal will, other things being equal, be more firmly connected with the situation, so that when it recurs, they will be more likely to recur; those which are accompanied or closely followed by discomfort to the animal will, other things being equal, have their connection with the situation weakened so that, when it recurs, they will be less likely to occur. The greater the satisfaction or discomfort the greater the strengthening or weakening of the bond."[39]

Sheer practice is not conducive to learning, Thorndike asserted, and rejected the notion that frequency is one of the main laws of association. "Practice without zeal—without equal comfort at success and failure—does *not* make perfect, and the nervous system grows *away* from the modes in which it is *exercised with resulting discomfort*. When the law of effect is omitted—when habit-formation is reduced to the supposed effect of mere repetition—two results are almost certain. By the resulting theory little in human behavior can be explained by the law of habit; and by the resulting practice, unproductive or extremely wasteful forms of drill are encouraged."[40]

The main law of learning was the law of effect. Successful steps in learning were rewarded, unsuccessful steps, eliminated. Pleasure or satisfaction will ultimately determine which responses will be learned.

Thorndike tried to avoid mentalistic terms and used a definition of pleasure worded in "objective" terms, as follows: "By a satisfying state of affairs is meant one which the animal does nothing to avoid, often doing things which maintain or renew it. By an annoying state of affairs is meant one which the animal does nothing to preserve, often doing things which put an end to it."[41] Thorndike believed that this definition put his theory in the realm of "objective psychology." Satisfaction and annoyance, as defined by Thorndike, were not mentalistic terms but empirical concepts derived from careful examination of animals' overt behavior.

Laws of Learning

In addition to the law of effect, Thorndike formulated other laws of learning, all of them corollaries of the law of effect. He criticized the associationist notion of the law of exercise but accepted this law as a subsidiary of the law of effect. He wrote: "When a modifiable connection is made between a situation and a response, that connection's strength is, other things being equal, increased." This is the law of use. Its counterpart is the law of disuse, which reads: "When a modifiable connection is not made between a

[39] Edward L. Thorndike, *Animal Intelligence: Experimental Studies*, Macmillan, 1911, p. 244.
[40] Thorndike, *Educational Psychology*, Teachers College, Columbia University, 1913–1914, Vol. II, *The Psychology of Learning*, p. 22.
[41] *Ibid.*, p. 2.

situation and a response during a length of time, that connection's strength is decreased."[42] The laws of use and disuse together form the *law of exercise*.

The *law of readiness* dealt with motivation for learning. It reads: "When any conduction unit is in readiness to conduct, for it to do so is satisfying. When any conduction unit is not in readiness to conduct, for it to conduct is annoying."

In addition to the three laws of effect, readiness, and exercise Thorndike suggested five subordinate laws. The *law of multiple response* was related to learning by *trial and error*. A new situation may lead to several responses until, after some experimentation, the right response brings the solution. Inability to make varied responses may prevent learning.

The *law of set* indicated that learning depends upon the learner's previous experiences and dispositions. Not every individual will "reset" in the same way to a given learning situation. Much depends on his "set,"or the "condition of man," and not on "the nature of the situation."

The *law of associative shifting* stated that it is quite easy to get *"any response of which a learner is capable associated with any situation to which he is sensitive."* [43] This law corresponds to Pavlov's conditioning, and Thorndike gradually attached more and more importance to it.

The *law of assimilation* or analogy states that "to any situation, man responds as he would to some situation like it, or like some element of it. In default of any bonds with it itself, bonds that he has acquired with situations resembling it, act."[44] This law is, in a way, the law of similarity of the early associationists.

The *law of prepotency of elements* indicated the selectivity in learning. The learner may select the important elements from a situation instead of responding in an unselected way, at random, to a given situation. This law can be considered a bridge between Thorndike's concepts of learning and the gestalt concept. Actually, in later years, Thorndike came even closer to the gestalt point of view.

Besides these laws of learning Thorndike was much interested in the problem of *transfer of training*. Faithful to his connectionism, he stated that "a change in one function alters any other only in so far as the two functions have as factors identical elements."[45]

The Revision

Thorndike's main laws of learning in 1913 were the laws of effect, of readiness, and of exercise and the five minor laws. In 1929, as a result of his

[42] *Ibid.*
[43] *Ibid.*, p. 15.
[44] *Ibid.*, p. 28.
[45] *Ibid.*, p. 358.

studies in human learning, he modified the basic laws and added six new laws.

A major revision in Thorndike's system was the rejection of the law of exercise. Experiments were made on blindfolded subjects who were instructed to draw several times a line of a certain length. Despite numerous repetitions, no improvement was noticed. However, when the subjects were told whether they did it right or wrong, a considerable improvement took place. In another study, Thorndike found that, although there is a slight improvement due to repetition of connections, the improvement due to reward is six times stronger.

In another experiment Thorndike asked the subjects to write down some nonsense words which were read to them. The spelling of these words was ambiguous. Each sound was repeated in the list of the nonsense words forty-nine times, and it was easy to find out whether the subjects tended to stamp in the sounds as a result of contiguity and frequency. For instance, a sound like the short *o* in the word *for* was repeated over and over again. In fact, almost all subjects wrote the short *o* as the vowel *o*. When the short *o* sound had been used ten times, it had been written down as the vowel *o* 8.37 times on the average. However, there was no significant increase in the use of the vowel *o* by the subjects; the third trial of ten gave the score of 8.61 and the fourth 8.06. Similar results were received with the sounds *a* and *s*, which showed no increase in preferred spelling despite contiguity and frequency.

In still another experiment, Thorndike proved that punishment (an annoyer) does not weaken the punished connection. He said: "There is no evidence that it takes away strength from the physiological basis of the connection in any way comparable to the way in which a satisfying after-effect adds strength to it."

The revision of Thorndike's theory brought it closer to its functionalistic origin. Trial and error played a lesser role in this new theory. A living organism is "set" on a certain activity and rewards have a "confirming influence" on association. The strengthening of responses by reward was now considered to be a product of the "direct confirmatory relation." This reaction is relatively independent of the affective strength of the satisfier; it is a function of drives or "overhead control in the brain." Thus, Thorndike's theory in its new version was a radical reductionist edition of functionalism. Men and animals act in accordance with their drives. "Their behavior is purposive, and directed by biological causation."[46]

Further studies led Thorndike to the conclusion that this "confirmatory relation" is probably "set up and controlled by large fractions of the 'higher' levels of the cortex, often by what corresponds to the general 'set' and purpose of the animal at the time."[47]

The shift from a *molecular-physiological* approach to a *molar* one with a

[46] Edward L. Thorndike, *The Fundamentals of Learning*, Teachers College, 1932, p. 312.
[47] Edward L. Thorndike, *An Experimental Study of Rewards*, Teachers College, 1933, p. 67.

functionalist and biological flavor was even more pronounced in Thorn-dike's later work. "The strengthening by satisfying consequences may have a biological causation. . . ." The over-all control "should be able to react to a certain stimulus by a reinforcement of whatever connection has most recently been active, and . . . the stimulus that sets off this 'confirming re-action' should be satisfying to the over all control."[48]

For years, Thorndike was criticized by gestalt psychologists. Finally, he yielded on some points. First, the "confirming reaction" was in itself a con-cession to gestalt. Instead of separate neurons, Thorndike introduced a sort of general cortex activity—"overhead control in the brain." This activity was supposed to be relatively independent of the affective value of the stimulus. Obviously, it was a function of the brain itself—and this interpre-tation brought Thorndike quite close to gestalt psychology (Chapter 12).

Another concession in the direction of gestalt was the *law of belong-ingness*. In one experiment, three thousand attempts were made to draw a line four inches long with closed eyes. No significant improvement was achieved toward the end of the experiment, and no learning took place despite the repetitions.

Thorndike found that mere repetition of stimuli in temporal contiguity does not lead to learning. He administered a group test in which ten sen-tences were read loudly ten times. The first and second words of each sen-tence were the name and surname of a person. The sequence of the last word in a sentence and the first word of the following sentence had the same frequency as the first and second words of each sentence. However, the subject usually recalled the second word after being given the first one but could not recall the first word of a sentence when given the last word of the preceding sentence. Thorndike concluded that repetition of items in temporal contiguity is not conducive to learning unless some other factors are involved. In the reported experiment it was the belonging to a sentence and belonging to a name which produced results in learning.[49]

In fact, the principle of learning by trial and error discards learning by repetitions, since futile and inefficient steps made by the animal are not being learned despite repetition and only those leading to the goal are learned.

Additional modification in Thorndike's theory was brought about by his experiments on the "spread of effect."[50] Subjects were asked to respond with numbers from one to ten to some words pronounced as stimuli by the experimenter. The responses were interpreted loudly by the experimenter as being either right or wrong. Since the number of words used by the ex-perimenter as stimuli was very large, it was practically impossible for the subjects to recall on further trials what they had actually said and how their statements were evaluated by the experimenter . After several trials Thorn-

[48] Edward L. Thorndike, *Man and His Works*, Harvard University, 1943, p. 33.
[49] Edward L. Thorndike, *Human Learning*, Appleton-Century, 1931, pp. 8 ff.
[50] Thorndike, *An Experimental Study of Rewards*.

dike found that the responses called "right" (the "rewarded" responses) occurred much more frequently than the others. Moreover, all responses which were given in proximity to a rewarded one were recalled better than the others. This phenomenon was called by Thorndike the "spread of effect." Obviously, these findings supported Thorndike's law of effect.

Intelligence

The idea of connectionism influenced Thorndike's work in other areas too. Most workers promoted the theory of intelligence conceived as a general mental ability of comprehension, adaptation, and problem solving. Spearman suggested a distinction between general intelligence (G) and specific abilities (S), and Stern defined intelligence as "a general mental adaptability to new problems and conditions of life."

Thorndike rejected the idea of an over-all mental capacity. "The mind is really but the sum total of an individual's feelings and acts, of the connections between outside events and his responses thereto, and of the possibilities of having such feelings, acts and connections."[51] He proposed a *quantity* or *synthesis theory*. Intelligence, according to him, depended on the "number of connections" in one's brain.

From a purely empirical point of view, one could distinguish three types of intelligence. *Abstract* intelligence dealt with symbols, words, and concepts. *Social* intelligence had to do with human relations and represented the sum of leadership, tactfulness, and other social abilities. *Mechanical* intelligence was related to objects, tools, and machinery and was the sum of manipulatory abilities with regard to physical objects.

Thorndike was opposed to Binet's tests because they were developed on the assumption of a general mental ability. Thorndike's tests, known as the Intellect CAVD (completion, arithmetic reasoning, vocabulary, directions), had a different rationale. There were four separate tests that were believed to measure four relatively independent abilities empirically recognized as representing abstract intelligence.

Thorndike emphasized hereditary factors in all kinds of intelligence. Notwithstanding environmental influences, some people have more nerve connections and are more intelligent.

Concluding Remarks on Thorndike

Forty years after Thorndike's *Animal Intelligence* was published, Tolman wrote: "The psychology of animal learning—not to mention that of child learning—has been and still is primarily a matter of agreeing or disagreeing with Thorndike, or trying in minor ways to improve upon him. Gestalt psychologists, conditioned-reflex psychologists, sign-Gestalt psychologists—all

[51]Thorndike, *Educational Psychology*, Vol. II, p. 367.

of us in America seem to have taken Thorndike, overtly or covertly, as our starting point."[52]

But even this statement does not contain the entire truth. Although Thorndike's efforts to synthesize objectivism and the pleasure principle, reductionism and mentalism, could not lead to the establishment of a consistent theory, it had provoked the thoughts of a whole generation.

Thorndike can be criticized on several points. First, there are many good reasons to distinguish between *antecedent* motivation and *subsequent* gratification. Undoubtedly they are closely related, but they are not identical. Seward's experiment can be used here for explanation of the differences between these two concepts. Seward divided the rats used in his experiment into two groups. Both groups had to press a bar in order to reach food; however, the first group was not given food, whereas the rats in the second group were promptly rewarded as soon as they pressed the bar. The rats who had been rewarded learned more and better (motivation and gratification), but the unrewarded rats learned too (motivation only). The ratio in the number of responses per animal per trial in all three days of the experiment was 41.7 to 33.3.[53]

Thorndike was often criticized on the ground that his law of *effect* is actually a law of *affect*. He tried to escape this accusation by introducing the term "O.K. reaction" as an effect of satisfiers. It is an "unknown reaction of neurones which is aroused by the satisfier and which strengthens connections on which it impinges." It strengthens connections whether they are pleasant and useful or wrong and useless.

Thorndike's law of effect has been open to criticism especially in relation to its supposedly retroactive influence. Since the effect comes after a given response, how can it possibly influence it and stamp it in? Thorndike's solution to this problem seems to be satisfactory. He assumed that the physiological connections do not disappear immediately after the response has occurred. They function simultaneously with the effect and can be influenced by it.

The weakest point in Thorndike's theory seems to be his strict reductionism. No evidence was offered in support of the theory of brain connections. All further studies done by several workers discarded the idea of brain connections as proposed by Thorndike.

What was stimulating in Thorndike's studies was his theory of learning, which even today is very much alive. The issue of reward still divides workers in this field into contiguity and reward theorists of learning (see Chapter 4. Section 8).

But, in the development of psychological theory, physiological reduc-

[52] Edward C. Tolman, "The Determiners of Behavior at a Choice Point," *Psychological Review*, 1938, *45*, 1–41.

[53] J. P. Seward, "An Experimental Study of Guthrie's Theory of Reinforcement," *Journal of Experimental Psychology*, 1942, *30*, 247–256.

tionism and the mentalistic pleasure principle could not be so easily combined. Some psychologists rejected mentalism; some rejected reductionism. Still others strove to attain a synthesis on a higher level of theory construction. Thorndike stood in the middle between the "old" and the "new" psychology. Perhaps more than anyone else, he paved the way for new psychological systems, but he himself did not enter the door which he helped to open.

2

Conditioned Reflexes

1. THE OBJECTIVE STUDY OF THE HIGHER NERVOUS PROCESSES

Pavlov's Postulates and Principles

None of the three "fathers" of contemporary psychology considered psychology his occupation. Freud was a practicing physician, Dilthey was a philosopher, and Pavlov was a pharmacologist and physiologist.

Ivan Petrovitch Pavlov never believed in a successful psychology. Although he did not suggest substituting physiology for psychology, he doubted whether psychology could ever develop into an independent discipline capable of objective and truly scientific research. He strongly recommended that psychologists relate their concepts to physiology; while physiology was building the "foundations," psychology was expected to build the "superstructure." However, since physiological concepts are "necessarily spatial" and psychology deals with "subjective states," Pavlov felt that the position of psychology as a science was "completely hopeless."[1]

For most of his life, Pavlov avoided mentalistic terms. He pursued his research in an empirical, inductive, and experimental way, as if humans were higher animals and nothing else. He repeatedly emphasized that his study was "absolutely excluding psychological conceptions,"[2] and that his study of the activity of the central nervous systems "has to do always with only objective facts—facts existing in time and space."[3]

A few principles, consistently applied by Pavlov, were repeatedly and emphatically stated, but no effort was made to prove them. These principles formed the very foundation of Pavlov's scientific outlook and an indispensable part of his philosophy as a natural scientist. He accepted them somewhat dogmatically with a certain degree of the optimistic naïveté of the nineteenth-century materialist philosophers.

Pavlov believed wholeheartedly and enthusiastically in the *monistic and materialist* philosophy. He believed that humans are a part of nature, nature

[1] Ivan P. Pavlov, *Lectures on Conditioned Reflexes*, Liveright, 1928, p. 219.
[2] *Ibid.*, p. 214.
[3] *Ibid.*, p. 192.

41

being interpreted as the sum of matter and energy. Whatever goes on in human life is going on in the nervous tissues and in the glands of inner secretion. Pavlov did not bother to take up the argument for or against introspection as other contemporary psychologists did. Therefore he easily avoided the pitfalls of behaviorism with its efforts to relate covert behavior to unperceivable motions of muscles or glands.

Pavlov's way was clear, simple, and safe. He did not deny psychology; he simply did not care much for it. He often admitted that the processes going on in human nature were physicochemical processes, which could be "subjectively" interpreted, but he did not attach much value to these subjective, nonscientific comments. In this attitude he resembled Marx's materialist philosophy, but ascribed even less importance to psychology than Marx did (cf. Section 6 of this chapter), for Pavlov's monism was a mechanistic and not a dialectic one.[4]

Pavlov applied the same mechanistic philosophy to the problems of causation. He subscribed to the theory of *mechanistic determinism* and professed a rigid, unviolable, necessary, and inflexible causation in animal and human behavior.

The third principle was a sort of *energetism*. Whatever goes on in the nervous system is a dynamic balance of energy with the processes of acquisition, discharge, stimulation, inhibition, irradiation, and concentration of energy. He wrote: "Let us take a certain reflex, i.e., there is excitation of a certain point in the central nervous system. If at the same time another reflex is evoked, another point in the central nervous system is stimulated, and the first reflex becomes weaker and may disappear. One may suppose that the exercise of the second reflex withdraws a certain amount of energy into its own centre at the expense of the energy of the first reflex centre; consequently less energy remains in the first reflex centre and its manifestation is weaker, or, if the diversion of energy is considerable, entirely absent. Other explanations can be given, but this one can not be gainsaid, as it corresponds well to the actual facts."[5] Obviously, all behavior was interpreted by Pavlov as a flow of energy regulated by a few relatively simple laws. The greater the energy of the stimulus, the strong is its effect; the more energy-charged a nervous center is, the more powerful its reaction to the stimuli.

The fourth principle, the principle of *equilibrium,* corresponds to and resembles Cannon's *homeostasis* and Freud's *constancy* principles. Pavlov wrote: "As a part of nature every animal organism represents a very com-

---

[4] Pavlov himself was definitely opposed to Marxism, and especially to its social philosophy. He believed that Marxism "is sheer dogmatism" (see footnote 42 in this chapter). But Pavlov's ideas on the relationship between psychology and physiology suggest that there is room for a bridge between Marxism (especially in Lenin's interpretation) and Pavlov. Soviet psychologists have been building this bridge (see Section 6 of this chapter). Though Pavlov never accepted Marxism, Soviet psychologists accepted Pavlov.

[5] Pavlov, *op. cit.,* p. 185.

plicated and closed system, the internal forces of which, at every given moment, as long as it exists as such, are in equilibrium with the external forces of its environment. The more complex the organism, the more delicate and manifold are its elements of equilibration. . . . All life, from that of the simplest to the most complex organism, including man WISE a long series of more and more complicated *equilibrations* with the outer world."[6] And further on he stated that through the two main activities of the nervous system, the analysis of the external stimuli (perception) and creating of new temporary connections between these stimuli and the functions of the organism (conditioning), "a complete equilibrium of the systems of energy and matter constituting the animal organism with the systems of energy and matter of the environment" is established.[7]

The Analyzers

Pavlov suggested a modification of the theory of brain function. It had been generally accepted that the central nervous apparatus consists of the centripetal-sensory part and the centrifugal-motor part. Pavlov believed that all achievements and perfections in the nervous activity are located in the receptor cells and all the "extraordinary intricacies" of function and the "complicated perfections" of the apparatus are situated in the centripetal part of the central nervous system, not in the centrifugal part.

According to Pavlov, the *reflex-arc* has to be divided into three parts. The first is called the *analyzer;* it begins in every "natural peripheral end" of the centripetal nerve and ends in the receptor cells of the central organ. The term "analyzer" is derived from the fact that the receptor cells decompose the external stimuli. The second part of the arc is the *connection* or lock between the receptors and effectors. The third part of the reflex-arc is the *effector* or the working part.

In 1910, Pavlov wrote that "the brain represents chiefly and probably exclusively (the last provisionally) the central end of the analyzers" or the "receptor centers," that is, the brain endings of analyzers; the motor region should be considered as a receptor center with "special relation to movement."[8]

Pavlov postulated distinct *physiological centers* such as the food center, the defensive center, the cold and heat centers, and the motor center. Each center represents a projection of the peripheral receiving apparatus and responds in a specific way to stimulation. This response is the unconditioned, or innate, reflex.

When several centers are stimulated, "the direction of stimulation is conditioned by the relative strength of the interacting centers. The food center is obviously a powerful physiological center; it is the protector of the

[6] *Ibid.,* p. 129.
[7] *Ibid.,* p. 242.
[8] *Ibid.,* pp. 117–118.

individual's existence. It is evident that in comparison with the food center, the defense center is of less importance. . . . During the struggle for food the different parts of the body are not specially defended; among animals there are fierce tussles and fights for food in which occur wounds and serious injuries."[9]

The relative strengths of the centers depend on the amount of energy at their disposal. Provided the respective centers are "fully charged," some of them have more, some less intense reflexes. However, a weak center with a heavy charge may produce a stronger response and inhibit a strong center having a small charge.

9/9

Excitation and Inhibition

"Nervous activity consists in general of the phenomena of excitation and inhibition. . . . I shall not commit a great error if I liken these two phenomena to positive and negative electricity," wrote Pavlov.[10] As said before, the nervous centers are "charged" with energy. If a certain center is stronger, the energy from the weaker centers passes over to this stronger center and the previously active center becomes entirely quiescent.

This conduction of energy from one center to another is called by Pavlov excitation; accordingly, the center which attracted energy becomes "excited." Three laws govern the processes of excitation. The first is the spread or *irradiation* of the stimulation in the cerebrum. A stimulation in a certain group of nervous cells irradiates over large parts of the cerebrum, and the excitation started in a certain cortical point spreads in a wave into surrounding areas. The second law is the law of *concentration* of excitation. The wave of irradiated excitation goes back to the starting point. Pavlov's idea of equilibrium is well represented by the third law, the law of *induction*. The term "induction" was borrowed from Sherrington. Concentration of both excitation and inhibition is effected by the reciprocal induction; once an area is stimulated and irradiates, the neighboring areas develop inhibition and force concentration of the stimulated area. This phenomenon is called positive induction. Once an area is inhibited and the inhibition irradiates, the neighboring areas develop stimulation and force concentration of inhibition. This is negative induction. In both cases "for the formation of the isolated foci of stimulation and inhibition in the cortex there is necessary, first of all, the presence of the corresponding stimuli; but once these foci have been formed, induction appears in the role of supporting mechanism for their maintenance and stability."[11]

Apparently the same three laws of irradiation, concentration, and induction apply to the second function of the central nervous system, *inhibition*. Pavlov remarked that "the cortical cells under the influence of the con-

[9] *Ibid.*, p. 188.
[10] *Ibid.*, p. 156.
[11] *Ibid.*, p. 324.

ditioned stimulus always tend to pass, though sometimes very slowly, into a state of inhibition." [12] The process of inhibition can be started by an internal or by an external agent. If during activity of one center another center is stimulated, an immediate diminution or even a complete cessation of action of the first center may follow. This is the case of external inhibition.

Internal inhibition is "the reverse side of excitation" and always follows excitation, in accordance with the law of reciprocal induction. What inhibition really is, Pavlov could not tell. "We must admit," he wrote in 1912, "that at the present time we know altogether nothing of the real nature of internal inhibition." However, his studies strongly indicate that both processes are processes in which some energy is being used, and probably both derive their energies from the same source. In another volume, Pavlov discussed in more detail the pathological states of mind. He observed that the decline of inhibitory processes is related to a decline of the general excitability of the brain which seems to indicate a general decline of vitality. [13] The extreme difficulty of establishing a conditioned response to food and a metronome in an old dog seems to indicate a lower irritability of the nervous centers. The same old dog had great difficulty in the process of differentiation, which obviously depended upon the process of inhibition.

Pavlov related excitation and inhibition to anatomic factors. He hypothesized that the cortical cells of the cerebrum contain some sort of "excitatory substances." Each individual is born with a "store of excitatory substances" in his cortical cells. Some individuals are poorly endowed with these substances or lose part of them during their life span, and their cortical cells tend to pass easily into the inhibitory stage. All cortical cells are very sensitive and destructible; they develop a special process of inhibition when threatened by a functional destruction or depletion of their excitatory substances. Thus inhibition is "conserving and economic," reduces the functional destruction of cells, and accelerates the restoration of expended excitatory substances.

Conduction and Connection

According to Pavlov, the main function of the nervous system is *reflex*. A reflex is usually started by an external agent producing stimulation in the *receptor*, which is, as said before, the ending of a centripetal, afferent nerve. When this stimulation is *conducted* along the path of the centripetal, afferent nerve to the central part of the nervous system, and then to the efferent or centrifugal nerve, a reaction takes place. Under certain circumstances a given stimulus provokes a definite, always the same, reaction. As a rule, the reflex follows the same nervous path. "A reflex is the mechanism of a definite connection by means of the nervous system between the phenom-

[12] Ivan P. Pavlov, *Conditioned Reflexes*, Oxford, 1927, p. 391.
[13] Ivan P. Pavlov, *Activity of the Cerebral Hemispheres* (Russian), Leningrad, 1926.

ena of the external world and the corresponding definite reactions of the organism."[14]

The nervous system is not only a conducting but a *connecting* system as well. Modification in the circumstances under which the stimulus is applied may lead to the formation of *new* connections. As a result of these new connections, a new functional union is formed in the path in which the excitatory process moves and a new reaction takes place. Under certain conditions, the usual stimulus–reflex path can be modified and a new, not innate but acquired, reflex can be established. This reflex is created, Pavlov hypothesized, by "intercellular membrane, if it exists," or by "fine ramifications between the neurons."[15] The site of this coupling is probably the synapses of the neurons, especially in the cortex of the cerebrum.

In Pavlov's experiments, the reaction was intended to be kept constant (salivation), while the stimulus was manipulated (food, metronome, whistle, light, etc.). This is classic conditioning research, as distinct from another type of research, later developed by Pavlov and several American research workers, in which the reactions of the animal were manipulated.

In 1922, Pavlov concluded that conditioned reflexes could be formed in the motor region, and that the motor region, like the eye or ear, had a *receptor* function. Accordingly, the entire cortex "is only a receptor apparatus which in various ways analyzes and synthesizes the incoming stimulations. These stimulations reach the purely effective apparatus by means of descending connecting fibres."[16] The motor region in the hemispheres is a receptor of the whole movement apparatus spread over the entire organism.

Several experiments with auditory and visual stimuli in which the temporal and occipital parts of the hemisphere were removed led Pavlov to repudiate the theory of a narrow localization of centers of perception. He believed that "each *peripheral receiving apparatus* (the 'sense' organ) has in the cortex a *special central territory*, its own *terminus*, which represents its exact *projection in the brain*. Here, owing to the special construction of this area (probably the more condensed distribution of cells, the more numerous connections between them, and the absence of cells with other functions) can be effected highly complicated stimulations (the highest syntheses), also their differentiation (this highest analyses). However, the given receptor elements *transcend this central area*, extending out over a great distance, probably throughout the entire cortex, but the farther they are from their center, the more unfavorably they are disposed (in regard to their function). In consequence of this, the stimulations become more elementary, and the analyses less refined."[17]

This broadly conceived theory of brain localization permitted Pavlov to

[14] Pavlov, *Lectures on Conditioned Reflexes*, p. 361.
[15] Ivan P. Pavlov, *Experimental Psychology and Other Essays*, Philosophical Library, 1957, Chapter 9.
[16] Pavlov, *Lectures on Conditioned Reflexes*, p. 301.
[17] *Ibid.*, p. 302.

accept the idea of the compensating ability of the organism. In his experiments with partial destruction of various regions of the cortex, he had several opportunities to observe how the remaining parts of the cerebral hemispheres take over the functions of the missing parts.

These are the physiological foundations of Pavlov's contribution to psychology.

2. CONDITIONING

ꮆꮮ   The Unconditioned Reflexes

Pavlov calls the basic element of interaction between the organism and the environment *reflex*. "Definite, constant, and inborn reactions of the higher animals to certain influences of the external world, reactions taking place through the agency of the nervous system, have for a long time been the object of strict physiological investigation, and have been named reflexes." [18]

These reactions are permanent and unchangeable. They are specific; that is, a certain external stimulus acting upon a peripheral ending of a centripetal nerve becomes transformed into a nervous process, reaches a certain center in the nervous system, and excites its activity.

The reflex is positive when the stimulus calls for a process of excitation, and negative when a process of inhibition is started. Some positive reflexes, such as food, sex, etc., provoke movement *toward* the stimulating object, whereas others provoke movement *away from* or *against* harming and destructive stimuli.

Pavlov saw no reason to distinguish between reflex and instinct. Both were considered by him innate patterns of behavior, the instincts representing, as a rule, more complex reflexes or a chain of them. Pavlov believed that one particular instinct or reflex is of fundamental importance, all other reflexes being its derivatives. All life is nothing but the "realization of one purpose, viz., the preservation of life itself, the tireless labor of which may be called the general *instinct of life*. This general instinct or reflex consists of a number of separate ones. The majority of these reflexes are positive movement reflexes toward the conditions favorable for life, reflexes whose object is to seize and appropriate such conditions for the given organism, grasping and catching reflexes." The chief grasping reflex is the food reflex, or grasping for the material necessary for "completing of our vital chemical processes." [19]

In all the various actions of the instinct or reflex of life there is a certain rhythm; one desires food, becomes satiated, and is abstinent from food for a while till a new desire appears. The same holds true for collecting of ob-

[18] *Ibid.*, p. 214.
[19] *Ibid.*, p. 277.

jects, for sex, etc. Pavlov wrote: "The reflex of purpose is of great and vital importance, it is the fundamental form of the life energy. Life is beautiful and strong only to him who during his whole existence strives toward the always desirable but ever inaccessible goal, or who passes from one purpose to another with equal ardor." [20] People can collect comforts of life, knowledge, discoveries, or even most trivial things. But as soon as the reflex of purpose becomes inhibited people can even commit suicide.

Pavlov distinguished several innate or unconditioned reflexes, all of them derived from the reflex of life and each of them connected with a definite sensory mechanism or analyzer and a center in the nervous system. He distinguished between food stimulations which call out the reaction of salivation and electric current stimulations which call out the defense reaction. Destructive stimuli or, according to the "psychological terminology," pain stimuli provoke the defense reflex. Food calls for a positive reaction—grasping of the substance and eating it.

Pavlov believed that the strongest reflex was the food reflex. When the dog eats, the food center is in a state of excitation; since this is a very strong center, according to "the law of conflict of centers" all other centers will be in a state of decreased irritability and stimulation of them will have little effect.

As mentioned before, Pavlov's experiments indicated that the defense reflex of skin is second in importance to the food reflex. An animal exposed simultaneously to an electric current acting upon his skin and to a food stimulus will respond not with defense but with food reaction. However, if the destructive stimulus is directed to the bones, the center for destructive stimulation of bones appears to be stronger than the food center.

Pavlov distinguished a great number of reflexes, among them the thermic ones. There is an easy irradiation between the cold and warm centers which seems to indicate that these two centers are closely interrelated. Among other reflexes, Pavlov mentioned the reflexes of sex, of freedom, of curiosity, etc., but more detailed analysis of this part of his work will be offered in connection with his theory of personality.

The "Temporary" Reflexes

Pavlov stated that reflex, being "a constant connection between certain phenomena and the action of certain organs," is a function of the lower part of the central nervous system, while formation of new and temporary connections is the main function of the higher parts of the central nervous system. The former connections are called *unconditioned reflexes* and the temporary connections are called *conditioned reflexes*.

A conditioned reflex is formed in the presence of certain conditions. Whenever some indifferent stimulus synchronizes with a stimulus producing a definite unconditioned reflex, then, after a certain number of such co-

[20] *Ibid.*, p. 279.

incidences, the formerly indifferent stimulus administered alone calls out the same reflex as the active stimulus which it previously accompanied.

Pavlov most often used two unconditioned stimuli, the food stimulus, which produced a positive reflex, and acid, which produced a negative one. In several carefully planned experiments, the salivary secretion was conditioned to metronome beats, to the sight of geometrical figures and letters, to cutaneous stimuli, and to the odor of camphor.

A conditioned reflex occurs when an object is placed in the mouth of the dog, and some of its properties excite the simple reflex apparatus of the salivary glands; for the production of the conditioned reflex, that action must be synchronized with the action of other properties of the same object influencing other receptive regions of the body. Just as the stimulus effects, owing to certain properties of an object placed in the mouth (unconditioned reflex), may coincide with a number of stimuli arising from other objects, so all these manifold stimuli can, by frequent repetition, be turned into conditioned stimuli for the salivary glands.

In most of Pavlov's experiments, the duct of the parotid gland in the dog was diverted by a small surgical operation. The saliva then flowed through an opening in the dog's cheek into a small glass funnel. A tuning fork was sounded and eight seconds later meat powder was given to the dog. After ten times of presenting the food and the sound, some slight salivation came after the sound, and after thirty tests the saliva appeared in greater quantities (sixty drops).

Pavlov believed that conditioning takes place in the cerebral cortex. In several experiments in which both hemispheres were removed, no conditioning took place. But in later experiments by Pavlov and his associates, auditory salivary conditioned reflexes were reestablished after the removal of both temporal lobes. Several other experiments have proved that conditioning in decorticated dogs is possible but that it is "primitive and diffuse."[21]

Pavlov manipulated the temporal relationships between the unconditioned and conditioned stimuli. In most experiments the conditioned stimulus was administered from a fraction of a second to five seconds *prior* to the unconditioned stimulus and continued *simultaneously*. In this type of experiment, the conditioned response followed immediately. In some other experiments, the conditioned stimulus started much earlier, sometimes even a few minutes before the unconditioned stimulus, and continued until the latter's start. In such a case, provided a simultaneous conditioned response was already established, a *delayed conditioned response* occurred.

In another series of experiments, conditioned and unconditioned stimuli did not overlap but were separated by a time interval. As a rule, the longer the interval, the more difficult it was to condition, but always the conditioned stimulus was administered *before* the unconditioned stimulus.

[21] Elmer Culler and Fred A. Mettler, "Conditioned Behavior in a Decorticate Dog," *Journal of Comparative Psychology*, 1934, *18*, 291–303.

Pavlov interpreted the nonsimultaneous conditioning by assuming that some *trace* of the stimulus persisted in the organism after the conditioned stimulus was discontinued. When the conditioned stimulus was administered ahead of time, its trace persisted until the unconditioned stimulus was administered. Thus, the traces of the conditioned stimulus and the unconditioned stimulus were simultaneous, and a reinforcement could take place in this *trace reflex*.

The already established conditioned responses can serve as unconditioned ones in further or "higher-order" conditioning. Once the sound of the metronome evoked salivation, a black square was held before the eyes of the dog for ten seconds and after an interval of fifteen seconds, the metronome was sounded again for another thirty seconds. Now the metronome was used as an unconditioned stimulus and the black square as the conditioned one.

This higher-order conditioning brought less salivation, and a more powerful stimulus was necessary for its establishment. Pavlov's interpretation pointed to the fact that the new stimulus often acted as an additional inhibitor; thus, a much more powerful original, or unconditioned, stimulus was necessary in order to produce a higher-order conditioned reflex.

The conditioned response is not to be considered identical with the unconditioned response, although they may be very much alike. In accordance with the division of the innate reflexes, the conditioned stimuli are divided into positive (i.e., provoking excitation) and negative (i.e., provoking inhibition) stimuli. Obviously the conditioned stimuli are related, like the unconditioned ones, to the various functions of the organism, such as food, sex, and defense, and all are subordinated to the main drive or reflex of purpose.

Generalization and Discrimination

A dog conditioned to secrete saliva in response to a metronome sounding 120 times per minute, also salivated in response to a quicker or a slower sounding. The conditioned stimulus became *generalized*, and the dog responded to a wider range of stimuli. Pavlov interpreted this phenomenon by irradiation. He quoted the study of the physiologists Fritsch and Hitzig, who proved that the contraction of a group of muscles might develop into tonic convulsions of the entire body, especially when the contraction was caused by a strong or continuous stimulation.

However, if in consecutive experiments with different metronome rates only one beating rate was reinforced by feeding, all other beating rates would gradually lose their effect and not produce any response. The dog became conditioned to a certain stimulus and *discriminated* between the various beating rates. A gradual bringing closer of the reinforced and nonreinforced stimuli indicated the *degree of discrimination*. Discrimination or differentiation was explained by the above-mentioned theory of concentration, which took place after irradiation, in accordance with the law of reciprocal induction.

In one experiment, two spots on the dog's leg were chosen. Food was offered whenever one spot was lightly scratched and never when the other spot was scratched. Thd dog became conditioned to discriminate between the scratches on the two distant spots on his leg and reacted with salivation to one of them only. Gradually the nonreinforced spot was moved closer to the reinforced one. When the two spots were very close to each other, the dog responded with salivation to each of them and no discrimination took place.

These processes of generalization and discrimination were described by Pavlov as follows: "If one chosen special agent is brought for the first time into connection with a definite physiological function, then the stimulation called out by this agent, coming to a certain point of the cortex, irradiates or spreads over the corresponding receptor centers; and thus not only the single point in the brain end of the given analyzer enters into the definite connection, but the whole analyzer or a greater part of it. And only later, owing to the opposition of the inhibitory process, does the field of influence of the stimulation become smaller until at last an isolated action is obtained."[22]

Reinforcement

Pavlov describes two kinds of processes, conditioning proper and reinforcement of conditioning. As a rule, the unconditioned stimulus (food in dog's mouth) provokes the unconditioned response (salivation). The conditioned stimulus alone does not produce this response. However, when the conditioned stimulus is repeatedly presented with the unconditioned stimulus, the conditioned response is evoked. Pavlov originally assumed that the conditioned and unconditioned responses were identical, although the unconditioned response was considered innate and the conditioned acquired.

The focal point in Pavlov's theory is the concept of *reinforcement*. Reinforcement takes place whenever the conditioned stimulus is presented simultaneously, or at least at an effective interval, with the unconditioned stimulus. Repetition of reinforcement is necessary for the establishment, strengthening, and continuation of conditioned responses.

Some psychologists believe that Pavlov's reinforcement was identical with Thorndike's "reward." Woodworth wrote: "It has become clear from all this work that Pavlov's 'reinforcement' and Thorndike's 'reward' are the same. They stand for the same positive factor in establishing an association."[23]

On a closer scrutiny of Pavlov's works, we find it difficult to agree with

[22] Pavlov, *Lectures on Conditioned Reflexes*, p. 172.
[23] Robert S. Woodworth, *Contemporary Schools of Psychology*, rev. ed., Ronald, 1948, p. 66.

Woodworth. Thorndike's explanation of reward was described before (Chapter 1) and it seems to have operated with an entirely different set of concepts and situations.

Pavlov has emphatically stated that the conditioned response must be started ahead of the unconditioned one. The conditioned stimulus must not coincide exactly with the unconditioned stimulus but must precede the latter by some seconds. Why?

The answer to this question can easily be inferred from the context of Pavlov's works. The inborn connections relate food to the food centers; thus, food used as an (unconditioned) stimulus acts as a powerful agent on the food center and provokes salivation and a proper motor action. If simultaneously with this powerful stimulus a weak and neutral stimulus, such as a metronome, whistle, or flashlight, is administered, it may have an immediate and partial inhibitory effect but cannot lead to a new excitation. However, if this neutral stimulus acts for a few seconds prior to the powerful unconditioned stimulus, it will cause some degree of excitation. The unconditioned stimulus, starting shortly afterwards, causes a much greater excitation in a more powerful center, which takes over the energy from the former weak center. This flow of energy from one center to another creates new paths, new couplings, new connections, called conditioned reflexes. The stimulation which entered one center passed over to the stronger center in accordance with Pavlov's mechanistic theory.

Pavlov made it clear that the conditioned stimulus must be "weaker" than the unconditioned one; otherwise no conditioning will ever take place. "During the action of the unconditioned stimulus the positive conditioned stimulus loses its effectiveness, becomes inhibited."[24] When the dog had already started to eat, the metronome lost all its effect on the dog's nervous system.

Pavlov said that one might substitute any accidental stimulus for food. Once it is presented simultaneously with food, it will call out the same motor and secretory reaction. However, this new signaling agent must be "to a certain extent indifferent, or at least not call out some other too strong reaction."[25]

Pavlov's theory is a theory of balance of energy, regulated by induction, irradiation, and concentration, and the principle of mechanistic determinism. The "bigger" the cause, that is, the stronger the load of energy, the more effect, that is, the more conditioning. The strong stimulus produces conditioning, while the weak one becomes inhibited. This reasoning has little in common with Thorndike's law of effect or with Hull's "need reduction" or with any other sort of theory of reward.

Moreover, Thorndike's theory of learning was developed in the satisfaction–annoyance dimension, which Pavlov definitely avoided. Pavlov dis-

[24] Pavlov, *Lectures on Conditioned Reflexes*, p. 362.
[25] *Ibid.*, translator's note, p. 372.

tinguished between food and destructive stimuli, usually referred to as pleasure and pain. However, these terms in Pavlov's context do not correspond to their use by Thorndike, or even Hull, Tolman, and Skinner (cf. Chapter 4). Pavlov conditioned the dogs to salivate when they were exposed to destructive electrical stimulation (pain). Despite the damage to their skin, the dogs salivated in expectation of food, whereas no salivation was produced under a mild acid stimulation. Pavlov's solution of this puzzle does not correspond to the pleasure–pain dimension. His frame of reference was the relative strength or the *energetic load* of the stimulus and of the center of the respective analyzer. "If a strong electrical destruction of the skin, usually provoking a marked defensive reaction, is always accompanied by feeding, there can be elaborated without special difficulty the food reaction with the complete disappearance of the defensive [one]."[26] Stimulation passes over to the stronger center. "You may cut, burn, or in any way destroy the skin, but instead of the defense reaction you see only the signs of the food reflex, or subjectively speaking, of a strong appetite."[27]

Pavlov remained faithful to his mechanistic theory of charges, discharges, and balances of energy. To him, it was always the *rhythm of life*, irradiation and concentration, excitation and inhibition, and the reciprocal induction—and nothing else.

Inhibition, Extinction, and Sleep

The question of motivation again came to the fore in the problem of inhibition and extinction. In the old associationism, the law of frequency was the basic law. The ancient Romans used to say *Repetitio mater studiorum est* ("Repetition is the mother of studies"), and for centuries educators believed in the usefulness of repetition. Thorndike, even in his revised theory, assigned a place of importance to the law of exercise.

Pavlov's experiments proved beyond doubt that the repetition of the conditioned stimulus led to a gradual decline and extinction of the conditioned response unless the conditioned stimulus was accompanied by the unconditioned stimulus. Without this reinforcement, extinction always took place. Each unreinforced trial increased the extinction and the shorter the interval of time between the experiments, the faster the extinction.

Pavlov distinguished between internal and external inhibition and enumerated several kinds of internal inhibition. The first type of internal inhibition was called *extinction*. "If a well elaborated and stable conditioned stimulus be repeatedly applied at short intervals alone, without being followed by the unconditioned stimulus, then it begins to decrease and gradually becomes inactive. This is not a complete destruction of the conditioned

[26]*Ibid.*, p. 284.
[27]*Ibid.*, p. 228.

reflex, but only a temporary suspension. That it is so, is proved by the spontaneous restoration of the reflex after an interval, unless during this time something acts unfavorably to its restoration."[28]

Another kind of internal inhibition was *retardation*. When the unconditioned stimulus was applied three minutes after the beginning of the conditioned one, the conditioned stimulus remained passive during the beginning of this action and produced a conditioned response with a delay.

Experiments with differentiation of stimuli explain the third type of inhibition. In experiments with differentiation of tones, the neighboring, nonreinforced tones became inhibited, and the reinforced tone became conditioned. This was *differentiated inhibition*.

The addition of an indifferent stimulus to a well-established conditioned stimulus with reinforcement created the fourth type of inhibition, the so-called *conditioned inhibition*.

These four types of inhibition belong to the category of internal inhibition. An external inhibition takes place whenever a new agent acting on the central nervous system struggles with other agents acting there already. Pavlov said: "Translating it into the language of neurology, we may say in the given case that a strongly excited point of the central nervous system decreases the irritability of all surrounding points."[29]

An inhibition may become *disinhibited* when an external stimulus acts on an inhibited conditioned response and removes the inhibition. For example, when a moderate stimulus is introduced during the time of action of a delayed reflex, the new stimulus attracts the animal's attention and inhibits the inhibition, and saliva begins to flow immediately.

As said before, the laws of irradiation and concentration apply to both excitation and inhibition. This fact was demonstrated by Pavlov in experiments in which several conditioned stimuli were connected with one unconditioned stimulus. When the experimenter extinguished one of the conditioned stimuli, all the other conditioned stimuli became partially or fully extinguished. This was apparently a result of irradiation of the inhibition. After a while all the stimuli regained their power and only the one which was extinguished remained inactive. The inhibition receded and concentrated at its initial point in accordance with the law of concentration.

The most general inhibition is sleep. Sleep is a widely irradiated internal inhibition. Pavlov believed that sleep serves as a means toward the establishment of an equilibrium between the processes of destruction and restoration. Sleep is an innate, unconditioned reflex, but it may become conditioned.

The laws of sleep were formulated by Pavlov as follows: "A more or less enduring stimulation falling on a certain part of the hemispheres, whether or not it is of vital significance (and especially if it is without such significance), and no matter how strong it may be,—every such stimulation,

[28] *Ibid.*, p. 206.
[29] *Ibid.*, p. 215.

if it is not accompanied by simultaneous stimulation of other points, or if it is not alternated with other stimulations, leads inevitably sooner or later to drowsiness and sleep. . . . Every monotonous and continuous stimulation leads to drowsiness and sleep."[30]

Any inhibition, said Pavlov, is a partial, localized, fragmentary sleep, confined within the boundaries of the opposite process of excitation. Sleep is an inhibition spread over the entire cerebrum or a great part of it or even into the lower centers. When the inhibition spreads, sleep starts, but when the inhibition process is limited by oncoming stimuli, sleep disappears.

In collaboration with L. N. Voskresensky, Pavlov observed the consecutive stages of sleep in dogs.[31] When the dog is awake, both secretory and motor reflexes are present. The dog responds to the conditioned stimulus with salivating and takes food as soon as it is offered. At the first phase of sleep the dog does not salivate but takes the food and eats it; the secretory reflex is inhibited. When the sleep becomes deeper, in the second phase, the dog salivates but does not take the food; now the motor reflex becomes inhibited and salivation disinhibited. In the third phase of sleep, in deep and complete sleep, both salivary and motor reflexes disappear.

Other experiments shed light on the nature of *suggestion* and *hypnosis*. At the transitory stage from the waking state toward sleep, the dogs responded better to weak stimuli than to strong ones. This *paradoxical* phase of sleep corresponds to hypnotic sleep, in which the strong stimuli of the external world become weak and the weak stimulus, coming from the hypnotizer, becomes powerful.

3. THEORY OF PERSONALITY

"Lust for Life"

Pavlov was "deeply and irrevocably convinced," as stated in the Preface to his *Lectures*, that the physiological "objective" research would bring "the final triumph of the human mind over its uttermost and supreme problem—the knowledge of the mechanism and laws of human nature."[32]

Human nature, he believed, could be presented as a series of analyzing, conducting, connecting, and effecting functions of the nervous system, in accordance with the principles of determinism and equilibrium between organism and environment, and interpreted as a chain of energetic processes. These energetic processes are excitation and inhibition, which follow the laws of induction, irradiation, and concentration.

Everything else is an application of and derivation from the aforementioned principles and laws. However, observing animal and human behav-

[30] *Ibid.*, p. 307.
[31] Pavlov, *Experimental Psychology and Other Essays*, p. 345 ff.
[32] Pavlov, *Lectures on Conditioned Reflexes*, p. 41.

ior, Pavlov was compelled to introduce some additional concepts which could not possibly be derived from his mechanistic theory.

The main reflex or instinct, said Pavlov, was the *instinct of life,* or the reflex of purpose, the purpose being the preservation of life. Pavlov was never able to offer a physical, chemical, or physiological interpretation of this statement, which could not be inferred from his system of postulates and laws. He observed, for example, that humans and animals collected objects. He concluded that this was an innate reflex or instinct, related to more a general instinct. The latter was the instinct of preservation of life or the instinct of purpose. This main reflex was not interpreted by Pavlov in terms of excitation, inhibition, irradiation, concentration, and induction. It stood on its own merits as an independent hypothesis, true or false, but not a mechanistic one. Once this main instinct or reflex was postulated, all the mechanistic rules could be applied to it.

All life, according to Pavlov, is realization of the main purpose, the preservation of life itself. The general instinct of life is composed of *positive-movement* reflexes toward conditions favorable for life and *negative-movement* reflexes guarding the organism against injury.

The positive-movement reflexes are grasping, catching, keeping, exploring, and acquiring. The food reflex is the main grasping reflex. "Every day we strive for certain substances necessary for us as a material for completing our vital chemical processes; we introduce this material into our bodies, become quiet for the time being, and strive again some hours later or next day to grasp a new portion of this material, *food.*"[33] The other grasping reflexes, such as the exploratory reflex, originated from the food reflex and were probably transmitted by heredity. The same applies to the collecting reflex.

All reflexive action develops in a certain periodicity, order, and rhythm of "striving toward an object." Attainment of the object brings "a quickly developing calm and indifference." This peculiar "rhythm of life" is related to the law of reciprocal induction.

Fear and Aggression

Inasmuch as Pavlov tried to avoid "mentalistic" terms he had to explain the fact that some dogs showed reactions strikingly similar to anger and fear in humans. Pavlov regarded the aggressive actions of the dogs as a "guarding" reflex. This is primarily an unconditioned reaction of the organism against injury. Some dogs showed much more hostility and aggressiveness than others.

The aggressiveness of the dogs could be increased by conditioning in three ways: first by putting the dog in a closed and isolated room; then by limiting the dog's freedom and tying him up in a harness; and last by the behavior of the experimenter. The more authoritative and dictatorial the ex-

[33] *Ibid.,* p. 278.

perimenter, the more aggressive became the dog toward strangers. The more restrained and reserved the experimenter, the less aggressive the dog's behavior (cf. Kurt Lewin's "social climate").

Pavlov distinguished passive-defensive (fear) reactions from active-defensive (anger) actions. He believed that dogs displaying a preference for passive-defensive reactions had a small reserve of excitatory substances or that these substances were extraordinarily destructible. Thus normal fear or pathological fears represent a case of predominance of inhibitory processes which indicate the weakness of the cortical cells.

Consciousness and Speech

One of the main difficulties of psychology, said Pavlov, is the fact that it does not deal with a continuous and unbroken series of phenomena, for the psychic life is composed in a checkered fashion of "conscious and unconscious elements."

Pavlov was not much concerned with the problem of consciousness. He believed that consciousness appears as a nervous activity of a certain part of the central hemispheres, possessing at the given momenet under the present conditions a certain optimal (probably moderate) excitability; owing to this state, new conditioned reflexes are easily formed and differentiation develops quickly and successfully. At the same time, the other outlying parts function in a stereotyped manner because of their decreased irritability. The activity of these areas is subjectively described as unconscious, automatic.

In the waking state a certain part of the cerebral hemispheres is in the state of consciousness, which facilitates the optimum of conditioning and discrimination in perception. In sleep, in dreams, and in hypnosis the highest cortical functions are inhibited and the subcortical and the spinal cord centers remain active. These lower nervous centers are the seat of the unconditioned stimuli and of the basic instincts and emotions.

The conscious does not seem to be the monopoly of humans, but humans operate on a higher level of development and use symbols as representatives of reality in perception and conditioning. The main difference between men and animals lies in speech. "In the animal reality is signalized almost exclusively by stimulations and by the traces they leave in the cerebral hemispheres. . . . This is the first system of signals common to man and animals. But speech constitutes a second signalling system of reality which is peculiarly ours, being the signal of the first signals."[34]

Experimental Neurosis and Mental Disorder

In some of the experiments with differentiation, Pavlov gradually raised the pitch of the low tones, making them more and more similar to

[34] Pavlov, *Experimental Psychology and Other Essays*, p. 642.

the high ones. At a certain point the difference became so small that the dog was no longer able to distinguish between them. In some cases, the dog broke down and started to bark and bite, apparently exposed to conflicting stimuli of excitation and inhibition. This state was called by Pavlov *experimental neurosis*. He described a similar case when a light circle used as a conditioned stimulus had to be distinguished from an ellipse. These two stimuli became undistinguishable when the semi-axes of the ellipse reached the ratio of 9:8. At that time, Pavlov reported, "the whole behavior of the animal underwent an abrupt change. The hitherto quiet dog began to squeal in its stand, kept wriggling about, tore off with its teeth the apparatus for mechanical stimulation of the skin. . . . On being taken into the experimental room the dog now barked violently. . . . In short it presented all the symptoms of a condition of acute neurosis."[35]

Some animals seem to succumb easily to stress while others show more resistance. Moreover, the different types of disorder developed under stress are related to the already existing differences in the behavior of animals. Some dogs easily form positive reflexes, but it is difficult to produce in them inhibitory reflexes. The same dogs are characterized by the prevalence of excitatory reflexes and are usually very aggressive. When exposed to two opposite processes of excitation and inhibition in an experiment which called for a differentiation that overtaxed their abilities, they broke down with a neurasthenia in which the inhibitory processes disappeared. Dogs which easily formed inhibitory reflexes were characterized by a quiet, timid, and submissive behavior. When exposed to the above-mentioned experiment, they faced a nervous breakdown of a hysterical type in which the inhibitory processes prevailed. The third type, the *central* or equilibrated, took strain well.

As a result of these observations Pavlov suggested a theory of personality types based on differences in behavior of the experimental animals, including their normal and disturbed behavior. In addition, Pavlov spent years in observing mental patients and developed a theory of types of nervous system which has been utilized in Soviet psychiatry.[36]

Temperaments: Types of Nervous Systems

Pavlov attempted to classify temperamental differences in relation to excitation and inhibition. His classification included the excitatory, the inhibitory, and the central or equilibrated type, the last of which could be divided into quiet and lively types. Accordingly, Pavlov divided all his experimental dogs into four categories and believed that humans could be

[35] Pavlov, *Conditioned Reflexes*, p. 291.
[36] Samuel A. Corson (Ed.), *Psychiatry and Psychology in the USSR*, Plenum Press, 1976, pp. 5–19.

classified in the same way. His division followed the four types suggested in ancient times by Hippocrates, namely, choleric and melancholic, which were the two extreme types, and sanguinic and phlegmatic, which were the two equilibrated types.

The excitable dog, that is, the *choleric*, responds quickly to positive stimuli, becomes easily conditioned, and is not easily inhibited. He is "pugnacious, passionate, and easily and quickly irritated." The choleric type corresponds to neurasthenia.

The inhibitory type is the *melancholic*. To him "every event of life becomes an inhibitory agent; he believes in nothing, hopes for nothing, in everything he sees the dark side."[37] The melancholic type corresponds to the hysterical.

Between these two extreme and pathological types there are the two equilibrated or central or healthy types, the *phlegmatic* and the *sanguinic*. The phlegmatic is "self-contained and quiet; persistent and steadfast." The sanguinic is "energetic and very productive" but without constantly new stimulations gets bored and falls asleep easily.

Schizophrenia is, according to Pavlov, a severe hysteria. Pavlov believed that the inhibitory hysterical dogs "have very weak cortical cells easily passing over into various degrees of a chronic inhibitory condition" and "the basic features of human hysteria are also a weakness of the cortex." Schizophrenia is "an extreme weakness of the cortex, as a marked degree of hysteria. . . . In our inhibitory, hysterical dogs, by applying the functional difficulties presented by our experiments, we can make completely isolated pathologic points and foci in the cortex; in schizophrenia, in the same manner, under the influence of certain experiences of life, acting perhaps on the already organically pathological condition, gradually and constantly there appear a larger and larger number of such weak points and foci, and by degrees there occurs a breaking up of the cerebral cortex, a splitting up of its normally unified function."[38]

Cyclic psychosis represents an extreme case of neurasthenia. Neurasthenics have periods of intense activity and then times of deep depression with curtailment of their activities and abilities.

Temperaments are determined mainly by the properties of the hemispheres and of the subcortical centers. Obviously, temperaments depend on innate qualities of the nervous cells. However, environmental influences may cause substantial modifications. Nature can be modified by nurture. Pavlov wrote: "As an animal from the time of its birth is subjected to the various effects produced by its environment . . . , the final nervous activity present in an animal is an alloy of the features peculiar to the type and of the changes wrought by the environment."[39]

[37] Pavlov, *Lectures on Conditioned Reflexes*, p. 377.
[38] *Ibid.*, p. 378.
[39] *Ibid.*, vol. II, 1941, p. 178.

4. CONCLUDING REMARKS ON PAVLOV

Pavlov's theory is basically a theory of the anatomy and physiology of the nervous centers. Applied to human behavior it represents a case in radical reductionism which relates psychological phenomena to a physiological theory. It is not surprising that psychologists became aware of the importance of this new theory; beginning with J. B. Watson, they incorporated Pavlov's method and findings into their respective systems. Pavlov's theory offered the missing link between human behavior and the nervous system. It was, undoubtedly, the best offer, and psychologists accepted it wholeheartedly, very much to Pavlov's amazement.

However, psychologists very quickly left the path paved by Pavlov. Since they were unable to prove or disprove the validity of the physiological interpretation, most of them dropped it. Hull, for example, did to Pavlov what Horney did to Freud: Horney continued psychoanalysis without libido;[40] Hull continued conditioning without the nervous system.

Although Watson accepted conditioning wholeheartedly, Pavlov could never have accepted behaviorism. Pavlov's intention was to study the nervous system, not to propose a psychological theory based upon his studies. He was opposed to the oversimplified application of his theory by Watson and his associates, and criticized E. R. Guthrie as follows: "The psychologist takes conditioning as a principle of learning, and accepting the principle as not subject to further analysis, not requiring ultimate investigation, he endeavors to apply it to everything and to explain all the individual features of learning as one and the same process."[41] The physiologist, however, proceeds in the opposite direction. The physiologist is opposed to the deductive method applied by the psychologist. Pavlov criticized behaviorism for indiscriminately putting psychology and physiology together. He never denied the legitimate study of "subjective" phenomena and never identified the conscious with the nervous system. From that point of view he came, in a way, close to the Marxian philosophy (see Section 6 in this chapter), in which the human psyche was seen as a product of physiological development, but also as a separate, nonphysiological entity.

Pavlov's physiological theory was never fully proved, but it has been accepted at face value by official Soviet science. Thousands of experiments in conditioning have been conducted in the Soviet Union and most of them have applied Pavlov's theory. "The technical quality of the experiments is of very high caliber," wrote a leading expert in conditioning and in Russian psychology.[42] Obviously, experiments cannot "prove" a theory, and the same data can be interpreted in a different way. "It is unlikely," wrote Gir-

---

[40] Benjamin B. Wolman, "Psychoanalysis Without Libido," *American Journal for Psychotherapy*, 1954, *8*, 21–31.

[41] Ivan P. Pavlov, "The Reply of a Physiologist to a Psychologist," *Psychological Review*, 1932, *39*, 91–127.

[42] Gregory Razran, "Soviet Psychology Since 1950," *Science*, 1957, *126*, 1100–1107.

den, "that learning, even of 'simple' conditioning, consists of synaptic switching of unit reflexes. The 'locus' of conditioning, as a consequence, can be expected to involve some integrating cerebral ('association') area outside of the specific pathways which mediate the conditioned and unconditioned stimuli and responses. . . . The association system may very well involve both cortical-subcortical recurrent pathways, or similar reverberatory circuits at either cerebral level alone. If these latter neurological mechanisms should be found to be essential in conditioning, the search for a *locus* is futile. The neurological correlate would be a pattern or circuit, rather than some change at a given synaptic center."[43]

This problem remains, at least for the time being, unsolved and rather controversial. The Russsian research workers, although faithful to Pavlov, are aware of the problem. In the Soviet Five-Year Plan for Medicine, Section Six on Physiology and Pathology of Nervous Activity, they wrote: "Morphology has up to now not solved the problem of the method of approach to the study of finer connections, particularly of the synapses, and this significantly hampers research. . . . The synaptic apparatus was studied only with difficulty in the sphere of the spinal cord connections. So far as the structure of the synaptic connections in the subcortical and especially in the cortical formations is concerned, we have at the present time only isolated researches of exploratory character."[44]

Now was the ages-old body–soul problem solved in Pavlov's laboratories. "I shall not touch on the problem," wrote Pavlov in 1913, "of how the brain substance creates subjective phenomena, etc." We can only endeavor to find out what sort of nervous processes go on in the hemispheres of the brain when we say we are "conscious" and speak of our "conscious" activity.

Thus, the entire issue of reductionism stands as it did before Pavlov. Pavlov rejected the naïve and crude reductionism of Watson and Bekhterev, but in his own cautious reductionism he had to face unsurmountable difficulties which could not be brushed away by semantics. For the avoidance of mentalistic terms does not solve the problem. If one uses the term "defensive reaction" in order to avoid the subjective and mentalistic terms "fear" and "anger," he does not offer any interpretation of the phenomenon under consideration, nor does he solve any significant problem. When Pavlov said "life is beautiful and strong only to him who during his whole existence strives toward the always desirable but ever inaccessible goal, or who passes from one purpose to another with equal ardor," his beautiful statement was as remote from physiology as Adler's *Geltungstrieb* or Lewin's level of aspiration or Freud's Eros.

In the last years of his life, Pavlov was less rigid in his avoidance of mentalistic terms. He stated that there was no basic difference between his

[43] Edward Girden, "Some Neurological Correlates of Behavior," in H. Helson (Ed.), *Theoretical Foundations of Psychology*, Van Nostrand, 1951, p. 121.
[44] Corson, *op. cit.*

own concept of conditioning and Thorndike's connectionism, although he would prefer to replace Thorndike's trial and error by a more objective term such as "chaotic reaction."[45] Moreover, he seems to have accepted the idea that conditioning and association are basically one and the same process. He wrote: "A conditioned connection is, apparently, what we call association by simultaneity. The generalization of a conditioned connection corresponds to what is called association by similarity."[46] And furthermore: "The temporary neural connection [the conditioned connection—B. W.] is the most universal physiological phenomenon in both the animal kingdom and in ourselves. At the same time it is a psychological phenomenon—that which psychologists call association, whether it be a combination of actions, impressions, letters, words, or thoughts."[47]

Yet the gap between physiology and psychology could not be closed even by Pavlov's theories. Pavlov pushed forward the frontiers of scientific research, and his findings are a milestone in the study of human nature. The soma–psyche dichotomy, although still unresolved, came closer to some solution, and definite progress was made both in the method and in the results of research.

5. VLADIMIR M. BEKHTEREV: REFLEXOLOGY

Materialistic Monism

Vladimir M. Bekhterev was Pavlov's contemporary. Independently of Pavlov, he developed a theory of conditioning and a psychological system based on physiology. In 1904, he published a paper,[48] and in 1907, a book, under the programmatic heading *Objective Psychology*. Bekhterev believed that the future of psychology depended on objective and external observation. His idea was to create a new and thoroughly scientific psychological system which would utilize physical and physiological data with the exclusion of mentalistic, subjective, and introspectionistic elements.

In order to develop such an objective and scientific psychology, Bekhterev accepted the principle of *mechanistic* and *materialistic monism*. This principle did not represent any innovation as far as the history of philosophy and psychology was concerned. The French Encyclopedists, Diderot, La Mettrie, Helvetius, d'Holbach, and others, had expressed similar materialistic ideas. La Mettrie, especially, should be credited with presenting man as a part of material nature. Prior to Darwin, he had introduced the princi-

---

[45]Pavlov, *Experimental Psychology and Other Essays*, pp. 578 ff.
[46]*Ibid.*, p. 261.
[47]*Ibid.*, p. 251.
[48]Vladimir M. Bekhterev, "The Objective Psychology and Its Subject Matter," *Vestnik Psikhologii* (Russian), 1904, pp. 660–666, 721–731.

ple of continuity in the animal world and stressed the anatomic similarity between men and monkeys. Vogt, Büchner, and Moleschott were even more emphatic in saying that man "is what he eats," or that "nutrition determines human nature," or that "thought is secreted" by the brain.[49]

Bekhterev offered the most radical solution to the body–soul problem. Physical energy—this was his answer to the problem which perplexed the greatest minds of mankind. Bekhterev's materialistic solution encompassed both organic and inorganic nature and presented matter and psyche as phenomena of the same mechanical energy. Causation and motivation, learning and thinking became reduced to a mechanistic model of the human organism which resembled the mechanistic part of Descartes's theory. Bekhterev's all-encompassing energetic principle was even more general and elaborated than Herbart's mechanistic metaphysical psychology.[50]

Conditioning

But Bekhterev was not a metaphysician. He was an empirical scientist who, simultaneously with Pavlov, discovered conditioned reflexes. In a series of well-planned experiments conducted on humans and animals, he administered an electrical stimulus to the skin which produced a defensive reaction. Then a neutral stimulus was administered simultaneously with the electrical stimulus and the same motor response was evoked. Obviously the acquired response was a conditioned reflex, named by Bekhterev the "associate reflex."

Bekhterev conducted several ingenious experiments. In one famous experiment, the "artificially associated respiratory motor reflex" was established. Whenever sudden cold is applied to the skin surface, an unconditioned breath-catching reflex occurs. In Bekhterev's experiments, the breath-catching reflex became associated or conditioned to neutral stimuli in humans and in animals as well.

In another experiment, Bekhterev elicited flection of the leg as a conditioned response. When the leg was immobilized in such a manner that no flection could take place, another limb responded to the stimulus with flection. Obviously, *generalization* took place.

Bekhterev's experiments covered a great many areas of conditioning. In contradistinction to Pavlov's, Bekhterev's experiments are varied and include a great number of motor responses. J. B. Watson and other learning theorists applied many of Bekhterev's findings, and Bekhterev's impact on the development of conditioning is second only to Pavlov's.

Bekhterev believed that speech is a highly complicated symbolic reflex which grew from simple reflexes under the influence of experience and ed-

[49] AS. A. Lange, *History of Materialism*, Harcourt, 1925.
[50] Michael Cole and Irving Maltzman (Eds.), *Handbook of Contemporary Soviet Psychology*, Basic Books, 1969.

ucation,[51] and symbolic conditioning became incorporated into the studies of several Soviet studies (see next section). Bekhterev interpreted his empirical data in physiological terms. The cerebral processes are processes of excitation and inhibition of energy. The energy used in organic chemical processes expresses itself in two kinds of phenomena, *objective* and *subjective*. The subjective processes are those usually called psychological. They are, as a rule, accompanied by the decomposition of phosphorus, by an increase of bodily temperature, and by electrodynamic phenomena. Whenever albumin is created, whenever organic life exists, subjective processes take place. Thus Bekhterev ascribed subjective or psychological processes to all forms, levels, and species of living matter. He believed the conscious, or consciousness, to be one of the states of energy. The cerebral process, he wrote in his book *The Objective Psychology*, is at the same time "a physical process and a subjective process."[52] Consciousness is not a result, or a correlate, or a derivative of physiological process. It is a state of physical energy, related to central inhibition and resistance in the cortical physiological processes. All mental or subjective processes are secondary to physical ones; all physiological processes, even in the lowest biological species, are accompanied by corresponding subjective processes which actually form an inseparable part of the physiological processes. To put Bekhterev's ideas in simple terms, one is tempted to say that the subjective processes form the other, and less important, side of the coin. They cannot be dealt with independently; they are secondary to physical processes.

All subjective processes are accompanied by a flow of energy in the nervous cells and tissues and, as said before, all objective processes are accompanied by subjective states. However, not all subjective states are conscious.

Concluding Remarks on Bekhterev

While Pavlov cautiously formulated his physiological theories and carefully avoided sweeping generalizations, Bekhterev was less modest and less cautious in his effort to build a bridge between physiology and psychology. One may say that Bekhterev's theory of energy ascribed mental functions to organic matter even in the lowest stages of evolution and reduced the higher mental processes to simple transformations of physical energy. Bekhterev assumed unity of physical and mental processes by raising the former and lowering the latter. This oversimplification of the problem does not help its solution, for mental functions are not interpreted better by substituting for them the physical term "energy." Energy in physics is just as logical a construct as libido in psychology; both can be operationally defined and both can be inferred from empirical data, but neither is an em-

[51] Vladimir M. Bekhterev, *General Principles of Human Reflexology*, International Publishers, 1932, p. 216.

[52] Vladimir M. Beckhterev, *Objektive Psychologie–Reflexologie*, Taübner, 1913, p. 45.

pirically observed fact. And on the other end of the bridge that Bekhterev believed he had built, primitive biological phenomena do not require any mentalistic interpretation whatsoever.

6. UNDER THE BANNER OF MARX AND PAVLOV

Naïve Materialism

Russian psychologists tried very hard to combine the philosophy of Marx, Engels, and Lenin with the experimental studies of Pavlov and Bekhterev. For a while there was some confusion as to how Soviet psychology should actually develop. Two tendencies were apparent. One was represented by an extremely mechanistic approach in which physiology was expected to be substituted for psychology. This crude mechanistic-materialistic philosophy, mostly influenced by Bekhterev, led to the belief that "consciousness is a product of the inhibitions of the capitalistic system and will wither under socialism."[53] This tendency went as far as the formation of groups under the leadership of a Soviet behaviorist, Yenchman. These clubs aimed at the "liquidation of the consciousness," which was "an illusory-deceptive product of the capitalist class system." Yenchman's club hoped that "through a correct socialist peripheral uninhibited living, consciousness could be more quickly liquidated."[54] Yenchman's ideas were apparently based on an oversimplification of Bekhterev's concept of consciousness.

In the early thirties most of the Soviet psychologists gave up naïve materialism and tried to develop a psychological theory based on the foundations of dialectic materialism as expounded in the works of Marx, Engels, and Lenin. After 1931, a new era started in the history of psychology in Russia, which was, according to a reviewer, an era of a "genuine dialectical psychology, a *Soviet* psychology, based on dialectical materialism."[55]

The efforts of Soviet psychologists to bring their studies in line with official Marxist-Leninist dialectic materialism started in 1923 with Kornilov's "call to arms in behalf of a Marxist psychology frankly based on dialectical materialism."[56] This was a criticism directed against Bekhterev's "vulgar materialistic mechanism," on the one hand, and all "idealistic" theories on the other.

Kornilov believed that Marxism considers psyche a property of most

[53] Razran, *op. cit.*, p. 1101.

[54] Gregory Razran, "A Note on London's Historical Survey of Psychology in the Soviet Union," *Psychological Bulletin*, 1950, *47*, 146–149.

[55] Ivan D. London, "A Historical Survey of Psychology in the Soviet Union," *Psychological Bulletin*, 1949, *46*, 241–277.

[56] K. N. Kornilov, "Psychology in the Light of Dialectic Materialism," in C. Murchison (Ed.), *Psychologies of 1930*, Clark University, 1930, pp. 243–278.

organized matter. Dialectic materialism does not reduce psychological processes to physiology; thus Kornilov proposed a theory of reactions of the psyche to the material world. This theory of *reactology* is the study of human reactions to stimulations coming from without. Psyche and conscious were mere "subjective reflection" of what was going on in the nervous tissues.

Kornilov's theory was exposed to bitter criticism. The critics maintained that, while Kornilov's opposition to Bekhterev was justified, his reactology failed to represent faithfully the Marxian point of view. It seems worthwhile, therefore, to explain Marx's approach to psychology.

Dialectic Materialism

R. S. Peters, who edited and abridged *Brett's History of Psychology,* explained the shift from biology toward the social sciences as follows: "Psychologists became increasingly aware that men were very different from animals not because they had a soul which animals did not have, but because they had a very complex social environment. They began to appreciate the large element of truth in Marx's saying that it is not the consciousness of man that determines his existence, but his social existence that determines his consciousness."[57]

However, Marx's influence on psychology is much deeper than is stated by Peters, because Marx's theory emphasized the two-way process in the man–nature relationship. "Marx is never weary of repeating that the distinctive character of social development as opposed to natural processes of development lies in the fact that human consciousness is involved," and human beings "actively participate in making their own history."[58] Putting it in terms of the dialectical triad, the natural environment is the thesis, human needs and desires, the antithesis, and the resulting human ideas and actions, the synthesis. Moreover, in Marx's own words, "by acting on the external world and changing it, man changes his own nature."[59]

Karl Marx was critical of mechanistic-materialistic theories. He wrote in 1845 as follows: "The materialist doctrine that men are products of circumstances and upbringing and that, therefore, changed men are products of other circumstances and changed upbringing, forgets that circumstances are changed precisely by men and that the educator himself must be educated."[60] In other words, there is a bipolar process. "Men are producers of their concepts. . . . Consciousness can never be anything else than con-

[57] R. S. Peters (Ed.), *Brett's History of Psychology,* Allen & Unwin, 1953, p. 702.
[58] Sidney Hook, *Toward the Understanding of Karl Marx,* Gollancz, 1933, p. 78.
[59] Karl Marx, *Capital,* Vol. I, p. 198.
[60] Karl Marx, "Theses on Feuerbach," in Emile Burns (Ed.), *A Handbook of Marxism,* Random, 1935, p. 229.

scious existence. . . . It is not consciousness that determines life but life that determines consciousness."[61]

Thought and consciousness, wrote F. Engels in 1877, "are products of the human brain and the man himself is a product of nature. . . . The products of the human brain, being in the last analysis also products of nature, do not contradict the rest of nature but are in correspondence with it."[62]

Friedrich Engels, wrote Lenin, "constantly and exclusively speaks in his works of things and their mental images of reflections (*Gedanken, Abbilder*)" and "mind itself is only the highest product of matter." According to Lenin, "Materialism in full agreement with natural science takes matter as the *prius,* regarding consciousness, reason and sensation as derivative, because in a well expressed form it is connected only with the higher forms of matter (organic matter)." For sensation "is connected with a particular kind of processes in matter organized in a particular way" and "there still remains so much to investigate, so much to find out about how matter, devoid of sensation, is related to matter which, though composed of the same atoms (or electrons), is yet endorsed with a definite faculty of sensation. Materialism, by putting clearly the problem, gives impetus to continual experimentation, thus making possible its solution."[63]

And this is precisely why Lenin, as the head of the Soviet government, was critical of Bekhterev and offered wholehearted support to Pavlov. While Bekhterev was obviously representative of a naïve materialism, Pavlov's theories were not identical with, but more acceptable to, Marxism. Pavlov dealt with nervous processes only but considered psychology the eventual function of higher organized organic matter.[64]

The correspondence between Lenin's and Pavlov's points of view becomes more evident from the following quotation from Lenin. "Engels opposed the 'vulgar' materialists, Vogt, Büchner and Moleschott because they assumed that thought is secreted by the brain as bile is secreted by the liver." "For every scientist . . . , as well as for every materialist, sensation is nothing but a direct connection of the mind with the external world; it is the transformation of energy of external excitation into a mental state."[65]

Natural science "holds that thought is the function of the brain, that perceptions, that is, the images of the external world, are effects of external objects on our sense organs. The materialistic elimination of the dualism of mind and body consists in this that the existence of the mind is shown to

[61] Karl Marx, "German Ideology," in Burns (Ed.), *A Handbook of Marxism,* pp. 212–213.

[62] Friedrich Engels, "Anti-Dühring," in Burns (Ed.), *A Handbook of Marxism,* p. 233.

[63] Vladimir I. Lenin, "Materialism and Empirico-criticism," in Burns (Ed.), *A Handbook of Marxism,* pp. 636, 654.

[64] Strangely enough, Bekhterev tried very hard to adjust his theories to Marxism, while Pavlov was always independent and intransigent. After a prolonged period of trial and error Soviet psychologists adjusted their theories to Pavlov's findings.

[65] Lenin, *op. cit.,* pp. 643, 647.

be dependent upon that of the body, in that mind is declared to be secondary, a function of the brain, or a reflection of the outer world."[66]

Psychology and Culture

In their effort to create a truly Marxist psychology, Vygotskii, Luria,
Leontyev, and others developed a psychological system related to the history of culture.[67] Their approach resembled that of Spranger and Dilthey,
but in the vein of the materialist philosophy of history of Karl Marx. While
the *Kulturwissenschaft* psychology (cf. Chapters 10 and 11) developed in an
atmosphere of the neo-Kantian philosophy with profound Hegelian influences, the Soviet "kulturpsychologists" tried to relate the development of
the human psyche to consecutive socioeconomic states of development. The
history of mankind in its economic aspects was regarded by Luria, Leontyev, Vygotskii, and others as the frame of reference for psychology. The
human mind was adapting itself to the economic development.

These studies utilized Marx's philosophy of history, the gestalt sign
theory, and Pavlov's conditioning, with the emphasis put on the Marxian
concept of the human psyche as a "superstructure" which reflects the more
basic material and economic foundations of life and, in return, influences
these foundations. To repeat Marx's rules in this issue: man is the product
of the environment but he can change the environment.

However, even this approach did not satisfy the critics because the
"cultural school" in Soviet psychology apparently failed in the solution of
the soma–psyche problem. Soviet psychologists were called to pay more attention to physiology, for, as Chernakov explained, "The Marxist conception of the psyche starts with a recognition of the fact that the psyche or
consciousness is a product of the brain and is a reflection of the outside
world; which means that psychic phenomena are derivative from, and dependent upon, physical reality, while the latter is independent of the
psyche and primary, because the outside world by its very nature is material and develops according to laws governing the movement of matter"[68]

This approach clearly indicated the direction in which the Soviet psychology had to go. Psyche is not a form of matter "but only a reflection of
matter," a reflection of objective reality, a reflection of the outside world.
But how could one develop a psychological theory within these limits?

The only open avenue was to relate psychological data to physiological
findings, and to develop a psychology which could serve as a "superstructure" to physiology. The physiological foundations for such a psychology

---

[66] *Ibid.*, p. 657.

[67] A. N. Leontiev and A. R. Luria, "The Psychological Ideas of L. S. Vygotskii," in B. B. Wolman (Ed.), *Historical Roots of Contemporary Psychology*, Harper and Row, 1968.

[68] E. T. Chernakov, "Protiv Idealisma Metafiziki v Psikhologii" ("Against Idealism and Metaphysics in Psychology"), *Voprosy Filosofii*, 1948, No. 3, quoted from J. Wortis, *Soviet Psychiatry*, Williams & Wilkins, 1950, p. 261.

were built by Sechenov and Pavlov. This is the direction psychological inquiry in the U.S.S.R. took, as represented in the writings of Rubinstein and, to an even greater extent, in the studies of the last ten years.

S. L. Rubinstein: Toward a Synthesis

One of the outstanding theorists who tried to combine Pavlovianism and Marxism with empirical studies in psychology was S. L. Rubinstein. Rubinstein is undoubtedly the most independent and original among the Soviet psychologists, and for a while he was the most accepted one.

Rubinstein distinguished two aspects in human personality: experience and perception. The term "experience," which indicates the influence of William Stern (cf. Chapter 11), represents the innermost and primary psychological fact. "The experiences of an individual comprise the subjective part of his real life, the subjective aspect of the way-of-life of one's personality." [69]

Experiences form the "dim background" out of which the consciousness emerges. There is no clear dividing line between the dim experiences and the conscious perception; drives and emotions "stem from a stimulation coming from the organism itself . . . drives reflect the organic need and their source is somatic." [70]

The unconscious drives and feelings originate in the inner organs of the body. "The nervous impulses which travel from the interoceptors to the central nervous system do not arrive in the majority of cases to the higher nervous centers in the cortex; thus they do not produce perceptions, although they do modify the functional state of the nervous system, mainly its sensory organs." [71]

Once these unconscious drives and emotions which stem from the interoceptors of the inner organs become directed toward the external world, they become conscious. The conscious is what is related to the perception of objects. However, even the perception of objects is not entirely a "reflection of the outer world" but is colored by emotions which are an "immediate experience." Emotions do not represent the "content of the object" but the subjective "state of the individual" and his "attitude" to the object. [72]

"When an individual becomes aware of the object which serves for the gratification of the urge and which is the aim of the drive, . . . the drive necessarily turns into a desire. . . . This transformation . . . brings about a change in the inner nature of the drive. . . . The drive becomes conscious." [73] In other words, an object-directed drive is no longer unconscious; the perception of objects is the sign of the conscious.

[69] S. L. Rubinstein, *Foundations of General Psychology* (Russian), Uchpedgiz, 1946, p. 7.
[70] *Ibid.*, p. 627.
[71] *Ibid.*, p. 199.
[72] *Ibid.*, p. 488.
[73] *Ibid.*, p. 628.

In this manner Rubinstein tried to develop a psychological theory based on empirical data, faithful to Marx's distinction between "reality" and "consciousness" and closely related to Pavlov's physiological findings. Undoubtedly Rubinstein came quite close to the theoretical interpretations of human behavior as developed by European and American psychologists, yet remaining faithful to Marx and Pavlov. Some of his critics were dissatisfied with this rapprochement. Chernakov criticized Rubinstein for a "compromise" with Western psychology and Freudian influence.[74] The latter seems to be undeniable.

Back to Pavlov

In 1950, the joint meeting of the Soviet Academy of Sciences and the Soviet Academy of Medical Sciences decided to "reconstruct on the basis of Pavlov's teachings: physiology, psychology, pathology, psychiatry. . . ." Since then, as pointed out by G. Razran in an excellent analysis of Soviet psychology, the entire field of psychological research in the Soviet Union has become subordinated to an orthodox Pavlovianism. "Like Marx, Engels, Lenin and (until recently) Stalin, Pavlov is now a Soviet classic, endowed with almost theologistic prescience of certainties and surely above criticism and impugnations—a doctrine which Pavlov himself, the thoroughgoing empiricist and antidogmatist, fought all his life, and indeed, considered ridiculous."[75]

The Russians felt that Pavlov and Marx could be reconciled. With the emphasis shifting to Pavlov, studies in conditioning moved into the foreground. But while in the United States conditioning developed mainly into a nonphysiological learning theory, in the U.S.S.R. the physiological elements in conditioning dominate the picture. Some highly specialized studies in conditioning of inner organs deserve to be mentioned.

These experiments dealing with the conditioning of inner organs serve as a bridge between the physiology of the inner organs and the psychology of the learning process. In a highly interesting experiment conducted by Balakschina and reported by Bykov, conditioned reflexes were formed in denervated kidneys and in kidneys with the hypophysis destroyed. When the kidneys were denervated and the hypophysis was destroyed, the conditioning took place. In such a case the kidneys function as a physical and not as a physiological apparatus.[76]

What is the difference between a physical and a physiological apparatus? Bykov believes that irradiation and concentration of excitation and inhibition, and the positive and negative induction, will be understood

[74] Chernakov, op. cit., p. 267.
[75] Razran, "Soviet Psychology Since 1950," Science, 1957, 126, 1100–1107.
[76] Konstantin M. Bykov, The Cerebral Cortex and the Inner Organs (W. H. Gantt, Trans. and Ed.), Chemical Publishing Co., 1957, pp. 36 ff.

with the progress of "the chemical dynamics of the mediating substances in the central nervous system." But this would mean not only that psychology could be replaced by physiology but that physiology could be replaced by chemistry. Is this bold reductionism possible today? Will it ever be possible? The statements of Pavlov and his disciples are hopeful, and the future will show whether they were justified.

Bykov and his associates (W. N. Tschernigowski, G. P. Konradi, and others) have proved the existence of inner receptors in practically all inner organs and have utilized their discovery for far-reaching research in interoceptory conditioning. They had to confront a problem which occupies one of the main positions in the American theory of learning (cf. Chapter 4), that is, the problem of pleasure and pain in conditioning. Bykov remarked that "the absence of pain sensations does not necessarily mean the absence of other receptors," and it "has been definitely proved that some organs . . . are devoid of pain sensibility."[77] Bykov found that several organs have receptors and that their functions could be conditioned, but there is a complete absence of any pain reaction. Among those organs are the *peritoneum viscerale*, the surface of the cerebral hemispheres, and probably some parts of the intestine.

The pain fibers terminate in the thalamus (the lateral dorsothalamic fasciculus). However, several experiments involving speech signals (Pavlov's "second order" conditioning) gave "convincing evidence of the role of the cerebral cortex in pain reception."[78] Some experiments were carried out with anesthesia (novocain) of the stimulated area. The unconditioned stimuli gave no pain reaction (zero plethysmogram), but in combination with the conditioned stimuli a reaction was evoked, namely, a constriction and dilation of vessels. Moreover, Bykov reports experiments conducted by Pshonik which proved that "the cortex has the capacity for inhibiting or annulling pain by turning pain sensations into subdolorotic sensations."[79]

Bykov tried to prove that there is no reason to distinguish between reactions to the impulses coming from without (*milieu extérieur*) and those coming from within the organism (*milieu intérieur*). Both kinds of receptor conditioning can take place.

The main differences between *interoceptors* and *exteroceptors* was stated by Bykov as follows: First, in the great majority of cases the stimulation of the exteroceptors has been accompanied by a subjectively perceived sensation, while the stimulation of the interoceptors is either not perceived subjectively at all or at least not accompanied by definite and localized sensations. The stimulation of exteroceptors may lead to variant actions not determined by the nature of the stimulus or the stimulated organ. The stimulation of interoceptors leads to a reaction which may be complicated but is

[77] *Ibid.*, p. 279.
[78] *Ibid.*, p. 344.
[79] *Ibid.*, p. 341.

invariably determined by the nature of the stimulus and the stimulated organ.[80] Moreover, "impulses conveyed from visceral receptors should be characterized as subthreshold impulses as compared to those conveyed from exteroceptors."[81] They may cause "subconscious" sensations.

Bykov and his associates have conducted experiments in which the existence of interoceptors in the stomach was proved. At the time of pouring water into a dog's stomach, his hindfoot was exposed to an electric current which led to a reflex of bending of the leg. Thereafter, pouring water into the stomach led to the foot reaction, which became a conditioned reflex. Obviously the walls of the stomach contain some receptory apparatus (analyzer) which is capable of communicating with the cerebral centers. In several other experiments, interoceptory conditioning was performed on kidneys, gall, and heart, and even inner secretion was increased or decreased. The inner organs became conditioned to tactile, electrical, chemical, vocal, and other stimuli.

Concluding Remarks on Soviet Psychology

With the growing emphasis on physiological factors, and improved and more precise methods of study, Soviet psychologists were able to enter such new areas of research as speech, learning, and perception.[82] In contradistinction to American psychologists, the Russians show conformity to one philosophy and they work within set limits of conceptualization centered around Marx and Pavlov, with Pavlov's influence dominating.

Within these limits they have achieved significant results in the direction of both interoceptive conditioning and "higher order" conditioning to words and symbols.[83] One wonders whether the results achieved are related to their philosophy or to a concentrated effort or to other factors. Whatever the reasons, the achievements in conditioning are considerable.

Soviet psychology has tried very hard to move toward the hoped-for solution of the soma–psyche dichotomy. There is no doubt that significant progress has been made as far as the physiological part is concerned; interoceptive conditioning offers new vistas in the study of unconscious processes and the pleasure–pain issue. But one cannot help wondering how much truth there is in what Pavlov said: that "the moment when the natural and inevitable joining and fushion of the psychological and physiological, of the subjective and the objective, will be accomplished is sure to come." Is this optimism justified? Is the answer near or at all possible? Are we coming close to crossing the soma–psyche bridge? Let us leave the discussion of this question to the last chapter of the book.

[80] *Ibid.*, p. 244.
[81] *Ibid.*, p. 277.
[82] Simon Brian (Ed.), *Psychology in the Soviet Union*, Stanford University, 1957.
[83] A. R. Luria, *The Nature of Human Conflicts or Emotion, Conflict and Will*, Liveright, 1932.

The following section describes the most recent developments in Soviet psychology.

7. CURRENT SOVIET PSYCHOLOGY

One can divide the history of Soviet psychology into three major periods. The beginning period (1917–1931) covers the years of Pavlov's classical experiments. The establishment of Marxist psychological theory took place in the years 1931 to 1945. Lastly, the present period is characterized by further developments of the philosophical-theoretical foundations of Soviet psychology. The first two periods have already been discussed in this chapter. At the end of the Second World War there was an emergence of new branches of psychology and a renewed interest in traditional fields of psychology. This interest took the form of utilizing concepts generated by disciplines somewhat related to psychology, such as cybernetics and information theory. Current psychological research in the U.S.S.R. has incorporated advanced statistical methods and the mathematical models of psychological functioning. Currently, educational psychology and engineering psychology have been given considerable attention and social psychology is gradually becoming more popular. Medical and forensic psychology, on the other hand, are rather neglected.[84]

R. M. Krauss, in discussing Soviet social psychology, pointed out that although much of Soviet psychology is not termed social psychology, it has always emphasized social determinants of behavior because this emphasis is such a crucial aspect of Marxist philosophy. Examples of this kind of social psychology can be seen in the work of psychologists such as Vygotskill, Leontyev, and Luria. In the field of social psychology proper there are four broad categories: (1) social psychological phenomena in large groups, (2) social psychological phenomena in small groups, (3) social psychological phenomena in special or specific groups, and (4) social psychological factors in personality development. In contrast to empirical preferences in social psychology in the United States, which deal less and less in terms of broadly based general theories, Soviet social psychology has a strong theoretical orientation based on the philosophical teachings of Marx and Lenin. Social psychology in the United States tends to focus on the consequences for social behavior of individual psychological processes, whereas Soviet social psychology focuses on social interactions. The greatest differences between the two countries lie in methodology. Psychologists in the Soviet Union rarely utilize the laboratory experiments which are so popular in the United States; rather, they conduct their studies in natural settings or do

[84] Josef Brozek, "Union of Soviet Socialist Republics: Psychology," in B. B. Wolman (Ed.) *International Encyclopedia of Psychiatry, Psychology, Psychoanalysis and Neurology*, Aesculapius, 1977, Volume 11, pp. 328–330.

conventional descriptive studies. Experimental designs in the U.S.S.R. are simple and rather infrequent; elaborate statistical analyses are rarely done.[85]

In the area of learning disabilities, the Soviet view of psychoeducational diagnosis follows largely from the Soviet model of human intellectual development, which differs from the model in the United States. The Soviet view of intellectual development is derived from a metatheory based on the notion of dialectics and remotely resembles Piaget's approach.[86]

L. S. Vygotskii's work in the area of thought and language is world renowned. His 1934 monograph was translated thirty years later. It represents an early study of psycholinguistics and the interrelations between intellective and verbal activity. Vygotskii theorized that thought and language were the keys to human consciousness; it is through words that thought develops, for words are the tools of mental activity. Through words the child internalizes overt behavior and external dialogue is transformed into inner speech or thought.

A. R. Luria, who was a close associate of Vygotskii, went on to state that, first, external speech and, later, internal speech represent the chief mechanisms of voluntary behavior. As the child develops the regulatory function of speech, he moves from words as direct impulses to action, toward a gradual use of words as carriers of meaning. Luria stated that by five, the child shifts from external to internal speech, which is crucial to both thought and voluntary behavior.[87]

Luria has made a significant contribution to the study of the impact of brain lesions on mental functions. He did not accept the concepts of traditional "morphopsychology" in which complex mental functions are either rigidly assigned to a specialized center or are believed to be the result of overall brain activity. Luria maintained that complex mental activities are carried out by a group of integrated structural units, both central and peripheral. He made extensive studies of brain injuries. Damaged brain cells do not regenerate, but there is a partial restoration of impaired brain function. Luria's studies covered the restoration process in movement, visual perception, speech, thinking, and motivation. According to Luria, there are three types of mechanisms involved in the restoration of brain function: (1) restoration of temporarily inhibited functions and restoration of synaptic transmission by pharmacological and/or psychological methods; (2) substitution of the one hemisphere by the other hemisphere; and (3) formation of

[85] Robert M. Kraus, "Social Psychology in the Soviet Union: Some Comments," in Samuel A. Corson and Elizabeth O. Corson (Eds.) Psychiatry and Psychology in the USSR, Plenum Press, 1976, pp. 59–82. See also Wolman, B. B. (Ed.) Historical Roots of Contemporary Psychology, Harper and Row, 1968.

[86] Robert H. Wozniak, "Intelligence, Soviet Dialectics and American Psychometrics: Implications for the Evaluation of Learning Disabilities," in Samuel A. Corson and Elizabeth C. Corson (Eds.) Psychiatry and Psychology in the USSR, Plenum Press, 1976, pp. 121–132.

[87] A. N. Leontiev and A. R. Luria, "The Psychological Ideas of L. S. Vygotskii," in B. B. Wolman (Ed.) Historical Roots of Contemporary Psychology, Harper and Row, 1968, pp. 338–367.

compensatory connections between different areas of the cortex.[88] These mechanisms facilitate the development of a new *functional system* evolved from areas of the brain which were not previously involved in the activity that was performed by the damaged brain areas.

Blyuma V. Zeigarnik, who wrote *The Pathology of Thinking*, is noted for her work in Soviet psychology and psychiatry. She defines thinking in a Marxist-Leninist framework as "a generalized and indirect reflection of the outside world" which is manifested in daily life as acquisition and assimilation of facts and utilization of knowledge. Thinking then entails the processes of analysis and synthesis in which both stages of sensory and rational cognition are integrated into a single activity. "Stressing the dialectical unity of these two stages of cognition (sensory and rational), the founders of Marxism-Leninism point out that it is the rational stage which makes it possible to probe in the essence of things and events in nature and society."[89]

Zeigarnik concentrated on thought disturbances in psychiatric patients. In her study, she grouped patients into nine categories and then, through the use of various tests, examined disturbances in three aspects of thinking: (1) abstraction and generalization, (2) logical trend of thought, and (3) the purposive and critical character of thought. Zeigarnik found that specific types of disordered thought are not strictly limited to particular nosological categories. Therefore, psychological examination of thought disorders can aid in diagnosis, but cannot be the sole basis for the determination of a specific diagnosis.[90]

[88] Alexander R. Luria, "Neuropsychological Analysis of Focal Brain Lesions," in B. B. Wolman (Ed.) *Handbook of Clinical Psychology*, McGraw-Hill, 1965, pp. 689–754.

[89] Josef Brozek, "Soviet Psychology," in M. H. Marx and W. A. Hillex (Eds.) *Systems and Theories in Psychology*, McGraw-Hill, 1973, pp. 521–548.

[90] Carson, *op. cit.*, pp. 126–127.

3

Behaviorism and Reductionism

1. JOHN B. WATSON: PSYCHOLOGY AS THE SCIENCE OF BEHAVIOR

Psychology without Consciousness

The man who crossed the bridge and closed the gap between the study of animal behavior and the study of human behavior was John Broadus Watson. Watson combined into one system the philosophical pragmatism of James, the psychological functionalism of Dewey, the experimental method of animal psychology of Yerkes, and the conditioning of Pavlov and Bekhterev.

Watson's system is based on *determinism, empiricism, reductionism,* and *environmentalism.* These four principles guided Watson's work and were incorporated with great consistency into his research. In Watson's own eyes his psychological system is such that "given the stimulus, psychology can predict what the response will be. Or, on the other hand, given the response, it can specify the nature of the effective stimulus."[1]

In accordance with radical empiricism Watson rejected anything that could not be observed from without. In his bias against unobserved phenomena, he outdistanced Pavlov, and in his zeal for a radical reductionism, he was matched only by Bekhterev.

"I do not wish unduly to criticize psychology," said Watson in 1913. "It has failed signally, I believe, during the fifty-odd years of its existence as an experimental discipline, to make its place in the world as an undisputed natural science. . . . The time seems to have come when psychology must discard all reference to consciousness; when it need no longer delude itself into thinking that it is making mental states the object of observation. . . ."[2]

Instead, Watson proposes a psychology, "which I should attempt to build up that would take as a starting point, first, the observable facts that organisms, man and animal alike, do adjust themselves to their environ-

[1] John B. Watson, *Psychology from the Standpoint of a Behaviorist,* Lippincott, 1919, p. 10.
[2] John B. Watson, "Psychology as the Behaviorist Sees It," *Psychological Review,* 1913, *20,* 158–177.

ment by means of hereditary and habit equipments. These adjustments may be very adequate or they may be so inadequate that the organism barely maintains its existence; secondly, that certain stimuli lead the organisms to make these responses. In a system of psychology completely worked out, given the stimuli the response can be predicted."[3]

Watson's psychology dealt with overt and observable behavior of the organism, its muscles, glands, and tissues. Watson hoped that all human behavior could be interpreted in physical-chemical terms. "Psychology, as the behaviorist views it, is a purely objective, experimental branch of natural science which needs introspection as little as do sciences of chemistry and physics. It is granted that the behavior of animals can be investigated without appeal to consciousness. . . . The position is taken here that the behavior of man and the behavior of animals must be considered on the same plane. . . .

"This suggested elimination of states of consciousness as proper objects of investigation in themselves will remove the barrier from psychology which exists between it and other sciences. The findings of psychology become the functional correlates of structure and lend themselves to explanation in physical-chemical terms."[4]

In his programmatic book Watson wrote as follows: "Psychology as a science of consciousness has no community of data. The reader will find no discussion of consciousness and no reference to such terms as sensation, perception, attention, image, will and the like. . . . I frankly do not know what they mean, nor do I believe that anyone can use them consistently."[5]

Nurture versus Nature

Watson's idea underwent a definite evolution. Until 1915, there was no mention of conditioning. In 1915, in his presidential address to the American Psychological Association, he took up the matter of conditioned reflexes. In his book in 1919, conditioned reflexes became very prominent; in 1920, he reported conditioning of fears in humans.

In 1919, Watson still admitted the existence of innate instincts and emotions but limited them to very few relatively simple responses—fear, rage, and love. In 1925, he completely discarded the instinct theory. He was undoubtedly under the influence of Z. Y. Kuo (see Chapter 5 Section 1), who believed that all human behavior is learned.

Watson took a radical environmentalistic stand in the nature–nurture controversy. He did not deny the fact that certain patterns of behavior were innate but said they were very limited in number and rather unimportant in comparison with the role of experience. "Give me a dozen healthy infants, well formed," he declared, ". . . to bring them up in and I'll guaran-

[3] *Ibid.*
[4] *Ibid.*
[5] Watson, *Psychology from the Standpoint of a Behaviorist*, p. xii.

tee you to take any one at random and train him to become any type of specialist I might select—doctor, lawyer, artist, merchant-chief and, yes, even beggar-man and thief, regardless of his talents, penchants, tendencies, abilities, vocations, and race of his ancestors."[6] Yet Watson did not reject the concept of instinct. He believed that instinct was "a hereditary pattern reaction, the separate elements of which are movements principally of the striped muscles. It might otherwise be expressed as a combination of explicit congenital responses unfolding serially under appropriate stimulation." Instinct is a system of inherited or unconditioned reflexes; instinctive activity is a complex response of a series of reflexes to "sensory stimuli in contact with the animal's body or at a distance in his environment."[7]

Theory of Learning

Watson was critical of Thorndike's annoyers and satisfiers, which had the flavor of subjectively perceived emotions and introspection. Of all the laws of association, Watson preferred the laws of frequency and recency. Most frequent and most recent acts were the successful ones; in animal learning, the proper interpretation of learning was the one offered by the laws of frequency and recency.

Bekhterev's and Pavlov's conditioning solved Watsons's difficulties. Watson admitted that the term "habit formation," which he had been using in his writings, was rather vague. The conditioned response offered a better way of interpreting learning and could be "looked upon as the unit of what we had been calling *habit*." And certainly, added Watson, from that point on he gave the master his due credit.

Yet Watson's theory of conditioning was never an exact translation and application of Pavlov's theory. Watson believed that the conditioned stimulus was a *substitute* stimulus for the unconditioned one. Such a statement was never made by Pavlov.

Experiments in conditioning in humans were first performed by Pavlov's disciple Krasnogorski. In the United States, Florence Mateer published in 1918 a volume in which she reported her experiments in conditioning in children. She used the method of placing a bandage over the eyes of the child as a conditioned stimulus before food was placed in the child's mouth.[8]

Conditioning, or association by contiguity, became incorporated into Watson's theory. Watson applied conditioning to most complex forms of learning. He considered trial-and-error learning a simple case in conditioning. Watson maintained that the right response was the most recent one and it occurred more frequently during the process of learning, since it ap-

[6] John B. Watson, *Behaviorism*, Kegan Paul, 1925, p. 82.
[7] *Ibid.*, p. 262.
[8] Florence Mateer, *Child Behavior, a Critical and Experimental Study of Young Children by the Method of Conditioned Reflexes*, Badger, 1918.

peared, at any rate, at least once on each trial. As said before, Watson incorporated Thorndike's sublaws of trial and error in his theory of learning while consistently rejecting Thorndike's law of effect.

Perception, Thought, and Speech

All human behavior was divided by Watson into *explicit* and *implicit*. Explicit behavior included all observable activities such as walking, talking, cutting wood, and smiling. Implicit behavior included the secretion of glands, some muscle contractions, and visceral and nerve functions.

Sensation and perception presented certain difficulties for behaviorism. Introspectionists tried to interpret these phenomena with the help of the descriptions given by the perceiving subject. Behaviorists, however, reject the notion of "sensation" because no one can observe another person's sensations. What can be observed is the response to a certain stimulus, be it visual, auditory, or olfactory. This is the method applied in animal psychology; the experimental animal responds to stimuli, and both stimulus and response are observable data.

In the controversy with the introspectionists, Watson suggested the *verbal report* as the way out. Speech is an act of overt behavior just like any other act. It is a movement of lips and tongue, push of air, sound, etc. Verbal report is a sort of motor response to sensory stimuli. It should be considered at its face value like any other motor response. When the subject says, for example, "I do not see," he has said that he does not see. The verbal report "registers" the stimulus just as the thermometer registers the temperature.

Even the range of perception, from the red to the violet end of the spectrum, for instance, could be studied objectively, and Watson suggested the following procedure: By the use of any wavelength and of an electric shock, a conditioned reflex could be established. "We then increase the length of the wave rather sharply and, if the reflex appears, we again increase the wave length. We finally reach a point where the reflex breaks down, even when punishment is used to restore it. . . ." A similar procedure should be applied to the violet end. "In this way we determine the individual's range just as surely as if we had stimulated the subject with monochromatic lights varying in wave lengths and asked him if he saw them."[9] The verbal report of the subject saying "I do not see," Watson believed, can safely be considered a part of the objective experimental procedure.

Watson went even further in his reductionistic endeavor: Perception is a function of sensory nerves which "register" the stimuli and transmit them to the brain hemispheres. In accordance with the physiological theory of conditioning, the brain is not only a conducting but a connecting apparatus. The nervous impulses coming from the sensory receptors are transferred to the motor centers and lead to a motor reaction. Human behavior

[9] Watson, *Psychology from the Standpoint of a Behaviorist*, p. 35.

can be reduced to a sensory-central-motor chain of stimuli and responses. The same applies to the processes of memory. They are created by residues or afterimages of sensory stimulations combined with kinesthetic elements of the muscles of the mouth in implicit speech processes.

The child learns to speak through his own unlearned vocalization. Words are acquired by conditioning. The child learns speech and through speech establishes a firm contact with his environment.

In the beginning, speech is overt behavior—"explicit," as Watson calls it. It is a sort of manipulation of the situation and environment by substituting words for overt manual movement. Not all movements are relegated to the larynx; shrugging the shoulders, nodding the head, frowning and grimaces, gestures and cries—all these are responses to a situation.

The most economic way of reaction is speech. Speech is thinking and thinking is speech. The overt expression of words, acquired by conditioning, becomes modified. As the child grows, he learns to avoid too much overt expression. He learns to speak subvocally, and no one can hear his voiceless speech. This voiceless speech, as well as vocal speech, is identical with thinking. The only difference between the two types of speech lies in the fact that the former is an implicit kind of behavior while the latter is explicit. Obviously, neither kind of speech requires any "consciousness" or introspection.

As a rule, verbal-language reactions accompany manual and visceral ones. Man controls his behavior by verbalizing it; it is easier to manipulate and experiment with words than to manipulate objects.

Emotions

"An emotion," says Watson, "is a hereditary 'pattern-reaction' involving profound changes of the bodily mechanisms as a whole, but particularly of the visceral and glandular systems. By pattern-reaction we mean that the separate details of response appear with some constancy, with some regularity, and in approximately the same sequential order each time the exciting stimulus is prescribed." [10]

Emotions stem from reflex activity in the erogenous zone. There are two kinds of this complex reflex activity called emotion. One leads toward movement; this is the *tumescence* reflex activity. The other type, the *detumescence* reflex, releases "the movements of avoidance."

Watson maintained that three innate emotions could be found in human infants: rage, fear, and love. These are the basic pattern-reactions which are inherited. Any other emotions or combinations of them are acquired by conditioning.

Watson produced what he believed to be empirical proof of the existence of these pattern-reactions in infants. "The *hampering of the infant's* movements is the factor which, apart from all training, brings out the movements characterized as rage. If the face or head is held, crying results,

[10] *Ibid.*, p. 195.

quickly followed by screaming. The body stiffens and fairly well-coordinated slashing or striking movements of the hands and arms result. The feet and legs are drawn up and down; the breath is held until the child's face is flushed." [11]

Fear is provoked in newborn infants by a violent noise or by a sudden removal of support. The reaction of love is produced by a gentle stroking of the genitalia.

Adult emotions are a product of the basic pattern-reactions but are largely modified by life experiences. "Apparently the hereditary pattern as a whole gets broken up. At any rate, it largely disappears (the parts never disappear), except under unusual conditions, and there can be noted only a reinforcement or inhibition of the habit and instinctive (exaggerated and depressed reflexes, for example) activities taking place at the moment." Especially "the implicit, mainly glandular and smooth muscular side of the pattern, remains. The emotionally exciting object releases important internal secretions which . . . reinforce or inhibit those actually in progress." [12]

All other emotions are derivations of the basic emotions developed by means of conditioning. Shame is connected with punishment for masturbation. Jealousy arises as a response to interference with the innate emotional response of the erogenous zone. The affected individual experiences muscular tension and flushing of face, moves away from his spouse, withdraws or assaults.

Personality

Personality is the end-product of our habit systems. It is the sum of "the individual's total assets (actual and potential) and liabilities (actual and potential) on the reaction side."

Behaviorism regards *personality* as a totality of behavioral patterns. These patterns are quite consistent but not unchangeable. Some conditioned reflexes can become extinct or reinforced and new ones can become established. No individual remains himself all his life. Usually individuals do not change rapidly; one's personality undergoes slow and gradual modification. At any moment personality can be compared to "an assembled organic machine ready to run."

In the study of personality, one has to consider the innate or unconditioned reflexes, the conditioned reflexes, and the physical and social environment and its influence on personality development.

The task of psychologists is *to know in order to improve*. Human life, human relations, and societies are not unchangeable. Patterns of behavior can be conditioned and unconditioned, reinforced and extinguished. Psychology is an applied science annd should be used for the betterment of mankind. [13]

[11] *Ibid.*, p. 200.

[12] *Ibid.*, pp. 197–198.

[13] It is interesting to note that Alfred Adler expressed similar optimism (Chapter 7).

It is up to men to make mankind happy and it is the task of the psychologist to be of help to mankind. Education which is nothing but conditioning is the powerful lever to be used by behavioristically oriented parents. "The universe will change if you bring up your children . . . in behavioristic freedom. . . . Will not these children in turn, with their better ways of living and thinking, replace us as society, and in turn bring up their children in a still more scientific way, until the world finally becomes a place fit for human habitation."[14]

Physiology or Psychology?

Watson believed that the motor pattern is a chain of movements; each movement arouses kinesthetic impulses which in turn produce the next movement. In his early studies on maze learning, he attributed the role of coordinating behavior to the kinesthetic processes. The latter offered Watson the necessary link between the observable stimulus and the observable response. Without them he was unable to explain what happens between stimulus and response. In the seventeenth century, Descartes had perceived human behavior as a result of the motion of a fluid from the sense organs to the brain along the nerves and back from the brain to the nerve endings in the muscles. The brain (more precisely, the pineal gland) was regarded by Descartes as the seat of the nonmaterial soul, which controlled both perception and motility.

Apparently, a mechanistic and materialistic interpretation of human behavior must *reduce* psychology to a branch of physiology and actually deny the existence of anything outside the realm of anatomy and physiology. This was exactly what Bekhterev tried to do and Yenchman did.

Watson could not accept these naïve theories. He was determined to apply the *methods* of the natural sciences but did not expect to attain satisfactory results by imitating their content. He did realize that between the two observable factors of stimulus and response, something was going on which could not be overlooked or denied.

The solution of this problem offered by Watson was, in fact, an evasion, but this evasion was committed in the best tradition of Hume's empiricism. Watson simply refused to deal with unobservable data. Psychology deals with what *is* or *can be* observed. What is observed is the *explicit* behavior and what can be observed is the *implicit* behavior. Watson's psychology, named by him "the science of behavior," was closely related to, and even overlapped, physiology but it never was physiology or a branch of it. "Behavior psychology" was not physiology because, as Watson put it, "nowhere in physiology do we get the organism, as it were, put back together again and tested in relation to its environment as a whole." Physiology deals with definite functions of the organism and "knows nothing of the total situations in the daily life of an individual that shape his action

14 Watson, *Behaviorism.*

and conduct,"[15] while the psychologist deals with the relationship of the organism as a whole to its environment.

This molar-physiological approach seems to be of great significance in Watson's system. To Watson, psychology is a natural science, a very close "scientific companion" of physiology, and the main difference between the two disciplines lies in the "grouping" of problems. While physiology deals with particulars, psychology, without neglecting "the functioning of these parts," is "intrinsically interested in what the whole animal will do from morning to night and from night to morning." Watson firmly points to the *molar* approach. "No matter what the human animal is doing, he does it as a whole." This physiological molar concept was the new point Watson endeavored to prove.

Concluding Remarks

The evasion of a problem is not the same as its solution. Suppose all experimental subjects of the behaviorist react to stimuli and nothing else happens. The subjects do not "feel," "perceive," "think," "empathize," or do anything which looks or sounds like a "mentalism." All well and good, but how does the behaviorist know what is going on within his subjects? If he were what his subjects are, he would discharge visual or auditory responses, make verbal reports, and do nothing else. How could the behaviorist interpret, reason, and develop any theory; how could he become convinced or believe in anything at all? *"L'homme machine"* of Descartes (with the exclusion of the soul) or La Mettrie (with some modifications) could not have developed any psychological theories, even mechanistic-materialistic ones. Obviously, the behaviorist seems to consider himself an exception to the push-and-pull model of behavioristic psychology.

Watson suggested eliminating from psychological investigation the "states of consciousness," because consciousness is the tool with which "all scientists work," and whether or not the tool is properly used at present by scientists is a "problem for philosophy and not for psychology."

But the "trouble with consciousness" started not because it had been included in some studies but because the entire field of inquiry was limited to consciously perceived phenomena, that is, to the surface of a volcano or to the smoke of a great fire. Thorndike, Watson, and all animal psychologists widened the field in one direction, Freud in another. Once psychology included behavior which was not perceived by the subject (Freud) and which could be seen by others (Watson), there was no more need to eliminate consciousness. Consciousness or the conscious is a legitimate, though limited, topic of psychological inquiry. Even the introspection method may be usefully applied in research, with some degree of caution.

Watson was unable to keep his programmatic promise. He promised a psychology in which, given the stimulus, the response could be predicted

[15] Watson, *Psychology from the Standpoint of a Behaviorist*, p. 20.

and in which only observable data were included. But by introducing the "verbal report," Watson opened the door for introspectionism. The idea of the "verbal report" does not stand the test of logic. If a verbal report is good in the case of sensation, why is it no good in other cases? If it is a reliable and objective method, why behaviorism at all? Let subjects report verbally what they have seen by self-observation and the clock of psychology will be turned back to introspectionism.

It seems advisable to distinguish between the methodological approach of behaviorism and behaviorism as a theory of human behavior. The first insists on avoiding statements which cannot be proved by controlled experiments or observation. This kind of behaviorism must reject introspection, psychoanalysis, Rorschach, etc., as unscientific methods. The other kind of behaviorism has erected a mechanistic model of human beings which gives little credit to heredity and explains practically everything by conditioning.

One may accept the first sort of behaviorism without approving the second. Watson tried to combine both, and hence, the apparent weakness of his system. Not all data are observable, and nonobservable data are not necessarily the same as observable ones. Any scientific inquiry comes to grips with nonobservable ones. Any scientific inquiry comes to grips with nonobservable data; Watson and Bekhterev went about it in rather a crude and naïve way. Bekhterev lumped all nonobservable data together under the vague and pseudomaterialistic name of energy. Watson was less naïve and his term "implicit behavior" covers a great variety of phenomena. However, in his effort to reduce psychology to a sort of generalized physiology, he reduced all unobservable data, such as thinking, feeling, and perceiving, to physiological facts of muscular tensions and glandular secretions which could not be observed but were believed to be observable in the future. One must ask at this point: What is the methodological advantage of shifting away from one kind of unobservable facts in an area under consideration to another unobservable group of facts without making sure that these two groups form a continuum? But Watson was not the first and maybe not the last to believe that inner secretion or electric waves are more self-explanatory than feelings or thinking and that physiological facts could be substituted for mental processes so that everything would be explained in a scientifically satisfactory manner.

2. THE EARLY BEHAVIORISTS

Albert P. Weiss: Biosocial Behaviorism

The reductionistic aspect of behaviorism was vigorously defended by Albert P. Weiss. In 1925 Weiss published a volume entitled *A Theoretical Basis of Human Behavior.*[16] The conscious, mentalism, and introspection

[16] Albert P. Weiss., *A Theoretical Basis of Human Behavior* (2nd ed.), R. G. Adams, 1929.

were banned from the realm of psychology. The entire functioning of the organism was interpreted in terms of physiochemical processes and interaction with the environment. Weiss propagated the most radical sort of reductionism. He believed that psychology could not deal with anything but the same elements of matter as physics did. The subject matter of any science is physical processes: psychology deals with those physical processes which take place in the nervous system. Protons and electrons are the elements of the physical world and there is no other world but the physical one.

Weiss emphasized the "biological and social components" of the behavioristic analysis. Through emphasis on social factors, Weiss could draw a line between psychology and physiology. Both study physical phenomena in the nervous system, but psychology concentrates on the interaction between the organism and its environment. Such an approach, in the best tradition of behaviorism, kept psychology within the realm of the natural sciences and yet enabled it to analyze social and cultural problems. Whatever a man does, Weiss implied, is done in accordance with the laws of nature, and psychology is a branch of biology which, in turn, is a branch of physics. There are indeed no other bodies, no other events, no other entities but those which form the subject matter of physics. However, the human organism is not only biological but social or, as Weiss put it, *biosocial,* and here new vistas open to the research worker.

Perhaps the newborn is a biological entity only, but as he grows and develops, his behavior undergoes changes. One of the most important tasks of psychology is to study the impact of social forces on human behavior. Human behavior is always biological and always social since other humans act as stimuli on our organism. New responses to the new and changing social situation are the main topic of psychological inquiry. Child development and learning are the proper areas of study, which has to apply observation and experimentation patterned on the natural sciences. Introspection, mentalistic terminology, the conscious, etc., will be of no avail in such an objective type of study as Weiss planned.

Weiss did not have the chance to implement his research program, which was both bold and consistent. But his emphasis on interaction between the organism and its social environment was well accepted and several research workers continued what he initiated.

Edward B. Holt: Unorthodox Behaviorism

Watson and many other behaviorists expelled the conscious from the realm of science and tried to represent the human organism as a physiological apparatus and nothing more. The problem of the conscious was dealt with in a different manner by E. B. Holt. He did not discuss the term "consciousness" or "conscious." He suggested relating it to *epistemological realism*, according to which, objects are as perceived even when they are not perceived by us. The conscious would mean an adjustment of the sensorimotor apparatus to the perceived object; it is a sort of photographic lens which reflects the correct picture of the reflected object. In the controversy between epistemological criticism and realism, the former, starting with Kant, ascribed to perceived objects elements stemming from the perceiving subject. In contradistinction to this point of view, the realists believe that we perceive the world correctly or almost correctly. At any rate, the nature of the world does not depend to any extent upon our perceptory apparatus. Holt, being a realist, logically concluded that the existence of the conscious was a function of the perceiving apparatus.

Holt took up Watson's idea that thinking is merely a matter of language mechanisms. Passive language habits or the response to words is nothing but conditioning. Pavlov named it "second-order conditioning." Holt believed that words can *substitute* for the unconditioned stimulus in the same manner as conditioning was interpreted by Watson. In representing the problem of language as a higher-order conditioning, Holt opened the way for future studies in verbal conditioning.

Holt's unorthodox behaviorism enabled him to take an attitude of keen interest in problems not directly related to academic psychology and to utilize a great variety of sources outside his main field of endeavor.[17]

Holt, like Watson, rejected the idea of heredity as far as human behavior was concerned. He was convinced that even the unconditioned reflexes were acquired either in prenatal life or soon after birth.

Behavior patterns are acquired in two ways. The first way is learning. Learning can take place when the organism is exposed to either outer or inner motivation. Outer stimulation corresponds to what Pavlov and Watson studied in the experiments on conditioning when their subjects were confronted with stimuli coming from without. However, the inner needs or drives, such as hunger, and thirst, can also force the organism to learn; "since their stimuli are contained within the organism, these cannot be avoided by ordinary avoidance response (locomotion, etc.) but will keep the organism restless until it acquires, by trial and error, very different and other intricate modes of response which will allay the internal stimulation."[18] Holt implied that learning may take place as a result of inner needs. In this way, he paved the road for the future development of learning theory by Hull (cf. Chapter 4) with the emphasis on drive reduction.

As mentioned before, Holt did not limit all human behavior to conditioning. He noticed that adults often preserve childish patterns of behavior even though some of these patterns have never been reinforced. Such behavioral preferences established in childhood and persisting into the later years of life were called by Holt (after Janet) canalization. Gardner Murphy

[17] Edward B. Holt, *The Freudian Wish and Its Place in Ethics*, Holt, 1915.
[18] Edward B. Holt, *Animal Drives and the Learning Process*, Holt, 1931, p. 125.

took up the idea of canalization and developed it into one of the main aspects of his theory of personality (cf. Chapter 16).

Walter S. Hunter: Anthroponomy

Hunter suggested substituting for the term "psychology" another name which would better represent the new science of human behavior. His choice was *anthroponomy*, in analogy to anatomy or astronomy, a science of the laws (*nomos*) that govern human behavior. He wrote: "Psychology, unlike the other sciences, has not found it possible to continue with the subject matter bequeathed it by philosophy." "For good or ill the onward march of experiment, which no mere speculation and controversy can halt, has carried psychology along the way of the objective study of human behavior." "Psychology seems to describe and explain, to predict and control, the extrinsic behavior of the organism to an external environment which is predominantly social." [19]

Hunter conducted experiments in *delayed responses* or *delayed reactions*. A light stimulus was directed toward the spot in which food was placed, but the experimental animals were prevented from moving in the right direction. Then the stimulus was removed and, after a lapse of time, the animals were permitted to move freely. Hunter's dogs, rats, and racoons reacted successfully to the original stimulus despite the lapse of time. This reaction was named by Hunter the delayed reaction.

Hunter was the first to use the *temporal maze*, in which motor learning processes were studied. The temporal maze had no blind alleys. Hunter's temporal maze represented a continuous pathway in the shape of a rectangular number 8 with 8 square corners. His experimental animals acted in the maze as if they were avoiding repetition. Their choices seemed to be highly selective and not sheer trial and error.

Following the environmental orientation of behaviorism, Hunter tried to substitute environment for the conscious. He believed that what comes from the outside (what we perceive) is nothing but the outer world. Therefore, he concluded, "I wish to point out that the consciousness, or experience for the psychologist, is merely a name which he applies to what other people call environment." [20]

With this presentation, Hunter was identifying the content of our perception with the function of perceiving. This naïve epistemological realism is characteristic of most of the early behaviorists. Hunter hoped to overcome the physical-mental dichotomy by overlooking the existence of mental factors, by replacing the fact that man perceives environment by the mere fact that environment is what is being perceived, and finally by confusing

[19] Walter S. Hunter, "The Psychological Study of Behavior," *Psychological Review*, 1932, 39, 1–24.
[20] Walter S. Hunter, "Anthroponomy and Psychology," in C. Murchison (Ed.), *Psychologies of 1930*, Clark University, 1930, p. 283.

the perceiving subject with the perceived object. It was indeed a regression to pre-Kantian reasoning, common to Bekhterev, Watson, and many other naïve materialists.

3. KARL S. LASHLEY: BRAIN MECHANISMS

Support of Watson

Lashley is one of the leading authorities on the physiology of the nervous system, and his adherence to behaviorism has added prestige to Watson's method of interpretation. Lashley's studies stand on their own merits; their implication for psychological theory parallels the studies of Pavlov, Bekhterev, and Bykov.

Lashley has been an outspoken follower of Watson. He wrote: "To me the essence of behaviorism is the belief that the study of man will reveal nothing except what is adequately describable in the concepts of mechanics and chemistry." And later: "The behaviorist denies sensations, images and all other phenomena which the subjectivist claims to find by introspection." Lashley was extremely critical of introspection, which is "an example of pathology of scientific method."[21]

Thus far, Lashley offered unconditional support to Watson. However, his own carefully planned experiments could not fit into Watson's theoretical framework. To begin with, Lashley, in contradistinction to Watson, did not accept uncritically Pavlov's theory of conditioning. In numerous and ingenious experiments he often came to conclusions not necessarily identical with those of Pavlov, and he disagreed with Pavlov on the issue of generalization. Lashley believed that generalization does depend to a lesser degree on the nature of the stimulus and to a much greater extent on the nature of the organism. Furthermore, the gradient of habit strength is not a result of spread or generalization of "connections," but depends on the stimulus threshold of the organism.[22]

Mass Action

As said before, behaviorism leaned heavily toward physiology. Watson saw the only difference between psychology and physiology in the psychological-molar versus physiological-molecular approach. Lashley's studies have shown the fruitfulness of the molar approach even in physiology.

In a series of experiments conducted by Lashley together with his former teacher, Shepherd I. Franz,[23] animals (cats and monkeys) were

---

[21] Karl S. Lashley, "The Behaviorist Interpretation of Conscious," *Psychological Review*, 1923, 30, 237–272, 329–353.

[22] K. S. Lashley and M. Wade, "The Pavlovian Theory of Generalization," *Psychological Review*, 1946, 53, 72–87.

[23] Shepherd I. Franz, *Nervous and Mental-Re-education*, Macmillan, 1923.

trained to escape from boxes similar to those used by E. L. Thorndike. After they had learned to escape, several parts of the cortex were cut away. Whenever the acquisition of the escape habit was recent, brain operations resulted in a complete loss of the acquired habit. However, whenever the habit was firmly established, the animals performed after the operation almost as well as before. In other experiments, the frontal lobes were severed and the animals learned without them as well as with them. Franz and Lashley summarized their conclusions as follows: "The experiments show that in the white rat the removal of large parts of the frontal portions of the brain does not greatly interfere with a learned reaction."[24]

In further experiments Lashley trained rats in the discrimination of light. After the rats had learned to discriminate brightness, Lashley operated on practically every part of the cortex, but in no case did the rats lose what they had learned prior to the surgical operations. Lashley was unable to prove that subcortical centers take over the function of the damaged cortical centers. The most justified conclusion was that the brain functions as a whole and that the remaining parts of the brain take over the function of the damaged parts. Obviously, these studies lend significant support to a holistic, molar point of view.

These and other experiments led Franz and Lashley to postulate two laws. The first was the law of *mass action*. Lashley was opposed to the theory of synapses within definite conduction units of the nervous system. Learning, he said, is not a product of the overcoming of synaptic resistances and establishing of new synaptic connections, as Sherrington[25] or Thorndike (cf. Chapter 1) implied. Lashley's experiment indicated that the retention of an established habit did not depend on any specific synapses or any specific intercellular connections. "The rate of learning of the four mazes reported in this study is clearly a function of the total mass of tissue and the evidence presented indicates that retentiveness as such for these habits is conditioned in the same way." The amount, or *mass*, of undestroyed tissues determines the degree of retentiveness irrespective of the area damage. Obviously, this conclusion was not in accordance with the theory of localization. Furthermore, Lashley's experiments prove that the "visual discrimination habit which normally involves only the occipital cortex, is formed with equal facility in the absence of this area."[26]

Equipotentiality

Actually Lashley was not entirely opposed to the theory of localization. What his experiments proved was the importance of the amount of intact nervous tissue for the learning process and the ability of those intact re-

[24] Shepherd I. Franz and Karl S. Lashley, "The Retention of Habits by the Rat after Destruction of the Frontal Portion of the Cerebrum," *Psychobiology*, 1917, 1, 3–7, 13–18.
[25] C. S. Sherrington, *The Integrative Action of the Nervous System*, Scribner, 1906.
[26] Karl S. Lashley, *Brain Mechanisms and Intelligence: A Quantitative Study of Injuries to the Brain*, University of Chicago, 1929, pp. 128 ff.

maining tissues to take over the functions of the destroyed tissues. This ability, named by Lashley *equipotentiality*, represents the second law in Lashley's theory, the first being *mass action*. In other words, the learning process is a process in which the entire *mass* of the nervous system participates and, if a part of the system is missing, the remaining parts are *equipotential* to carry on the activity which might be primarily a function of a certain area. Even when the visual area was removed and the rats lost the ability of pattern vision, they could still discriminate the intensity of light, avoid obstacles, follow the light signal, and obtain food.

Lashley's experimental studies in neurosurgery brought him close to gestalt theory (cf. Chapter 12). Lashley found that relational properties do not depend on such factors as size and area of stimulus; square or rectangle is perceived as such under any circumstances.[27]

These and other studies brought Lashley to emphasize the gestalt ideas in perception and learning. But it would be rather difficult to include him with field theorists or gestaltists, for Lashley was highly critical of Köhler's field theory of excitation and never gave up his qualified but persistent adherence to the Watson–Pavlov theories.[28]

Apparently Lashley was gradually putting more emphasis on "central" elements in the learning process; he did it much more than Hull, Tolman, or Skinner did. Even when Lashley concluded that only the dominant elements in stimuli will become conditioned, he was still more in accord with Pavlov than with Köhler. Actually, Pavlov's studies imply that only the stronger stimulus will become conditioned, the term "stronger" being related either to the strength of the stimulus proper or to the strength of the stimulated center (cf. Chapter 2). The idea of set, or selective conditioning, was developed by G. Razran, who never was a gestaltist but always has been a brilliant and original interpreter of Pavlov.

Lashley emphasized the factor of *organization* in learning: In support of Krechevsky's theory,[29] which maintained that rats do not act at random but are selective in their choice of clues, Lashley wrote: "The mechanism of nervous integration is such that when any complex of stimuli arouses nervous activity, that activity is immediately organized and certain elements or components become dominant for reaction while others become ineffective. In any trial of a training series, only those components of the stimulating situation which are dominant in the organization are associated. Other stimuli which excite the receptors are not associated because the animal is not set to react to them."[30]

[27] Karl S. Lashley, "The Problem of Cerebral Organization," in H. Klüver (Ed.), *Visual Mechanisms*, Cattell, 1942, pp. 301–322.

[28] Cf. Ernest Hilgard, *Theories of Learning*, Appleton-Century-Crofts, 1948, pp. 296–297.

[29] I. Krechevsky, "A Study of the Continuity of the Problem-Solving Process," *Psychological Review*, 1938, *45*, 107–133.

[30] Karl S. Lashley, "An Examination of the 'Continuity Theory' as Applied to Discriminative Learning," *Journal of General Psychology*, 1942, *26*, 241–265.

Reductionism

Thus, Lashley can still be classified as a behaviorist, but not as an orthodox follower of Watson. Lashley explained his attitude as follows: "I became glib in formulating all problems of psychology in terms of stimulus–*response* and in explaining all things as conditioned reflexes. . . . [However], the conditioned reflex turned out not to be a reflex, not the simple basic key to the learning problem. . . . The nature of the stimulus and of the response is intrinsically such as to preclude theory of simple point-to-point connection in reflexes."[31]

Lashley was always consistent and persistent in his reductionism. In 1941, the great neurophysiologist Sherrington stated the pessimistic view that brain and mind are still far apart and that there is no way to bridge the gap between the fact of brain and the experience of mind. He wrote: "The two for all I can do remain refractorily apart."[32]

Both Pavlov and Lashley expressed strong disapproval of this view. Lashley wrote: "With this statement the greatest living neurophysiologist despairs of finding a common ground between the sciences of the brain and of the mind. He seems to have missed a solution of the problems by no more than the turning of the page. In the same lectures he has faced the problem of the nature of life and found that life is not a thing attached to this or that substance or chemical action, but is organized activity, varying in character with complexity of structure and ranging without discoverable discontinuity from the neatly crystalline simplicity of the filterable virus to the elaborate organization of the mammalian body. He has just missed seeing that mind also is not a thing attached to life, a unique form of existence, but is a term including an indefinite number of complex structures or relations."[33]

Concluding Remarks on Lashley and the Early Behaviorists

Lashley's theory represents a fruitful combination of a persistent empiricism with a daring and consistent materialistic philosophy. Lashley is undoubtedly the most scientific of the behaviorists and the best equipped to handle the difficult problems created by the ardent reductionism of the behavioristic school.

Having conducted firsthand experimental studies in brain physiology, Lashley is less prone to generalize than any other behaviorist. Some of the early behaviorists oversimplified the problems instead of solving them.

[31] Karl S. Lashley, "Cerebral Cortex versus Reflexology: A Reply to Professor Hunter," *Journal of General Psychology*, 1931, 5, 3–20.
[32] Charles S. Sherrington, *Man on His Nature*, Macmillan, 1941, p. 312.
[33] Karl S. Lashley, "Coalescence of Neurology and Psychology," *Proceedings of the American Philosophical Society*, 1941, 84, 461–470.

They believed they could reduce human behavior to the overt functions of the organism and its interaction with environment, and hoped to be able to present psychology in physiological terms. Obviously, they dealt with but a fraction of the phenomena, and even these phenomena were never put in physiological terms in a scientifically sound manner. No wonder that behaviorism in its orthodox form quickly lost ground.

Lashley was never an orthodox behaviorist. He deviated from Watson and Pavlov and came fairly close to Goldstein (cf. Chapter 5). In his later studies Lashley was no longer "glib"; he became a cautious, thorough, and persistent worker who tried very hard to find the continuity of organic life from "the neatly crystalline simplicity of the filterable virus to the elaborate organization of the mammalian body" and toward the human mind. Lashley never said that *"der Mensch ist was er isst"* ("Man is what he eats"). He is one of those great minds who believe in the soma–psyche continuity and who avoid sterile speculations, but whose empirical research brings more and more evidence of such a continuity. Whether this will be ultimately successful no one can predict.

4. DONALD O. HEBB: ORGANIZATION OF BEHAVIOR

Hebb's Position

It may seem unjustified to discuss the theory of D. O. Hebb in the same chapter with J. B. Watson and A. P. Weiss. It will probably seem less strange if our analysis of the writings of Hebb follows that of Lashley and both of them are included in the same chapter. As mentioned before, we follow in this book the principle of "common roots" rather than of "common roofs," and Hebb's original contribution to psychology shares its roots with the early behaviorists, with their bold efforts to expel mentalism and to derive psychology from physiological data. There are deep differences between Hebb and Watson, yet both represent the same reductionism and empiricism, both emphasize the neurological aspects of psychology, and both pursue their studies in the spirit of associationism in contradistinction to gestalt and psychoanalysis.

Hebb's system is closely related to, and at the same time definitely opposed to Lashley's theory. Hebb emphasizes the local actions of cells and their more complex units and challenges Lashley's principle of equipotentiality. Hebb's writings display a certain effort to contradict both Lashley and Köhler. Hebb tried to develop a reductionistic system of psychology closely related to the observable data of neurology. However, instead of synaptic connections between neurons, he postulated organizational units allied to each other by synchronization of actions. Undoubtedly he is indebted to the gestalt theorists for his "organizational" deviation from associationism.

Assembly and Complex

Hebb's starting point is a group of sensory and motor neurons working together as a unit called an *assembly*. The cells which participate in an assembly are interconnected by several pathways and synapses. The discharge of energy ("firing") in these cells is coordinated and synchronized, so that they form a functional unit and act as a unit in the sensory and motor responses to oncoming stimuli.

Assemblies are formed by perceptual processes. If a person looks at an object, the cortical cells participating in this act become interconnected. They may be both afferent-sensory and efferent-motor cells, the latter directing the movement of eyes in the case of visual perception. In Hebb's words, "When an axon of cell A is near enough to excite a cell B and repeatedly or persistently takes part in firing it, some growth process or metabolic change takes place in one or both cells such that A's efficiency as one of the cells firing B is increased."[34]

The assembly of cortical neurons can undergo changes through either *fractionation* or *recruitment*. Fractionation takes place whenever some cells "fall out of line" and lose their synchronization with the assembly. Such a cell soon drops out. When neighboring cells join the assembly and become a part of it, recruitment takes place.

When our eye shifts from one item of an object to another, more assemblies are formed and these become interconnected. For instance, when we look at a triangle, we may first notice a definite part or angle. Several experiments with chimpanzees reared in darkness and with humans who see for the first time in their life after removal of a congenital cataract have shown that perception proceeds from parts to the whole. The human subjects noticed parts first, and only after prolonged training could they grasp the figure. Hebb maintained that the perception of figures is not innate; it must be learned. Obviously his finding contradicts the findings of Köhler (cf. Chapter 12).

These associationistic ideas, which Hebb shared with Pavlov and Watson, in contradistinction to gestalt, led him to postulate the *t* factor or the *superordinate system*. Whenever the separate assemblies become so well coordinated as to enable the individual to combine the respective elements perceived by him into a "distinctive whole," a *t* system of the assemblies has been formed. In looking at a triangle, our eye rests first on one of the *a* or *b* or *c* angles of the triangle. An assembly unit comes into being in our cortex. Then our eye shifts in the direction of the other two angles and two additional assembly units are formed. This shifting is reported as *phase sequence*. Any excitation "in one of the assemblies a, b, c and t is an unstable equilibrium which moves readily into another phase. The stability of a perception is not in a single pattern of cerebral activity but in the tendency of the phases of an irregular cycle to recur at short intervals."[35]

---

[34] Donald O. Hebb, *The Organization of Behavior*, Wiley, 1949, p. 62.
[35] *Ibid.*, p. 100.

Since the assemblies function almost simultaneously, or at least are overlapping, their timing in the discharge of energy becomes synchronized and they form a *system* or a *complex* of assemblies. The superordinate t is defined by Hebb "as being whatever determinate, organized activity results from repeated activity in the earlier-developed or subordinate structures giving rise to it."[36] The t factor is instrumental in the formation of complexes.

Learning

Sometimes one assembly facilitates another and any a may facilitate a b or c. Attention is the "central facilitation" of perceptual activities, or the tendency to form new complexes of assemblies.

Learning is a process in which *facilitations* are established in such a way that a certain neural unit, an assembly or a complex of cell assemblies, facilitates the oncoming of some other units. Once something has been learned, a given stimulus starts a series of well-established phase sequences. Once a definite cortical pattern has been established, on successive trials the same stimulus will set off the same phase sequences.

Simple relationships are as easily perceived by animals as by humans. In order to perceive more complex entities, the acquisition of the perception of the whole becomes important. Higher organisms are more capable of abstraction and generalization. Even if some elements of the totality are missing, they can still activate the t factor and perceive a triangle as a triangle despite the fact that the angles are not closed. This idea, the perceiving of a whole or of a figure despite missing elements, brings Hebb closer to the gestalt theory of *Prägnanz* (cf. Chapter 12) and K. Goldstein's figure–ground theory (cf. Chapter 5). However, one must admit that Hebb's theory stands on its own ground in its original approach to learning, and the gestalt element in it is always secondary and never considered to be an innate feature of living organisms.

Motivation

In Hebb's theory, motivation and emotionality are related to the phase sequences of assemblies of cells and complexes of assemblies. Motivation is related to the *persistence* with which phase sequences take place. Since mental integration is a question of timing, "metabolic changes, by altering time relations in neural firing, must tend to disrupt behavior. . . . If a metabolic change affects one cell much more than other cells in the system, it must drop out; if enough cells drop out, the assembly does not function. If, instead, all the cells in an assembly are affected to about the same extent, the system would continue to function; but the facilitation delivered to

[36] *Ibid.*, p. 98.

other assemblies might be modified in a way that would disturb, or re-direct, the phase sequence (that is, the sequence of assembly actions)."[37]

This is Hebb's interpretation of "disturbance of behavior" resulting from the changes of blood content, such as take place in hunger or pain. Sleep is "the extreme case of a loss of motivation";[38] sleep is the opposite of motivation. Each phase sequence needs new content to maintain its organi-zation and persistence. In order to maintain "motivation" or persistence in organization, new combinations of assemblies, new ideas, new perceptions must take place.

Pleasure is a transient state in which "a new synthesis in assembly ac-tion [is] being achieved." It is "a direct *growth* or *development* in cerebral organization."[39]

Hebb accepted Watson's theory of the three basic emotions, rage, fear, and love, with certain reservations, but he believed that learning took place even in these emotions. He believed that the sudden disruption of an es-tablished neural connection in the cortex causes fear. Animals and children fear the unknown and are frightened by a sudden change. "The immediate source of fear is a disruption of a coordination, principally acquired in the timing of cellular activities in the cerebrum. The disruption may be due to conflict, sensory deficit or constitutional change. With disruption there at once occur processes tending to restore the integration of cerebral activities; in fear these include either liminal or subliminal activation of processes, de-termining avoidance. Optimally, avoidance tends toward completely avert-ing the cerebral disruption, and at this stage avoidance without fear would be said to occur."[40]

Fear, like any other emotion, is actually a sort of neurological distur-bance, said Hebb. It is a disruption of timing in the activity of neurons. This disruption may be caused by a conflict in phase sequences, by a lack of sensory support for a given phase sequence, such as darkness, or by changes in metabolism.

Concluding Remarks

Hebb's system, briefly described here, is a product of a thoroughgoing investigation and bold speculation. The investigation is psychological; the speculation is neurological. Strangely enough, Hebb tried to subordinate his empirically sound observations of human behavior to a neurological model borrowed from modern physics. "What Hebb has done . . . is to apply some relatively recent notions from physics, notably of reverberating circuits, to the nervous system and to test the fit for a number of psycho-

---

[37] *Ibid.*, p. 197.
[38] *Ibid.*, p. 223.
[39] *Ibid.*, p. 232.
[40] Donald O. Hebb, "On the Nature of Fear," *Psychological Review*, 1946, 53, 259–276.

logical phenomena," writes Adams.[41] Adams suspects that this may be "good neurology," but he warns that "what appeared to some as an *extension* of psychological theory construction seems to be already becoming another strait-jacket."[42]

What Hebb is actually doing is relating good empirical studies of human behavior (usually called psychology) to some fictitious model (never tested in the realm of physiology) of the actions of the nervous system. Of course, iron is stronger than wood, but who would substitute very thin pieces of iron for good solid lumber in building a house? With all respect to neurology (to a thoroughly empirical neurology), what's the good of relating observable psychological phenomena to imaginary physiological models?

Moreover, despite his great erudition and sophistication, Hebb could not have avoided the pitfalls of radical reductionism. In his book, he used phrases such as: "Pleasure is . . . fundamentally a directed *growth* or *development* in cerebral organization" (p. 232); "The factor of *interest* or *motivation* which is provisionally translated into the stability and persistence of the phase sequence" (p. 223); "The kind of activity *throughout the cerebrum* which we call consciousness . . ." (p. 219).

It is not at all easy to translate motivation into a phase sequence of the synchrony in neural firings. These two languages do not convey the same things. It is Hebb's idea to relate phenomena reported in mentalistic terms, such as interest and motivation, to phenomena reported in physiological terms, such as neurons, synapses, and firing. No useful purpose is served by saying that what has to be proved (and what no one has ever been able to prove) is simple and self-evident. For no one has ever proved that any activity of the cerebrum *is* consciousness. By "calling" it consciousness no one could serve the cause of scientific progress nor could he solve any of the perennial problems of science.

Analogously, no "growth" of the cerebral organization *is* pleasure; and if it is, it has to be proved; if such a proof is possible at all, it should be offered.

From that point of view, the critical evaluation of Hebb's work must relate his method of reasoning to Watson's radical reductionism, with all credit given to Hebb for his originality and ingenuity in theory formation. As is the case with Lewin (cf. Chapter 13), Hebb's experiments stand on their own merits. Does his theory also? Let us leave that question open to future research and evidence.

[41] Donald K. Adams, "Learning and Explanation," in *Learning Theory, Personality Theory and Clinical Research. The Kentucky Symposium,* Wiley, 1954, p. 74.
[42] *Ibid.,* p. 75.

4

Neo-Behaviorism and Learning Theory

1. Edwin R. Guthrie: Learning by Contiguity

Radical Empiricism

The most persistent advocate of conditioning is undoubtedly E. R. Guthrie. Guthrie considers association by contiguity in time, or "simultaneous conditioning," the most general law in psychology. "Stimuli acting at the time of a response tend on their recurrence to evoke that response," he says. Any other type of behavior can be derived from simultaneous conditioning. Especially the processes of learning represent the general law of simultaneous conditioning or association by contiguity in time of stimuli and responses. "The outstanding characteristics of learning which have been expressed in forms of frequency, intensity, irradiation, temporary extinction, conditioned inhibition, forgetting, forward and backward conditioning, and so on, are all derivable from this more general law,"[1] Guthrie believes.

Guthrie was very much aware of the importance of theory. He wrote: "It is theories that endure, not facts. Events are ephemeral and their descriptions also may be ephemeral. It is theory that lasts for years or for generations. It is theory rather than fact that leads to new controls over nature and events."[2]

The business of scientific inquiry is to predict and control the events of nature. The aim of scientific research is the discovery of scientific laws leading to the anticipation of natural events. The validity of scientific laws, including psychological laws, is "measured by their success in prediction.

Scientific laws deal with observable phenomena only. Guthrie's radical empiricism was uncompromising. "The laws of science describe the *observ-*

---

[1] Edwin R. Guthrie, "Pavlov's Theory of Conditioning," *Psychological Review*, 1934, 41, 199–206.

[2] Edwin R. Guthrie, "Psychological Facts and Psychological Theory," *Psychological Bulletin*, 1946, 43, 1–20.

able conditions under which certain classes of events take place."[3] He rejected Thorndike's theory of synapses as an unnecessary and speculative assumption not supported by observable data. He was critical of the gestalt "theory of the brain as a dynamic electrical field in which any change in detail alters the whole pattern. The theory is quite safe, of course, from experimental verification or disproof by any technique so far developed and as an attempt to state the circumstances under which action or learning occurs it is quite useless because it calls on unobservable determinants."[4]

Guthrie had definite ideas concerning theory formation in psychology. Theories "enable men to confront new facts and deal with them successfully. Furthermore, theories are required to direct the search for relevant facts. . . . It is theory rather than fact that leads to new controls over nature and events. From theory inferences can be made and applications devised. Facts are likely to be local and temporary. Their applications are limited. . . . Theory [must] be continuously produced and continuously used to guide the collection of fact." However, as much as facts have to be related to theory, theory must also be related to facts. Guthrie continued: "Facts may accumulate without theory; but they will prove to be unstable and of little profit in the end. Theories may flourish, if their basis lies not in scientific fact but in opinions and presentations acceptable only to the members of a limited faction; but they will be bad theories."[5]

Guthrie's methodological position is that of a radical empiricist reluctant to delve into matters beyond our sensory perception. Apparently this kind of empiricism does not conflict with the reductionism inasmuch as psychological data could be related to observable facts in any other field of science. However, models or constructs are excluded from Guthrie's theory; he prefers to stick to observable phenomena of behavior and hence his outspoken anti-reductionism. His anti-reductionism does not reject physiology as such; it is merely opposed to relating observable data in psychology to presumably interpretive theories which deal with "invisible" elements of the nervous system and the cortex.

Learning

The organism responds to stimuli by contraction of muscles or secretion of glands. These responses are the basic elements of behavior. The specific patterns of motor and glandular actions are called by Guthrie *movements*. Pavlov's conditioning was mostly concerned with movements.

Guthrie distinguishes between *acts* and movements. Any act is a movement but not vice versa. An act is a movement or a series of movements which brings end results. The achievement of the end result of an act is

---

[3] Edwin R. Guthrie, *The Psychology of Learning,* Harper, 1935, p. 187.
[4] *Ibid.*, p. 195.
[5] Guthrie, "Psychological Facts and Psychological Theory," *Psychological Bulletin,* 1946, 43, 1–20.

"dependent on the acquisition, through learning, of a specific stereotyped movement or set of movements for the accomplishment of the effect that defines the act."[6] Learning deals with movements, not with acts, and the association of stimuli and response movements is explained by contiguity. Thorndike's law of effect concerns acts and not movements. Thus, Guthrie concludes, Thorndike does not deal with the basic laws of learning.

Guthrie was highly consistent in rejecting the ideas of Thorndike. He explained his position as follows: "Our position is that what is associated is a stimulus and a response. It would perhaps be more exact to say that what is associated is some stimulation of sense organs and a corresponding muscular contraction or glandular secretion. By calling them associated we mean that the stimulation has become the occasion for the response because of a past association of the two."[7]

An ingenious experiment was designed by Guthrie and Horton in order to prove that learning is a process of association and of nothing else.[8] In the Guthrie–Horton experiment, a cat had to learn how to get out of a box; a small pole in the middle of the cage floor was the release mechanism. Whenever the cat touched the pole, from whichever side and in whatever way, the door opened and the cat could escape and eat the food prepared outside the cage.

Guthrie's cat did not have to work as hard as Thorndike's cat did. The cat found the solution immediately. When put in the box again, he repeated his behavior. Whenever the cat acted the first time by pushing the pole with his back, the same kind of behavior was repeated again and again. If the cat escaped from the box by use of claws, the same action was repeated again and again. There have been very few deviations from this rule. Guthrie felt that he could safely state that what any animal would do at any moment was most securely based on a record of what he did the first time.

Guthrie believed that all principles of learning could be reduced to one, namely *contiguity in time*. He enumerated ten such principles, some of which we shall discuss, but he hoped to prove that there is actually only one principle of learning. The first principle is conditioning itself, and Guthrie considered the possibility of reducing all other principles to this one. The second principle is inhibitory conditioning or conditioned inhibition; Guthrie believed that inhibitory conditioning is essentially the conditioning of inhibiting responses and behaves like any other conditioning. The third principle, remote or delayed conditioning, deals with "delayed" or "trace" reflexes which, in Guthrie's opinion, are not direct conditioning at all. In these cases the conditioned stimulus precedes the unconditioned.

[6] Edwin R. Guthrie, "Personality in Terms of Associative Learning," in J. McV. Hunt (Ed.), *Personality and the Behavior Disorders*, Ronald, 1944, Vol. I, p. 51.
[7] Edwin R. Guthrie, "Conditioning: A Theory of Learning in Terms of Stimulus, Response, and Association," in *The Forty-First Yearbook of the National Society for the Study of Education*, University of Chicago Press, 1942, p. 43.
[8] Edwin R. Guthrie and G. P. Horton, *Cats in a Puzzle Box*, Rinehart, 1946.

Guthrie explained that a new stimulus which follows the stimulus for a particular act might easily be simultaneous with the proprioceptive stimulation involved in the act itself and hence become a conditioner of the act. Improvement as a result of practice is the fourth principle. Guthrie believed that conditioning should take place after a single trial. He wrote: "It is entirely possible that if Pavlov could have controlled all stimuli instead of a very few, conditioning would be definitely established with one trial instead of fifty or more."[9] The "strengthening" of a stimulus–response connection by repetition was regarded by Guthrie as a result "of the enlistment of increasing numbers of stimuli as conditioners, and not the result of the 'strengthening' of individual connections." Association, said Guthrie, could occur after one connection and last forever. Forgetting is not a matter of decay of old impressions and associations but a result of inhibition of old connections by new ones.

Guthrie had little difficulty in explaining forgetting, extinction, and unconditioning. He assumed that a stimulus pattern gains its full associative power on the occasion of its first pairing with a response. This statement corresponds to Thorndike's minor law of recency, but in Guthrie's theory it becomes the focal issue.

Guthrie explained extinction of a given conditioned response as an inhibition of this response by a new stimulus–response association. Any learned response will exist forever unless it is inhibited by a new response which is incompatible with the former one. A response is unlearned, not by extinction resulting from lack of reinforcement, but by inhibition. In Guthrie's theory there is no room for reinforcement.

Nevertheless, Guthrie agreed that repetition improves learning, because learning of a skill requires association of more than one activity. The more varied the stimuli, the more repetition is needed. This explains the fact that, although an association between a single stimulus and a single response is established in a single coincidence, learning usually requires more than one trial. It is the complex structure of the stimulus that requires several trials before the response becomes associated with all the exteroceptive, proprioceptive, and interoceptive elements of the stimulus situation. A simple movement does not require repetitions, but a complex function composed of several movements will be learned through repetitions which enable all the separate movements to become associated.

The last response is usually the lasting response. Guthrie believed that the concepts of reward and punishment could be replaced by the principle of the last response. In a "reward" situation the last successful response either removes the animal from the learning situation or changes the situation to such an extent that no new associations related to the stimulus can be formed. These two facts can be readily explained. In a puzzle box, success means escape from the box; in a maze situation success means feeding,

[9] Edwin R. Guthrie, "Conditioning as a Principle of Learning," *Psychological Review*, 1930, *37*, 412–428.

which removes the drive-stimulus or at least reduces it substantially. In both cases, new associations with the stimulus are rendered impossible. In other words, not the feelings caused by reward or punishment but the specific, overt actions caused by reward or punishment become conditioned and learned.

Motivation and Intentions

Little room was left in Guthrie's system for anything besides the overt stimulus and the overt response. The problem of motivation is rather circumvented by Guthrie. Hunger may become a factor in conditioning only through the act of eating. "The hunger dies when eating occurs. . . . [The] elements of the consummatory response tend to be present throughout a series of actions driven by a maintaining stimulus."[10] Hunger, food, etc., do not "reinforce" behavior; they simply introduce a new situation and in this way prevent unlearning. Obviously there is no room in Guthrie's theory for "annoyers" and "satisfiers" or for reinforcement interpreted as "need reduction."

Yet the idea of purposefulness or *intention* found its way into Guthrie's theory. Guthrie borrowed from Sherrington the idea of two consecutive steps, preparatory and consummatory.[11] But even the preparatory actions, such as salivation in anticipation of food, are conditioned. The *intention*, explains Guthrie, is "a body of maintaining stimuli which may or may not include sources of unrest like thirst or hunger but always includes action tendencies conditioned during a past experience . . . and in each case a readiness not only for the act but also for the previously rehearsed consequences of the act."[12]

However, Guthrie did not believe "that all stimulus-response associations are dependent on conditioning. Maturation of the nervous system appears to be the principal determiner of many classes of acts."[13] Guthrie admitted that certain differences in behavior are related to the differences between different biological species and gave ample consideration to the innate physiological factors. The internal stimuli stemming from glandular and muscular tensions are potent factors in conditioning; they are the *maintaining* stimuli.

Concluding Remarks

Guthrie's system has enchanted many psychologists by its simplicity and aversion to cumbersome theory building. The question is whether Guthrie's parsimonious approach has been fruitful in yielding the expected

[10] Guthrie, *Psychology of Learning*, p. 152.
[11] Charles S. Sherrington, *The Integrative Action of the Nervous System*, Yale, 1906.
[12] Guthrie, *Psychology of Learning*, p. 205.
[13] *Ibid.*, p. 38.

results in predictability. The main test of the system must be an experimental one.

In such a theory-testing experiment by John P. Seward, two groups of rats were used.[14] Both groups had to press a bar in order to get food. However, only the first group was permitted to eat the food; the second group was promptly removed without being able to eat any food at all. Though both groups learned to press the bar, the rewarded group learned much better. Obviously, Seward's experiment brings evidence contrary to Guthrie's assumptions; for both groups, the stimulus situation was changed either by eating-reward or by removal, yet the rewarded rats showed far superior results as compared to the unrewarded. Seward believed that his experiments challenged the validity of Guthrie's propositions.

E. R. Hilgard, in his excellent book on theories of learning, quotes the experimental study of Sheffield and Roby[15] in which the nonnutritive taste of saccharin was used as a reward. Hilgard seems to believe "that the empirical support for Guthrie derives from the fact that the rat's behavior changes strikingly after the saccharin is ingested."[16]

However, the quoted experiment can only disprove the theory of need reduction of reinforcement; it cannot disprove, for example, Thorndike's law of effect or Pavlov's reinforcement by a stronger stimulus. Saccharin may be a "Satisfier"; it may be a second-rank conditioned stimulus already associated with sugar. Thus the Sheffield and Roby experiment does not necessarily support Guthrie's theory of contiguity.

On the other hand, one must admit that Guthrie's theory covers at least a certain part of the empirical data and that it stands very well against the Thorndike law-of-effect criticism. For, as several workers have proved, conditioning may take place without satisfiers or annoyers. Bykov's studies (cf. Chapter 2, Section 6) are convincing on this point. Guthrie's studies show that there is no need for perceiving reinforcement as a "reward," or "pleasure," or "need reduction." Moreover, conditioning on the first contiguity and with a single contiguity is not an unusual phenomenon.

As things stand now, one wonders whether Guthrie's theory is a *general* theory of learning or is representative of a certain group of phenomena. Obviously, it cannot represent a general theory, for it does not answer the question *why* in certain experiments learning takes place on the first contiguity and in others it does not.

Guthrie went very far in his generalizations. In his overzealous empiricism he denied any reinforcement whatsoever. Reinforcement, as formulated by Pavlov, is the key construct in the physiological theory of con-

[14] John P. Seward, "An Experimental Study of Guthrie's Theory of Reinforcement," *Journal of Experimental Psychology*, 1942, *30*, 247–256.
[15] F. D. Sheffield and T. B. Roby, "Reward Value of a Non-Nutritive Sweet Taste," *Journal of Comparative and Physiological Psychology*, 1950, *47*, 349–354.
[16] Ernest R. Hilgard, *Theories of Learning* (2nd ed.), Appleton-Century-Crofts, 1956, p. 59.

ditioning. It represents the victory of a "stronger" stimulus, the connotation of "stronger" being a given quantity of neurological energy.

Guthrie dropped the construct of reinforcement because he did not care for any constructs at all. "Why does conditioning take place?" is the question asked by the *theorists* of learning. Guthrie did not answer this question. In his ardent empiricism, following in the footsteps of David Hume,[17] he discarded the problem of causation. His theory follows Hume in presenting learning not in a *propter quod* (because of which) but in a *post quod* (after which) continuity. Thus, one may wonder whether Guthrie's theory explains anything at all. His system is a description of *how* events take place without dealing with the question of *why* they happen. It is more presentation than explanation (cf. Chapters 14 and 15).

Some time ago an effort was made to "formalize" Guthrie's theory.[18] One cannot help wondering why Guthrie's clear and beautiful English prose should have been translated into a series of less understandable and less lucid, though very elaborate statements. As far as the content of Guthrie's findings is concerned, no additional areas of study could be included, nor could the causation problem be handled better. Even after the remarkable work of formalization, Guthrie's system leaves the causal questions unanswered.

Guthrie's radical empiricism deserves attention for its relentless rejection of logical constructs which are not derived from empirical studies. One feels, however, that he went a bit too far and that his rejection of any unobservable elements is more a hindrance than a help in theory construction. A theory cannot overlook the truth that some facts are still (or will be forever?) not given in an empirical observation and yet that their impact on observed facts cannot be denied (see Chapter 15).

2. Clark L. Hull: Deductive Behaviorism

The Hypothetico-Deductive Method

Clark L. Hull occupies a distinguished position in contemporary psychological theory. No one else, perhaps with the exception of Kurt Lewin, was so keenly devoted to the problems of scientific methodology. Few psychologists have had such a mastery of mathematics and formal logic as Hull had. Hull applied the language of mathematics to psychological theory in a manner used by no other psychologist. Whatever exists, Hull believed, exists in a certain quantity; whatever relationships can be discovered by science, must be present in mathematical equations.

Hull discerned four methods leading to the discovery of scientific truth.

[17] David Hume, *A Treatise of Human Nature*, Clarendon, 1896, Vol. III.
[18] Virginia W. Voeks, "Formalization and Clarification of a Theory of Learning," *Journal of Psychology*, 1950, *30*, 341–362.

The first method is simple, unplanned observation. The second is systematic, planned observation. The third is the experimental testing of some specific and mutually nonrelated hypotheses. The hypotheses come from intuition or observation and are scrutinized by a carefully planned experimentation.

All these methods have been quite fruitful, but Hull believed that the most fruitful method was the fourth. It is a three-step method of research that applies a rigorous deduction from a priori set principles. First, a system of definitions has to be introduced. Then a series of highly conceptualized postulates (tentatively stated laws) is proposed. From these definitions and postulates a series of detailed theorems is rigorously deduced. The totality of definitions, postulates, and thorems form a systematic and integrated theory. This theory should be tested by carefully controlled experimentation. Any part of the theory which does not pass the experimental test has to be modified according to the experimental evidence.

A scientific theory constructed in such a manner represents a set of logical deductions from definite postulates of what should be observed under specified conditions. Any scientific theory should permit the observational determination of its truth or falsity.

Hull was not opposed to empirical generalizations or to the inductive method of research. He felt that the *hypothetico-deductive method* "reaches independently through a process of reasoning the same outcome with respect to (secondary) principles as is attained through the process of empirical generalizations." [19]

The advantage offered by a deductive method was apparent to Hull. Only mathematical and formal logical statements have unlimited generality. If psychology, in accordance with the behavioristic program, is to become an objective science patterned after other natural sciences, the deductive-mathematical method seems to be the most appropriate one.

In his preference for the hypothetico-deductive method, Hull was influenced by *logical positivism* as promoted by the *Viennese circle* (cf. Chapter 14). The logical positivists, or physicalists, accepted David Hume's views on induction and causation and emphasized the importance of logical analysis. Moreover, some of them, such as R. Wittgenstein, R. Carnap, and others, saw the main test of philosophy in the clarification of language and the development of a system of symbolic signs free from inner contradictions (the *immanent* truth). The more moderate M. Schlick insisted upon checking this system against perceptible evidence (*transcendent* truth). The even more moderate French mathematician and philosopher, H. Poincaré, the father of *conventionalism*, suggested that although any system of postulates can be proposed, it should be modified according to the results of empirical testing (cf. Chapter 15).

Hull was influenced by the moderate wing of logical positivism and by

[19] Clark L. Hull, *Principles of Behavior*, Appleton-Century, 1943, p. 2.

conventionalism. He attached great importance to formalization of scientific language and believed, as the physicalists did, that one may start from any set of postulates and axioms, provided they are not mutually contradictory (the immanent truth). A theory, said Hull, "is a systematic deductive derivation of secondary principles of observable phenomena from a relatively small number of primary principles or postulates, much as the secondary principles or theorems of geometry are ultimately derived . . . from a few original definitions and primary principles called axioms." [20] And further on: "An observed event is said to be explained when the proposition expressing it had been logically derived from a set of definitions and postulates coupled with certain observed conditions antecedent to the event." [21] The postulates and axioms have to be checked against "observed conditions" in accordance with the principle of the transcendent truth (cf. Chapter 15).

Hull proposed four criteria for a scientific theory. The first concerns definitions and postulates. Definitions and postulates have to be (1) clearly defined, (2) mutually consistent, that is, not contradicting each other, (3) formulated in such a manner as to permit deductions of theorems, and (4) as few as possible.

The second criterion concerns the implications and inferences to be deduced from the main definitions and postulates. All deductions have to be (1) clear, (2) exhibited, that is, without tacit assumptions, and (3) detailed.

Hull's third and fourth criteria deal with the relationship between the theorems and experiments (the criteria of transcendent truth). Theorems usually represent the anticipated outcome of experimental studies, which should verify the theorems. The third criterion proposed by Hull required that theorems should be closely related to empirical data; otherwise there is no way of checking them experimentally. "Metaphysics does not permit this continuous check on the validity of the deductions," but scientific data should be testable by experimentation. The fourth criterion deals with the experimental proof of the theory.

Hull suggested a laissez-faire policy in regard to postulates. Only the law of inner consistency (the immanent truth) and the law of parsimony should be observed. If a set of postulates is really bad, said Hull, it will sooner or later come into conflict with results obtained by experiments and be modified or abandoned.

A theory constructed in such a manner must encounter a certain difficulty in its efforts to define precisely the terms to be used. However, since the "definition of a term always requires the use of one or more other terms, it follows that in any formal system there must be a number of terms which are not really defined at all. . . . Once an adequate set of such primi-

[20] Ibid.
[21] Ibid., p. 5.

tive concepts or undefined notions is available, the remaining critical terms employed in the system may presumably be defined with precision."[22] Obviously, the definitions dealing with "unobservables" must belong to the category of undefined notions or primitive concepts.

Even the most formalized system must apply nonformalized concepts, and even a mathematical system must use nonquantitative statements. "Since it appears probable that everything which exists at all in nature exists in some amount, it would seem that the ultimate form of all scientific postulates should be quantitative. Nevertheless it is a fact that many scientific principles, at least when first stated, are qualitative or, at most, only quasi-quantitative."[23]

Three steps lead to quantification. First, one variable has to be stated as a mathematical function of at least one other variable, usually in the form of an equation. Second, at least one factor in the equation, for example, the g in the physical law of gravitation must be constant. Third, if measurement has to take place, a unit of measurement should be available.

In 1940, Hull presented his system in quasi-quantitative terms. By 1952, his system was almost entirely quantified.

The Biological Frame of Reference

Human behavior, according to Hull, is an interplay between organism and environment. In this interaction, the stimulus is provided by the environment and the response is given by the organism. These two facts are observable, but the totality of the interaction must be viewed in some broader context which is not entirely an observable stimulus–response situation.

This broader frame of reference is the *biological adaptation* of the organism to the environment. The concept of adaptation in Hull's theory formation is "useful in making a preliminary survey in the search of postulates, but . . . once the postulates have been selected they must stand on their own feet . . . [and] must be able to yield deductions in agreement with observed detailed phenomena of behavior."[24]

Biological adaptation facilitates *survival of the organism*. Whenever the survival of the organism is not facilitated, the organism is in a state of *need*.

Hull defined need as a state of the organism in which a deviation of the organism from the optimum of biological conditions necessary for survival took place. When a need arises, the organism acts and this action brings a reduction of the need. Any behavior is therefore goal directed, and this goal is the reduction of the need, which serves to promote optimal conditions for survival.

Drive (D) is a general condition of privation in the organism; it is "a

---

[22] Clark L. Hull, "The Hypothetico-Deductive Method," in M. Marx (Ed.), *Psychological Theory*, Macmillan, 1951, p. 220.
[23] *Ibid.*, p. 226.
[24] Hull, *Principles of Behavior*, p. 66.

common denominator of all primary motivations, whether due to food privation, water privation, thermal deviations from the optimum, tissue injury, the action of sex hormones, or other causes."[25]

Under the pressure of needs and drives the organism undertakes adaptive actions. The patterns of actions which lead to reduction of a need become predominant or reinforced. Apparently, this is exactly what Thorndike had in mind with his "stamping in" concept in the law of effect (cf. Chapter 1, Section 3).

A stimulus which leads to a need-reducing action may become associated with another, originally neutral, stimulus. This is conditioning as described by Pavlov. Hull believes that no conditioning will take place unless there is need reduction. Reinforcement is need reducing, and conditioning takes place only when there is reinforcement. In Hull's frame of reference, "the conditioned reaction is a special case of the law of effect."

Reinforcement is explained by Hull as follows: "Whenever a reaction (R) takes place in temporal contiguity with an afferent receptor impulse ($\dot{s}$) resulting from the impact upon a receptor of a stimulus energy (S), and this conjunction is followed closely by the diminution in a need (and the associated diminution in the drive, D, and in the drive receptor discharge, s_D, there will result an increment, Δ ($\dot{s} \rightarrow R$), in the tendency for that stimulus on subsequent occasions to evoke that reaction."[26]

This tendency for a given stimulus to "evoke that reaction" on subsequent occasions is called *habit*. Habits are reinforced conditioned-response patterns; they are persistent patterns of behavior acquired by reinforcement. Once the reinforcing need is removed, habits may become inhibited, weakened, or extinguished. Habits are "set up by virtue of the law of reinforcement." Whenever habits do not lead to the biological adaptation of the organism and do not help survival, they become subject to *experimental extinction* and gradually disappear.

Molar or Molecular

Most of Hull's explanations are stated in two languages, one the empirical description and the other using neurophysiological terms. Stimulus (S) is defined by Hull in terms of physical energy such as mechanical pressure, sound, light, etc. When the organism is exposed to stimulus energy, an *afferent neural receptor* impulse (s) evokes a reaction (R). This process is described by Hull as follows: "When a stimulus (S) impinges on a suitable receptor organ, an afferent neural impulse (s) is generated and is propagated along connected fibrous branches of nerve cells in the general direction of the effector organs, via the brain. During the continued action of the stimulus energy (S), this afferent impulse (s), after a short latency, arises quickly to a maximum of intensity, following which it gradually falls to a

[25] *Ibid.*, p. 239.
[26] *Ibid.*, p. 71.

relatively low value as a simple decay function of the maximum. After the termination of the action of the stimulus energy (S) on the receptor, the afferent impulse (s) continues its activity in the central nervous tissue for some seconds, gradually diminishing to zero as a simple decay function of its value at the time the stimulus energy (S) ceases to act."[27]

Hull's presentation relates behavior to nervous cells, brain, etc. Moreover, Hull seemed to believe that conditioning was influenced by chemical factors which he never explained. He believed that in the final analysis all behavior could be reduced to physicochemical factors. He wrote: "It appears probable that when blood which contains certain chemical substances thrown into it as the result of states of need, or which lacks certain substances as the result of other states of need, bathes the neural structures which constitute the anatomical basis of habit ($_sH_R$), the conductivity of these structures is augmented through lowered resistance either in the central neural tissue or at the effector end of the connection, or both."[28]

In other words, conductivity is probably influenced by the chemistry of the blood. Hull could not go beyond this point because "neuroanatomy and physiology have not yet developed to a point such that they yield principles which may be employed as postulates in a system of behavior theory." Therefore, "any theory of behavior is at present, and must be for some time to come, a molar theory." Molar is opposed to molecular; "the latter would presumably deal with the action of the ultimate nerve cell, the protoplasmic molecules making up the neuron or perhaps the atoms constituting the molecule, or even the electrons, protons, neutrons, etc., constituting the atom. Thus the term *molar* as here used corresponds approximately to the term *macrocosmic*, or *coarse-grained*."[29] The molar approach deals with the organism as a whole, the molecular with the detailed, fine, and exact elements of action of the nervous system. As said before, Hull preferred the molecular approach but, he stated, "Students of the social sciences are presented with the dilemma of waiting until the physio-chemical problems of neurophysiology have been adequately solved before beginning the elaboration of behavior theory. . . . There can be hardly any doubt that a theory of molar behavior founded upon an adequate knowledge of both molar and molecular principles would in general be more satisfactory than one founded upon molar considerations alone. . . . It is conceivable that the elaboration of a systematic science of behavior at a molar level may aid in the development of an adequate neuro-physiology and thus lead in the end to a truly molecular theory of behavior firmly based on physiology."[30]

It seems that Hull's approach can be defined as a "not-yet reduc-

[27] *Ibid.*, p. 47.

[28] *Ibid.*, p. 241.

[29] Clark L. Hull, "The Problem of Intervening Variables in Molar Behavior Theory," *Psychological Review*, 1943, 50, 273–291.

[30] Hull, *Principles of Behavior*, p. 20.

tionism." Hull's main definitions and postulates are not firmly rooted in physiology or in any other science. His empirical and experimental data are not physiochemical, physiological, or neurological. His empirical data are derived from and defined in terms of the overt behavior of the organism. The unobservable data, such as need, drive, etc., are defined in neurophysiological terms. Thus, a certain ambiguity is noticeable in Hull's writings which stems probably from his hoped-for but not-yet-proved correspondence between behavioral and neurophysiological terms.

Hull's not-yet reductionism is not a matter of principle but is dictated by the lack of "an adequate neurophysiology." His heart was with reductionism and, whenever it seemed possible, he introduced neurophysiological concepts. Moreover, his way of thinking was always influenced by his desire to use the physiological–molecular frame of reference. The fact remains that he operated with behavioral elements while having in mind the nervous system. Hull's frame of reference is one of interpreting behavior in terms of a living organism interacting with environment through the medium of the nervous system, in accordance with the behavioristic tradition.

Conditioning and Reinforcement

Hull's system underwent definite modifications from the programmatic paper published in 1935,[31] through the comprehensive presentation in a series of papers and in the monumental *Principles of Behavior* (1943), toward its final revision in the *Essentials of Behavior* (1951) and in the posthumously published *A Behavior System* (1952). The main trend of modification was in the direction of a more rigorous formalization and quantification. Initially, Hull worded his postulates in quasi-mathematical terms. Gradually, as experimental data permitted, the postulates were modified till Hull felt that he could incorporate in them the quantitative results of the experiments and formulate them as mathematical equations with the use of probability calculations.

Here we quote verbatim Hull's postulates and corollaries[32] with comments and interpretations whenever necessary.

POSTULATE I. UNLEARNED STIMULUS-RESPONSE CONNECTIONS ($_sU_R$)

Organisms at birth possess receptor-effector connections ($_sU_R$) which under combined stimulation (S) and drive (D) have the potentiality of evoking a hierarchy of responses that either individually or in combination are more likely to terminate a need than would be a random selection from the reactions resulting from other stimulus and drive combinations.

[31] Clark L. Hull, "The Conflicting Psychologies of Learning—A Way Out," *Psychological Review*, 1935, 42, 491–516.
[32] All quotations taken from *A Behavior System*, Yale University Press, 1952, pp. 5–14.

Postulate II. Stimulus Reception (S and s)

A. When a brief stimulus (S) impinges upon a suitable receptor there is initiated the recruitment phase of a self-propagating molar afferent trace impulse ($\dot{s}'$), the molar stimulus equivalent ($\dot{S}'$) of which rises as a power function of time (t) since the beginning of the stimulus, i.e.,

$$\dot{S}' = 465{,}190 \times t^{7.6936} + 1.0 \tag{1}$$

$\dot{S}'$ reaching its maximum (and termination) when t equals about .450″.

B. Following the maximum of the recruitment phase of the molar stimulus trace, there supervenes a more lengthy subsident phase (s'), the stimulus equivalent of which descends as a power function of time (t'), i.e.,

$$S' = 6.9310(t' + .01)^{-1.0796} \tag{2}$$

where $t' = t - .450''$.

C. The intensity of the molar stimulus trace (s') is a logarithmic function of the molar stimulus equivalent of the trace, i.e.,

$$s' = \log S' \tag{3}$$

Postulate III. Primary Reinforcement

Whenever an effector activity (R) is closely associated with a stimulus afferent impulse or trace (s) and the conjunction is closely associated with the rapid diminution in the motivational stimulus (S_D or s_G), there will result an increment (Δ) to a tendency for that stimulus to evoke that response.

Corollary i. Secondary Motivation

When neutral stimuli are repeatedly and consistently associated with the evocation of a primary or secondary drive and this drive stimulus undergoes an abrupt diminution, the hitherto neutral stimuli acquire the capacity to bring about the drive stimuli (S_D), which thereby become the condition (C_D) of a secondary drive or motivation.

Corollary ii. Secondary Reinforcement

A neutral receptor impulse which occurs repeatedly and consistently in close conjunction with a reinforcing state of affairs, whether primary or secondary, will itself acquire the power of acting as a reinforcing agent.

Postulate IV. The Law of Habit Formation ($_sH_R$)

If reinforcements follow each other at evenly distributed intervals, everything else constant, the resulting habit will increase in strength as a positive growth function of the number of trials according to the equation,

$$_sH_R = 1 - 10^{-.0305\dot{N}} \tag{4}$$

where $\dot{N}$ is the total number of reinforcements from Z. Z is the absolute zero of the reaction potential.

The first three postulates represent, in a final and quantified form, Hull's main concepts. The organism functions under definite, innate needs, and responds to stimuli in a manner in which the needs will be terminated. As experimental studies have shown, the most favorable interval between the conditioned stimulus and the unconditioned one was about .450 seconds, when the maximum after-effect of the conditioned stimulus meets with the start of the unconditioned response.[33]

Hull's law of reinforcement as formulated in 1943 closely resembled Thorndike's law of effect: "Whenever a reaction takes place in temporal contiguity with an afferent receptor impulse resulting from the impact upon a receptor of stimulus energy, and this conjunction is followed closely by the diminution of a need (and the associated diminution in the drive and in the drive receptor discharge), there will result an increment in the tendency from that stimulus on subsequent occasions to evoke that reaction. This is the 'law' of primary reinforcement."[34]

In its final formulation (in 1952, as quoted above in the third postulate), Hull preferred to use drive-stimulus (S_D) instead of drive proper (D). It seems that the drive-stimulus is more observable than the drive proper.

In a way, Hull has reversed Pavlov's principles of conditioning. Things become conditioned, says Hull, because of reinforcement and not vice versa. A logical continuation of the third postulate is offered in the two corollaries. Once a certain stimulus has been associated with a certain drive, it becomes, itself, a (secondary) drive. For example, fear, curiosity, etc., can easily become drives once they become associated with hunger or pain or any other primary drive. Moreover, if this secondary drive causes a reduction in the intensity of the stimulus, it acts as a secondary reinforcement (Corollary ii). In Hull's words, "It follows that any stimulus consistently associated with a reinforcement situation will through that association acquire the power of evoking the conditioned inhibition, i.e., reduction in stimulus intensity, and so of itself producing the resulting reinforcement. Since this indirect power of reinforcement is acquired through learning, it is called *secondary reinforcement*."[35]

In contradistinction of Guthrie, Hull believed that the number of reinforcements strengthens the stimulus–response connection or the habit strength (Postulate IV). Habit strength, which is the persistence of the conditioning (the opposite to extinction), is a function of reinforcement.

[33] Gregory A. Kimble, "Conditioning as a Function of the Time between Conditioned and Unconditioned Stimuli," *Journal of Experimental Psychology*, 1947, 37, 1–15. See also Gregory A. Kimble, "Hypothetico-Deductive Method," in B. B. Wolman (Ed.), *International Encyclopedia of Psychiatry, Psychology, Psychoanalysis, and Neurology*, Aesculapius Publishers, 1977, Vol. 5, p. 465.

[34] Hull, *Principles of Behavior*, p. 71.

[35] Clark L. Hull, *Essentials of Behavior*, Yale, 1951, pp. 27–28.

Motivation, Inhibition, and Generalization

Let us start with Hull's fifth and sixth postulates.

POSTULATE V. PRIMARY MOTIVATION OR DRIVE (D)

A. Primary motivation (D), at least that resulting from food privation, consists of two multiplicative components: (1) the drive proper (D'), which is an increasing monotonic sigmoid function of h, the number of hours of food privation; and (2) a negative or inanition component (ϵ), which is a positively accelerated monotonic function of h decreasing from 1.0 to zero, i.e.,

$$D = D' \times \epsilon \tag{5}$$

where

$$D' = 37.824 \times 10^{-27.496} \frac{1}{h} + 4.001$$

and

$$\epsilon = 1 - .00001045 h^{2.486}$$

B. The functional relationship of drive (D) to one drive condition (food privation) is: during the time from h = 0 to about h = 3, drive rises in a linear manner until the function abruptly shifts to a near horizontal, then to a concave-upward course, gradually changing to a convex-upward course reaching a maximum of 12.3σ at about h = 59, after which it gradually falls to the reaction threshold ($_sL_R$) at around h = 100.

C. Each drive condition (C_D) generates a characteristic drive stimulus (S_D), which is a monotonic increasing function of this state.

D. At least some drive conditions tend partially to motivate into action habits, which have been set up on the basis of different drive conditions.

POSTULATE VI. STIMULUS-INTENSITY DYNAMISM (V)

Other things constant, the magnitude of the stimulus-intensity component (V) of reaction potential ($_sE_R$) is a monotonic increasing logarithmic function of S, i.e.,

$$V = 1 - 10^{-.44 \ \log \ S} \tag{6}$$

POSTULATE VII. INCENTIVE MOTIVATION (K)

The incentive component (K) of reaction potential ($_sE_R$) is a negatively accelerated increasing monotonic function of the weight (w) of food or quantity of other incentive (K') given as reinforcement, i.e.,

$$K = 1 - 10^{-a \sqrt{w}} \tag{7}$$

Postulate VIII. The Constitution of Reaction Potential ($_sE_R$)

The reaction potential ($_sE_R$) of a bit of learned behavior at any given stage of learning, where conditions are constant throughout learning and response-evocation, is determined (1) by the drive (D) operating during the learning process multiplied (2) by the dynamism of the signaling stimulus trace (V_1), (3) by the incentive reinforcement (K), and (4) by the habit strength ($_sH_R$), i.e.,

$$_sE_R = D \times V_1 \times K \times {}_sH_R \qquad (8)$$

Corollary iii. Delay in Reinforcement (J)

A. The greater the delay in reinforcement of a link within a given behavior chain, learning and response-evocation conditions remaining constant, the weaker will be the resulting learned reaction potential of the link in question to the stimulus traces present at the time.

B. The greater the delay in the receipt of the incentive by groups of learning subjects, learning and response-evocation conditions remaining constant, the weaker will be the resulting learned reaction potentials ($_sE_{R_d}$), the shape of the gradient as a function of the respective delays being roughly that of decay with the lower limit of the extended gradient passing beneath the reaction threshold, i.e.,

$$J = {}_sE_{R_d} = D \times V_2 \times K \times {}_sH_R \times 10^{-.15d} \times V_1 \qquad (9)$$

where

$$d = \log S' \text{ of } V_1 - \log S' \text{ of } V_2$$

Corollary iv. The Summation ($\dotplus$) of Habit Strengths

If two stimuli, S' and S, are reinforced separately to a response (R) by N' and $\dot{N}$ reinforcements respectively, and the $_{s'}H_R$ generalizes to S in the amount of $_sH'_R$, the summation ($\dotplus$) of the two habit strengths at S will be the same as would result from the equivalent number of reinforcements at S, i.e.,

$$_sH_R \dotplus {}_sH'_R = {}_sH_R + {}_sH'_R - {}_sH_R \times {}_sH'_R \qquad (10)$$

Corollary v. The Summation ($\dotplus$) of Reaction Potentials

If two stimuli, S' and S, are reinforced separately to a response (R) and $_{s'}H_R$ generalizes to S in the amount of $_sE'_R$, of the two reaction potentials will summate at S as would the equivalent number of reinforcements in an original learning, i.e.,

$$_sE_R + {}_sE'_R = {}_sE_R + {}_sE'_R \frac{_sE_R \times {}_sE'_R}{M} \qquad (11)$$

where M is the asymptote of $_sE_R$ by distributed trials.

Corollary vi. The Withdrawal ($\dotdiv$) of Habit Strength

If a smaller habit strength ($_sH'_R$) is to be withdrawn ($\dotdiv$) from a larger habit strength (C), the result will be:

$$C \div {}_sH'_R = {}_sH_R = \frac{C - {}_sH'_R}{1 - {}_sH'_R} \tag{12}$$

Corollary vii. The Withdrawal ($\div$) of Reaction Potential

If a smaller reaction potential (${}_s\underline{E}'_R$) is to be withdrawn ($\div$) from a larger reaction potential (C), the result will be:

$$C \div {}_s\underline{E}'_R = {}_sE_R = \frac{M(C - {}_s\underline{E}'_R)}{M - {}_s\underline{E}'_R} \tag{13}$$

Corollary viii. The Problem of the Behavioral Summation ($\dotplus$) of Incentive Substances (K)

If two incentive substances, f and a, have $A\sqrt{w}$ and $B\sqrt{m}$ as the exponential components of their respective functional equations, the second substance will combine ($\dotplus$) with the first in the production of the total K according to the following equation:

$$K_{f+a} = 1 - 10^{-A\sqrt{w + m \times \frac{B_2}{A_2}}} \tag{14}$$

Postulate IX. Inhibitory Potential

A. Whenever a reaction (R) is evoked from an organism there is left an increment of primary negative drive (I_R) which inhibits to a degree according to its magnitude the reaction potential (${}_sE_R$) to that response.

B. With the passage of time since its formation, I_R spontaneously dissipates approximately as a simple decay function of the time (t) elapsed, i.e.,

$$I'_R = I_R \times 10^{-.018t} \tag{15}$$

C. If responses (R) occur in close succession without further reinforcement, the successive increments of inhibition (ΔI_R) to these responses summate to attain appreciable amounts of I_R. These also summate with ${}_sI_R$ to make up an inhibitory aggregate ($\dot{I}_R$), i.e.,

$$\dot{I}_R = I_R + {}_sI_R \tag{16}$$

D. When experimental extinction occurs by massed practice, the $\dot{I}_R$ present at once after the successive reaction evocations is a positive growth function of the order of those responses ($\dot{n}$), i.e.,

$$\dot{I}_R = 1.84(1 - 10^{-.0434\dot{n}}) \tag{17}$$

E. For constant values of superthreshold reaction potential (${}_s\underline{E}_R$) set up by massed practice, the number of unreinforced responses (n) producible by massed extinction procedure is a linear decreasing function of the magnitude of the work (W) involved in operating the manipulanda, i.e.,

$$n = 3.25(1.1476 - .00984W) \tag{18}$$

Corollary ix. Conditioned Inhibition

Stimuli and stimulus traces closely associated with the cessation of a given activity, and in the presence of appreciable I_R from that response, become conditioned to this particular non-activity, yielding conditioned inhibition ($_sI_R$) which will oppose $_sE_R$'s involving that response, the amount of Δ_sI_R generated being an increasing function of the I_R present.

Corollary x. Inhibitory Potential ($\dot{I}_R$) as a Function of Work

For a constant value of n, the inhibitory potential ($\dot{I}_R$) generated by the total massed extinction of reaction potential set up by massed practice begins as a positively accelerated increasing function of the work (W) involved in operating the manipulandum, which gradually changes to a negative acceleration at around 80 grams, finally becoming asymptotic at around 110 grams.

Corollary xi. Inhibitory Potential ($\dot{I}_R$) as a Function of the Number of Responses

For a constant value of the work (W) involved in operating the manipulandum, the inhibitory potential ($\dot{I}_R$) generated by the total massed extinction of reaction potential set up by massed practice is a negatively accelerated increasing function of the total number of reactions (n) required.

Postulate X. Stimulus Generalization ($_s\overline{H}_R$, $_s\underline{E}_R$, and $_s\dot{I}_R$)

A. In the case of qualitative stimuli, S_1 and S_2, the effective habit strength ($_s\overline{H}_R$) generates a stimulus generalization gradient on the qualitative continuum from the simple learned attachment of S_1 to R:

$$_{S_2}\overline{H}_R = {}_{S_1}H_R \times 10^{-.0135d} \tag{19}$$

where d represents the difference between S_1 and S_2 in j.n.d.,s, and

$$_{S_2}\underline{E}_R = D \times K \times V_2 \times {}_{S_2}\overline{H}_R \tag{20}$$

and where $D \times K \times V_2$ is constant.

B. A stimulus intensity (S_1) generalizes to a second stimulus intensity (S_2) according to the equation

$$_{S_2}\overline{H}_R h_{S_1}H_R \times 10^{-bd} \times V_1 \tag{21}$$

where d represents the difference between S_1 and S_2 in log units and

$$_{S_2}E_R = D \times K \times V_2 \times {}_{S_2}\overline{H}_R \tag{22}$$

and where $(D \times K)$ is constant and V_2 is the stimulus-intensity dynamism at S_2.

C. In the case of qualitative stimulus differences, ordinary conditioning and extinction spontaneously generate a gradient of inhibitory potential ($_sI_R$) which is a negative growth function of $_sI_R$ and d, i.e.,

$$_{S_2}\dot{I}_R = {}_{S_1}I_R \times 10^{-ad} \tag{23}$$

and in the case of stimulus-intensity differences,

$$_{S_2}I_R = {}_{S_1}I_R \times 10^{-bd} \times V_2. \tag{24}$$

Corollary xii. The Generalization of $_sH_R$ and $_sE_R$ on S_D as a Continuum

When a habit is set up in association with a given drive intensity (S_D) and its strength is tested under a different drive intensity, there will result a falling gradient of $_s\bar{H}_R$ and $_sE_R$.

POSTULATE XI. AFFERENT STIMULUS INTERACTION

All afferent impulses (s's) active at any given instant mutually interact, converting each other into š's which differ qualitatively from the original s's so that a reaction potential ($_sE_R$) set up on the basis of one afferent impulse (s) will show a generalization fall to $_šE_R$ when the reaction (R) is evoked by the other afferent impulse (š), the amount of the change in the afferent impulses being shown by the number of j.n.d.'s separating the $_sE_R$'s involved according to the principle

$$d = \frac{\log \dfrac{_sE_R}{_šE_R}}{j} \tag{25}$$

In Hull's theory motivation plays the most important role. There cannot be learning without reinforcement, and reinforcement brings a reduction of drive or of drive-stimulus (S_D). Postulates V, VI, VII, and VIII represent the relationship between the strength of the drive and the resulting reaction potential ($_sE_R$). Obviously $_sE_R$ is a function of the drive (D) and of reinforcement or "habit strength" ($_sH_R$). In addition Hull introduced (in the eighth postulate) two variables, the dynamism of the signaling stimulus trace (V) and the incentive reinforcement (K). He arbitrarily assigned to each of them a decimal value, with a maximum of 1.00, which was a way out of the difficult problem of measurement of D (cf. summary on Hull in this chapter). Drive is the main factor in conditioning; it provides primary and secondary reinforcement and facilitates the transformation of habit strength into reaction potential.

The problem of goal and teleology was one of the controversial issues between McDougall and Watson. Hull took a definite stand on this issue in the early stages of his work on theory formation[36] and included it in Corollary iiiB. The first type of time gradient is created by the rising and declining stimulus trace in classical conditioning (Pavlov). The second type was geared to operant conditioning (Skinner).

What happens when two stimuli become associated with the same response by independent, separate reinforcements? Hull's answer, given in

[36] Clark L. Hull, "The Goal Gradient Hypothesis and Maze Learning," *Psychological Review*, 1932, *39*, 25–43.

Corollaries iv, v, vi, and vii, is represented in the form of mathematical equations which show that the sum obtained is less than the total of the two separate stimuli. Corollary viii gives the mathematical formula for summation of two incentive substances used in conditioning.

The problem of *inhibition* is handled by Hull (Postulate IX) in a manner entirely different from that of Pavlov. Hull distinguished between the *reactive inhibition* (I_R) and the *conditioned inhibition* ($_sI_R$). Inhibition is empirically observed as a lessening or disappearing of the conditioned response. It is an *extinction* of the association between the conditioned stimulus and the conditioned response. Reactive inhibition is the reaction of the organism to effort; it is the aftereffect of a response caused by pain, fatigue, etc. The more that reactive inhibition accumulates, the greater is the likelihood for this inhibition to become conditioned ($_sI_R$). Both types of conditioning together form $_sI_R$, the *inhibitory potential* (Corollaries x and xi).

Postulates X and XI and Corollary xii remind one of Thorndike's spread of effect. The greater is similarity between stimuli (in Thorndike's language, the more "identical elements"), the better are chances for a substitution of one by the other. Hull's *gradient* of generalization (Postulate X) is actually a quantitative elaboration of the aforementioned principle of Thorndike.

Postulate XI is an interesting application of the gradient of generalization which is represented by j, a constant determined by this gradient. In Hull's explanation, this equation defines the amount of reduction of the reaction potential ($_sE_R$) in a way which brought Hull quite close to the gestalt theory of perception (cf. Chapter 12).

Reaction Potential and Secondary Reinforcement

The remaining postulates and corollaries deal mainly with the oscillations of the reaction potential ($_sE_R$) and secondary reinforcement. In 1939, Hull experimented with a trial-and-error type of learning, and his experimental data confirmed his theory of *alternation cycles*. In Thorndike's study of trial-and-error learning the incorrect answers were not eliminated at once but came back occasionally in the later trials. Hull was able to derive a probability equation of oscillations in behavior (Postulate XII), which was experimentally confirmed.[37]

POSTULATE XII. BEHAVIORAL OSCILLATION ($_sO_R$)

A. A reaction potential ($_sE_R$) oscillates from moment to moment, the distribution of behavioral oscillation ($_sO_R$) deviating slightly from the Gaussian probability form in being leptokurtic with β_2 at about 4.0; i.e., the distribution is represented by the equation

---

[37] Clark L. Hull, "Simple Trial-and-Error Learning–An Empirical Investigation," *Journal of Comparative Psychology*, 1939, 27, 233–258.

$$Y = Y_0 \frac{1}{\left(1 + \dfrac{X^2}{\alpha^2}\right)^m}$$

B. The oscillation of $_sE_R$ begins with the dispersion of approximately zero at the absolute zero (Z) of $_sH_R$, this at first rising as a positive growth function of the number of subthreshold reinforcements to an unsteady maximum, after which it remains relatively constant though with increasing variability.

C. The oscillations of competing reaction potentials at any given instant are asynchronous.

Corollary xiii. Response Generalization

A. The contraction of each muscle involved in a habitual act varies its $_sE_R$ from instant to instant ($_sO_R$) about a central reinforced region of intensity which is approximately normal (leptokurtic) in distribution; this constitutes response-intensity generalization.

B. Where several muscles jointly contract to produce a given habitual act, the contraction of each muscle varies more or less ($_sO_R$) independently of the others, producing a qualitative deviation from the central tendency of the joint result of the muscular contractions originally reinforced; this constitutes qualitative response generalization.

POSTULATE XIII. ABSOLUTE ZERO OF REACTION POTENTIAL (Z) AND THE REACTION THRESHOLD ($_sL_R$)

A. The reaction threshold ($_sL_R$) stands at an appreciable distance (B) above the absolute zero (Z) of reaction potential ($_sE_R$), i.e.,

$$_sL_R = Z + B \tag{26}$$

B. No reaction evocation (R) will occur unless the momentary reaction potential at the time exceeds the reaction threshold, i.e., unless,

$$_s\dot{\overline{E}}_R > {}_sL_R \tag{27}$$

Corollary xiv. The Competition of Incompatible Reaction Potentials ($_s\overline{E}_R$)

When the net reaction potentials ($_sE_R$) to two or more incompatible reactions (R) occur in an organism at the same instant, each in a magnitude greater than $_sL_R$, only that reaction whose momentary reaction potential ($_s\dot{\overline{E}}_R$) is greatest will be evoked.

POSTULATE XIV. REACTION POTENTIAL ($_sE_R$) AS A FUNCTION OF REACTION LATENCY ($_st_R$)

Reaction potential ($_sE_R$) is a negatively accelerated decreasing function of the median reaction latency ($_st_R$), i.e.,

$$_sE_R = 2.845(_st_R)^{-.483} \tag{28}$$

Postulate XV. Reaction Potential ($_sE_R$) as a Function of Reaction Amplitude (A)

Reaction potential ($_sE_R$) is an increasing linear function of the Tarchanoff galvanic skin reaction amplitude (A), i.e.,

$$_sE_R = .02492A \tag{29}$$

Postulate XVI. Complete Experimental Extinction (n) as a Function of Reaction Potential ($_sE_R$)

A. The reaction potentials ($_sE_R$) acquired by massed reinforcements are a negatively accelerated monotonic increasing function of the median number of massed unreinforced reaction evocations (n) required to produce their experimental extinction, the work (W) involved in each operation of the manipulandum remaining constant, i.e.,

$$_sE_R = 4.0(1 - 10^{-.0110n}) + .46 \tag{30}$$

B. The reaction potentials ($_sE_R$) acquired by quasi-distributed reinforcements are a positively accelerated monotonic increasing function of the median number of massed unreinforced reaction evocations (n) required to produce their experimental extinction, the work (W) involved in each operation of the manipulandum remaining constant, i.e.,

$$_sE_R = .1225 \times 10^{.0647n} + 2.114 \tag{31}$$

Postulate XVII. Individual Differences

The "constant" numerical values appearing in equations representing primary molar behavioral laws vary from species to species, from individual to individual, and from some physiological states to others in the same individual at different times, all quite apart from the factor of behavioral oscillation ($_sO_R$).

Corollary xv. Secondary Reinforcement by Fractional Antedating Goal Reaction ($r_G \rightarrow s_G$)

When a stimulus (S) or a stimulus trace (s) acts at the same time that a hitherto unrelated response (R) occurs and this coincidence is accompanied by an antedating goal reaction (r_G), the secondary reinforcing powers of the stimulus evoked by the latter (s_G) will reinforce S to R, giving rise to a new S→R dynamic connection.

Postulates XIII, XIV, XV, and XVI and Corollary xiv deal with the problem of the conditioned response or potential of reaction ($_sE_R$). Postulate XIII, which sounds like one of the axioms of Euclid, states that the threshold of reaction must stand above the zero point of the potential of reaction. Obviously, the higher the reaction potential, the more unreinforced evocations are necessary to produce experimental extinction. This mathematical relationship is formulated in the sixteenth postulate.

The seventeenth and last postulate deals with the problem of individual differences, a problem which could not be evaded by any psychological study. Pavlov (cf. Chapter 2, Section 3) distinguished between various "temperaments." Hull was aware of the problem of individual differences but he did not go beyond the programmatic statement that individual differences "between species and species, individual and individual, and the same individual at different times" require proper consideration in psychological studies.

In the fifteenth and last corollary quoted, attention is again paid to the reinforcing power of an "antedating goal reaction." In the later chapters of the *Essentials of Behavior* Hull added two more corollaries. The sixteenth corollary explains generalization both in conditioning and in extinction in a case when "substantially the same muscles" are used in different negative or positive responses. The seventeenth corollary describes what happens when the anticipated goal reaction is frustrated. A frustrated anticipation may lead to an increase in drive (D) and result in a higher reaction potential $(_sE_R)$.

The seventeen postulates and seventeen corollaries are followed by 133 theorems in which the theoretical statements are formulated in a manner that permits "the observational determination" of the truth or falsity of the theory. The method chosen by Hull for observational determination was laboratory experimentation.

Experimental Verification

All his life Hull was modifying his theory in an effort to keep it in accord with the experimental evidence. He was stating hypothetical postulates and putting them to an experimental test; obviously, the experimental procedure was geared to the main goal of his research, which was to prove, to disprove, or to adjust his hypotheses in accordance with the observational evidence. Some of these experiments, representative of Hull's method of theory construction, will be described here briefly.

In 1934, Hull tested the goal-gradient hypothesis.[38] In a specially constructed runway, rats were trained to run to the food compartment. The experiment indicated "positive acceleration"; the closer the rats came to the goal, the faster they ran.

Several other experiments in the same vein were conducted by Hull and his associates. In 1947, Arnold trained rats in a special push-button apparatus with food reward.[39] Then the rats had to make a choice to press one

[38] Clark L. Hull, "The Rat's Speed-of-Locomotion Gradient in Approach to Food," *Journal of Comparative Psychology*, 1934, *17*, 393–422.
[39] William J. Arnold, "Simple Reaction Chains and Their Integration. I. Homogeneous Chaining with Terminal Reinforcement," *Journal of Comparative and Physiological Psychology*, 1947, *40*, 349–363.

out of four buttons. All four buttons started a car in motion but no food appeared; after all four buttons had been pressed, the food pellet appeared. No single push-button action was reinforced, but reinforcement was given to the entire series of four push-button actions.

Obviously at the start of the experiment with four buttons the rats had already had some $_sE_R$. The experimenter found an increase of speed in pushing buttons with a remarkable gain at the last button, the nearest to the reinforcement. In this case, the results obtained by theoretical deductions and empirical experimentations were very close to each other, and Hull could rightly say that "This degree of agreement between experiment and theory is, perhaps, as close as may reasonably be expected in the present early stage of the science."[40]

Another experiment, reported by Hull in 1939, dealt with the fact observed by Thorndike, that the "stamped out" responses occasionally came again. In order to find out the quantitative relationship in the alternation of right and wrong answers Hull constructed a special box which was a modification of the Skinner box (cf. this chapter, Section 3). The experimental animals, white rats, had to press either a horizontal or a vertical bar, both bars being reinforced in the earlier stages of the experiment. In the final stage of the experiment, reward was offered to earlier reinforced and weaker vertical bar pressing. All experimental animals showed alternation cycles. Hull drew a curve in which this alternation was marked.[41] A strikingly similar curve was derived by him from his theoretical postulates. Again experiment and theory stated the same truth.

In 1937, Hovland carried out a series of experiments on generalization using human subjects. His studies led to quantitative statements related to the stimulus generalization of the galvanic skin reaction to excitation by auditory vibration.[42] The experiments yielded a "primary stimulus generalization gradient of extinction" fully corroborated by Hull's experimental and theoretical research.

Hull believed that 121 out of 178 theoretical statements included in the book *Behavior System* were experimentally tested, and 87 percent of them were substantially validated.

Concluding Remarks

The strength or weakness of Hull's system does not depend so much on his being right or wrong on a certain issue. The focal problem is that of theory construction, to which we shall return in Chapter 15.

[40] Hull, *A Behavior System*, p. 165.

[41] Hull, "Simple Trial-and-Error Learning—An Empirical Investigation," *Journal of Comparative Psychology*, 1939, 27, 233–258.

[42] C. I. Hovland, "The Generalization of Conditioned Responses," *Journal of General Psychology*, 1937, 17, 125–148.

The hypothetico-deductive system in geometry was developed by Pieri. Critical of the intuitive factors in classical geometry, which uncritically assumed certain facts and relationships, Pieri tried to "objectify" geometry and develop a nonempirical branch of science based on only two undefined and uncritical assumptions: point and motion. Anything else should be deduced by a rigid logical procedure.

It is still open to discussion whether Pieri's method is applicable to empirical sciences and, if so, whether it is the best method for theory construction in psychology. Some critics of Hull seem to be enchanted by the indisputable thoroughness of his endeavor, but feel that it would be rather too early to develop a hypothetico-deductive psychology.

It seems that some of the critics, as, for example, S. Koch in his highly sophisticated analysis of Hull's theory, fail to do justice to Hull. Koch's main effort was directed to a presentation of Hull's theory in an independent, dependent, and intervening variables continuum as suggested by E. Tolman. Although Hull accepted Tolman's idea, still Hull's theory was not constructed in such a continuum. Koch himself noticed that in Hull's *Principles of Behavior* "the terms 'independent variable' and 'dependent variable' are not explicitly used."[43] As Koch remarked, in Hull's theory only the independent and dependent variables are operationally defined, which is in accordance with Hull's policy of using operational terms on observable data only.

Hull's theory did not follow exactly the three-variable continuum. It comes much closer to some sort of applied geometry patterned after Pieri, in which the first part, the bulk of truthful statements, is axiomatically stated, and everything else is derived by a logical inference from the postulates. The second, the applied part, is the testing of the system by experimentation and checking the a priori statements (postulates) against the a posteriori experimental results. Hull kept his promise of transcendent truth. As soon as the quantitative data obtained in experimentation became available, he transformed his postulates into quantitative statements.

However, on this point Hull is most open to criticism. Koch[44] brought sufficient proof that Hull's $_sE_r$ scale value differences were not "expressible on the same scale and in terms of the same unit." Moreover, Hull's "calibration" experiments did not fully justify the calibration. Koch maintains that Hull's quantified postulates are based on "remote inferences by *combining* arbitrary calculations," and he seems to have a point in his criticism.

One is tempted to say that Hull became, to a certain extent, a victim of his zest for mathematics. He knew mathematics and he loved it. Whenever the opportunity came, he quantified his statements, sometimes pursuing

[43]Sigmund Koch, "Clark L. Hull," in W. K. Estes, S. Koch, K. MacCorquodale, P. E. Meehl, C. G. Mueller, Jr., W. N. Schoenfield, and W. S. Verplanck, *Modern Learning Theory*, Appleton-Century-Crofts, 1954, p. 26.

[44]*Ibid.*, p. 128.

the issue *ad absurdum;* for example, the seventh postulate of his general
theory of behavior deals with the quantity of food necessary for conditioning in rats, and the thirteenth postulate represents the rat's reaction time as
a general law of behavior. The generality of such statements has been repeatedly questioned by several critics.

Hull's position on reductionism requires some clarification. His frame
of reference was biological and he always related his theory to the living organism and the nervous system. Undoubtedly, this simultaneous use of
two languages, the language of observed psychological phenomena and the
language of assumed physiological factors, is a source of ambiguity. Moreover, despite Hull's constant reference to neurophysiology, his theory does
not make much use of physiological findings. Like most learning theorists,
Hull did not include in his reasoning the physiological theory of conditioning offered by Pavlov (cf. Chapter 2). Nor did he develop his own physiological theory. Energy meant to Pavlov physical energy; excitation and inhibition are related by Pavlov to definite nervous substances; reinforcement
was a product of greater *amount* of excitation.

Hull always had the greatest admiration for physiology and an unlimited faith in it, but he did not *operate* with physiological terms. His love for
physiology reminds us of Lewin's (cf. Chapter 13) love for mathematics.
Neither of them fully utilized his much professed scientific preferences.

Hull's position could be described as a *proposed* but *not too well practiced reductionism.* One can easily read his works and understand his theory
in terms of the observable psychological data and the system of postulates
from which the data are derived. Naturally, there is the broad frame of reference of the living organism and its physiological needs, but even the
most radical anti-reductionist could not deny the fact that mental phenomena are somehow related to the living matter. As far as methodology of
research is concerned, Hull's method, in contradistinction to Pavlov's, is
non-reductionistic or, as we have named it above, *not-yet-reductionistic.*

Hull accepted the *molar* or *macroscopic* or *coarse-grained* way of interpretation against his own convictions. He believed that ultimately a molecular
theory based on a detailed knowledge of nerve cells could be developed.
Until such time as anatomy and neurophysiology are sufficiently developed, "at the present, and for some time come," the theory of behavior
must be molar. Again Hull expressed his preference for something which
he was unable to implement.

In summary, one feels that Hull's contribution to psychological theory
was probably much greater than Hull's own theory could be. Psychologists
may accept or reject this or that part of Hull's theory or even reject it entirely. But there is a deep feeling of respect and admiration for the house
that Hull built. His theory is entrenched with numerous and ingenious experiments conducted in a most rigorous manner by himself and his brilliant
friends, followers, and disciples, among them J. S. Brown, J. Dollard, C. I.

Hovland, G. E. Kimble, N. E. Miller, O. H. Mowrer, K. W. Spence, and H. G. Yamaguchi (to mention only a few), and some of them assumed for themselves a leading position in the contemporary theory of learning. Hull's way of reasoning is impeccable, his explanations are lucid, and his constant double-check of theory against empirical evidence invites emulation. Some questions still remain open, among them the questions of the generality of his statements and of the general validity of his quantifications and, the most general problem, whether psychology should be studied in the manner in which Hull studied it.

3. B. F. Skinner: Inductive Behaviorism

Operationism

In one respect, Skinner is diametrically opposed to Hull. Hull's main endeavor was to postulate a theory a priori and check the theorems against empirical evidence. Skinner avoided theory. He preferred to start from empirical data and gradually, if at all, proceed toward tentative generalization. Hull represents the *deductive* method in psychological research; Skinner represents the *inductive* method as it was introduced and developed by Francis Bacon, John Stuart Mill, and others (cf. Chapter 15).

Skinner's positivism is closely related to the positivism of Auguste Comte (cf. Chapter 15). Skinner insists on dealing with observable behavior only and rejects any method of inquiry which is not based upon sensory observation or its application. The observed *data* have to be *identified* and stated in clear, unambiguous terms. The next step in research is to put the known facts into *classes* or categories and state *laws* representing their interrelations. Then comes the third and last step, the development of high-order, general *concepts*.

Skinner's system "confines itself to description rather than explanation. Its concepts are defined in terms of immediate observations and are not given local or physiological properties. A reflex is not an arc, a drive is not the state of a center, extinction is not the exhaustion of a physiological substance or state. Terms of this sort are used merely to bring together groups of observations, to state uniformities, and to express properties of behavior which transcend single instances. They are not hypotheses, in the sense of things to be proved or disproved, but convenient representations of things already known. As to hypotheses, the system does not require them—at least in the usual sense."[45]

The influence of Mach and the neo-positivist is apparent in Skinner's works. Psychology, as a scientific discipline, "must describe the event not

[45] B. F. Skinner, *The Behavior of Organisms*, Appleton-Century-Crofts, 1938, p. 44.

only for itself but in its relation to other events"; and, in point of satisfaction, it must *explain*. These are essentially "identical activities," believes Skinner, who accepts "that more humble view of explanation and causation which seems to have been first suggested by Mach," in which "explanation is reduced to description and the notion of the function substituted for that of causation. The full description of an event is taken to include a description of its functional relationship with antecedent events."[46]

The scientist describes what he sees and as much as he can see and seeks functional relations between a given phenomenon and the antecedent and consecutive phenomena. This, Skinner believes, is the only, and the total task of scientific inquiry.

Skinner believes that the "terms 'cause' and 'effect' are no longer widely used in science. . . . The terms which replace them, however, refer to the same factual core. A 'cause' becomes a 'change in an independent variable' and an 'effect' a 'change in a dependent variable.' The new terms do not suggest *how* a cause causes its effect; they merely assert that different events tend to occur together in a certain order."[47]

Skinner's philosophical convictions led him to reject the necessity of any postulates or any variables beyond observable data of the environment and the behavior of organisms. The external variable of which behavior is a function "provides for what may be called a causal or functional analysis. We undertake to predict and control the behavior of the individual organism. This is our 'dependent variable'—the effect for which we are to find the cause. Our 'independent variable'—the causes of behavior—are the external conditions of which behavior is a function."[48]

This attitude brought Skinner close to *operationism*, which is a current trend in the methodology of scientific inquiry. While we shall postpone the detailed and critical analysis of operationism to Chapter 15 of the present volume, a brief description of operationism might be helpful in understanding Skinner's position.

Operationism is a sort of radical empiricism which rejects any speculative approach to the scientific inquiry. As its name indicates, it emphasizes the necessity of keeping an open eye on the operations performed by the scientist. Operationism forces the scientist to abandon the position of naïve realism and to view critically his own research work. Moreover, operationism assumes that the only scientific statements are those which report the results of the scientific inquiry in terms of the deeds done by the research worker, that is, the research operations.

To Skinner, operationism is "the practice of talking about (1) one's observations, (2) the manipulative and calculational procedures involved in

[46] B. F. Skinner, "The Concept of the Reflex in the Description of Behavior," *Journal of General Psychology*, 1931, 5, 427–458.

[47] B. F. Skinner, *Science and Human Behavior*, Macmillan, 1953, p. 23.

[48] *Ibid.*, p. 35.

making them, (3) the logical and mathematical steps which intervene between earlier and later statements, and (4) *nothing else*."[49]

The Problem of Reductionism

A small part of the environment or of the independent variables is enclosed within the organism. It is "private." A private event is distinguished by its limited accessibility to research and by nothing else. "We have no reason to suppose that the stimulating effect of an infected tooth is essentially different from that of, say, a hot stove," wrote Skinner.[50] In studying behavior, we may have "to deal with the stimulation from a tooth as an inference rather than as a directly observable fact."

Skinner was fully aware of the body–mind problem. He wrote: "Modern science has attempted to put forth an ordered and integrated conception of nature. . . . The picture which emerges is almost always dualistic. The scientist humbly admits that he is describing only half the universe, and he defers to another world—a world of mind or consciousness—for which another mode of inquiry is assumed to be required. Such a point of view is by no means inevitable. . . . It obviously stands in the way of a unified account of nature. The contribution which a science of behavior can make in suggesting an alternative point of view is perhaps one of its most important achievements."

The traditional solution of the problem was based on the admission of certain "private events" into the body of scientific inquiry. "It is usually held that one does not see the physical world at all, but only a nonphysical copy of it called 'experience.' When the physical organism is in contact with reality, the experienced copy is called 'a sensation,' 'sense datum' or 'percept'; when there is not contact, it is called an 'image,' 'thought' or 'idea.' Sensations, images, and their congeries are characteristically regarded as psychic or mental events, occurring in a special world of 'consciousness' where, although they occupy no space, they can nevertheless often be seen."[51]

Skinner was strongly opposed to the use of terms which refer to "supposed nonphysical events," such as sensation, image, drive, habit, and instinct. If one assumes that there are such nonphysical events, these events are "private," inaccessible to the public and to objective study.

Skinner's position can be defined as a methodological anti-reductionism. The task of the psychologist is to relate observable data of behavior to the environment in which it takes place. Skinner saw no reason to relate his data to data arrived at an another level of observation by other sciences. Although behavior is correlated to physiological factors, human behavior

[49] B. F. Skinner, "The Operational Analysis of Psychological Terms," *Psychological Review*, 1945, *52*, 270–277, 291–294.
[50] Skinner, *Science and Human Behavior*, p. 258.
[51] *Ibid.*, p. 276.

cannot be described in physiological terms or related to physical or chemical data. Skinner was opposed to explanations of observed facts of behavior "which appeal to events taking place somewhere else, at some other level of observation, described in different terms, and measured, if at all, in different dimensions."[52]

The only task of scientific inquiry is to find the relationship between the stimulus controlled by the experimenter, other experimental variables, and the response of the experimental subject. What is considered today a "private" event, inaccessible to scientific research, will eventually, with the progress of research technique, become amplified and accessible to objective, public, and scientific study.

Reflexes

Psychology is the science of behavior. Behavior is defined by Skinner as "the movement of an organism or of its parts in a frame of reference provided by the organism itself or by various external objects or fields of force. It is convenient to speak of this as the action of the organism upon the outside world, and it is often desirable to deal with an effect rather than with the movement itself, as in the case of the production of sounds."[53]

The simple unit of behavior is *reflex*. Skinner uses the term "reflex" in an unorthodox fashion. To him, reflex is just any "observed correlation of stimulus and response." "The reflex as an analytical unit is actually obtained in *practice*. The unit is a fact, and its validity and the validity of the laws describing its changes do not depend upon the correctness of analytical assumptions or the possibility of a later synthesis of more complex behavior."[54] In later writings, Skinner preferred to identify the elements of a response instead of a response as a whole. He seemed to believe that each response consisted of smaller "atomic" units.

Behavior was related by Skinner to some general "biological advantage" which is not too precisely analyzed. Reflex responses are executed by the smooth muscles, such as the muscles in the walls of the blood vessels and the glands. Reflexes are "intimately concerned with the well-being of the organism. The process of digestion could not go on if certain secretions did not begin to flow when certain types of food entered the stomach. Reflex behavior which involves the external environment is important in the same way. If a dog's foot is injured when it steps on a sharp object, it is important that the leg should be flexed rapidly so that the foot is withdrawn. . . . Such biological advantages 'explain' reflexes in an evolutionary sense: individuals who are most likely to behave in these ways are presumably likely to survive and to pass on the adaptive characteristics to their

[52] B. F. Skinner, "Are Theories of Learning Necessary?" *Psychological Review*, 1950, 57, 193–216.
[53] Skinner, *Behavior of Organisms*, p. 4.
[54] *Ibid.*, p. 29.

offspring."[55] Conditioned reflexes also have "survival value," helping the organism to modify its behavior and to adjust to changing conditions.

Since reflex is the basic unit of observable behavior, the scientific inquiry has to discover the natural laws governing the reflexes. Skinner distinguished between *static, dynamic,* and *interaction* laws.[56]

THE LAWS OF BEHAVIOR

Static Laws

1. *The Law of Threshold.* The intensity of the stimulus must reach or exceed a certain critical value (called the threshold) in order to elicit a response.
2. *The Law of Latency.* An interval of time (called the latency) elapses between the beginning of the stimulus and the beginning of the response.
3. *The Law of Magnitude of the Response.* The magnitude of the response is a function of the intensity of the stimulus.
4. *The Law of After-Discharge.* The response may persist for some time after the cessation of the stimulus.
5. *The Law of Temporal Summation.* Prolongation of a stimulus or repetitive presentation within certain limiting rates has the same effect as increasing the intensity.

Dynamic Laws

6. *The Law of the Refractory Phase.* Immediately after elicitation the strength of some reflexes exists at a low, perhaps zero, value. It returns to its former state during subsequent inactivity.
7. *The Law of Reflex Fatigue.* The strength of a reflex declines during repeated elicitation and returns to its former value during subsequent inactivity.
8. *The Law of Facilitation.* The strength of a reflex may be increased through presentation of a second stimulus which does not itself elicit the response.
9. *The Law of Inhibition.* The strength of a reflex may be decreased through presentation of a second stimulus which has no other relation to the effector involved.
10. *The Law of Conditioning of Type S.* The approximately simultaneous presentation of two stimuli, one of which (the "reinforcing" stimulus) belongs to a reflex existing at the moment at some strength, may produce an increase in the strength of a third reflex composed of the response of the reinforcing reflex and the other stimulus.
11. *The Law of Conditioning of Type R.* If the occurrence of an operant is followed by presentation of a reinforcing stimulus, the strength is increased.
13. *The Law of Extinction of Type R.* If the occurrence of an operant already strengthened through conditioning is not followed by the reinforcing stimulus, the strength is decreased.

The Laws of Interaction

14. *The Law of Compatibility.* Two or more responses which do not overlap topographically may occur simultaneously without interference.

---

[55] Skinner, *Science and Human Behavior,* p. 54.
[56] Skinner, *Behavior of Organisms,* pp. 12–33, 105, 170, 228, 229. By permission of Appleton-Century-Crofts, Inc.

15. *The Law of Prepotency.* When two reflexes overlap topographically and the responses are incompatible, one response may occur to the exclusion of the other.
16. *The Law of Algebraic Summation.* The simultaneous elicitation of two responses utilizing the same effectors but in opposite directions produces a response the extent of which is an algebraic resultant.
17. *The Law of Blending.* Two responses showing some topographical overlap may be elicited together but in necessarily modified forms.
18. *The Law of Spatial Summation.* When two reflexes have the same form of response, the response to both stimuli in combination has a greater magnitude and a shorter latency.
19. *The Law of Chaining.* The response of one reflex may constitute or produce the eliciting or discriminative stimulus of another.
20. *The Law of Induction.* A dynamic change in the strength of a reflex may be accompanied by a similar but not so extensive change in a related reflex, where the relation is due to the possession of common properties of stimulus or response.
21. *The Law of Extinction of Chained Reflexes.* In a chain of reflexes not ultimately reinforced only the members actually elicited undergo extinction.
22. *The Law of the Discrimination of the Stimulus in Type S.* A reflex strengthened by induction from the reinforcement of a reflex possessing a similar but not identical stimulus may be separately extinguished if the difference in stimuli is supraliminal for the organism.
23. *The Law of the Discrimination of the Stimulus in Type R.* The strength acquired by an operant through reinforcement is not independent of the stimuli affecting the organism at the moment, and two operants having the same form of response may be given widely different strengths through differential reinforcement with respect to such stimuli.
24. *The Law of the Operant Reserve.* The reinforcement of an operant creates a single reserve, the size of which is independent of the stimulating field but which is differentially accessible under different fields.

Operant and Respondent Behavior

Whenever behavior is correlated to "specific eliciting stimuli," it is *respondent* behavior, and whenever no such stimuli are present, it is called *operant* behavior. Any modification of the environment is called a stimulus, and a correlated part of behavior a response. The observed relation between them is called reflex. A respondent reflex is regarded as a correlation of stimulus and response. The operant reflex is "a functional part of behavior"; it is spontaneous; it does not originate in the environment. "An operant behavior is an identifiable part of behavior of which it may be said, not that no stimulus can be found that will elicit it (there may be a respondent the response of which has the same topography), but that no correlated stimulus can be detected upon occasions when it is observed to occur."[57] Obviously the term "reflex" originally applied to respondent be-

[57] *Ibid.*, p. 21.

havior only; however, Skinner believes an operant "may and usually does acquire a relation to prior stimulation."

There are two kinds of conditioning. Skinner says the S type of conditioning applies to respondent behavior and the R type is conditioning of operant behavior. In Pavlov's experiments, the reinforcer was paired with the stimulus. In Skinner's experiments, the reinforcer is contingent upon the response. In Skinner's experiments with pigeons, food is the reinforcer. Presenting food when the pigeon raises its head is reinforcement. "The change in frequency with which the head is lifted . . . is the process of operant conditioning. . . . Through operant conditioning the environment builds the basic repertoire with which we keep our balance, walk, play games, handle instruments and tools. . . ." Operant reinforcement "improves the efficiency of behavior." [58]

Skinner revised Thorndike's *law of effect.* "Instead of saying that a man behaves because of the consequences which *are* to follow his behavior, we simply say that he behaves because of the consequences which *have* followed similar behavior in the past. This is, of course, the Law of Effect or operant conditioning." [59]

The term "operant," wrote Skinner, emphasizes the fact that the behavior *operates* upon the environment to generate consequences. In his standard lever-pressing experiment in the specially devised box for experiments with rats (the Skinner box), whenever the pellet of food was produced in the presence of an additional stimulus (such as light or sound) and was not produced without it, discriminatory conditioning took place.

In operant conditioning, the response comes first and then it becomes reinforced. Not only can the stimulus be *discriminatory,* but also the response can be *differentiated.* In a series of experiments with rats Skinner successfully trained the experimental animals to act in different, new, and never before practiced ways.

The Nature of Reinforcement

Thorndike believed that reinforcing stimuli produced either pleasure or pain. Hull substituted drive reduction for pain and pleasure. Pavlov related reinforcement to the amount of energy discharged by the stimulating factor. Skinner's non-reductionism prevented him from accepting Pavlov's interpretation, and the positivistic-inductive method did not allow him to go beyond observable data. The observed data were merely that the more hungry the animal was, the better was his response to the reinforcing stimuli of food; thus, reduction of deprivation was very often reinforcing. Skinner did not go beyond this inductive statement and did not accept its generality or universality. His experimental data show that conditioning

[58] *Ibid.,* p. 66.
[59] *Ibid.,* p. 87.

might have taken place without reduction of deprivation. Skinner was rather undecided as to what really takes place in conditioning. Why does "reinforcement reinforce? . . . The connection between reinforcement and satiation must be sought in the process of evolution. We can scarcely overlook great biological significance of the primary reinforcers. Food, water, and sexual contact, as well as escape from injurious conditions are obviously connected with the well-being of the organism. . . . It is tempting to suppose that other forms of stimulation produced by behavior are similarly related to biologically important events . . . A biological explanation of reinforcing power is perhaps as far as we can go in saying why an event is reinforcing. Such explanation is probably of little help in a functional analysis, for it does not provide us with any way of identifying a reinforcing stimulus as such before we have tested its reinforcing power upon a given organism."[60]

While Skinner felt unable to explain the nature of reinforcement, his experimental studies were a profound contribution toward the understanding of the problem. He could not find the answer to the problem of why reinforcement reinforced, but he did offer a detailed and precise description of reinforcement.

In a series of ingeniously planned experiments with pigeons, Skinner studied *interval* and *ratio* reinforcement; these two types of reinforcement are included in the category of intermittent reinforcement. In experiments related to interval or periodic reinforcement, reinforcements were given at more or less fixed intervals, a definite number of times per hour. The results of this interval reinforcement were rather stable and constant and highly resistant to extinction.

In experiments with ratio reinforcement, the reinforcement was administered not at certain time intervals, but after a certain number of responses. The less frequent the reinforcement, the quicker the response. The ratio of unreinforced responses to reinforced ones, called the *extinction ratio*, was 20:1 in the interval reinforcement and 200:1 in the ratio reinforcement. The implications for education are quite obvious.

An originally neutral stimulus can become reinforcing through repeated association with a reinforcing stimulus. The neutral stimulus acquires a reinforcing value of its own, and may be called a conditioned, secondary, or derived reinforcement. A secondary reinforcement can be extinguished when repeatedly applied to a response for which there is no ultimate primary reinforcement.[61]

Secondary reinforcements can become easily generalized. Whenever they become associated with several primary reinforcers, they can stimulate many various activities. Money, for instance, being associated with the

[60] Skinner, *Science and Human Behavior*, pp. 81–84.
[61] B. F. Skinner, *Contingencies of Reinforcement: A Theoretical Analysis*, Appleton-Century-Fox, 1969.

acquisition of food, clothes, etc., is a good example of a secondary reinforcer which became quite generalized and stimulated a great number of activities.

When operant behavior is not reinforced by delivery of food, the process of extinction starts. The total number of operant responses prior to complete extinction indicates the "reserve" of responses or *reflex reserve*—the number of responses which could be emitted without additional reinforcement.

The *reflex reserve* was originally defined by Skinner as the "*available activity,* which is exhausted during the process of repeated elicitation of which the strength of the reflex is at any moment a function." The reflex reserve indicates the spontaneous recovery from fatigue in respondent reflexes. In operant reflexes it is related to the "strength of reflex," which is proportional to the reserve. "All operations that involve elicitation affect the reserve directly, either to increase or to decrease it. Conditioning increases it; extinction and fatigue decrease it. . . . Facilitation and certain kinds of emotion increase the strength, while inhibition and certain kinds of emotion decrease it without modifying the reserve. The operations that control the drive also affect the proportionality factor. Without altering the total number of available responses, a change in drive may alter the rate of elicitation of an operant from a minimal to a maximal value."[62]

In his later writings, Skinner apparently abandoned this concept. It became superfluous and, in accordance with his philosophy of parsimonious induction, he did not use it any more.

Drives

It was quite easy to find that the number of hours of food deprivation was related to reinforcement. In an experiment with eight rats, Skinner found that the group of rats which suffered a severe food deprivation gave double the number of responses given by the group exposed to mild deprivation. However, deprivation was not correlated to extinction.

Deprivation can be measured; it is an operational term. The term "drive" is not. In his persistent avoidance of going beyond empirical data, Skinner used the term "drive" only as an abbreviated name for the operations by which the rate of responses could be measured. The term "drive," says Skinner, is "simply a convenient way of referring to the effects of deprivation and satiation and of other operations which alter the probability of behavior in more or less the same way. . . . There are many ways of changing the probability that an organism will eat; at the same time, a single kind of deprivation strengthens many kinds of behavior. The concept of hunger as a drive brings these various relations together in a single term. . . . A drive is a verbal device with which we account for a state of

[62]Skinner, *Behavior of Organisms,* pp. 26–27.

strength, and it cannot answer experimental questions. We cannot control the behavior of an organism by directly changing its hunger, its thirst, or its sex drive. In order to change these states indirectly, we must deal with the relevant variables of deprivation and satiation and must face all the complexity of these operations."[63]

Thus, in the spirit of operationism, Skinner did not deal with drive as a cause of behavior; he prefered to discuss deprivation and satiation and to omit the term "drive." For instance, one could say that the eating of salty hors d'oeuvres makes a person thirsty and that the thirst then drives him to drink. It is simpler, in both theory and practice, to restrict ourselves to the fact that consuming salty hors d'oeuvres leads to drinking.

When Skinner comes to the question how many drives there are, he asks instead in how many ways an organism could be deprived. The problem of satiation and deprivation should be dealt with in terms of the functional analysis and the question should read: How many kinds of behavior vary in strength independently of one another?

Apparently, reinforcement strengthens behavior in a given state of deprivation. The effect of deprivation can be experimentally tested.

Emotions

Skinner took a similar operationistic approach to the problem of emotionality. "The emotions are an excellent example of the fictional causes to which we commonly attribute behavior. We run away because of 'fear' and strike because of 'anger' etc.," ridicules Skinner.

Skinner saw in emotions "predispositions to act in certain ways. The 'angry' man shows an increased probability of striking, insulting, or otherwise inflicting injury. . . . The man 'in love' shows an increased tendency to aid, favor, be with. . . . The names of the so-called emotions serve to classify behavior with respect to various circumstances which affect its probability. . . ." Emotion can be defined as "a conceptual state, in which a special response is a function of circumstances in the history of the individual. . . . But so defined, an emotion, like a drive, is not to be identified with physiological or psychic conditions."[64]

In accordance with Skinner's theory of reinforcement, the emotional responses are reinforced by their consequences, or feedback mechanism. Food is reinforcing to a hungry organism and damage inflicted upon an opponent reinforces anger. Some emotional responses, as already observed by J. B. Watson, are not conditioned. An angry child may strike or bite without prior conditioning. Adults possess, as a rule, a "full fledged repertoire" of conditioned responses of angry behavior, verbal and otherwise.

Motivation (drives) and emotions overlap. An extreme deprivation is

[63] Skinner, *Science and Human Behavior*, p. 144.
[64] *Ibid.*, pp. 162–163.

usually an emotional operation. The starving man is almost necessarily frustrated and afraid, and nostalgia includes both a drive and an emotion, said Skinner.

Emotions could be defined "as a particular class of strength or weakness in one or more responses induced by any one of a class of operations" and should not be perceived as causes of behavior. The causes are the stimuli. The so-called emotions are indicators of probability of the strength of certain responses.

"As long as we conceive of the problem of emotion as one of inner states, we are not likely to advance a practical technology. The behavior observed during an emotion is not to be confused with emotion as a hypothetical 'state' any more than eating is to be confused with hunger. An angry man, like a hungry man, shows a disposition to act in a certain way. He may never act in that way, but we may nevertheless deal with the probability that he will do so. Just as we infer from a history of deprivation that a man is probably hungry even though he is unable to eat, so we infer that he is probably angry by showing that he generally behaves in an angry fashion upon similar occasions."[65]

Skinner consistently avoided the mentalistic terms "pleasure" and "displeasure." He preferred to discuss behavior in terms of *positive* vs. *negative* reinforcers. Positive reinforcers add something to the existing situation, for example, food or water. Negative reinforcers remove something from a given situation, for example, removal of an electric shock or extreme heat. In experiments with both types of reinforcers the probability of response was increased.

One could translate Skinner's reasoning and say that the positive reinforcers procure pleasure and the negative reinforcers remove pain. But this translation is exactly what Skinner avoided all his life. A positive reinforcer, he wrote, is any stimulus, the presentation of which strengthens the behavior on which it is made contingent. A negative reinforcer is any stimulus the withdrawal of which strengthens behavior.

An aversive stimulus can be withdrawn to reinforce behavior. In non-Skinnerian language, the withdrawal of the stimulus reduces tension or drive. In Skinner's operationist description, it merely increases behavior or reinforces. For instance, shaming someone into an effort is a presentation of an aversive stimulus; withdrawal of the shame, if effort is made reinforces the behavior. Obviously, any stimulus which consistently precedes the aversive withdrawal of a positive reinforcer can come to act as a conditioned negative reinforcer.

Anxiety is a result of conditioning. Whenever "a stimulus characteristically *precedes* an aversive stimulus by an interval of time sufficiently great" certain *effects* or behavioral changes take place. These resulting changes are called anxiety. Any single aversive stimulus, such as the death of a friend, may be followed by the "feeling of doom," or similar anxiety

[65] *Ibid.*, p. 168.

states. Naturally, Skinner's term "anxiety" is not an "inner state" but "a set of emotional predispositions attributed to a special kind of circumstance."[66]

Skinner offered a highly illuminating analysis of the psychology of punishment, which was applied in an experimental study by W. K. Estes.[67] The positive reinforcers, in lay language, are rewards; the withdrawal of an aversive, negative reinforcer is a reward too. Punishment is the application of a negative stimulus or the withdrawal of a positive one. Punishment stops a certain response by eliciting an incompatible response. When a child giggles in church, pinching the child will elicit pain and stop the giggling. A severe punishment may suppress, although not permanently, the occurrence of the punished behavior in the future. The third effect of punishment corresponds to what Freud called repression. Skinner, using terms of overt behavior, said that punishment may establish aversive conditions which are avoided by the organism.

The unfortunate by-products of punishment are reduction of the efficiency of the punished organism and generation of rage and fear. Instead of punishment, Skinner suggests extinction and positive conditioning of incompatible behavior.

Making Decisions

A functionally unified system of responses is often called *self*. However, this concept represents a presumably coherent system of responses and indicates consistencies of behavior which can be doubted. Behavior is a function of environment, and "the pious churchgoer on Sunday may become an aggressive, unscrupulous businessman on Monday. He possesses two response systems appropriate to different sets of circumstances, and his inconsistency is no greater than that of the environment which takes him to church on Sunday and to work on Monday," wrote Skinner.[68] Decisions made by an individual are a function of environmental stimuli, just as any other responses are.

Skinner rejected the idea of an "innerself," will power, or any other construct put between the independent and dependent variables. All areas of behavior, he believed, could and should be handled in the same manner of cautious, objective, and "public" observation.

In decision making, some variable are "private events" within the organism. Skinner saw in decision making a preliminary behavior responsible for the action decided on, and believed that even this complex problem could be handled without resolving to "inner factors."

The behavior of decision making helps one to escape from indecision.

[66]*Ibid.*, pp. 180–181.
[67]William K. Estes, "An Experimental Study of Punishment," *Psychological Monographs*, 1944, 57, No. 263.
[68]Skinner, *op. cit.*, p. 286.

The oscillation between incomplete forms of response is time consuming, and therefore, aversive. The behavior which puts an end to this conflict by withdrawing the aversive stimulus is reinforcing. Socially administered reinforcement increases the probability of making decisions.

Thinking and problem solving can be defined as behavior "which, through the manipulation of variables, makes the appearance of a solution more probable. . . ." Whenever an organism is in a state of deprivation or aversive stimulation, one possibility is to manipulate stimuli until those stimuli are found which control the response which brings the solution to the problem. One increases the chances of a solution by looking over the problem carefully and arranging and rearrranging all the relevant stimuli until the solution comes. Another method of problem solving consists of a review of tentative solutions.

Concluding Remarks

Among psychologists, Skinner is the most persistent in the application of inductive empiricism. His method of rigorous observation and experimentation is, indeed, impressive. If a prize were offered for sober generalization and parsimonious use of concepts, it would be surely given to Skinner.

Skinner never accepted easy solutions offered by shallow reductionism nor did he indulge in farfetched dualistic hypotheses. Whenever observations warranted it, new generalizations were introduced. Accordingly, Skinner introduced such concepts as operant behavior, positive and negative conditioning, and intermittent reinforcement. Whatever Skinner said was related to observed phenomena and their interrelationships.

And yet, what would one say if a chemist or a physicist confined his study to the observable data only? Did Einstein deal with an empirically perceptible fourth dimension? Did Mendeleyev observe all the chemical elements?

Skinner refused to deal with the crucial problem of motivation because "we cannot control the behavior of an organism by directly changing its hunger, its thirst, or its sex drive. In order to change these states indirectly, we must deal with the relevant variables of deprivation and satiation and must face all the complexity of these operations."[69]

Actually, we cannot control the behavior of human organisms even indirectly. No psychologist would try to produce experimentally sexual craving, or homosexuality, or the desire to rob or kill. The psychological laboratory works within a limited scope of experimentation. As far as human drives and emotions are concerned, the range of experimentation is very restricted.

Should this exclude human drives and emotions from the scope of psy-

[69] Ibid., p. 144.

chological inquiry? If stars and moons do not fit laboratory work, should we change the subject matter or the method of scientific inquiry?

What Skinner studied, he studied thoroughly and precisely. But what he omitted, could represent some important problems of human behavior. Skinner says that "a child is made more likely to drink milk by restriction of his water intake." Any psychiatrist or child psychologist would contest this statement and present empirical evidence contrary to Skinner's, for human motivation is not simply a matter of supply and deprivation.

Skinner was strongly opposed to the "traditional pattern of looking for a course of human behavior inside the organism." He believed that this "pattern of an inner explanation of behavior is best exemplified by doctrines of animism. . . . The traditional procedure has been to invent an inner determiner, a 'demon,' 'spirit,' 'homunculus' or 'personality' capable of change of course or of origination of action." [70] Skinner seems to have taken a radical behaviorist stand, even more radical than J. B. Watson's.

Moreover, clinical and experimental studies of conversion hysterias, anorexias, and psychosomatic medicine cannot avoid this "inner" explanation so carefully avoided by Skinner.

Like many other scientists, Skinner tried to avoid the "bifurcation of nature into physical and psychic" by assuming that the organism "simply reacts" to environment. But it is not that simple. The reaction of the human organism to the environment is not the same as the reaction of amoebas. There must be some "inner causes." These may or may not be proved to be physiological, but they cannot be dismissed. The business of science is to study *all* facts, even if they do not fit into some particular frame of reference.

However, it has to be said that what was observed by Skinner was observed very carefully, and a great many psychoanalytic findings fit well into his system. Skinner explained with great clarity such phenomena as repression, symbols, and reaction formation, without using Freud's "mechanisms." As a keen observer, he could not have overlooked the contribution of another keen observer. What he resented was the freedom with which Freud introduced models between observable independent and dependent variables.

The greatness of Skinner's system lies in his refusal to answer the questions of why aversive stimuli are aversive and why positive stimuli are reinforcing. To have done so would have meant to deal with the so-called "private events." This is what Freud did. It was Freud's greatness that he had the courage to go beyond the observable data. One may say that both Skinner and Freud were looking on the same object: Skinner from the outside, Freud from the inside. Their findings cannot be mutually contra-

[70] B. F. Skinner, "Critique of Psychoanalytic Theory," in H. Feigl and M. Scriven (Eds.), *Minnesota Studies in the Philosophy of Science*, University of Minnesota, Vol. 1, 1958, p. 79. Also, B. F. Skinner, *About Behaviorism*, Knopf, 1974.

dictory (cf. Chapter 6 on Freud and Chapter 15 on the scientific method), although they do report on different sides of observed phenomena.

4. EDWARD C. TOLMAN: PURPOSIVE BEHAVIORISM

Is Tolman a Behaviorist?

K. W. Spence suggested dividing all theories of learning into two groups.[71] To the first, the stimulus–response (S-R) group, belong the theories of Thorndike, Hull, Guthrie, Miller, Dollard, and Spence. To the other, the stimulus–sign (S-S) group, belong Köhler, Koffka, Lewin, Tolman Adams, and Zener. The stimulus–response group relies heavily on associationism, while the stimulus–sign group relates learning to the processes of perception.

Actually, Tolman's system defies classification. Tolman has been no more influenced by Lewin than by Watson or Pavlov, no less by Freud than by McDougall or Woodworth. Tolman's system is unique in its deep consideration of the problems of theory construction and its emphasis on the need to develop a stimulus–response type of theory interpolated by theoretical interpretation of nonobservable factors. The authors of an excellent volume devoted to the scientific analysis of learning theories have been much influenced in their method of analysis by Tolman's methodology.[72] When Estes, Koch, and others critically reviewed contemporary psychological theory, they related their findings to the triple factors of independent, dependent, and intervening variables as postulated by Tolman. Tolman's *operationism*, which insisted that psychological concepts be testable by "concrete repeatable observations," influenced an entire generation of psychologists, and Tolman's eclecticism invited a large number of intersystemic studies.

We have decided to include Tolman in this chapter, which deals with neo-behaviorism, because of our principle of "common roots." We may doubt whether Tolman's system was "genuine behaviorism," as Hilgard said,[73] but we have no doubts that Tolman's system was rooted in behaviorism. Tolman originally deviated from Watson on two issues, purposivism and molar behavior.

Tolman, like most contemporary neo-behaviorists, is a methodological non-reductionist. "Psychology, like physics, must take immediate experience for granted and then proceed to develop maps, rules and equations for finding one's way about. Physics develops one type of such a map and psy-

[71] Kenneth W. Spence, "Theoretical Interpretations of Learning," in S. S. Stevens (Ed.), *Handbook of Experimental Psychology*, Wiley, 1951.

[72] W. K. Estes, S. Koch, K. MacCorquodale, P. E. Meehl, C. G. Mueller, Jr., W. N. Schoenfeld, and W. S. Verplanck, *Modern Learning Theory*, Appleton-Century-Crofts, 1954.

[73] Ernest R. Hilgard, *Theories of Learning* (2nd ed.), Appleton-Century-Crofts, 1956.

chology another, and the two maps are ultimately to be fitted together as to make complete prediction—complete finding of our way out—possible," wrote Tolman in 1936.[74]

The ultimate goal of this science is the development of both psychological and physiological behaviorism. The facts and laws of physiology will presumably explain the facts and laws of psychology; however, "psychology cannot be explained by a physiology until one has a psychology to explain." Thus, psychology must use its own methods and tools and develop its own set of testable concepts, which eventually should be "fitted together." The observable acts of behavior are the legitimate subject matter of psychology in accordance with the behavioristic tradition.

Independent Variables

According to Tolman, what can be observed and operationally assessed are the initiating causes of behavior and the final resulting behavior itself. The initial causes of behavior consist of five *independent variables*, namely (1) the environmental stimuli (S), (2) physiological drive (P), (3) heredity (H), (4) previous training (T), and (5) maturity or age (A). Behavior (B) is a function (f) of S, P. H, T, and A.

$$B = f_1(S, P, H, T, A)$$

The function (f_1) has to be broken down into a set of mental processes which will figure "in the guise of objectively definable *intervening variables.*"

The environmental stimulus (S) and the physiological drive (D) are the *releasing* variables. They "set behavior going." Heredity (H), previous training (T), and a given age or maturity (A) are *guiding* variables, for they do not initiate behavior, but do determine to a great extent the final character of behavior which is initiated by S and P.

The stimulus (S) and the drive (D) can be observed and measured. The stimulation can be determined by the experimenter and easily described in operational terms. The physiological drive can be presented operationally and measured by the amount of deprivation in an experimental situation, as it was by Warden's measurement of the time since the last feeding.[75]

The list of independent variables stated in *Purposive Behavior in Animals and Men* (1932) was revised in 1937 to include the following independent variables, divided into two groups. The first group includes the *individual difference* variables heredity (H), age (A), previous training (T), and some organic factors such as endocrine and vitamin conditions (E). The ex-

[74] Edward C. Tolman, "The Intervening Variable," in M. H. Marx (Ed.), *Psychological Theory*, Macmillan, 1951, p. 88.

[75] C. J. Warden, *Animal Motivation, Experimental Studies on the Albino Rat*, Columbia University, 1931.

perimental independent variables include the *sum of preceding occasions* (ΣOBO) in which a certain stimulus complex (O) was followed by a certain behavior (B) and this behavior was followed by another stimulus complex (O). The other independent variables are the *maintenance schedule* (M), meaning the state of the drive at a given time, the appropriateness of the *goal object* (G) which describes the incentive, the *stimuli* (S), the types of *motor response* required (R) by the experimenter in his experimental design, and finally, the *pattern* of the preceding and succeeding maze units (P), which represents the experimental tools and setup.[76]

Dependent Variables: Molar, Docile, and Purposeful Behavior

The *dependent variables* include the observable behavior of the organism. In maze experiments with rats, Tolman proposed the *behavior ratio* as the measurable dependent variable. The behavior ratio is the frequency of the turns of the rat into the right alley divided by the total frequency of all right and wrong turns.

On the whole, behavior of organisms is active and selective. In Tolman's experiments, the rat "often has to look actively for the significant stimuli in order to form his map and does not merely passively receive and reset to all the stimuli which are physically present."[77]

Although behavior is a stimulus–response affair, it is not a mechanistic S-R relationship. Tolman distinguishes two types of behavior. The first is *simple reflex* or *tropism*. The lower the organism, the more physiological its response. All behavior is "disturbance and quiescence," but only some of it is reflex. The simple reflexes, like the spinal reflex, are *molecular*.

Docile, or teachable, behavior is *molar*. It is the function of the organism as a whole. Whenever the organism as a whole does something, such an action is goal directed and not a mechanistic stimulus–response connection.

Tolman's system deals with docile behavior. Docile behavior is *purposive* and *cognitive* and presents the problems of hierarchy of demands, sign–gestalt, readiness, and expectation. Docile behavior is molar; it does not break up into atomistic reflexes and it has a meaning. It is determined by the goal-directed perceptions of the totality of the situation, or the *sign–gestalt expectations*.

The sign–gestalt expectation, in simple language, represents a combination of perception and motivation. There are three "modes" of expectation: (1) perception, (2) memorization, and (3) inference, which can be

[76] Edward C. Tolman, "The Determiners of Behavior at a Choice Point," *Psychological Review*, 1938, 45, 1–41.
[77] Edward C. Tolman, *Purposive Behavior in Animals and Men*, Appleton-Century Crofts, 1932, p. 201.

translated to (1) cognition of the environment, (2) retention of perceived data, and (3) deriving of conclusions by inference in future and similar situations.

Tolman's main idea is that behavior is not a sequence of causes and effects but a chain of goals and actions leading toward the goal object. The experimental animals in Tolman's experiment follow neither Thorndike's trial and error nor Pavlov's and Skinner's conditioning. They have a "goal" and behave as if they were following some "signs" which made them "expect" to reach the goal. Perception and motivation are the main elements in Tolman's theory. The organism learns through the perception of the stimulus, the sign which leads to a purposeful action of the organism. Thus the sign–gestalt expectation, which represents a combination of motivating and perceptory elements, must be considered the main concept in Tolman's theory.

Intervening Variables

Between the observable independent variables and the observable dependent variables, Tolman postulates a set of inferred and non-observed factors.

These *intervening variables* are the determinants of behavior. They are divided into (1) immanent purposive and cognitive determinants, (2) capacities, and (3) behavior adjustments. They cannot be directly observed, but they can be inferred from behavior. "They are to behavior as electrons, curves, or whatever it may be, are to the happenings in inorganic matter."[78]

The original list of intervening variables (1937) included six factors coordinated to the independent variables. The intervening variable *observed* was correlated to the maintenance schedule; *appetite* to the appropriateness of goal object; *differentiation* to the types and modes of stimuli provided; *motor skill* to the types of motor responses required in the experiment; *hypotheses* to the cumulative nature and number of trials; *biases* to the pattern of preceding and succeeding maze units.

In 1952, Tolman revised his list of intervening variables and suggested the following three main variables: (1) the *need-systems*, which depend on the physiological deprivation or drive situation at a given moment, (2) the *belief-value* motives, representing the degree of preferences of certain goal objects and their relative strengths or "values" in gratification of needs or deprivation, and (3) the *behavior-spaces*, a term obviously borrowed from K. Lewin (cf. Chapter 13). Behavior, says Tolman, takes place in the behavior-space; the acting organism or the actor "moves" in the space. Some objects attract him—i.e., they have a *positive valence*. Some repel him—for they have a *negative valence*. The term "valence" is used by Tolman in the frame-

[78] *Ibid.*, p. 414.

work of perception; some objects are *perceived* as to be sought or to be avoided.[79]

Motivation

"Behavior goes off, in the last analysis, by virtue only of certain final physiological quiescences, which are being sought, or of certain final physiological disturbances, which are being avoided. . . . Organisms are provided innately, at least vaguely, with sign-gestalt-readinesses as to how to get thus to and from, and also with the necessary accompanying demands to make them actually try thus to get to and from. Organisms are innately ready, provided they are also suffering at the moment from appropriate initiating organic states or excitements, to demand certain quiescences to-be-reached and certain disturbances to be avoided. And they expect that positive or negative commerces with the objects presented by stimuli will, or will not, get them to and from."[80]

Following in the steps of W. Craig,[81] Tolman distinguishes appetites and aversions. The ultimate goal of appetites is the "state of physiological quiescence to be reached by commerce with the consummatory object." The ultimate goal of aversion is the state of physiological quiescence to be reached when the disturbing stimulus ceases to act upon the organism. Appetites and aversions are "states of agitation."

Tolman believes that the consummatory and avoidance responses of the organism are "usually docile and not wholly blind and reflex." The states of agitation, or the "initating organic states of excitement," are both purposive and cognitive.

An appetite or an aversion has three phases, as follows: (1) a *physiological state* metabolically determined, which gives rise to (2) a *demand* for action leading to a physiological quiescence and (3) a "sign-gestalt-readiness" as to the type of stimulus object to be sought to achieve the demanded quiescence.

Appetites, such as hunger and sex, follow a metabolic cycle or rhythm. Aversions, such as fear or pugnacity, tend to be enduring and constant.

Following the example set by McDougall (cf. Chapter 5), Tolman set up a list of human appetites and aversions. Tolman distinguished six appetites: food hunger, sex hunger, excretion hunger, specific contact hunger, rest hunger, and sensory–motor hunger (aesthetic and play hunger). The initiating physiological state of each appetite is the state of disequilibrium in the organism. When this disequilibrium is in force, a demand is released

[79] Edward C. Tolman, "A Psychological Model," in T. Parsons and E. A. Shils (Eds.), *Toward a General Theory of Action*, Harvard, 1951.

[80] Edward Chace Tolman, *Purposive Behavior in Animals and Men*, The Century Co., 1932, p. 271.

[81] W. Craig, "Appetites and Aversions as Constituents of Instincts," *Biological Bulletin*, 1918, *34*, 91–107.

for a state of physiological quiescence. The demand is accompanied by a sign–gestalt readiness that the demanded quiescence lies in a certain means–end relation with a certain goal object. In the case of food hunger, the demand for alimentary satiation is accompanied by the sign–gestalt readiness that certain types of food are appropriate to reach satiation. In the case of contact hunger, the demand is for the quiescence of the physiological disequilibrium of bodily contacts such as thumb-sucking and bed-wetting. Tolman was not sure whether these needs formed a part of sex hunger, as suggested by Freud (cf. Chapter 6), or were an independent appetite.

There are two aversions, said Tolman: fright and pugnacity. Fright is avoidance of injury and pugnacity is avoidance of interference. In fright, the demand is to avoid the physiological disturbance of pain or injury and the sign–gestalt readiness is that a certain fright-evoking object will lead to such pain or injury. In pugnacity, the interference with one's activities is the physiological disturbance to be avoided.

As said before, the *motivators* of all behavior, with the exception of "pure reflexes and tropisms," are the innate appetites and aversions. Appetites lead toward physiological quiescences, aversions lead away from physiological disturbances. In both cases the organism "is provided innately with certain more or less vague sign-gestalt-readinesses as to how to get thus to and from. In the case of an appetite he is provided innately with some vague sign-gestalt-readiness as to the type of consummatory object and consummatory response which will lead to the given quiescence—and also, it would seem, with some vague subordinate sign-gestalt-readiness as to how to explore in order to get the consummatory objects. That is, when the appropriate stimuli are provided he tends to 'perceive' the appropriate consummatory and subordinate objects and to respond more or less correctly to them." [82]

The appetites and aversions, together called *first-order drives,* are docile, that is, capable of modification. In addition to these drives, humans are motivated by *second-order drives,* such as curiosity, gregariousness, self-assertion, self-absement, and imitativeness. The second-order drives are "in some measure due to their own innate initiating physiological states," so they are relatively independent of the first-order drives. However, being weaker than the first-order drives, the second-order drives usually become subordinate to them.

At this point, Tolman quoted Dunlap and Kempf. Dunlap related the dominance–submission pattern to disturbances in the tissues of the circulatory and respiratory systems. [83] Kempf developed a theory of drives, relating them to the viscera and skeletal muscles controlled by the autonomic nervous system. [84] Although, to quote Tolman, these are "arm-chair specu-

[82] Tolman, *Purposive Behavior,* p. 287.
[83] Knight Dunlap, *Elements of Scientific Psychology,* Mosby, 1922, pp. 324 ff.
[84] Edward J. Kempf, *The Autonomic Functions and Personality,* Nervous & Mental Disease Publishing Co., 1918.

lations," still, he believes, they perhaps do justify the notion that the second-order drives could have their own physiological initiating states and their own definitive quiescences and disturbances.[85]

In the controversy between heredity and environment, or instincts and learning, Tolman took a moderate stand. He disagreed with the attacks on the theory of instincts, as follows: "Every response when it appears, represents a convergence between the effects of both inherited dispositions and past environmental media. Responses cannot, therefore, it is said, be subdivided into the two neat categories: instinct, or the primarily hereditarily induced, on the one hand, and habit, or the primarily environmentally induced, on the other. There can be no behavior purely dependent upon innate endowment and none purely dependent upon past training,"[86] and the first- and second-order drives, being innate, "qualify as instincts."

The second-order drives "seem to be aversions" for they "appear to be evoked primarily by external situations." They are not cyclical or spontaneously aroused, as are the appetites.

Some combinations of first- and second-order drives create *personality mechanisms*, such as phobias, compulsions, sex perversions, and the "somewhat less certain," psychoanalytically conceived processes of Oedipus complex, transference, sublimation, compensation, and symbolisms. Tolman believed that all these personality mechanisms are modifications of sign–*gestalt* expectations and readinesses released by drives of the first and second order. The main mechanisms, he believed, are repression, fixation, and sign–magic.

Repression causes the repressed material to be insulated from new experiences. Once the repressed material is brought into consciousness, its sign–gestalt sequences become exposed to new experiences and break up. Thus the phobia, which is a combination of fixation and repression, will be cured as soon as it is brought into the consciousness.

Theory of Learning

Tolman believed that the behavior of organisms is docile. With the exception of tropism and the simplest reflexes, all patterns of animal and human behavior can be modified by experience. Thus, learning plays a prominent role in Tolman's theory.

There are three types of learning theory, said Tolman: trial and error, conditioning, and gestalt. Tolman considered his own theory a subvariety of gestalt.

According to Tolman, Pavlov's dog acquired "a sign-gestalt-expectation to the effect that 'waiting' in the presence of the sign-object, color or sound, would lead to the significate, food. . . . The response originally made the significate was also appropriate to the sign, as a temporal signal of this

[85] Tolman, *Purposive Behavior*, p. 293.
[86] *Ibid.*, p. 304.

coming significate. . . . The response made after learning to the total sign-gestalt-expectation is the same as the response made before learning to the significate object by itself."[87]

Tolman was opposed to Thorndike's S-R connectionism. Experiments in latent learning, especially those by H. C. Blodgett, contradict Thorndike's law of effect (cf. Chapter 1). In these experiments "the animal is presented initially with alternative response situations, under conditions of no reward or, at the most, of relatively slight reward for the one response as against the others. As the result, he acquires 'apparently only a very slight propensity to take what is later to be a correct route. Yet a very considerable 'latent learning' does take place—a learning which manifests itself as having taken place, the moment a real differential award is introduced."[88]

What actually takes place in so-called trial-and-error learning is a refinement or building up of sign–gestalts. When the organism tries both correct and incorrect responses, the respective consequences of these responses are discovered. Accordingly, the appropriately differentiated sign–gestalts are built or refined, said Tolman.

Learning, according to Tolman, is "an affair of sign–gestalt formation, refinement, selection and invention." The laws of learning should be divided into (1) *capacity laws* and (2) *stimulus laws*. The stimulus laws can be related either to the *material* of learning or to the manner of *presentation*.

The description of the laws of learning follows.[89]

Capacity Laws (Conditioned Reflex Learning)

The capacity laws are to be conceived in general as listing certain fundamental traits, capacities, aptitudes, the possession of which in the given individual or species will favor learning.

(a) Formal means-end-capacities (i.e., capacities for simple differentiation and prediction) are obviously essential even to such simple sign-gestalt formation as is involved in conditioned reflex learning. An animal must, then and there, be capable of differentiating the given sign, significate, and means-and-relation from others and of forming the connecting predictive relations. And the quicker and more facile he is at such differentiation and such prediction, the better he will be at such conditioned reflex learning.

(b) Dimensional means-end-capacities and discriminanda- and manipulanda-capacities. The animal must be capable also of achieving correct expectations with respect to the specific sorts of dimensional material—space, time, gravitation, social relations, or what not—constituting the stuffs of the given sign, the given significate and the given means-end-relations. And the greater his capacities for such materials, again the better he will be at the given conditioned reflex learning.

(c) Retentivity. Finally, the animal must be capable of "retaining" these differentiations and predictions from trial to trial. And the better he is at retaining, the sooner he will thus learn.

---

[87] *Ibid.*, p. 331.

[88] *Ibid.*, p. 343.

[89] All quotations taken from Tolman's *Purposive Behavior*, pp. 374–388. Certain parts of Tolman's presentation have been omitted.

CAPACITY LAWS (TRIAL AND ERROR LEARNING)

(d) Formal means-end-capacities, alternativeness, roundaboutness, final common pathness, etc. It seems quite obvious that, since trial and error learning is, as we have seen, not merely a discovery of what the individual paths lead to, but also an eventual selection among those paths, trial and error learning will be especially favored by the capacity for the more general field-relationships of alternativeness, roundaboutness, final common pathness, etc.

(e) Consciousness-ability plus ideation-ability. We are assuming that consciousness-ability, i.e., the capacity to run back and forth in a disinterested fashion over the elements of the field, and also ideation-ability, the capacity to "adjust" to such runnings-back-and-forth, are not involved to any appreciable extent in simple conditioned reflex learning. The animals that are conscious probably do not acquire conditional reflexes any more rapidly than the animals that are not thus conscious. (An interesting experiment to try in this connection would be to see whether simple conditioned reflexes could be acquired in sleeping conditions as readily as in waking ones.) We shall assume, however, that, when it comes to trial and error learning, this being conscious or this ideating is of very considerable advantage. The more the given animal, or species of animal, can "hold up" his practical behavior in order to reinforce by "actual" or "adjustmental" runnings-back-and-forth relative to the predictive and differentiative relations in the total field, the more rapidly, we must suppose, he will be able to build up a total field and the relations among the alternatives within such a field.

CAPACITY LAWS (INVENTIVE LEARNING)

(f) Creativity (creative instability). It seems obvious that a capacity to break out into new lines of behavior, ideationally or actually, will be fundamental for inventive learning. Two individuals of one and the same species may be exactly equal in formal and dimensional means-end-capacities, in consciousness-ability, ideation-ability, retentivity, etc., and yet the one is more inventive than the other. The less inventive will "understand" the matter, once it has been shown to him, with facility equal to that of the other. But he will be less likely to "hit upon" this matter initially and for himself. The more inventive will be better at inventive learning solely by virtue of being endowed with a larger dose of something to be called creativity, or perhaps even creative instability. This more inventive individual will be one who, for some reason, is especially prone to break out into new differentiations and predictions. He will break out, into responses which, as far as the given type of situation is concerned, have never occurred with him before. This inventive individual will be the one who is liable and "unstable." He will by virtue of some sort of internal breakdown, tend to do something "queer" and "foreign" in any given situation. He will have a large dose of creativity.

STIMULUS LAWS: LAWS RELATIVE TO THE NATURE OF THE MATERIAL (CONDITIONED REFLEX LEARNING)

Given the necessary formal dimensional means-end-capacities and discriminanda- and manipulanda-capacities and the necessary retentivity, then simple conditioned reflex learning consists, as we have declared, in the acquisition of single sign-gestalt-expectations and -readinesses. What now are the conditions in the "stimulus" material itself which will affect the formation and retention of such sign-gestalts? We seem to find three such conditions which we shall summarize under the heads of the Law of Togetherness and the Law of Fusibility and Other Gestalt-Like Laws.

(m) The Law of Togetherness (i.e., of sign, significate, and means-end-relation) would state that in order that a specific sign-gestalt-expectation may be acquired readily, the parts of that gestalt, i.e., the specific sign, means-end-relation and significate, must be presented by the environment in some sort of a "togetherness" fashion which sets them off as a unit or "figure" from the total background of surrounding experience. Or, in other words, the given sign, means-end-relation and significate must vary together concomitantly, whatever the changes or lack of changes in the other surroundings. The dog will not learn to secrete saliva for the given color unless this color, together with the subsequent fact of its leading on to food, are actually placed by the experimental conditions into a single temporal "togetherness," which makes them stand out from all the million and one other concurrently bombarding stimuli. And the rat that learns to take the white side of the discrimination box as the sign for coming food, will not learn to do so unless again these parts—whiteness, entering, getting food—are, as such, placed "together" spatially, temporally and sequentially, or whatever it may be. This fact of the need of a "togetherness" for learning has indeed been prettily illustrated by Thorndike. He has called it the principle of "belongingness."

Or, in our own terms, it appeared that quite without any motivation on their part, the subjects did tend to connect the pairs into sign-gestalt wholes whereby the presentation of the first member of a pair did lead the subject then to expect the second member of that pair. Some sort of a "togetherness" of the members of a pair against the rest of the numbers and words as background caused them to form sign-gestalt wholes in which the first-coming word of each pair became the sign for the later-coming number of the same pair.

But indeed this fact of some sort of a "togetherness" as the essential condition for the formation of "organizations" (gestalts) is perhaps the main burden of the contributions of Gestalt Psychology to the problems of learning and memory. Köhler in particular seems to have emphasized this point.

(n) The Law of Fusibility.—The second gestalt law which seems to us to be involved even in Conditioned Reflex Learning—i.e., single sign-gestalt formation—we have designated as the Law of the Fusibility of sign, significate and signified means-end-relation. And what we mean by this law is that certain characters of signs, means-end-relations and significates will undoubtedly fuse together into single sign-gestalt wholes more readily than will others. It appears, in short, that there will be stronger dispositions toward gestalt-formation when the characters of the parts have certain relations to each other than when they have other relations. Some characters will organize themselves into gestalt wholes more readily than will others.

In the case of the conditioning of simply physiological reflexes this would mean, say, that certain types of to-be-conditioned stimuli, perhaps odors, should come to evoke salivary secretions, i.e., become a sign for coming food, more readily than will others. Whereas other types of stimuli—say, perhaps, noises—will more readily come to evoke avoidance responses. And, in the case of rats learning mazes, it would mean, perhaps, that it should take fewer trials to establish the running-on response to food than, say to acquire the response of merely waiting in a detention-chamber for food or the like.

Again, however, it is to be noted that this law of the greater fusibility of some characters than others into single sign-gestalts is in a sense merely a further extension of the preceding law of "togetherness." The Law of Togetherness as worded above stated that some sort of temporal and spatial, or other, "togetherness" was essential to easy "gestalting," whereas this Law of Fusibility adds the further point that certain types of "qualitative togetherness" will also make for easier gestalting than will others.

(o) Other Gestalt-like Laws. Finally, it may be pointed out that probably certain other gestalt-like laws ought to be included by us somewhere about here,—viz., laws concerning the career of the sign-gestalt-expectations in the course of forgetting. For the gestalt psychologists have brought it now to the attention of us all that the process of forgetting is not a simple one of mere weakening or dimming but is, rather, one tending to involve also actual changes and rearrangements in the qualities of the material which has been learned. Their doctrine is that, with the passage of time, the remembered material tends to be modified always in the direction of Prägnanz—that is, in the direction of "better," "clearer," "more stable," ("more pregnant") gestalts.

LAWS RELATIVE TO THE NATURE OF THE MATERIAL
(TRIAL AND ERROR LEARNING)

Under this head there has been listed only one new law—

(p) Interrelations among the spatial, temporal and other characters of the alternatives. We present this as an additional law because, although this law has not yet, as far as we know, been demonstrated, it seems to us indubitable that the future must discover such a law. The field as a whole is a gestalt which grows out of the minor gestalts corresponding to the individual trials and errors. It seems probable, therefore, that there will be some especially gestalt-favoring relationships whereby such bigger wholes will most readily appear. Certain temporal, spatial, or qualitative interrelations between the alternatives will undoubtedly be more favorable to the building up of such total field-wholes, than will others.

LAWS RELATIVE TO THE NATURE OF THE MATERIAL
(INVENTIVE LEARNING)

(q) We have designated it rather vaguely as the Law of Presentations and Characters favoring new closures and expansions of the field. Inventive learning differs from trial and error learning in that, whereas trial and error learning involves merely the building up of a total means-end-field out of alternative parts, all of which are actually experienced, inventive learning requires the extrapolation of such a field to parts never actually enjoyed. Such inventive learning will, therefore, be favored by whatever conditions, of content and the like, the gestalt psychology discovers as favorable to such extrapolations. There will, that is, no doubt be conditions in the placement—and order—and character-interrelations of the parts of the field, already given, which will be especially favorable to the invention of the required new parts. An instance of this would be the discovery by Köhler that in the case of the apes' learning to use a stick to rake in food, the solution came sooner when the stick lay on the ground near the food.

(u) [Frequency and recency are what] we designated as the correct use of the "law of exercise." For it is obvious that the more frequently and more recently the actual sequence of sign, means-end-relation and significate has been presented, the stronger, other things being equal, this resulting sign-gestalt will tend to be.

(v) Revival after Extinction, Primacy, Distributed Repetitions. Under this single, rather omnibus, heading, we have sought to gather together a variety of further conditions which, no doubt, still need more investigation but all of which have to do with the temporal relations of the presentation. It has been seen that the simple conditioned reflex, after it has been made to wane on a given day because of lack of confirmation, will nevertheless tend to revive on a subsequent day. And this, it seems, is closely related to the old doctrine of primacy, viz., the doctrine that those connections which are established early have an undue tendency to persist and revive. And again there is also the well-established orthodox finding that temporally spaced repetitions are better than temporally concentrated ones. We are concerned here, that is, with the various temporal conditions of presentation, and with the laws whereby some such temporal conditions are more favorable than others.

(w) Motivation (?). Next, as a third law under the head of conditioned reflex learning, we should suggest (with a question mark) the law of motivation. We should suggest, that is, that in so far as the significate is either a strongly to-be-got-to or a strongly to-be-got-from object, by virtue of a given appetite or aversion or by virtue of some established subordinate drive, that the formation of the given sign-gestalt-readiness and -expectation will tend to be facilitated. The evidence on this point is, however, by no means clear.

When we recall the latent learning experiments, we remember that they indicated that latent learning conditions (in which the food box was not strongly to-be-got-to) seemed, as far as pure learning was concerned, to lead to the requisite sign-gestalt-formations just as rapidly as and perhaps more rapidly than did the control conditions in which the rewards were always present.

It appears possible, therefore, that learning without any very obvious motivation can occur. But, on the other hand, it might also be contended that in such cases the learning would not have occurred, if it had not been for some "general" motivation of curiosity, or the like, which made all paths to some degree interesting. Obviously further experiments and further analysis are needed.

(x) Not "Effect" but "Emphasis." Finally, it now appears that, irrespective of whether or not the Law of Motivation holds, there is a Law of Emphasis which does hold. Any strongly inciting situation, good or bad, accompanying either the sign or the significate, or both, does tend to facilitate learning. Pleasant or repulsive odors, electric shocks and the like seem always to aid learning. And, further, it is to be noted that this seems to be all that we have left of the old, orthodox Law of Effect. The significate or the sign must, probably, have some "interest," positive or negative, to the animal (though perhaps not too much) if he is to respond to it and its relations at all. But it makes no difference whether this "interest" is due to its "goodness" or its "badness." In fact, if there be any differential effect at all, it may well be that the "bad," "unpleasant" consequences will "stamp in" the sign-gestalts leading to them more rapidly than "good" or "pleasant" consequences will stamp in the contrasted sign-gestalts.

Laws Relative to the Manner of Presentation
(Trial and Error Learning)

There is only one new law relative to the conditions of presentation which seems to appear when we pass from conditioned reflex learning to trial and error learning.

(y) It may be labeled the Law of Temporal Orders and Sequences in the presentation of the alternatives. There is perhaps as yet no very good experimental evidence as to this law. But it seems more than probable that, since, in trial and error learning, the animal has to build up a grasp of the interrelations in a total field, certain orders and successions in trying out these alternatives should be more helpful than others. If, for example, there are only two paths to be distinguished between, it may well be that alternate trying of the one and then the other may be less helpful in building up the total relationships than a concentrated bunch of takings of first the one path, followed by a concentrated bunch of takings of the second path. (Or it may be that just the reverse holds.) But in any case, it seems indubitable that there will be some law of this general sort, if we can but discover it.

Laws Relative to the Manner of Presentation
(Inventive Learning)

Finally, turning to inventive learning, we find but one more law. We have designated it:

(z) Temporal relations between the presentation of certain of the already given alternatives and the true solution. We have in mind here the undoubted fact that a final solution (i.e., the new sign-gestalt-readiness and -expectation) will be hit upon more successfully as a result of a recent dwelling upon certain of the other already given sign-gestalts than as a result of a recent dwelling upon others of them. We recall again in this connection the experiments of Brown and Whittell. It must be noted that these investigators found that the difficulty of any given multiple choice problem depended very much upon what problems had just preceded it.[90]

Theory of Learning: Experiments and Modifications

In highly interesting experiments with chimpanzees, the experimental animals acted as if they had expectancy of the goal and made choices definitely leading to a rewarding achievement of the goal.[91] This *reward expectancy* represents one type of learning as seen by Tolman.

Learning is usually facilitated by hunger and food, that is, by "drive and the possibility of its satisfaction." But learning itself, says Tolman, is the bringing together and organizing of perceptual experiences, and nothing else. In several experiments, inference or insight in rats was examined. A special maze was constructed in which three paths of different lengths led to the food box. In preliminary training, the shortest path, number one,

[90] From *Purposive Behavior in Animals and Men*, by Edward Chace Tolman. Copyright, 1932, The Century Co. By permission of Appleton-Century-Crofts, Inc.

[91] John T. Cowles and Henry W. Nissen, "Reward Expectancy in Delayed Responses of Chimpanzees," *Journal of Comparative Psychology*, 1937, 24, 345–358.

was blocked and the rats developed preference for the use of the second shortest path, number two. The first two paths had a common segment. When this segment leading to the food compartment was blocked, the rats chose the third path, which was the longest one and the least chosen in preliminary training. The rats behaved as if they were in possession of a *cognitive map*. This *place learning* was considered by Tolman to be indicative of the importance of cognitive processes in learning, in contradistinction to mechanistic trial and error and to the conditioning theories.[92]

In experiments with *latent learning*, the rats were allowed to run through the mazes without food. When, later on, the food reward was introduced, the rats who had had the chance to "explore" the maze learned much faster than those who had not. In an interesting experiment, one food-rewarded group, one not-rewarded group, one experimental group which was fed only once in the maze, and two control groups were employed; the experimental group was in the maze ten times, being fed there only once; when it was fed on the eleventh day, it matched in performance the group which was fed every day. Tolman's interpretation was that some "latent training" took place as a result of exploration without food reward.[93]

Tolman believed that learning depended primarily on the expectancy of achievement and on confirmation of the expectancy. The experimental animals seem to make predictions as to which step will lead to the expected solution. These predictions are usually in a considerable degree of agreement with the real probabilities.[94] On the basis of past experiences, the animal develops a *cognitive structure*. This cognitive structure (analogous to K. Lewin's field) is a system of hypotheses as to what are the best means leading toward the end.

Motivation, such as hunger or thirst, determines which parts of the situation will be *emphasized* and therefore included in the cognitive structure. Whenever the expectations are confirmed, learning takes place. Thus, in Tolman's system, emphasis replaces effect, and confirmation replaces reinforcement. In Tolman's system, the confirmation of an expectancy by an experience corresponds to the role of reinforcing reward in Hull's system.

Tolman summarized his position as follows: "We shall designate the remembered food (or distant maze feature) as the signified-objects, or *significates*. Secondly, we shall designate the immediate maze features, the stimuli for which are now *re*-presented, as the sign-objects or *signs*. And finally, the direction-distance-relations involved in the manner in which, on previous occasions, the commerces with the signs led on to the commerce with significates, we shall designate as the signified means-end-relations.

---

[92] Edward C. Tolman and Charles H. Honzik, " 'Insight' in Rats," *University of California Publications in Psychology*, 1930, *4*, 215–232.

[93] Edward C. Tolman and C. M. Honzik, "Introduction and Removal of Reward and Maze Performance in Rats," *University of California Publications in Psychology*, 1930, *4*, 257–275.

[94] Egon Brunswik, "Probability as a Determiner of Rat Behavior," *Journal of Experimental Psychology*, 1934, *25*, 175–197.

The process of learning any specific maze is thus the building up of, or rather a refinement of and correction in, the expectations of such specific (*sign, significate* and *signified means-end-relation*) wholes, or, as we may hereafter call them, sign-gestalts."[95]

In a revision of his theory of learning in 1949, Tolman distinguished six types of learning as follows:

1. *Cathexis* stands for connection or attachment of specific types of final positive goal objects or of final negative "disturbance objects" (disturbance object–negative goal) to basic drives. It is a connection for example, between a given type of food and the corresponding drive of hunger. "The learning of cathexis is the acquisition by the organism of positive dispositions *for* certain types of food, drink, sex-object, etc. or of negative dispositions *against* certain *types* of disturbance-object."[96]

2. *Equivalence belief* is a connection between "a positively cathected type of disturbance-object and a type of what may be called a sub-disturbance object."

3. *Field expectancy* takes place when one organism is repeatedly and successfully presented with a certain environmental setup. The organism usually tends to acquire such a "set" that "upon the apprehension of the first group of stimuli in the field, he becomes prepared for the further 'to come' groups of stimuli and also for some of the interconnections or field relationships between such groups of stimuli."

4. *Field-cognition modes,* so called by Tolman, are the new modes of perceiving, remembering, and inferring which, in addition to new field expectations, are acquired in the course of usual learning experiments.

5. *Drive discrimination* is based on C. L. Hull's and R. W. Leeper's experiments, in which there is a definite relationship between the type of deprivation and the way the animals learn. In the reported experiments hunger-motivated rats responded in a different way from thirst-motivated rats.

6. *Motor patterns,* Tolman admits, are most simply conditioned by contiguity (as suggested by Guthrie).

Concluding Remarks

Tolman has combined Watson's behaviorism and Pavlov's conditioning with Thorndike's law of effect and McDougall's purposivism and the gestalt

95 Tolman, *Purposive Behavior*, pp. 135–136.
96 Edward C. Tolman, "There Is More Than One Kind of Learning," *Psychological Review*, 1949, 56, 144–155.

theory of perception, colored by Lewin's field theory. Tolman is not, however, in opposition to Freud or, perhaps, to anyone at all.

But Tolman's theory is not a mere conglomeration. It is behaviorism in so far as it insists on the study of observable behavior. It is gestalt in its learning theory. It is purposivism in its general idea of behavior.

Tolman himself offered an interesting analysis of the affinities of his system of purposive behaviorism to behaviorism, purposivism (the hormic psychology), and gestalt.[97] He accepts the definition of behavior as a "stimulus-response affair," but rejects Watson's way of interpreting behavior by a "premature neurologizing." Tolman considers behavior a means–end relationship, that is, purposive. However, he rejects McDougall's theory of instincts and "mentalism" and calls his own system "an objective, behavioristic purposivism." He relates his system to gestalt theory because he believes that behavior is molar and meaningful. He disagrees with gestalt theory on the issue of psychophysical parallelism between psychological gestalt and neurological gestalt (the gestalt principle of isomorphism is discussed in Chapter 12). Moreover, Tolman does not confine his studies to gestalt only, and his theory is purposive in contradistinction to gestalt theory.

Tolman's theory raises two more penetrating questions in regard to theory construction in psychology. Why do the same (probably?) rats behave in different ways? Tolman's rats seemed to show much more insight, goal expectancy, intelligence, and abilities than Thorndike's or Skinner's animals.

The second question is: Are Tolman's conclusions applicable to all organisms or only to those put to an experimental test? For example, Tolman's dove will not continue to avoid the loud sudden noise when it is "proved" to him that a "specific and particular loud noise threatens no final physiological disturbance."[98] How would Skinner's dove behave? Does the necessity of logical proof apply to Skinner's dove or does Skinner's dove only need "reinforcement"? How would a snake, a turtle, or a snail react to the same situation? And how much of all that, if it is applicable to humans, is applicable, let us say, to an imbecile, a moron, an average or a gifted child? Tolman, being somewhat programmatic, left more questions than answers.

Yet credit must be given to Tolman for his emphasis on perception and motivation in learning. Anyone who has taught school children or college students could not possibly deny it. Undoubtedly, as Tolman said, there is more than one kind of learning.

Tolman suggested that learning can take place on lower and higher levels. Although his own studies were chiefly confined to the sign–gestalt learning, he considered the learning of simple motor patterns simple conditioning. Obviously, different animals can be conditioned by different meth-

[97] Tolman, *Purposive Behavior*, pp. 417 ff.
[98] *Ibid.*, p. 273.

ods. Moreover, the same animal can learn in different ways. But the solution of this problem was not offered by Tolman.

5. GREGORY RAZRAN: EVOLUTIONARY LEVELS OF LEARNING

The Evolutionary Approach

In the above-mentioned study by K. W. Spence, all contemporary learning theories have been grouped according to "necessary conditions," as follows: (1) reinforcement or law of effect theories, which include Thorndike and Hull; (2) theories that do not hold reinforcement to be necessary for learning—to this group belong Guthrie, Tolman, Lewin; (3) "To the third group belong two-factor theories which assume that there are two basically different learning processes, one governed by reinforcement and the other occurring independent of reinforcement."[99] To this group, Spence believes, belongs G. Razran.

Actually, Razran's theory transgresses the borders of the two-factor theories. Razran has introduced a new approach to the theory of learning which opens new vistas in psychological theory and offers the possibility of a rapprochement between Freud and Pavlov.

Razran's scientific equipment was enormous. Himself an experimentalist, Razran closely watched the 1500 conditioning experiments in Russia and drew useful comparisons between American and Russian research. Razran's erudition in his own field led to an objectivity and a sense of proportion between the respective "schools" in psychology and enabled him to utilize the contributions of scholars using approaches different from his own.

Razran did not deny that there is room for cognition in *some* processes of learning, or that there is room for a Thorndike-type reward learning. But cognition, reward, or contiguity are not the only types of learning. It all depends on whom you condition and how.

Razran introduced the evolutionary point of view to the theory of learning. Conditioning of lower biological species such as paramecia,[100] or of decorticated and curarized animals,[101] or of visceral reflexes (cf. Chapter 2, Section 6, studies reported by K. M. Bykov), clearly indicates that "primitive" conditioning depends directly on "some source of specific biological energy." Some conditioning requires verbalization and/or cognition, some

---

[99] Kenneth W. Spence, "Theoretical Interpretations of Learning," in S. S. Stevens (Ed.), *Handbook of Experimental Psychology*, Wiley, 1951, pp. 692 ff.

[100] S. Tchakhotine, "Réactions conditionnés par Micro-puncture ultra-violette dans le Comportement d'une Cellule isolée (*Paramecium caudatum*)," *Archives d'Institute Prophyl.*, 1938, 10, 119–133.

[101] Edward Girden, "Conditioned Responses in Curarized Monkeys," *American Journal of Psychology*, 1947, 60, 571–587.

does not. Some requires Thorndike's reward or Skinner's reinforcement, some does not.[102]

According to Razran, all three types of learning theory, as represented by Pavlov, Thorndike–Skinner, and Tolman, contain a great deal of scientific truth. They should not be counterposed to one another. Actually each of them represents the process of learning on a certain level of the evolution of the organic world. The three ways of learning represent three consecutive stages in the evolution of organisms and their ever-growing flexibility and adjustability to the environment.

On the lowest levels, as far as primitive organisms and viscera are concerned, classic conditioning takes place. Responses are conditioned "when one of the responses is a response to a powerful biological need—hunger, thirst, sex, fear, damaging stimulus." The conditioning of the viscera is unconscious. It corresponds to Freud's id.

Thorndike's cats and Skinner's pigeons learned by reward, or "reinforcement" as conceived by Skinner. Razran does not see much difference between these two concepts. Tolman's experimental animals and Razran's subjects used perception in learning. This is the higher level of learning. It is "cognitive" learning. All three types of learning should be related in one all-embracing psychological system.

The Inductive Method

In the methodological controversy between facts (Skinner) and theory (Hull), Razran takes a moderate view. He believes, like Skinner, "that the primary task of the psychology of learning is to discover low-level (directly observable) facts and to array them into low-level functional relationships (parameters, laws) with a use of low-level concepts, and that this task may be—and often is—hampered and misled by 'transcendent' theories and concepts that are only loosely and fragmentarily anchored to empirical bases."[103] Hull accepted the facts of classical conditioning and developed on it an independent superstructure of his own theories on motivation and effect and mathematico-logical methodology. This is why Hull's "pillars-postulates need so much continual propping and are indeed in danger of crumbling altogether."

On the other hand, Razran is critical of Skinner's bias against theory. "Blunders in the history of science are not confined to unempirical rationalists and intuitionists. Mach, the chief theoretician of 'descriptionism' whom Skinner quotes and to whom he has been likened, opposed, as is well known, for descriptive reasons, the atomic theory of matter."[104]

---

[102] Gregory Razran, "Second Order Conditioning and Secondary Reinforcement," *Psychological Review*, 1955, *62*, 327–332.

[103] Gregory Razran, "The Dominance-Contiguity Theory of the Acquisition of Classical Conditioning," *Psychological Bulletin*, 1957, *54*, 1–46.

[104] *Ibid.*, p. 14.

What Razran proposes and practices in his experimental and theoretical work is a cautious inductive empiricism. Psychological research must start from the discovery of directly observable facts. These facts should be related to each other and presented in a series of simple, low-level, functional relationships, parameters, and laws. After this empirical systematization of an area of low-level facts has been achieved, "theories are necessary," primarily as aids in "search for high-level facts to 'explain' the lower-level ones."

This is the inductive method, which proceeds from facts to generalizations, concept formations, and theoretical structures based on firm empirical foundations. Razran wrote in a critical vein about the deductive method: "I am unfriendly towards the wholesale physics-like and engineering-like deductive conceptualization and mathematicalization that has gripped the American academic psychology in the last two decades or so. I don't think that what is good for physics is necessarily good for psychology. . . . Psychology is to me a top of a pyramid of sciences, and oversimplified mathematical models are in it no more justified—really less justified—than in physiology, pathology, biology, or biochemistry. I consider myself primarily an inductive theorist, this meaning that good theory must be preceded by a thorough empirical systematization. I am not an empty-organism positivist, liking as I do to anchor my concepts in the nervous system, and hoping that eventually the matter of psychological generalizations at neural levels will become not only an inferable but also an observable enterprise." [105]

Man Is Not Only a Machine

Razran takes a definite stand on the issue of reductionism. He is definitely opposed to reducing psychology to geometry, to physics, to physiology, or to neurology. He does not subscribe to Pavlov's not parsimonious and not empirically tested specific neurological theories of induction, irradiation, concentration, and typology (cf. Chapter 2). Nonetheless, he believes Pavlov is basically right and classical conditioning is a good method for studying the activities of the cortex. The "neural view of conditioning as 'strong brain centers attracting weak ones' could obviously be regarded as a pictorial way of expressing a theory of neural dominance." [106]

Razran states that "whatever extra constructs the behaviorial psychology of learning may need, they must be grounded in and modeled after neural action rather than merely fashioned in the form of logical relations. True, the neural constructs have no predictive cash value . . . at the macro-

[105] Gregory Razran, "Evolutionary Psychology: Levels of Learning—and Perception and Thinking," in B. B. Wolman (Ed.), *Scientific Psychology: Principles and Approaches*, Basic Books, 1965, pp. 207–253.

[106] Razran, "The Dominance-Contiguity Theory of the Acquisition of Classical Conditioning," *Psychological Bulletin*, 1957, 54, 1–46.

behavioral level of conditioning proper, and are at present only promissory notes . . . at the microbehaviorial level of neural action. Yet—to continue the analogy—the debtor, the nervous system, is quite real, of known location and unquestioned solvency, and has paid off on a number of occasions. Hence, a formal neural systematization of classical CR acquisition (as a supplement to the behaviorial systematization) would seem worth attempting." [107]

And this is exactly what Razran is trying to do in his experimental and theoretical works. Without giving up behaviorial data to the "debtor," the nervous system. For, it is Razran's conviction, "Man is not a machine should mean that he is not only a machine, and not that he is never a machine and not even that he is not often a machine. A contrary view mistakes and mistakes not only the evidence of the laboratory but also, I should say, the wisdom of the ages." [108]

The First Level: dg Learning

Learning is defined by Razran as a more or less permanent modification of one reaction by another. If the modifying action is designated by g or G (the capital letter indicating greater and the small letter lesser strength), then, in a simple case, $g + d$ gives rise to a dg, dg indicating d modified by g. G imparts some of its characteristics to d.

This is what happened in Pavlov's conditioning when the reaction to the metronome assumed characteristics of reactions to food. The same applies to conditioning with infants. When an infant, nursed by a woman in a black robe, starts sucking movements at the sight of the robe, it is the dg type of learning.

In Pavlov's experiments, the power of the conditioning stimulus and the power of the center determine the power of the conditioned response (cf. Chapter 2, remarks on reinforcement). The dG mechanism, says Razran, seems to be what Ukhtomski, the Russian neurophysiologist, called *dominance* or *prepotence*. The modification is caused by the action of a sheer neural strength with "no regard for reality and adaptiveness, no benefit of cognition, and little account of affectivity. . . ." Dominance is a principle of sheer "force," wrote Razran. [109]

This theory was introduced for the first time in 1930, [110] and fully developed later on. Contiguity, wrote Razran, is a necessary, but not a sufficient condition for the acquisition of conditioning. The amount of neural energy, the "strong get stronger," determines the process of conditioning.

The evidence for the dominance principle is drawn from three phases

[107] *Ibid.*, p. 14.
[108] Razran, "Evolutionary Psychology."
[109] *Ibid.*
[110] Gregory Razran, "Theory of Conditioning and Related Phenomena," *Psychological Review*, 1930, *37*, 25–43.

in conditioning which "seem to need specific translation into neural terms. First, there is the unmistakable finding that the lower limits of conditionability are considerably higher in the UR than in the CS continua, which, in conjunction with the fact that typical USs produce in general greater neural changes than CSs, clearly suggests the neural generalization that for conditioning to be effected the value of the US-initiated neural event must be considerably greater than that of the CS-initiated neural event, that is, the former must 'dominate' the latter. Second, . . . conditionability varies directly with the values of both the US-initiated and the CS-initiated neural events. Third, . . . beyond certain points the US- and the CS-initiated neural events interfere in some manner with each other and . . . by all signs this interference varies directly with the interfering variate and inversely with the interfered one."[111]

Razran himself stated that his theory is "most closely related to what may be found in the writings of Pavlov." Although Razran neither subscribes to Pavlov's theory of such brain mechanisms as excitation, inhibition, and irradiation, nor accepts Pavlov's animal typology, Pavlov's system, states Razran, has "a very wide empirical base."

Contiguity is a necessary, but not a sufficient condition for the acquisition of conditioning, says Razran. Moreover, "Guthrie's insistence that all CRs gain full associative strength in one trial appears to the writer also to have a philosophical rather than an empirical flavor. There is, of course, no denying that the classical conditioning of *some* reactions in higher animals and in men may be effected under some favorable conditions in one trial and that increments with repetition often stem merely from the enlistment of more 'conditioners'—or the involvement of more favorable conditions. But this is a far cry from any generalization that there is no efficacy difference in the very basic unit of learning between men and paramecia and among the vast hierarchy of responses of different levels in human beings and in higher animals."[112]

Razran is opposed to Hull's theory of learning for its "indiscriminate combining data from classical conditioning, operant conditioning, maze learning and even verbal learning." Hull's reinforcement "in the sense of drive reduction is neither a sufficient nor a necessary condition for classical conditioning, and motivation (drive strength) is only a general energizer or an indirect or more or less approximate UR *indicator* rather than a direct and independent CR *determiner*."[113]

Razran's review of 618 experiments with classical conditioning led him to reject the idea of food deprivation (usually equated with drive strength) as being of ubiquitous importance. *"Variations in US-magnitude* (or *US-intensity*) and in duration of food deprivation are *both* well reflected in the

---

[111] Razran, "The Dominance-Contiguity Theory of the Acquisition of Classical Conditioning," *Psychological Bulletin*, 1957, 54, 12.

[112] *Ibid.*, p. 17.

[113] *Ibid.*, p. 10.

variations of UR-*magnitude*, and thus are of any specific value only *when information on the latter is not available*. Otherwise, they are operationally superfluous. What correlates with variations in CR-efficacy are variations in UR-magnitude, and it seems to matter little whether these magnitude variations are produced by differences in US-magnitudes, differences in the duration of food deprivation . . . or something else. Hence, a concept like drive strength is, as far as classical conditioning is concerned, of little heuristic and predictive value (the situation is quite different in operant conditioning). And if there is no value in drive strength, there is no meaning in drive reduction." [114]

The Second Level: dD Learning

The second "level" of learning takes place when g does not impart any of its characteristics to d, but does strengthen d. The d becomes more frequent and more stable; the d becomes D. A good example is given in the dog's lifting the paw while receiving food and then lifting it quicker and better. Lifting of the paw did *not* take on the characteristics of eating but did become stronger. In classical conditioning, the reaction to neutral stimuli became very much like the reaction to the meat powder, that is, the d turned into dG. In second-level conditioning, d did not change; flexion of the leg did not become similar to the food reaction. The d became stronger; it became dD.

This type of learning encompasses what Thorndike called "reward" and Skinner "reinforcement." It falls well in line with some post-Pavlovian experimentation in Soviet Russia, for example, the experiments of Ivanov–*Smolensky* with children pressing rubber balls to obtain candies.

"The law of effect," maintains Razran, "is a special higher form of conditioning that may best be called qualitative conditioning, in which a quality, a detection, a tendency, an affect—a vector or a valence, if you prefer— is the chief conditioning datum. . . . This qualitative conditioning, unlike typical quantitative or mere linkage conditioning, operates only within a special group of responses and manifests a number of characteristics that are not predictable or derivable from facts of quantitative or mere linkage conditioning." [115]

Comparing the results obtained in Pavlov-type and Skinner-type conditioning, Razran noticed that classical conditioning required a reinforcement–trial ratio of 1:3, while in Skinner-type experiments, the ratio 1:50 was sufficient. In Pavlov's laboratories the extinction scores rarely exceeded a few dozen nonreinforced trials, while in Skinner-type experiments the scores run into hundreds or even thousands of trials. The great efficacy of the operant conditioning observed by Razran led him to the conclusion that

[114] *Ibid.*, p. 5.

[115] Gregory Razran, "The Law of Effect or the Law of Qualitative Conditioning," *Psychological Review*, 1939, *46*, 445–463.

Skinner-type conditioning is a different kind of learning. It is the second type, the dD type of learning, which "extracted from common sense reward, traditional hedonism, and Thorndike's law of effect goes in the current behavioristic literature . . . often under the name of instrumental or operant conditioning."[116]

This second type of learning does not extend to autonomic reactions. It is a more efficient but less universal type of learning. The strengthening of the reaction by a reward given subsequently does not apply to primitive animals, decorticated animals, or to viscera. It seems that the second type of learning (dD) might be related to the pleasure–pain centers in the brain.

At a certain level of evolution, the organism "behaves and not only reacts, he influences the environment and not only is influenced by it." This kind of learning by reward, as studied by Thorndike and Skinner, "applies to the cat and organs which come in a direct contact with the environment. This kind of learning takes place whenever the man or the animal acts and influences the environment, i.e., in the external motor actions of animals and in motor-verbal actions of men. . . . This learning does not apply to the viscera nor does it apply to the animals in the lower stages of evolution such as most of the invertebrates. This learning represents a higher level than conditioning. Experiments prove that this learning is more efficient, faster and more lasting than learning by conditioning."[117] This learning is called reward and punishment, or positive and negative reinforcement. From Razran's point of view, there is not much difference between the two sets of terms.

The Third Level: M(dg) Learning

On the highest evolutionary level, a new type of learning takes place. It is creative learning. "This learning is confined to our verbal-semantic or symbolic actions mainly. This is the learning of perception, reasoning and imagination. . . . One may call it also the intellectual learning," wrote Razran in 1957.[118].

The classical dg conditioning is the most universal, starting at the lowest stages of animal life. The second level the dD, is less universal and more efficient. The third level, $M(dg)$, is the least universal and the most efficient. "A knowing subject may, on one hand, show complete unextinction, continue to give a conditioned reaction despite numerous non-reinforcements or he may, on the other hand, show immediate extinction and withhold a conditioned reaction despite hundreds of reinforcements. Cog-

---

[116] Gregory Razran, "Operant Vs. Classical Conditioning," *American Journal of Psychology*, 1955, *68*, 489–490.

[117] Gregory Razran, *The Psychology of Learning—Theory and Implications* (Hebrew), Teachers College (Boston), 1957, p. 14.

[118] *Ibid.*, p. 15.

nition in the form of presumed M reactions enters the picture and begins taking control—at least part control," wrote Razran.[119]

Razran studied the influence of set and purpose in configural conditioning.[120] He administered the same conditioned stimuli to two groups of subjects. The conditioned stimuli were green and red lights. One of the groups had to solve a bolthead maze, while eating. The green light was a sign that they had done the right thing in the maze problem; the red light signalized errors. The other group was just sitting and eating when lights were flashed.

Both groups were conditioned to the lights and both responded with salivary responses to single lights as well as to the composed pattern of lights. The group that had to solve the maze task responded better to the single lights, since the single lights guided them in their maze task. The other group, with no task assigned, responded better to the light pattern as a whole.

The experiments in configural conditioning served as evidence that sets and attitudes lead to more permanent learning in humans than sensory stimuli. In other experiments, Razran conditioned the subjects to the sentence "Poverty is degrading" and received good transfer to the sentence representing a similar idea, "Wealth is uplifting," but not to the sentence "Poverty is not degrading." The element of cognition and meaning was decisive in this conditioning.[121]

Razran never accepted the gestalt theory in its orthodox form, but he gives credit to Lashley and Tolman for the distinction of the cognitive or relational or semantic or conscious learning. A knowing subject may continue to give a conditioned reaction despite numerous nonreinforcements, or may withhold a conditioned reaction despite hundreds of reinforcements.

In neurological terms, dG learning is the opening of a new neural pathway and dD learning is the strengthening of a pathway. $M(dG)$ learning must be conceived as the opening of a new neural territory, the realm of meaning. It is the fastest, the most efficient, and the most lasting type of learning. As said before, it is also the least universal.

All three types of learning "coexist" in humans and they often interact and conflict. Phylogenetic and ontogenetic studies show that the simple, classical, dG conditioning is the most universal phenomenon. It can be found in invertebrates, in infants, in decorticated animals, and in various visceral organs.

In Razran's own experiments, the human subjects always reacted in ac-

---

[119] Razran, "Evolutionary Psychology."

[120] Gregory Razran, "Studies in Configural Conditioning. II. The Effects of Subjects' Attitudes and of Task Sets upon Configural Conditioning," *Journal of Experimental Psychology*, 1939, 24, 95–105.

[121] Gregory Razran, "Conditioning and Perception," *Psychological Review*, 1955, 62, 83–95.

cordance with Pavlov's classical theory of conditioning, provided they were uninformed about the aims and ideas of the experimenter. The "naïve" human subjects acted like Pavlov's dogs.

In man, *dg* learning brings about "significant changes in a wholly mechanical, machine-like, largely non-adaptive and, we may say, primordial biological way, an evolutionary continuation of the mesozoic era. . . . Pavlovian conditioning is at best adaptive in only an embryonic inchoate fashion. What adaptive sense is there in continuing to secrete saliva at the sound of a buzzer without food for 30 or 40 times and continuing to do so through spontaneous recovery for weeks or even months. The adaptive way would seem to be no food, no saliva . . . which is what happened on the third level. . . .

". . . Again there is the second evolutionary and more recent level of learning: . . . Man as a reward, pleasure, and pain sensitive organism. . . .

"And finally . . . the third and last type of learning, cognitive, volitional, semantic. . . . I have no objection to calling this learning rational, meaningful, logical. . . ." [122]

Concluding Remarks

Freud, Bühler, and Razran all emphasized the evolutionary point of view, but each did it in his own way. Razran's evolutionary levels are mainly phylogenetic, with wide applications to ontogenesis, and they emphasize the adaptability of the organism to the environment.

Razran's evolutionism leads toward bridging the gap between experimental psychology and experimental physiology. Razran was too cautious to be carried into a shallow and not-too-empirical reductionism. Although a disciple of Pavlov, he did not accept uncritically all the physiological theories of Pavlov, nor did he ever substitute physiological models for psychological observations.

Moreover, by introducing the fruitful idea of evolutionary levels of learning, Razran has offered a solution to the so-called contiguity vs. reinforcement controversy. Razran accepted both of them and assigned a place to each in his evolutionary levels of learning. With one stroke the controversy was removed and the experimental data were put together in an orderly system of theoretical explanation.

At the top of the ladder Razran put cognitive learning. Now the S-S theories could find their place among the other learning theories and the road lay open for a general theory of learning.

Some questions, pointed to or singled out by Razran, still await further empirical research and theoretical formulation. In Razran's theory, the lowest, the *dg*, type of learning does not need reward. The second does. What about the third one? Furthermore, Freud apparently overlooked the

122 Razran, "Evolutionary Psychology," pp. 214 ff.

mechanical, nonpleasurable aspects of behavior (cf. Chapters 6 and 16). But visceral learning, as Razran emphasized, is unconscious and does not require reward. Razran believes in scientific convergencies and seems to expect Pavlov's and Freud's data to be utilized in an over-all system. Razran has indicated some possibilities but has not yet presented his findings in a fully developed theory.

While Razran's approach to the problem of reconciliation with psychoanalysis is a very cautious one, some of Hull's disciples have tried to incorporate psychoanalytic concepts directly in their theories.

6. Learning Theory Influenced by Psychoanalysis

John Dollard and Neal E. Miller: Innate Drives

In his excellent volume, Hilgard divided the present-day post-Hullian theorists of reinforcement into two groups, each of them subdivided as follows: [123]

1. Single-factor theories
   a. Contiguity only (Sheffield, Seward)
   b. Drive reduction only (N. E. Miller)
2. Dual theories
   a. Drive reduction for instrumental acts only (Mowrer)
   b. Drive reduction for classical conditioning only (Spence)

We shall analyze one theory of each group, namely, the theories of N. E. Miller and O. H. Mowrer. Our choice of Miller and Mowrer, as in other cases throughout the present volume, was dictated by our preference for systems and theoretical formulations conceived in terms of general psychology rather than for specific psychological problems.

Dollard and Miller can be classified as Hull's disciples, although they have introduced definite modifications in Hull's theory of learning. Some stimuli come from without, some from within the organism. Any stimulus which is strong enough to cause a motor reaction is a *drive*. The motor reaction aims at the reduction of the drive stimulus. Hunger, thirst, pain, and sex are *primary drive stimuli* which elicit actions of the organism leading toward the gratification or reduction of the drive stimulus. The primary drives are, as a rule, closely related to the physiological processes of the organism.

The neonate is endowed with primary drives which force him to act but which do not determine the course of his actions. The other factors which influence the activities of the child are specific reflexes, initial hierarchies of responses, and learning.

The specific reflexes are innate responses to certain stimuli. The initial

[123] Ernest R. Hilgard, *Theories of Learning* (2nd ed.), Appleton-Century-Crofts, 1956, p. 422.

hierarchies of responses are innate also, and indicate certain preferences of reactions to stimuli. One child may cry, another may push away an unpleasant stimulus. The child's first response to any new stimulus is not a matter of chance but a part of the child's natural endowment.

All the innate factors, the primary drives, the specific reflexes, and the initial hierarchies, can be modified by experience. This modification of behavior by experience is *learning*. All learning is association between stimulus (cue) and response, and this association is named *habit*. Personality is a system of innate and acquired responses (habits). Since habits can be formed, changed, and extinguished, personality is not a rigid structure but a fluctuating system of innate and acquired behavioral patterns.

In contradistinction to many learning theorists, Dollard and Miller included in their theory the processes of natural growth and developmental stages as suggested by Sigmund Freud. Moreover, they incorporated into their research great portions of Freud's theory (cf. Chapter 6) and believed that the infant's mind was unconscious. All drives, cues, and responses are largely unconscious even in adults. "The child is urgently, hopelessly, planlessly impelled, living by moments in eternal pain and then suddenly finding itself bathed in endless bliss. The young child . . . has just those symptoms that we recognize as psychosis in the adult. . . . Savage drives within the infant impel to action. . . . The higher mental processes (the Ego) cannot do their benign work of comforting, directing effort and binding the world into a planful sequence. . . . These are the tumultuous circumstances in which severe unconscious mental conflicts can be created." [124]

Behavior is related to five gradients. The gradient of *approach* indicates the increasing tendency to move toward the goal as one comes nearer to it; the nearer one is to the goal, the stronger is the desire to reach it. Analogously, the gradient of *avoidance* indicates that the nearer the negative stimulus comes, the greater is the tendency to avoid it. The third gradient indicates that avoidance is more powerful than approach. The fourth gradient indicates that the increase of drive-stimulus increases the strength of approach or avoidance. The fifth gradient states that in the case of conflict, the stronger response will win.

On these foundations of innate factors and developmental stages, much resembling psychoanalytic propositions, Miller and Dollard built their theory of learning, also leaning heavily on C. L. Hull's theory.

"Learning takes place according to definite psychological principles. . . . The learner must be driven to make the response and rewarded for having responded in the presence of the cue. This may be expressed in a homely way by saying that in order to learn one must want something, notice something, do something, and get something. Stated more exactly, these factors are drive, cue, response, and reward. These elements in the learning process have been carefully explored, and further complexities

[124]John Dollard and Neal E. Miller, *Personality and Psychotherapy: An Analysis in Terms of Learning, Thinking and Culture*, McGraw-Hill, 1950, pp. 130–131.

have been discovered. Learning theory has become a firmly knit body of principles which are useful in describing human behavior." [125]

This four-factor distinction does not deviate substantially from Hull's theory. As said before, any strong stimulus which elicits a motor reaction is called drive. The primary drives are rooted in the physiology of the living organism.

A cue is a stimulus which determines the nature of the response of the organism. The same stimulus may serve both as a drive and as a cue. Cues can be auditory, visual, olfactory, or tactile. A visual cue such as a blinding flash of light may elicit blinking of the eyes. An auditory cue may elicit a different reaction. Cues differ both in their quality (auditory, visual, etc.) and in their magnitude or intensity (strong, weak, etc.). The cues determine when and where the organism will respond as well as which response will be given.

The initial response to a certain cue is a result of the innate and initial hierarchy of responses which is found in every newborn organism. This hierarchy undergoes changes according to the individual's experiences. A given response may or may not be reinforced. Once it is reinforced a new *resultant* hierarchy of responses develops.

Reinforcement is the reduction of the intensity of the stimulus. Food introduced through the mouth brings quicker learning results than food introduced directly into the stomach fistula, avoiding the mouth. Mouth intake serves as a secondary reinforcement, but the fact that reduction of hunger is reinforcing is considered by Miller to be evidence for the stimulus-reduction theory of reinforcement as postulated by Hull. [126] Reward and reinforcement are identical in the theory of Dollard and Miller, but reward cannot take place without drive stimuli. Rewards reduce the intensity or strength of drive stimuli up to a point where further reduction becomes impossible. Thus reinforcement is always a stimulus drive reduction.

Nonreinforced responses are subject to extinction. A response repeated without reward becomes extinguished gradually, and spontaneous recoveries may take place. If not reinforced for a long period of time, the S-R bond, the habit, or the tendency to respond in a certain way will become completely extinguished.

Dollard and Miler related Thorndike's spread of effect to the *gradient of reinforcement*. Responses contiguous to the reward or in an immediate priority to it become more strongly linked to the cue. The gradient of generalization relates to the gradation of cues in the degree of their similarity; the more similar the cues, the more chances for generalization in the responses.

At this point, Dollard and Miller believed they had come close to psy-

---

[125] Neal E. Miller and John Dollard, *Social Learning and Imitation*, Yale, 1941, pp. 1–2.

[126] Neal E. Miller and M. L. Kessen, "Reward Effects of Food Via Stomach Fistula Compared with Those of Food Via Mouth," *Journal of Comparative and Physiological Psychology*, 1952, 45, 555–564.

choanalysis. Reinforcement, being a reduction in the drive stimulus, corresponds to Freud's pleasure principle, and generalization corresponds to Freud's displacement. The latter statement underwent experimental testing.

In a series of experimental studies, Dollard and Miller tested the hypothesis that the psychoanalytic concept of displacement can be presented as stimulus generalization. In one study, they proved that frustrated individuals turn their aggression against inanimate nature or innocent individuals.[127] In other experiments, Miller has shown the possibility of generalization from hunger stimuli to pain and fear, which, he believes, corresponds to Freud's theory of the interchangeability of drives.[128] The logic of this reasoning seems to be highly convincing.

One of the learned patterns of behavior is repression. (The term "repression" is used here in the same way Freud used it; cf. Chapter 6, Section 6.) Repression is the response of "do-not-think about certain things." This response halts the reduction of fear in thinking about them; the repressing response is drive-reducing and reinforced. Once more Freud's theory is believed to fit well in the framework of the theory of learning.

The secondary or learned drives, which "are acquired on the basis of the primary drives, represent elaborations of them, and serve as a façade behind which the functions of the underlying innate drives are hidden."[129] The basic mechanism of reinforcement (a reduction in strong stimulation) is the same for primary and learned rewards.

Let us consider fear. Fear is basically an innate or primary drive, for it acts as a stimulus for action which brings a reduction in fear and is reinforcing. Fear could become a secondary drive if the fear responses are linked to cues which initially are not fear producing. Animals exposed to a shock in white compartments (cue), may later respond with fear reactions whenever they are put into these compartments, even without being exposed to shocks. Thus, fear can also be a secondary or acquired drive.

Acquired drives may act as cues. Some responses are *cue producing* or leading to other responses. Language is a system of such cue-producing responses. Giving names to objects and to events is cue producing.

Words may be used as rewards, that is, reinforcements. Verbal representations are helpful in reasoning. The immediate responses to the drive stimulus and cue must be inhibited or at least delayed. Only when a child has learned to speak and to think can he learn to wait and to "construct future in a controlled way." In reasoning, we use symbols for testing the possible outcome of our actions, thus reducing the necessary amount of trial and error in learning. Reasoning helps in finding out the best way toward future action.

[127] J. Dollard, L. W. Doob, N. E. Miller, O. H. Mowrer, R. R. Sears, C. S. Ford, C. I. Hovland, and R. T. Sollenberger, *Frustration and Aggression*, Yale, 1939.
[128] Neal E. Miller, "Theory and Experiment Relating Psychoanalytic Displacement to Stimulus Response Generalization," *Journal of Abnormal and Social Psychology*, 1948, 43, 155–178.
[129] Dollard and Miller, *Personality and Psychotherapy*, p. 32.

Language is a social product, and Miller and Dollard are much concerned with social factors in learning. It is not easy to predict a human's behavior without knowing his social environment. "Culture, as conceived by social scientists, is a statement of the design of the human maze, of the type of reward involved, and of what responses are to be rewarded. It is in this sense a recipe for learning." [130]

Miller and Dollard developed a theory of socialization of the child based on learning and imitation, in accordance with their theory of conditioning and reinforcement. There are three distinct elements in this process: (1) The infant is initially motivated by an internal *drive*. (2) The infant sees problems of behavior which serve as *cues* for imitation. (3) The infant acts and achieves, and is *rewarded* for his achievement. The reward is drive reducing and the acquired pattern of behavior is reinforced.

Dollard and Miller embarked on a daring enterprise in psychological theory. Always keen experimentalists, they put psychoanalytic findings to work for learning theory. It is rather too early to judge how successful the outcome is (cf. Chapter 8, Section 5). However, no one can doubt that certain psychoanalytic concepts are testable and that learning theory may be enriched by the experiences of clinicians.

O. Hobart Mowrer: Two-Factor Learning Theory

Is all learning reinforced by drive reduction? Mowrer's starting point was the same as Miller's and Dollard's, but he soon modified his position and introduced the two-factor theory.

In his experimental studies in avoidance learning, the reduction of fear was the reinforcing factor. Fear (or anxiety) stems from pain. Anxiety was the conditioned response, pain the unconditioned one. Avoidance learning was acquired by tension reduction. Mowrer explained his viewpoint as follows:

> There are clinical, experimental, logical, and common sense considerations which all suggest that there are two fundamentally different learning processes, which may be simply referred to as *solution learning* and *sign learning*. In the one case the subject acquires a tendency to action, an action which is the *solution* to some problem, be that problem either a primary drive or a secondary one. In the other case the organism acquires what may be most inclusively referred to as an *expectation, predisposition, belief* or *set*. . . . Solution learning is problem solving, drive reducing, pleasure giving; whereas sign learning, or conditioning, is often—perhaps always—problem making. In terms of the effector systems and neural tracts involved and the conditions under which they occur, these two forms of learning appear to be basically different. [131]

Sign learning corresponds to contiguity. In sign learning, the autonomic nervous system participates. For instance, pain and fear are involuntary responses controlled by the autonomic nervous system. "Condition-

[130] Miller and Dollard, *Social Lerning and Imitation*, p. 5.
[131] O. Hobart Mowrer, *Learning Theory and Personality Dynamics*, Ronald, 1950, p. 5.

ing, it now appears, must be restricted to the process whereby emotions, meanings, attitudes, appetites, and cognitions are acquired, with 'solution learning' applying to all cases of overt instrumental habit formation." [132]

Mowrer's sign learning comes close to Guthrie's contiguity, and his solution learning corresponds to Skinner's instrumental learning. It deals with the skeletal responses largely under the control of the central nervous system. In solution learning the rewarding reinforcement is the decisive factor.

Mowrer tested several Freudian concepts in the laboratory setting and seems to have reversed Freud's position as far as the pleasure and reality principles are concerned. In Freud's theory, the pleasure principle is the innate and primitive principle of immediate gratification while the reality principle involves postponement and modification of gratification, acquired by experience (cf. Chapter 6). Mowrer relates the pleasure principle to the rewarding reinforcement in instrumental learning, presumably controlled by the central nervous system. He relates the reality principle to Pavlov's classical conditioning, for in such conditioning the animal learns "not what is pleasurable and relieving, but what is actual, true, real." [133]

Mowrer developed his own theory of neurosis in contradistinction to Freud's. Freud, said Mowrer, made the assumption that parental punishments produce repressions. Freud's id corresponds to the primary drives, ego to solution learning, and superego to social conditioning or sign learning. Expressing his own theory in Freudian terms, Mowrer said that "neurosis arises, not when an excessively severe superego develops and overpowers the ego, thus forcing a repudiation or repression of id forces, but rather when the ego, which is initially under the *complete* sway of the id, remains essentially id-dominated and directs repressive action *against the superego*. In terms of two-factor theory, this alternative view holds that the neurotic individual is one in whom the primary drives not only had but still have major control over the problem-solving processes and cause these to be directed toward the blocking, inhibition, or nullification of the secondary, acquired drives of guilt, obligation, and fear." [134] Repression is, Mowrer believes, the learning of how not to learn. Neurosis starts whenever the individual uses his problem-solving abilities to avoid new emotional learning or to paralyze existing emotional reactions.

Mowrer's two-factor theory takes into consideration the fact that some conditioning does not require reward and some does. This conviction Mowrer shares with G. Razran. However, while Razran places the three types of learning in an evolutionary order, Mowrer prefers to relate reward to pleasure and non-reward to higher processes. It seems that Mowrer was

[132] O. Hobart Mowrer, "Two Factor Learning Theory: Summary and Comment," *Psychological Review*, 1951, *58*, 350–354.

[133] Mowrer, *Learning Theory and Personality Dynamics*, p. 6.

[134] O. Hobart Mowrer, *Psychotherapy, Theory and Research*, Ronald, 1953, p. 145.

at this point misled by the ambiguity of Freud's pleasure principle (cf. Chapter 8, Section 5).

Mowrer's theory is not a sheer compromise between Hull and Freud. Mowrer deviates from Hull as much as he deviates from Freud, and his theoretical work, although still incomplete, leads to the development of new conceptual tools and new ideas on human behavior.

Robert R. Sears: Dyadic Units

R. R. Sears has widened the horizons of learning theory both in the area of social psychology and in the direction of psychoanalysis. Sears participated in the frustration–aggression study with Miller, Dollard, Mowrer, and others. He accumulated a great deal of experimental evidence in support of the psychoanalytic prepositions and wrote an excellent report on what was done in this field.[135] Some of his own experiments will be reported in Chapter 8, Section 3.

As far as his own theoretical position is concerned, Sears tried to incorporate psychoanalytic and social psychological findings into the framework of a stimulus–response theory analogous to that of Miller and Dollard. A wealth of psychoanalytic observations was utilized by Sears, with a definite leaning toward Sullivan's theory of interpersonal relationships (cf. Chapter 9, Section 4).

Most psychologists are concerned with what is going on with a single individual—with, that is, *monadic* units of behavior. Sears pointed to the fact that interpersonal behavior, or *dyadic* units, may be even more important. Consider an infant crying. The cries of the child are a cue stimulus for the mother. The mother picks up the child; this is her response to the stimulus. The infant smiles. The smiles of the infant reduce the mother's stimulus drive; it is drive reducing, or rewarding and therefore reinforcing. The mother's behavior can be understood in its totality only in interaction with the infant. The instrumental act of an individual, in this case the mother, is not a closed unit, for it includes interaction with environmental factors.

Sears presented his theory of interpersonal relations as follows:

> The behavior of each person is essential to the other's successful completion of his goal-directed sequence of action. The drives of each are satisfied only when the motivated actions of the other are carried through to completion. The nurturant mother is satisfied by the fully loved child's expression of satiety, and the child is satisfied by the expressions of nurturance given by his mother.[136]

---

[135] Robert R. Sears, *Survey of Objective Studies of Psychoanalytic Concepts*, Social Science Research Council, Bulletin 51, 1943.

[136] Robert R. Sears," Social behavior and Personality Development," in T. Parsons and E. A. Shils (Eds.), *Toward a General Theory of Action*, Harvard, 1952, p. 471.

Action does not exist in a vacuum. Each individual has certain potentialities or properties that determine what kind of behavior he will produce under any given set of circumstances. Personality is a description of
those properties. A description of personality has to include reference to
motivation, expectations, habit structure, and the individuals and actions
in the person's environment.

Sears believes that personality factors are antecedents of individual and
group behavior; on the other hand, personality development itself is a
result of learning. Therefore there is a need for a theory "that has the following properties: its basic reference events must be *actions;* it must combine both *dyadic* and *monadic* events; it must account for both *ongoing action*
and *learning;* it must provide a description of personality couched in terms
of *potentiality for action;* and it must provide principles of personality development in terms of *changes in potentiality for action."* [137]

Concluding Remarks on Dollard, Miller, Mowrer, and Sears

These studies of Dollard, Miller, Mowrer, and Sears have opened new
avenues for cooperation between experimental and clinical psychology.
Each of the two methods has its faults and virtues. The experimentalist con-
ducts precise, controlled, and quantified studies, but the scope of his research is necessarily limited to issues which fit laboratory testing.

From this point of view the above-mentioned workers introduced important innovations. Their research methods have been strictly experimental and their experimental designs beyond reproach. Their assumptions
were rooted in the studies of Pavlov, Watson, and Hull. Yet they did not
overlook the tremendous wealth of empirical (but not experimental) observations accumulated by Freud and related systems. Miller, Dollard,
Mowrer, and Sears are not eclectics, and their acceptance or rejection of
psychoanalytic propositions was dependent upon experimental testing. In
fact, none of them has fully accepted or incorporated psychoanalytic theory.
The frame of reference of all of them is the S-R bond, but all have selectively
utilized certain psychoanalytic propositions. Mowrer went furthest in the
effort to modify psychoanalysis in order to make it fit his two-factor learning theory.

7. SOME PROBLEMS IN THE THEORY OF LEARNING

Pavlov's Neurology Neglected

Pavlov's theory of conditioning was based on (1) observations of overt
behavior of animals, (2) observations of overt behavior of animals combined with surgically induced variations in the nervous system, and (3) in-
[137] *Ibid.,* p. 477.

terpretation of behavior in terms of physiology of the nervous system. Right or wrong, this was a cautious and well-designed scientific procedure.

Now let us see what learning theories have done with Pavlov's conditioning. By all definitions, learning is a modification of behavior brought about by experience. Accordingly, conditioning represents either all learning or at least some category of learning.

The apparent weakness of psychology prior to the development of the theory of learning is probably related to its "static" nature and its efforts to perceive behavior in rigid terms of definite patterns. The theory of adjustment as promoted by the functionalists stimulated the search for determinants of adjustment. What makes organisms change?—that was the question which made history in psychology.

Two types of answers were given to this question, one by the giant of educational psychology, E. L. Thorndike, the other by the giant of physiology of the nervous system, I. P. Pavlov. Each proceeded in his own orbit; there was practically no clash between them, as there cannot be a clash of opinion between a scientist saying, "Mr. A is angry" and another saying, "Mr. A has an accelerated blood circulation." However, since both of them were talking about something which took place at a certain time in a certain organism, it would be worthwhile to explore the relationship between the circulation of blood and the feeling of anger.

This exploration could proceed in more than one way, and there is no reason to expect that ultimately one would prove that blood circulation *is* anger. What could be reasonably expected is that *some* relationship will be discovered indicative of the *continuity* of living matter, in contradistinction to Descartes's radical dualism.

We have to admit that such a discovery has not yet taken place. No one has been able to find the method by which physiological data can be translated into psychological phenomena or vice versa. The creators of the great psychological systems, Pavlov and Freud, have been extremely cautious on this issue and have avoided the pitfalls of an easy reductionism. Some workers, especially Watson and Bekhterev, denied the existence of the difficulty, assumed that psychology is a sort of physiology, and avoided the problem instead of facing it. At the other extreme, Dilthey and Spranger also denied the existence of the difficulty, but assumed that psychology dealt with immaterial and cultural issues, and had nothing to do with living matter, they avoided the other part of the problem instead of facing it (cf. Chapter 10).

The learning theorists tried very hard to solve the problem. Being influenced by two different sources of information, Thorndike and Pavlov, they have faced an almost unsurmountable task. Pavlov dealt with irradiation and concentration of energy in the cortical centers. Thorndike discussed the impact of annoyers and satisfiers. These are *not* the same. Thorndike's law of effect is related to Palov's reinforcement; probably they both deal with similar or overlapping phenomena, but there is a great difference in the approach to the description. The same dollar bill will be described differently by an economist, to whom it represents a financial document, a chemist, to whom it represents a chemical composition of a certain kind, and a painter, who will be attracted by the figures and colors on the surface of the bill.

Learning theorists tried to move in both dimensions, which is undoubtedly a legitimate procedure. Errors have been made, such as equating reinforcement and effect identical. And the difficulties in relating the physiological terms of Pavlov to the psychological terms of Thorndike have led most learning theorists not only to give up neurological studies but not to make any use of Pavlov's neurological theories. This did not happen because learning theorists did not care for physiology; on the contrary, even C. L. Hull constantly related his findings to the organism, its drives, and its physiological needs. Hull's system sounds like a reductionistic system, but it is a strange type of reductionism, for the omission of empirical neurological data is rather conspicuous.

Something similar happened to many learning theorists, whether they related their data to the living organism or not. Learning theorists took Pavlov's findings and omitted Pavlov's neurology; thus, they have applied a *truncated theory of conditioning.* Undoubtedly, Hull, Tolman, Skinner, and others introduced precision, refinement, and sophistication into the study of conditioned reflexes. But the unrelatedness of their findings to neurological data seems to call for additional, neurologically oriented research. This is a good point to mention Hebb's neurological speculations and Razran's evolutionary levels.

Motivation

Another source of difficulty in present-day learning theory is related to motivation. What makes a person learn?

One group of theories is represented by Pavlov and orthodox Pavlovians (cf. Chapter 2, Section 1). It is characterized by a consistent presentation of the problem in terms of nervous energy undergoing the processes of excitation, inhibition, and induction. It is, in Razran's definition, the principle of sheer force; the more energy, the more learning. Reinforcement, as presented by Pavlov, is not reward.

Another group of theories, represented by Guthrie and his followers, is contiguity, or pure associationism. However, contiguity as the only factor in conditioning has been widely contested.

The confusion of reinforcement with effect, and drive reduction with pleasure, caused a great deal of superfluous controversy. After elminating the Pavlov–Ukhtomski–Bykov–Razran (on the lowest level only in Razran's theory) term "reinforcement" from further discussion, the controversy continues over whether Hull's drive reduction and Thorndike's annoyers and satisfiers are one and the same thing. Obviously, drive reduction is reduction of a drive, such as hunger, or thirst whether it is pleasurable or not. Deprivation–action–satiation—this is Hull's frame of reference. Pleasure–displeasure, whether reducing or not reducing drives, is Thorndike's frame of reference. These two terms are not identical.

Sheffield and Roby [138] proved that the non-nutritive saccharin could be a reinforcing agent. This is very possible and does not necessarily contradict Hull's theory. One may hypothetically state that learning can take place with and without pleasure, with and without drive reduction. Some conditioning, as the Russian workers have definitely proved, can take place without feelings of pleasure. Undoubtedly, as Razran explained it, this is true in regard to visceral conditioning.

Thorndike's annoyers and satisfiers and Skinner's type of reinforcement probably apply to a certain category of learning, when pain and pleasure determine the amount of learning. Miller and Kessen's experiments, in which learning was faster when food was given by mouth instead of being introduced directly to the stomach (cf. this chapter, Section 6), do not refute Sheffield's data. In Miller's experiment, reinforcement was given both ways, by drive reduction and by pleasure.

Ultimately, one may feel that a promising solution was offered by Razran in his evolutionary levels. We are tempted here to suggest some modification: All learning is related to *neurological* factors, and there should be, in the future, a possibility of relating all, even the higher levels, of learning to neurological processes—autonomic, subcortical, or cortical (cf. Chapter 15, Section 1).

As far as the *modes* of learning are concerned, we are inclined to believe that the problem is how to find the evolutionary ladder leading up from simple conditioning to learning with perception.

But *motivation* is still another problem. One may observe that learning can take place on pre-hedonic, hedonic, and post-hedonic levels. More about this problem will be said in the last chapter of this book (Chapter 16).

8. The Current Status of Learning Theory

Reinforcement

The status of learning theory was critically examined in 1973 by B. F. Ritchie,[139] who wrote: "During the past 20 years untold millions of dollars have been spent in support of research devoted to the study of learning in both animals and men. This expenditure has produced a tremendous mass

[138] Frederick D. Sheffield and Thornton B. Roby, "Reward Value of a Non-Nutritive Sweet Taste," *Journal of Comparative Physiological Psychology*, 1950, *43*, 471–481.
[139] Benbow F. Ritchie, "Theories of Learning: A Consumer Report," in B. B. Wolman (Ed.) *Handbook of General Psychology*, Prentice-Hall, 1973, pp. 451–460.

of facts about a wide variety of behavioral phenomena." However, "in the field of learning there are no theoretical explanations that are not challenged by many equally plausible alternative explanations."

Let us consider reinforcement, which is one of the crucial concepts in learning theory. According to Ritchie, the vagueness of the idea of reinforcement has made many learning hypotheses untestable. Ritchie[140] quotes the following definitions of reinforcement:

> S. A. Barnett: A positive reinforcer may be defined as a stimulus which increases the strength of a response. (1963, p. 167)
>
> D. E. Broadbent: Anything we do to an animal which makes its immediately preceding action more probable, can be regarded as a reward. (1961, p. 164)
>
> W. K. Estes: A class of outcomes which produce increments in probability of response A is represented by element E in the set of "reinforcing events." (1959, p. 459)
>
> G. A. Kimble: A reinforcer is an event which, employed appropriately, increases the probability of occurrences of a response in a learning situation. (1961, p. 203)
>
> S. A. Mednick: Operationally defined, a reward is an event that immediately follows a response and increases the likelihood of that response. (1964, p. 22)
>
> George A. Miller: Reinforcement: strengthening. In discussions of conditioning, a reinforcement is any outcome of an act that tends to increase the likelihood of that act under similar circumstances in the future. (1962, p. 352)
>
> N. E. Miller: I have defined rewards as events empirically found to have the effect of strengthening cue–response connections. (1959, p. 240)
>
> James Olds: Reward: a positive response selector; anything which increases the frequency of a response or response series which it follows. (1955, p. 75)
>
> Murray Sidman: Any event, contingent upon the response of the organism, that alters the future likelihood of that response, is called a reinforcement. (1960, p. 396)
>
> K. W. Spence: Environmental events exhibiting this property of increasing the probability of occurrence of the responses they accompany constitute a class of events known as reinforcers. (1956, p. 32)

Ritchie[141] suggested a new set of rules that must be followed in order to obtain an adequate definition of reinforcement:

> 1. The definition must provide us with an exact distinction between two classes of response-produced stimulation: the reinforcers and the nonreinforcers. Only if this distinction is exact can we test statements about the effects of reinforcers on behavior. If the distinction is so vague that frequently we cannot decide whether or not a certain rps is a reinforcer, then the definition must be rejected as unsatisfactory.
> 2. This distinction not only needs to be exact but it also needs to be practical in the sense that both classes of rps (the reinforcers and the nonreinforcers) must in fact have members. Because there are in fact no rps that are sufficient to improve performance, the distinction between those rps that are sufficient and those that are not is exact but wholly impractical.

---

[140]*Ibid.*, pp. 456–457.
[141]*Ibid.*, p. 458.

3. The distinction must not only be exact and practical but it must also be relevant to the rough common sense distinction between rewards and non-rewards which it seeks to replace. This rough common sense distinction regards rewards as rps that somehow are sufficient to support the performance of the responses that produce them. Thus, a satisfactory definition must specify in what sense reinforcers support such performance.

It is, however, dubious whether all researchers and theoreticians would accept Ritchie's rules.

The Concept of Drive and Hull's Theory

The concept of "drive" has often been interpreted as a result of or a sign of *status of deprivation*. One may raise the question whether drive should be identified with deprivation at all, or whether it is a result of deprivation or a sign of deprivation. Hull [142] proposed a hypothetical construct D, *drive strength*, which should be understood as a *function* of the time of deprivation of a needed object, or of the strength of an incentive, or of both. This goes far enough because a functional relationship does not necessarily involve a caused relationship.

An activity that reduces the deficiency is implicitly "reducing the drive." According to Webb, [143] drives relevant to learning situations are those that have been *rewarded* by the learning, that is, reduced by the response. A state of deficiency, called drive, elicits a certain activity which "rewards," that is, reduces the deficiency. Apparently, Webb is going further than Hull, maintaining that drive is a function not of deficiency but of the deprivation itself. Wolman's [144] *Dictionary* quotes thirteen different definitions of drive:

> Drive   1. An impelling force, push, or pressure. 2. An inner urge that stimulates or prevents action. 3. (W. B. Cannon) A special localized sensation determined by organ stimulation, e.g. the hunger drive is hunger-sensation, pangs caused by the contraction of the stomach. 4. (S. Freud) Drive (Trieb) is an innate force, synonymous to instinct, that facilitates or prevents the discharge of energy; see instinct. 5. (C. L. Hull) A general energizer whose reduction is reinforcing. If the reinforcement takes place without learning, the drive is primary; if the reinforcement takes place after prior learning, it is a secondary drive. Thus the primary drives are the unlearned sources of energy in the organism. 6. (N. E. Miller and J. Dollard) Drive is a stimulus that impels the organism to make responses to cues in the stimulus that have been rewarded; thus reward is drive reducing. Primary drives, such as hunger and thirst, are based on physiological processes. Secondary or acquired drives are based on the primary drives. 7. (C. T. Morgan) See Central Motivating State. 8. (B. F. Skinner) Skinner uses the term drive as "a verbal device," a convenient way of referring to the effects of deprivation and satiation. 9. (W. Stern) Drive is an innate disposition towards the implementation of one's own goals. There are four types of drives, namely: (1) self-preservation, (2) self-development, such as self-adornment, (3) social drives, and (4) human drives such as intellectual

[142] C. L. Hull, *Principles of Behavior*, Appleton, 1943.

[143] W. W. Webb, "The Motivational Aspect of an Irrelevant Drive in the Behavior of the White Rat," *Journal of Experimental Psychology*, 1949, *39*, 1–14.

[144] Benjamin B. Wolman, *Dictionary of Behavioral Science*, VanNostrand Reinhold, 1973.

and idealistic strivings. 10. (P. Teitelbaum) Drive is activation of unlearned behavior, in contradistinction from motive, which implies activation of learned behavior. 11. (C. J. Warden) A behavioral tendency activated by an arousal stemming from deprivation and/or incentive. 12. (R. S. Woodworth) Woodworth introduced the term drive in 1918 as a factor motivating human behavior. 13. (P. T. Young) The energy of behavior; the sum of energy released in behavior.

This lack of agreement in defining the concept of drive has affected the interpretation of the concept of reinforcement. Hull interpreted reinforcement as drive reduction. According to Miles,[145] Hull's theory has been supported so far by experiments/studies using *time-dependent* measures of performance strength. However, his theory must be revised when one takes into account *time-independent* experiments. Apparently, the vagueness of the concept of drive has left open the question of whether drive reduction is valid. But time-linked experiments, in which the so-called drive reduction is measured by hours of deprivation can support Hull's ideas.

Spence[146] rejected Hull's idea that reinforcement is a product of need reduction. He believed that a nonreward that is nonreinforcing plays an active part in determining the inhibitory factors. Reinforcement and delay in reinforcement were key concepts in Hull's system as the determinants of habit strength, whereas to Spence they were merely motivational variables.

Spence[147] also introduced a new viewpoint concerning discriminatory learning. He emphasized the necessity to learn what "to look at" and then to develop differential responses to the cues one looks at.

Spence made the assumption that anxiety is a state of drive:[148]

> In Hullian theory the effect of drive (D) is to multiply habit strengths (sHr) to heighten performance (see Learning-performance distinction). Thus, if strong anxiety means high drive, a high level of anxiety should improve performance under certain circumstances. The conditions where this should not happen are considered below. Tests of this general idea were made with experimental subjects differing in their levels of anxiety.
>
> Presumably as a result of different early experiences, some individuals acquire a chronically high level of anxiety while others develop a lower level. These differences can be measured by a paper and pencil test that asks about anxiety in a variety of situations. On the basis of scores on this Manifest Anxiety Scale (MAS) it is possible to identify groups of high- and low-anxiety subjects and to compare their performances in a variety of learning situations.
>
> Some of the most important of these tests were carried out with eyelid conditioning. In the eyelid conditioning experiment, a weak tone or light serves as the CS and a puff of air delivered to the cornea about 0.5 seconds later is the US. The conditioned response (CR) and the unconditioned response (UR) are both blinks. A typical experiment involves a series of 60 to 80 pairings of CS and US. In such experiments the almost universal finding has been that high-anxiety subjects con-

---

[145]Raymond C. Miles," Animal Learning: An Overview," in B. B. Wolman (Ed.), *Handbook of General Psychology*, Prentice-Hall, 1973. pp. 461–482.

[146]Kenneth W. Spence, *Behavior Theory and Conditioning*, Yale University Press, 1956.

[147]Kenneth W. Spence, *Behavior Theory and Learning*. Prentice-Hall, 1960.

[148]Gregory A. Kimble, "Anxiety and Conditioning," in B. B. Wolman (Ed.), *International Encyclopedia of Psychiatry, Psychology, Psychoanalysis and Neurology*. Aesculapius, 1977, vol. 2.

dition to a higher level than low-anxiety subjects. The Hullian interpretation is that learning (habit strength) is the same for both groups, but the higher drive of the high-anxiety group increases their level of performance.

According to Amsel,[149] no behavior theory should survive twenty years of experimental testing, and Hull's theory has been tested more vigorously than any other psychological theory. Amsel maintains that the Hull–Spence approach represents merely a collection of separate thought-related theories rather than a unified system. Moreover, the Hull–Spence approach is far better suited for integrating the phenomena of "non-intentional, goal directed learning." Furthermore, Amsel wrote, "While Hull's theory of 1943 or its 1949 revision or even the more recent revisions by Spence of the theory cannot be expected to handle the phenomena they were not intended to handle, we certainly can expect extensions of these ideas to more complex phenomena."

Current research has brought a galaxy of new research, new ideas, and great many revisions of the old ideas. The following pages will describe some of them.

Classical Conditioning

Research in animal conditioning has discovered hitherto unexpected complexities in the Pavlovian-type classical conditioning.[150] Several research workers have discovered new categories of classical conditioning. For instance, Konorski[151] pointed to additional Pavlovian categories of conditional responses (CR) beyond Pavlovian salivation or leg flection. Licking and jaw movements in response to food or water, as well as eye blinking or nictitating membrane closure in reaction to aversive unconditioned stimuli (US) belong to what Konorski called *consummatory conditioned responses*. Konorski also introduced the term *preparatory conditioned responses*, which become conditioned to conditioned stimuli of long duration; they are responses to a motivational state rather than to a particular instantaneous stimulus.

Konorski's research is only one of many new avenues of classical conditioning. Several new research areas have contributed to a widening scope of classical conditioning. In a review of animal conditioning, Dickinson and Mackintosh[152] wrote:

> Two phenomena that have received intensive study during the last decade, autoshaping and taste-aversion conditioning, have, however done most to reshape our

[149] Abram Amsel, "On Inductive Versus Deductive Approaches and Neo-Hullian Behaviorism," in Benjamin B. Wolman and Ernest Nagel (Eds.), *Scientific Psychology: Principles and Approaches*, Basic Books, 1965, pp. 187–206.

[150] A. R. Wagner, J. W. Rudy, and J. W. Whitlow, "Rehearsal in animal conditioning," *Journal of Experimental Psychology*, 1973, 97, 407–426.

[151] J. Konorski, *Integrative Activity of the Brain: An Interdisciplinary Approach*, Chicago University Press, 1967.

[152] A. Dickinson and N. J. Mackintosh, "Classical Conditioning in Animals," *Annual Review of Psychology*, 1978, 29, p. 591.

current views about the domain of classical conditioning. . . . But it is perhaps of even greater long term significance that general approach and withdrawal behavior may be conditioned by purely classical contingencies. Pigeons will not only peck at a localized visual stimulus paired with the delivery of food; they will also approach such a stimulus even though it takes them away from the food magazine itself. . . . But since it must be to an animal's general advantage to approach (and investigate and manipulate) stimuli associated with appetitive reinforcements and to withdraw from stimuli or places associated with danger, it is now clear that classical conditioning plays an unexpectedly important role in modifying an animal's behavior.

Suppression

Experiments with omission of contingency imply that omission schedules suppress the probability of response. However, if an omission of contingency is added to a classical contingency between a conditioned stimulus (CS) and an aversive unconditioned stimulus (US), the performance of the conditioned response (CR) enables the subject to avoid the unconditioned stimulus (US).[153]

S-R versus S-S Theories

One of the main controversies in learning theory has been the S-R concept versus the S-S concept. In the S-R approach, represented by C. L. Hull, the unconditioned stimulus (US) produces the unconditioned response (UR) in temporal contiguity with the conditioned stimulus (CS). In other words, the CS and UR are directly associated.

The S-S position is represented by E. C. Tolman, who postulated an association between the conditioned stimulus (CS) and the unconditioned stimulus (US). According to Tolman, the conditioned response (CR) represents the "expectancy" or anticipation of the occurrence of US whenever the CS is introduced.

In 1973 and 1974, Rescorla[154,155] reinterpreted the S-S theory. According to Rescorla, after conditioning, the conditioned stimulus (CS) evokes the memory of the unconditioned stimulus (US). The CR (conditioned response) is the reaction of the organism to this memory.

Moreover, in the same two papers, Rescorla indicated that the S-R versus S-S controversy is closely related to the differences in the procedures of conditioning, and either theory could be right within the framework of a particular conditioning technique.

With the spread and diversification of research, bridges have been built between the various theories of learning. As mentioned in Chapter 3, the

[153] W. K. Estes (Ed.), *Handbook of Learning and Cognitive Processes*, Earlbaum, 1975.

[154] R. A. Rescorla, "Effect of US Habituation Following Conditioning," *Journal of Comparative and Physiological Psychology*, 1973, *82*, 137–143.

[155] R. A. Rescorla, "Effect of Inflation of the Unconditioned Stimulus Value Following Conditioning," *Journal of Comparative and Physiological Psychology*, 1974, *86*, 101–106.

traditional distinction between the *classical conditioning* originated by Pavlov and the *instrumental conditioning* originated by Thorndike was based mainly on the nature of contingencies. When the contingency involves two stimuli, namely the unconditioned stimulus and the reinforcer, and this contingency becomes learned, it is a classical learning process. When the contingency is between a response and a stimulus, specifically, a reinforcing stimulus, and this relationship is learned, it is an instrumental learning process.

However, Rodgers[156] has pointed out that instrumental learning may take place even when the experimental contingencies are classical, and, on the other side, classical learning may take place when the contingencies are instrumental.

The above-mentioned suppression experiments are based on intentional interaction between classical and instrumental conditioning.[157] In the conditioned suppression experiments, the experimenter stands with classical conditioning and the unconditioned stimulus is paired with a conditioned stimulus; for example, a tone is paired with electric shock. This is followed by instrumental procedures, for example, learning to press a bar is rewarded by food.

One-Trial Learning

The processes of learning and memory are intrinsically related one to the other. Murdock[158] distinguished three phases in the processes of memory: registration, retention, and retrieval. Rock's experiments shed light on the relationship between the three phases of memory. Rock[159] conducted experiments in paired-associate learning. He proved that subjects can learn a paired associate in one trial. Apparently, repetition carries little importance for learning; it is, however, useful for retention and eventual retrieval.

According to Bugelski,[160] the importance of Rock's results for present theory is their relation to the postulate of attention and the corollary of time. "It is obvious that anyone who can hear and speak can repeat a pair-associate unit as soon as he hears. One trial is all that is required to learn that much." Apparently, there is much more to learning processes than was thought by the theorists described in Chapter 3, and vigorous research continues unabated.

[156] James P. Rodgers, "Conditioning: Classical–Instrumental Interactions," in B. B. Wolman (Ed.), *International Encyclopedia of Psychiatry, Psychology, Psychoanalysis and Neurology,* Aesculapius Publishers, 1977, Vol. 3, p. 316.

[157] *Ibid.,* p. 317.

[158] Bennet B. Murdock, "Remembering and Forgetting," in B. B. Wolman (Ed.), *Handbook of General Psychology,* Prentice-Hall, 1973, pp. 530–546.

[159] Irvin Rock, "The Role of Repetition in Associative Learning," *American Journal of Psychology,* 1957, 70, 183–193.

[160] B. R. Bugelski, "Human Learning," in B. B. Wolman (Ed.), *Handbook of General Psychology,* Prentice-Hall, 1973, p. 527.

5

Hormic and Holistic Theories

1. WILLIAM McDOUGALL: HORMIC PSYCHOLOGY

Vitalism

It may seem unjustified to include William McDougall in the part of our book which deals with behaviorism and conditioning. It seems to be even less justified to include K. Goldstein in the very same chapter. All his life, McDougall was opposed to behaviorism, and Goldstein has little, if anything, in common with McDougall.

However, both theories are derivatives of functionalism and both have roots in common with behaviorism. Functionalism dealt with psychological phenomena as functions of the living organism. The position taken by functionalists led to two kinds of interpretation. One was pursued by behaviorists. It was the method of objective study of behavioral phenomena considered as functions of the living organism. Behaviorists strongly endorsed the physiological point of view in a mechanistic, deterministic manner.

Functionalism also opened the door to another type of interpretation. Living organisms are the subject matter of biology. While some biologists have accepted a mechanistic point of view, other biologists, called *vitalists*, have introduced the molar and teleological point of view. Driesch, for example, has observed the ability of organisms to adjust to a changing environment and to regenerate lost parts. Thus, the principle of *entelechy*, or of goal-directed behavior, gained strong support in natural science.[1]

McDougall went even further. He assumed that some purposive and hormic tendencies were characteristic of the inorganic world as well; otherwise the continuity of evolution would be disrupted. Therefore he hypothetically postulated some "trace of mental nature" in inorganic matter. McDougall clearly distinguished between inanimate nature and its inertia—locomotion being caused by external forces—and living matter, which "actively behaves." Psychology is the science of behavior and behavior

---

[1] Hans Driesch, *The Science and Philosophy of the Organism*, Gifford Lectures, Aberdeen, 1908.

is characterized by its being terminated when a goal is reached, in contradistinction to the inertia of inanimate nature. "The striving to achieve an end is, then, the mark of behavior; and behavior is the characteristic of living things."[2]

McDougall's theories were based on three main assumptions: (1) Behavior is purposively, or hormic. (2) Each individual is endowed with certain purposeful behavioral tendencies called instincts or propensities. (3) The entire behavior is determined by instincts or their derivatives called sentiments or tastes.

As mentioned before, the holistic and purposivistic ideas of McDougall clashed with the mechanistic and deterministic behaviorism of Watson, yet both were the legitimate progeny of psychological functionalism. McDougall was as much a disciple or follower of functionalism as Watson was; perhaps McDougall was even more a functionalist than Watson was. Its adversaries accused functionalism of being purposivistic and therefore unscientific, just as the mechanistic school in biology was critical of vitalism. The giants of the theory of evolution such as Darwin, Galton, and Wallace were mechanistically minded. But Spencer's pleasure principle could be explained both in a mechanistic–causal and in a vitalistic–teleological manner.

Physiological Foundations

McDougall strove to combine a teleological theory of evolution with a physicochemical frame of reference. Behavior is discharge of energy, McDougall said, and he formulated his thoughts in terms of a psychophysical reductionism. The basic energy is stored in the tissues in a chemical form and can be accumulated, discharged, and transformed into any other type of energy.

A certain type of this energy was called by McDougall *instinctive energy.* Its task was to "liberate and direct" the stored, or potential psychophysical energy. This instinctive energy enabled the "conversion of potential energy stored in the tissues in a chemical form, into the free or active form, kinetic or electric or what not," McDougall explained.[3]

Patterns of behavior must be related to the psychophysical disposition. Any action is a discharge or redistribution of energy, action being a discharge and inhibition being a redistribution or "drainage" of energy. All behavior is a function of the nervous system. Just as the reflex action implies the presence in the nervous system of the reflex nervous arc, so instinctive action implies "some enduring nervous basis whose organization is inherited, an innate or inherited psycho-physical disposition which, anatomically regarded, probably has the form of a compound system or sensori-motor arcs," wrote McDougall.

[2]William McDougall, *Psychology, The Study of Behavior*, Holt, 1912, p. 20.
[3]William McDougall, *Introduction to Social Psychology* (23rd ed.), Methuen, 1936, p. 32.

Horme

The basic construct in McDougall's theory is *horme*, the urge to live, the desire to survive. All living organisms "behave," that is, act on purpose, and their main purpose is to survive. "The hormic theory holds," says Mc-Dougall, "that where there is life there is mind; and that if there has been any continuity of the organic from the inorganic, there must have been something of mind, some trace of mental nature and activity in the inorganic from which such emergence took place."[4] For acting on purpose is a sign of mind, be it even so primitive as it is in the protozoa.

Behavior is not always a product of external forces or a mere response to a stimulus. Certain activities start from within; they are spontaneous. Behavior is purposeful and serves adjustment to life and conservation of life, which is the main goal of all living organisms. Organic nature is endowed with the urge or propensity or instinct to live.

The general theory of horme leads to more specific postulates. The continuity of purposeful development is implemented by the heredity of certain dispositions which direct the behavior of the organism. These dispositions, called instincts, are inherited psychophysical dispositions which determine their possessor "to perceive or to pay attention to objects of a certain class, to experience an emotional excitement of a particular quality upon perceiving such an object, and to act in regard to it in a particular manner, or at least to experience an impulse to such action."[5]

Heredity

McDougall, following in the footsteps of Lamarck, assumed that acquired modes of behavior could be transmitted through genes to the next generation. This assumption is one of the fundamental principles of McDougall's theory. Unchangeable and inflexible instincts could hardly explain anything. Human behavior could not be interpreted unless learning was taken into consideration. But this was just what McDougall opposed. The only way out was to assume that acquired or learned patterns of behavior could be transmitted by heredity from one generation to another, in accordance with Lamarck's theory. McDougall trained twenty-three generations of rats in the following way. He placed the rats in a tank with two exits; whenever the rats tried to escape by the more illuminated exit, they received an electric shock. McDougall reported that the control group made 165 errors in learning how to escape by the right exit and avoid the shock, while the twenty-third generation of the trained rats made only twenty-five errors.

These and other experiments which dealt with the heredity of acquired patterns of behavior stirred up a great controversy. As things stand now, it

4 *Ibid.*, p. 462.
5 *Ibid.*, p. 25.

seems that heredity of acquired traits was never proved by McDougall or anyone else. Kuo proved with cats that environment and not heredity determines behavior.[6] Agar's experiments with rats have repeated McDougall's experiment with decisively negative results.[7]

Theory of Instincts

The best-known, and most controversial, concept in McDougall's theory is *instincts*, defined by him as inherited psychophysical dispositions which cause the individual "to perceive or to pay attention to objects of a certain class, to experience an emotional excitement . . . and to act in regard to it in a particular manner."[8]

"It is not any one kind of movement that defines the instinct but the general tendency of using different and variously combined movements to bring about a result of a kind common to the species and of nature to contribute to the welfare of the individual," explained McDougall.[9]

Instincts were often described by McDougall as "release mechanisms or just easily exploding containers of energy." We might, he said, regard each instinct "as containing a store of potential energy which is liberated and directed into the appropriate channels when the instinct is excited, and which leaks or overflows in that restlessness which we have seen to be characteristic of *appetite*."[10]

McDougall was aware of the ambiguity of the instinct concept, which represented both a releasing mechanism and a storage of energy. Therefore, on the same page he added that perhaps it would be better and more justified to postulate a general "store of energy" and regard the several instincts of an animal as somehow drawing upon a common store of reserve energy.

Instinct, says McDougall, is "a concrete fact of mental structure, which in the main we infer from the facts of behavior and of experience. . . ."[11] One has to distinguish between facts of "mental structure" and facts of "mental activity or functioning." The instinctual patterns of behavior were inherited, or at least based on inherited predispositions. Instinctive action implies, says McDougall, "some enduring nervous basis whose organization is inherited, an innate or inherited psycho-physical disposition which, anatomically regarded, probably has the form of a compound system of sensori-motor arcs."[12]

In McDougall's theory, instinct indicates three kinds of functions: per-

[6] Z. Y. Kuo, "The Fundamental Error of the Concept of Purpose and the Trial and Error Fallacy," *Psychological Review*, 1928, *35*, 414–433.

[7] Quoted by F. V. Smith, *The Explanation of Human Behavior*, Constable, 1951, p. 115.

[8] McDougall, *Introduction to Social Psychology*, p. 25.

[9] *Ibid.*, p. 415.

[10] William McDougall, *Outline of Psychology*, Scribner, 1923, p. 107.

[11] *Ibid.*, p. 103.

[12] McDougall, *Introduction to Social Psychology*, p. 32.

ceptual, emotional, and motivational, that is, cognitive, affective, and conative.

The perceptual factors in instincts were emphasized in some of McDougall's later writings. "The instinct is not defined by the kind or kinds of bodily activity to which it impels the animal, but rather by the nature of the objects and situations which evoke it and, more especially, by the nature of the goal, the change in the situation, in the object or in the animal's relation to it, to which instinct impels." [13]

The central and main part of instinct is the emotional part, such as tenderness in parenthood or the feeling of fear in the escape instinct. This emotional part is inherited and cannot be modified by experience, whereas the sensory and motor parts of instincts can be changed by learning.

It has to be emphasized that McDougall's theory of instincts is not hedonistic, that the term "satisfaction of needs" does not correspond to, let us say, Freud's pleasure principle. "Each animal species is so constituted that it seeks or strives for certain natural goals, the attainment of which satisfies corresponding needs of the animal. Since these needs and the tendencies to satisfy them, to strive towards the corresponding goals (such as food, shelter and mate) are inborn and transmitted from generation to generation in all members of the species, they are properly called instinctive." [14] Then, "it is the teaching of this book that human behavior is built upon a basis of innate tendencies which are in all essentials very similar to the instinctive tendencies in animals." [15]

When McDougall substituted the term "propensity" for "instinct" he did it rather unwillingly, under the pressure of criticism of his theory of instincts. Actually, the list of propensities as published by McDougall in *The Energies of Men* is, with minor exceptions, the same as that published formerly under the heading of instincts in *An Outline of Psychology* and *An Introduction to Social Psychology*. McDougall explained that since the word "instinct" cannot be used without provoking controversy and needless difficulties, it is perhaps better to avoid it; and "perhaps the best word to use here is the good old word 'propensity' . . . which is the name given in these pages (in accordance with an old usage) to any part of the innate constitution whose nature and function is to generate upon occasion an active tendency." [16]

As mentioned before, the emotional part of instinctual behavior cannot be modified by experience or learning. The urge to eat, to fight, or to escape is inherited, but the ways humans behave in seeking gratification for their instinctual desires is subject to change and can be learned and unlearned. For example, the instinct of pugnacity is an inherited pattern of behavior, "but its modes of expression have changed with the growth of civilization;

[13] *Ibid.*, p. 417.
[14] William McDougall, *The Energies of Men* (2nd ed.), Methuen, 1933, p. 26.
[15] *Ibid.*, p. 70.
[16] McDougall, *Outline of Psychology*, p. 110.

as the development of law and custom discourages and renders unnecessary the bodily combat of individuals, this gives place to the collective combat of communities and to the more refined forms of combat within communities."[17]

Animal behavior is both instinctive and intelligent, said McDougall, pointing to the possibilities of learning from experience. While every act of any animal is to some extent prescribed by the inherited constitution, that constitution itself provides the capacity for adaptation, for adaptive deviation from the pattern common to the species.

Classification of Instincts and Emotions

In 1908, McDougall described twelve instincts in humans, but in 1932, his list contained seventeen main instincts. The number of instincts and their classification was often a target for criticism, and McDougall's classification of instincts underwent, accordingly, several modifications, until finally "seven primary instincts" became the core of his theory. The choice was based on the respective role played by each instinct in the life of the higher mammals and humans.

Each instinctive process, as mentioned before, is composed of three elements, the cognitive, the affective, and the conative. While the cognitive (afferent) and conative (efferent) depend on experience, the affective element forms the central and invariable essence of the instinct. Each primary instinct is permanently accompanied by a primary emotion.

Here is the list of the seven basic instincts matched by the seven primary emotions:

Instinct	Emotion
Escape	Fear
Combat	Anger
Curiosity	Wonder
Repulsion	Disgust
Self-assertion	Elation, positive self-feeling
Self-abasement	Subjection, negative self-feeling
Parental	Tender Emotion

Several other instincts were considered by McDougall to be of considerable importance: craving for food, mating, gregariousness, constructiveness, and acquisitiveness. The additional five instincts or propensities were sleeping, avoiding discomfort, migrating, crying, and laughing—altogether, seventeen instincts. Besides these seventeen "propensities," Mc-

[17] McDougall, *Introduction to Social Psychology* (5th ed.), Methuen, 1912, p. 20.

Dougall mentioned such "desires" as sneezing, coughing, and catching breath, none of them included in the list of instincts.

Several instincts related to the same object can become united into a *sentiment*. For example, the social behavior of humans and their involvement in groups and organizations is not solely a product of the instinct or propensity of gregariousness. The social sentiment may be a combination of love, tenderness, self-assertion, or possessiveness. The instincts are inherited, but their combinations, the sentiments, are derived from instincts under the influence of circumstances and experience.[18]

Concluding Remarks

McDougall's critics have repeatedly pointed to his inability to provide adequate proof for his theories. Such failure cannot be excused in a scientific theory. McDougall failed to prove the theory of heredity of acquired patterns of behavior; his method of experimentation and the way in which he presented his data have often received sharp criticism. The ideas of horme and purposive behavior were attacked not so much for their content as for the dogmatic way in which they were introduced. McDougall's reasoning was not too convincing in regard to his main hypothesis, and one can not help wondering whether this was the best way in which the empirical data could be interpreted. When McDougall introduced his list of instincts, his ideas were attacked on two points. Critics questioned the scientific usefulness of the concept of instinct and wondered whether it did not lead back into the pitfalls of the old faculty psychology: a man eats because he has the eating faculty and he fights because he possesses the faculty or instinct to fight. More criticism was aroused by the apparently arbitrary way in which the list of instincts could be compiled.

McDougall's method includes serious shortcomings in theory construction. His system presented insolvable difficulties for anyone who tried to test it. One earnest critic wrote: "In McDougall's system an innate neural organization is held to prescribe the form of perception or the significance which a given situation may have for the organism. The percept is then associated with a particular form of emotional excitement, which in turn is associated with a particular impulse to action, and this finally with the action which may persist until the condition of emotional dis-equilibrium and the experience of the associated impulses is alleviated. Neural organization, which would be difficult to demonstrate, and felt impulses and emotional excitement, which are difficult to describe and assess, both qualitatively and quantitatively, are causally associated with observable activity."[19]

McDougall ascribed mind to nature, related neural processes to physi-

18 H. G. McCurdy, "William McDougall," in B. B. Wolman (Ed.), *Historical Roots of Contemporary Psychology*, Harper & Row, 1968, pp. 111–130.
19 F. V. Smith, *The Explanation of Human Behavior*, Constable, 1951, p. 185.

cal ones, attached behavior to innate patterns—and all this with the ease of a man who deals with simple, self-explanatory, and generally accepted principles. Unfortunately, this is not the case and most of McDougall's statements are concerned with highly complicated and most controversial issues.

Yet psychology has to give credit to McDougall for his searching spirit and for his daring effort to understand human behavior. His emphasis on emotional and irrational elements in human behavior introduced a refreshing breeze in psychological research. His idea of purposeful behavior was taken up by G. Allport and many outstanding behaviorists such as Hull and Tolman. Although not too many contemporary psychologists are McDougall's disciples, very many are indebted to him for the wealth of ideas and problems that he has introduced into contemporary psychology.

2. KURT GOLDSTEIN: HOLISTIC SYSTEM

Holism

Goldstein believed that the only legitimate scientific procedure for gaining facts is the study of single phenomena or the *atomistic* method. But, he said, the organism is not a sum of parts which can be studied separately and then combined into a science of the whole organism. He clearly distinguished between the physical and biological sciences. Both sciences deal with symbols and signs that transcend the empirical facts. In physical science, symbols may correspond to partial processes and sometimes operate with a system of fictitious science. This, Goldstein said, is not permissible in biology, because "biological knowledge needs a more complete image of an individual concrete character which must match as closely as possible the particulars from which we build it up. . . . In biology, symbols, theoretical representations, must in principle include quality and individuality in all their determinations. Biological descriptions must exhibit a definite qualitative organization, the symbol must have the characteristics of a Gestalt."[20]

Goldstein did not ascribe gestalt to inorganic nature. He found the "qualitative organization" in the living organism, which is a "whole." This is why biological knowledge cannot be advanced by "adding more and more individual facts. The facts which are gradually included in the 'whole' as parts can never be evaluated merely quantitatively, in such a way that the more parts we are able to determine the firmer our knowledge becomes. In biology every fact always has a qualitative significance."

With this statement, Goldstein promoted a definite methodological position. Physical sciences operate with quantities; biological sciences, in-

[20] Kurt Goldstein, *Human Nature in the Light of Psychopathology*, Harvard, 1940, pp. 28–29.

cluding psychology, operate with qualitative organizations. Accordingly, Goldstein did not make much use of statistics and preferred to concentrate on a detailed study of single cases.

As stated before, Goldstein was fully aware of the fact that the organism is composed of cells and tissues as a house is composed of bricks. Yet no architect would try to construct a house by adding a brick to a brick, and no psychologist should try to interpret the organism by adding a cell to a cell. The picture of the whole organism and its *gestalt* should be interpreted in its totality, in a *holistic* manner.

Even from the methodological point of view, the study of separate parts is inadvisable, because the separate, "isolated" parts of human behavior cannot be properly understood or perceived in perspective. Actually each single reflex, innate or conditioned, is a fraction of a totality of action and a partial expression of the functioning of the organism as a whole. To pay attention to a particular motion without considering the total situation can lead to an erroneous interpretation. "Only knowledge of the whole organism leads us to understand the various reactions we observe in isolated parts."[21]

Equalization of Energy

Goldstein's psychological theory is based on the principle of constancy, or *equalization of energy*. This principle corresponds to Cannon's homeostasis, Pavlov's equilibrium, and Freud's constancy principle. Goldstein assumed that whatever goes on in the human organism is an accumulation, distribution, and/or discharge of energy. Energy cannot perish, cannot be lost, cannot disappear. It is transformed and transmitted from one part of the organism to another or discharged when a state of hypertension is created.

As a rule, in a normal organism the amount of energy is fairly constant and evenly distributed, and a normal or *average* state of tension exists. Whenever this average state of tension is disturbed by inner or external stimuli, the organism tends to restore the balanced or average state. The functions of eating when hungry, escaping when frightened, fighting when assaulted are examples of this process of return to the average. Goldstein called this process the *equalization of energy*. In normal life, excitation which has been changed by a stimulus returns after a period of time to its former state; that is, if no new stimulation occurs, it returns to a state of equilibrium.[22]

Goldstein's principle of equalization or constancy does not imply any release or removal of tension. "Freud," says Goldstein, "fails to do justice to the positive aspects of life. He fails to recognize that the basic phenomenon of life is an incessant process of coming to terms with the environment;

[21] *Ibid.*, p. 123.
[22] *Ibid.*, p. 14.

he only sees escape and craving for release. He only knows the lust or release, not the pleasure of tension."[23]

Goldstein believed that living matter cannot be at complete rest. Life is constant tension, but this tension must be kept within certain limits. Equalization means the restoration of the "average" state of tension, which is usually the optimal state of the organism. Equalization enables the organism to function in the most efficient way, for life is possible only within certain limits of stimulus; overstimulation and understimulation jeopardize the organism's chances for survival.

Equalization is established by an interaction between the organism and its environment. The organism responds to stimuli in a selective manner. When a noise is sounded, the ear responds to it. A stimulus which is beyond the capacities of the organism is not perceived by it. The organism simply *ignores* the stimulus and no equalization is needed.

Some stimuli cannot be ignored; they are too powerful to be dismissed. The organism reacts to these with disorganization if no way of adjustment and equalization can be found. In such a case, the organism feels a task is beyond its capacity. Sometimes other parts of the organism take over and the excitation spreads over a large area. And sometimes the too powerful stimuli disrupt the functioning of the organism and create a state of shock, which is experienced as anxiety.

Self-Actualization

The level of tension at which the organism is balanced varies from case to case. Perfect equalization would be the state of the organism in which its function can be performed most efficiently, most smoothly, and most economically. Goldstein emphasizes two vital functions of the organism, and the law of equalization applies to both of them.

These two main functions are the realization or *actualization* of self and the adjustment to or *coming to terms with the environment*. Both functions serve survival; both offer the best possible chances for the organism in its efforts to stay alive and to live at its best.

Human life has an implicit goal, a purpose, and a direction. It strives to completeness, to perfection, to full development. Goldstein's completeness or *becoming a whole* resembles the principle of *Prägnanz* of the gestalt psychologists (cf. Chapter 12), but in Goldstein's theories the craving for completeness and the striving toward a full life are the main issue. On this point, Goldstein comes quite close to McDougall's teleological concepts of life; Goldstein's emphasis on the zest for life and on the affirmative, creative, assertive elements of human nature resembles McDougall's horme and Pavlov's instinct of life.

Striving toward completeness is the main motive of human nature. It is the striving for *self-actualization*. "We assume only one drive, the drive of

[23] Kurt Goldstein, *The Organism*, American Book, 1939, p. 333.

self-actualization, but are compelled to concede that under certain conditions the tendency to actualize one's potentiality is so strong that the organism is governed by it." [24] In a normal organism, "the tendency toward self-actualization is acting from within, and overcomes the disturbance arising from the clash with the world, not out of anxiety but out of the joy of conquest." [25]

Each organism has several potentialities for development and improvement. They are usually expressed in interests, preferences, and aptitudes. As a rule, one likes best what one does best, for in doing things well, one finds his way toward completeness. "The organism has definite potentialities and because it has them it has the need to actualize or realize them. The fulfillment of these needs represents the self-actualization of the organism," explained Goldstein. [26]

But no organism lives in a vacuum. One must consider the environment to which it has to adjust or with which it must "come to terms."

Coming to Terms with the Environment

As mentioned before (in the section on equalization), the organism reacts to stimuli in a selective manner. The stimuli disturb the existing balance and the organism reacts to them in a manner which should reestablish equilibrium.

This constant interaction between organism and environment requires from the organism a certain degree of flexibility. This is the ability "to come to terms with the environment." The organism must find the best possible means of self-preservation and self-realization while facing the problems and challenges posed by the environment.

The functioning of the organism in relation to the environment can be flexible or inflexible, or in Goldstein's terminology, *abstract* or *concrete*, respectively. If the organism accepts the environment as it is and passively adjusts to the given situation, it takes the *concrete* attitude. This leads to a rigid and inflexible type of behavior; the organism accepts the present, concrete situation and acts accordingly, without any effort to change the situation or to modify its own methods of behavior. Concrete behavior is repetitious and constricted and lacks initiative. *Abstract* behavior is behavior in which the organism perceives the situation in its potentialities, adjusts to it accordingly, and modifies the environment or its own behavior or both.

Abstract behavior is "not determined directly and immediately by a stimulus configuration but by the account of situation which the individual gives to himself. The performance is thus more a primary action than a mere reaction, and it is a totally different way of coming to terms with the

24 Goldstein, *Human Nature*, p. 144.
25 Goldstein, *The Organism*, p. 305.
26 Goldstein, *Human Nature*, p. 146.

outside world. The individual has to consider the situation from various aspects, pick out the aspect which is essential, and act in a way appropriate to the whole situation."[27]

Normal behavior includes both concrete and abstract parts. In some situations we act in a concrete manner, without thinking or even realizing what we are doing. However, the general mental set of normal individuals is the "abstract attitude," that is, the ability to act actively, to have initiative, to consider the total situation, and to prepare themselves for activity.

Most cases reported by Goldstein in his classic study on brain injury, however, have lost their ability for abstract behavior.[28] It seems that those individuals function on their possible best, in a "concrete" manner.

Figure and Ground

Adjustment to the environment requires proper organization of the organism. It is the *figure–background* or foreground–background problem. "There is a continuous alteration as to which 'part' of the organism stands in the foreground. . . . The foreground is determined by the task which the organism has to fulfill at any given moment, i.e., by the situation in which the organism happens to find itself, and by the demands with which it has to cope. The tasks are determined by the 'nature' of the organism, its 'essence,' which is brought into actualization through environmental changes that act upon it."[29]

What is figure and what background is determined by the "task" which the organism has to fulfill at a given time. To a hungry person, food is the figure and everything else is the background.

The ability of the organism for holistic functioning and perceiving things as figures in accordance with needs or tasks can be impaired in childhood, especially when the child is exposed to excessive demands which are above his capacities.[30]

Ordered and Disordered Behavior

Goldstein distinguished two types of behavior. In situations of success, a person appears poised, calm, in a good mood, and well adjusted. This type of behavior is called *ordered behavior*. When a person fails in his task and is unable to overcome his difficulties, his behavior becomes anxious, agitated, distressed, and often frightened; sometimes the entire organism

---

[27] *Ibid.*, p. 60.

[28] Kurt Goldstein, *After-Effects of Brain Injuries in War*, Grune & Stratton, 1942.

[29] Goldstein, *The Organism*, p. 111.

[30] It is worthwhile to note that this writer has arrived at similar conclusions using the Freudian frame of reference. See S. Arieti, G. Derner, K. Goldstein, Z. Piotrowski, B. B. Wolman, "The Deterioration of the Ego in Schizophrenia," Symposium, Eastern Psychological Association, 1958.

shows signs of disorder. Behavior in situations of failure was defined by
Goldstein as *disordered* or *catastrophic behavior*.[31] This applies especially to
abnormal individuals, but even normal individuals go through states of
disorder and catastrophe.

Brain injury can incapacitate an individual's abstract behavior. However, even the damaged organism tries to come to terms with the environment. The undamaged parts of the brain take over the functions of the damaged parts and compensate for the loss. When a certain function is seriously
impaired, regression or *dedifferentiation* takes place; the organism regresses
to earlier, less differentiated patterns of behavior. Very often the organism
develops "protective" mechanisms such as withdrawal from a situation in
which failure seems to be inevitable.[32]

Goldstein defined disease as "a shock to the existence of the individual
caused by the disturbance of the well regulated functioning of the organism. . . ."[33] The goal of therapy is to restore health or at least to enable
the patient to exist despite his defects. Therefore, simple symptoms have to
be considered in their "functional significance" for the total personality, for
the *organism as a whole*.

Goldstein believed that the observation of sick individuals offers a better opportunity for understanding normal behavior than the observation of
normal behavior itself. Pathological behavior is usually simplified behavior,
and deficiencies of some kind reveal the interrelationships in behavior. The
sick organism tries to make some adjustment in order to survive. These
desperate efforts are easier to observe than are the usual adjustment processes in normal individuals.

Concluding Remarks

Goldstein's approach was monistic and free of unnecessary models,
which often complicate and obscure the picture. His theory is a good example of a well-balanced empiricism which utilizes as few constructs as
possible. His distinction between the physical and biological sciences, with
the emphasis in psychology on the *case study*, deserves the greatest attention by psychologists.

Goldstein shared with Pavlov and Freud a simplicity and clarity of
reasoning and a cautious economy in introducing new concepts. The idea
of equilibrium is also common to all three of them. A keen observer like
Goldstein could not miss the apparent effort of living organisms to stay
alive. In this respect, Goldstein was close to Freud's eros and Pavlov's "instinct of life."

Goldstein's reservations as far as quantification and experimentation
are concerned were moderate and realistic. He preferred to study organisms

[31] Goldstein, *The Organism*, pp. 35 ff.
[32] See footnote 30.
[33] Goldstein, *Human Nature*, p. 6.

in a natural environment. He did not dismiss experiment, but preferred observation of the cases in a realistic life setting.

Goldstein dealt with the organism as a whole and considered both physiological and psychological functions as functions of the same organism. He did not put consciousness under the category of physiology, but presented it as one of the functions of the organism. Thus, he came close to Pavlov's cautious approach in contradistinction to Watson's and Bekhterev's naïve and radical reductionism.

Goldstein's theories were derived from his empirical studies on brain injuries, which brought him world fame, yet he is not a reductionist in the usual connotation of the word, as Watson, Bekterev, Hull, and Hebb are. He did not try to force his psychological data into a strait jacket of physiology even though he was a leading authority in the field of neurology.

Dealing so much with injured organisms, Goldstein became fully aware of the two sides of their functioning, the physical and the mental. He did not try to substitute one for the other. Neither did Pavlov or Freud. Pavlov used non-mentalistic terms but left the door open for a psychology based on (but not reduced to) physiology. Freud created a psychological system, but he was fully aware of the fact that mental life, while being a part of organic life, cannot be reduced to physiology. Goldstein dealt with the total organism and used both approaches to the organism. Consciousness, he explained, is a person's awareness of a situation, of his own activity and purpose. It is a function of the organism, but it cannot be reduced to cerebral synapses. Goldstein's theory has something of Spinoza's philosophy; there are two sides to the coin, the physical and mental. Both together form the whole organism.

3. Jacob R. Kantor: Organismic Psychology

Interbehavior

J. R. Kantor is undoubtedly indebted to Adolf Meyer, who introduced the idea of the mind–body unity and considered the human mind not as independent "mind-stuff," but as a function or action of the higher, organized, living organisms. Psychology is a natural science like all other natural sciences and deals with the functions of the organism. Hence the name introduced by Meyer: *psychobiology*. [34]

These ideas were taken up by Kantor. Living organisms are not just objects or things. They live; they adjust to environment by interaction or *interbehavior*, which includes all actions of the organism, physical and mental alike.

The organism, stated Kantor, responds to stimuli and can store up energy. Its main actions serve the "maintenance of the individual." Psy-

[34] Adolf Meyer, *Common Sense Psychiatry*, McGraw-Hill, 1948.

chological organisms are at the same time physical and biological objects. However, "psychology has its own subject-matter-specific interactions between organisms and stimulating objects."[35]

Kantor was opposed to the molecular approach in psychology. He believed that the organism is one psychological entity and acts always as a whole. The individual as a whole reacts to stimuli and interacts with the sources of stimulation. Therefore, the study of the organism treated as an isolated entity may lead to many misconceptions. The organism functions not in a vacuum but in a definite environment, and the subject matter of psychology is the interbehavior of the organism with objects, events, and other organisms. The "field" of this interaction is the subject matter of psychological inquiry.

Kantor made a strong plea for a non-reductionistic psychology. "All sciences constitute investigative enterprises for the purpose of ascertaining the nature of specific events. . . . It is assumed that nature comprises an intricate manifold of events—fields in which things (particles, waves, organisms, etc.) operate in certain ways and change under specific conditions. Each science including psychology isolates some phase of this manifold for its special object of study. The data and methods of psychology are therefore homogeneous with those of all other sciences. . . . All sciences are coordinate. . . . Psychology, then, does not require any specific neural or general biological guarantee for the reality of its data."[36]

Psychology must develop its statements on two levels. The first level is the description of observable phenomena. Such a description is the result of "investigative contacts of the scientist with the events." The second level of the scientific inquiry is the interpretation of data. In the construction of interpretations, the psychologist cannot incorporate anything which is "not derived from an original operation upon data. For example, when a psychologist observes an organism discriminate a red from a green square, he cannot regard the color quality as a psychic or neural middle term between the stimulation—regarded as operation of light rays—and the response—considered as the operation of muscular processes. . . . Constructions should not only be derived from and made applicable to original events, but also . . . whenever it is necessary to build upon prior constructions such building must be carefully controlled. . . . What must be guarded against is building psychological constructions out of prior biological (muscle action) and physical (energy) constructions as though these were preanalytic investigative events."[37]

This methodological anti-reductionism reflects Kantor's position. Kantor did not deny the fact that mental processes are functions of living matter. He was, however, strongly opposed to the idea that fictitious physio-

[35] Jacob R. Kantor, *A Survey of the Science of Psychology*, Principia, 1933, p. vii.
[36] Jacob R. Kantor, "Interbehavioral Psychology," in M. H. Marx (Ed.), *Psychological Theory*, Macmillan, 1951, pp. 318–319.
[37] *Ibid.*, pp. 320–321.

logical models or constructs are any better than psychological ones. He was adamant in his opposition to the uncritical borrowing of concepts from foreign areas instead of developing them out of observable psychological data. Psychology, he believed, can function on its own merits just like any other empirical science and does not need any "support" from physiology.

As a matter of fact the physiological theories related to the functioning of the nervous system are biased and dualistic, and not prepared to offer sufficient explanation in their own realm. Kantor described in detail the physiological counterparts of psychology. In a volume published in 1947 he exposed to a thorough and severe criticism several theories which tried to reduce psychology to physiological phenomena and localize mental functions in the cortex.[38] Kantor never denied the fact that mental functions are accompanied by physiological ones, and he made a plea for an "authentic" physiological psychology. Such a psychology would by no means represent the entire truth, for the subject matter of psychology is not the organism only but the "field" of "interbehavior" between organism and environment. Therefore, the description of organic or physiological factors in psychology cannot replace the description of psychological data. "The most elaborate description of such participating biological factors cannot cover the essential features of the psychological event," wrote Kantor.[39] However, an "authentic" physiological psychology could be very helpful.

Kantor's studies are a significant contribution to the methodology of psychological inquiry. His methodological anti-reductionistic point is well taken and clearly elaborated, and his theory of organism–environment interaction brings him close to K. Goldstein and K. Lewin.

4. SOME NEW IDEAS ON PURPOSIVISM

E. C. Tolman

In 1932, E. C. Tolman published his book *Purposive Behavior in Animals and Man*. He was considered to be a behaviorist because he rejected the assumption that purposes are manifestations of voluntary intentions of conscious agents. Yet he was different from other behaviorists, such as Watson, in that he believed that behavior in the global sense is both purposive and goal oriented. " 'Behavior,' " he wrote, "reeks of purpose."[40] In his work, he tried to develop a systematic psychology which would reject the observable variables described by behaviorism while also demonstrating the existence of purposiveness in behavior. He felt that purposive aspects

[38] Jacob R. Kantor, *Problems of Physiological Psychology*, Principia, 1947.
[39] *Ibid.*, p. 337.
[40] Paul McReynolds, "Purpose and Purposivism," in B. B. Wolman (Ed.), *International Encyclopedia of Psychiatry, Psychology, Psychoanalysis and Neurology*, Aesculapius, 1977, *9*, p. 331.

of behavior could be deduced from objective aspects of behavior, for example, in the way that rats running mazes will eventually develop the most efficient path. This kind of interpretation of purposive behavior does not mean that a mentalistic type of purpose could be attributed to the rats.[41]

Current Concepts

The concept that man is purposeful in his behavior, that is, that he intentionally moves toward certain aims or goals—as opposed to moving mechanistically—is debated in various terms. It would seem that one might take the concept of purpose for granted. But the discipline of philosophical psychology has approached this problem in a methodologically sophisticated fashion. Philosophically oriented behaviorists, as well as cognitive and personality psychologists, address themselves to the concepts of purpose, agent, and attention. The philosopher Charles Taylor asserted that teleological concepts are crucial to the issue of purpose, and were inappropriately discarded by the positivist movement. Taylor stated that purpose implies both a teleological explanation and also a description of the way in which the agent or person with the purpose sees his situation.[42]

Willard Day, a radical behaviorist, has proposed a description of purposive behavior that includes the notion of intention, thus avoiding mentalistic concepts.[43]

[41] *Ibid.*, pp. 331–332.
[42] *Ibid.*
[43] *Ibid.*

Summary of Part I

Part I includes various psychological theories brought together by their common start in the controversy over introspection. The first chapter sets the stage and describes the dominating trend of *structuralism*, based on introspection. Both Wundt in Germany and Titchener in the United States were experimental psychologists who, under the influence of nineteenth-century physiologists, introduced the experimental method into psychology.

Another group of psychologists, most of them in the United States, felt that the biological theory of evolution offered a more fruitful stimulation. James, Dewey, Angell, Woodworth, and others preferred to look on mental activities from the perspective of adjustment to life. These psychologists, called *functionalists*, perceived consciousness not as a receptor–motor machine but as a weapon of the living organism in its fight for survival. This point of view, influenced by the American philosophy of *pragmatism*, undermined the status of consciousness as the only subject matter of psychology and challenged introspection as the main method in psychology.

The rapidly expanding study of animal psychology led to an ever increasing criticism of introspection. Thorndike's *neo-associationism*, called *connectionism*, built a bridge leading from studies based on introspection to the new and objective psychology. Thorndike never burned the bridge, and his writings serve as a link between the "old" structuralism, functionalism, and associationism on one side and the "new" *behaviorism* and *conditioning* on the other.

The second chapter is devoted to I. P. Pavlov and his school. Starting with I. M. Sechenov, Russian physiologists and neurophysiologists embarked on the most fruitful research in the physiology of the nervous system and its relationship to behavior. Pavlov's main principles were monism, empiricism, conservation of energy, and determinism. Pavlov did not intend to develop a psychological theory. He believed that a scientific psychology based on physiology (but not reduced to it) still had to come. Meanwhile, the physiological foundations were laid by Pavlov.

Whatever is going on in overt behavior, according to Pavlov, is related to connections in the nervous system and conduction of energy along the nerve paths. Some connections are innate, some acquired. The acquired ones are the conditioned reflexes, acquired in accordance with the dynamics of irradiation and concentration of energy.

A new world was opened up to psychology, a world based on a definite theory relating observable behavioral data to a physiological theory well supported by experimentation.

Pavlov's contemporary, Bekhterev, discovered conditioning simultaneously with Pavlov and conducted ingenious experiments which led to the so-called *instrumental conditioning*. Bekhterev believed that physical and mental processes can be presented in one physical continuum of energy.

Soviet psychologists, seeking guidance from the sources of Marxist philosophy, have been greatly influenced by the giants of neurophysiology, Pavlov and Bekhterev. In recent years, the pendulum has swung in the direction of Pavlov, and the precision experiments in conditioning of covert behavior (interoceptive and proprioceptive) by Bykov and others are quite impressive. Soviet psychology continues to lean heavily both on Marx's dialectic materialism and on Pavlov's neurophysiology. These two theories are not irreconcilable, as the studies of Rubinstein, Luria, Smirnov, and others indicate.

The third chapter introduces *behaviorism* and *programmatic reductionism*. A psychologist might or might not try to reduce psychology to physiology; this is merely one aspect of his theory. But some psychologists seemed to believe that psychology must be reduced to physiology (Watson) or must not (Spranger). Then the issue becomes programmatic.

Independently of Pavlov and Bekhterev, some American psychologists were searching for a "scientific," objective psychology. This programmatic rebellion against introspection was introduced by J. B. Watson.

Watson incorporated *conditioning* into his theory. Psychology was to him either a science of behavior or not a science at all. According to Watson, the only difference between physiology and psychology was that psychology dealt with the behavior of the "whole" organism. Apparently, his point of view was *molar*.

The early Watsonians, Weiss, Holt, Hunter, and Lashley, developed their own theories, perhaps with more sophistication in the body–mind problem. A new system of reductionistic psychology was developed by the neurophysiologist Lashley, who introduced the principle of equipotentiality.

Hebb went even further. A keen observer and experimentalist, he developed his own full-fledged neurological theory of behavior, opposed to Lashley's, and emphasized the local actions of the nervous calls.

The fourth chapter is the longest chapter in the book. It is devoted to the neobehaviorists and contemporary learning theorists. It starts with Guthrie's uncompromising theory of learning by mere contiguity in time, supported by several carefully planned experiments.

The second section is devoted to the man who introduced the *hypo-thetico-deductive* method into the realm of psychology. C. L. Hull's method is an excellent example of theory construction in psychology. Hull utilized Pavlov's empirical findings on conditioning but replaced Pavlov's energetic principle of reinforcements by his own theory of drive reduction. Hull's theory is a result of deductive reasoning checked against rigorous experimentation.

The analysis of B. F. Skinner's works follows. Skinner's work is a case of *radical empiricism*, a most carefully applied inductive method and an avoidance of theory. Skinner preferred description to explanation, observable data to postulates, mathematical functions to causality. He is an operationist. He introduced the distinction between the classical and instrumental conditioning based on modification of the method of experimentation.

The fourth section of this chapter is devoted to E. C. Tolman, the man who introduced the distinction between the independent, intervening, and dependent variables. Tolman's theory is still a branch of the tree that Watson planted, but it is a very remote branch, indeed, much intertwined with the perception theory of the gestalt psychologists and purposivism.

A solution to the controversy between the various theories of learning was offered by G. Razran. Razran ordered the levels of learning using evolutionary steps in phylogenetic development. On the lowest level, learning is performed by sheer neural strength. On the next level, reward is the reinforcing factor. On the highest level, cognitive learning takes place.

Dollard, Miller, Mowrer, Sears, and others introduced psychoanalytic concepts into learning theory. All of them started with Pavlov and Hull but gradually modified their points of view and developed new and original theories.

The last sections of the chapter point to the neglect of neurophysiological aspects of learning and to a certain confusion in the present-day theory of motivation in learning.

The fifth chapter is devoted to alternative solutions to the problem posed by the functionalists. Adjustment to life was interpreted by biologists both in a *mechanistic* and in a *vitalistic* fashion. The same happened in psychology.

W. McDougall offered a theory of behavior dramatically opposed to Watson's. Watson's device was causation; McDougall's teleology. Watson emphasized environment; McDougall heredity. Watson believed in learning; McDougall in instincts. McDougall's entire prolific work was an elaboration of this theory of instincts.

Yet both Watson and McDougall have "common roots" in James and Dewey, and both deal with the role of the mind in adjustment. Both lean heavily on physiology and both are mainly concerned with the overt behavior of organisms.

The other two *purposivistic* and *holistic* theories belong to K. Goldstein and J. R. Kantor. Goldstein's excellent studies in brain injury brought him world fame, and his thought-provoking theory of equalization of energy, self-actualization, and adjustment to environment was based on painstaking observations. Kantor turned against reductionism and introduced the idea of interbehavior between the organism and the environment.

PART II
Psychoanalysis and Related Systems

6

Psychoanalysis

1. METHODOLOGY

Sapere Aude

Psychoanalysis and related schools became a part of contemporary psychological theory after a long and complicated process of development. Psychoanalysis cannot be traced from the philosophical discussion about the human soul, nor was it born in the atmosphere of the academic *Wissenschaft* of psychological laboratories. It started in medicine and it was, and partially still is, a part of the medical discipline that grew exceedingly slowly in its endeavor to understand and treat mental disorder. While official medicine rigorously pursued the path of anatomy, histology, and physiology, rebellious psychoanalysis followed in the footsteps of "unscientific," "mentalistic," and "metaphysical" concepts repudiated by the official science, and studied the irrational and even parapsychological aspects of human life. Freud and his followers introduced into the area of irrationality the rational method of scientific inquiry and proved beyond doubt that being scientific is not identical with choosing a rational phenomenon but depends upon the method applied in the study of empirical phenomena, irrespective of their being rational or irrational.

Originally Freud did not intend to create a full-fledged psychological theory, but in the end he developed even more than a psychological system. All psychological theories started from a certain area, covered it thoroughly, and gradually expanded to other fields. Pavlov studied conditioned reflexes. Watson applied conditioning to the study of several aspects of overt behavior. Skinner studied complicated learning problems. Goldstein started with brain injuries. Freud studied mental disorder, primarily, and went on to an analysis of etiological factors. His etiological research shed light on child psychology and the laws of human growth and development. Then came a general theory of personality dynamics; then a study of human nature through the ages and a theory that dealt with the impact of society, culture, and religion on personality; finally, psychoanalysis, originally meant as a psychotherapeutic technique, became a great psychological

theory encompassing almost every area of normal and abnormal personality
theory and entering into the fields of sociology, anthropology, history, education, and the arts.

Rarely has any theory been exposed to so much bitter, and sometimes
unfair, criticism as has psychoanalysis. In medical circles, Freud was criticized for neglecting organic factors. Academic psychologists criticized him
for being unscientific; philosophers, for being unethical and degrading the
dignity of men.[1] On one issue, however, friends and foes had to agree: they
could not help admiring the great moral courage of Freud, who dealt with
the most controversial problems in a frank and forthright manner, despite
social pressures and taboos. Freud attacked the issues of love and hate, of
sexuality and destructiveness, of life and death. He unmasked bigotry and
hypocrisy, and with unabated zeal penetrated the areas of mental health
and illness, of an individual's growth and decline, of religion and crime, of
creative arts and destructive wars. Nothing could stop him in the ardent
pursuit of the truth; neither his personal biases nor even his own former
statements were spared by his critical mind. He was anything but conservative or opportunistic; he had the courage to acknowledge his mistakes and
to revise his theories drastically, even reverse them completely in some issues. He can serve as a noble example of scientific honesty that shuns
compromise with the truth. Of Freud it can be said that he possessed the
great virtue of a research worker: *Sapere Aude*.

His theories were taken up, either accepted or criticized, by research
workers and philosophers. Psychology and medicine, sociology and anthropology, history and philosophy, art and literature, political science and
social and religious philosophy are indebted to the indefatigable and
searching mind of Sigmund Freud.[2]

Empiricism

Freud was brought up in an atmosphere characterized by rapid progress in the natural sciences. He was born in 1856 and studied medicine. The
natural sciences were celebrating, at that time, their great triumphs in several fields. The glorious progress of biology, physics, chemistry, anatomy,
and physiology filled human hearts with the hope that the riddles of the
universe and of human nature would soon be solved, and that the searching mind, armed with adequate tools, would soon penetrate the areas still
belonging to philosophy or religion.

This optimistic outlook of the era of Darwin and Spencer enhanced

[1] There have been several excellent presentations of Freud's work. Some authors (E. Jones, G.
Murphy, R. S. Woodworth, and others) preferred to analyze Freud's work in a historical way,
emphasizing the development of Freud's ideas. Many others (O. Fenichel, D. Rapaport, and
others) chose the systematic way and organized Freud's theories around certain topics. This
writer prefers to use the systematic way.
[2] The *International Encyclopedia of Psychiatry, Psychology, Psychoanalysis and Neurology*, edited
by B. B. Wolman (Aesculapius, 1977) has over one hundred articles on Freud and his works.

Freud's preference for an empirical approach to psychology and instilled in him a strong dislike for any sort of speculation. Freud started by observing phenomena of overt human behavior in a clinical setting.

Originally he was more a neurologist than a psychiatrist, but at that time psychiatry was organically oriented. In 1885, Freud went to study in France with the great Charcot and was introduced to the enigmatic phenomena of suggestion, hypnosis, and hysteria. Back in Vienna, and together with Breuer, he embarked on the study of these phenomena, a study that bears witness to the empirical method employed by both of them.[3]

Freud's scientific method was a direct descendant of British and French empiricism, represented by Francis Bacon's criticism of bias and "idols" and John Stuart Mill's "canons." In the best tradition of empirical inquiry, Freud proceeded from observable phenomena to generalization and interpretation. He was not a naïve empiricist, nor did he refrain from inquiry into unobservable phenomena. He developed far-reaching hypotheses that had to be verified by observation. Whenever his clinical observations did not corroborate his hypotheses or his hypotheses failed to interpret the empirical data, he changed his hypotheses accordingly.

Freud's method of investigation can be demonstrated by his approach to the study of dreams. He said: "If the dream is a somatic phenomenon it does not concern us; it can only be of interest to us on the hypothesis that it is a mental phenomenon. So we will assume that this hypothesis is true in order to see what happens if we do so. The results of our work will determine whether we may adhere to the assumption, and uphold it, in its turn, as an inference fairly drawn."[4] Freud believed that the objective of scientific inquiry is to understand the phenomena, to establish the connection between them, and to gain control over them. "Reality will always remain 'unknowable.' What scientific work elicits from our primary sense perceptions will consist of an insight into connections and interdependences which are present in the external world, which can somehow or other be reliably reproduced or reflected in the external world of our thoughts, and the knowledge of which enables us to 'understand' something in the external world, to foresee it and possibly to alter it. Our procedure in psychoanalysis is exactly similar."[5]

Scientific Truth

In the epistemological discussion concerning the terms of scientific evidence, Freud was consistently a realist who believed in transcendent truth, that is, the dependence of truth upon experience. Scientific thought, he

[3] Joseph Breuer and Sigmund Freud, "The Psychical Mechanism of Hysterical Phenomena," *Neurologisches Zentralblatt*, 1893; Joseph Breuer and Sigmund Freud, *Studies in Hysteria*, Vienna, 1895.

[4] Sigmund Freud, *A General Introduction to Psychoanalysis*, Perma Giants, 1949, p. 90.

[5] Sigmund Freud, *An Outline of Psychoanalysis*, Norton, 1949, p. 106.

said, endeavors "to eliminate personal factors and emotional influences, carefully examines the trustworthiness of the sense perceptions, manages to have new perceptions unobtainable by usual means, and isolates the determinants of these new experiences by purposely varied experimentation. Its aim is to arrive at correspondence with reality, that is to say, with what exists outside of us and independently of us. . . . This correspondence with the real external world we call truth. It is the aim of scientific work. . . ."[6]

This principle of correspondence with external reality puts Freud in the camp of positivism as developed by Auguste Comte and against the sort of idealism initiated by Immanuel Kant. Freud's empiricism is based on the assumption that scientific inquiry is based on sensory perception. Sensory perception itself, although it can be improved and should be improved by the microscope, telescope, or other tools is a perception of the things that exist, independent of our perception.

There is not much in common between Freud's sterm adherence to the principles of external truth (called the principle of *transcendent truth,* cf. Chapter 15) and the neo-positivists or logical positivists or physicalists, who emphasized the principles of *immanent truth.* Freud probably had them in mind when he called some of his contemporary philosophers, nihilists and anarchists. "According to this anarchistic doctrine there is not such a thing as truth, no assured knowledge of the external world. . . . Ultimately we find only what we need to find, and see only what we desire to see. We can do nothing else. And since the criterion of truth, correspondence with an external world, disappears, it is absolutely immaterial what view we accept. All of them are equally true and false. And no one has a right to accuse any one else of error," Freud wrote about these philosophers.[7]

Theory Construction

Psychology, like any other empirical science, must go beyond empirically observable data. A series of correct observations is a preliminary step in scientific inquiry, but science must go farther and discover the temporarily unobservable data and interpret all the data in some coherent system of relationships and interdependencies.

The study of these relationships, as well as a tentative presentation of the facts that are temporarily not accessible to scientific inquiry, forms a legitimate part of any theory formulation. Theory is, in an oversimplified statement, a series of hypotheses, postulates, and models, that connect the empirical data into such a system as permits understanding of their interrelationships and the prediction of future development.[8]

[6] Sigmund Freud, *New Introductory Lectures in Psychoanalysis,* Norton, n.d., p. 233.
[7] *Ibid.,* p. 240.
[8] Benjamin B. Wolman, "Historical Laws—Do They Exist?" *Proceedings of the Xth International Congress of Philosophy,* Amsterdam, 1948 (abstract).

One can present psychoanalysis as a stimulus–response theory. The stimuli act upon the organism; then some action takes place. What goes on within the organism between the stimulus and the response forms the subject matter of psychoanalytic study. Freud developed a system of hypotheses or constructs that enables one, given the stimulus, to understand and predict the response or, given the response, to state correctly what was the stimulus. Every practicing psychoanalyst applies these hypotheses. Once the patients tell him their life history (the stimulus or the independent variable), the psychoanalyst applies psychoanalytic theory to an understanding of the patients' symptoms, and in many cases he is able to predict them. Or vice versa: when the patients describe their symptoms, the psychoanalyst can, to some extent, visualize their life history as a stimulus that caused the symptoms (the response, or the dependent variable).

"We have adopted the hypothesis of a physical apparatus, extended in space, appropriately constructed, developed by the exigencies of life, which gives rise to the phenomena of consciousness only at one particular point and under certain conditions," wrote Freud. "This hypothesis has put us in a position to establish psychology upon foundations similar to those of any other science, such as physics. In our science the problem is the same as in the others: behind the attributes (i.e., qualities) of the object under investigation which are directly given to our perception, we have to discover something which is more independent of the particular receptive capacities of our sense organs and which approximates more closely to what may be supposed to be the real state of things. There is no hope of our being able to reach the latter itself, since it is clear that everything new that we deduce must nevertheless be translated into the language of our perceptions, from which it is simply impossible for us to get ourselves free. But in this lies the nature and limitation of our science." [9]

These are the objective difficulties of theory construction in psychology. Freud did not believe that psychology could be presented as a series of mathematical equations (like physics or chemistry). The main difficulty in psychological theory remains the fact of the consciousness. But "conscious processes do not form unbroken series which are complete in themselves, so that there is no alternative to assuming that there are physical or somatic processes which accompany the mental ones and which must admittedly be more complete than the mental series, since some of them have conscious processes parallel to them but others have not." In addition, every science is "based upon observations and experiences arrived at through the medium of our psychical apparatus. But since *our* science has as its subject that apparatus itself, the analogy ends here. We make our observations through the medium of the same perceptual apparatus, precisely by the help of the breaks in the series of (conscious) mental events, since we fill in the omissions by plausible inferences and translate them into conscious material. In this way we construct, as it were, series of conscious events complementary

[9] Freud, *Outline of Psychoanalysis*, p. 105.

to the unconscious mental processes. The relative certainty of our mental science rests upon the binding force of these inferences."[10]

Scientific laws are established in inference. The processes which psychology deals with "are in themselves just as unknowable as those dealt with by the other sciences, by chemistry or physics, for example; but it is possible to establish the laws which those processes obey and to follow over long and unbroken stretches their mutual relations and interdependences—in short, to gain what is known as an 'understanding' of the sphere of natural phenomena in question. This cannot be effected without forming fresh hypotheses and creating fresh concepts."[11] And this is exactly how Freud developed his theory.

2. POSTULATES

Causation

One can hardly understand Freud without being aware of the basic principles underlying his research. These principles could not be directly proved by Freud or by anyone else. They did not emerge out of empirical research, nor could they be represented as conclusions drawn from successful experimentation. They were assumed, postulated as guiding principles of research. Any new bit of factual data, any new experiment, any success in exploration strengthens the belief that these principles are useful for the furtherance of knowledge and represent a highly generalized truth.

The necessity to postulate principles applies not only to psychology but to practically all empirical sciences. Any empirical study that deals with some fraction of the world makes certain assumptions as to the nature of the world. Then, in accordance with the usual scientific procedure, it tries to prove or, what is usually much more easily done, to disprove the postulated principles by data supporting or contradicting the assumptions.

Freud postulated some general principles such as causation, monism, mental energy, mental economy, the pleasure principle, and the biogenetic evolution of the human mind. It is still doubtful whether any of these principles can be empirically proved. Yet as long as no contradictiory data are available and as long as empirical study brings in more and more data that fall in line with the postulated principles, these principles should be considered scientifically useful working hypotheses, and their value *is* being constantly increased by further research.

One of the principles is the principle of *causation*. Natural sciences, especially contemporary physics, struggle with the difficulties arising from

---

[10] *Ibid.*, pp. 36–37.
[11] *Ibid.*, p. 36.

a strict application of the causation principle.[12] No such difficulties have been encountered in any of the areas of scientific psychology. All students of psychology have to accept a more or less strict deterministic point of view. Freud accepted a most rigorous determinism that says, "no causes without effects, no effects without causes," and this is the most general research principle of psychoanalysis.

This determinism cannot be finally proved; it is, however, a principle that more and more is being corroborated by research. Once accepted or postulated, it forces the research worker to continuous efforts in finding causes and predicting results. Any success serves as evidence that one is on the right track and encourages further efforts that promise to bring additional proof. Lack of success indicates that one has to check and double-check his methods and look for additional data. This strict determinism helped Freud in the study of the most irrational areas of dreaming and symptom formation in neuroses. The principle "whatever is, has its causes" forced Freud to give up the theory of sex vs. ego instincts, to assume the existence of destructive instincts, and to be on constant guard in searching for minute details that might have been partial causes in mental development and mental disorder.

The Problem of Reductionism

All his life Freud was faithful to the *monistic* philosophy and conception of the unity of man and nature. His entire education was guided by the monistic and materialistic concepts of the human organism.

Freud was influenced by Charcot and his attention gradually shifted to psychogenic factors; yet, he never gave up the search for organic equivalents of mental disturbance. It is not surprising that Freud's model of personality was influenced by physics, that his theory of libido was modeled on electrical concepts, and that human actions were represented by him as discharges of energy.

In 1894, Freud wrote that it is "scarcely possible to avoid picturing these processes as being in the last resort of a chemical nature." He never gave up this belief; even when he introduced several non-reductionistic concepts, he kept referring to the future research which would probably close the gap between physicochemical and mental facts.

Among the first principles he postulated was the concept of *energy*. All mental activities and everything that psychology deals with are discharges of mental energy analogous to, or some derivative of, physicochemical energy. However, Freud did not try to close the gap between physical and mental processes by a simple reductionism that overlooked the differences

[12] Benjamin B. Wolman, "Concerning Psychology and the Philosophy of Science," in B. B. Wolman (Ed.), *Handbook of General Psychology*, Prentice-Hall, 1973, pp. 22–48.

between these two realms. He was very much against such a naïve reductionism.

In his last work, in which he tried to bring together the doctrines of psychoanalysis and to state them, as it were, dogmatically—in the most concise form and in the most positive terms—Freud wrote:

> We know two things concerning what we call our psyche or mental life: firstly, its bodily organ and scene of action, the brain (or nervous system), and secondly, our acts of consciousness, which are immediate data and cannot be more fully explained by any kind of description. Everything that lies between these two terminal points is unknown to us and, so far as we are aware, there is no direct relation between them. If it existed, it would at the most afford an exact localization of the processes of consciousness and could give us no help toward understanding them.[13]

Freud never rejected the organic foundations of the mental life. Id, he said, contains "everything that is inherited, that is present at birth, that is fixed in constitution." But he never ran into a shallow reductionism. At best, he believed, one can assume, and never more than assume, that mental processes utilize some kind of energy that is at the disposal of the living organism. This energy is analogous to any other energy, and that is all we know. "We assume, as the other natural sciences have taught us to expect, that in mental life some kind of energy is at work; but we have no data which enable us to come nearer to a knowledge of it by analogy with other forms of energy."[14]

This is as far as Freud went in his reductionism. A consistent reductionism would have lead to naïveté or to an arid although "highly scientific" tautology, and be of "no help toward understanding" of the mental phenomena.

Freud was a monist and never gave up the hope for a monistic interpretation that would combine both physical and mental processes. But, as things stand now, one has to reject reductionism for methodological reasons and to develop some new hypothetical constructs independent of the physical sciences. This is what Freud actually did. He was fully aware of the fact that the new constructs were non-reductionistic and non-reducible to any of the constructs of physics or chemistry. He felt that the future might prove that some chemical substances were influencing the amount of energy and its distribution in the human mind. Such an assumption today would be, to say the least, useless. Today, psychology must develop its own hypotheses and concepts.

The processes with which psychology is concerned "are in themselves just as unknowable as those dealt with by the other sciences, by chemistry or physics, for example; but it is possible to establish the laws which those processes obey and follow over long and unbroken stretches their mutual relations and interdepencences. . . . This cannot be effected without fram-

13 Freud, *Outline of Psychoanalysis*, pp. 13–14.
14 *Ibid.*, p. 44.

ing fresh hypotheses and creating fresh concepts. . . . We can claim for them the sense value as approximations as belongs to the corresponding intellectual scaffolding found in the other natural sciences, and we look forward to their being modified, corrected and more precisely determined as more experience is accumulated and sifted. So too it will be entirely in accordance with our expectations if the basic concepts and principles of the new science (instinct, nervous energy, etc.) remain for a considerable time no less indeterminate than those of the older sciences (force, mass attraction, etc.)." [15]

Fenichel, one of the leading thinkers in psychoanalysis, summarized the scientific task of psychoanalysis as follows:

> Scientific psychology explains mental phenomena as a result of interplay of primitive physical needs . . . and the influences of the environment on these needs. . . . Mental phenomena occur only in living organisms; mental phenomena are a special instance of life phenomena. The general laws that are valid for life phenomena are also valid for mental phenomena; special laws that are valid only for the level of mental phenomena must be added. . . . Scientific psychology investigates, as does any science, general *laws*. It is not satisfied with a mere description of individual psychic processes. . . . Its subject is not the individual but the comprehension of general laws governing mental functions." [16]

Mental Energy

Once the principle of monism is established and causation is accepted as a binding law, some dynamic factors producing change must be postulated. The psychologist Kurt Lewin (cf. Chapter 13) preferred to introduce the concept of forces. Freud, dealing with the organism as a whole and considering mental phenomena a part of the functions of the living organism, found the concept of energy more useful and more in accordance with the monistic principle. This postulate of *mental energy* enabled Freud to relate mental processes to physicochemical processes.

He made the assumption that there is but one energy in nature and that all the observable types of energy are variations or transformations of that basic energy, be it electrical or any other. If this is true in physics, it must be true in chemistry, biology, and psychology. It does not mean that human thoughts *are* electrical processes, or that they can be reduced to quantities represented by amperes or watts or volts, or measured by encephalographs. Mental processes cannot be reduced to anything which is not mental. However, Freud believed, they somehow stem from the same physical source as anything else in the world. Mental energy is energy in the physical meaning of the word, that is, probably something that can be transformed into another kind of energy analogous to the transformation of mechanical into thermic energy. Energy is not perishable; it can be accumulated, preserved, discharged, dissipated, blocked—but it cannot be

---

[15] *Ibid.*, p. 36.

[16] Otto Fenichel, *The Psychoanalytic Theory of Neurosis*, Norton, 1945, p. 5.

annihilated. This postulate of preservation of mental energy, its trans-formability, its functioning in close analogy to physical energy, is one of the guiding principles of psychoanalysis.

"Among the psychic functions there is something which should be dif-ferentiated (an amount of affect, a sum of excitation), something having all the attributes of a quantity—although we possess no means of measuring it—a something which is capable of increase, decrease, displacement and discharge, and which extends itself over the memory-traces of an idea like an electric charge over the surface of the body. We can apply this hypoth-esis . . . in the same sense as the physicist employs the conception of a fluid electric current."[17]

One may, therefore, postulate that psychic energy is not anything en-tirely new or different from other types of energy. Since electricity can be transformed into light or into thermic or dynamic energy, this serves as evi-dence for the physicist that the different types of energy are basically one energy only. It may also hold that psychic energy is a transformation of somatic energy. "The visceral excitation will then actually develop continu-ously, but only when it reaches a certain height will it be sufficient to over-come the resistance in the paths of conduction to the cerebral cortex and express itself as a psychical stimulus." And later: "Once it has reached the required level, the somatic sexual excitation is continuously transmuted into psychical excitation."[18]

The Constancy Principle and Repetition Compulsion

One of the most important postulates of psychoanalysis is the principle of *constancy*. Whatever goes on in the human mind and whatever psychol-ogy deals with are related to energy. Energy is the explanatory principle behind all mental phenomena, and the distribution of energy is the second leading principle of Freud's theory.

Mental processes can be explained as follows: Any organism, including the human organism, is capable of responding or reacting to inner and outer stimuli. This capability of reaction to stimuli, or *irritability*, is a gen-eral feature of living, organic matter. When an organism is stimulated, a tension or disequilibrium takes place. Prior to the action of the stimuli one must postulate a state of equilibrium or, as Freud called it, Nirvana. Once the organism has been stimulated, the disequilibrium tends to terminate it-self, and the organism tends to restore its former balance. This can be ac-complished by discharge of energy. It is as if the mental apparatus tries to keep the quantity of excitation as low as possible or, at least, to keep it con-stant, and as if the increasing excitation were jeopardizing the existence of the organism. This tendency to restore equilibrium, or homeostasis, is called by Freud the *principle of constancy*.

[17] Sigmund Freud, *Collected Papers*, Hogarth, 1924, Vol. I, p. 75.
[18] *Ibid.*, pp. 97–98.

Freud felt that heredity and embryology bear witness to the compulsion of organic life to repeat. Instincts express the conservative nature of the living substance. An instinct, Freud wrote, "is a compulsion inherent in organic life to restore an earlier stage of things which the living entity has been obliged to abandon under the pressure of external disturbing forces." [19]

Freud quoted Plato's theory of the origin of love that "traces the origin of an instinct to a need to restore an earlier state of things." In Plato's *Symposium*, Aristophanes tells about primeval men who had two faces, four hands, four legs, and so on. Zeus cut them in two. But then Aristophanes tells, "the two parts of man, each desiring his other half, came together, and threw their arms about one another eager to grow into one." [20]

The same theory of the origin of love is found in the Indian *Upanishads*. The Atman was the only man. "But he felt no delight. Therefore a man who is lonely feels no delight. He wished for a second. He was so large as man and wife together. He then made this his Self to fall in two, and thence arose husband and wife. Therefore Yagnavalkya said: 'we two are thus (each of us) like half a shell!' Therefore the void which was there is filled by the wife." [21]

One may hypothetically assume that the living substance was torn apart into small particles "which have ever since endeavored to reunite through sexual instincts." If this were true, said Freud, then several biological processes could be interpreted by the tendency to restore an earlier state of things.

The principle of pleasure related to mental economy raises additional implications in two directions. Since the restoration of the former status is in itself pleasurable, then, by implication, the instinctual forces are bound to produce continuous repetitions of a disturbance until the balance is restored. When an individual suffers a traumatic experience and is unable to regain his prior balance, he will be prone to relive emotionally this unpleasant experience. This is what Freud called *repetition–compulsion*.

Freud and his followers often noticed that an individual who suffered some highly unpleasant, damaging, or humiliating experience tended to act as if he were interested in repeating it, either by his overt behavior, leading to self-defeat, or in dreams. Usually the individual was unaware of this compulsion for repetition of tensions. However, once the tensions were resolved in the course of psychoanalytic therapy, they did not come back again.

The other implication deduced from the pleasure principle as a reduction of tension was the idea of Nirvana or of the perfect sleep. Once the tensions are removed, the infant falls asleep. Sleep is the escape from overstimulation and perfect sleep is perfect satisfaction. But if this is the truth,

[19] Sigmund Freud, *Beyond the Pleasure Principle*, Liveright, 1950, p. 47.
[20] *Ibid.*, pp. 79–80.
[21] *Ibid.*, pp. 79–80.

death may be considered the perfect rest, balance, and happiness. This led Freud, as will be explained in the next section, to develop a theory of death instinct.

Principle of Economy

Energy is nonperishable. Various objects can be invested with it; it can be transformed; or it can be released or accumulated. Once some amount of energy is put into something, the latter becomes loaded or charged with mental energy as bodies become charged with electricity. This process of charging *ideas or objects* with mental energy was called by Freud *cathexis*, and objects or ideas invested with energy were cathected. Cathexis can be applied to external objects as well as to one's own organism.

Energy is transformable and displaceable. Mental processes are processes of *mental energy economics*, that is, *quantitative* processes of investment, discharge, accumulation, transformation, of mental energy. Some processes are more energy consuming, some less. Often an individual does not do anything and yet a great amount of energy is being consumed. When strong instinctual drives urge immediate discharge of energy, a great amount of energy is needed to prevent it. Individuals who have strong inner conflicts cannot be very efficient because too much of their energy is being tied up, and they can feel very tired even if they do not do anything.

Mental economy depends on the strength of the stimuli, of the instinctual drives, and of the inhibitory forces. One may, in a simplified form, present human behavior as a series of reflex-arcs. A stimulus acts on the organism, causing a disequilibrium (perceived as a tension). Tension leads to an action, that is, to a discharge of some amount of energy. The discharge of energy restores the equilibrium and is perceived as relief or relaxation.

However, this simple presentation does not contain the entire truth. Between the tension and discharge of energy, something happens in the organism. Two contradictory types of forces step in, one type facilitating the discharge of energy which brings relief, the other preventing or postponing this discharge. The forces that urge and facilitate discharge are called by Freud *drives* or *instincts*. The instincts or instinctual drives press for discharge or energy, for lowering of the level of excitation and reduction of the tension in the organism. These forces help to restore the equilibrium. Since the tendency to keep equilibrium or homeostasis seems to be a general tendency of living matter, the instinctual drives must be basic, innate, and primary biological forces. The counterforces oppose the immediate discharge, ward it off, or *repress* it. These inhibitory forces stem originally from outside the organism, but in the process of an individual's growth and development they become internalized. The neonate is endowed with instinctual forces that are the guardians of the mental equilibrium. The adult's mental mechanism is far more complicated. Between the stimulus and the response a complicated process of interaction between instinctual and inhibitory forces takes place.

Pleasure and Relief

The idea of pleasure and unpleasure as related to the mental economy of excitation was borrowed by Freud from Fechner, whom he quotes as follows: "In so far as conscious impulses always have some relation to pleasure or unpleasure, pleasure and unpleasure too can be regarded as having a psycho-physical relation to conditions of stability and instability. This provides a basis for a hypothesis . . . [that] every psychophysical movement crossing the threshold of consciousness is attended by pleasure in proportion as, beyond a certain limit, it approximates to complete stability, and is attended by unpleasure in proportion as, beyond a certain limit, it deviates from complete stability; while between the two limits, which may be described as qualitative thresholds of pleasure and unpleasure, there is a certain margin of aesthetic indifference."[22]

Actually, Freud inferred the ideas of constancy and economy from his observations on pleasure and unpleasure. From the logical point of view, the pleasure principle follows the principle of constancy. The mental apparatus endeavors to keep the quantity of excitation low, and any stimulus that increases the stimulation is felt as unpleasurable.

"We have decided," wrote Freud in 1920, "to relate pleasure and unpleasure to the quantity of excitation that is present in the mind but is not in any way 'bound'; and to relate them in such a manner that unpleasure corresponds to an *increase* in the quantity of excitation and pleasure to a *diminution*."[23] This is how pleasure and unpleasure are experienced by an infant. Any excessive stimulation coming from without, such as noise or light, or from within, such as hunger or pressure in bowels or bladder, is experienced as unpleasure. Once the excitation is removed the infant falls asleep in a feeling of happiness (bliss).

The stimulation of the organism by inner or external factors causes disbalance of energy or tension. Tension is experienced by humans as unpleasure, and, as said before, the instinctual forces press for an immediate discharge of energy so as to reestablish the equilibrium that existed prior to the disturbance. This discharge of energy brings relief and is experienced by the individual as pleasure or gratification of the instinctual demands. The perfect pleasure is the perfectly balanced state of the organism.

The sexual drives exemplify tension experienced as pleasure and discharge of energy as pleasure. The most profound feeling of gratification is associated with orgasm, which restores the equilibrium in the system. However, it is well known that sexual tension itself is often perceived as

[22] *Ibid.*, pp. 3–4.
[23] *Ibid.*, p. 2.

pleasurable. It is as if the expectation of relief is a pleasure in itself, and building up of this expectation by sexual foreplay is pleasant as a promise of the forthcoming complete gratification. It is the pleasure of a good appetite.[24]

3. THE UNCONSCIOUS

Mesmer and Hypnotism

For years, psychology was the science of the human conscious. Psychology dealt with conscious processes, defined by introspectionists as the processes observed by the experiencing individual or "given in his inner experience." Processes of which the individual was aware, and nothing else, were considered the legitimate area of psychology.

Several phenomena apparently belonging to the realm of psychology, such as dreams, amnesias, and hypnotism, were left out by the psychology of the conscious. But it was rather arbitrary to dismiss the amazing mental phenomena of dreams, which captured the imagination of poets and prophets in ancient times. Far more difficult was it to overlook the strange lapses of memory that occurred in everyday life and in everyone's experience. Even more puzzling were the discontinuities in memory and the conscious caused by emotional disorders, known even in ancient times.

Ultimately, psychology was forced to recognize suggestion and hypnosis as unusual, but nevertheless true, phenomena of the human mind. When Mesmer demonstrated his "animal magnetism" and "magnetic fluid," official medical science censured him. A special committee appointed by the Académie des Sciences and the Faculty of Medicine in Paris concluded that since "the magnetic fluid could not be noticed by any of our senses therefore, such fluid does not exist."[25] Mesmer believed in this "magnetic fluid" that fills the universe, and a balance of this fluid in the human organism was believed to be a prerequisite for good health. The magnetizer could restore this equilibrium by touching the patients and thus magnetically controlling this fluid. A British surgeon, James Braid, rejected the idea of "magnetic fluid" but accepted the idea of influencing people's minds in a strange way which he named *hypnotism*. A French physician, A. Liebeault, published a book in 1864 about the influence of "moral factors" on the human body and described his methods of treatment with the use of hypnotism. In 1882, the well-known neurologist Charcot presented at the Académie des Sciences a paper based on a comprehensive practice and research of neurological changes artificially induced in hysterical patients.

[24] Gardner Murphy, *Personality* Harper, 1947; see Chapter 5, on preparatory and consummatory responses, pp. 102 ff.
[25] Gregory Zilboorg and George W. Henry, *A History of Medical Psychology*, Norton, 1941, p. 345.

Freud came to grips with hysterical symptoms at Charcot's clinic at Salpêtrière in 1885. Charcot proved that hysterical symptoms can be produced and removed by hypnotic suggestion. Charcot himself interpreted hypnosis by a physiological theory which considered psychogenic disturbance a by-product of organic factors possibly related to heredity.

At the same time, also in France, Pierre Janet developed a new theory of mental disorder. Although Janet insisted that mental disorder stems from degeneration, his theory was thoroughly psychogenic and dealt with a non-organic "automatism," named by Janet the "unconscious."

In 1889, Freud attended Bernheim's experiments in hypnosis in Nancy. The hypnotized subject was made to experience several hallucinatory experiences. When he woke up, he maintained that he could not recall anything. Bernheim urged the subject to recall what happened to him and assured him that he could recall everything. Surprisingly, the subject gradually recalled everything.

This experiment convinced Freud that an individual may not know that he knows. It was as if a part of mental life was concealed, not available to consciousness. Bernheim's studies finally did away with the common belief that humans are always aware of what they are doing and are always capable of making conscious decisions. The old-fashioned "faculty of will" was finally disposed of, and human beings were seen as they really are: torn by emotions, often perceiving reality erroneously, sometimes hallucinating, and occasionally being pushed by some "irresistible impulse."

The psychological conception of man as a rational being controlled by an intellectual "will power" was at an end. The time had arrived when human nature, with its irrational elements, unconscious mental life, and highly complicated mental structure, was open for research.

Joseph Breuer and the Cathartic Method

Prior to his study in Salpêtrière under Charcot, Freud had been under the influence of a distinguished Viennese neurologist, Joseph Breuer. Back from France, Freud cooperated with Breuer and together they cured hysterical patients by having them recall past experiences under hypnosis. The reliving of a trauma was the cure of the neurosis.

"The fundamental fact was that the symptoms of hysterical patients are founded upon highly significant but forgotten scenes in their past lives (traumas); the therapy founded upon this consisted in causing them to remember and reproduce these scenes in a state of hyponosis (catharsis); and the fragment of theory inferred from this was that these symptoms represented an abnormal form of discharge for quantities of excitation which had not been disposed of otherwise (conversion." [26]

In 1895, Breuer and Freud published a volume entitled *Studies in Hysteria*. These studies reported successful treatment of hysterical symptoms by a

[26] Freud, *Collected Papers*, Vol. I, p. 289.

method called *catharsis*. The assumption was made that emotional conflicts could lead to a transfer of some quantity or energy, together with its emotional content, from the conscious part of the mind to the unconscious part. This is *repression*. By helping a patient to relive the conflict, the therapists opened the way for discharge of the repressed energy with its emotional content, the mind was cleared (catharted) of the unconscious emotional load (often called *complex*), and the neurotic symptoms were removed.

The success of the cathartic method was regarded by Freud as evidence of the existence of the *unconscious*. What had once been conscious, was made unconscious by repression and conscious again by catharsis. Freud said that he was accustomed to dealing with the unconscious part of the mind as with "something actual and tangible." Some of the symptoms of obsessional neurotics give the impression, even to the patients themselves, of being "powerful visitors" from another world.

Obsessive symptoms, Freud said, indicate a sphere of mental activity "cut off from the rest of the world." This sphere is the unconscious. Neurotic symptoms are produced in the unconscious and as soon as the related conflict is made conscious, the symptoms must vanish. Breuer and Freud arrived at these conclusions in their clinical practice. They had actually removed neurotic symptoms by making their patients conscious of the unconscious meaning of the symptoms.

Conscious, Preconscious, and Unconscious

Freud's theory of the unconscious was derived from experiences in hypnotism and catharisis. The spectacular phenomenon of *amnesia* and the restoration of memory in therapy called for the assumption of a continuum in which memories, loss of memories, and regaining of memories could be presented. Freud believed that the more "obscure and inaccessible" areas have to be studied by the "least rigid hypothesis." This was his methodological strategy. But he did not consider the unconscious a theory or an a priori postulate; the unconscious, he said, is "a stock taking of the facts of our observation."

Even perceptions and mobility are not necessarily conscious. One may perceive objects without being aware of doing so, as in hysterical blindness, and one may move around unconsciously, as in somnambulism.

The newborn infant probably has no conscious but is undoubtedly "sensitive," that is, he perceives and reacts to pain and pleasure. These perceptions and reactions are believed to leave memory traces. The unconscious stores memories which are inaccessible in the waking state, for example, the memories of early childhood experiences. Many childhood wishes are unrealizable and yet imperishable; many happenings are registered in the infant's mind and yet are uncommunicable. It is exceedingly difficult to study the deep and preverbal layers of the unconscious. What Freud actually did was to make an indirect analysis of the unconscious; in this analysis the observable phenomena of dreams, free association, slips of the tongue, and symptoms of mental disorder were studied as representatives of the great mental province of the unconscious.

In accordance with the homeostatic principle, Freud believed that the infant's mind avoids overstimulation by falling asleep. The infant wakes up only when the pressure of stimuli such as hunger, bowel or bladder discomforts, or loud noise, becomes unbearable. As soon as he can get rid of the stimulus, he sleeps or is half-awake.

Even when awake, the infant hallucinates rather than perceives, dreams rather than sees. But the external stimuli do not permit the pleasure of sleep to be perpetuated. The tension-provoking stimuli force the infant to perceive them, to cope with them, and to try to master them. This is probably the origin of the conception of reality, and this is the way the conscious emerges out of the unconscious. Tension leads to the development of the *conscious*.

The development of the conscious depends on the infant's growing ability to utilize his memories. The memories accumulate, as it were, on the "surface" of the unconscious, easily accessible, and easily becoming conscious. This part of the unconscious forms the *preconscious*.

Thus, the unconscious is divided into two parts: the preconscious and the unconscious proper. Some unconscious processes can become conscious without any difficulty. They can be recalled and the individual can easily become aware of them. They resemble conveniently stored goods, easily accessible. What is conscious, is actually conscious for a short while only, and can easily pass into the preconscious. On the other hand, the mental processes of the preconscious can become conscious "without any activity on our part."

The preconscious is what is unconscious at a given time but can easily become conscious; it is *latent* or temporarily unconscious. Slips of the tongue, forgetting of well-known names and places, errors, and misplacement of objects belong to this category. In contradistinction to the preconscious layer, the deeper layers of the unconscious are less accessible and may never become conscious.

The individual is conscious or aware of only a small fraction of his mental processes at a given time. Thus, the conscious (or consciousness) must be a result of a selective process. The unconscious tends to become preconscious and eventually conscious, but only a part of it actually becomes conscious. Some impulses and perceptions may become preconscious or conscious for a while and then to be thrown back to the unconscious. Originally, Freud ascribed to the conscious and unconscious dynamic properties, but finally he relegated all dynamics to instincts and the the "mental agencies" of id, ego, and superego (see Section 6 of this chapter). Thus, the terms "conscious," "preconscious," and "unconscious" do not indicate any dynamic forces in personality but, as Freud finally concluded, the *mental provinces*. They are topographic concepts indicating the "depth" of the mental processes, their relative distance from the surface. What the individual is aware of is conscious; what he is not aware of but may become so at any time is preconscious; what he cannot become aware of without definite effort or cannot become aware of at all is unconscious.

Repression and Resistance

Freud distinguished between the rejection of an impulse (sometimes called suppression) and repression. In suppression, the energy put at the disposal of the impulse that is seeking to "convert itself into action" has been withdrawn. The impulse has no more energy attached to it; it becomes powerless and exists merely as a memory.

Repression is "a vehement effort" that has been exercised to prevent the mental process in question from penetrating into the conscious, and as a result it has remained unconscious. Repression is an act by which either a mental act is prevented from entering into the preconscious and is forced back into the unconscious, or a mental system which belongs to the preconscious is thrown into the unconscious. Repression is a "topographic–dynamic" conception.

What has been repressed tends to find outlets for discharge. Freud was always consistent in regard to the energetic principle (cf. Section 2 of this chapter). All mental processes are processes in which some energy is accumulated, stored, blocked, or discharged. Some forces, whether conscious or unconscious, prevent the discharge of energy. The very same repressing forces, later called "defense mechanisms," forever resist the discharge of repressed energy. A person undergoing psychoanalytic therapy usually unconsciously "resists" the efforts of the therapist aimed at the discharge of blocked energies and the removal of tension. *Resistance* is nothing but the continuation of repression. It requires a special therapeutic skill to undo the resistance and to release the repressed energies.

Dream Interpretation

Dreams are the main mechanisms by which the unconscious manifests itself and is accessible to research. The interpretation of dreams was considered by Freud to be the strongest point in his studies. Dream is a part of sleep, and sleep is a temporary refusal to face the outside world. Freud believed that our relationship with the world which we entered so unwillingly seems to be endurable only with intermission; hence, we withdraw periodically into the condition prior to our entrance into the world; that is to say, into intra-uterine existence. At any rate, we try to bring about conditions—warmth, darkness, and absence of stimulus—characteristic of that state. Some of us still "roll ourselves tightly up into a ball resembling the intra-uterine position."

Sleep starts with the wish to withdraw from reality. With this relaxing withdrawal, the individual regresses to more primitive modes of activity and the controlling forces of the conscious are more and more reduced. The floor, so to say, is open to the voice of the unconscious—to the dream.

Dreams are a reaction of the mind to external or internal stimuli that act upon the organism in sleep. In dreams the individual attributes objective reality to the imagery that forms the material of the dreams. "A dream, then, is a psychosis with all the absurdities, delusions and illusions of a psychosis," said Freud. It is a consciously willed, temporary withdrawal from the external world and a regression to the state of mind that preceded the development of the conscious.

Dreams represent demands or wishes stemming from the unconscious; these wishes are usually repressed demands for instinctual gratification. Often the demands arise in the preconscious and are residues of the day's activities in the waking state. These demands may be related to a decision that has to be made or to a conflict that has to be resolved. The dreams of one night usually represent together one context; mostly, each dream is the precondition of the following one.

These unconscious or preconscious demands are pressures coming up against the conscious part of personality, which represses the unconscious wishes. Later on, Freud introduced a division of personality into three parts, each of them being a separate mental agency: the *id, ego,* and *superego* (see Section 6). The ego is the guardian of sleep, and all the pressures are pressures on the ego. The sleeping ego, Freud said, is focused on the wish to maintain sleep; it regards a demand as a disturbance and seeks to get rid of the disturbance. The ego achieves this "by what appears to be an act of compliance: it meets the demand with what is in the circumstances the innocent fulfillment of a wish and thus disposes of the demand. This replacement of a demand by the fulfillment of a wish remains the essential function of dream-work." [27]

The *dream-work* transforms the unconscious or preconscious wish, which is the *latent* dream thought, into what the dreamer perceives, that is, into *manifest dream content.* To use Freud's examples, if a doctor has to wake up in the morning to be in a hospital on time, which is a case of a preconscious wish, he may continue to sleep and to dream that he is already in the hospital as a patient who does not have to get up early in the morning. The latent dream material is the conflict about getting up. The sleeping ego protected the sleep by means of the dream-work, which transformed the wish into the manifest dream content of being already in the hospital as a patient, thus disposing of the conflict.

Dreams protect one's sleep. All dreams deal with wishes which, for some reason, cannot be accepted in the conscious and waking state. Every dream is an attempt "to put aside a disturbance of sleep by means of a wish-fulfillment." This *wish-fulfillment* of a repressed impulse is toned down because the path to motor discharge is closed in sleep. The repressed

[27] Freud, *Outline of Psychoanalysis,* p. 55.

impulse that presses toward motor discharge has "to content itself with an hallucinatory satisfaction." The latent dream thoughts are therefore turned into a collection of sensory images and visual scenes.[28]

Not all dreams represent a simple wish or a wish-fulfillment. Many dreams are rather unpleasant and some of them are horror-stricken nightmares. All dreams represent rejected or repressed wishes but some of them carry a violent inner conflict. What represents a gratification for the unconscious id may be perceived as a threat to the preconscious or conscious ego. In anxiety dreams, the latent dream material has undergone little change and the demands are too great to be warded off. Sometimes, when the threat to the ego is very great, as it is in nightmares, the individual gives up sleep and returns to a waking state.

Dream-work results in *dream-distortions*. Dream-work, as said before, is a result of a compromise between the unconscious forces that press for a discharge of energy and the opposing forces of the ego, the *dream-censor*, which inhibits, restrains, and counteracts these pressures. The dream-censor is the same force that represses the unconscious wishes, keeps them repressed, and resists their expression in free associations necessary for dream interpretation in psychoanalytic therapy.

The interpretation of dreams is based on a deterministic assumption that everything has a cause and an effect. This strict determinism is conducive to a thorough investigation of the manifest content of the dream. The continuity of human mental life is established when one accepts the Freudian idea that the dream is an expression of unconscious material. Irrational and nonsensical as the dream may sound, it always represents some unconscious processes which the dreamer does not know he knows and thinks he does not.

Analysis of dreams enabled Freud to discover the laws that govern the *primary*, unconscious processes and to find the differences between them and the *secondary*, conscious processes. In the unconscious the thought elements that in a waking state are kept apart are combined or *condensated* into larger units. One thought element of the manifest dream may represent a cluster of unconscious and latent dream thoughts. Usually, as dream analysis proves, the brief manifest content of a dream, or what the dreamer perceives, is an *allusion* to a great amount of unconscious thoughts and wishes.

Another law governing the unconscious processes is *displacement*. In the waking state, instinctual energies are invested or cathected in definite objects. In dreams, those cathexes or mental energy loads are easily shifted from one object to another. Sometimes, very significant latent dream elements are barely mentioned or only alluded to in the manifest dream content, while unimportant unconscious elements may be represented in the manifest dream in a very clear manner.

As dream analysis implies, the unconscious uses its own language. It is

[28] Freud, *New Introductory Lectures in Psychoanalysis*, p. 32.

the grammarless language of illogic, where contradictory elements are applied, and compromise is reached between mutually exclusive statements. Yes and no, true and false, reality and imagination are brought together in utter disregard for inner consistency.

There is no logic in dreams. In the *secondary elaboration,* nonrelated elements may be put together and represented as a whole. An idea may be represented by its opposite; a causal relationship may be replaced by a merely temporal sequence. What is impossible in waking life can become possible and come true in a dream.

Dreams apply symbols, usually pictorial. Some symbols are universal, such as a house, which symbolizes the human body. When it is smooth, it symbolizes a man. When there are balconies and ledges, it represents a woman. Parents appear in dreams as kings and queens, siblings as little animals or vermin. Birth is represented by water, death by a journey. Most symbols applied in dreams relate to sexual organs and functions. The female sexual symbols are pockets, flower pots and vases, receptacles, bags, purses, drawers, jars and boxes, doors and gates; rooms and stores symbolize the uterus; watches and clocks symbolize periodic processes and intervals; snails and mussels symbolize women; a diamond represents the open female genitals; buildings such as chapels and churches symbolize women; apples, peaches, and oranges represent breasts. A landscape with rocks, woods, and water represents female organs.

A cloak and a hat symbolize a man. Sticks, keys, knives, poles, pencils, guns, snakes, trees, and hammers symbolize the male sexual organ. A bridge represents the male organ that connects parents during sexual intercourse. In symbolic meaning, a bridge may indicate birth or death, or transitions from life to death or womb to birth. Airplanes and balloons symbolize erection. Machinery represents masculine organs. The number 3 represents the penis and testicles.

A spider usually symbolizes the aggressive, phallic mother, and fear of a spider represents fear of incest and abhorrence of the female sexual organs.

Sliding and gliding usually represent masturbatory activities, as does pulling off branches. Climbing, riding, shooting, dancing, mounting stairs or a ladder, and rhythmical and violent motions represent sexual intercourse. Falling out and extraction of teeth symbolizes castration as a punishment for masturbation.

All these symbols are used in folklore, mythology, manners and customs, fairy tales, and popular jokes. To be rescued from water, as in the stories of Sargon, King of Akkad, and Moses, means to give birth.[29] Going away on a journey is, in dreams, a symbol of dying; it is akin to such figurative expressions as "the last journey," "passed away," and "gone away."

When a patient describes a dream, the psychoanalyst's efforts aim at

[29] Sigmund Freud, *Moses and Monotheism,* Knopf, 1939.

discovering the latent dream thoughts. He asks the dreamer to free himself from the impression of the manifest dream, to switch his attention from the dream as a whole to individual parts of its content, and to tell unreservedly all that occurs to him in connection with these parts. This is the technique of *free association* which is based on the assumption that, once the controlling mental apparatus is eliminated, the subject's hidden thoughts will appear in his associations in a flood of memories, ideas, questions, and arguments. The free associations are not exactly the latent dream thoughts; rather, the latent thoughts are contained in the associations, but not completely contained. It is as if the associations themselves were selective; some of them flow easily, and sometimes the dreamer seems to be thwarted; often he goes a long way around toward the latent thoughts and sometimes he conceals his thoughts entirely. The forces of resistance may prevent the expression of the latent dream thoughts. Thus the interpretation of dreams requires considerable skill and resembles, in a way, the solving of a puzzle where the final solution is verified by the fact that all partial solutions fit well together.

Psychology of Error

Unconscious wishes find outlets in several ways besides dreams. Everyone commits errors in daily life. Some errors are annoying because they express the opposite of the conscious wish of the individual. One kind of error is *slips of the tongue*. Often we wish to say one thing and say something entirely different; for example, a soldier says to a friend, "I wish there were a thousand of our men *mortified* on that hill, Bill," when he meant to say *fortified*. Or a woman complains that she has an "incurable *infernal* disease" instead of saying *internal* disease. Or a professor says in his introductory lecture, "I am not inclined (*geneigt* instead of *geeignet* = "fitted") to estimate the merits of my predecessor." Or the Speaker of a parliament opens a session with the words "Gentlemen, I declare a *quorum* present and herewith declare the session closed."[30] In all these cases the unconscious wish was expressed.

Other types of errors are mislaying things, losing things, forgetting things and names, mistakes in writing, misreading and mishearing, and erroneously carried out actions. An individual takes the wrong train, or forgets his umbrella, or cannot recall the address of a person whom he has visited several times, or cannot find a book he received as a gift from his wife. In practically all of these cases, some hidden forces are acting. In a special treatise, Freud analyzed the psychology of error and found the source of the errors to be in the conflict between unconscious wish and conscious censorship. Nothing ever happens by chance, and the errors indicate

[30] Freud, *General Introduction to Psychoanalysis*, pp. 31 ff.

the effort to block a wish which somehow succeeds in finding expression despite the repressing forces.[31]

The Unconscious and Symptom Formation

The maintenance of certain internal barriers or defenses is a *sine qua non* of normality. Lowering of these barriers, with a consequent pressing forward of unconscious material, takes place regularly in the state of sleep and thus brings about a necessary precondition for the formation of dreams, wrote Freud. In sleep, all of us behave as if we were psychotics. But if, in the waking state, unconscious becomes conscious and the individual's way of thinking, speaking, and acting is seriously regressed and includes condensations, displacements, secondary elaborations, and other unconscious elements, he is apparently psychotic.

The study of symptom formation in mental disorder shed additional light on the nature of the unconscious. Neurotic symptom formation, said Freud, is a result of a compromise between the unconscious demands or impulses and the reality-oriented, conscious censorship. The symptom comes into being as a fulfillment of an unconscious wish, distorted by the forces that oppose the wish-fulfillment. Here is a significant difference between symptom formation and dream formation. "The preconscious purpose in dream-formation is merely to preserve sleep and to allow nothing that would disturb it to penetrate consciousness. It does not insist upon confronting the unconscious wish-impulse with a sharp prohibiting 'No, on the contrary.' It can be more tolerant because a sleeping person is in a less dangerous position; the condition of sleep is enough in itself to prevent the wish from being realized in actuality."[32]

What are the dynamic forces pressing for a discharge of energy and what are the repressing, barrier-creating factors—these questions have to be answered in connection with Freud's theory of instincts and personality structure.

4. THEORY OF INSTINCTS: EROS AND THANATOS

Instincts

The ultimate cause of all activity is called by Freud *Trieb* or drive, usually translated into English as "instinct." The source of instincts is the chemophysical state of the organism. In Freud's theory, instincts represent the bridge between the physical and the mental worlds; while rooted in the human body, they are the forces that release mental energy.

[31] A. A. Brill (Ed.), *The Basic Writings of Sigmund Freud*, Random, 1938, pp. 35 ff.
[32] Freud, *General Introduction to Psychoanalysis*, p. 315.

"The instincts are mythical beings superb in their indefiniteness. In our work we cannot for a moment overlook them, and yet we are never certain that we are seeing them clearly," wrote Freud in 1933.[33]

Instincts are psychological concomitants of biological processes. They are borderline concepts between the mental and the physical and represent the demand "made upon the mind in consequence of its connection with the body."

Instincts arise from sources of stimulation within the body. They operate as a constant force. A person can escape an external stimulation, but he cannot escape the inner stimulation caused by instinctual forces. Instincts have a source, an object, and an aim. The source is some excitation within the body caused by deficiency (such as hunger) or any other disturbance of the inner balance. The aim of any instinctual activity is to remove the excitation and to restore the inner equilibrium by a discharge of energy. The instinctual activity can be pictured as "a certain sum of energy forcing its way in a certain direction."

The aim of the instinct is always the restoration of equilibrium, which is accomplished by somatic change and is perceived as satisfaction. This aim requires some object by which it can be satisfied. The object can be one's own body or an external object.

There is a great possibility for the modification of instinctual aims and objects, and for the transformation, fusion, and substitution of instinctual gratifications. "The evidence of analytic experience," said Freud, "proves conclusively that instinctual impulses from one source can join on to instinctual impulses from another and share their further vicissitudes, and that in general the satisfaction of one instinct can be substituted for the satisfaction of another. . . . The relations of an instinct to its aim and to its object are also susceptible to alterations; both can be exchanged for others, but the relation to the object is the more easily loosened of the two."[34] In other words, the energy at the disposal of an instinct can be cathected in (invested in, attached to) a certain object and under certain circumstances removed from this object and invested in another one.

Sometimes the instinctual drive comes to a stop and renounces its full gratification. This takes place when the instinctual drive becomes too powerfully cathected in a certain object. For instance, affection represents a case of permanent object cathexis which expresses itself in a constant care for the subject without sexual gratification. This process of suspension of gratification was named by Freud *aim inhibition*.

Instincts are capable of another modification when the aim and object are changed in a manner that makes them socially valuable. This modification is *sublimation*. Freud believed that works of art represent the process of sublimation. The energies put originally at the disposal of instincts may be

[33] Freud, *New Introductory Lectures in Psychoanalysis*, p. 131.
[34] *Ibid.*, p. 133.

turned into creative art; in such a case, both the aim and the object of the instinctual drive have been replaced by an entirely different aim and object.

The Sexual Instincts

All living organisms act in accordance with two purposes, self-preservation and the preservation of the species. Accordingly, Freud distinguished self-preservation or ego instincts and sexual instincts. These two instinctual forces are often in conflict with each other. The sexual instincts are more flexible than the self-preservation instincts; they can be held in suspense (aim-inhibited), sublimated, diverted into new channels, distorted, and perverted; their gratification can be denied or substituted for and their objects can be easily changed. Freud said: "The popular view distinguishes between hunger and love, seeing them as representatives of the instincts that aim at self-preservation and reproduction of the species respectively. In associating ourselves with this very evident distinction we postulate in psychoanalysis a similar one between the self-preservative or ego-instincts on the one hand and the sexual instincts on the other; the force by which the sexual instinct is represented in the mind we call 'libido'—sexual longing—and regard it as analogous to the force of hunger, or the will to power, and other such trends among the ego-tendencies." He added: "We have defined the concept of libido as a quantitatively variable force which could serve as a measure of processes and transformations occurring in the field of sexual excitation. We distinguish this libido in respect of its special origin from the energy which must be supposed to underlie mental processes in general, and we thus also attribute a qualitative character to it." [35]

Freud did not postulate a single urge that leads to fertilization and preservation of the species. He believed that there are a great number of relatively independent instincts that stem from various somatic sources. All of them strive toward gratification in their respective somatic zone, that is, toward *organ pleasure*. In the process of ontogenetic development, some of them merge with the sexual instinct proper that originates in the genital organs; some of these instincts will eventually be repressed, some partially incorporated in the final organization of the adult sexual functions.

Freud distinguished between source, object, and aim in sexuality. The source is a stimulation arising in some part or zone of the organism. The parts of the body that are capable of reacting to sexual stimuli are called *erotogenic zones*. The main erotogenic zone is the genitals, but many other parts of the body such as the mouth or the anus can in certain cases, serve as erotogenic zones in the pregenital phases of a child's development.

The usual *object* of sexual urge is a person of the opposite sex, but

[35] James Strachey (Ed.), *The Standard Edition of the Complete Psychological Works of Sigmund Freud*, Hogarth and the Institute of Psycho-Analysis, 1953, Vol. VII, p. 217.

often, as in homosexuality, a person of the same sex or, as in masturbation, the individual himself is the sexual object.

Freud broadened the concept of sexuality to include perversions and infantile sexuality, which do not lead to the usual aim of sex—fertilization and reproduction. In fact, perversions were never excluded from the realm of sexuality. A perverse sexual relation usually ends with orgasm and ejaculation just as does normal sexual intercourse, which can lead, in addition to orgasm, to fertilization and reproduction. Sexual activities of persons considered to be normal include several elements which, if performed exclusively and in place of normal intercourse, would be considered perverse. Kissing, for example, is an indispensable part of the sexual foreplay in normal individuals, but actually kissing gives a pleasurable arousal by a contact of two oral zones. Undoubtedly the mouth is an erotogenic zone, that is, an area capable of producing sexual excitation. Some individuals achieve orgasm by kissing or some modification of it such as "deep kissing" (introducing the tongue into the partner's mouth) or by oral-genital contacts. Whenever kissing is a part of sexual foreplay which leads to the union of the genital organs, it is considered normal. Only when kissing takes the place of intercourse and excludes the union of genital organs does it become a perversion. Obviously, normal and perverse sexuality have much in common. Freud believed that normal sexuality grows out of something very similar to perversions and develops through modification of some elements, discontinuation of other elements, and incorporation of yet other elements.

The same applies to any sexual deviations. Onlooking, gazing, or touching of erotogenetic zones are generally accepted and widely practiced parts of sexual foreplay. If these practices take the place of intercourse, and exclude the union of genitalia, the foreplay becomes a perverted voyeurism. Or, fixation of erotic interest on an object of clothing, for example, instead of on the genital organs, is fetishism.

Perverse sexuality points to the fact that sexuality is not limited to reproduction or to the function of genital organs, nor is it necessarily heterosexual. There are several possibilities in regard to the source, aim, and object in sex. The genital organs may be replaced by the other organs for the purpose of gratification, as in the normal kiss, or by perverse practices, or by conversion symptoms of hysteria.

Once Freud assumed that both normal and abnormal sexuality stem from the same source, he had to conclude that sexual deviations are some sort of retardation or thwarting of sexual development. This was a far-reaching hypothesis. Comparative studies in biology and embryology led him to believe that Haeckel's biogenetic theory could be readily applied to sexual development. "Ontogenesis is a repetition of phylogenesis," Haeckel said, and Freud, in his essays about sex, accepted this theory and assumed that the child's sexual development is a recapitulation of the main phases in the evolution of sex in organic nature.

The study of sexual perversions in adults and the biogenetic principles led to the study of infantile sexuality. "The child is psychologically father of the man," Freud said. Infantile sexuality contains all the potentialities for future development, which may lead in any direction—either into a normal or into an abnormal sexuality. Normal development takes place when the source, the object, and the aim of sex are combined in a consistent effort toward unification of genital organs of two persons of opposite sex. The normal sexual source is the genitals; the object, an adult person of the opposite sex; the aim, heterosexual intercourse. The normal individual passes through developmental stages and if, for some reason, he retains the characteristics of one of them (remains "fixated"), he is considered abnormal. What is normal in infancy is abnormal in adulthood. A sexually abnormal individual is a sexually retarded individual. The infant is "a polymorphous pervert" that may or may not eventually become a well-adjusted adult.

The Self-Preservation Instincts

The entire activity of men is, according to Freud, "bent upon *procuring pleasure and avoiding pain.*" This activity is controlled by the *pleasure principle.* "We may venture to say that pleasure is *in some way* connected with lessening, lowering, or extinguishing the amount of stimulation present in the mental apparatus; and that pain involves a heightening of the latter. Consideration of the most intense pleasure of which man is capable, the pleasure in the performance of the sexual act, leaves little doubt upon this point."[36]

Sexual instincts always follow the pleasure principle. Self-preservation instincts, sometimes called ego instincts, as a rule do the same. However, the task of avoiding pain forces them to postpone, or sometimes even renounce, pleasure. This ability to compromise with reality and to consider what could be done and what price has to be paid for pleasure is the *reality principle.* The reality principle is a modified pleasure principle; it approves of pleasure, but not at any price or at any time. The reality principle is the striving for pleasure combined with the avoidance of pain; it is the ability to sacrifice one kind of pleasure for another.

The consideration of circumstances apparently makes a great difference between the two groups of instincts. Through ego instincts, we learn to comply with reality. Sex instincts are less concerned with reality. The reality principle usually gets an early hold on ego instincts; sexual instincts are not so easily controlled and it takes years before they become at least partially subordinated to the reality principle.

The other difference between sex and self-preservation instincts relates to their flexibility. The self-preservation instincts have a limited flexibility. One cannot change the zones or indefinitely postpone the gratification of hunger or thirst, nor is there any way to substantially change the objects that satisfy hunger or thirst; all the objects that satisfy the basic needs for

[36] Freud, *General Introduction to Psychoanalysis,* p. 311.

air, food, and fluids must contain respectively oxygen, nutritional elements, and water. The sexual instincts can be modified in regard to zone, aim, and object, and they are open to a great number of deviations, perversions, substitutions, and conflicts. This latitude does not apply to the self-preservation instincts.

Narcissism

In 1914, Freud revised his theory of instincts. Originally he felt that the libido or love instincts had to be distinguished from the ego or self-preservation instincts. After several years of clinical experience, he discovered that libido may be directed to oneself and not necessarily to external objects only. Love for oneself precedes love for others; the newborn is not capable of loving other people.

Infants learn to divert part of the love primarily cathected (invested) in themselves and to cathect it in their mothers. This self-love was called by Freud *narcissism* after the Greek legendary hero Narcissus, who fell in love with himself.

Narcissism or self-love is a never terminated phenomenon. It starts probably in prenatal life and accompanies us until the last day of life. At the earliest stage of life, it is the only channel of libido cathexis; all the energies at the disposal of the love instincts are invested in oneself in a stage called by Freud *primary narcissism*. Later in life, in cases when the object love is being thwarted, the libido may turn back to one's own person and *secondary, morbid narcissism* may develop.

The discovery of the phenomenon of narcissism destroyed the barriers separating the libido from the ego instincts. The ego instincts had to be considered from now on as a special case of libido cathexis, namely, as an investment of libido in one's own person. Now Freud arrived at a monistic interpretation of instinctual life: there is but one instinctual force, the force of love, the libido.

The conflict that often takes place between sex and self-preservation instincts could now be interpreted in a different way. It is narcissism versus object love. In well-adjusted individuals there is a balance of cathexis in oneself and in others which permits the individual to protect himself and to take care of those whom he loves. In some individuals this balance is disturbed; some develop secondary and morbid narcissism after they have been seriously thwarted in the development of object cathexis. Some are unable to take care of themselves owing to insufficient narcissism or abundant object cathexis.[37]

Freud united under the name "Eros" all the forces that serve pleasure and enhance the vital functions of the individual. Eros encompassed all sex-

---

[37] Cf. Paul Federn, *Ego-Psychology and the Psychoses*, Basic Books, 1952; Benjamin B. Wolman, "Explorations in Latent Schizophrenia," *American Journal of Psychotherapy*, 1957, *11*, 560–588.

ual and egoistic drives, and libido became the name for all the energies that are at the disposal of the Eros.

Thanatos

In 1920, Freud again revised his theory of instincts. He wrote about this revision as follows: "After long doubts and vacillations we have decided to assume the existence of only two basic instincts, *Eros* and the *destructive* instinct. . . . The aim of the first of these basic instincts is to establish ever greater unities and to preserve them, thus—in short, to bind together; the aim of the second, on the contrary, is to undo connections and so to destroy things. We may suppose that the final aim of the destructive instinct is to reduce living things to an inorganic state. For this reason we also call it the death instinct."[38]

This new hypothesis of separate aggressive and destructive instincts was derived mainly from the study of sadism and masochism. The sexual gratification of a sadist depends on pain and suffering inflicted by him on his love object, and of a masochist on pain inflicted on him by his love object. It was exceedingly difficult to interpret sadism in terms of libido theory, and the existence of a masochistic wish to suffer formed a most serious challenge to the libido theory.

Freud had to look for additional factors, which would make people wish to inflict or to accept pain. This factor could not be related to libido and Eros. The only possible solution was to assume another driving force or another instinctual power that leads men to cause pain to others in an object-directed situation or to inflict pain on themselves in a self-directed situation. Such an instinctual force could be held responsible for the desire to hurt, to humiliate, and to destroy. The existence of this force was sufficiently proved by daily experience and by the testimony of human history. Humans are born lovers and haters; as much as there is energy (libido) at the disposal of the love instinct, there is no less energy (called *mortido* by Federn) at the disposal of the aggressive instinct. The final aim of the love instinct is to create life and the final aim of the aggressive instinct is to destroy life and to go back to inorganic nature.

When aggressiveness against the outer world becomes thwarted and cannot find satisfaction, it may, in certain circumstances, turn inward. It may, said Freud, increase the amount of self-destructiveness. An impeded aggression entails most serious dangers; it seems that we have to destroy things and people in order not to destroy ourselves. In order to protect ourselves from the tendency toward self-destruction we must find some external channels for aggressiveness.

All instincts, as stated before, are directed toward the reinstatement of an earlier state. As soon as a given state of things is upset, an instinct arises to re-create it. This tendency was called by Freud *repetition–compulsion*. It

[38] Freud, *Outline of Psychoanalysis*, p. 20.

may become even stronger than the pleasure principle and often overcomes it. Repetition–compulsion explains the tendency to reproduce in dreams unpleasant and often trumatic experiences.

Life developed from inorganic matter. Once life started, an instinct was born that aimed at reinstatement of the inorganic state and the destruction of life. This is, according to Freud, the origin of the destructive instinct, whose final aim is death or the reestablishment of inanimate nature. Life and death are interwoven; construction and destruction are inseparable. No vital process can be free from the death instinct. The erotic instincts try "to collect living substance together into ever larger unities," and the death instincts act against this "and try to bring living matter back into inorganic condition. The cooperation and opposition of these two forces produce the phenomena of life to which death puts an end."[39]

This idea of the interrelationship between life and death was not a new one. Freud mentioned in this context the influence of the philosopher Arthur Schopenhauer and the Indian Nirvana. Another philosopher and scientist, Herbert Spencer, elaborated the idea and postulated a continuum of consecutive development and decline, evolution and disolution, accumulation and dissipation.[40]

In the life of an individual, *Eros* and *Thanatos* may combine their resources, but they often fight each other. Eating is a process of destruction with the purpose of incorporation, and the sexual act is aggression that aims at the "most intimate union." Most of the impulses of sexual life are rarely purely erotic; usually sexual impulses are a combination of erotic and destructive instinctual demands.

In extreme cases, when the destructive instincts become the stronger part in the fusion of the two kinds of instincts, sadism or masochism results. In sadism, aggressive impulses thrust the sexual aims away and the aim of hurting the love object is substituted for the normal sexual aim. Sexual gratification becomes possible only if pain is inflicted on the sexual object. In masochism the aggression is self-directed, and sexual gratification depends on pain and humiliation inflicted by the love object.

When an individual is overwhelmed by the forces of Thanatos directed to the outer world, he becomes hateful and destructive, spreading pain and death around. When these forces are directed to himself, suicidal attempts may take place.

5. DEVELOPMENTAL STAGES

The Neonate

To be born is a traumatic experience that disrupts the well-balanced life in the uterus. Birth as the first trauma is the prototype of all anxiety feelings

[39] Freud, *New Introductory Lectures on Psychoanalysis*, pp. 146–147.
[40] Herbert Spencer, *First Principles* 1860–1862.

in later life. The organism is flooded by stimuli, tensions come to a peak, and the helpless organism is exposed to the shock of being born.

After birth, the newborn's mental apparatus is exposed to stimuli far beyond his capacity to handle. The natural tendency is therefore to restore the mental economy through a withdrawal from reality by falling asleep. Once an unpleasant tension such as hunger is removed, the infant falls asleep with a feeling of profound happiness and bliss. Only when stimulated by hunger or cold or some other discomfort is he awake.

The neonate is thoroughly narcissistic. In this stage of primary narcissism, outer objects are barely noticed. The gratification of the infant's needs come immediately and he is unable to distinguish between wish and reality, self and the outer world. He may feel as "omnipotent" when his wish is gratified (after receiving food or after eliminations) as he felt miserable when the tension arose.

The earliest signs of the neonate's attitude to the outer world can be characterized as an objectless longing for something or some sort of unconscious craving for unification with the outer world. This foggy longing is called by Freud the *oceanic feeling*. It is as if the infant were longing to go back to the uterus or, even farther, to nonexistence. Eros and Thanatos are united in the striving toward the all-encompassing and soothing passivity which ultimately means death.

The first pleasure-giving objects the infant meets are the nipples of the mother's breast or the bottle. The first somatic zone that experiences the pleasurable sensation of sucking is his mouth. Thus the oral stage of instinctual development starts immediately after birth.

The Oral Phase

The biogenetic principle was one of the main reasons for Freud's assumption that the child's sexuality is polymorphously perverse and leads through developmental stages to adult and normal sexuality. Additional reasons for this assumption are derived from clinical studies indicating that normal and perverse sexuality develop from the same source, infantile sexuality. Both normal and perverse sexuality aim at the same goal—orgasm. Both stem from the unorganized infantile sexuality where various wishes and desires exist independently. In adult sexuality, one component becomes dominant and the entire sexual activity becomes concentrated in one area, other areas being excluded or relegated to secondary roles. In normal adults the genital zone is dominant, in perversions, some other zone. In childhood, all areas or any area may strive for its own pleasure. Some adults whose sexuality remains infantile remain polymorphously perverse.

The development of each individual depends on (1) innate instinctual forces, (2) biologically determined developmental stages, and (3) environmental influences. Freud never underestimated the environmental factors. How quickly, how successfully, how completely the individual passes through these stages, how much of them is carried over into his adult life, depends mainly on the interaction of the child with his environment.

The earliest sexual life of an infant represents a series of independent activities of single-component impulses each seeking pleasure in a bodily organ, that is, organ pleasure. These various organs are *erotogenic zones*. They serve as centers for sexual gratification in the pregenital stages of libido development, prior to the subordination of all the sexual component instincts under the primacy of the genital zone.

The infant's first sexual excitations are connected with the feeding process. As the infant falls asleep at the breast, completely satisfied, "it bears a look of perfect content which will come back again later in life after the experience of the sexual organ." The infant may continue to suck even if he does not take any food; he is sucking for the pleasure of sucking.

Sucking for nourishment is the "prototype of every later sexual satisfaction." The desire to suck includes the desire for the mother's breast, which is therefore the first *object* of sexual desire. Love is attached to hunger, and sucking brings gratification both of hunger and of love. At first, the child does not distinguish between the mother's breast and his own body. As he turns to sucking for pleasure, the breast is given up as a love object and is replaced by a part of his own body; he sucks his own thumb or tongue, and his own body is his love object.

Whether the child was breast-fed or bottle-fed, weaned early or late, he always longs for the mother's breast and the mother as a whole, and she stays in his memory as his first love object and prototype of all love relations, whether he is a boy or a girl.

During the oral phase of libido organization, object love is ambivalent and contains both Eros and Thanatos. The longed-for object is assimilated by eating or swallowing and annihilated at the same time. The infant wishes to swallow what he loves and his love leads to swallowing, that is, to destruction of love objects. It is a cannibalistic tendency; a cannibal, said Freud, has "a devouring affection" for his enemies and devours people of whom he is fond.

Once the milk is swallowed, the infant does not care for it any more. Once tension is removed, he falls asleep and discontinues the contact with the outer world. This is a primitive kind of love—a love for a while, a love that terminates itself immediately after gratification.

Some adults who do not outgrow the oral stage can retain these destructive elements in their love in adult life. They love their love object inasmuch as they can exploit it and love only as long as the exploitation goes on.

One of the earliest emotional ties to the outer world is *primary identification*. It is the wish to be like the other person, and it antecedes a true *object relationship*, which is the wish to possess the other person. Identification is not necessarily love: "It can turn into an expression of tenderness as easily as into a wish for someone's removal."[41]

[41] Sigmund Freud, *Group Psychology and the Analysis of the Ego*, Liveright, 1949, p. 61.

Identification is accomplished by *introjection*. At the oral stage the infant takes things into his mouth and incorporates whatever he loves. Once he incorporates the object, he may believe himself to be like the beloved object. Since to love something at this stage is identical with the wish to incorporate it or to introject it, the oral introjection is the means for primary identification.

Primary identification, which is a general phenomenon in earliest childhood, has to be distinguished from what Freud called *secondary identification*, which takes place in pathological cases at a later developmental stage. Sometimes a loss of love object causes desexualization of it and giving up of object cathexis; the mourner "introjects" his love object, and his object relationship gives way to a regression to identification with the lost love object.[42]

One of the brilliant associates of Freud, Karl Abraham, suggested dividing the oral phase into *oral-passive* and *oral-aggressive*.[43] The oral-passive phase extends over several months of the first year of life; toward the second (often well into the second) year of life the oral-aggressive phase of libido development takes place. The oral-passive or oral-dependent stage is characterized by pleasure derived from sucking. At this stage the infant may not be able to distinguish clearly between himself and the external world and perceives in the sucking a self-gratifying and taken-for-granted experience.

The oral-aggressive phase usually coincides with teething. The infant becomes aware of the fact that the mother's breast is not a part of himself, that is, it is not always available as he wishes it to be. He can no longer take the breast for granted. When frustrated, he forces his way through, he grabs and bites, he tries to receive his oral gratification by acts of aggression.

Eros and Thanatos are combined in the entire oral stage in its cannibalistic tendencies of swallowing. However, at the oral-passive stage the infant is basically not aggressive and takes for granted the supply of milk. At the oral-aggressive stage aggressiveness is being utilized as a weapon in procuring gratification. The infant swallows as before, but in addition he may spit and bite, and these are definitely aggressive patterns of behavior.

The Anal Phase

The second stage of libido development was called by Freud *anal-sadistic*. In the second and often third year of life, the child derives considerable pleasure from excretion and learns to increase the pleasure by retaining feces and stimulating the mucous membranes of the anus.

> Infants experience pleasure in the evacuation of urine and the content of bowels, and they very soon endeavor to contrive these actions so that the accompanying excitation of the membranes in these erotogenic zones may secure them

---

[42] Karl Abraham, *Selected Papers*, Basic Books, 1954, p. 433.
[43] *Ibid.*, pp. 393 ff.

the maximum possible gratification. . . . The outer world steps in as a hindrance
at this point, as a hostile force opposed to the child's desire for pleasure. . . . He
is not to pass his excretions whenever he likes but at times appointed by other
people. . . . In this way he is first required to exchange pleasure for value in the
eyes of others.[44]

The child values his feces as "part of his own body and is unwilling to
part with them." He may offer resistance to the social pressures and feel
that the feces are his property and no one may exercise control over them.
He may act aggressively by elimination; libido and hate are combined in
anal eroticism in the pleasure of defecating and the sadistic "getting rid" of
feces. When the child resists bowel training and holds back feces, he expresses in another way his opposition to adults.

The anal stage is ridden with another ambivalence aside from the expulsion–retention one. Masculinity and femininity are distinguished at this
stage by activity and passivity, respectively. Masculine impulses are *scop-
tophilia* (gazing), onlooking, curiosity, and the desire to manipulate and to
master, which easily develops into cruelty and sadism. Active expulsion of
feces is masculine. Feminine impulses represent a passive desire connected
with the anal and hollow erotogenic zone. The rectum can be easily stimulated by acceping a foreign body that enters it. The anal ambivalence of
masculine-active expulsion and feminine-passive reception of a foreign
body may lead to bisexual tendencies in later life.

The child's sexual interest is primarily diverted to the problem of birth,
usually caused by the birth of a sibling. Many children believe that babies
are born by bowel and are eliminated as a piece of feces. Children's fantasies develop around the mystery of birth. The mother's gain of weight in
pregnancy is often interpreted by children as an oral intake analogous to
food intake that will be terminated in anal elimination of the newborn
baby.

Abraham suggested subdividing the anal stage into anal-expulsive and
anal-retentive phases. In the early and expulsive phase the child does not
care for the external object and enjoys the sadistic expulsion of feces. Folklore and slang bear witness to these anal-aggressive tendencies, which are
often kept alive in teen-agers and adults.

At the late anal or anal-retentive stage, the child may develop affection
for the feces, which becomes his love object. He may try to keep and to
preserve them. Feces are the first possession that the child parts with out of
love for the person who cares for him. Feces are the prototype of a gift, and
subsequently, of gold and money. On the other hand, feces symbolize
babies since most children believe that childbirth is a process similar to
defecation. Often the penis is regarded by children as analogous to the col-
umn of feces that fills the mucous tube of the bowel. The anal-retentive
phase is considered the source of tenderness. Freud accepted Abraham's
suggestions on this point and elaborated on the concept of tenderness in
contradistinction to the oral type of love.

[44] Freud, *General Introduction to Psychoanalysis*, p. 276.

Tenderness stems from the wish to keep and to preserve the object that gives gratification and to take care of it. Only very small babies do not care for, and tend to destroy, objects that give them pleasure.

As the child grows, he cares more for pleasurable objects and wishes them to stay and to continue to serve as a source of pleasure. This new attitude to objects starts with his consideration for the breast or bottle. Then it grows into a consideration for his mother, whom he wishes to keep and preserve as a source for a future and continuous flow of gratification. Toward the end of the anal stage, as Abraham found, "retention pleasure" outweighs "elimination pleasure."

Later on, as the object cathexis grows, the child cares for his property and pets, and handles them carefully and with tenderness. The sexual instinct becomes *aim-inhibited*. The wish to perpetuate the existence of the love object can take the place of the wish to possess it. In well-adjusted adults, the wish to possess and the wish to preserve are merged in marriage.

The Urethral Phase

The urethral developmental stage is an introductory period to the phallic stage, when genital organs become the main avenue of libido gratification. In both male and female the urinary tracts are closely related to the genital tracts, and children's sexual fantasies often confuse urine with semen and sexuality with urination.

Urethral eroticism is mainly autoerotic, for one's own body becomes the love object. This eroticism turns toward other objects through fantasies about urinating on them or being urinated on by them.

Urethral eroticism in girls sometimes develops into a retentive pattern, but usually it is aimed at the expulsion of urine and at the pleasure derived from emptying the bladder. The urination itself may be active and aggressive such as urinating on someone. In boys, this leads to normal and active genital eroticism. In girls, it leads to a conflict about their sex role and later on becomes associated with penis envy. The passive nature of urination, felt as "let it flow," or loss of control over the bladder, leads in boys to confusion about their sex, and quite often one may find feminine tenderness in men who have been bed-wetters in their childhood.

Training for bladder control often leads to conflicts with parents. Lack or delay in assuming this control is often punished by parents in a manner that hurts the child's self-esteem and provokes feelings of *shame*. Bedwetting children often develop *ambitious* strivings in the struggle against this shame.

The Phallic Phase and the Oedipus Complex

Usually around the age of four the child enters the phallic stage of his libidinal development. The name "phallic" is derived from *phallos*, which means penis in erection. At this age the pleasurable sensations in the genital organs procured by manual stimulation assume the dominant role. The libido is being "placed" now in the genital organs, but it takes time for all sexual excitement to become concentrated in the genitals and discharged by them.

The most important development that takes place at the phallic stage is the *Oedipus complex*. Greek mythology, and later the great Greek writer Sophocles, told the story of a young prince, Oedipus, who killed his father, married his mother, and became the king. Oedipus did not know that it was his father whom he had killed and his mother whom he had married. In Greek mythology, the deeds of Oedipus were not a result of his malevolence, but an inevitable fate. When Oedipus' crime was discovered, he repented of it and punished himself by pulling out his eyes. This legendary story was regarded by Freud as a symbolic story of the prehistorical development of human society, which, in accordance with the biogenetic principle, is reexperienced by children.

Something similar to the Oedipus drama, Freud said, happens to the four- or five-year-old boy. Often he desires to possess his mother physically "in the ways which he has derived from his observations and intuitive surmises of sexual life and tries to seduce her by showing her the male organ of which he is the proud owner." The boy tries to take over his father's place; he considers his father a competitor and develops ambivalent feelings toward him. Although he loves and admires his father, at the same time he hates him intensely and wishes to annihilate him.

At this stage, the penis becomes a source of pleasurable sensations. In contradistinction to the urethral desire to be fondled, there is a definite need for active push and thrust with the penis. It becomes a most precious source of gratification and pride.

The mother usually notices the masturbatory activities of the little boy, forbids him to play with his penis, and may threaten that unless he stops masturbating, she will take away his penis. Often she warns the boy that she will tell the father, and that the father will cut the penis off.

The little boy is aware of his vulnerability and inferiority in relation to the father, whose penis is larger. He is afraid the father may punish and castrate him. If he has had a chance to notice the difference between male and female organs, the castration threat becomes something very realistic and shocking. He believes that all people have had a penis but that in some cases it was cut off by the omnipotent father. This castration fear is much stronger than the oral fear of being eaten or the anal fear of losing the body content.

The castration fear forces the boy to abandon his incestuous wishes. He may give up masturbation altogether and develop a passive attitude of a nature ascribed by him to his mother. This passive attitude conceals his increased fear of and hatred for his father, which sometimes develops later on into a defiant attitude against all men in authority. Nor does the boy give up his affection for his mother, which often turns into a dependence relationship, into a need to be loved. This attitude, with its strong feminine components and partial identification with the mother, may lead to a submissive attitude toward women.

In some cases, the love for the father is stronger, and the little boy represses his phallic strivings toward his mother. Instead he develops a passive, pregenital sexual desire for his father. This *negative Oedipus complex* can lead to homosexuality.

In girls, the Oedipus complex proceeds in a reverse order. In boys, it causes castration fears that lead to its resolution; in girls, there are no castration fears. As soon as the little girl realizes the organ differences between the sexes, she develops the *penis envy* which leads to love for the father. This is the feminine Oedipus complex, called the *Electra complex*.

Originally, the little girl believes that everyone is built the way she is. But as soon as she discovers that some people have penises, she wishes to have one and it occurs to her that she had a penis but lost it. "She begins by making vain attempts to do the same as boys and later, with greater success, makes efforts to compensate herself for the defect—efforts which may lead in the end to a normal feminine attitude."[45] Often, she masturbates, using the clitoris as a penis substitute. If the little girl clings to her wish to have a penis, she may develop masculine tendencies and become domineering and aggressive, and sometimes homosexual. However, things can develop in another direction. She may become hostile to her mother because her mother did not give her a penis or took it away from her and because the mother possesses the father. The girl's wish to annihilate her mother and to possess her father's penis is typical for the feminine Oedipus complex. Love to the mother turns into hate; she is no longer a love object, and the girl reacts to the loss of the love object by *identifying* herself with it. She wishes to take her mother's role and instead of having a penis desires to be given a baby, which is a penis substitute. Her role now becomes passive and receptive; the road is paved for normal feminine sexuality.

The sexuality of the girl at this stage is focused in the clitoris. Clitoral masturbation is typical for this age, and it is sometimes accompanied by masculine fantasies in which the clitoris plays the role of a penis. In the case of a negative Electra complex, a girl may dream about taking the role of the father and inserting her clitoris into the mother's vagina and having a baby with her.

In normal cases, the love for the father, or positive Electra complex, leads to giving up the wish for a penis, identification with the mother, acceptance of the feminine–receptive role, and the wish to have (to "incorporate") a baby.

The differences between masculine and feminine traits are described by Freud as follows: "When you say 'masculine,' you mean as a rule 'active' and when you say 'feminine' you mean 'passive'. . . . The male sexual cell

45 Freud, *Outline of Psychoanalysis*, p. 97.

is active and mobile; it seeks out the female one, while the latter, the ovum, is stationary, and waits passively. This behavior of the elementary organisms of sex is more or less a model of the behavior of the individuals of each sex in sexual intercourse. The male pursues the female for the purpose of sexual union, seizes her and pushes his way into her."[46]

But, Freud remarked, in some animals the female is the stronger and more aggressive party. Even the function of care for the infant is not always feminine. The function of feeding, caring for, and protecting the infant, usually performed by mothers, is not a passive waiting.

The best method for studying the differences between the sexes is to observe the way in which men and women develop out of the bisexual disposition of infants. In the earliest stages, little girls are more dependent and docile and learn earlier to control bowels and bladder. In the anal-sadistic stage, girls are no less sadistic than boys. In the phallic phase girls behave as if they were little men, and all their masturbatory activities concentrate around the clitoris, which is a penis equivalent at this stage.

The boy does not have to change his love object, which is always the mother, nor the erotogenic zone, which is the penis. The girl, on the other hand, has to change both. To become a woman she has to substitute father for mother as a love object and vagina for clitoris as the erotogenic zone.

In the pre-Oedipal stage, girls are attached to their mothers just as boys are, with all the ambivalent feelings of love and hate of the oral, anal, and phallic stages. The turning away from the mother in the post-Oedipal phases may develop into a bitter resentment against her. The main reason is that the girl holds her mother responsible for her lack of a penis.

The difficulties and hazards of the phallic phase in girls are summarized by Freud: "The discovery of her castration is a turning-point in the life of the girl. Three lines of development diverge from it; one leads to sexual inhibition or to neurosis, the second to a modification of character in the sense of masculinity complex, and the third to normal femininity. The little girl . . . finds her enjoyment of phallic sexuality spoilt by the influence of penis envy. . . . She gives up the masturbatory satisfaction which she obtained from her clitoris, repudiates her love towards her mother, and at the same time often represses a good deal of her sexual impulses in general."[47]

The Latency Phase

The intensity of these feelings and conflicts depends on the quantitative relation between the conflicting forces and the amount of pressure exercised by them on the child's mind. The child is usually protected from external dangers by his parents, and the loss of parental love means the loss of security. Fear of this loss of support, combined with the castration fear,

[46] Freud, *New Introductory Lectures in Psychoanalysis*, p. 156.
[47] *Ibid.*, p. 172.

reinforced by primeval sources, forces the child to give up his Oedipal incestuous wishes. He "introjects" the parental prohibitions and usually identifies himself with the parent of the same sex. This identification with parental wishes and acceptance of parental standards leads to the establishment of *conscience* and *superego* (see Section 6).

At the next developmental stage, called by Freud the *latency period,* the Oedipal incestuous and aggressive feelings are repressed and forgotten. Part of the instinctual forces is put behind the parental prohibitions and used as anti-instinctual forces. The *internalized* parental prohibitions, which form the superego, threaten the child with severe punishment and keep under severe control his repressed Oedipal cravings. The child has identified himself with the threatening parental figure, which in normal cases is the parent of the same sex. The sexual interest of the child subsides considerably, mainly through inhibitions and sublimations. His love for his parents becomes desexualized and aim-inhibited. Although the sexual-sensual elements are preserved in the unconscious, the sensual goals of his sexuality become inhibited and the child's feelings toward the parents are rather tender than passionate.

As a result of the inhibition of the Oedipal cravings, children give up their interest in persons of the opposite sex. During the latency period, usually between six and eleven, boys play with boys, and girls play with girls. The children tend to associate and identify with the parents, adults, and peers of the same sex, and develop interests that increase their identification with and feeling of belonging to their own sex.

Puberty

At the time of puberty, the libido finally becomes detached from its former relation to parents. In order to become psychologically and socially adjusted, the boy has to direct his libido away from his mother to an external love object, and to resolve the conflict with his father. This development takes place, as a rule, in the teen-age.

Physiological changes bring to full-scale development the sexual urge and lead to new interpersonal relationships. In the period of rapid physical growth and glandular changes, the genitalia becomes the main erotogenic zone and the desire for heterosexual contacts becomes dominant. Identification with the proper sex was accomplished in the latency period; now the adolescent strives toward action patterned on the actions of the parent of the same sex.

In most cases, the sensual and the "tender" undercurrent of love unite at puberty. The adolescent learns to combine the uninhibited and bursting sensual urge with deeply inhibited feelings of care, tenderness, and consideration for his love object. He grows into adulthood and becomes gradually more ready for marriage.

Often, the unification of these two elements does not take place or is retarded or partially unsuccessful. In such cases, the adolescent, and later on the adult, keeps separate his tender feelings and admiration for women who do not arouse him sexually, and becomes aroused and potent with women for whom he has neither respect nor any tender feelings. The maturation is in such cases far from complete; the tender and aim-inhibited attachment to the mother, normal for the latency period, was not overcome in the teen-age and continues to act as a disturbing factor in adulthood.

In some cases, when the unresolved Oedipus complex remains in a highly intense fixation, the adolescent, instead of giving up the desire for his mother, identifies himself with her. The renounced love object becomes introjected into the ego, and severe emotional disorder may develop.

Fixation and Regression

The development of libido is a biological process, and the consecutive stages represent some innate tendencies to proceed in accordance with the laws of development. The idea of developmental stages was borrowed by Freud from biology, especially from Darwin and Haeckel. The concept of gradual development as a natural process was strongly supported later by independently conducted observations of children. Gesell in America and Piaget in Switzerland developed theories of child development independently of Freud.[48] Gesell established the *structure–function* principle, which implies that a certain pattern of activity may not start until the organism is ready for it. Piaget went even further, suggesting definite developmental stages, some of them strikingly similar to those proposed by Freud.

Some critics of Freud have accused him of being too biological-minded and not sociological-minded enough. However, biology has never overlooked environmental factors and ecological considerations. Nor was Freud blind to social influences on libido development. Biology is not the opposite of sociology, and environment seems to be the determining factor in variations in the development species.

"Owing to the general tendency to variation in biological processes it must necessarily happen that not all these preparatory phases will be passed through and completely outgrown with the same degree of success; some parts of the function will be permanently arrested," wrote Freud. The usual course of development can be "disturbed and altered by current impressions from without."[49]

These variations in libido development are caused by environmental factors. Parts of the libido, or of its component impulses, sometimes become arrested at an early phase of development. This arrest was called by Freud *fixation*. The fact that some portions of the libido become fixated,

[48] Arnold Gesell, "Maturation and the Patterning of Behavior," in C. Murchison (Ed.), *Handbook of Child Psychology*, Clark University, 1933; Jean Piaget, *The Language and Thought of the Child*, Harcourt Brace, 1926; cf. other works of Piaget.
[49] Freud, *General Introduction to Psychoanalysis*, p. 297.

increases the danger that in a later stage, when facing obstacles, the libido may *regress* to those fixations.

Actually, libido development is never perfect and rarely proceeds smoothly from one stage to the next. Fixations are often formed; regressions often take place. While the main body of the libido progresses from one stage to another, some units of it may become fixated. If, owing to unfavorable circumstances, the fixations are substantial, the main body of the libido becomes weakened and less capable of overcoming the external obstacles in development. Neurotic disturbances result from regression to an early developmental stage of the libido.

There are two types of regressions of the libido. The first type takes place when the libido returns to its early love objects. Obviously this regression revives the incestuous wishes. The other type takes place when the entire libido falls back to an early developmental stage.

Frustration may cause regression. Sexual urge seems to be much more flexible than hunger or thirst, and there are many ways to endure sexual frustration. Libido can be displaced; its objects can be easily changed; if one component of sexuality is frustrated, another may be satisfied.

Another way of handling frustration is *sublimation*. Sublimation is a diversion of a part of the sexual energy into nonsexual activites. Freud ascribed creative art to a sublimating of libidinal energies, putting them at the disposal of the creative talent.

It would be rather impossible to sublimate the total amount of libido and there are some definite limitations as to how much sexual deprivation one may take. The measure of unsatisfied libido that the average human being can take upon himself is limited, said Freud. Sublimation is not always possible, and it discharges only a part of the libidinal energies.

The danger of regression under stress depends on the strength of the fixation and on the amount and duration of stress to which one is exposed. The fixation of libido is the internal, predisposing factor, while frustration is the external, environmental, and experimental factor. The development of the libido, with all its unavoidable fixations, represents the *predisposing* factor. This is the *sexual constitution* of the individual. On the other hand, the events and frustrations experienced by the individual are powerful factors in causing regressionand neurosis. The relative importance of constitution and constellation or of fixations and frustrations varies from case to case.

6. THEORY OF PERSONALITY

Constitution and Constellation

In 1921, Freud introduced a new model of personality structure based on economic, topographic, and dynamic considerations.[50] It dealt with the

[50] Sigmund Freud, *The Ego and the Id*, Hogarth, 1947.

distribution, balance, and mutual interdependence of the two instinctual forces, Eros and Thanatos, and the energies at their disposal, the libido and the destructive energy—or the *economy of mind;* it dealt with the three mental provinces, the unconscious, preconscious, and conscious—or the *topography of the mind;* and it dealt with the three mechanisms of personality, the id, the ego, and the superego—or the *dynamics of the mind.*

"The determining causes of all the varying forms of human mental life are to be found in the interplay between inherited dispositions and accidental experiences," wrote Freud.[51] One instinct may be "innately too strong or too weak," or one capacity may be "stunted or insufficiently developed in life." The totality of the innate elements forms the *constitution* of an individual.

On the other hand, each individual is exposed in his life span to external situations. The totality of those situations forms the *constellation.* Some constellations are more, some less favorable to the development of an individual, but one has to bear in mind that what the constitution of one individual can easily handle could prove an unmanageable task to another.

Among constitutional factors, the somatic structure is the first thing to consider. For example, anatomical and physiological sexual differences are of great importance for the psychological development of men and women. The instinctual forces are another constitutional factor and they form a bridge between the physical and the mental apparatus.

Constitution includes not only what is given at birth but also the biologically determined developmental phases. These phases Freud related to the phylogenetic development. He assumed, in accordance with Haeckel's biogenetic principle, that hereditary disposition enables the infant to grow into a civilized adult and to pass through an immensely long stretch of human development "in an almost uncannily abbreviated form."

This growth is impossible without parental and other educational influences. Whether the child will pass safely through the developmental stages or remain fixated on one of them depends primarily on his experiences and his interaction with the physical and social environment. Freud never proposed rigid and universal developmental phases. He suspected that in different cultures these phases must undergo far-reaching modifications. The growth of human personality depends on life experiences, which may or may not encourage inherited potentialities, may foster or prevent growth, may stimulate development or thwart and cripple it. Mental health and disease are only partially dependent on innate constitution. The environment, the constellation, and not the constitution, usually has the final say about personality structure, whether normal or abnormal.

The Id

The new personality model introduced a division of personality into three parts, the *id,* the *ego,* and the *superego.* The neonate has only the id;

[51] Freud, *Outline of Psychoanalysis,* p. 81.

the ego and superego develop later in life. Whatever is inherited or fixed in the constitution, above all the instincts which orginate in the somatic organization, finds its first mental expression in the id. The id is the link between somatic and mental processes; it is "somewhere in direct contact with somatic processes, and takes over from them instinctual needs and gives them mental expression, but we cannot say in what substratum this contact is made."[52]

The id expresses the true purpose of the individual organism's life, namely, the immediate satisfaction of its innate needs. No such purpose as that of keeping itself alive or of protecting itself from dangers by means of anxiety can be attributed to the id. The id knows no precautions to insure survival. In fact, an immediate and unconditioned gratification of instinctual demand, forcefully pursued by the id, can lead to a dangerous clash with the external world and to death of the organism.

The entire mental energy is stored in the id. This energy is primarily put at the disposal of the organic instincts, which are composed of fusions of the two primal forces, Eros and destructiveness. The only endeavor of all the instincts related to the various somatic organs is satisfaction or immediate discharge of energy to remove tension and bring relief. This is what Freud meant by the *Lustprinzip* (usually translated as the *pleasure principle*); it is the urge for an immediate discharge of energy that brings an immediate relief and pleasure.

The id is entirely *unconscious* and therefore, at the beginning of an individual's life, everything is unconscious. Owing to the influence of the external world, part of the unconscious material of the id develops into preconscious material and the ego emerges. Not all the preconscious material remains a permanent property of the ego; part of it is lost, part repressed. In adults, the id's unconscious material is composed both of the original, unaltered, and almost inaccessible unconscious nucleus, and of a relatively younger and more easily accessible material that has been repressed by the ego and thrown back into the id.

The mental processes in the id, the so-called *primary processes,* are not subject to the laws of logic. They may or may not help the survival of the individual. The id is cut off from the external world but performs perceptory functions in its own interior. The very fact that the id is governed by the *pleasure principle* and acts always in the direction of procuring pleasure and avoiding unpleasure indicates that the id is capable of perception. Self-directed perceptions and coenesthetic feelings disclose the economy of inner tensions and the balance of the mental apparatus. Whenever the economy or the equilibrim of the mental apparatus is disturbed, the instinctual forces react by striving for immediate discharge of energy. As said before, the id blindly obeys the pleasure principle. It knows no values, no right or wrong, no moral standards, no considerations for other people. It is a "cauldron of seething excitement," Freud said. "Instinctual cathexes seek-

[52] Freud, *New Introductory Lectures in Psychoanalysis,* p. 104.

ing discharge"—that is all the id contains. The id's energy is unbound, fluid, capable of quick discharge, easily condensated and displaced.

Id does not change. "Conative impulses which have never gotten beyond the id, and even impressions which have been pushed down into the id by repression, are virtually immortal and are preserved for whole decades as though they had only recently occurred."[53] The repressed remains unaltered by the passage of time. In dreams, long-forgotten infancy memories come back, and in mental disorder, early childhood experiences play a decisive role. All other "agencies of the mind" or mechanisms of personality such as ego and superego grow out of and become separated from the id. All are ruled by the same principles of economy and pleasure.

It remains certain, Freud wrote in the last summary of his theory, "that self-perceptions—coenesthetic feelings and feelings of pleasure-unpleasure—govern events in the id with despotic force. The id obeys the inexorable pleasure principle. But not the id alone. It seems as though the activity of the other agencies of the mind is able to modify to the pleasure principle but not to nullify it; and it remains a question of the greatest theoretical importance, and one that has not yet been answered, when and how it is ever possible for the pleasure principle to be overcome."[54]

The energies stored in the id are the unbound, undirected, and uncontrolled resources of an individual's vitality. The id leads the individual to the most irresponsible type of actions, resembling those of a neonate. Imagine an adult–neonate with all the power and skill of an adult governed by a "cauldron of seething excitement" and one has a picture of a man ruled by the id.

When the other mental agencies, the ego and the superego, develop, their energies are borrowed or derived from the id. It has to be emphasized again that the only source of mental energies, both of Eros and Thanatos, is the id, and parts of its energies become vested in the higher mental agencies.

The Archaic Ego

The neonate is exposed to stimuli but is unable to perceive clearly what is going on, or to move voluntarily, or to master the excitations created by inner and outer stimuli. These three functions—perception, voluntary motility, and control of tensions—will eventually become the functions of the emerging ego.

But the newborn has no ego. He is exposed to excitations which he cannot master. He becomes somehow dimly aware of them and feels uncomfortable and unhappy. Hunger, thirst, cold, noise, and other tension-producing stimuli flood his mental apparatus and produce a state of anxiety.

[53] Ibid, p. 104.
[54] Freud, Outline of Psychoanalysis, p. 109.

The first mental tendency that develops in the infant is to get rid of the disturbing stimuli. The infant himself is unable to do so. He is helpless and cannot survive without being taken care of. Help comes from without, and the disturbing stimulus of hunger disappears with the satisfaction of hunger.

The neonate's mental apparatus, as seen by Freud, resembles a body floating in water. Its surface is exposed to the other world and receives external stimuli and discharges motions. Originally, the entire apparatus is id. Under the influence of environmental forces, acting on the surface of the id, this surface undergoes substantial changes and gradually develops into a separate part of the mental apparatus called *ego*. It must be emphasized that the influence of the environment produces changes in the external part of the id. The unconscious material of the id becomes transformed into the *preconscious ego,* in which the primary mental processes give ground to the emerging secondary processes.

This infantile, "archaic" ego knows and loves only itself. It is narcissistic. At this stage of primary narcissism, the infantile ego is only dimly aware of the external world. The infant is wrapped up in himself and in his needs; when his needs are gratified and tension is removed, he falls asleep or drowses in a feeling of bliss and omnipotence.

The gratification of needs comes from outside. Hunger is satisfied by mother's milk. In this early stage, the craving for an object and the craving for removal of unpleasant stimuli seem to be identical. The cessation of hunger tension restores the narcissistic state and feeling of omnipotence. The supply of food regulates the supply of self-esteem. The desire for milk and the gratification of this need regulate the infant's self-esteem, which is so significant for the future growth of his ego. The feeling of self-esteem and omnipotence is attained in a state of complete relaxation and satisfaction.

This leads to some sort of inner contradiction. When the infant is free from disturbing stimuli, he falls asleep. Then the stimuli come again: there is hunger, pressure in the bowels and bladder, irritation of skin, and the infant craves objects. At the earliest stage of life, the infant craves reality and tries to get rid of it. "This is the point at which a contradiction of basic importance in human life arises, the contradiction between longing for complete relaxation and longing for objects (stimulus hunger)," said Fenichel, a leading psychoanalyst.[55]

As the years go by, the child is forced to give up his narcissistic feeling of omnipotence and ascribes omnipotence to the outer world which satisfies his needs. The adults around him seem to have unlimited power and the child may hope to share this omnipotence by fantasies about incorporating them or being incorporated by them.

Love of oneself by incorporation, or secondary narcissism, expresses itself in longing for unification with the omnipotent adults or other external

[55] Fenichel, *Psychoanalytic Theory of Neurosis,* p. 35.

forces which are believed to be omnipotent. The infantile ego is unable to distinguish clearly between self and other objects, and narcissistic love and object love are not yet separated.

As the child grows, his ego becomes gradually more capable of protecting the organism against threats coming from within and without. In well-adjusted adults the ego is the main mental agency controlling behavior. The better developed and stronger the ego, the better balanced and more adjusted the individual is.

The Tasks of the Ego

The main task of the ego is self-preservation of the organism. It performs this task in regard to the external world by becoming "aware of the stimuli from without, by storing up experiences of them (in memory), by avoiding excessive stimuli (through flight), by dealing with moderate stimuli (through adaptation) and, finally, by learning to bring about appropriate modifications in the external world to its own advantage (through activity). In regard to internal events and in relation to the id, the ego performs its task by gaining control over the demands of the instincts, by deciding whether they shall be allowed to obtain satisfaction, by postponing that satisfaction to times and circumstances favorable in the external world or by suppressing their excitations completely. Its activities are governed by consideration of the tensions produced by stimuli present within it or introduced into it. The raising of these tensions is in general felt as *unpleasure* and their lowering as *pleasure*. . . . The ego pursues pleasure and seeks to avoid unpleasure. An increase in unpleasure which is expected and foreseen is met by a *signal of anxiety*." [56]

The ego is concerned with discovering the most favorable and least perilous method of obtaining satisfaction. In this endeavor, the ego takes into consideration the external world. The ego, too, is ruled by the pleasure principle. But in contradistinction to the id, the ego is capable of calculating the *consequences* of its behavior. This id is blind and bound upon immediate gratification of the instinctual demands while the ego is capable of logical reasoning, of considering causal relations, and of learning by experience.

Owing to these intellectual activities (which will be explained later) the ego applies a modified pleasure principle. Ego clings to the task of self-preservation and postpones or suppresses instinctual demands that threaten the existence of the organism. Ego does not object to the gratification of instincts but it guards the existence of the organism, which is the prerequisite for any pleasurable experience. For the ego, safety is prior to pleasure. To put it in other terms, the id does not care for life which does not offer pleasure, and the ego does not care for pleasure which jeopardizes life. The id clings to instinctual cravings notwithstanding future results; the

[56] Freud, *Outline of Psychoanalysis*, p. 15.

ego clings to reality and pursues the cause of pleasure provided there is no danger in it. This modified and limited pursuit of pleasure was called by Freud the *reality principle*.

The Functions of the Ego: Reality Testing

The ego is the part of the mind that adjusts the organism to the external world. Several functions are performed by the ego, and one of them is the contact with reality. The ego perceives inner and external stimuli, weighs the possibilities of successful (maximum pleasure and minimum displeasure) gratification of the instinctual impulses, and takes into consideration the totality of inner resources (abilities, etc.), the totality of circumstances. The ego can be compared to the driver of a car on a crowded road. The driver (1) perceives what is going on outside the car, (2) perceives (or knows) the resources of his car, that is, power, size, weight, roadability, and brakes, and (3) weighs the chances of swiftly moving along the road, considering the necessary adjustment of his own speed and maneuvering of the car in view of the external conditions (the road being wet, slippery, other cars moving, etc.) and the conditions of his own car, (4) exercises proper control of his own car, and (5) moves on the road in the direction of his goal trying to make the best possible time and the safest and most economical ride. One has to add here that the task of the ego is complicated by the fact that the id is not an engine, but a bursting volcano that cannot always be controlled, and in the car, symbolizing the organism, there is a back-seat driver, the superego.

As said before, the first and most important task of the emerging ego is the contact with the outer world, that is, the *perception of objects*. The narcissistic perception of one's own body is the first step in this direction. The infant dimly perceives some tensions stemming from within as from "inside something." This leads to the formation of his own body image, which emerges out of pleasant and unpleasant sensations of his own body. The perception of one's body as a definite object is an important step forward in the direction of perception of the outer world.

In the beginning, perceptory and motor functions are diffused and intertwined. The newborn organism is flooded by stimuli and is unable to control them. The passive experiencing of excitation is gradually replaced by observation, retention of perception (*memory*), and motor responses. The growing ego becomes an organized entity with differentiated functions, one of them being protection against too many or too strong stimuli.

The ego endeavors to control the incoming stimuli. When this is impossible, it regresses into the id by falling asleep or fainting. *Regression* is a result of failure to master reality; it is a sign that the ego is too weak and is unable to protect the organism against painful stimulation.

The process of perception of external objects starts with the primary, archaic *identification* with the perceived objects. Several functions are in-

cluded in this archaic identification performed by the emerging ego. The
infant puts the perceived things into his mouth, introjecting his first love
objects. The *oral introjection* of the object indicates that perceptory, motor,
and emotional processes are, at this stage, still undifferentiated from each
other. Identification involves imitation of the perceived objects; it is an effort to master the too intensive stimuli by adjusting one's body to them.

As said before, the vague conception of the outer world is accompanied
by a feeling of omnipotence. Once perception improves, the child becomes
aware of his limitations and realizes that satisfaction of his needs depends
upon external factors.

The early perceptions are vague, inexact, and undifferentiated. Objects
are perceived in a diffuse manner and often overlap each other. Sometimes
external objects are perceived as part of the body (introjection) or parts of
the self are ascribed to the external world (projection). The child is prone to
ascribe pleasant stimuli to his own body and unpleasant stimuli to the
outer world. Objects are perceived in relationship to the child's needs. They
are classified as "good" when pleasurable and as "bad" when threatening.
It seems that the child perceives himself as the center of the universe with
all other objects revolving around him.[57]

The "surface" part of the mental apparatus is the perceptual-conscious
or *Pcpt-cs* system. This system "is directed on to the external world, it med-
itates perceptions of it, and in it is generated, while it is functioning, the
phenomenon of consciousness. It is the sense organ of the whole apparatus,
receptive not only of excitations from without but also of such as proceed
from the interior of the mind."[58]

The mature ego has at its disposal this mental apparatus. The mature
ego is capable of *reality testing,* that is, checking the content of its perceptions against the outer reality and eliminating from the picture of the external world any elements that may stem from the "inner sources of excitation." Reality testing takes place by performing an action related to a
perception. If the action, such as closing one's eyes in visual perception or
putting cotton in the ears in auditory perception, removes the perception, it
is evidence that the perception comes from the outer world. If visual or auditory perception is not affected by the action, then its source must lie
within the organism itself.

The Functions of the Ego: Speech and Reasoning

The ability to talk is of crucial importance in the development of the
ego. The use of words permits a better communication with other people
and a better reality testing. In very early childhood, and in cases of severe
mental deterioration, the individual applies his own autistic vocal expres-

---

[57] Piaget arrived at similar results using a different research method. See Jean Piaget, *Judgment
and Reasoning in the Child,* Humanities Press, 1930, and other works.
[58] Freud, *New Introductory Lectures to Psychoanalysis,* p. 106.

sions, understandable only to himself, while normal speech is a means of interpersonal communication.

Speaking enables the child to think. Undoubtedly, there is a preverbal way of thinking as there is a preverbal consciousness and a preverbal perception. However, logical thinking requires verbal symbols that can be applied in several forms of logical manipulation, such as generalization or abstraction.

The earliest way of thinking, archaic thinking, tolerates contradictions, is ruled by emotions, and is controlled by wish and magic beliefs. It is unorganized; it puts together things that are unrelated to each other; it takes parts for wholes, similarities for identities, and it confuses self with the outer world. Archaic thinking operates with primitive symbols, pictures, distortions, and substitutive figures. The symbols are pictorial, visualizing definite objects rather than classes of objects.

When, later in life, the ego takes over control of the thinking process, the pictorial-symbolic, prelogical way of thinking is retained in dreams and other unconscious processes. In cases of severe mental disorder, the individual may regress to these primitive, prelogical forms of thinking and become disconnected from verbal expression. In psychoanalytic therapy, the unconscious material becomes verbalized and is thus moved from the unconscious to the conscious.

In the process of thinking the residues of past experiences, stored up in memory, are utilized. "Thinking is an experimental dealing with small quantities of energy, just as a general moves miniature figures about over a map before setting his troops in motion," said Freud.[59] The ego brings together, unifies, and organizes the mental processes, eliminates contradictions and develops into a coherent and well-functioning unit that keeps an open eye on what is going on, checks and controls the correctness of perceptions, and steers the entire mental system, avoiding unnecessary risks. Instead of the infant's hallucinatory images, a precise picture of reality is put at the disposal of the individual, enabling him to adjust better and to be more successful in life.

The Functions of the Ego: Motor Control

Mastery of the environment is one of the main tasks of the ego. This can be accomplished by action, and the adult ego controls the motor apparatus. Simultaneously with the development of sensory apparatus and with an increasingly better use of it, the growing ego learns to master, that is, to inhibit and regulate, the motor functions of the organism. Originally, stimuli provoked immediate and unorganized mass reaction of the organism. One of the earliest and most important functions of the ego is to *bind* the instinctual impulses and to convert their mobile cathectic energy into a predominantly quiescent, tonic cathexis.

[59] *Ibid.*, p. 124.

The ego learns to postpone reaction and to abide by the *reality princi-ple*. This principle was first mentioned by Freud in 1911.[60] As mentioned before, it is not contradictory to the pleasure principle; it is rather a devel-opment of the latter. The ego pursues pleasure as much as the id does, but the ego is concerned with the avoidance of displeasure and preventing of disastrous consequences of a blind pursuit of pleasure. Ego seeks the best way to procure a maximum of pleasure with a minimum of unpleasure.

Before responding to a given stimulus, the ego weighs the possible consequences of the action. It learns to control the functions of the body, to withstand some amount of tension, and to discharge the energy in a way that provides the best possible (i.e., the least risky) gratification of needs.

Three milestones in this direction are the acquisition of the ability to walk, to talk, and to control the bowel movements. The functions of walk-ing and talking increase contact with the external reality. By the process of walking the child can reach new objects, meet new people, and experience new situations. The narcissistic and self-centered world of the infant gives way to a new world of many objects and people; instead of a passive and hallucinatory imagination and expectation, the child moves around, be-comes an active explorer of reality, and tries to master it. With the develop-ment of the speech function, the child exchanges communication with the outer world and rapidly enlarges his field of knowledge. He begins to antic-ipate the reactions of adults, and his growing ego learns to avoid unplea-surable experience stemming from the instinctual wishes.

The ego "controls the path of access to motility, but it interpolates be-tween desire and action the procrastinating factor of thought, during which it makes use of the residue of experience stored up in memory. In this way it dethrones the pleasure principle, which exerts undisputed sway over the processes in the id, and substitutes for it the reality principle, which prom-ises greater security and greater success."[61] The ego carries out the inten-tions of the id but only under conditions that guarantee a successful fulfill-ment.

The Functions of the Ego: Control of Inner Tensions

In a normal and stable state of mind, the frontiers of the ego are firmly safeguarded against the id by *anti-cathexes*, or charges of energy that control impulses. The superego can hardly be distinguished from the ego, for the cultural values of the well-balanced individual are in harmony with his per-ception of reality. The ego in harmony with the superego invests or cathects energy in warding off some instinctual demands that are socially undesira-ble or dangerous for the survival of the organism.

In sleep the ego withdraws its cathexes from the sensory organs and

[60] Freud, "Formulations Regarding the Two Principles in Mental Functioning," *Collected Pa-pers*, Vol. IV.
[61] Freud, *New Introductory Lectures in Psychoanalysis*, p. 106.

severs the contact with the external world. The withdrawal of inhibitory anti-cathexes, usually directed against the id, is harmless, since the ego controls the movements of the organism. In sleep, the reduction or withdrawal of inhibitions allows the id considerable but harmless freedom; the wishes that are warded off in the waking state now "occupy the stage" and expose themselves in dreams. In some pathological cases, such as somnambulism, the motor apparatus performs unconscious actions of which the individual is unaware.

The neonate does not have the ability to control the impulse for immediate discharge of energy, and the archaic ego is unable to master excitation. The growing ego acquires the ability to tolerate greater amounts of excitation and to control the tendency for panic reactions by the use of anti-cathexes.

This defense apparatus grows from several sources. The child, driven by the id's demand for immediate gratification, is often exposed to painful consequences stemming from his physical or social environment. "The burned child dreads fire," says the proverb. The social environment, parents and other persons, may inflict pain on the child and force him to consider the dangers resulting from his urge for immediate gratification.

As soon as memories are stored in the preconscious and become easily accessible to the conscious, the ego develops *defense mechanisms*, not directed against the instinctual demands, but aimed at controlling them. The stronger the ego, the higher the tolerance of strain, whether the strain is created by outside sources or by inner pressures.

When the organism is exposed to external danger, the ego reacts with *fear*. When the inner pressure stemming from the unconscious threatens the ego, the feeling of *anxiety* serves as a signal of danger.

Anxiety

Originally Freud regarded anxiety as a result of thwarted sexual urge. Unsatisfied libido and undischarged excitation cause anxiety neurosis. It seemed, said Freud, as if the unsatisfied libido were directly transformed into anxiety.

In 1926, in a monograph entitled "The Problem of Anxiety" Freud developed a new theory of anxiety. It did not contradict the former theory but reduced it to a special case only. Anxiety, said Freud, stems from the infant's inability to master excitations. The infant's system is unavoidably exposed to powerful stimulations beyond his coping ability. These traumatic experiences create in the child the feeling of desperate helplessness. This is the painful, horrible feeling of *primary anxiety*. The first experience of this kind is the birth trauma, in which the main characteristics of anxiety such as the accelerated action of heart and lungs play a decisive role in the child's survival. Later in life, separation from the mother is anxiety producing; in the phallic stage, castration fear; in the latency period, the fear of superego.

   The state of painful helplessness or the anxiety may be revived in later life under trying circumstances. The feeling of being helplessly flooded is one of the main symptoms in practically all neurotic disturbances and especially in a traumatic neurosis. Inability to control excitation, whether it stems from sexual or aggressive impulses, creates the state of anxiety, which is always experienced as inability to master excitation. By this interpretation, the early theory of anxiety becomes a part of the later and more broadly conceived theory, which says that any anxiety can be traced back to situations of external danger. Sooner or later the ego realizes that the satisfaction of some instinctual demands may create one of the well-remembered danger situations. Then the ego must inhibit the instinctual wishes. A strong ego accomplishes this task easily; a weak ego has to invest more energy into a counter-cathectic effort to ward off the repressed impulse.

   Anxiety, said Freud, is an affective state characterized by a specific unpleasurable quality, by efferent or discharge phenomena, and by the perception of these. Anxiety is "a specific state of unpleasure accompanied by motor discharge along definite pathways."[62]

   There are three types of anxiety-producing situations in childhood, but they can be reduced to one. These are the situations of (1) being left alone, (2) being in the dark, and (3) finding a strange person in place of the mother. All these situations represent the feeling of loss of the loved person. Anxiety seems to be a reaction to the perception of absence of or separation from the loved object and is probably experienced by an infant in birth trauma, in the weaning from the mother's breast, and later, in castration fears. In all these situations, privation causes an increased tension and an economic disturbance demanding some action, some discharge of energy.

   In Freud's words: "If the infant longs for the sight of the mother, it does so surely, only because it already knows from experience that she gratifies all its needs without delay. The situation which the infant appraises as 'danger' and against which it desires reassurance, is therefore, one of not being gratified, of an *increase of tension arising from nongratification of its needs*—a situation against which it is powerless."[63]

   Anxiety is a sign of the ego's weakness. When the ego is hard pressed by external reality, it develops *reality anxiety*. When it is pressed by the superego, which creates a feeling of guilt and inferiority, the so-called *moral anxiety* appears. When the pressures of the id threaten to disrupt the ego, a *neurotic anxiety* develops.

   Objective or reality anxiety is a reaction to external danger. It is a reaction to an anticipated threat. *Anxiety-preparedness* may develop in one of the two following manners: Either the old experience called anxiety devel-

[62] Sigmund Freud, *The Problem of Anxiety*, Psychoanalytic Quarterly Press and W. W. Norton, 1936, p. 70.
[63] *Ibid.*, p. 76.

opment is reexperienced as a signal of danger and the individual faces the danger by a proper action of flight or fight, or the past danger is reexperienced in its totality with all its paralyzing effects leading to an utter failure in counteracting the present danger.

Neurotic anxiety is experienced in three ways. One is the *anxiety neurosis,* usually felt as some sort of general apprehensiveness, dreadful expectancy, and uneasiness. The anxiety neurosis is usually caused by undischarged excitation and the unsatisfied libido energy is transformed into anxiety.

Another type of neurotic anxiety takes place in *hysteria* and in some other severe neuroses. The ideas attached to libido become repressed and distorted, and the energy, whether libidinal or destructive, turns into anxiety.

The first neuroses of childhood are *phobias.* An internal danger or fear of one's own libido or death instinct becomes transformed into a fear of external dangers. It is as if the neurotic anxiety became externalized and perceived as objective anxiety or fear of an external threat. The neurotic transforms the fear of his own libido (or death instinct), from which there is no flight, into an external danger that can supposedly be warded off by obsessive behavior.

Moral anxiety is a reaction to pressure which is exercised by the superego. It is experienced as feelings of *guilt* or *shame* or a feeling of one's inferiority and inadequacy. The factual threat to an organism does not necessarily produce anxiety. Anxiety can be produced by an imaginary threat, by inner tension, or by any other factor that is experienced as a threat.

In the final analysis, it is not the danger itself that causes anxiety; accordingly, the pleasure principle is not identical with self-preservation. Freud said:

> What is it that is actually dangerous and actually feared in such a danger situation? It is clearly not the objective injury which need have absolutely no importance psychologically, but it is something which is set up in the mind by it. Birth, for example, our prototype for the state of anxiety can hardly in itself be regarded as an injury, although it may involve a risk of injury. The fundamental thing about birth, as about every danger situation, is that it evokes in mental experience a condition of tense excitation which is felt as pain and which cannot be mastered by discharge. . . . The operation of the pleasure principle does not guarantee us against objective injury but only against a particular injury to our mental economy. . . . The magnitude of the excitation turns an impression into a traumatic factor which paralyses the operation of the pleasure principle and gives significance to the danger situation.[64]

Defense Mechanisms

The term "defense mechanisms" was introduced by Freud in 1894 but was not used for some thirty years. This is the name for techniques by

[64] Freud, *New Introductory Lectures in Psychoanalysis,* pp. 130–131.

which the ego wards off the instinctual demands of the id or the pressures of the superego. With the exception of sublimation, all defense mechanisms indicate an inner conflict.

One of the most important defense mechanisms is *rationalization*. In its attempt to mediate between the id and reality, the ego is often forced to ascribe rationality to the irrational demands of the id, to display a "pretended regard" for reality and, with "diplomatic dishonesty," assume that the id accepts reality while it actually distorts it. Rationalization is basically a fallacious reasoning which serves to represent over-irrational motivation as if it were rational and, at the same time, to protect self-esteem. It is used to cover up mistakes, misjudgments, and failures and it tries to justify behavior by reasons that seem to be rational.

A more serious distortion of reality is the mechanisms of *undoing*. The individual seems to believe that he can undo or nullify his former actions that make him feel guilty. Expiation, for example, is a belief that one may nullify his former deeds; whenever this belief is applied in the struggle of ego, the mechanisms of undoing is being used. It is a kind of magic, said Freud, to "blow away" not only the consequences of an event but the event itself.

One step further away from reality is the mechanism of *denial*. When reality becomes too painful or too dangerous to cope with, the infantile ego withdraws from any contact with it and refuses to acknowledge its existence. Memory and perceptions prevent unlimited denial or reality, but in some pathological cases the hard-pressed ego gives up reality testing and applies the mechanism of negating the unpleasant experience.

Introjection was mentioned in our description of the oral phase of development. It is the desire to swallow the love object and it is the prototype of any object relations. It represents the primitive and ambivalent attitude in which love and destruction are combined in incorporation of the love object and in identification with it. When in later life the individual is unable to develop more mature object relationships, the hard-pressed ego may set primitive introjection as an instinctual aim and accept identification as the only possible object relationship.

The opposite to introjection is *projection*, just as the opposite to swallowing is spitting out. In the early stages of development the ego draws a line between "something to be swallowed," which is pleasurable and belongs to the ego, and "something to be spit out," which is unpleasurable and belongs to the outer world.

The defense mechanism of *isolation* is often used in compulsion neuroses. This defense mechanism separates an emotional content from idea into which the emotion was cathected, thus separating two parts of the same experience. In cases of "split ego" or "dual personality" part of an experience is kept separate from the rest of one's ego; usually it is a very unpleasant part that cannot be accepted by the ego. Isolation consists of a "transposition" of a refractory period during which nothing more is allowed to happen—no perception is registered, no action performed. It usually takes place after an unpleasant experience. The ego, unable to face pain or humiliation, stops functioning for a while.

One of the most important defense mechanisms is *reaction formation*. It is related to repression. When a wish or desire is repressed, the ego tries to prevent its reappearing. One of the methods used is to keep down the repressed impulse by developing a wish opposite to the original and repressed one. An individual who hates his father and is very unhappy about it may develop a ritual of affection directed toward his father; an individual torn by an impulse toward dirt may develop compulsive cleanliness.

Regression is applied by the ego in its struggle against the demands of the libido, usually against the pressures caused by the Oedipus complex. In compulsion neurosis, the genital organization proves to be too weak to face the conflict between Oedipus desires and castration fears. When the ego undertakes the measures of defense just referred to, the first result achieved is that the genital organization (of the phallic stage) is wholly or partially pushed back to the earlier anal-sadistic stage. Regression is always related to fixation and may be limited to the erotogenic zone (e.g., regression to oral wishes) or may be an over-all regression to primary narcissism.

The successful and normal defenses against objectionable instinctual wishes are called *sublimation*. Sublimation is a cathexis of instinctual energy into a substitute aim or object, or both, and a channeling of the instinctual demands into new and desexualized strivings.

Repression and Resistance

The unconscious exclusion from the consciousness of objectionable impulses is called *repression*. Objectionable wishes or ideas are usually removed from the conscious and forgotten; the ego "pushes them down" into the unconscious and acts as if they are now extinct.

Once the ego has repressed the instinctual impulses, it endeavors to keep them repressed forever. Whenever the repressed material comes close to the surface and threatens to come back into the conscious, the ego's defense mechanisms push it down, back into the unconscious. It is kept repressed by powerful counter-cathexes stemming from the ego and preventing it from becoming conscious again. The same forces that cause repression keep the repressed material under close guard and resist its unearthing. This action of the ego is called *resistance*.

The repressed material remains in the unconscious. It may be very active there and find outlets in dreams or slips of the tongue. Sometimes it creates neurotic tensions. In psychoanalytic therapy it is important to remove the inhibitions, to "unmask" the neurotic symptoms and dispose of the energy attached to the repressed instinctual demands. This *catharsis*, which originally formed the main method of psychoanalytic therapy, meets the unconscious resistance of the patient; resistance is actually a continuation of repression.

The "Quality" of the Ego

In order to perform this vast variety of tasks—learning from experience, sizing up the present situation, foreseeing future consequences, and being capable of control, postponement, and suppression of the instinctual demands—the ego must be a highly complicated apparatus. It has to control the entire sensory apparatus of perception, it has to master the motor apparatus, and it has to be able to withstand pressures coming from within and without.

Most of the ego "has the quality" or belongs to the "mental province" of the preconscious. It has access to the conscious and it can easily become conscious without any effort. On the other hand, the ego is "linked" with verbal residues, and the "presence of speech gives a safe clue to the preconscious nature of a process."

A considerable part of the ego is unconscious, notably that part which may be described as its nucleus or its original part. Freud wrote: "Conscious processes on the periphery of the ego and everything else in the ego unconscious—such would be the simplest state of affairs that we might picture." This is probably the situation in animals. In men, internal processes in the ego can also acquire the quality of consciousness. This complication is produced by the "function of speech, which brings the material in the ego into a firm connection with the memory-traces of visual and more particularly of auditory perceptions." Ego can be stimulated from within even more than from without. Ideas and other intellectual processes can become conscious. The simple equation "perception = reality (external world)" no longer holds, since perception may stem from within, from memories, and from inside the body. During the early stages, the ego confuses inner stimulation with stimuli coming from the external world. These confusions are called *illusions* and *hallucinations*, and they take place whenever the ego is not fully alert in early childhood and in dreams and psychotic states in adults. Owing to reality testing, the mature ego is able to distinguish between inner and outer stimulation, between memory traces associated with verbal residues and actual, external reality.

The ego borrows its energy from the id. The instinctual demands of the id lead to investment of parts of its energy in objects. This object cathexis enables the ego to draw some amounts of energy from the id by means of various devices, one of them being identification. By identifying itself with the cathected objects the ego "recommends itself to the id in the place of the object and seeks to attract the libido of the id on to itself. . . . In the course of a person's life the ego takes into itself a large number of such precipitates of former object–cathexes."[65]

The Superego

Freud said: "The picture of the ego which mediates between the id and the external world, which takes over the instinctual demands of the former in order to bring them to satisfaction, which perceives things in the latter and uses them as memories, which, intent upon its self-preservation, is on guard against excessive claims from both directions, and which is governed in all its decisions by the injunctions of a modified pleasure principle–this picture actually applies to the ego only up to the end of the first period of childhood, till about the age of five."[66]

A new mental agency, the *superego*, develops as a result of weakness of the infantile ego. During the anal stage the child faces conflict with parents in matters of toilet training. The fear of punishment and the need for affection and protection force him to accept the parental admonitions, to *internalize* them, that is, to consider them his own. For example, the little child may develop a dislike for playing with feces because his parents dislike him to do this.

These internalized prohibitions and self-restraints are the "forerunners of the superego." Obviously they are very weak and, when no one is looking, they are easily disregarded by the child. However, these "forerunners" contain the main elements of the future superego, namely, fear of punishment and conformity with parental demands.

The actual development of the superego takes place toward the end of the phallic period. The fear of punishing parents comes to its peak in the Oedipus complex. The little boy, shocked by castration fear, is forced to give up his mother as a love object. The little girl, under the threat of losing her mother's love, is forced to abandon the father as her love object. The frustrated child of either sex regresses from object relationship to identification by introjection. Introjection of the love object is a common phenomenon in the oral stage and apparently oral regression takes place in the formation of the superego.

The introjected parental figures are idealized and seem to be more powerful and more glorious than they might be in reality. In most cases, the father's image plays a greater role in the child's superego, which usually encompasses the images of both parents. The superego is originally a new element added to and introjected into the ego and forms a part of the ego; it develops later into a separate mental agency, often opposed to the ego.

The superego represents the "voice of the parents" and their moral standards as perceived by the child. Thus, the superego may be irrational

[65] *Ibid.*, p. 108.
[66] Freud, *Outline of Psychoanalysis*, p. 121.

and childish, imposing rigid restrictions which persist into adulthood without much consideration for the present situation. One of the elements of the superego is the *ego–ideal*. The ego–ideal stems from an expression of admiration for the parents, to whom the child ascribes perfection. It is a striving toward perfection and an effort to live up to the expectations of the parents. Freud described it as follows: "The ego–ideal comprises the sum of all limitations in which the ego has to acquiesce, and for that reason the abrogation of the ideal would necessarily be a magnificent festival for the ego, which might then once again feel satisfied with itself. There is always a feeling of triumph when something in the ego coincides with the ego-ideal. And the sense of guilt (as well as the sense of inferiority) can also be understood as an expression of tension between the ego and the ego-ideal."[67] Freud often used the ego–ideal as the equivalent of what he later called superego; in the later works, however, ego–ideal refers to a part of the superego which represents the strivings for perfection as an important function of the superego.

The energy used by the ego for its inhibiting and anti-instinctual functions is drawn from the id. The anti-instinctual forces of the superego are also derivatives of the instinctual forces of the id. The superego is mostly *unconscious* and is composed of both instinctual forces, love and hate, often with hate predominating.

It is quite obvious that the child's aggressiveness against his parents cannot find satisfactory discharge. His love for his parents, or the parental strictness, or something else may thwart the discharge of aggressiveness. The superego becomes endowed with a great part of the child's aggressiveness originally directed against the parents, and now, in the superego, directed against the child's own ego.

The ego's attitude to the superego resembles the child's attitude toward his parents. The ego needs affection and forgiveness. Its self-esteem depends on the approval of the superego. When the ego lives up to the expectation of the superego, the superego reacts with a feeling of joy and pride. When there is a conflict, the aggressive forces stored in the superego turn against the ego with accusations creating feelings of guilt and depression. *Depression* is self-directed aggression; it is the result of the ego's being torn down by the superego, in resemblance to parental criticism of the child's behavior.

In manic-depressive disorder, the individual oscillates between the joy and happiness resulting from the all-approving superego and the tortures of guilt feeling and depression when the superego becomes sadistic. In manic-depressive disorder, the superego "becomes over-severe, abuses, humiliates, and ill treats his unfortunate ego, threatens it with the severest punishments, reproaches it for long forgotten actions which were at the time regarded quite lightly, and behaves as though it had spent the whole interval in amassing complaints and was only waiting for its present increases in

[67] Freud, *Group Psychology and the Analysis of the Ego*, pp. 105–106.

strength to bring them forward and to condemn the ego on their account. The superego has the ego at its mercy and applies the most severe moral standards to it; indeed it represents the whole demands of morality and we see all at once that our moral sense of guilt is the expression of the tension between the ego and superego."[68]

In latent schizophrenia, the ego is at the mercy of a severe and demanding superego. The introjected parental images assume a despotic control over the entire mental apparatus until the hard-pressed ego gives up the struggle and submerges itself in the unconscious in a psychotic breakdown.[69]

In well-adjusted adults, the superego plays the role of self-observer and represents conscience and moral standards; it is the social and moral frame of reference of the individual. The adult superego differs considerably from the superego established at the end of the phallic period by means of identification with the parents. The parents' influence at that time includes

> not merely the personalities of the parents themselves but also racial, national, and family traditions handed on through them as well as the demands of the immediate social *milieu* which they represent. In the same way, an individual's superego in the course of his development takes over contributions from later successors and substitutes of his parents, such as teachers, admired figures in public life, or high social ideals.[70]

As the individual grows, his superego gradually draws away from the infantile images of the parents and becomes more impersonal, more related to the objective social and ethical standards to which he subscribes. In well-balanced adults there is no conflict between the moral standards of the society as represented by the superego and the realistic consideration of self-protection and survival as represented by the ego and the reality principle.

Parapsychology

The description of Freud's theory of personality cannot be completed without a few remarks about occult phenomena. Despite objection raised by friends and foes, despite the apparent danger of being ridiculed, Freud wrote: "We intend to treat these things in just the same way as we treat any other material for scientific investigation. First, we have to establish whether these processes really occur, and then, but only then, when there is no doubt as to their actuality, we can set about their explanation."[71]

Unfortunately, said Freud, there is no way to prove or to disprove tales of wonderful happenings and miracles in the past, and séances of occultists with their media remind one of "children's pranks or conjurors' tricks." This sad state of things should not deter scientists. All phenomena of the

---

[68] Freud, *New Introductory Lectures in Psychoanalysis*, pp. 87–88.
[69] Wolman, *Call No Man Normal*, International Universities Press, 1973, Chapter 7.
[70] Freud, *Outline of Psychoanalysis*, p. 17.
[71] Freud, *New Introductory Lectures in Psychoanalysis*, p. 48.

human mind should be open for scientific research, irrespective of their rational or irrational character and disregarding the fact that nonscientists might have had erroneous ideas about these phenomena.

Freud believed that one occult phenomenon, *telepathy*, is more accessible to scientific inquiry than any other. Telepathy was defined as an alleged fact that an event which occurs at a specific time comes more or less simultaneously into the consciousness of a person who is spatially distant, without application of any of the known methods of communication. In such a case, two persons must be mutually emotionally involved. Freud quoted a case of a middle-aged man who dreamt that his daughter gave birth to twins, and the twins actually were born.

A similar case is the *thought transference* of some fortunetellers, who often express the secret wishes of their clients. The question is, how could the fortunetellers possibly know about the hidden thoughts of their clients? But there is no doubt that these individuals often express the wishes of their clients without having any known access to or source of information about their clients' thoughts.

Another instance of thought transference was brought out by Freud in connection with psychoanalytic treatment; one of his patients told him about foresight a few minutes after a Dr. Forsyth had called on Freud. This phenomenon of thought transference between patient and therapist in situations when the deep emotional involvement of transference has been established, has been reported by several psychoanalysts.

The anticipation of future risks and dangers is another metapsychological problem. Freud has noticed that certain individuals seem to have access to their own unconscious and are somehow aware of their own unconscious feelings about themselves and about others. They display a considerable degree of *foresight* which cannot be explained in terms of objective perception and logical reasoning.

Psychoanalytic therapy is believed to increase one's ability to "see through himself" and to give him an access to mental phenomena which are usually repressed and inaccessible. Actually, one of the main tools of psychoanalytic therapy is the ability of the therapist to feel or empathize or somehow perceive intuitively what is on the patient's mind.

Since these phenomena are not too accessible to scientific study, room is left for speculation. The knowledge of hidden thought has often been ascribed to magicians and mystics, and it has been a widespread belief that the occult may shed light on what has been unknown. "It can easily be imagined," wrote Freud, "that certain practices of mystics may succeed in upsetting the normal relations between the different regions of mind, so that, for example, the perceptual system becomes able to grasp relations in the deeper layers of the ego and in the id which would otherwise be inaccessible to it. Whether such a procedure can put one in possession of ultimate truth, from which all good will flow, may be safely doubted. All the same, we must admit that the therapeutic efforts of psychoanalysis have chosen much the same method of approach." [72]

This part of the personality, unconscious thought and perception, remains the least understood and the least accessible problem for scientific inquiry. Prior to Freud, dreams and symptom formation in neurosis were overlooked by the scientific inquiry. But it would be entirely unjustified to neglect some areas of human life simply because they do not fit into some logical system. Whatever goes on in the human mind is a legitimate object of psychological research. Undoubtedly, the deeper the layer and the more obscure the symptom, the more caution is required. But no part of reality is unscientific, and all phenomena should be subject to a rigorous scientific inquiry (cf. Part IV).

Character and Characterology

In psychoanalytic literature the term *character* indicates the more permanent and consistent patterns of overt and covert behavior. Character represents the totality of ways in which the individual meets frustrations, faces hardships, forms ideas, and relates to other individuals. The character of a man is influenced by social factors. By stressing different values and applying different educational methods, each society encourages different elements in the development of the individual.

Fenichel believes that the term "character" is almost identical with the term "ego." However, a closer scrutiny of Freud's writings shows that these are two different, although closely related, terms established on different levels of description. Ego is a "dynamic" term, that is, part of the dynamic apparatus that contains, besides the ego, the superego and the id. The term "character" deals not with the mental apparatus but with the behavior of an individual; it is related to the history of his libidinal development, his fixations and regressions, his defense mechanisms and adjustments, and the totality of interactions between himself and his environment. Character is not a function of the ego, although it certainly overlaps the ego. It is not entirely as Fenichel says: "Character, as the habitual mode of bringing into harmony the tasks presented by inner demands and by the external world, is necessarily a function of the constant, organized, and integrating part of the personality which is the ego. The question of character would be thus the question of when and how the ego acquires the qualities by which it habitually adjusts itself to the demands of instinctual drives and of the external world, and later also of the superego." [73]

The psychoanalytic theory of character has been, to a certain extent, influenced by Dilthey and Spranger (cf. Chapter 11). Accordingly, character

[72] *Ibid.*, p. 111.
[73] Fenichel, *Psychoanalytic Theory of Neurosis*, p. 467.

represents in psychoanalysis the quality, the "how" of personality. Each personality contains various elements, but how they all work together, how the individual functions in life, and in what way he differs from other individuals—these depend on his character.

In psychoanalytic theory, the problem of interaction between the various mental forces and agencies is of primary importance. Character is determined mainly by the relative strength of the id, ego, and superego, which are in turn influenced by education and other environmental factors.

The ego can deal with the instinctual impulses either in a cathectic or in an anti-cathectic manner. In well-balanced individuals the instinctual demands find proper outlets, that is, they are cathected. The instinctual energies are cathected in the natural functions of the organism and in the objects of these functions. This type of behavior, the *cathectic character,* perpetuates the instinctual demands and finds avenues of gratification in which the demands of the id, the ego, the superego, and the external world are brought into harmony. The cathectic character type finds ways to handle those instinctual demands which jeopardize this harmony. Either they become "successfully repressed" or their energies are sublimated, that is, directed into new and more acceptable channels. Usually, it is the Oedipal situation that leads to sublimation; in favorable circumstances the child gives up the object and aim of his Oedipal wish, and the energies related to the wish are not blocked but cathected in a substitute aim and object. The libidinal energy continues to flow but becomes desexualized. Successful sublimation, which depends on the strength of the ego and on the chances of identification with the parents, helps the individual to function smoothly while the unacceptable instinctual aims and objects are given up. In children, some sublimations can be noticed in games in which sexual and aggressive impulses are harmlessly acted out.

The ego is not always capable of a cathected type of behavior, and often anti-cathectic, that is, reactive or defensive, behavior develops. In the *reactive type* of character, the ego wards off the instinctual demands by counter-cathexis. This expenditure of energy obviously impoverishes the mental economy and reduces the individual's efficiency. There is a continuous need for repeated counter-cathexes to ward off the unacceptable impulses. Anxiety accompanies the conflict between the ego and the repressed impulses and limits the ability of the individual to obtain full satisfaction in life.

The main mechanisms used in the reactive character type are reaction formations and phobias. Both defense mechanisms develop into habitual behavior patterns or character traits. Some reactive character types seem to be frigid, as if they had a "feeling phobia" or a fear of letting themselves experience the usual human emotions. Others seem to be "hyperemotional" as a reaction formation against emotions. Some develop reaction formations against reaction formations. The reactive character traits seem to be a kind of armor used by the ego in its struggle against both instincts and environment.[74]

Apparently, character somehow depends on the individual's history of libidinal development. Accordingly, character types can be distinguished. Freud and Karl Abraham, one of the earliest and most capable associates of Freud, have suggested the following character types, related to the developmental stages and points of fixation.[75] Oral fixation results in *oral character* traits. This fixation is a result of either an abundant or an insufficient oral satisfaction. In the first case, the individual may develop an overdependent but optimistic attitude; in the case of oral deprivation depressive and aggressive tendencies may develop. In both cases, orally fixated individuals demand narcissistic supplies from without, are self-centered, and wish to be helped by others. The oral-erotic character types are compulsive eaters, drinkers, smokers, and talkers, unless these tendencies are hidden by reaction formations or successfully resolved by sublimations. All oral character types are selfish "takers," always "hungry" and acquisitive, and desirous of "swallowing" more food or more love objects or more knowledge, depending on the specific nature of reactions and sublimations of their oral cravings.

Abraham suggested distinguishing between the early oral, or oral-passive, and the late oral-sadistic or oral-aggressive phases. The oral-passive fixation relates to sucking in the first months of the child's life. The oral-passive character type is passive and overdependent. He is easily disappointed when his cravings are thwarted and he does not take frustrations too well. He seems to believe that the world owes him maternal support and affection, and in his optimistic moods he hopes to receive it. The oral-aggressive type is related to frustrations in nursing, to biting and chewing; he is usually sarcastic, pessimistic, and cannibalistic and he tends to destroy his love objects. He seems to believe that the world owes him support and affection, but he doubts whether he will get what he wants. He often alienates his friends and displays disagreeable and offensive behavior as if trying to force them to give him the love and affection that the world owes him.

The *anal-erotic character* type has been subdivided by Abraham into anal-expulsive and anal-retentive; in both substages the conflict around toilet training leads toward peculiar anal fixations.[76] Orderliness, parsimony, and obstinacy are the three main anal character traits. Training for cleanliness may lead to compulsive behavior in washing, cleaning, and keeping one's own body and possessions extremely neat. Parsimony develops usually in the anal-retentive stage. Parsimony is an expression of the tendency to retain what one possesses. Feces are the prototype of transfer-

[74] William Reich, *Character Analysis*, Orgone Institute, 1945.
[75] Karl Abraham, *Selected Papers on Psychoanalysis*, Hogarth, 1927.
[76] Sigmund Freud, "Character and Anal Eroticism," in *Collected Papers*, Vol. II, pp. 45–50.

able possession and at the anal-retentive stage the child is prone to postpone elimination and to enjoy retention. Anal character types are often stingy and unwilling to part even with useless objects. Obstinacy characterizes the anal-sadistic period. It is the child's first rebellion against the mother. The child refuses to give her the feces or he expresses the wish to eliminate indiscriminately in disregard of her toilet-training demands.

The *urethral character* type is ambitious, impatient, and envious. It includes oral traits and a tendency toward passivity. The urethral personality types have usually been punished for *enuresis* by being put to shame. The bed-wetter would like to hide his deeds and to avoid shame; hence the "burning ambition" not to be shamed anymore by anyone and the feeling of envy toward anyone who has been successful and has not been humiliated. The urethral personality type lacks, however, the persistence necessary for being successful. He often expects, in an oral fashion, that some outside forces will help him to attain success and glory.

The *phallic character* type develops as a reaction formation to castration fear. Self-assuredness, boastfulness, and aggressiveness are the main phallic personality traits, combined with a narcissistic self-love, vanity, and sensitiveness. Exhibitionistic and overtly aggressive behavior is a reaction formation to castration fear. The ambivalent feelings of need and fear of love, of courage and timidity, are symptomatic for the phallic character, who tries to overcompensate by aggressiveness and to cover up his inner fear of castration and doubts concerning his own masculinity. Overtly daring and boisterous behavior is the façade behind which timidity and anxiety are hidden.

In girls, penis envy may be either resolved or sublimated, or it may lead to reactive character traits. Penis envy may be elaborated either into a wish-fulfillment and assumption of a masculine role or into a vindictive feminine type with a tendency toward being humiliated and toward humiliating men.

Normal adulthood is characterized by the *genital character.* The supremacy of the genital zone over other erotogenic areas, the subordination of all genital aims to the normal heterosexual urge, and the proper choice of a heterosexual love object are the main elements of the genital character.

In accordance with the economic principle, sublimation is facilitated when great quantities of excitation are discharged. When too much instinctual energy is blocked, sublimation is almost impossible, and reaction formations usually take place. In the genital character, sexual energy finds proper outlets; emotions are not warded off but used by the ego. Pregenital impulses are partly subordinated to the normal heterosexual function and serve as a forepleasure; they become partially sublimated. The ego becomes the master of the total mental apparatus. The diversified instinctual impulses become coordinated, the Oedipus complex is resolved, and harmony is established between id, ego, and superego. The more harmonious is the character, the more normal and better adjusted is the individual.

7. SOCIETY AND CULTURE

The Socialization of the Individual

Freud's starting point was the individual, always the individual. The neonate, Freud believed, is neither social nor antisocial. He is asocial or presocial. His first feelings and motions turn toward himself in a narcissistic love. Soon the child becomes aware of the presence of need-gratifying objects and persons and part of his libido becomes invested (cathected) in them.

Pleasure-procuring objects and persons facilitate the development of object love, which is the prototype of any social relationship. The development of the child depends on social forces; in unfavorable environmental circumstances, the development of object love and social relations may be impaired and severe narcissistic fixations may occur. In normal cases, the child develops primitive and ambivalent social feelings in the oral stage. The first object love is ambivalent. The child tends to swallow what he loves and to love what he swallows; love and hate are combined in "cannibalistic" feelings.

Incorporation and identification represent the early, archaic pattern of interpersonal relations. A new type of relation starts with the development of consideration of the loved object, which begins at the anal stage. The child begins to see the love object as an independent entity and not as something that has to be swallowed and incorporated, or that may swallow and incorporate him. The sensual aim becomes inhibited, and the child seems to have given up the wish to possess the object. Instead, he begins to care for the survival of the object in order to preserve it. This new feeling of "tenderness" usually starts the anal stage, when, according to Karl Abraham, retention pleasure becomes stronger than elimination pleasure.

Tenderness and aim inhibition are fundamental factors in adult social relations, although some individuals never become fully capable of consideration of other persons and take their friends for granted, and others are unable to develop aim-inhibited and desexualized friendly attitudes. The normal adult, however, is capable of having consideration for other individuals and of developing aim-inhibited and friendly feelings toward them.

Aim-inhibited feelings enable individuals to relate to one another in a nonsexual manner. The child–parent relationship, after the resolution of the Oedipus complex, becomes aim-inhibited and tender. The same applies to the normal parent–child relationship. Aim-inhibited impulses are the main factor in friendship between individuals. Since these impulses, wrote Freud,

> are not capable of really complete satisfaction, they are especially adapted to create permanent ties; while those instincts (drives) which are directly sexual incur a loss of energy each time they are satisfied and must wait to be renewed by a fresh accumulation of sexual libido, so that meanwhile the objects may have

been changed. The inhibited instincts (drives) are capable of any degree of ad-
mixture with the uninhibited. . . . It is well known how easily erotic wish develops out of emotional relations of a friendly character, based upon appreciation
and admiration.[77]

As mentioned before, aim-inhibited feelings start at the anal stage but
become more fully developed at the end of the phallic period. Individuals
with powerful phallic fixations are boisterous and not very considerate of
other persons. In order to become well adjusted and capable of sharing
social norms and responsibilities, an individual has to renounce his parents
as love objects and identify himself with their norms and standards.

No one is socially adjusted without a fully developed superego, which
is the carrier of social norms and values within one's mental system. As
explained before, the superego is born toward the end of the phallic stage
as a result of the Oedipus conflict. The image of the beloved parent becomes internalized in the child's mind and forms the superego. Very often
the beloved parent stands as a symbol of perfection and as a model to be
imitated, thus facilitating an idealistic pattern of social behavior.

In some cases

the object serves as a substitute for some unattained ego ideal of our own. We
love it on account of the perfections which we have striven to reach for our own
ego, and which we should now like to procure in this roundabout way as a means
of satisfying our narcissism. . . . The ego becomes more and more unassuming
and modest, and the object more and more sublime and precious, until at last it
gets possession of the entire self-love of the ego, whose self-sacrifice thus follows
as a natural consequence. The object has, so to speak, consumed the ego. Traits of
humility, of the limitation of narcissism, and of self-injury occur in every case of
being in love; in the extreme case they are only intensified, and as a result of the
withdrawal of the sensual claims they remain in solitary supremacy.[78]

This kind of attitude is more than just aim-inhibited. The aim-
inhibited object (or person) becomes a model for imitation, an image of
perfection, and a symbol of a goal to be attained. Such an attitude is found
in adult life in admiration for heroes, in submissiveness to leaders, and in
readiness for self-sacrifice for a lofty ideal.

The Origin of the Social Order

In 1912, Freud published a volume entitled *Totem and Tabu* in which he
introduced a hypothesis concerning the primitive forms of human society.
In accordance with Darwin, Freud suggested that primitive society was a
horde governed by a despotic male, the "father" who "owned" all females
in the horde. The primal father prevented his sons from gratification of
their sexual needs. After the father's death, the youngest son, the mother's
favorite, became the father's successor as the head of the horde or tribe.

The beginning of totemism was traced from the rebellion of all males

[77] Freud, *Group Psychology and the Analysis of the Ego*, p. 119.
[78] *Ibid.*, pp. 74–75.

against the tyrant. The paternal horde was transformed into a brotherhood of sons who killed the father, cut his body in pieces, and decided that no one would take his place. In order to preserve the new social order and to prevent another tyranny, the brothers established totem prohibition. Apparently, they could not prevent each other from forming new families with the male as the head of the family. But now, instead of one large family with a tyrannical father, there were several families whose fathers had to come to terms with one another.

Prior to the killing of the father, the sons lived under a permanent castration threat. After he was killed, the castration threat became "internalized" in the form of guilt feelings. Rituals are then related to the castration complex. Freud discusses this problem as follows: "Castration has a place, too, in the Oedipus legend, for the blinding with which Oedipus punished himself after the discovery of his crime is, by the evidence of dreams, a symbolic substitute for castration. The possibility cannot be excluded that a phylogenetic memory-trace may contribute to the extraordinarily terrifying effect of the threat—a memory-trace from prehistory of the human family, when the jealous father would actually rob his son of his genitals if the latter interfered with him in rivalry for a woman. The primeval custom of circumcision, another symbolic substitute for castration, is only intelligible if it is an expression of subjection to the father's will (compare the puberty rites of primitive people). No investigation has yet been made of the form taken by the events described above among races and in civilizations which do not suppress masturbation among children."[79]

To Freud, culture meant restraint. Social order developed out of restrictions imposed on the two driving forces: sex and destruction. Incest and murder were forbidden. The killed father became totem, and all the females inside the tribe became taboo.

The Origin of Leadership

Freud assumed definite analogies between ontogenesis and phylogenesis, and he traced the origin of any human group from the primal horde. Primitive men ascribed to their chieftain magic and uncanny power. They were afraid of their leader and believed that it was dangerous to contradict him or to disobey his orders, or sometimes even to look straight into his eyes.

The same type of relationship applies in hypnosis, when the hypnotist takes over the father role and reactivates in the subject the arachaic inheritance of subservience to the father, to whom the subject surrenders his own will. Some uncanny and coercive elements can be found in the relationship of group members to their leader. In the minds of the group members, the leader takes over the role of their superego. Freud believed that "a group is a collection of individuals who have introduced the same person in their

[79] Freud, *Outline of Psychoanalysis*, pp. 92–93, footnote.

superego, and on the basis of this common factor have identified themselves with one another in their ego. This naturally only holds for groups who have a leader."[80] The group is patterned on a family with the head as a father substitute and the group members united in their admiration for and obedience of the primal father. They are acting under the assumption of being equally loved by the powerful father. "The indestructible strength of the family as a natural group formation rests upon the fact that this necessary presupposition of the father's equal love can have a real application in the family,"[81] said Freud. Accordingly, the phenomena of transference and hypnosis are explained by the fact that the therapist is perceived by the patient as the loving and omnipotent father who takes over their superego and controls their behavior.

Freud was influenced by Le Bon's study of the crowd and accepted the idea that individuals behave in a group as if they were under the spell of a coercing force and not as separate and independent entities.[82] Le Bon introduced the concept of group spirit, which was not accepted by Freud. Instead Freud introduced the concepts of the primal father and of transference.

Two main features of collective behavior were singled out by Freud. The inhibition of intellectual functions, such as criticism, judgment, and logical reasoning, and the intensification of emotions, both hate and destructiveness and love and devotion, are the outstanding characteristics of group behavior. These two symptoms are typical for the transference situation in psychoanalytic therapy. Once the patient sees in the therapist the parent substitute, his intellectual functions become partially inhibited and his emotions intensified. This regression facilitates the emotional reeducation which is the aim of psychoanalytic therapy. Group behavior can be interpreted in a similar manner: in the transference relationship to the leader, the members of a group admire him and obey his orders while their capacity for criticism is reduced and their emotionality increased.

The Price of Civilization

Society cannot permit full freedom of action of each individual because absolute freedom for one could mean slavery for others. Some curtailing of individual freedom and inhibition of instinctual wishes is necessary for the survival of the society. Social norms grew out of this necessity. It is quite easy, wrote Freud, for a barbarian "to be healthy: for a civilized man the task is a hard one. The desire for a powerful and uninhibited ego may seem to us intelligible, but, as it is shown by the times we live in, it is in the profoundest sense antagonistic to civilization. And since the demands of

[80] Freud, *New Introductory Lectures in Psychoanalysis*, p. 96.
[81] Freud, *Group Psychology and the Analysis of the Ego*, p. 95.
[82] Gustave Le Bon, *The Crowd: A Study of the Popular Mind*, Fisher & Unwin, 12th impression, 1920.

civilization are represented by family education, we must remember to find a place too in the etiology of the neuroses for this biological character of the human species—the prolonged period of its childhood dependence."[83] The long childhood of humans and the inability of the human child to face the exigencies of life call for protective and restrictive actions of the parent. The parental restraint of the child's freedom and the thwarting of his instinctual wishes must lead to an inner conflict in the child's mind.

At this point, Freud concluded: "We cannot escape the conclusion that neuroses could be avoided . . . if the child's sexual life were allowed free play, as happens among many primitive races." But, on the other hand, this early repression must effect one's readiness for cultural growth, because "The instinctual demands, being forced aside from direct satisfaction, are compelled to take new directions which lead to substitutive satisfaction . . . and may become desexualized." One may conclude "that much of our most highly valued cultural heritage has been acquired at the cost of sexuality and by the restriction of sexual motive forces."[84]

The restriction of the destructive instincts is even more important than the restriction of sex. No society could ever have survived without imposing definite prohibitions on the use of force. Inner conflicts and fights could destroy the social organization, so taboos have been imposed on the use of force within the boundaries of family and tribe. The thwarted aggressiveness becomes internalized and stored in the superego, where it may turn against one's own person in acts of self-destructiveness. Freud explained this danger as follows: "When the superego begins to be formed considerable amounts of the aggressive instinct become fixated within the ego and operate there in a "self-destructive fashion. This is one of the dangers to health to which mankind becomes subject on the path to cultural development. The holding back of aggressiveness is in general unhealthy and leads to illness. A person in a fit of rage often demonstrates how the transition from restrained aggressiveness to self-destructiveness is effected, by turning his aggressiveness against himself. . . ."[85]

Religion

In his studies of sociology and anthropology, Freud could hardly evade the problem of religious feelings. He event went so far as to publish a volume on the origin of Judaism and the monotheistic religions.[86] Since this monograph goes far beyond the scope of psychology, we shall not deal with it here but rather confine ourselves to presenting Freud's view on religion as a social-psychological phenomenon.

[83] Freud, *Outline of Psychoanalysis*, p. 85.
[84] *Ibid.*, p. 114.
[85] *Ibid.*, p. 23.
[86] Freud, *Moses and Monotheism*.

Freud regarded religious feeling as a craving for protection and power. In early narcissism, the child has the feeling of omnipotence. Gradually he must give up this feeling and instead ascribe it to his parents, who, so he believes, are omnipotent. Unsatisfactory object relations and frustrations lead to a secondary narcissism, which is the need for regaining the feeling of omnipotence and the wish for a reunion with the omnipotent beings. This is, Freud says, the source of religious feelings. The powerless individual strives to attain power by introjecting the powerful figures or a part of them or being incorporated by them.

Religion is, in Freud's judgment,

> an attempt to get control over the sensory world in which we are placed by means of the wish-world which we have developed inside us as a result of biological and psychological necessities. But it cannot achieve its end. Its doctrines carry with them the stamp of the times in which they originated, the ignorant childhood days of the human race. Its consolations desire no trust. Experience teaches us that the world is not a nursery.[87]

Any religious group is based on the "illusion"[88] that there is a sublime spiritual being who loves all the members of his group with equal love. This head is the father surrogate for all the group members, who consider themselves brothers in their faith. Several religious rites imitate brotherhood and sisterhood, and gods are called by the name of father. Religious feelings contain the elements of regression to childhood and a wish to be taken care of by a loving parent or parent surrogate and to live in a childhood paradise united with family members in the love and admiration for the protecting father.

People who do not belong to the community of believers, who do not love the head or the god and whom he does not love, stand outside this tie. "Therefore, a religion, even if it calls itself the religion of love, must be hard and unloving to those who do not belong to it. Fundamentally indeed every religion is in this same way a religion of love for all those whom it embraces; while cruelty and intolerance towards those who do not belong to it are natural to every religion." But their love within the group and hate to outsiders applies to any other group which is based on libidinal ties. In fact, religious groups today represent less of love and hate, and more of inhibition of libido. "If today that intolerance no longer shows itself so violent and cruel as in former centuries," Freud said, "we can scarcely conclude that there has been a softening in human manners. The cause is rather to be found in the undeniable weakening of religious feelings and the libidinal ties which depend upon them. If another group tie takes the place of the religious one—and the socialistic tie seems to be succeeding in doing so—then there will be the same intolerance towards outsiders as in the age of the Wars of Religion; and if differences between scientific opin-

[87] Freud, *New Introductory Lectures in Psychoanalysis*, p. 229.
[88] Sigmund Freud, *The Future of an Illusion*, Liveright, 1928.

ions could ever attain a similar significance for groups, the same result would again be repeated with this new motivation."[89]

Religion, Freud said, satisfies man's desire for knowledge and competes with science. Religion assures men of protection in the face of the dangers and mishaps of life and promises them a happy end to their misfortunes. No science can do that. Science tries to help people to avoid misery or to alleviate it, but no science can offer a panacea for all human discomforts. A third task of religion is to guide men by a system of directions and prohibitions. Science cannot do that either. The business of science is to discover facts and to find their interrelationships. Some recommendations for behavior can be deduced from scientific facts and theories, but science cannot offer directions for behavior. Religion combines teaching of the origin and nature of the universe with ethical precepts, and with assurances of protection and happiness as a reward for fulfillment of these precepts.

Thus, Freud contended that "the religious man's picture of the creation of the universe is the same as his picture of his own creation." This is why the idea of cosmogony of the God–Creator–Father is combined with ethical commandments and promises of comfort and protection. The Father, the symbol of parenthood, is the creator of life, the source of ethical norms, and the punishing and protecting force.

8. PSYCHOANALYSIS AS A PHILOSOPHY OF LIFE

With the analysis of the role of civilization and religion, psychoanalysis crossed the boundaries of the empirical sciences and entered the realm of speculation. This seems to be the logical and inevitable outcome of psychoanalytic inquiry. Once Freud embarked on the study of the problems men face in life, he could hardly stop at the gates of problems hitherto considered the domain of philosophy. Psychoanalysis had to cross this border too.

Freud seemingly avoided ethical and philosophical problems but could not evade them. He suggested that the psychoanalytic therapist remain neutral and noncommittal on ethical issues. It would not be proper for a psychoanalyst to impose his moral standards on his patients or to offer them a definite set of values. Psychoanalytic therapy aims at helping the individual to overcome infantile fixations and regressions and to become a mature adult. Moralizing would not help.

Moreover, one of Freud's endeavors was to discover the truth about human beliefs and attitudes; the moral foundations of human behavior have been scrutinized by psychoanalytic investigation. Freud rejected the idea of a superhuman origin of the moral conscience. He wrote: "The philosopher Kant once declared that nothing proved to him the greatness of

[89] Freud, *Group Psychology and the Analysis of the Ego*, pp. 50–51.

God more convincingly than the starry heavens and the moral conscience within us. The stars are unquestionably superb but, where conscience is concerned, God has been guilty of an uneven and careless piece of work, for a great many men have only a limited share of it or scarcely enough to be worth mentioning."[90]

Morality starts in childhood as a part of personality development. Small children are notoriously amoral. The first source of their morality is an external power, the parental authority which inhibits their pleasure-seeking impulses. Parents influence their children by affection and punishment; punishment acts in two ways—as a threat of pain and as a loss of love. Fear of punishment and of loss of love and reward for compliance are the main sources of children's compliance with the moral demands of their parents. To be bad means to do things that annoy parents and invite their grief and to be good means to do things that win their approval.

This state of affairs is carried over by adult men into their religious beliefs. Men believe that there is a superior, father-like power that rewards people for good behavior, punishes wickedness, and protects human life. This belief derives from the experiences of early life when, Freud says, each child is "brought up to know its social duties by means of a system of love-rewards and punishment, and in this way it is taught that its security in life depends on its parents (and subsequently other people) loving it and being able to believe in its love for them."[91]

The same applies to phylogenetic development. The primitive man was forced by society to restrain his pleasure-seeking impulses. The norms established by the society for the protection of its members became internalized in the minds of individuals. Conscience is basically the fear of society; it is the inner restraint, imposed on himself, of the individual who is "virtually an enemy of culture." But moral and cultural restraints stem from without and the majority of men obey the cultural prohibitions "only under the pressure of external force . . . as long as it is an object of fear. This also holds good for those so-called moral cultural demands."[92]

There is another source of moral behavior—love for the other person. "Love for oneself knows only one barrier—love for others, love for objects. . . . Love alone acts as the civilizing factor in the sense that it brings a change from egoism to altruism."[93] Once people share the satisfaction of their needs, the libido chooses them as its objects. Members of a group primarily established for narcissistic purposes begin to like each other and cathect libido in each other. This object cathexis necessarily limits the narcissistic love of oneself.

On this point Freud's conclusions are quite similar to those arrived at independently by Piaget in his study of the child's morality.

[90] Freud, *New Introductory Lectures in Psychoanalysis*, p. 88.
[91] *Ibid.*, p. 224.
[92] Freud, *Future of an Illusion*, p. 19.
[93] Freud, *Group Psychology and the Analysis of the Ego*, p. 57.

Scientific Weltanschauung

Freud was a staunch follower of empiricism and positivism. It was quite possible, he said, that at the time of early animism, men had more self-confidence than we have today; although the demons of animism were hostile to men, men had considerable self-confidence derived from magic practices. In their fight against the forces of nature they used magic, which is "the first forerunner of our modern technology." They believed in the omnipotence of their thoughts and ascribed magic power to the spoken word. It took quite a long time for men to learn to observe natural phenomena and interpret them with scientific caution. Scientific inquiry gradually replaced magic, empirical observation took the place of anthropomorphic images, and criticism and logic were introduced to replace the wishful thinking of the early ages. Science is never as certain as magic. Unfortunately, the philosophy of our times has still preserved "essential traits of animistic modes of thought such as the over-estimation of the magic of words and the belief that real processes in the external world follow the lines laid down by our thoughts. It is, to be sure, an animism without magical practices," wrote Freud.[94] Apparently, Freud was opposed to the idealistic German philosophy, especially to Kant and Hegel, and rejected the idea that the universe is ruled by the laws of logic.

The only source of human knowledge is a verified observation of empirical data. The results of these observations can be "intellectually manipulated" and put together into a system of generalizations and laws that represent the results of empirical research.

"It is inadmissable to declare," said Freud, "that science is one field of human intellectual activity, and that religion and philosophy are others at least as valuable, and that science has no business to interefere with the other two, that they all have an equal claim to truth, and that everyone is free to choose when he shall draw his convictions and in what he shall place his belief. Truth cannot be tolerant and cannot admit compromise or limitations, and scientific research must adopt an uncompromisingly critical attitude towards any other power that seeks to usurp any part of its province."[95]

Interpretation of History

History has attracted the attention of several psychologists. One can consider historical events as adventures in human nature and apply psychology to the interpretation of history or utilize historical data for psychological studies.[96]

Freud felt that economic factors cannot be the sole determinants in

[94] Freud, *New Introductory Lectures in Psychoanalysis*, p. 226.
[95] *Ibid.*, p. 219.
[96] B. B. Wolman (Ed.), *Psychoanalytic Interpretation of History*, Harper-Torchbooks, 1973.

human societies. He criticized Karl Marx for overlooking cultural and psychological factors and said that Marxism in Russia had acquired "an almost uncanny resemblance to what it was opposing," that is, to the Czarist autocracy. Freud would agree that economic factors play a considerable role in history, but human nature has always been the driving power in history.

In 1933, Freud wrote: "It is probable that the so-called materialistic conceptions of history err in that they underestimate this factor. They brush it aside with the remark that the 'ideologies' of mankind are nothing more than resultants of their economic situation at any given moment or superstructures built upon it. That is the truth, but very probably it is not the whole truth. Mankind never lives completely in the present; the ideologies of the superego perpetuate the past, the traditions of the race and the people, which yield but slowly to the influence of the present and to new developments, and, so long as they work through the superego, play an important part in man's life, quite independently of economic conditions." [97]

Freud offered a psychoanalytic interpretation of history. History is made by men. Men and their instincts, emotions, inhibitions, reaction formations, and sublimations determine the course of history. The two great instinctual forces, Eros and Thanatos, live forever. Men have always been lovers and haters and the power of hatred has never ceased to incite men to wars.

There are two sources of hostility. One is the primary force of threats, of instinct of death and destruction, which may be directed either against the self or against the other man. The other source is self-love or narcissism. Narcissism works for the self-assertion of the individual and, in group processes, for the aggressive attitudes of groups toward people who do not belong.

This is why, said Freud, "closely related races keep one another at arm's length. . . . We are no longer astonished that greater differences should lead to an almost insuperable repugnance. . . ." One could not be too optimistic about the future of mankind, nor expect some miraculous solution of human conflicts.

Freud was highly critical of the interpretation of history by some sort of "obscure Hegelian philosophy." The truth is that man and his instinctual forces determine the course of historical events. Man and not *"der absolute Geist,"* men and not dialectics, men and not logical systems make history. Can men harness their instinctual forces and make them work for peace?

The future of mankind, said Freud, depends on "whether and to what extent the cultural process developed in it will succeed in mastering the arrangements of communal life caused by the human instinct of aggression and self-destruction. In this connection perhaps the phase through which we are passing at this moment deserves special interest. Men have brought their powers of subduing the forces of nature to such a pitch that by using them they could now very easily exterminate one another to the last man.

[97] Freud, *New Introductory Lecture in Psychoanalysis*, pp. 95–96.

They know this—hence arises a great part of their current unrest, their dejection, their mood of apprehension. And now it may be expected that the other of the two 'heavenly forces,' the eternal Eros, will put forth his strength so as to maintain himself alongside of his equally immortal adversary."[98] This task can be accomplished, if ever, by means of education.

Education

"One of the most important social tasks of education is to restrain, confine, and subject to an individual control (itself identical with the demands of society) the sexual instinct when it breaks forth in the form of reproductive function. . . . Without this [restraint—B. W.] the instinct would break all bounds and the laboriously erected structure of civilization would be swept away," wrote Freud.[99] Later on, as he developed the theory of the death instinct, emphasis was put on the need to restrain both instincts, especially the aggressive one.

Civilization is built up at the cost of aggressive and sexual impulses, which must be partly repressed and partly sublimated. Each society demands that individuals limit aggression and mitigate sex. No society can survive without inhibition of instincts. The child must be educated in a way that will enable him to live in a society.

Freud wrote:

> The child has to learn to control its instincts. To grant it complete freedom, so that it obeys all its impulses without any restriction, is impossible. . . . The function of education, therefore, is to inhibit, forbid and suppress, and it has at all times carried out this function to admiration. But we have learned from analysis that it is the very suppression of instincts that involves the danger of neurotic illness. Education has therefore to stem its way between the Scylla of giving the instincts free play and the Charybdis of frustrating them. . . . If we can find an optimum of education which will carry out its task ideally, then we may hope to abolish one of the factors in the etiology of neurotic illness, viz. the influence of accidental infantile traumas.[100]

9. CONCLUDING REMARKS ON PSYCHOANALYSIS

The Areas Covered

Three periods in Freud's work can be distinguished. In the first stage, Freud, as a practicing psychiatrist, was mostly interested in neurosis and other aberrations from normal behavior. In the second stage, which started around 1900 and lasted until about 1920, Freud developed a highly complex psychological theory. Although this theory was derived from clinical expe-

---

[98] Sigmund Freud, *Civilization and Its Discontents*, Hogarth, 1930.
[99] Freud, *General Introduction to Psychoanalysis*, p. 273.
[100] Freud, *New Introductory Lectures in Psychoanalysis*, p. 204.

rience, it eventually became a general theory of personality rather than a study of mental disorder. In the third stage, after 1920, while Freud kept modifying his clinical theories and techniques, his main interest shifted toward the most general and universal problems of humanity, such as war and peace, civilization, and religion.[101]

It is, indeed, difficult to believe that all this was done by one man. Judged by the areas covered by his research, by its dimensions and diversity, Freud's work is impressive and perhaps unique. It could not be expected, however, that such a grandiose undertaking could represent a uniform and equal degree of accomplishment in all the various areas covered by Freud's searching and indefatigable mind. Although Freud was quite consistent in his method of theory construction, he treated some problems rather perfunctorily, and in some fields his conclusions do not seem to be a necessary inference from empirical data.

Some Unresolved Problems

One of the areas insufficiently clarified by Freud is perception. Freud said that the ego controls the motor apparatus, and that the images of the external world are communicated to the id by the perceptual system. But the nature of both the motor apparatus and the perceptual system requires further clarification. The relationship between them and the ego is still another unresolved problem.

Another problem related to perception is the question of the perceptory functions of the id. The id is supposed to be "blind" and incapable of perception. It might well be asked whether the neonate, whose mental apparatus consists of the id only, is capable of perceiving. It is worth while to mention here Sullivan's hypothesis (cf. Chapter 9) concerning the "modes" of perception. The neonate's perceptions are probably diffused and often hallucinatory, but still there are some perceptions. It is also an unresolved problem whether empathy, telepathy, and other unconscious processes are functions of the id or of the archaic ego and what they actually are.

There has been some research in which Freud's clinical findings have been related to experimental psychology and learning theory, but there is still the unresolved question of the relationship between learning, on one side, and fixation, regression, repression, on the other (cf. Chapter 8).

Environmental Factors

Some writers, such as Clara Thompson,[102] maintain that Freud turned away from environmental factors to organic constitution. Thompson explains that originally Freud related hysteria to premature sexual experience.

---

[101] In 1914, Freud wrote: "Psychoanalysis has never claimed to provide a complete theory of human mentality as a whole." *Collected Papers*, Vol. I, p. 338.

[102] Clara Thompson, *Psychoanalysis: Evolution and Development*, Hermitage, 1953.

Later, he discovered that stories of childhood seduction were often fantasies or wishes of the patients themselves.

Actually, Freud never turned away from environmental forces. Constitution and constellation, nature and nurture, were always considered by Freud to be the two indispensable factors working together in shaping human fate. The instinctual forces are inherited and the developmental phases are embedded in the life of human organisms. What will ultimately evolve in human life is determined by the forces of environment that facilitate or prevent frustrations, fixations, and regressions, that make out of the "polymorphous pervert" which the infant is, a normal and well-adjusted individual or an adult pervert. Freud strongly emphasized the impact of environment upon mental health and disorder. The sociologically oriented schools of psychoanalysis have some important ideas and observations, but their criticism of Freud is not always justified (cf. Chapter 9).

The Principle of Constancy

Freud's constancy principle can serve as the broadest framework for any theory of motivation. It represents a tension–relief continuum which is wittingly or unwittingly accepted by practically all psychologists. Horney's "safety and satisfaction" theory can be viewed as an effort to emphasize the social influences (safety) in obtaining gratification, that is, in restoring the equilibrium. Adler's theory of compensation is more broadly conceived and represents the same striving to restore the balance. Sullivan's theory can be seen, in this respect, as an elaboration of the Adler–Horney concepts of environmental influences that either create euphoria (the Freudian "bliss") by approval, or arouse anxiety by disapproval. Actually all psychoanalytic schools represent variations of the "constancy–homeostasis" principle.

The non-psychoanalytic schools utilize the same principle. Pavlov's reinforcement and extinction fall well in line with it. Hull's need-reduction theory and Tolman's physiological quiescence are applications of the same law. Goldstein's theory is par excellence a theory of homeostatic functioning of the human organism. Lewin's tension–relief theory is another example of the same principle.

An additional methodological advantage in acceptance of the principle of constancy relates to its universality. It would be in accordance with the scientific tradition to assume that the human mind is a part of nature and the general laws of the universe apply also to that fraction of the universe which psychology deals with.

Criticism of the Pleasure Theory

The subjective experience of this equilibrium was named by Freud pleasure–unpleasure. This part of his theory is quite vulnerable, but not because scientific psychology must reject any subjectivistic or mentalistic or introspectionistic data. It would be, so this writer believes, extravagant to throw away the introspectively perceived data in order to satisfy some arbitrarily set principles of "pure science." Psychology cannot afford to give up this treasure and be left with the limited material produced by the rigorous method of external observation and experimentation.

However, there are some important reasons for doubts concerning the pleasure theory. Pleasure is, by definition, a mental process perceived, sensed, or experienced by the organism. As long as the organism is somehow aware, even dimly aware on the conscious, preconscious, or unconscious level, pleasure is a process to be accounted for.

But what happens if the organism is completely unaware of it and if nothing of the kind can be registered by the organism itself or by any observer? In such a case the pleasure principle becomes a hypothesis that evades proof. No evidence of any sort can be brought to prove it nor can any logical inference be applied in support of it. Freud assumed, for example, that the neonate reacts with pleasure or unpleasure to stimuli. This can be inferred from the bulk of psychoanalytic theory and practice and, to a certain extent, it has been empirically proved by J. B. Watson, W. Stern, C. Bühler, and others.

Can the same be proved in regard to the lower functions of the human organism? In the discussion between the classical and neo-conditionists. Thorndike, Hull, Tolman, and Skinner seem to be in a stronger position than Pavlov, Watson, and Guthrie.

However, studies of conditioning in visceral organs conducted recently in Russia do not seem to give any indication of reward or pleasure in visceral conditioning (cf. Chapter 2), and they are quite convincing. In other words, one may hypothetically conclude that at a certain point of phylogenetic, and probably ontogenetic, development the feeling of pleasure makes its appearance.

There is no evidence for, and there are good methodological reasons against, a universality of the pleasure principle. Would anyone assume that fertilization of plants, which corresponds biologically to sexual intercourse in mammals, is accompanied by any kind of sensation of pleasure?

Apparently the hedonic principle can explain only a part of human behavior; certain phenomena require an interpretation on an *ante-hedonic* level. On the other hand, certain human actions are probably *post-hedonic*, such as those involving moral responsibility, feeling of duty, idealism, self-sacrifice, and all other deeds of men in which not one's own happiness but the happiness of his fellow man is the motivating force.[103]

Freud was aware of these types of object relationships and found in them aim inhibition, tenderness, and sublimation. No new principle was introduced by Freud at this point, although new phenomena were observed. Obviously, the pleasure and reality principles cannot be used here.

[103] The writer's point of view is presented briefly in Chapter 16. More research is in progress and will be reported elsewhere.

Freud felt the necessity to go beyond the pleasure principle in relation to repetition–compulsion, sadism and masochism, and suicide. However, repetition–compulsion can be easily explained by the constancy principle, and the instinct of death can hardly explain idealism. When a mother gives away the last piece of bread to her hungry child, or when she runs into a fire to save her child, she does not do it for self-destructive purposes. Her only aim is to save the child and she is willing to risk pain and destruction. Neither pleasure nor the reality principle nor the death wish can be applied in this case. Analogously, when men sacrifice their lives for their religious or political convictions, when they fight for freedom and justice, it is neither for pleasure nor out of self-hate. Some other, post-hedonic interpretation should be introduced.

The Death Instincts

Freud's theory of death instincts has stirred a great deal of controversy. Even the orthodox Freudian Fenichel has been critical of Freud and said that "the speculative basis is the conservative character of the instincts, as characterized by the constancy principle, namely the fact that instincts tend toward getting rid of tensions. But there is also a phenomenon that seems to run contrary to the constancy principle, namely a hunger for stimuli, seen mostly in the sexual instincts." [104]

Moreover, Fenichel said, the idea of a death instinct is "neither necessary nor useful" and there is no need to assume "two basically opposite kinds of instincts, the aim of one being relaxation and death, the aim of the other being of binding to higher units." "The thesis of an instinct source that makes the organism react to stimuli with drives toward 'instinct actions' which then change the source in an appropriate manner, cannot be applied to a death instinct." [105]

Several other hypotheses have been introduced and some of them will be discussed in the following chapters. One thing is certain: there is a great deal of aggressiveness and destructiveness in human behavior, and practically all mental disorder entails profound destructive tendencies. [106]

Freud's Method

One may find more shortcomings and more unresolved problems. Some of them have been taken up by Freud's disciples and resolved in a manner which would not have been approved by Freud. A great deal of criticism has come from experimental psychology.

Yet Freud's work is undoubtedly the single greatest contribution to

[104] Fenichel, *Psychoanalytic Theory of Neurosis*, p. 58.
[105] *Ibid.*, p. 60.
[106] Benjamin B. Wolman, "Psychotherapy with Latent Schizophrenics," *American Journal of Psychotherapy*, 1959, 13, 343–359.

psychology. While some investigators have limited their study to mental phenomena visible from within (introspectionists) and others to phenomena observable from without (behaviorists), Freud dealt with the totality of mental life including the most obscure and inaccessible regions of the mind. It seems that Freud, luckily for himself and for generations of psychologists, avoided the mistake of speedily erecting rigid theoretical structures. Herbart (cf. Chapter 1) is the best example of such a hurry; having a few unproved observations, Herbart developed a series of mathematical functions which were supposed to explain the most complex mental processes. Some contemporary scientists, even men of such stature as Hull or Lewin, have also tried to present the complexity of mental life in a series of rigid mathematical propositions.

Was not the unprecise, nomathematical, nonexperimental, and nonrigorous Freud more sound, more scientific, more knowledge-producing, more promotive of scientific inquiry than anyone else? Freud's scientific policy was cautious approximation. In discussing, for example, the problem of pleasure and unpleasure, he wrote in 1920: "This is the most obscure and inaccessible region of the mind, and, since we cannot avoid contact with it, the least rigid hypothesis, it seems to me, will be best."[107] And, inasmuch as any scientific inquiry strives toward quantification and experimental proof, Freud's cautious empiricism may prove to be the most rewarding method.

[107] Freud, *Beyond the Pleasure Principle*, p. 2.

7

Individual and Analytic Psychologies

1. ALFRED ADLER: INDIVIDUAL PSYCHOLOGY

The Early Schism

Adler and Jung represent the schism in psychoanalysis as it was formulated before the outbreak of the First World War. While the main body of psychoanalytic theory continued to grow, the separate branches grew too. Today, the common past forms the main link between the splinter groups of Adler and Jung and the main body of the psychoanalytic movement. Each theory went far in its own direction, and today there are deep differences among the three psychological theories. Though all three have common roots, they no longer form one body of data, nor do they have much in common in their concepts and theory.

Yet it is rather difficult to understand Adler or Jung outside of the context of their rebellion against Freud. Most of Adler's and Jung's ideas are related to their controversies with Freud, as if they were repeatedly saying, "On this point I agreed with Freud and on that I disagreed."

In the years 1911–12, Freud's theory was formulated in terms of libido–*sex* and ego–self-preservation instincts. The theory of the death instinct, of the superego, and the further development of the theory of ego, anxiety, and defense mechanisms came later. Adler's rebellion started with the problem: What is the driving power in man? Is it the hedonistic libido? Or the self-preservation instinct? And for these crucial questions, Adler's answer was entirely different from Freud's.

Adler was faithful to Freud in the emphasis on the role played by early childhood in personality development. Adler believed that all significant attitudes of a man could be traced back to early childhood, and that the nursery years are the formative years for all man's future attitudes. But Adler rejected Freud's theory of developmental stages and did not approve of the universality of the Oedipus complex.

Adler owes to Freud the idea of unconscious motivation, dream interpretation, and symptom formation. However, Adler did not accept Freud's theory of "mind topography."

The Impact of Kulturwissenschaft

Freud's theory was built on the foundations laid by the natural sciences, especially biology. Charles Darwin's theory of evolution and adjustment, Ernst Haeckel's principle of biogenetics, the theories of preservation of energy and homeostasis, and a strict determinism form the bases of psychoanalysis (cf. Chapter 6, Section 1). Although Freud embarked on a methodological non-reductionism and formulated a full-fledged psychogenic theory of mental disorder in contradistinction to neurological theories, he postulated that mental energy was a sort of unexplained derivative of the energy that activates all living substance.

Adler's rebellion was directed against the biological orientation of psychoanalysis and led in the direction of the *Kulturwissenschaft* (cf. Chapter 1, Section 1 and Chapter 10, Section 2). Freud considered men as a part of animate nature and traced the instinctual forces from man's ancestors. The instincts, said Freud, were the bridge between physiology and psychology; they are the driving power in men.

Adler leaned heavily on the *Kulturwissenschaft* and believed that men were driven by a *creative power*. It is a purely human force, not derived from biological factors. Adler, like all "understanding" psychologists (cf. Chapter 10), believed in the uniqueness of human nature and in the uniqueness of each individual. In the division of the sciences into natural and cultural sciences, as proposed by Windelband (cf. Chapter 10), Freud belongs to the first category, Adler to the second.

According to Adler, each individual is a unique case, an idiophenomenon:

> Types, similarities, and approximate likenesses are often either entities that owe their existence merely to the poverty of our language, which is incapable of giving simple expression to the nuances that are always present, or they are results of a statistical probability. The evidence of their existence should never be allowed to degenerate into the setting up of a fixed rule. Such evidence cannot bring us nearer to the understanding of the individual case. It can only be used to throw light on a field of vision in which the individual case in its uniqueness must be found.[1]

Adler took up the discussion of the problem as it was presented by Dilthey and Windelband.

The Creative Power

Each individual always manifests himself as unique, be it in thinking, feeling, speaking, or acting. Even when two individuals do the same thing,

[1] Heinz L. and Rowena R. Ansbacher, *The Individual Psychology of Alfred Adler*, Basic Books, 1956, pp. 193–194.

it is still not the same. Each is endowed with an individual *creative power*, considered by Adler to be a third factor besides heredity and environment; the creative power combines the innate potentialities and environmental influences into a movement toward overcoming of obstacles in one's path of life.

Thus, the decisive factor in one's life is his *law of movement*. Adler believed that the establishment of the law of movement was the greatest step in the development of his theory. It is the way the individual arrives at the solution of his problems. It is the manner in which he goes about overcoming the obstacles in his life. The law of movement is entirely individual and unique for each person. Each individual can be characterized and recognized by his law of movement.

The child is born with a free creative power. This innate power is exposed to influences stemming from the child's organism and his environment. As a result of the interaction between his free creative power and these factors, the child chooses a path in life and a style of life. The free creative power is no longer free; it becomes involved in the total structure of the individual personality. It is the main determinant of personality because it utilizes the individual's heredity and environment.

Purposivism versus Causality

The first principle of individual psychology is *teleology*. Adler rejected the deterministic and mechanistic causation of Freud and moved in the direction of finality. This approach was shared by McDougall, Goldstein, and Tolman.

Adler wrote: "All psychic activities are given a direction, a previously determined goal. . . . *Every psychic phenomenon, if it is to give us any understanding of a person, can only be grasped and understood if regarded as a preparation for some goal.*" Consider the case of poor memory. "After excluding the possibility of all organic causes, we would ask ourselves what the objective of this weakness of memory is? . . . We should then have unmasked this weakness of memory as tendencious and could understand its importance as a weapon against a contemplated undertaking. In every test of ability we should then expect to find the deficiency due to the secret life plan of an individual."[2]

The final goal alone is a sufficient explanatory principle for anything the individual does, strives, feels, and thinks.

Adler accepted the validity of causality in the natural sciences but believed that "In psychology we cannot speak of causality or determinism. . . . Even organ inferiorities are effective only to the extent that we wish. Man can raise these inferiorities to rank and dignity; he can make them a cause. A large number of people cannot resist the tendency to do so. A child born with serious shortcomings is likely to take a timid, hostile atti-

---

[2] Alfred Adler, *The Practice and Theory of Individual Psychology*, Routledge & Kegan Paul, 1929, pp. 4–5.

tude toward life, but this is not causally determined, for we know that the attitude can pass if we make things easier for him."[3]

Adler's teleology corresponds to a certain extent to Freud's theory of primary and secondary gains. In Freud's theory an individual may wish to get sick to avoid tension (primary gain) or to win social approval (secondary gain). Adler's teleological philosophy is borrowed from Vaihinger's ideas.[4] According to Vaihinger's idealistic positivism, man's life is guided by certain ideas or goals. Man acts upon these ideas "as if" they were true. These ideas are not necessarily true representatives of reality; they may be fictitious; yet they exercise an irresistible power over man's actions.

Man's actions, said Adler, are related to causes, but they are dictated by goals. The history of mankind is not an account of causes and effects; it is a history of ideals, beliefs, and strivings. "The final goal alone can explain man's behavior," wrote Adler.

Goals may be conscious or unconscious. They are a teleological device of the "soul which seeks orientation." When an infant cries he cries not only because he is hungry but in order to get food or win sympathy.

Even dreams are subordinated to the general goal of life. "The dream strives to pave the way towards solving a problem by a metaphorical expression of it, by a comparison, an 'as if.' . . . In dreams we produce those pictures which will arouse the feelings and emotions which we need for our purposes, that is, for solving the problems confronting us at the time of the dream in accordance with the particular style of life which is ours."[5]

The Aggressive Drive

In the beginning, Adler believed that the main driving force in men was the drive for self-assertion. In 1908 he wrote as follows:

> From early childhood, we can say from the first day (first cry), we find a stand of the child toward the environment which cannot be called anything but hostile. If one looks for the cause of this position, one finds it determined by the difficulty of affording satisfaction for the organ. This circumstance as well as the further relationships of the hostile, belligerent position of the individual toward the environment indicate a drive toward fighting for satisfaction which I shall call "aggressive drive." . . . Fighting, wrestling, beating, biting, and cruelties show the aggression drive in its pure form. . . .[6]

The aggressive drive leads men into several occupational choices.

> The occupations of judge, police officer, teacher, minister, physician, and many others are taken up by persons with a larger aggression drive and often show continuity with analogous children's games. . . . Whereas the aggression drive so often withdraws from our perception through turning against the self and through refinement and specialization, it becomes altogether a hidden-figure

---

[3] Ansbacher, op. cit., p. 91.
[4] Hans Vaihinger, Philosophy of "As If," Harcourt, Brace, 1925.
[5] Ansbacher, op. cit., p. 82.
[6] Ibid., pp. 34–35.

puzzle in the reversal into the antithesis of the aggression drive. Charity, sympathy, altruism and sensitive interest in misery represent new satisfactions on which the drive, which originally tended toward cruelty, feeds.[7]

When Adler introduced the aggressive drive in 1908, Freud objected to it. Twelve years later Freud himself introduced the theory of the instinct to death and destruction, but in the meantime, Adler had reversed his position.

Adler was exposed to criticism for replacing Freud's libido theory by the aggressive drive. Gradually, Adler relegated aggressiveness and antisocial strivings to the role of neurotic signs. The neurotic strives toward personal superiority while the normal individual strives toward the perfection which benefits all, wrote Adler in 1933.

Inferiority Complex

Adler's theory of aggressiveness was related to his studies of organ inferiority. The first issue he considered was penis envy in women, as found by classic psychoanalysis. Adler generalized his findings. Whenever an individual has an organ inferiority, be it in the sensory apparatus or the digestive or respiratory tract, there is a tendency to restore the equilibrium by compensatory action. The unsatisfied demands increase until the deficit is made up through growth of the inferior organ or of some other organ which may serve as a substitute. According to Adler, approximately 70% of the students of painting have been found to suffer from some optical disorder. Many orators, such as Demosthenes and Demoulins, originally were stutterers, and many great musicians, such as Beethoven and Robert Franz, had ear afflictions.

These were Adler's ideas in 1908. Two years later, Adler was already critical of Freud, although he broke away one year later, in 1911. In a paper published in 1910, Adler wrote: "For children with inferior organs and glandular systems . . . their growth and functioning show deficiencies and that sickness and weakness are prominent especially in the beginning." "These objective phenomena frequently give rise to a subjective feeling of inferiority. . . ." "Such children are thus often placed in a role which appears to them unmanly. . . . The renunciation of masculinity, however, appears to the child as synonymous with femininity. . . . Any form of uninhibited aggression, activity, potency, power, and the traits of being brave, free, rich, aggressive, or sadistic can be considered as masculine. All inhibitions and deficiencies, as well as cowardliness, obedience, poverty and similar traits, can be considered feminine."[8]

Adler shifted from the innate aggressive drive to the drive of overcoming one's feeling of inferiority. Submission to inferiority is feminine, rebellion against it is masculine. This aggressive rebellion was called by Adler

[7] Ibid., p. 36.
[8] Ibid., pp. 46–47.

der männliche Protest ("masculine protest"), and from now on this term was substituted for the aggressive drives. The masculine protest was, according to Adler, a normal and general phenomenon of compensation. Overcompensation is pathological. When the individual fears defeat in a useful compensation, he may, in a neurosis, prefer a useless, antisocial compensation.

The more intense is the deprivation, the stronger the urge for compensation. The entire life of the child, his dreams, wishes, and play are filled with his goal to be a man, to be big and strong.

Both concepts, the inferiority and the protest, underwent changes in Adler's writings. In 1933, Adler emphatically stated that "to be human means to feel inferior," for every child is inferior in the face of life and of adults. The weakness of the child, his ever-present inferiority feeling, became now the main problem in Adler's theory.

The masculine protest was gradually transformed into a general striving for adequacy (*Vollwertigkeit*), for meaning something in life (*Geltungstrieb*), for security. The child is born weak and within his first four or five years a goal is set. This goal is compensatory, and the striving toward it is a striving to "security, power, and perfection." It is no longer striving for sheer power but for *overcoming* the difficulties of life and of one's own inferiority feelings.

Thus, compensation is no longer limited to any specific organic or social deficiency or inadequacy. We all, wrote Adler, strive to attain a goal which will make us feel strong, superior, perfect.

Striving for Superiority

Human volition is usually interpreted in two ways. The first is the pleasure–pain antinomy and the other the survival–death antinomy. Adler did not deny the importance of seeking pleasure, but he denied that this is the guiding principle in human life.

Nor did Adler agree that self-preservation or preservation of the species is the main driving force in men. We act, he said, every minute in violation of these two principles. We may wish to die when in pain and give up the attainment of pleasure when we or our self-esteem are threatened. The overemphasis of either principle is neurotic. Some neurotics overvalue pleasure in their effort to compensate for their organ inferiority, and some overvalue life in compensation for their fear of death. The main guiding principle is the advancement of self-esteem, the overcoming of inferiority feelings, the *striving for superiority*. Pleasure or displeasure are only ancillary rewards on this great road to the final goal of man.

This striving for superiority is innate. It is a basic urge in man, comparable to Freud's instinctual forces of Eros and Thanatos. It is primordial, inherent in our nature. It is the continuous effort toward a better adaptation between man and world.

Said Adler: "Whether a person desires to be an artist, the first in his profession, or a tyrant in his home, to hold converse with God or humiliate other people; whether he regards his suffering as the most important thing to which everyone must show obeisance, whether he is chasing after unattainable ideals or old deities, over-stepping all limits and norms, at every part of his life he is guided and spurred on by his longing for superiority, the thought of his godlikeness, the belief in his special magic power. In his love he desires to experience his power over his partner. In his purely optional choice of profession the goal . . . manifests itself in all sorts of exaggerated anticipations and fears."[9]

On this point Adler's thinking ran ahead of Freud's. As early as 1908, Adler emphasized the importance of aggressive impulses. However, while in Freud's writing aggressiveness was a function of the death instinct, in Adler's theory it is the most general human striving, "an intrinsic necessity of life itself. It is at the root of all solutions of life's problems and is manifested in the way in which we meet these problems. All our functions follow its direction. They strive for conquest, security, increase, either in the right or in the wrong direction. . . . Whatever premises all our philosophers and psychologists dream of—self-preservation, pleasure principle, equalization—all these are but vague representations, attempts to express the great upward drive."[10] This upward drive, which stems from the *feeling of inferiority*, is the cause of human culture and progress.

Sociability

Freud was always aware of the impact of environment on personality structure. The instinctual innate forces and the developmental stages are significant factors, yet the final outcome depends a great deal on the individual's interaction with his environment. All of us, said Freud, have innate impulses and all of us go through developmental stages. But fixations and regressions, formations and malformations of the ego and the superego depend on our environment.

What could Adler add to this? Adler presented the issue in sharper lines, in a focal position, and in a different light. Freud perceived the individual as a separate entity and then exposed him to the restraining or encouraging social forces. Adler, the contrary, emphasized that community precedes the individual life. Man has always been in a society, never outside of it. Adler saw the basic fact as social life, not as the individual's socialization.

Sociability in men is a phylogenetic and ontogenetic necessity, a *conditio sine qua non*. Adler stated that

> Darwin already pointed out that one never finds weak animals living alone. Man
> must be included among these, particularly because he is not strong enough to

---

[9] Adler, *op. cit.*, p. 7.

[10] Alfred Adler, "Individual Psychology," in C. Murchison (Ed.), *Psychologies of 1930*, Clark University, 1930, p. 398.

live alone. He has only little resistance against nature, he needs a larger amount
of aids to live and preserve himself. . . . Man could maintain himself only when
he placed himself under particularly favorable conditions. These, however, were
afforded to him only by group life.[11]

This is the phylogenetic point of view. From the ontogenetic point of
view, the need for group life is no less imperative. Newborn children are
weak and their weakness makes child care a necessity.

Adler believed that the social interest or social feeling of an individual
is an evaluative attitude toward life (*Lebensform*). It is the ability to "see
with the eyes of another person."

Social interest coincides, at least partially, with empathy, identification, understanding of the other man, which makes us capable of friendship, sympathy, and love. Identification is defined by Adler as the ability to
understand the other person and to see with the other person's eyes.

This ability for cooperation with others, the social interest or sociability
(*Gemeinschaftsgefühl*), is an innate potentiality. But in order to attain the
high degree of cooperation necessary for survival, this innate potentiality
must be developed far beyond its initial stage. Moreover, the desire for superiority must be coordinate with sociability and even subordinated to it.

Even in 1908, Adler emphasized the *need for affection* in infants. While
Freud, starting from the individual, emphasized the individual's need to
give love, Adler took up the other side of the problem, the need to receive
love. On this point, Horney and Sullivan (Chapter 9, Sections 2 and 4) are
Adler's disciples. This need became incorporated in the later writings of
Adler into the *social interest*.

Adler was opposed to Freud's idea of primary narcissism. He said that

when other schools of psychology maintain that the child comes into the world a
complete egoist with 'a drive for destruction' and no other intention than to foster
himself cannibalistically on his mother, this is an erroneous inference based on
incomplete observation. . . . These schools overlook in the relationship the role
of the mother who requires the cooperation of the child. The mother with her
milk-filled breasts and all the other altered functions of her body . . . needs the
child just as the child needs her.[12]

According to Freud, social development in childhood is a product of
the biologically determined developmental stages and the interaction between the child and his environment. Adler discarded the developmental
stages. The biological background of personality, heredity, and physique,
played a secondary role in his theory. Although at the beginning Adler
ascribed a great deal of importance to the innate "organic inferiority," later
on he did not regard any inferiorities, organic or social, as determinants of
behavior. They became incorporated into the over-all life plan of the individual.

According to Freud, social development is a function of libido development. Adler was opposed to this idea. He wrote that it would not be possible to maintain that every drive has a sexual component. Adler separated

[11] Ansbacher, *op. cit.*, p. 129.
[12] *Ibid.*, p. 137.

sociability and sexuality. The social interest or sociability is "an innate potentiality which has to be consciously developed."

Accordingly, Freud's ideas of socialization of the child through repression, reaction formation, aim inhibition, envy, and superego formation became superfluous in Adler's frame of reference. Humans are born with the "innate potentiality." The Oedipus complex, is according to Adler, not a universal pattern of development, but merely an error in the upbringing of children.

In opposition to Freud, Adler believed that the child's initial and innate impulses of affection are directed toward others and not toward himself. Freud believed the newborn child to be a narcissist; Adler believed that self-boundedness is an artifact imposed on the child by his education and by the present state of our social structure. The creative power of the child is misled toward self-boundedness instead of being guided into the normal channels of cooperation with other individuals.

In normal development the striving for superiority is blended with the social interest. All the actions of the individual should be useful to the society. In pursuing his own end, the individual is interested in others.

Conscious and Unconscious

Conscious and unconscious are not two opposites. As soon as we understand the unconscious, it becomes conscious; wherever we fail to understand the conscious, it becomes unconscious.

Unconscious is that part of our conscious which we have not fully understood. We tend to put aside thoughts which stand in our way and accept those that help us. "All individuals consider for the most part only things which are useful for their view and attitude. In other words, that becomes conscious which advances us, and that remains unconscious which might disturb our argumentation." [13]

When the child is about five years old his attitude to his environment is already firmly established. His personality evolves around his goal, and he perceives the world in the perspective of his own strivings. "The child builds up his whole life, which we have called concretely style of life, at a time when he has neither adequate language nor adequate concepts. When he grows further . . . he grows in a movement which has never been formulated into words and therefore, unassailable to criticism, is also withdrawn from the criticism of experience. We cannot say that something has not been understood or that this is a repressed unconscious. Rather we must say that something has been withheld from the understanding," wrote Adler in 1929. [14]

Sullivan's concept of "selective inattention" (cf. Chapter 9, Section 4) sounds pretty much like Adler's reasoning. The similarity is even more striking in the following passage:

[13] Ibid., p. 233.
[14] Alfred Adler, Problems of Neurosis: A Book of Case-Histories, Kegan Paul, 1929, p. 152.

Because the individual adopts a certain particular approach, a certain attitude, a certain relation toward the problems of the outside world . . . , anything that does not fit this early-adopted attitude is more or less excluded . . . and is interpreted in accordance with the individual's view of the world. The same thing happens with regard to the inseparably associated emotional factors and the attitudes growing out of them. We can observe in the whole life . . . the direction selected by the individual for his striving. What is left over after this process of elimination by the life style remains as a part of the mental life and operates "unconsciously" . . . or "not understood." [15]

Sullivan did not add much to it.

Style of Life and Personality Structure

Adler presented the essence of human personality as follows: Human beings are born weak; they face hardships and feel insecure. The feeling of inferiority stimulates them to movement and action aimed at overcoming it. Such persistent movement toward superiority is called the *style of life*.

All men strive toward superiority but each strives in a different way. No individual adjusts mechanically to his environment. The style of life is the expression of one's individuality, for each individual sees the goal of superiority in an individual, unique way.

The style of life controls the totality of the child's behavior. All aspects of life become coordinated with and subordinated to this over-all plan. The style of life represents the unity of the personality expressed in all facets of the individual's life: in his conscious and unconscious, in his thinking and feeling, in acting and resting, in sex, and in social interest.

In the first four or five years of life, the child absorbs the impact of his own body and environment. Then the creative activity or the style of life begins. In contradistinction to Freud, Adler assumed that the ego or the goal-directed creative power is formed after the first four or five years of life. Moreover, once the Adlerian ego or self or creative power of striving toward the goal is formed, the total personality is under its perfect control. The ego represents the *unity of personality*.

Adler thus shifted the focus of psychological inquiry from id and superego toward ego. Anna Freud did the same but within the theoretical framework of psychoanalysis.[16] Freud himself accepted her ideas and incorporated them into his theory of personality. To Freud, the ego was an outgrowth of the id and the superego was an outgrowth of the ego. Freud's concept of ego assumed continuity between the innate id and its outgrowths, the ego and superego. Adler's ego was the innate creative force, as soon as it became goal bound.

Adler compared heredity to a "supply of bricks" of various quality used by each individual in a different way in building his style of life. What matters most is not what one has inherited but *what one does* with

[15] *Ibid.*
[16] Anna Freud, *The Ego and the Mechanisms of Defense*, Hogarth, 1948.

what he has. Even art and genius are not undeserved gifts of nature or inheritance but the individual's own creation.

An analogous reasoning applies to the environment. Adler strongly emphasized environmental influences but rejected the idea of an environmentalistic determinism. We are neither machines nor dictaphones. No experience, not even a traumatic one, is a cause of future success or failure in one's life. Men give meaning to situations in accordance with their goals and life styles. Happy or unhappy experiences influence one's life not by their happening but through the meaning one attaches to them. It is not the experiences that determine the individual's course of action but the conclusions he draws from them. His learning, remembering and forgetting are selective, guided by the promise of success of his life style.

Besides the creative force there are two important determinants of personality, the *social interest* and the *degree of activity*. This term resembles Edward Spranger's (Chapter 11) *Kulturformen*, that is, the individual's attitude to the problems of life, which are, according to Adler, always social in nature. Adler's "degree of activity" reminds one of similar ideas expressed at about the same time by K. Lewin (cf. Chapter 13). Adler wrote in 1937: "It would be a tempting task for a psychologist to show graphically the extent and form of the individual life-space." [17] Adler's "degree of activity" is well represented by the actions of a boy who runs away from home or starts a fight on the street as compared to a boy who sits home and reads a book. K. Lewin's indebtedness to Adler is quite obvious.

The psychological life of a person is oriented toward the final act, like that of a character created by a good dramatist. "The fictional, abstract ideal is the point of origin for the formation and differentiation of the given psychological resources into preparatory attitudes, readiness, and character traits. The individual then wears the character traits demanded by his fictional goal, just as the character mask (*persona*) of the ancient actor had to fit the finale of the tragedy." Moreover, the ego or self or creative force guides the individual toward the ideal of himself. "In every case the point of the self-ideal (*Persönlichkeitsideal*) posited beyond reality remains effective. This is evidenced by the direction of the attention, of the interests, and of the tendencies, all of which select according to points of view given in advance." [18]

Adler's self-ideal corresponds to Freud's ego-ideal and later superego, but it plays a less important role in Adler's personality structure as compared to Freud's fully developed personality model. The way the self-ideal was worded by Adler indicated his unwillingness to consider this "ideal" as a part of the mental apparatus. It indicates a striving rather than an accomplishment. No wonder Karen Horney is indebted to Adler in her concept of self-image (cf. Chapter 9, Section 2).

In the striving toward the goal, character traits and complexes are formed. "The character traits are . . . the outer forms of the movement line of

[17] Ansbacher, *op. cit.*, p. 164.
[18] *Ibid.*, p. 94.

a person. As such they convey to us an understanding of his attitude toward the environment, his fellow man, the community at large, and his life problems. They are phenomena which represent means for achieving self-assertion. They are devices which join to form a method of living."[19]

Character traits are acquired. Individuals seem to believe that they lead them toward their goals of superiority. For instance, envy or distrust, ambition or laziness is such a trait acquired by an individual in the hope that it will bring him closer to his goal.

Emotions are intensifications or accentuations of character traits; they are forms of psychological movement, limited in time. They are purposeful; they serve the purpose of improving the situation of an individual. Joy, anger, fear, and sorrow lead to an intensified movement of the individual, who makes an effort to come closer to his goal.

Complexes characterize the individual as schemata or personality traits do. The complex is a useful concept, helpful as an explanation of the individual's attitude to the tasks presented by the environment. The individual moves toward his goal and in so doing faces tasks. Failures of movement represent the various forms of the inferiority complex. The compensation is the *superiority* complex. The *redeemer* complex represents the desire to save someone. The *proof* complex represents the fear of failure and the desire to be always right. The *predestination* complex expresses itself in the belief that whatever happens to the individual is inevitable.

This goal directedness applies to the human body also. The body has its own language, the *organ dialect*. Enuresis is an expression of hostility to parents or a means of attracting their attention. Insomnia is an expression of ambition. Organic disorders usually express the craving for power. Usually each emotion has its own somatic expression and is expressed in the organ dialect. The choice of the organ usually depends on the individual's childhood experiences subordinated to his craving for overcoming his inferiority feeling. A healthy individual may desire to become sick if the illness could bring him more superiority than health does.

Adler believed that the style of life can exert a permanent influence on the somatic development of the individual. "A courageous individual will show the effects of his attitude in his physique."[20] Body and mind are parts of a whole, and there is constant reciprocal influence between the two.

Typology

Adler believed, in accordance with Windelband's theory of idiophenomena (cf. Chapter 10), that human beings cannot be divided into classes or types. Although the goal of superiority and success is universal, each individual's attitude toward his goal is unique, and success has a different meaning for each individual. Classification is necessarily an unfruitful

[19] *Ibid.*, p. 219.
[20] Alfred Adler, *What Life Should Mean to You*, Little, Brown, 1931, p. 40.

method. Therefore, Adler said, his classification or typology is merely an educational device, introduced "for teaching purposes" only.

In 1927, Adler interpreted Hippocrates' four temperaments, the sanguine, choleric, melancholic, and phlegmatic. The *sanguine type* is the most healthy, believed Adler. Since the sanguine person is not subjected to severe deprivations and humiliations, he has little if any inferiority feeling. He is capable of striving toward superiority in a happy and friendly manner.

The *choleric* is tense and aggressive. His striving for superiority and power involves a great expenditure of energy. He goes about attaining his goal in a direct, aggressive manner. His social adjustment is rather poor.

The *melancholic* is overwhelmed by his inferiority feeling to such an extent that he lacks initiative in overcoming his obstacles. He is worrisome and undecided and lacks self-confidence and courage to take risks. He is not antisocial, but does not participate very much in social interaction.

The *phlegmatic* has lost contact with life. He is depressed, slow, sluggish, not impressed by anything, and unable to make an effort for improvement.

In 1935, Adler introduced his own typology,[21] utilizing his concepts of degree of activity and the social interest as the two guiding principles in the grouping of personality types.

The first type displays a great deal of activity in pursuing his goal, but lacks social interest. His lack of consideration for others makes him act in an antisocial manner. He is the *dominant* or *ruling* type. This type corresponds, obviously, to Hippocrates' choleric type.

The second type is the *getting* type. He lacks both activity and social interest and expects others to take care of him. He himself lacks initiative and consideration for others. The similarity between the getting type and the phlegmatic type is quite apparent.

The third type is the *avoiding* one. Instead of struggling for success and superiority, he stands still, undecided. Both his activity and his social interest are very small. The avoiding type resembles the melancholic.

The fourth type is the *socially useful* one. He is active, but his activity is in harmony with the needs of others and beneficial to them. The useful type closely resembles the sanguinic.[22]

Concluding Remarks

Adler's revolt against Freud was based on more than one difference. The place of psychology in the realm of science is one of the most important controversies. Should psychology use observation, measurement, experi-

---

[21] Alfred Adler, "The Fundamental Views of Individual Psychology," *International Journal of Individual Psychology*, 1935, 1, 5–8.

[22] It is worth mentioning that Pavlov believed that sanguinics and phlegmatics were the normal types (cf. Chapter 2, Section 3).

ment, and become one of the natural sciences or should it be classified among the humanities, like history or aesthetics? Adler was strongly impressed by E. Spranger's *Lebensformen* (Chapter 11, Section 1). Adler rejected the materialistic concept of energy, as K. Lewin did later. Both of them operated with the concepts of space, movement, and goal, but Lewin went much further in styling psychology (cf. Chapter 13).

Adler's theory is more optimistic than Freud's. Freud saw man as torn between the forces of life and love, Eros, and the forces of death and destruction, Thanatos. The road to a peaceful coexistence of men is undermined with the dynamite of hate. No wonder many abhor seeing men as Freud saw them.

Adler believed in innate *Gemeinschaftgefühl*, that is, a general sociability. Moreover, this sociability can be taught, fostered, and improved. Adler, the humanist and humanitarian, could not help believing in men.

The most important thing, wrote Adler, was to understand the individual as a whole. The over-all goal permits one to understand the meaning of the various separate actions of an individual and to perceive them as parts of a whole.

The goal of superiority, said Adler, is the governing principle, the source of unity of personality. But is superiority the governing principle of mental life?

Adler was never a very systematic or consistent thinker. He went a long way from the aggressive drive and organ inferiority to the creative power which, as a goal-bound force, becomes the leading factor, the ego, the self. His presentation left many questions unanswered. What is this creative force? Why does it become goal directed? How does it involve heredity and environment? Why don't people become reconciled to their feeling of inferiority? Are all people striving to superiority? Are all people so worried about their weakness in comparison to the universe that all their life is one continuous effort to overcome it, to become superior, and to gain self-esteem? How general is this rule? Do experimental and clinical studies bring evidence in support of the generality of inferiority feeling and drive toward superiority?

Adler's holistic and purposivistic approach creates insurmountable difficulties. The goal of life is either immanent in each individual, or set by external forces, or chosen by the individual. Adler rejected the first choice, which inevitably leads to a deterministic heredity. He rejected the second choice, which would make a "dictaphone" out of a man. He repeatedly stated that man himself creates his life plan. But what shapes man's mind in such a way that he would make this or that choice?

It is, probably, the deterministic bias of the present writer that forces him to be critical of any indeterministic theory. The universe seems to function in a pretty organized and ordered manner, and the rejection of the causal principle seems to be against empirical evidence (cf. Chapter 15).

Adler's opposition to causation does not sound too convincing. He stated that "each individual acts and suffers in accordance with his peculiar teleology," which sounds rather deterministic. Or, in the same passage, he stated that the springs of this teleology "may be traced to his earliest childhood, and nearly always we find that they have been diverted into false channels by the pressure of the earliest situations in the child's life,"[23] which implies even more causation. When Adler said that things could have taken another turn, and therefore were not causally determined, he probably committed a logical error. With additional causal factors, the picture would change; changed causes create new effects. Furthermore, teleology does not exclude causation, for there are causes which lead men to set goals.

Adler's analysis of human nature contains many brilliant observations and suggestions and it has to be said that Adler's influence is much greater than is usually admitted. The entire neo-psychoanalytic school, including Horney, Fromm, and Sullivan, is no less neo-Adlerian than it is neo-Freudian. Adler's concepts of sociability, self-assertion, security, self, and creativeness permeated the theories of the neo-analysts.

Clara Thompson says about Adler that "he anticipated by several years a more general acceptance of several similar ideas. He was a pioneer in applying psychoanalysis to the total personality. . . . He was the first person to describe a part of the role of the Ego in producing neurosis and to show that the direction in which a person is going, that is, his goals, significantly contribute to his neurotic difficulties."[24]

Adler's emphasis on the conscious part of the personality, the ego, was exceedingly helpful in the development of psychoanalytic theory proper. It was stimulating even outside the borders of the psychoanalytic schools and therapeutic clinics. In the words of Gardner Murphy, "the mass of data relative to the problems of the ego that has come to us from Adler and his school is tremendously rich; we shall remain forever indebted for the ruthlessness and simplicity with which such problems were described in an era when Adler was generally ridiculed by the analysts and ignored by 'hard-headed' medical men. Adler did as much as any individual to make clear that the ego's problems are as central as sex or any other problems . . . indeed that for most civilized men they are the most burning problems of all."[25]

2. CARL GUSTAV JUNG: ANALYTIC PSYCHOLOGY

Irrationality as a Method

Carl Gustav Jung was the first president of the International Psychoanalytic Association, founded by Freud in 1910, and continued in this position

---

[23] Ansbacher, op. cit., p. 93.
[24] Clara Thompson, Psychoanalysis: Evolution and Development, Hermitage, 1951, pp. 160–161.
[25] Gardner Murphy, Personality: A Biosocial Approach to Origins and Structure, Harper, 1947, p. 593.

until 1914, when he resigned his presidency and withdrew his membership.

He broke away from Freud soon after Alfred Adler. Both Adler and Jung disagreed with psychoanalysis as it stood prior to the First World War. They rebelled against Freud's theory of libido with its sexual connotation. Later on, Freud himself completely revised his theory of libido (cf. Chapter 6, Section 4), but Adler and Jung were already far from the original point of controversy and the gulf was never closed. The differences kept growing, and in the end Adler and Jung shared with Freud only those concepts which were acceptable to them before they broke away.

Adler, as discussed in the previous section of this chapter, was more concerned with the conscious processes than Freud was. Adler's theory is, to a great extent, a theory of what Freud called the ego. Jung moved in the opposite direction. His main interest and his numerous works were concerned with the unconscious processes. Freud distinguished between the parts of the unconscious which were conscious and became repressed, and the parts which had never been conscious. Jung's works deal mainly with the deepest layers of the human unconscious. Freud believed that in well-balanced individuals the rational ego exercises a reasonable degree of control over the id and superego. Jung advocated some sort of cooperation between the rational conscious and the irrational unconscious.

Apparently Jung not only followed Freud into the realm of the unconscious but also became enchanted by it. The primitive beauty of the primary-primordial mental resources, studied by Jung in psychotherapeutic practice as well as in anthropological and cultural-historical research, was tempting indeed. Jung progressively ascribed to the unconscious more and more importance. Freud saw human nature in the perspective of unconscious, preconscious, and conscious, with the conscious as the controlling force. Jung definitely rejected the rule of the conscious.

Jung also disagreed with Freud on more issues. This disagreement was, first of all, a methodological one. Freud persistently applied scientific analysis to all "mental provinces," including the unconscious. A great deal of his work was devoted to the primary processes, but he always used the rational method and empirical observation. It was always the conscious part of Freud's mind that analyzed dreams.

Jung was deeply involved with unconscious phenomena and bluntly refused to apply to them the method of scientific analysis. He insisted that we must make sure that "we do not foist conscious psychology upon the unconscious," for the unconscious cannot be represented in such terms as thinking or reasoning. Jung refused to accept the idea that the unconscious processes could be perceived by and represented in terms of the conscious mind.

In a sense, Jung violated the Freudian principle of reality testing by saying that the unconscious "affects us just as we affect it. In this sense the world of the unconscious is commensurate with the world of outer experience." [26]

[26] Carl G. Jung, *Two Essays on Analytical Psychology*, Dodd, Mead, 1928, p. 198.

The conscious or consciousness, says Jung, is "the most unfavorable object imaginable for psychology. The essence of consciousness is the process of adaptation which takes place in the most minute details. . . . The unconscious is generally diffused, which not only binds the individuals among themselves to the race but also unites them backwards with the peoples of the past . . . and is . . . the object of a true psychology."[27]

Freud was a determinist and Adler a purposivist. For a long time, Jung seems to have accepted both principles. The human mind, he said, is guided by both, for, on the one hand, it is a "precipitate of the past," and, on the other hand, the psyche "creates its own future."

Jung's discussion of this problem was devoted less to the search for truth and more to the analysis of the possible implications of causation and teleology for human attitudes to life. Jung was not sure that either causation or purpose could be proved or disproved; he accepted somewhat the Kantian position and believed that both principles are methods of cognition rather than laws of nature. The acceptance of causation would, however, make men feel unhappy, pessimistic, and unable to undo their past, while purposivism leaves more freedom to the individual. Consequently, decided Jung, man lives by aims as well as by causes. Jung did not see any contradiction in these two principles. Moreover, while he was opposed to deterministic causalism, he introduced a fatalistic predestination theory through the eternal factors of ancestral history, which influence the actions of each individual.

In 1955, Jung introduced the idea of synchronicity and interpreted such phenomena as clairvoyance and telepathy by this principle. An unconscious idea may appear simultaneously in the physical world of happenings and in the mind of the individual. None of these phenomena is either a cause or an effect.[28]

The Libido

In 1912, Jung published his ideas concerning libido. In a volume entitled *The Psychology of the Unconscious*, he introduced the concept of primal libido, which indicated the totality of undifferentiated psychic energy, analogous to Henri Bergson's *élan vital*. According to Jung, libido is the general energy of life, the "energy of the processes of life." He used the term "libido" in another, more limited, connotation as psychic energy, perceived as a part of the broader concept of vital energy.

Jung maintained that human behavior is dominated neither by the all-powerful sexual libido of Freud nor by the mastery drive of Adler. There is only "undifferentiated life energy," which expresses itself at one time in the pursuit of sensual pleasure and at another time in the striving for superiority, artistic creation, play, and other activities.

Mental energy, or libido, is used basically for self-preservation and preservation of the species. When these biological needs are satisfied, it is

[27] Carl G. Jung, *The Psychology of the Unconscious*, Dodd, Mea, 1916, p. 199.
[28] Carl G. Jung, and W. Pauli, *The Interpretation of Nature and the Psyche*, Pantheon, 1955.

available for the pursuit of other goals, such as the cultural, social, or creative needs of the individual.

Jung accepted the idea that mental energy is a continuation of physical energy and that each of the two types of energy could be transformed into the other. "Life takes place through the fact that it makes use of natural physical and chemical conditions as a means to its existence. The living body is a machine that converts the amounts of energy taken up into its equivalents in other dynamic manifestations. One cannot say the physical energy is converted into life, but only that the transformation is the expression of life." And further on: "All the means employed by an animal for the safeguarding and furthering of his existence, not to speak of the direct nourishment of his body, can be regarded as machines that make use of natural potential in order to produce work. . . . Similarly, human energy, as a natural product of differentiation, is a machine; first of all a technical one that uses natural conditions for the transformation of physical and chemical energy, but also a mental machine using mental conditions for the transformation of libido." [29] In later writings, Jung concluded that both material and psychic energy stem from a third, prematerial, *brute* element.

One of the main principles of Jung's theory is the *principle of opposites*, or dialectics. Life is construction and destruction, creation and decay, waking and sleeping. It is a cosmic principle, reminiscent of the tenets of the ancient Greek philosopher Heraclitus and the idealistic German philosopher Hegel. It is the dialectic law of development through opposites, through the swinging from one extreme to the other, from a thesis to its antithesis. After oscillation comes stability; the deeper the conflict, the more profound the stability.

This law serves as the guiding principle of the human mind. "Everything human is relative, because everything depends on a condition of inner antithesis; for everything subsists as a phenomenon of energy. Energy depends necessarily on a pre-existing antithesis, without which there could be no energy. There must always be present height and depth, heat and cold, etc., in order that the process of equalization—which is energy— can take place. All life is energy, and therefore depends on forces held in opposition." [30]

The greater is the conflict between the opposites, the more mental energy comes out of them. Discharge of energy is caused by the state of inner conflict within a given system. The distribution of mental energy follows the principles of equivalence and entropy. The principle of conservation of energy, or *equivalence*, states that energy removed from one area will appear in another. Jung's theory is a faithful exposition of this principle. His principle of *entropy* is borrowed from the second law of thermodynamics. If one part of the personality is charged with a heavy load of libido, and another with a low load, libido will move from the former toward the latter.

[29] Carl C. Jung, *Contributions to Analytical Psychology*, Harcourt, Brace, 1928, p. 46.
[30] Jung, *Two Essays on Analytical Psychology*, p. 78.

The two main rules of libido movements are *progression* and *regression*. When the opposite forces within the system are balanced and the psyche is in a state of equilibrium, the libido moves smoothly from the unconscious layers of personality toward the conscious in the process of progression. "During the progression of the libido the pairs of opposites are united in the coordinated flow of psychical processes. Their working together makes possible the balanced regularity of these processes, which, without this reciprocal action, would be one-sided and unbalanced." The individual whose libido is in state of progression experiences the feeling of pleasure, happiness, and well-being. Jung calls it the "vital feeling."

In some situations the progression of the libido is thwarted. Dammed up, its flow is stopped. The opposites united in the flowing libido fall apart. Inner conflict mounts, great amounts of energy are generated, and "the vital feeling that was present before disappears and in its place the psychic value of certain conscious contents increases in an unpleasant way; subjective contents and reactions press to the fore and the situation becomes full of affect and favorable for explosions."[31]

Symbols

Psychic energy, the libido, can be utilized in more than one way. Freud saw the basic drive in sex. Jung saw it in self-preservation. Food intake, according to Jung, is the primary factor. The child enjoys sucking not because sucking is a presexual function, but because it is necessary for self-preservation. The child's interest in the mother is not sexual but nutritional, as the mother is the child's provider.

Jung did not deny the analogy between the rhythmical movements in sucking and in intercourse. However, he drew a clear-cut line. Food intake is the primary function of sucking; here Jung was at great variance with Freud.

Mental energy is used primarily for survival functions, but once biological needs are satisfied, the surplus libido is transformed into cultural and spiritual phenomena. "The psychological machine which transforms energy is the symbol." "Symbols are the manifestation and expression of the excess libido. At the same time they are transitions to new activities, which must be specifically characterized as cultural activities in contrast to the instinctive functions that run their course according to natural law."[32]

The symbol is a *libido analogue*, or libido equivalent, which transforms libido from its biological, physiological service of the organism into cultural activities.

Signs and words communicate what is already known. Symbols interpret the unknown. One may use the cross as a sign representing divine love, but "the interpretation of the Cross is Symbolic, which puts it above all imaginable explanations, regarding it as an expression of an unknown

[31] Jung, *Contributions to Analytical Psychology*, p. 35.
[32] *Ibid.*, p. 53.

and yet incomprehensible fact of a mystical or transcendent, i.e., psychological character, which simply finds its most striking and appropriate character in the Eros." [33]

Symbols emerge in the unconscious part of the human psyche. They
are formed spontaneously, never thought out consciously. They may come
to the conscious by the force of intuition or revelation and, if accepted by
the ego, may become a major guiding force in the individual's cultural activities and creativeness.

The Conscious

The psyche is composed of three parts: the conscious, the personal unconscious, and the collective unconscious. The conscious and the unconscious are opposites that balance each other in *reciprocal relativity*. The tension between the conscious and unconscious parts of the mind sets free
psychic energy.

In our times, the conscious part of the personality has been unduly
overstressed, said Jung. The conscious forms the upper floors of a sky-
scraper, while the unconscious forms its lower floors. Conscious without
unconscious would be suspended in the air and dangerously detached from
the basic unconscious elements of human personality. A nervous breakdown is inevitable in such a case.

The conscious in Jung's theory plays a secondary role as compared to
the unconscious. The conscious is useful in adjustment to the environment.
"The essence of consciousness is the process of adaptation which takes
place in the most minute details. On the other hand, the unconscious is
generally diffused, which not only binds the individuals among themselves
to the race but also unites them backwards with the peoples of the past and
their psychology." [34]

The central part of the consciousness is endowed with a high degree of
continuity, and is called by Jung the *ego*. The ego represents the conscious
and fairly consistent attitudes of the individual toward the outer world.

Dreams and the Personal Unconscious

The personal unconscious is the superficial layer of the unconscious. It
encompasses all the forgotten memories, subliminal perceptions, and suppressed experiences. In addition, it contains "fantasies (including dreams)
of a personal character, which go back unquestionably to personal experience, things forgotten or repressed." [35]

[33] Carl G. Jung, *Psychological Types*, Harcourt, Brace, 1923, p. 502.
[34] Jung, *Psychology of the Unconscious*, p. 199.
[35] Carl G. Jung and Carl Kerenyi, *Essays on a Science of Mythology*, Bollingen Series, XXII,
    Pantheon, 1949, p. 102.

Dreams represent both the personal and the collective unconscious. Freud believed that dreams represent a repressed wish; Adler introduced the idea that dreams foreshadow our future actions. Jung accepted both interpretations, but apparently his favorite interpretation went even beyond Adler's theory and he often interpreted dreams as prophetic anticipations of the future.

Jung developed the method of study of the unconscious by *free word association*. His "discrete-stimulus" method consists of an analytical study of the significance of individual associations. He used a list of one hundred stimulus words chosen and arranged in such a manner as to stir the most common emotions.

The subject is told to respond to each word with the first word that comes to his mind. The examiner records the response as well as the time required for the response. If the stimulus word is not connected with an emotional complex in the individual, he will be able to respond quickly with some other word.

Certain types of responses were regarded by Jung as indicative that the stimulus had aroused an emotional response. Even normal persons in a test with one hundred words would show some emotional reactions, but too many unusual reactions indicate an unstable person. Further analysis of these unusual reactions may give an indication concerning the emotional complexes. The reactions that are supposed to be indicators of emotional tensions are as follows:

1. A *delayed reaction* to a stimulus word indicates that a complex has been touched. A person who is excited cannot think, not because he is incapable of thinking, but because the excitement interferes.

2. *Multiple responses*, that is, responses which use many words, show the inability to control reaction. Some examples of this type of response are:

STIMULUS WORD	RESPONSES
To quarrel	Angry—different things—I always quarrel
To marry	How can you marry?—reunion—union
To sin	This idea is quite strange to me—I do not recognize it

The subject responds quickly with a word, then he fears he may give the experimenter some clue to his excitement, so he attempts to cover his confusion with other responses; people often chatter when they are confused.

3. A *personal response* to an objective stimulus shows a tendency to extend the ego. The following illustrate personal responses:

STIMULUS WORD	RESPONSE
To dance	Love it
Luck	Don't believe in it
Money	Poor, wish I had some

4. *Repetition of the stimulus word* in the association experiment indicates that the word has struck some complex and that the repetition is a defense, a pause to regain poise before a response is made.

5. *Perseveration* means giving the same response to the most varied stimulus words. This indicates that there is a dominant complex which many irrelevant words set off. For example, in the list of one hundred words a patient gave the response *long* ten times to the stimulus word when it was not at all logically connected with the word. Investigation showed that the word *long* was related to her difficulty. She and her husband worked a *long* time to save money to build a home. When they began building after a *long* period of time, they lost their money. They would have to wait a *long* time before saving enough money again. But she was getting old and it would not be *long* before she would be too old to enjoy a home.

6. When the stimulus word strikes a complex, the subject may defend himself by responding with a *superficial association;* the subject may name anything that happens to be in sight.

7. Probably as significant as any of the complex indicators is the *failure to respond* at all. When the patient waits a number of minutes and finally says that he cannot think of a thing, it is fairly good evidence that a definite emotional blocking has been encountered.

8. *Failure of reproduction* often shows emotional tension. It is useful to go through the entire list of one hundred words a second time in order to determine the number of responses that are different on the second trial. When a response is different, the indication is that an emotionally accentuated complex has been touched. A person very easily forgets what he has said under an emotional stress and is even likely to contradict a statement so made. Jung stated that in his experience a normal person has no more than 20 percent different responses on the reproduction test, while abnormal persons have from 20 to 40 percent.

9. *Accessory emotional reactions*—stammering, blushing, clearing the throat, sighing, weeping, laughing, acting surprised—indicate that a complex has been touched off. The meaning of the particular emotional reaction is not usually apparent, however, and care should be exercised in drawing an inference from it.

Jung's method is used to throw light on the nature and significance of the different unconscious complexes.

The Complexes

In Freud's theory and cathartic method there was room for a concept representing a load of energy attached to an unconscious wish. It was the *complex,* such as the Oedipus complex or the Electra complex.

Jung went farther in assigning independent, "autonomous life" to the complexes. The conflict between the conscious and unconscious parts of the psyche generates psychic energy; this energy cannot be placed under the control of the consciousness, and units so loaded with mental energy thus start their independent life.

These units of energy, set free, attract ideational content and form independent entities or constellations, or *complexes*. Complexes are *autonomous partial systems* in the human mind; they form split personalities within a given personality; they indicate relatively independent inclinations within the same individual.

In dreams, these separate inclinations appear in the disguise of characters. It is as if the dreamer were experiencing the various characters that exist in his mind beyond his control. These "psychic splits" are universal; each individual is composed of several relatively independent individualities. Only when thse complexes get too far apart from each other and from the rest of psyche is mental health jeopardized. When a complex reactivates elements of the deepest layers of the unconscious, the archetypes, and takes over control of the personality, a psychosis has developed.

One of these complexes is *persona*. *Persona* is Latin for "mask." Actors had to wear different masks for different plays; analogously, said Jung, each individual wears different masks playing different roles in relation to different people. The same man is a son to his father, a husband to his wife, an employer to his employees, a father to his children. In each situation he puts on a different mask. He can never be the totality of all his conscious and unconscious forces, and in each situation another part of his personality comes to the force. The various relationships elicit different responses, and the degree of consistency in the different masks of one person depends on the inner integration.

It is worthwhile to mention here that Jung's persona resembles James's social self and also G. H. Mead's social roles, J. L. Moreno's role playing, and H. S. Sullivan's self (cf. Chapters 9 and 16). Jung's persona represents the conscious attitude of the individual, the mask that he wears when he faces others. It is balanced by the unconscious; whoever tries to be too moral experiences powerful pressures from the opposite unconscious forces. Whenever the persona moves too far from its unconscious foundations, the unconscious forces will burst out and overthrow it.

The persona represents the conscious attitudes of the individual toward the outer world. It must be, therefore, related to the ego. But the *ego* in Jung's theory is merely a certain "condition of consciousness." It is a "complex of representations which constitutes the centrum of any field of consciousness and appears to possess a very high degree of continuity and identity." Accordingly, the ego forms the kernel of one's *persona*, which represents the attitudes of the individual toward the outer world. The strong, domineering qualities in the individual gather together in the conscious ego and the ego is drawn into the persona. In some cases the entire "conscious area as seen by others, i.e., the persona, becomes identical with the ego. This is the case with individuals whose entire life is guided by a certain focal idea or talent."[36]

The weak and least adapted tendencies also gather together to form an unconscious complex, the *shadow*. The shadow contains the urges and wishes which cannot be approved of by the conscious ego. It is a personality within a personality. The shadow represents the forbidden sexual and aggressive impulses; it forces the individual to irresponsible and dangerous actions; it embarrasses the ego by tactless and stupid blunders; it gives the individual unpleasant, often weird feelings. The shadow has its own psychic energy. If strong enough, it may pierce the conscious and take over control. In such a case, a mental disorder develops.

One of the main tendencies of the shadow is projection. "We still attribute to the 'other fellow' all the evil and inferior qualities that we do not like to recognize in ourselves. That is why we have to criticize and attack him."[37]

The shadow is the opposite of the ego and usually functions on the level of the personal unconscious. The deeper the shadow penetrates into the unconscious, the more opposite it becomes to the ego. The ego of a man is represented in his persona as a male figure; his shadow takes on the female form, becomes the feminine component in his personality, his *anima*. All men have feminine elements in their psyche and all women have masculine elements. The unconscious, the shadow, of a woman is represented, accordingly, by the male component, or *animus*.

The Collective Unconscious

Jung believed that acquired traits and cultural patterns are transmitted by heredity. In each individual, he wrote, there are hidden "the great 'primordial images,' those potentialities of human representations of things, as they have always been, inherited through the brain structures from one generation to the next." Jung did not deny that besides these collective deposits, which contain nothing specifically individual, the psyche may also inherit "memory acquisitions of a definite individual stamp."

These primordial images are called *archetypes*. Jung was much influenced by the French social scientists Émile Durkheim and Lucien Lévy-Bruhl and was especially impressed by the idea of *l'esprit du corps* ("collective spirit"). This collective spirit must be unconscious and manifests itself through the individual mind.

The contents of the archetype nature are manifestations of the collective unconscious. "They do not refer to anything that is or has been conscious, but to something *essentially unconscious*. In the last analysis, therefore, it is *impossible* to say *what they refer to*. . . . The ultimate core of meaning may be circumscribed but not described. Even so, the bare circumscription de-

[36] Jung, *Psychological Types*, p. 564.
[37] Carl G. Jung, *Modern Man in Search of a Soul*, Harcourt, Brace, 1933, p. 163.

notes an essential step forward in our knowledge of the pre-conscious structure of the psyche, which was already in existence when there was as yet no unity of personality."[38]

The archetypes represent the memories of a race and are unconscious forces in the deep layers of the mentality of the members of a race. Since Jung believed in the heredity of acquired traits and culture patterns, he ascribed to certain races inherited patterns.[39] In German patients, he observed archetypes stemming from the pre-Christian era; the symbol of the ancient German god Wotan which expresses violence and cruelty was found in the unconscious of German people.

In later writings, Jung came out with the idea that the psychic did not develop out of organic matter but that there is a primal, cosmic, prematerial, prephysiological level. At this level the cosmic elements gradually developed into material and spiritual, biological and psychic elements. At this prematerial and prepsychological level, autonomously functioning systems developed the archetypes.

These autonomous, functioning systems are deeply seated in human nature. They are never conscious. When the total mental structure breaks up, they "possess" the mind.

In normal cases, these systems are expressed by symbols. Symbols can move up to the conscious, carrying the elements of the archetypes and the collective unconscious, as expressed in mythology. Mythology contains the dreams of mankind. Jung called the collective symbols *motifs* and believed that the motifs were the links between the individual and the cosmos.

The archetypes form the core of autonomous partial systems, independent of consciousness. Once an archetype is stirred up, it develops into an autonomous partial system and takes "possession" of an individual; the individual is mentally sick. These autonomous systems are *demons* and overwhelm the mind with their irresistible power.

Archetypes play an important part in Jung's theory of personality. An archetype is a universal idea that makes up part of our collective unconscious. It is always an inherited idea.

God is an archetype. We do not know the ultimate derivation of this archetype any more than we know the origin of the psyche, which is our total personality. Men always worshiped the sungod who gives warmth and light. Jung did not prove or disprove the existence of God; the archetype of the hero does not prove the actual existence of a hero. Jung believed that all religions are different methods of stating the same idea of God as a symbol of the psychic energy which carries a tremendous load of libido.

There are many archetypes, appearing under different names in the various mythologies; among them are the archetype of the mother, the Old Wise Man, which personifies past experience, and the birth archetype.

[38] Jung and Kerenyi, *Essays on a Science of Mythology*, p. 104.
[39] Jung has been often accused of a friendly attitude toward the racist philosophies of the Nazis.

One of the archetypes is the child hero. The child Moses is saved out of the waters of the Nile; the child Christ was hidden by Mary and Joseph. The child symbolizes the emergence of the self; the libido regresses into the unconscious, enters the womb (in a symbolic analogy to sex), and emerges again in childbirth. "The 'child' is born out of the womb of the unconscious, begotten out of the depths of human nature, or rather out of Living Nature herself. It is a personification of vital forces quite outside the limited range of our conscious mind; . . . a wholeness which embraces the very depth of Nature. It represents the strongest, most ineluctable urge in every human being, namely the urge to realize itself."[40]

The Self

Jung was indefatigable in the development of his theory, and his later writings add so much to his earlier works that one wonders whether his work can be presented as one logical system.

In two erudite volumes, entitled *Aion* and *Psychologie und Alchemie*, Jung apparently accepted the idea that alchemists knew more psychology than any psychologists could have known. Jung believed that the "base" and "noble" metals in alchemy stand for base and noble elements in the human mind, that is, unconscious and conscious respectively. Just as the alchemists tried to transform the base metals into gold, the human psyche performs the *unifying function* of merging unconscious and conscious.

This unifying function is relegated in Jung's later works to the anima. In his former writing, anima was just one of the complexes; later it became the symbol of the entire unconscious and of all archetypes.

Whenever the individual is capable of raising the unconscious, powerful, libido-loaded, miraculous, *mana*-like anima from the unconscious into the conscious, the total personality undergoes deep and profound changes. The anima, elevated from unconscious into conscious, loses its tremendous load of libido. It becomes depotentiated and loses the power of *possession*.

The mental energy released by the now conscious anima is free, unbound. It is a tremendous quantity of energy which is neither conscious nor unconscious. This libido becomes the central point of personality between the conscious and the unconscious and is called *self*. The self, said Jung is his *Two Essays*, "has come into being only very gradually and has become a part of our experience at the cost of great effort. Thus the self is also the goal of life."[41]

The conflicting elements of conscious and unconscious come to harmony in the self. This integration of personality through the emergence of self is found in the art and religion of several people, especially of the Far East. It is represented by the *Mandala* symbol, in the form of a square or a circle with a central point. Mandala, according to Jung, represents the reconciliation of opposites, the fusion of the conscious and the unconscious.

[40] Jung and Kerenyi, *Essays on a Science of Mythology*, p. 123.
[41] Jung, *Two Essays on Analytical Psychology*, p. 268.

The various complexes and systems within the personality strive toward expansion and expression. If one of them attracts too much libido, the other centers will oppose it and stir inner conflict. In normal individuals proper outlets are provided for the various aspects of personality. The process by which development of the respective parts of the personality is facilitated is called *individuation*. The aim of individuation is "to free the self from the false wrappings of the Persona on one hand, and from the suggestive power of the unconscious image (i.e., the anima) on the other."[42]

This diversifying individuation is a step forward toward integration of the personality and development of the *self*. The *transcendent function* takes place by which the *already differentiated systems unite into one whole*.

"If we picture the conscious mind with the ego as its center, as being opposed to the unconscious, and if we now add to our mental picture the process of assimilating the unconscious, we can think of this assimilation as a kind of approximation of conscious and unconscious, where the center of the total personality no longer coincides with the ego, but with a point midway between the conscious and unconscious. This would be the point of a new equilibrium, a new centering of the total personality, a virtual center which, on account of its focal position between conscious and unconscious, ensures for the personality a new and more solid foundation."[43]

No individual is born with the self. The self gradually develops out of inner conflicts, in the years of trial and experience. Jung rejected Freud's theory of developmental stages but suggested dividing the span of human life as follows:

1. The first five years of life are the years of self-protection. The libido is invested in the growth and development of the basic skills, like walking and talking, necessary for survival.
2. Around the age of five, libido flows into the sexual values, reaches its peak around the teen age, and leads the individual in choosing a mate, forming a family, and establishing himself in his bread winning occupation. The individual is extraverted, vigorous, outgoing.
3. In the late thirties or early forties, great changes take place. The individual turns gradually toward spiritual and philosophical values; he becomes introverted, and interested in religious, moral, and spiritual values.

Four Functions

Life energy can take the form of *rational* processes determined by what Jung called "objective values," that is, activities which are verifiable in terms of logical anaylsis. Or it may take the form of *irrational* processes, determined chiefly by "accidental perceptions," chance, and more or less il-

[42] *Ibid.*, p. 185.
[43] *Ibid.*, p. 219.

logical associations. Both cases are manifestations of the movements of the libido.

The rational process is divided into two fundamental functions: *thinking* and *feeling*. In parallel fashion, the irrational is divided into *sensation* and *intuition*. The former functions are dominated by reasoning and judgment, the latter by intensity of perceptions but not by rational judgment. Sensation is the first reaction of the individual to the outer world; then comes *thinking* or "interpretation of that which is perceived"; next comes *feeling* or "evaluation of the perceived object"; last comes *intution* or the "immediate awareness of relationships." Furthermore, "sensation establishes what is actually given, thinking enables us to recognize its meaning, feeling tells of its value, and finally inutition points to the possibilities of the whence and whither that lie within the immediate facts. In this way we can orientate ourselves with respect to the immediate world as completely as when we locate a place geographically by latitude and longitude."[44]

Thinking and sensation are masculine personality traits, while intuition and feeling are feminine, but each individual is capable of all four functions. Usually one of them is *dominant* in a given individual. The dominant function is carried by a great load of the libido energy into the conscious part of his personality and eventually, through fusion with his ego, becomes the guiding principle in his life. The entire mental life of an individual revolves around the dominant function. For example, all men use feeling for setting up the evolution criteria, but the "feeling type" will relate his entire life to this function. The dominant function occupies the center of the conscious, and its opposite, in this case "thinking," becomes necessarily unconscious. Any function on the unconscious level is undifferentiated, merged with other functions, and diffused. When the function is carried by the libido from the unconscious into the conscious it becomes *differentiated*, that is, purified, separated from the opposite function. Usually the function which guarantees the most success, a talent, becomes dominant and differentiated.

The opposite function loses its load of energy to the dominant function. If, as a result of the drain of energy by the dominant function, the opposite function becomes exceedingly impoverished, it goes deep down to the lowest levels of the unconscious, stirs the archetypes, and leads toward mental disorder. The autonomous partial systems will then take possession of the human mind.

Introversion and Extraversion

"When the orientation to the object and to objective facts is so predominant that the most frequent and essential decisions and actions are determined not by subjective values but by objective relations, one speaks of an

44 Jung, *Modern Man in Search of a Soul*, p. 107.

extraverted attitude. When this is habitual, one speaks of an extraverted type. If a man so thinks, feels and acts, in a word, so *lives,* as to correspond *directly* with objective conditions and their claims, whether in a good sense or ill, he is extraverted.

"His entire consciousness looks outwards to the world, because the important and decisive determination always comes to him from without. But it comes to him from without only because that is where he expects it. . . ."[45]

In extraversion the libido moves toward the outer world. Accordingly, the extravert is guided by the impression the external world leaves on him. All interests, values, and attitudes are directed toward his physical and social environment.

The introvert, on the contrary, "selects the subjective determinants as the decisive ones. This type is guided, therefore, by that factor of perception and cognition which represents the receiving subjective disposition to the sense stimulus. . . . Whereas the extraverted type refers pre-eminently to that which reaches him from the object, the introvert principally relies upon that which the outer impression constellates in the subject."[46] Accordingly, the introvert is self-centered and much involved with his inner world.

Extraversion and introversion can be organized around one of the fourfold features: thinking, feeling, sensation, and intuition. A brief description of each type of individual follows.

1. *Extraverted Thinking Type.* Accepts the world from the senses and uses his sensory impressions as a basis for logical analysis and construction of his reality. He is concerned with facts and their classification.

2. *Extraverted Feeling Type.* Determined by the feeling for the external object. The individual tends to feel and act according to the demands and expectations of the situation; he is able to establish friendship with others.

3. *Extraverted Sensation Type.* Conditioned by and oriented to the sensory and/or concrete features of a given object. He is the "realist" and "materialist."

4. *Extraverted Intuition Type.* The external object does not so much control his perception or sensation as offer him a suggestion for elaborating the possibilities of the object at the moment as something to manipulate and control.

5. *Introverted Thinking Type.* Marked by ideational patterns which have been almost completely organized subjectively until they suit the individual (so that he tends to become indifferent). He can have some success in social contacts.

[45] Jung, *Psychological Types,* p. 417.
[46] *Ibid.,* p. 472.

6. *Introverted Feeling Type.* Dominated also by the "subjective factor." This individual lives within his own internal world of emotions and feelings. He is the daydreamer or the silent person who is at peace with the world.
7. *Introverted Sensation Type.* Though attending to the external world, his perceptions are dominated by his subjective internal state. The creative artist may have this kind of character make-up.
8. *Introverted Intutiion Type.* Directs his attention to imagery. These images are clues to his activity. He lives within himself and may be the so-called dreamer, religious prophet, fanatical crank, or artist.

Jung stated that type differences can be modified, as when a natural-born introvert is forced by circumstances into extraversion, but he believed that such transpositions are rather superficial.

Most people display both extraversion and introversion. They are called *ambiverts.* According to Jung, the four functions of thinking, feeling, sensation, and intuition appear in all individuals, but one of these modes predominates. A particular person's response to the world and to himself might be said to be typically or characteristically in this or that modality, which does not imply an absence of the other features. Which of these extremes one should strive for is a question of norms and values. In our society, despite the culturally approved stimuli to become extraverted, we find a place for some introverts—though we are likely to consider them a bit "queer" or perhaps divergent from the "best" in our values; doubtless the majority of people fall into the middle range of so-called ambiverts.

History and Culture

The eternal archetypes appear in each epoch in a different guise, but they are always the same primordial images of mankind. Men cannot rid themselves of these archetypes. Historical symbols "arise directly from dreams or at least are inspired by them," especially the deep, great dreams, in which the archetypical symbols appear again and again. The archetypes may become conscious through symbolization. Then they are called *motifs.*

When the archetypes or motifs or autonomous systems penetrate the psyche of groups they cause psychic epidemics or mass psychoses. Mass psychoses revive the deep-rooted archetypes common to a given race and embedded in the unconscious layers of its members.

In support of this theory of the racial unconscious, Jung referred to delusions and hallucinations of the insane, dreams of normal people, and widespread belief in superstition and magical influences. During periods of mental illness, the thinking of modern man tends to be of a prelogical, primitive nature. During sleep, when the lower levels of consciousness are permitted greater expression, the contents of our dreams are not only unreal and illogical but resemble certain bizarre thoughts of primitive man. We converse with animals, fly through the air with ease, and destroy our enemies by a simple gesture. In spite of our present-day rationalism, most of us are inclined to relate our misfortunes to having seen a black cat cross our path. The content of dreams and hallucinations, said Jung, is the same for all members of a given race. So it must be inherited.

Mythology is the anamnesis of a cultural group, a race. It represents the collective memory of a racial and cultural group. Just as a dream relates to the individual's past, mythology relates to the early childhood of a race. The common archetypical elements incorporated in the culture developed by a race, the Etruscans or the Germans, for example, are called *demons*. The demons are archetypes, historical symbols which draw individuals together "as if by a magnetic force, and thus a mob is formed; and its leader will soon be found in the individual who has the least resistance, the least sense of responsibility. . . . He will thus let loose everything which is ready to break forth, and the mob will follow with the irresistible force of an avalanche."[47]

Religion starts as an autonomous system of an archetypical nature. It binds people together in their unconscious. People "live" and experience their religious symbols. The main archetype of religion is God. This archetype symbolizes the life energy and, accordingly, a great amount of mental energy is invested in it.

Under normal conditioning, the conscious and the unconscious, the ego and the shadow are in harmony. Neurosis is a dissociation of personality, a war between the conscious and the unconscious. Neurosis is a downward, regressive moment of the libido. If it goes very deep and stirs the autonomous forces in the unconscious, a psychosis may develop.

Religion, by harmonizing the various aspects of personality, is an important factor in mental health. Modern man is beset by conflicting values and is often unable to reconcile them. Religion represents the unconscious, archetypical elements in harmony with the conscious elements of personality and society.

Concluding Remarks

Of all psychoanalytic theories, Jung's have been the most criticized. For example, in an illuminating and quite objective description of the history of psychoanalytic thought, Clara Thompson wrote about Jung that "his thinking becomes more mystical and he creates a conception of personality which sounds like a rigid obsessional system."[48]

But Jung's method is all but rigid. It seems to be rather inconsistent, often whimsical, and almost haphazard. Jung introduced concepts with an ease which defied any principle of parsimony. In the beginning, the ego was the focal point of the consciousness, but later it became a sort of satel-

[47] Carl G. Jung, *Essays on Contemporary Events*, Kegan Paul, 1947, p. xi.
[48] Clara Thompson, *Psychoanalysis: Evolution and Development*, Hermitage, 1957, p. 168.

lite rotating around the self "very much as the earth rotates around the sun." The persona was originally a conscious complex, the anima an unconscious one. Later on, persona and anima stood for the two entire zones of the conscious and the unconscious respectively. Originally, Jung postulated, the conscious and the unconscious; later he introduced a twilight area, a sort of "demilitarized" zone between the two, where they merge in a rather unexplained way.

Jung originally accepted both causation and purposivism, but in 1955 he added a third category, *contemporariness* of events which supposedly occur at the same time and yet are not casually interrelated.

Jung very often used inconsistent and circular definitions. "The psychological machine which transforms energy is the symbol," he wrote. And later on, "Symbols are the manifestations and expression of the excess libido."[49]

Or consider Jung's definition of the ego: "By ego I understand a complex of representations which constitutes the centrum of my field of consciousness and appears to possess a very high degree of continuity and identity." But, "by consciousness I understand the relatedness of psychic contents to the ego in so far as they are sensed as such by the ego."[50]

Jung's theory was often criticized for being exceedingly involved. In his defense one may say that simplicity does not necessarily correspond to empirical data, nor does complexity necessarily contradict them. Although one may be amazed at each new "Copernican revolution" of the same author, this is still not a reason for refutation of his theories.

The criticism raised against Jung is mainly directed against his arbitrarily, almost dogmatically, set system, which was changed several times almost at will. Despite his tremendous erudition in anthropology and history of culture, Jung displayed a great eagerness to accept analogies as scientific evidence. Consider his enthusiasm for alchemy. Alchemy merges elements, and the human mind merges elements; thus, Jung concluded, alchemy offers the key to psychology. Jung's inquiry into human behavior was guided by the acceptance of mystical beliefs and of what some human had perceived at certain times as being the true picture of the universe.[51]

Jung's greatness lies in the wealth of his studies in the history of mysticism and irrational thinking. His apparent weakness lies in his uncritical enthusiasm for his discoveries. Instead of applying the rational tools of scientific inquiry to the irrational phenomena of the human mind in its ontogenetic and phylogenetic development, Jung accepted these phenomena as scientific truth. One could say that Mandala, alchemy, and pictorial symbolism are products of the human mind; perhaps they represent how the primitive and regressed human mind pictures itself. A schizophrenic may say that his mind *is* a television set controlled by his relatives, whose minds

[49] Jung, *Contributions to Analytical Psychology*, pp. 50, 53.
[50] Jung, *Psychological Types*, pp. 535, 540.
[51] Edward C. Whitmont, *The Symbolic Quest*, Putnam, 1969.

are a sort of remote-control apparatus. The business of scientific inquiry is to find out what made the psychotic think that way or how much symbolic, archaic thought is involved in that presentation. There is no reason to dismiss the statements made by a morbid mind; but it is even less rational to accept them as scientific truth. Freud looked into mythology, analyzed it, and found in it the products of sick and primitive minds. Jung was enchanted by mythology and accepted it as an authentic photographic copy of the human mind. Freud found an analogy between the prelogical thinking of mythology, of psychopathology, and of infancy. Jung accepted the content of mythology as scientific evidence in psychology. Freud exploited myth for scientific purposes; Jung accepted myth as scientific evidence.

In this volume we have carefully avoided saying which theory is true and which false. Actually, no theory is true in the empirical sense (cf. Chapter 15). The aim of this book is the analysis and criticism of the methods used by the various psychologists in ascertaining empirical data and their interpretation. And from this point of view, Jung represents a unique case in contemporary psychological theory, for he and only he accepted intuitive and irrational phenomena on their face value.

Yet Jung undoubtedly offered some valuable observation into the darkest spots of the human mind. His studies in mythology and in mental disorder, especially schizophrenia, contain a wealth of important data. Those acquainted with the way the schizophrenic mind works cannot deny that Jung came across very important archaic elements in the human mind, where psychological factors so easily produce physiological disturbances and vice versa.[52]

Jung observed these phenomena and tried to report them. He reproduced them in the language of schizophrenic thought, using terms such as "possessed," "cosmic," "live symbols," and "demons." He took his findings literally—and left open the questions of whether his observations were correct and whether his interpretations corresponded to scientific analysis.

[52] Albert Kreinheder, "Jung's Contribution to Psychology," in B. B. Wolman (Ed.), *International Encyclopedia of Psychiatry, Psychology, Psychoanalysis and Neurology*, Aesculapius, 1977, Vol. 5, pp. 254–258. See also Benjamin B. Wolman, *Children without Childhood: A Study of Childhood Schizophrenia*, Grune & Stratton, 1970.

8

New Theories in Psychoanalysis

1. Psychoanalysis Modified by Clinical Experience: Orthodox and Unorthodox

Adler's and Jung's disagreements with Freud were on matters of theory and principle. Both Adler and Jung rejected the concepts of Eros and Thanatos, the theory of developmental stages, and the personality model based on the id, ego, and superego.

When Adler and Jung left the ranks of the psychoanalytic movement, psychoanalysis became very much a "school" united in the acceptance of Freud's method and set of principles. Now the entire system, as developed by Freud and his faithful disciples, was put to a continuous clinical test. Freud's theory grew and developed in a clinical setting; it was primarily a system of hypotheses related to growth, development, and malformations in the human personality. Armed with Freud's theoretical and technical principles, scores of psychoanalysts tried to help people. The task was a tremendous one. Psychoanalysis was considered the only method by which human problems could be solved. The clinic was the laboratory and success or failure in the practical task of curing mental patients was considered equivalent to an experimental verification of the theory.

The difficulties faced in therapeutic efforts forced Freud to recast his theoretical assumptions. His associates also had to introduce modifications based on clinical experience. Growing numbers of practicing psychoanalysts joined the ranks of research workers. Each new "case" presented new problems; each unsuccessful therapy called for a revision, or at least a checking of the underlying principles. The area covered by clinical research has been constantly growing, and the empirical data derived from the scrutiny of thousands of life histories have expanded rapidly.

The clinical and theoretical studies went in all directions. Freud did not intend to develop an all-encompassing psychological theory, but the logic of the psychoanalytic system forced his disciples to apply psychoanalysis to practically all aspects of human life. As Gardner Murphy said, "the insights of Freud, with reference to human motivation, impulse control, reality test-ing, and much else besides, are among the most profound ever vouchsafed to an investigator."[1] Motivation, control of emotionality, and perception were the main areas in which new developments took place.

Freud himself was not always in favor of the new developments. Some of them (such as O. Rank's and W. Reich's theories) he overtly rejected. Even before his death in 1939 psychoanalytic theory had been developing and growing, partially along more or less orthodox Freudian lines, and par-tially along non-orthodox lines. Fenichel, Jones, Glover, Anna Freud, Fe-dern, Hartmann, Loewenstein, Kris, and scores of other prominent workers in this field have continued psychoanalytic research in accordance with the main ideas of Freud. Some other disciples of Freud introduced so many and such far-reaching modifications that their theories could no longer be placed under the roof of Freud's theory. What they have in common with contemporary psychoanalysis is common roots only. In accordance with the policy of this book, priority will be given to the new and original theories.

2. EARLY MODIFICATIONS IN PSYCHOANALYTIC THEORY

Anna Freud

Anna Freud's extensive work with children and adolescents enabled her to test psychoanalytic hypotheses about early development. By studying both normal and disturbed individuals she has provided valuable informa-tion regarding metapsychological processes and their relationship to actual behavior.[2]

While Freud had introduced and developed the concept of defense mechanisms in 1894, it was Anna Freud who described these mechanisms in detail.[3] In 1936, she published *The Ego and the Mechanisms of Defence* in which she systematized Freud's concept of repression as well as defining nine other mechanisms of defense. These included regreession, reaction formation, undoing, introjection, identification, projection, turning against the self, reversal, and sublimation (displacement of instinctual aims).[4]

From her own work ". . . Anna Freud introduced and made familiar such constellations as the 'identification with the aggressor,' the asceticism

[1] Gardner Murphy, "The Current Impact of Freud upon Psychology," *American Psychologist*, 1956, *11*, 663–672.
[2] Mark Kanzer and Harold Blum, "Classical Psychoanalysis since 1939," in B. B. Wolman (Ed.), *Psychoanalytic Techniques*, Basic Books, 1967, pp. 94–95.
[3] Benjamin B. Wolman (Ed.), *Dictionary of Behavioral Science*, Van Nostrand Reinhold, 1973, p. 91.
[4] Gertrude Blanck and Rubin Blanck, *Ego Psychology: Theory and Practice*, Columbia University Press, 1974, p. 23.

and altruistic surrender of the adolescent, and phase-specific aspects of denial through fantasy, word, and action."[5]

Otto Rank

Among those who started as orthodox and faithful disciples, but ended in open rebellion and defiance of the basic principles of Freud, was Otto Rank. Rank regarded birth as the most traumatic event in human life and as the major source of an overwhelming anxiety. Any other anxiety in later life was presented by Rank as an outcome of the basic birth anxiety. Since birth is separation from the mother's body, any future separations would revive this anxiety.

The male's desire for intercourse was regarded by Rank as a craving for the mother's womb, but the sight of the birth-giving female organs is also fear producing. The figure of the Sphinx in the Oedipus myth represents the mother symbol, the mother toward whom the man strives and of whom he is afraid, with a fear of being enclosed. The Oedipus complex, says Rank, is a repetition of the primal birth anxiety. "The hero, who is not swallowed by the Sphinx, is enabled, just through the overcoming of anxiety, to repeat the unconscious wish in the pleasurable form of sexual intercourse with the mother."[6]

Both male and female abhor female sexual organs because of association with the birth trauma. If they are not able to overcome this fear, homosexual reactions develop. According to Rank, all homosexuals reexperience the asexual, but libidinal, mother–child, womb–embryo relationship. The masochist seeks to convert the pain of birth into a pleasure by fantasies of being bound and beaten. The sadist has the "unquenchable hatred" of one who has been expelled and he violently forces his way back. The exhibitionist wants to return to a "paradisical" state of nakedness.

Prior to birth, the individual was a whole and united with his mother. He was "bound inseparably with a greater whole" and experienced the feeling of totality and wholeness.

In his postnatal life, the individual has to accept himself as an independent, whole, and "real" entity. What he fears is the fear of life, the fear of becoming an individuality. This fear of *individualization* is the fear of being himself, of making himself different from others.

The striving for independence and the fear of it, the fear of growing and the fear of going back to the womb are, respectively, the fear of life and of death. "This ambivalent primal fear which expresses itself in the conflict between individuation and generation is derived on the one side from the experience of the individual as a part of the whole, which is then separated from it and obliged to live alone (birth) and on the other side from the final

[5] Kanzer and Blum, "Classical Psychoanalysis," p. 95.
[6] Otto Rank, *Trauma of Birth*, Harcourt Brace, 1929, p. 149.

necessity of giving up the hard won wholeness of individuality through total loss in death."[7] Apparently, Erich Fromm is heavily indebted to Rank's idea of the fear of living and being independent.

Paul Federn

Federn was a close associate of Freud's. Federn made a distinction between consciousness and those feelings of unity in continuity, contiguity, and causality in the experience of the individual which he called *ego feelings*. These ego feelings represent the energy that Federn called *ego cathexis*. An aspect of mental content is cathected and felt as *I*. The ego is separated from nonego (id, internal processes, external reality, etc.) by a boundary. Moreover, the ego itself is composed of various states with boundaries separating them. Stimulation which crosses this ego boundary is experienced as object, with the ego or ego feelings being subject. Thus, the ego boundary becomes crucial to the experience of reality. When there is deficient ego cathexis invested in the ego boundary, the self is not able to distinguish between self (subject) and other (object). There is a sense of estrangement from the outside world; the individual is vulnerable to depersonalization states.[8]

This concept of inadequate or weak ego boundaries was a significant contribution to the treatment of mental disorders. Federn was very successful in treating schizophrenia. He found that, contrary to Freud's notions, schizophrenics do develop transference. Freud had postulated that schizophrenia represented a regression to narcissism, a withdrawal of libido from objects and a loss of contact with reality. Federn, on the other hand, believed that schizophrenia was not a withdrawal of object cathexis. He felt that schizophrenics have poorly cathected ego boundaries which prevent an accurate perception of reality. They tend to overcathect objects at the expense of their own egos, which then become impoverished.[9] Therefore, the therapist must help the patient to strengthen his ego boundaries so as to once again perform accurate reality testing and also to repress the id material which has flooded the ego. "He described this process as 'psychoanalysis in reverse,' or the re-repressing of that which was overwhelming the weakened ego."[10]

Federn would interpret the process which caused the patient to misperceive reality rather than interpreting the content of the unconscious material in order to strengthen the capacity for reality testing. Moreover, he

[7] Otto Rank, *Will Therapy and Truth and Reality*, Knopf, 1947, p. 134.
[8] John G. Watkins, "Psychotherapeutic methods," in B. B. Wolman (Ed.), *Handbook of Clinical Psychology*, McGraw-Hill, 1965, pp. 1161–1162.
[9] Benjamin B. Wolman, "Schizophrenia and Related Disorders," in B. B. Wolman (Ed.), *Handbook of Clinical Psychology*, McGraw-Hill, 1965.
[10] Watkins, "Psychotherapeutic Methods," p. 1162.

would help strengthen the ego boundaries by providing the patient with "mother–helper" figures to provide the kind of support and nurturance that enables the infant to develop a normal balance of ego and object cathexis.[11]

Sandor Ferenczi: A New Theory of Instincts

Ferenczi suggested four stages in the development of reality perception. In the prenatal stage, all wishes of the child are gratified; this, therefore, is the stage of *unconditional omnipotence*. The neonate probably feels that all his wishes are satisfied; he has only to wish and the wish will immediately be fulfilled. This is *hallucination–magic omnipotence*. Day by day, the child faces reality and experiences disappointments and frustrations. Gradually, he learns to overcome them by crying and gestures, and *magic gestures omnipotence* develops. Later, the child believes in the *magic of thoughts and words*.[12]

Normally, the child gradually gives up the feeling of omnipotence as the stimuli coming from the outside world, which he cannot master, bring with them some feelings of limitation.

While these observations were accepted by the main psychoanalytic school, Ferenczi made another suggestion, this time diverging from Freud. He mentioned that the patient's attitude toward the analyst is not only a product of transference but reflects a *real* relationship that takes place between the two persons. Thus, the so-called *participation* technique developed.

Freud's therapeutic technique could not be discussed in this book, but it forms an integral part of his system. Transference meant to Freud cathexis of instinctual energy in a state of regression. The patient loves and hates his analyst as if he were a child and the analyst the parental figure. Any other interpretation of the patient–analyst relationship is not merely a modification of the therapeutic technique but a serious deviation from Freud's theory. Obviously, Rank's ideas about will therapy and Ferenczi's participation therapy bring us close to Sullivan's theory.

Ferenczi also deviated from Freud in the interpretation of sexual behavior. Freud clearly distinguished between life and death instincts. To Ferenczi, and after him French and Alexander, sexuality is the channel for all "free-floating pleasure tensions of all organs." Ferenczi distinguished between the "utility function" of each organ and its surplus energy, which is shifted to the genital organ for discharge. According to Ferenczi, sexuality is merely a discharge of all those "accumulated amounts of unpleasure which, side-tracked during the utility functioning of the organs, were left undealt with, undisposed of." And "whenever an organ fails to indulge its pleasure tendencies directly but renounces these in favor of the organism as a whole, substances may be secreted from this organ or qualitative innerva-

[11] *Ibid.*
[12] Sandor Ferenczi, *Contributions to Psychoanalysis*, Badger, 1916.

tions be shifted to other organs and eventually to the genital, it being the task of the latter to equalize in the gratificatory act the free-floating pleasure tensions of all the organs." Therefore, "in ejaculation all those autonomic tendencies (tendency to get rid of a part of the body) are summated, the carrying out of which was neglected by utility functioning." [13]

Apparently, Ferenczi distinguished between useful purposes on one side and useless sexuality on the other. All organs function in a useful way. Their surplus excitation, which cannot be put to any useful purpose, is discharged through sexuality.

Ferenczi's theory replaces Freud's theory of love and hate with a theory of useful and free-floating discharge of energy. Pleasure that serves the needs of the organism is put on one side, and sexual pleasure, which is for its own sake, is put on the other. Furthermore, Ferenczi distinguished between two ways in which the organism satisfies its needs. The first way is the *autoplastic*, or the change of the organism itself. Both ontogenetic and phylogenetic development bear witness to adjustment through inner changes. Living organisms adjust to such conditions as external temperature and external threats to the supply of food by undergoing changes in themselves (their structure, color of skin, actions, etc.). Certain organisms adjust in an *alloplastic* manner, that is, they modify their environment (by digging holes, building houses, etc.).

Apparently, Ferenczi has many keen observations to offer. One may say that in certain situations sexual discharge alleviates a general tension in the organism. What this writer doubts is that Ferenczi's observations justify his generalizations.

The study of the psychoanalytic type of psychological theory is quite impressive for its wealth of data, but it is threatened by its not too rigorous application of the principles of scientific inquiry. This problem will be discussed at length in Chapter 15 of this book, but it must be said here that the ease with which Freud's foes and friends introduce new concepts represents a violation of the principles of scientific caution and thoroughness. Freud himself was quite aware of this danger and was exceedingly cautious in building his personality model. But if Freud's scientific method is open to criticism, the methods of Adler, Jung, Rank, Ferenczi, Klein, Alexander, Horney, Sullivan, Fromm, and others seem to be even more vulnerable (cf. Chapter 15).

Melanie Klein

Melanie Klein, a leading British psychoanalyst of children, accepted Freud's theories but emphasized the aggressive impulses and believed that the formation of the personality structure takes place in the first year of a child's life, in contradistinction to Freud's developmental schedule.

Klein emphasized the importance of the second part of the oral stage,

[13] Sandor Ferenczi, *Thalassa: A Theory of Sexuality*, Psychoanalytic Quarterly Press, 1938.

the oral-aggressive or oral-sadistic. She presented the picture of "an infant from six to twelve months trying to destroy its mother by every method at the disposal of its sadistic tendencies—with its teeth, nails, and excreta and with the whole of its body, transformed in imagination into all kinds of dangerous weapons." [14]

The infant accepts objects by swallowing them or rejects them by spitting them out. Pleasure-producing objects are introjected. This oral sadism of an infant may become intensified by frustrations.

According to Klein, the aggressive impulse is originally directed at oneself. The mechanism of projection enables the child to ascribe his own hostile feelings to his parents. A *paranoid posiition* develops in which the infant acts out his hostile feelings toward his mother.

If the mother gratifies the child's instinctual needs, she helps him to overcome his aggressive impulses. Love and fear combined lead to the formation of the superego. Freud said that the superego develops in the phallic stage; Klein believed that one part of the id turns against the other and inhibits it and that the earliest introjected objects form the core of the superego.

The fear of one's own destructive impulses leads to projection. The child fears the supposedly hostile mother and wishes to swallow her. A new crisis develops, called by Klein the *depressive position*. The infant comes to realize that his mother is both "good" and "bad." After introjection of his love object, the infant must go through a mourning and depressive mood as described by Freud and Abraham. Klein believed that the infant internalizes the "good breast" and the "bad breast." All pleasure is attributed to the good breast, all frustration to the bad, persecuting breast. Oral frustration may elicit the Oedipus complex even at that early stage of human life. Moreover, Klein assumed that at that stage the ego already was able "to project, deflect and distribute desires and emotions, as well as guilt and the urge to make reparations on new objects and interests." [15]

The main area of disagreement between Klein and the other Freudians relates to the former's deviation from that part of Freud's theory which deals with the development of the mental apparatus of id, ego, and superego. It has been a highly controversial issue between Klein and Anna Freud, for Anna Freud's main contribution to the psychoanalytic theory was her volume on the defense mechanisms of the ego. [16]

Apparently, Klein's interpretation of early childhood phenomena goes far beyond empirical evidence. It is, at the present level of evidence, rather difficult to ascribe to an infant awareness of sexuality and Oedipus complex. Moreover, Klein's clinical evidence stems from her work with older children; neither she nor anyone else actually observed the kind of behavior she ascribed to one-year-old infants. Klein's deviation from Freud is an in-

[14] Melanie Klein, *The Psychoanalysis of Children* (2nd ed.), Hogarth, 1937, p. 187.
[15] *Ibid.*, p. 224.
[16] Anna Freud, *The Ego and the Mechanisms of Defense*, International Universities Press, 1946.

teresting speculation rather than an observation, and has to be viewed as such.

W. Ronald Fairbairn

Fairbairn was particularly impressed with Klein's concept of the early structuring of the mind, especially her concept of internalized objects. Based on his own work with schizoid patients, Fairbairn proposed that Freud's libido theory be replaced by a theory of personality development in which the individual's functioning is seen in terms of ego structures created out of experience with objects. Fairbairn maintained that the ego is present from birth but remains relatively unstructured prior to interaction with the environment. Contrary to Freud's definition of libido, Fairbairn felt that libido is the innate tendency of the ego to seek objects and that instincts represent patterns of ego action. For example, aggression is a reaction to frustration and is therefore shaped by the nature of the individual's object relations. Anxiety is a direct, innate response to the absence or loss of an object.[17]

Fairbairn further proposed that unsatisfactory experiences with the mother and her breast leads to the creation of an internal structure or *imago* of the desired "good object." This good object then becomes a means of defense against frustration. However, this internalized object or imago has two aspects, which form two separate internal objects; the satisfying or good object and the rejecting or bad object correspond to the two kinds of experiences that the infant has with the mother. These two object structures are split off from the core of the original unitary ego of the infant, which is still actively involved with the originally internalized good object. The split-off systems are repressed and therefore become relatively closed systems which can then become the basis for future pathological development, depending on the degree of attachment to them and the various ways they are dealt with.[18]

Concluding Remarks on Object Relations Theory

Object relations theory differs from classical Freudian theory on several points. Freudian theory proposes that the ego begins as an undifferentiated structure which becomes unified through development. Object relations theory, on the other hand, states that the ego is whole at birth and becomes deunified, or split, as a result of early negative experiences with objects, particularly with the mother. The object relations theory regards libido as a primary life drive which provides the ego with the energy it needs for

[17] J. D. Sutherland, "Fairbairn, W. Ronald D. (1890–1964)," in B. B. Wolman (Ed.), *International Encyclopedia of Psychiatry Psychology, Psychoanalysis, and Neurology*, Aesculapius, 1977, Vol. 4, pp. 449–450.
[18] *Ibid.*

research of its relatedness to objects, which in turn fosters development. Aggression is not seen as an innate drive but rather as a natural reaction to frustration of the libidinal drive. Finally, the ego structure that emerges after the break up of the original unified ego represents a pattern of ego splitting and the resulting formation of internal ego–object relations.[19]

Object relations theory, with its shift in emphasis to the external environment and the impact of objects on development, became the basis for the work of many British psychoanalysts, such as Michael Balint and Donald Winnicott.[20]

In 1952, before the Medical Society, Winnicott proclaimed that there is no such thing as a baby!

> If you show me a baby you certainly show me also someone faring for the baby, or at least a pram with someone's eyes and ears glued to it. One sees a "nursing couple" . . . before object relations the state of affairs is this: that the unit is not the individual, the unit is an environment-individual set-up. The center of gravity of the being does not start off in the individual. It is in the total set-up. By good-enough child-care, technique, holding and general management the shell becomes gradually taken over and the kernel (which had looked all the time like a human baby to us) can begin to be an individual.[21]

3. EGO PSYCHOLOGY

Heinz Hartmann and His Collaborators

As it became apparent that instinct theory alone could not adequately explain behavior, there was increasing interest in the psychoanalytic investigation of the ego and its functions.[22] In this investigation, Heinz Hartmann has become a central figure and is considered to be the father of modern ego psychology.[23] Hartmann began his theoretical work with the concept of *adaptation*. In his book *Ego Psychology and the Problem of Adaptation*, he defines adaption as "primarily a reciprocal relationship between the organism and its environment."[24] In the context of this relationship, there are two forms of adaptive activity—*autoplastic activity*, or the capacity of the organism to act on itself, and *alloplastic activity*, which is the capacity to ef-

[19] W. W. Meissner, John E. Mack, and Elvin V. Semrad, "Classical Psychoanalysis," in A. M. Freedman, H. I. Kaplan, and B. J. Sadock (Eds.), *Comprehensive Textbook of Psychiatry* (2nd ed.), Williams and Wilkins, 1975, p. 482.

[20] *Ibid.*

[21] Masud Kahn, "Winnicott, Donald W. (1896–1971)," in B. B. Wolman (Ed.), *International Encyclopedia of Psychiatry, Psychology, Psychoanalysis, and Neurology*, Aesculapius, 1977, Vol. 11, pp. 424–425.

[22] Gertrude Blanck and Rubin Blanck, *Ego Psychology*, Columbia University Press, 1974, p. 22.

[23] *Ibid.*, p. 24.

[24] Heinz Hartmann, *Ego Psychology and the Problem of Adaptation*, International Universities Press, 1958, p. 24.

fect responses from the environment.[25] In order to describe autoplastic activity, Hartmann states that "Mental development is not simply the outcome of the struggle with instinctual drives, with love objects, with the superego, and so on. For instance, we have reason to assume that this development is served by apparatuses which function from the beginning of life."[26] Hartmann called these the *apparatuses of primary autonomy*, and with this construct he proposed a major revision in psychoanalytic theory. Freud had described the ego as arising out of that aspect of the id which comes into contact with the outside world. In contrast, Hartmann, with his construct of apparatuses of primary autonomy, was postulating the existence of inborn ego apparatuses such as perception, intention, object comprehension, thinking, language, recall phenomena, productivity, and motor development. In other words the ego (or at least its forerunners) is, like the id, present at birth. Hartmann called these forerunners the *undifferentiated matrix*. "Strictly speaking, there is no ego before the differentiation of ego and id, but there is no id either, since both are products of differentiation."[27] Freud suggested this concept of an undifferentiated matrix in his paper "Analysis Terminable and Interminable," yet it was Hartmann who expanded this suggestion into a logical system.[28]

Hartmann further postulated that with normal development, these inborn apparatuses function in a *conflict-free sphere*, and that only under traumatic circumstances do they become expressive of conflict. In considering normal versus pathological development, Hartmann proposes that normal development is fostered by what he calls the *average expectable environment*, in which the mother, with her need to perform maternal functions, reciprocates the infant's needs in such a way as to prevent traumatic overstimulation. The infant, on his part, brings to this environment his own particular constitutional make-up. Growth then becomes a function of *maturation*, the term Hartmann used for those processes which are purely biological, and *development*, which he delineated as processes which are biological and psychological.[29]

As the organism grows, he engages in what Hartmann refers to as a process of progressive *internalization*, whereby there is increasing independence from the environment as "reactions which originally occurred in relation to the external world are increasingly displaced into the interior of the organism."[30] With this concept of internalization, Hartmann maps out the process by which the infant is gradually able, through participation in the mother–child dyad, to differentiate himself as a self in relation to a world of objects.

[25] Blanck and Blanck, *Ego Psychology*, p. 27.
[26] Hartmann, *Ego Psychology and the Problem of Adaptation*, p. 15.
[27] *Ibid.*, p. 12.
[28] Blanck and Blanck, *Ego Psychology*, p. 28.
[29] *Ibid.*, p. 29.
[30] Hartmann, *Ego Psychology and the Problem of Adaptation*, p. 40.

Through the process which Hartmann called *structuralization*, the various internalizations are organized with the aid of thought processes. These structures are then, in turn, vulnerable to *intrasystemic* conflict as opposed to *intersystemic* conflict.[31]

Another crucial concept introduced by Hartmann is that of *neutralization*. He defined neutralization as the process whereby both libidinal and aggressive energies are transformed from the instinctual to the noninstinctual mode, a transformation which renders these energies available to the ego. This concept is a logical extension of Freud's concept of neutralization. "The capacity to neutralize drive energy, working in a circular, expanding interaction with the capacity to delay drive discharge, places energies for ego building (structuralization) and expanding ego functions at the disposal of the infant."[32] This capacity for neutralizing instinctual energies is already active in an infant as young as three months. The infant "uses the sensation of hunger in conjunction with memory traces of past gratification to summon his mother by his cry, which, by then, has changed from the objectless cry of the neonate to a purposeful one."[33] Object relations are thus developed out of a transformation of energy which has been invested in the drives, to energy available to the ego for investment in negotiation with the environment.[34]

The concept of neutralization further clarified theories of psychosis. While Freud had felt that psychosis represented conflict between the ego and reality, Hartmann proposed that it represented a failure of neutralization, which in turn hindered the ego's ability to organize its various functions and to mediate between the drives and reality. For example, neutralized aggression would be the source of energy for the defensive mechanisms of the ego.[35]

Hartmann further proposed that the development of object relations is a progressive one moving from the objectless stage of primary narcissisms, to the stage in which the object is experienced only in terms of its capacity to fulfill the needs of the infant, to the final, most mature level, the level of object constancy. When object constancy is obtained, the infant maintains a constant mental representation of the object, regardless of its state of need; that is, the mother remains herself regardless of the infant's particular need state.[36]

Starting in the late 1940's, Hartmann worked with Ernst Kris and Rudolf Loewenstein to extend ego psychology in such a way as to further delineate ego functioning beyond its defensive function. To the three existing aspects of Freudian metapsychology—the dynamic, the topographic,

[31] Blanck and Blanck, *Ego Psychology*, p. 33.
[32] *Ibid.*, pp. 33–34.
[33] *Ibid.*, p. 33.
[34] *Ibid.*, p. 34.
[35] *Ibid.*
[36] *Ibid.*, pp. 34–35.

and the economic—they added a fourth, the *genetic*. "Genetic propositions describe why, in past situations of conflict, a specific solution was adopted, why the one was retained and the other dropped, and what causal relation exists between these solutions and later developments."[37] In this way, they addressed themselves to the interactive effects of innate characteristics and life experience.

They enlarged the concept of identification by proposing that in addition to its defensive properties, it is also a part of normal development. They demonstrated that identification is a process of internalization of aspects of objects which enables the individual gradually to achieve independence from the object as internal structures are able to take on more and more of the functions of the object proper. Finally, Hartmann, Kris, and Loewenstein made substantial contributions to the understanding of the superego and its development.[38]

René Spitz

René Spitz is perhaps best known for his studies of hospitalized infants, in which he found that marasmus and death are the fate of the unmothered infant. He has made many contributions to ego psychology. Grounded in a knowledge of animal psychology and ethology, which he has combined with psychoanalytic theory and his own observational data, Spitz concluded that the neonate's innate equipment is "quickened" through interaction with the mother.[39] "From the beginning of life, it is the mother, the human partner of the child, who mediates every perception, every action, every insight, every knowledge."[40] Furthermore, there are critical nodal points in development. At these points asynchronous maturation of the infant's innate equipment demands a complementary adaptive development of psychic structures. If there is a failure in this necessary development, deviant psychic organization results. Failure can be effected by biological factors but the role of the environment is also crucial. Observed forms of infant pathology can be correlated with failures of what Spitz called phase-specific development.[41]

Spitz introduced the term *indicator* to designate those external signs indicating that internal shifts in the infant's organization are taking place. For example, the smiling response is seen when the infant's psyche is organized in such a way that the infant can link affect to intentionality. Stranger anxiety, or the fearfulness exhibited by the infant around the age of eight months in response to a face other than that of the mother, is another indicator; it indicates the attainment of a greater level of object

[37] *Ibid.*, p. 35.
[38] *Ibid.*, pp. 36–37.
[39] *Ibid.*, p. 41.
[40] René Spitz, *The First Year of Life*, International Universities Press, 1965, p. 96.
[41] Blanck and Blanck, *Ego Psychology*. pp. 41–42.

relations whereby the infant can distinguish its mother as separate and distinct from others. With these observations and hypotheses, as well as many others, Spitz demonstrated that mothering is crucial not only to development but to life itself. It was up to another investigator and theorist, Margaret Mahler, to explore and clarify the role of the child in this mother–child dyad.[42]

Margaret Mahler

Through extensive observational studies of mothers and their children, Mahler found a wide variation in individual children's capacities to respond to the mother. On one extreme, there are those infants who cannot engage in the dyadic experience at all, while on the other extreme, there are children who are able to extract essential psychological supplies from an emotionally impoverished environment. Mahler delineated three phases of development culminating in the establishment of identity in approximately the fourth year of life. These are the *autistic*, the *symbiotic*, and the *separation–individuation* phases. During the first weeks of life, the infant is in a state of primitive hallucinatory disorientation in which he experiences his needs, as well as their satisfaction, as part of his own omnipotent *autistic* orbit. He is, in effect, "objectless" and unable to distinguish his own tension-reducing efforts from those of the mother. Gradually, the infant begins to distinguish pain from pleasure. During approximately the second month of life, the infant becomes dimly aware of the presence of a need-satisfying object. This awareness represents the beginning of the *symbiotic* phase.[43] "The essential feature of symbiosis is hallucinatory or delusional, somatopsychic omnipotent fusion with the representation of the mother and, in particular, the delusion of a common boundary of the two actually and physically separate individuals."[44] The autistic and symbiotic phases are regarded as two aspects of that phase which Freud had called primary narcissism.

During the third month of life, the infant becomes more clearly aware that his needs are gratified by the object, or mother, and symbiosis proper begins. Mahler states that optimal symbiotic gratification is essential to development. There can, in some instances, be such an extreme communicative mismatching between mother and infant that the child becomes psychotic. Yet in contrast to theories which focus on the mother as the source of the pathology, that is, the schizophrenogetic mother, Mahler stresses that there are infants who are not able to engage in the symbiotic unit. Under normal conditions, however, there is an adequate symbiotic experience and ego building occurs. The infant is gradually able to disting-

[42] *Ibid.*, p. 52.
[43] *Ibid.*, pp. 52–54.
[44] Margaret Mahler, *On Human Symbiosis and the Vicissitudes of Individuation*, International Universities Press, 1968, pp. 7–8.

uish between inner and outer reality, and the ego operations, such as the capacity to tolerate frustration, develop.[45]

At the point that optimal symbiosis has been achieved, the *separation–individuation subphases* begin to emerge. These subphases are *differentiation, practicing, rapprochement,* and *separation–individuation proper,* or the formation of a discrete identity, separateness, and individuality. Separation, as Mahler uses it, refers not to physical separation but to the child's sense of psychological separateness from the mother. Differentiation begins to occur when the child, supported by the "safe anchorage" of the symbiotic unit and propelled by maturational forces such as those involved in locomotion, begins to move beyond the symbiotic unit. Then, from about ten to sixteen months, the child now fully engaged in exploring his environment with greater and greater physical mobility experiences more and more physical separation from the mother. Mahler calls this subphase practicing. By approximately eighteen months, the child is experiencing an increasing awareness of physical separateness. He enjoys his autonomous capacity and his ability to engage in semantic communication, and representational thought leads to the experience of object constancy. This experience interrupts the child's relative obliviousness to his mother's presence and he enters the rapprochement subphase in which he seeks to reassure himself of the continuation of the mother's love and concern for him. If the mother has come to enjoy the increased freedom accompanying the child's independence during the practicing subphase and rebuffs the child's efforts toward rapprochement, a lifelong pattern of disappointment and depression can begin. Failure to successfully undergo the separation–individuation subphases can produce borderline personally organization. If, however, the symbiotic phase and the separation–individuation subphases are experienced adequately, the child will be seen to achieve a stable, separate identity, and the only form of pathology to which the child may still be vulnerable is neurosis.[46]

Edith Jacobson

Edith Jacobson's theoretical work is along different lines than that of Spitz or Mahler. She attempted to enlarge on the concept of the *undifferentiated matrix* which exists prior to the development of the ego proper. She makes a distinction between the *ego*, which is a structure, and the *self*, which is the totality of the psychic and bodily person, and *self representations*, which are "the unconscious, preconscious and conscious endopsychic representations of the bodily and mental self in the system."[47] Jacobson uses the term representations to distinguish between self and object as they are experienced and self and object as they exist in reality. The

[45] Blanck and Blanck, *Ego Psychology*, pp. 54–58.
[46] *Ibid.*, pp. 58–60.
[47] Edith Jacobson, *The Self and the Object World*, International Universities Press, 1964, p. 19.

infant forms his self images in response to the pleasurable or unpleasurable quality of his experiences with the environment. The same holds true for object representations, and it is not until more mature structuralization occurs that these representations become stable and unified. When this stabilization and unification fails, healthy development is impaired.[48]

Otto Kernberg

Otto Kernberg has focused his work on the description and exploration of the various types of pathology which are determined by abnormal development of internalized object relations, a position which connects him with the work of Hartmann and the other theorists described in this section. He is rapidly becoming a leading writer in the area of personality disturbance which he calls the borderline personality organization. In his work, he has attempted to develop a theoretical position which integrates psychoanalytic instinct theory with ego psychology.

Instincts are first expressed as inborn behavior patterns, while the functions of the mothering object and interpersonal interactions result in the internalization of object relations which in turn organizes structuralization. Kernberg postulates four stages of development that take place during this process. The first stage precedes the development of undifferentiation of self–object. It corresponds closely to stage which others have called primary narcissism, nondifferentiation, or autism. Pathological arrest or cessation during this period would lead to psychosis.

During the second stage, there is a consolidation of the undifferentiated, all-good self–object image which corresponds to positive experience. Simultaneously, there arises out of painful experiences a separate all-bad self–object representation. But there is not yet any differentiation between self and object, and only rudimentary ego boundaries exist. Fixation or regression to this stage would also result in psychotic symptomatology, but with a potentially better prognosis than fixation or regression to the first stage.

In the third stage of development, ranging from six to eighteen months of age, there is a differentiation between self images and object images which allows for the development of integrated ego boundaries and facilitates the differentiation between self and others. There is also a primitive idealization of the all-good mother object which is used as a defense against the experience of contamination of this image by the all-bad image. While the splitting of the object into all-good versus all-bad is normal during this phase, it interferes with further integration of self and object representations if it persists. Indeed, continued, and thus pathological, splitting is the central defensive mechanism of the borderline personality organization.

In the fourth stage of development, the all-good and all-bad self and object representations are integrated into a stable and consistent concept of

[48] Blanck and Blanck, *Ego Psychology*, pp. 61–62.

self and object. The individual who manifests the borderline personality organization is unable to enter this stage because of predominance of primitive aggression which is defended against through the mechanism of splitting.[49]

Heinz Kohut

Heinz Kohut, like Kernberg, has focused on preneurotic personality disturbances. He is noted for introducing the concept of narcissistic personality disturbance. This disturbance represents an arrest of development in which a cohesive grandiose self and a cohesive idealized object have been formed. Under normal development conditions, the grandiose self is absorbed and integrated into the overall adult personality, while the idealized object becomes internalized as part of the superego. However, when severe narcissistic trauma such as the loss of or rejection by a parent occurs, the "grandiose self does not merge into the relevant ego content but retains its unaltered form and strives for the fulfillment of his archaic aims."[50] Similarly, if the idealized parent becomes a source of disappointment, the existing idealized self–object is not transformed into an internalized, self-regulating aspect of the ego structures. Traumatic disappointment occurs in such instances as when the mothering figure is unable to empathize adequately with the infant, to serve as an auxiliary stimulus barrier, to act as a tension-relieving regulator, or to give the infant the necessary stimulation and gratification to enable him to experience himself as a person. In a healthy mother–child relationship, there is a development of internal structures which perform those functions which the maternal object had originally performed. When severe trauma occurs, development of these structures is impaired.[51]

4. PSYCHOANALYSIS AND STUDIES OF CULTURE

Polyculturalism

Sociological and anthropological considerations form the common denominator of the entire neo-psychoanalytic movement. Almost all neo-psychoanalysts have shifted the emphasis from hereditary aspects to environmental aspects of personality, from the genetic factors toward situationism, and from a monocultural analysis of mankind toward polyculturalism.

Freud himself envisaged the future interest in studies in comparative anthropology and paved the road for them in his volume on *Totem and*

---

[49] *Ibid.*, pp. 74–79.
[50] Heinz Kohut, *The Analysis of the Self*, International Universities Press, 1971, p. 28.
[51] Blanck and Blanck, *Ego Psychology*, pp. 79–83.

Tabu. The interest in cultural anthropology was quite profound among the early Freudians, and as early as 1909, Karl Abraham, Freud's most orthodox and perhaps most brilliant disciple, published a monograph devoted to anthropological studies.[52]

An important contribution to the development of psychoanalytic anthropology is the field studies of B. Malinowski. While conducting his research independently of Freud, Malinowski offered definite support to psychoanalysis. Malinowski studied the culture of the Trobriand Islanders. He found that their Oedipus complex differs from that found in patriarchal families. In the societies described by Freud, Abraham, and others, the son desired the mother and considered the father his rival. In the Trobriand Islands, the father, *tama*, yields his role to his brother-in-law, *kadaju*, the mother's brother. "As soon as the child begins to grow up and take an interest in things outside the affairs of the household and his immediate needs, certain complications arise and change the meaning of tama for him. He learns that he is not of the same clan as his tama, that his totemic appellation is different, and that it is identical with that of his mother. . . . Another man appears on the horizon and is called by the child kadaju (my mother's brother). . . . He also sees as he grows up that the mother's brother assumes a gradually increasing authority over him, requiring his services, helping him in some things, . . . while the father's authority and counsel become less and less important."[53]

Malinowski's studies provided an important support to Freud's theory and at the same time broadened the horizons of psychoanalysis. The empirical studies of primitive cultures corroborated the main concepts of psychoanalytic theory, but they clearly indicated that Freud's developmental stages are greatly dependent on cultural factors.

They raised the question of whether the developmental stages could be modified by one's life experiences within a given culture, as Freud believed, or were merely a product of cultural influences. As will be shown, there is no consensus of opinion on this issue.

The anthropologists Margaret Mead and Gregory Bateson are not psychoanalysts, but they applied the psychoanalytic approach to the study of the Balinese culture. Bateson and Mead described a symbolic courtship dance which reflects the knowledge of the Balinese male that he will eventually "marry a woman whose attitude toward human relations will be exactly that of his mother." Apparently, Freud's theory of the Oedipus complex received strong support in this study. Moreover, "There is a conflict which recurs in each generation in which parents try to force the children of brothers to marry each other; to stay withing the family line and to worship

[52] Karl Abraham, *Dream and Myths*, Nervous and Mental Disease Monograph Series, No. 15, 1913.
[53] Bronislaw Malinowski, *The Sexual Life of Savages in North Western Melanesia*, Routledge, 1929, pp. 5–6.

the ancestral gods while the young people themselves rebel and, if possible, marry strangers. Fathers and brothers may help a boy to carry off a girl who is not kin but no male relative of the girl herself can admit complicity in any such scheme. An abduction elopement is staged . . . dramatized in a frequent plot; that of the prince who attempts to abduct a beautiful girl but through accident gets instead the ugly sister," wrote Bateson and Mead.[54] Always the Balinese man marries a woman who resembles his domineering mother.

Wilhelm Reich: The Character

The man who broke the ground for asciocultural deviation from Freud was Wilhelm Reich. Reich won fame with his studies of the neurotic "character" and "armor," which had a definite sociological slant. He was more Freudian than Freud himself in regard to the importance of libido. To Reich, sexual potency was a criterion of mental health, and sexuality was the main factor in personality structure.

Yet Reich paved the road for a definite deviation from Freud and, for a while, believed in a rapprochement between psychoanalysis and Marxism. Reich noticed that the development of personality types, or characters, depends on the socioeconomic system. Thus, one may consider him the forerunner of Horney, Kardiner, and Fromm. "In connection with the sociological function of character formation we must study the fact that certain social orders go with certain average human structures, or to put it differently, that every social order creates those character forms which it needs for its preservation. In class society, the ruling class secures its position with the aid of education and the institution of the family, by making its ideologies the ruling ideologies of all members of the society. But it is not merely a matter of imposing ideologies, attitudes and concepts on the members of society. Rather it is a matter of a deep-reaching process in each new generation, of the formation of a psychic structure which corresponds to the existing social order in all strata of the population," wrote Reich in 1933.[55] But the man who subordinated personality structure to the economic system was Abraham Kardiner.

Kardiner and Linton: Economic Determinism

In accordance with Freud, Kardiner maintained that the individual's attitudes and values, called by him the "projective system," are shaped in early childhood. The child's early experiences are his child–parent experi-

---

[54] Gregory Bateson and Margaret Mead, *Balinese Character*, New York Academy of Science, Special Publication, Vol. 2, 1942, p. 36.

[55] Wilhelm Reich, *Character Analysis*, Orgone Institute, 1945, Chapter 18 (first published in 1933).

ences. Hitherto, child-rearing practices play the decisive role in shaping personality.[56]

Child-rearing practices are "culturally patterned." Parents apply educational methods formed in their environment which reflect the culture of their environment. Hence, the child-rearing methods used by members of a given society "tend to be similar." This similarity in the parent–child relationship must influence the children and develop in them similar "personality configurations." Personalities of individuals growing in different cultural settings must therefore differ one from another, while in a given society, the members share similar early experiences and develop a similar personality type, called by A. Kardiner and R. Linton the *basic personality type*.

A culture, said Kardiner, consists of an organized collective of humans who have fixed modes of thoughts and behavior commonly accepted by them, such as traditions, religious practices and beliefs, means of earning a livelihood, rules and laws, and child-rearing methods. These fixed modes of thought and behavior are known as *institutions*. Deviation from the common acceptance of these institutions creates disturbance in the individual and in his group.

There are a great many cultures, all of which have institutions that are unique. Yet, different cultures have institutions that are similar to one another, for all these institutions attempt to satisfy definite needs of humans. For instance, the infant's need to be nursed and cared for by the mother is met by all cultures with some degree of uniformity, although the duration of such care varies and the technique of rearing children differs widely. The institution of marriage is universal, although the regulations as to whom and how one marries differ in different cultures.

Apparently, the individual is creator, carrier, and perpetrator of all institutions. An individual in a culture learns about the institutions in his culture by means of contact with other individuals. Thus, Kardiner attempted to discover and analyze the effects of institutions on individuals. How institutions satisfy or frustrate basic human needs and how an individual adapts himself to these institutions were Kardiner's main concerns.

One of the most useful and informative means of obtaining data for these questions is to make systematic and detailed studies of the institutions of several different cultures.

These studies, in which the combined method of projective techniques and life histories was applied, led to a definite deviation from Freud. Although the starting point of Kardiner's studies was psychoanalysis, his conclusions are not psychoanalytic. Consider for example, the impact of social relations on personality structure. Among the Marquesans, the number of men is much greater than the number of women. This situation was conducive to a more favorable position of women, and, accordingly, led to a different development of the male and female personality types.

[56] Abraham Kardiner, *The Individual and His Society*, Columbia University, 1939.

The Oedipus complex, concluded Kardiner, cannot be universal, for in Marquesan society, the father is the protector and caretaker of children of both sexes. The rejecting mother is often regarded as a competitor who takes away the beloved father. Again, the Tanala of Madagascar respect their parents; their repression of hostility resembles the puritan. This is interpreted by Kardiner as the result of an early and strict sphincter control. Tanala babies are carried by their mothers without diapers and if they soil the mother's clothes they are punished. Thus, they arrive at sphincter control at the age of six months. In a study of the people of Okinawa, Moloney found that flexible, permissive, and affectionate infant-feeding methods result in a friendly, cheerful, and secure personality type.[57] Kardiner's conclusion was that personality structure depends on environmental factors rather than on developmental stages.

Oral mastery, wrote Kardiner, does not result from frustration of sucking needs. Finger-sucking and other oral manifestations are not found among the Marquesans, despite the fact that they are usually weaned after a few weeks of sucking. Their mothers are anxious not to lose the beauty of their breasts by prolonged nursing of their babies. According to Kardiner, oral mastery seems to develop from *economic anxiety*. The child who fears famine and is not sure that he will be supported by his parents may develop oral patterns of behavior.

Thus, socioeconomic factors play quite a prominent role in Kardiner's theory. The idea of universality of the developmental stages is replaced by the idea of adjustment to the physical and social environment. Geza Roheim, a leading psychoanalytic anthropologist, remarked that Kardiner oscillates between an economic and a psychological determinism.[58]

Actually, Kardiner did not oscillate, and his point of view was clearly explained. The sexual instinct in man, he wrote, has well-defined characteristics: (1) The satisfaction of the sexual craving can be deferred. (2) It can be vicariously gratified. (3) Its energy (according to Freud) can be deflected into channels other than sexual (by sublimation). However, the need for food cannot be substituted for; its satisfaction cannot be deferred very long; and it is not capable of the process of sublimation.

As Kardiner showed, *food anxiety* plays a leading role in many cultures, and a great many institutions or mores have been elaborated with regard to eating. These mores have influence on *what* kind of food is eaten in a culture, *when* it shall be eaten, and *how* it shall be eaten.

Food anxiety will materially influence the behavior of individuals in any society. The problem is further complicated by the fact that economic pressures are never found singly. That is, there is no guarantee that the same pressure will produce the same effects in different cultures. The reaction to food anxiety may have several elements. Rational efforts may be

[57] J. C. Moloney, *The Magic Cloak*, Montrose, 1949.
[58] Geza Roheim (Ed.), *Psychoanalysis and The Social Sciences*, Vol. I, International Universities, 1947, p. 30.

made to get food, food may be taken from some other person, or hallucinatory gratification of hunger may be obtained by fantasy or dreaming. Several other anxieties may appear, such as the fear of being eaten up.

In our culture there is no generalized food anxiety because the means of production and exchange are under complete control and food is well distributed. The technique for procuring food is part of those social pursuits of the individual which we call "economic." The reaction to food anxiety in our culture is highly individualized because of the differentiation in economic pursuits.

In several cultures food anxiety is a definite problem. There was food anxiety among the Marquesans because the islands on which they lived are subject, from time to time, to droughts which lead to serious crop failures and shortages of drinking water. The rational method for dealing with this food anxiety consisted of storing food in great communal pits and the entire yield of the first crop went into these pits. This kept the Marquesans well prepared for emergencies most of the time. Nevertheless, there is evidence of an exaggerated anxiety about food, according to the anthropologist Ralph Linton. There was, first of all, an overevaluation of eating itself. The emphasis fell on bulk and not on quality of food.

Cannibalism was an important evidence of this food anxiety. There was also a fear of being eaten, which was expressed in many ways and led to a great many different kinds of institutions, the purposes of which were to relieve this fear. It was fear of being eaten which undoubtedly increased the hostility between tribes and the practice of cannibalism.

Although there was eating of enemies because of revenge obligations, there was also plain meat-hunting of enemy tribes for food, especially at times of food shortage. Linton, who collected all this material during a stay of nearly one year in the Marquesas, from 1920 to 1921, stated that there was another indication that cannibalism was not merely ceremonial or practiced for revenge obligations; the Marquesans ate everything, from infants up. Also, there was ordinarily no cannibalism within the tribe, but in time of extreme famine, a priest might designate certain victims who would be killed and eaten.

Marquesan eating habits, and everything else associated with food, showed the effects of the periodic food shortages and the tremendous value placed upon food. For instance, at the age of ten every child went through the ceremony of sanctifying his or her hands. After this, he could prepare food for himself and others. Food was prepared separately for men and women, even cooked at different fires and in different utensils. There were a number of taboos on food. Certain foods could not be eaten by people in certain occupations. Food was one of the few things subject to theft; members of the family would steal food from one another but nothing else.

It can be readily seen, therefore, that food scarcity in the Marquesans led to the development of hypochondriacal characteristics within the personality structures of the individuals in that culture.

The Tanala of Madagascar, with a system of dry rice cultivation, showed little evidence of food anxiety. Linton was in Madagascar in 1928 and made a study of these people. The country in which they live had an elevation of 300 to 400 feet. There were no navigable streams, but the country was well watered. Sufficient soil was available, although it was poor and required ten to fifteen years of fallowing. There was no incentive for any family to raise more than it needed in the way of crops, for crops could be neither sold nor hoarded.

The rice crop was stored by the family. Yet, although there was no famine, every household was equipped with a series of measures of various sizes used to apportion the daily rations to the family members. The old crop always carried over until the time of the next harvest. Though the Tanala had neither ceremonial attitudes nor magic connected with food, there was a rice ceremony which consisted of a small family offering made to the ancestors at the time of harvest. Also, charms were kept in certain villages in the hope of preventing hailstorms and locusts from destroying the rice crops.

Eating habits were quite simple. One meal a day was served in the afternoon. The personal cleanliness of these people was noteworthy. They washed their hands and mouth before and after eating. Each individual had his own eating spoon. However, at meal time the father sat apart in an elevated position and was served separately. His food dish had to be elevated above that of the other members of the family. For this purpose elaborate stands of basketry were made. The oldest son, from the age of four onward, was also served separately. The mother and the other children ate from a common dish. Meat was rarely eaten. In fact, the dream of cutting meat was a bad omen indicating a funeral in the family. Milk was taken only when the cow had more than her calf could use. Even the manure of a cow was not employed in agriculture.

There was little evidence of food anxiety among the Tanala. Their confidence in their ability to control their food supply came mainly from the certainty of their social and organizational aspects. Each individual was so trained in his social role, as well as in the techniques which required no special skill, that he was bound in a system of sanctions and punishments. The father and oldest son of a family exacted subsistence and prestige from the labor of the younger sons. The younger sons were a dependable factor in the system of production, and their diligence was guaranteed by the threat of disapproval of their father. The level of prestige, standing, and status for the younger sons depended on their competing with each other in winning the father's favor. Thus, there was almost complete immobility in status for the younger sons of a family. This created, obviously, tension between the younger brothers against each other and against the oldest son. However, the father's position was too strong for any open hostility. Thus, only two attitudes toward the father were possible, hatred and submission. The hatred was easy to suppress in view of the father's ability to confer favors and the son's ability to collect them. Aggression would usually emerge only when the rewards for submission were withdrawn.

Kardiner's theory represents an application of Freud's principles leading to a definite deviation from Freud's conclusions. Kardiner is still Freudian as far as the personality structure of unconscious, conscious, and preconscious goes and partially so in regard to the mental apparatus. However, Freud's theory of libido underwent most radical changes in Kardiner's studies.

Erik H. Erikson

Erik Erikson is a German psychoanalyst who was analyzed by Anna Freud and who studied with such noted psychoanalysts as Helene Deutsch, Heinz Hartmann, August Aichorn, Edward Bibring, and Ernst Kris. He graduated from the Vienna Psychoanalytic Institute in 1933. Erikson worked as a psychoanalyst of children in Boston at the Harvard Psychological Clinic, and had research appointments at both Harvard Medical School and Yale School of Medicine. His work included observations of "normal" children at the Institute of Child Welfare of the University of California and of Sioux and Yurok Indian children. He worked in collaboration with the anthropologists Scudder Mekeel and Alfred Kroeber and during this period he began to develop his now classic epigenetic, developmental overview of not only childhood but also what he came to see as the whole "life cycle." In his book *Childhood and Society*, he presented his investigations of ego psychology, normal as well as pathological, cross-cultural aspects of development as well as observations of middle-class children, and the nature of the relationship of the individual to his social, economic, and historical environments.[59]

In 1950, Erikson joined the staff at Austen Riggs Center in Stockbridge, Mass. It was out of his work here that his second book *Identity: Youth and Crisis* emerged. In it he outlined his observations of the ways in which adolescents develop a continuous sense of themselves, built on private and individual experiences, biological inheritance, social and cultural history, and the various conditions, both supportive and pathological, of a particular historical era. This book was particularly important in that it proposed that adolescence is more than just an extension of childhood, that it is a crucial period when identity is consolidated.[60]

One of Erikson's most notable contributions is his theory of *eight basic stages of ego development*, covering the entire span of life from birth to death. While roughly paralleling the psychosexual stages proposed by Freud, Erikson's concepts include both the negative and positive aspect of each stage, and he maintains that personality continues to grow and change

---

[59] Robert Coles, "Erikson, Erik Homburger," in B. B. Wolman (Ed.), *International Encyclopedia of Psychiatry, Psychology, Psychoanalysis and Neurology*, Aesculapus, 1977, Vol. 4, p. 370.
[60] *Ibid.*

throughout the eight stages. Moreover, how well the individual masters the problems of one stage will determine how well he is equipped to deal with subsequent stages. A failure to master the problems of one stage can, however, be corrected in subsequent stages, if environmental conditions are positive enough to support this mastery. For example, in the first stage, the oral–sensory stage which spans the first year of life, the infant will, based on his experiences, develop a dominant feeling of trust or mistrust in relation to his environment.

Erikson endeavored to relate child development to sociocultural factors. He sought to identify the criteria "by which the individual demonstrates that his ego, at a given stage, is strong enough to integrate the timetable of the organism with the structure of social institutions."[61]

Erikson characterized the eight stages of man as follows: (1) basic trust versus basic mistrust, (2) autonomy versus shame and doubt, (3) initiative versus guilt, (4) industry versus inferiority, (5) identity versus role confusion, (6) intimacy versus isolation, (7) generativity versus stagnation, and (8) ego integrity versus despair.

Erikson believes that "to understand either childhood or society, we must expand our scope to include the study of the way in which societies lighten the inescapable conflicts of childhood with a promise of some security, identity, and integrity."[62]

During the *first stage* of life, an infant needs continuous care and protection that will enable him to attain a peaceful satisfaction of his basic needs as related to, for instance, the intake of food, bowel movements, and sleep. Motherly care can provide the necessary comfort. "Consistency, continuity and sameness of experience provide a rudimentary sense of ego identity."[63]

The presence or absence of the feeling of security or, as Erikson calls it, trust, is an important factor in mental health. Parents must convey to children the basic feeling of trust. The amount of trust does not depend on the quantity of food given to the child, nor on demonstrations of love, but on the quality of maternal care that "combines sensitive care of the baby's individual needs and a firm sense of personal trustworthiness within the trusted framework of their culture's life style."[64]

The *second stage* ("autonomy versus shame and doubt") is related to muscular maturation of the capacities of holding and letting go (Freud's retention and expulsion). Holding can mean care and protection, but it can also mean restraint and cruelty. Toilet training can lead to a tender care of the infant, or to shaming and doubting him.

> This stage, therefore, becomes decisive for the ratio of love and hate, cooperation and willfulness, freedom of self-expression and its suppression. From a sense of

---

[61] Erik Erikson, *Childhood and Society* (2nd ed.), Norton, 1963, p. 246.
[62] *Ibid.*, p. 277.
[63] *Ibid.*, p. 247.
[64] *Ibid.*, p. 249.

self-control without loss of self-esteem comes a lasting sense of good will and pride; from a sense of loss of self-control and of foreign over-control comes a lasting propensity for doubt and shame.[65]

In the *third stage* ("initiative versus guilt"), the emphasis is on attack and conquest in boys; it is the "phallic–intrusive" mode. In girls, it is making oneself attractive and endearing and, in more aggressive modes, it is "catching."

> Infantile sexuality and incest taboo, castration complex and superego all unite here to bring that specifically human crisis during which the child must turn from an exclusive, pregenital attachment to his parents to the slow process of becoming a parent, a carrier of tradition. Here the more fateful split and transformation in the emotional powerhouse occurs, a split between human potential, human glory and potential total destruction. For there the child becomes forever divided in himself. The instinct fragments which before had enhanced the growth of his infantile body and mind now become divided into an infantile set which perpetuates the exuberance of growth potentials, and a parental set which supports and increases self-observation, self-guidance, and self-punishment.[66]

The *fourth stage*, "industry versus inferiority," corresponds to the child's school age, and the Freudian latency period.

> This is socially a most decisive stage: since industry involves doing things beside and with others, a first sense of division of labor and of differential opportunity, that is, a sense of the technological ethos of a culture, develops at this time. wThere is aE danger threatening individual and society where the schoolchild begins to feel that the color of his skin, the background of his parents, or the fashion of his clothes rather than his wish and will to learn will decide his worth as an apprentice, and thus his sense of *identity*—to which we must now turn. But there is another, more fundamental danger, namely man's restriction of himself and constriction of his horizons to include only his work to which, so the Book says, he has been sentenced after his expulsion from paradise. If he accepts work as his only obligation and "what works" as his only criterion of worthwhileness, he may become the conformist and thoughtless slave of his technology and of those who are in a position to exploit it.[67]

The *fifth stage*, adolescence, is called by Erikson, "identity versus confusion." Physiological revolution is but one aspect of the dangers typical of this stage. The ego has to integrate childhood identifications with the vicissitudes of the libido, with endowed aptitudes, and with social roles and opportunities related to the prevailing culture. The adolescent has to develop his sense of identity in his sociosexual role and in group identification.

The *sixth stage*, "intimacy versus isolation," reflects the problems of young adults. Freud was once asked what a normal person should do well. His answer was short: *lieben* and *arbeiten*; that is, a normal adult is capable of loving and of working. "Satisfactory sex relations," Erikson wrote, "make sex less obsessive, over-compensation less necessary, sadistic controls superfluous."

[65] *Ibid.*, p. 254.
[66] *Ibid.*, p. 256.
[67] *Ibid.*, pp. 260–261.

The *seventh stage* presents the conflict between "generativity and stagnation," or productivity and aridity. An individual's mature age can lead to stagnation, or it can open the best chances for productive work and creativity.

The full realization of oneself in the *eighth stage* is presented dramatically by Erikson as "ego integrity versus despair." Lack of ego integration is signified as fear of death. Integrity of the ego is "a postnarcissistic love . . . he partakes."[68]

Robert Jay Lifton

Robert Jay Lifton, who traces his influences to the psychoanalytic tradition of Erik Erikson and the anthropological and sociological work on national character of Mead, Benedict, and Riesman, has attempted to combine depth psychological and historical perspectives to a description of what he calls "self-process." Lifton states that his emphasis is on change and flux and he therefore objects to words such as character or personality, which he feels are suggestive of permanence. He sees Erikson's use of identity as an attempt to avoid this connotation of fixity or permanence, but Lifton has chosen "self-process" because it emphasizes the notion of flow. The notion of identity does not, for Lifton, describe a state of inner stability, which is no longer possible in a world such as ours in which stability or permanence in the traditional sense no longer exists.[69]

Therefore, influenced by his cross-cultural studies with young Chinese and Japanese, Lifton has become convinced that a universally shared style of self-processing is emerging. This process is derived from three general determinants of human behavior: ". . . the psychobiological potential common to all mankind at any moment in time; those traits given special emphasis in a particular cultural tradition; and those traits related to modern (and particularly contemporary) historical forces. My thesis is that this third factor plays an increasingly important part in shaping self-process."[70]

5. INTERACTIONAL PSYCHOANALYSIS

Benjamin B. Wolman's interactional theory, albeit rooted in Freud's system, introduces several far-reaching modifications in (1) the theory of motivation, (2) the theory of social relations, (3) developmental stages, (4) structural theory, and (5) psychopathology.[71]

[68] *Ibid.*

[69] R. J. Lifton, "Protean Man," in B. B. Wolman (Ed.), *The Psychoanalytic Interpretation of History*, Harper Torchbook, 1973, p. 33.

[70] *Ibid.*, pp. 33–34.

[71] Benjamin B. Wolman, *Call No Man Normal*, International Universities Press, 1973.

Critique of the Death Instinct

Freud's concept of Thanatos, the death instinct, was based on the assumption that each organism wishes to die only in its own fashion. The living organism struggles most energetically against events (dangers, in fact) which might help it to attain its life's goal rapidly—a kind of short-circuit.[72] Freud's theory of the death instinct implies an innate death-wish. He maintained that "the vital process of the individual leads for internal reasons to an equalization of chemical tensions, that is, to death."[73]

It is Wolman's contention that equalization of chemical tensions does not mean death, nor does death put an end to all *biochemical* processes such as decay, decomposition of cells, and other changes in body chemistry. Death does stop certain biological processes, but it does not convert organic matter into inorganic matter. Moreover, the decline of life brings an organism closer to death, but death itself is not a definable process; it is something which cannot be described in a meaningful manner, for death signifies a zero point, nothingness. The statement, "Mr. A. is dead," is a negative statement, it means that Mr. A is "not-alive." There is no inner, innate, instinctual force that releases energy to produce death in the way that the Eros releases libidinal energy.

Life can be a state of equilibrium or disequilibrium, of action or rest, of a waking state or sleep, of tensions or reliefs. Life is a process of oxidation, input and output, and metabolism. Every living organism can be in a balanced or disbalanced state. The *principle of constancy* implies the tendency to restore the balance of life, the balance of the living organism. The constancy principle applies to living organisms only.

Life and death are concepts of energy. Life contains a certain amount of energy; death contains none. Life is power; decline of life is the decline of power. Death comes when all the energy is exhausted or its source or flow is destroyed. Charles Darwin formulated the fundamental law of biology: *fight for survival*.

The issues of life and death are connected with love and hate, for love means support of life and hatred leads to its destruction. Those who love and create are called good; those who hate and destroy are called evil. Freud's theory of Eros and Thanatos closely corresponds to this antinomy of life and love versus death and hatred, and his own writings support, not a suicidal death instinct, but an object-directed destructive instinct. It was his belief that[74]

> From the earliest times it was muscular strength which decided who owned things or whose will shall prevail. Muscular strength was soon supplemented by the use of tools; the winner was the one who had the better weapons or who used them the more skillfully. From the moment at which weapons were introduced,

[72]Sigmund Freud, "Beyond the Pleasure Principle," *Standard Edition of Complete Psychological Works of Sigmund Freud*, Hopedale Press, 1962, Vol. *18*, p. 51.
[73]*Ibid.*, p. 76.
[74]Sigmund Freud, *New Introductory Lectures on Psychoanalysis*, Norton, 1933, pp. 274–275.

intellectual superiority already began to replace brute muscular strength; but the
final purpose of the fight remained the same.

Wolman maintains that at the onset of prehistory, man's *libido* was self-directed, while *destrudo* was object-directed. There was no death instinct, but there was plenty of fighting for survival.[75]

According to Freud,[76] when outward aggression is unable to find adequate gratification in the external world, it may "turn back and increase the amount of self-destructiveness within." It would seem, therefore, "as though it is necessary for us to destroy some other thing or person in order not to destroy ourselves, in order to guard against the impulsion to self-destruction."

Freud's theory of Thanatos implies that suicidal tendencies occur earlier than do genocidal tendencies, in both the phylogenetic and ontogenetic sense. Were this true, animals would have eaten themselves up before they ate one another, and babies would have hurt themselves before they began to suck their mothers' breasts.

Certainly there are cases of self-directed hostility. But according to Freud, the self-directed hostility is seated in the superego, the last to develop of the three systems of the mental apparatus, while according to Wolman's interactional theory, the object-directed hostility is primary and self-directed hostility is secondary.

Self-Preservation

The main thesis of Wolman's interactional theory reads:[77]

> All living matter is endowed with biochemical energy derived from the universal energy that, in turn, as explained by Einstein, is a derivative of matter. At a certain evolutionary level this biochemical energy is transformed into mental energy [which] serves survival. The apparatus of discharge, call it drive, instinct or instinctual force, reflects the most universal urge to stay alive. It is the "lust for life," the wonderful craving of all living matter to live.

Self-preservation is the most general and best known empirical fact pertaining to living matter. The various functions that serve self-preservation may be divided into intake of oxygen, food and water, flight, fight, etc. One may call oxygen, food, and water *needs*, defining "need" as a condition for survival. Deprivation of one of these, or another, biological needs motivates the organism to act in a way which leads to the satisfaction of the need. Unsatisfied needs represent a state of deprivation, that is, disequilibrium, and lead toward an action aimed at the restoration of equilibrium. Every organism has a certain quantity of energy at a certain time. The fact that matter, in accordance with Einstein's formula $E = mc^2$, is a peculiar ac-

[75] Benjamin B. Wolman, "Human Belligerence," *International Journal of Group Tensions*, 1972, 2, pp. 48–66.
[76] Freud, *op. cit.*, p. 105.
[77] Wolman, *Call No Man Normal*, p. 37.

cumulation of energy does not contradict this line of reasoning. The energy is discharged, in accordance with the principle of equilibrium, whenever the organism is exposed to internal or external stimulation.[78]

Lust for Life

The energies of a living organism, the basic driving forces, or "lust for life," can be used in two directions, either toward the promotion of life or toward its destruction. When they are positively directed, they are called *Eros* or love. When they are channeled into destructiveness, they are known as *Ares*. The drives of love and hostility indicate the *direction* in which the mental energy is used, but it is important to remember that there is only *one energy*.

Apparently, Ares is a more primitive and phylogenetically older drive than Eros, and is probably a more powerful one. This theory is borne out by the fact that Pavlov's dogs did not copulate when their skin was burned, but they did continue to salivate.[79] However, when Pavlov tried to crush the dogs' bones, even salivation stopped. Hungry animals can bear minor wounds, but bone breaking means death, and in the face of death all energy is mobilized for self-defense.

Both Eros and Ares have an impetus, a source, an object, and an aim. Ares' impetus is the amount of destructive energy (*destrudo*) that is discharged. Its source is a threat to the individual's own life. Its aim is the complete or partial destruction of enemies. Its object can be the self or any other organism.[80]

Pavlov[81] believed that hostile behavior is a *guarding reaction* against real or threatened injury. Experimental studies by Dollard and his colleagues[82] and Lawson,[83] stressed the fact that frustrated individuals tend to become hostile.

Love, Sex, and Power

This shift of emphasis from Eros, libido, and sexuality to survival and adjustment to life follows, to a certain extent, the ideas of Kardiner, Hartmann, and Erikson. But Wolman's interactional theory reinterprets psychosexual development and sexual behavior in the light of the fundamental "lust for life" drive. In phylogenetic development, the fight for survival is

[78] Benjamin B. Wolman, "Mind and Body," in B. B. Wolman (Ed.), *Handbook of Parapsychology*, Van Nostrand Reinhold, pp. 861–882.

[79] Ivan P. Pavlov, *Lectures on Conditioned Reflexes*, Liveright, 1928, p. 228.

[80] B. B. Wolman, "Violent Behavior," *International Journal of Group Tensions*, 1973, 3, pp. 127–141.

[81] I. P. Pavlov, *op. cit.*, pp. 255 ff.

[82] J. Dollard, L. Doob, N. E. Miller, O. H. Mowrer, and R. R. Sears, *Frustration and Aggression*, Yale University Press, 1939.

[83] R. Lawson, *Frustration*, MacMillan, 1965.

the earliest and most fundamental driving force, while sexual procreative urges appear much later in the process of evolution. With very rare exceptions, the urge to live is more powerful than the urge to love, and sexual behavior is secondary to the more basic need to survive.[84]

According to Wolman, Freud's ideas concerning sexuality were based on observations of particular phenomena in a particular cultural–historical setting, and must be reviewed in a broader perspective of biological and sociocultural factors. The biological factors have to be stated in terms of the *primacy and universality of the fight for survival*, thus presenting sexuality as a second order issue greatly colored by the primary biological drive for survival. The sociocultural factors must be related to everchanging morals and to the inevitably limited empirical studies.[85]

Social Relations

Compared to other species, humans are quite belligerent; human history is a succession of genocidal incidents.[86] No other animals wage preventive wars or spend their entire lives accumulating material possessions, nor do any other animals make preparations against remote or nonexistent threats to their lives. And humanity is the only species obsessed by the fears of not having enough to eat and/or falling prey to real or imaginary enemies. These fears provide the species with its strongest motive: the desire to be strong, that is, *the universal wish for power.*

If power is defined as the ability of an organism to defend itself and to obtain food sufficient for survival, then its chances for survival become an indicator of its power. An organism is strong when it possesses the tools and weapons for acquisition of food and protection against enemies; it is weak when it is poorly equipped to carry out these tasks. To bring this theory to its logical conclusion, the peak of power would be omnipotence—the ability to satisfy all needs and ward off all threats. All living organisms operate on a continuum of greater or lesser amounts of power; the more power an organism has, the better its chances of survival.

Sociopsychological Concepts

Wolman's experimental research in group dynamics has led to a classification of human interaction according to the aims of the participants in the interaction. Thus, when the main purpose of an interaction is the satisfaction of one's own needs, Wolman calls the relationship *instrumental*. When the aim is to meet the partner's needs, he terms it *vectorial*; when the

---

[84] B. B. Wolman, "Psychology of Women," in B. B. Wolman (Ed.), *Psychological Aspects of Gynecology and Obstetrics*, Medical Economics, 1978.

[85] *Ibid.*

[86] B. B. Wolman, "Sense and Nonsense in History," in B. B. Wolman (Ed.), *Psychoanalytic Interpretation of History*, Basic Books, 1971.

goal is to meet the needs of both partners in the interaction, then the relationship is *mutual*.[87]

Human life starts as a parasitic process: the infant must receive all that is necessary for his or her survival. Thus, the infant's relationship to its mother is the prototype of instrumentalism, whereas parenthood is the prototype of vectorialsm. Parents protect the child and take care of it, irrespective of looks, health, or intelligence.

A well-adjusted adult is balanced in social interaction: he or she is *instrumental* in the struggle for survival, *mutual* in relationships with friends and in marriage, and *vectorial* in regard to children and those who need help, that is reasonably selfish (instrumental), reasonably mutual, and reasonably vectorial.[88]

Wolman tried to relate his theory of the three types of interindividual relations to psychoanalytic theory by introducing the concept of *interindividual cathexis*. While there are no neurological or physiological counterparts to this concept, it could be analogous to Pavlov's explanation of reflex. An external stimulus, wrote Pavlov,[89] is

> transformed into a nervous process and transmitted along a circuitous route (from the peripheral endings of the centripetal nerve, along its fibers to the apparatus of the central nervous system, and out along the centrifugal path until, reaching one or another organ, it excites its activity).

Pavlov's description can be explained in terms of the Freudian cathexis of physical energy: the external stimulus transmits a part of its energetic load into the peripheral endings of the centripetal nerve, thus cathecting the nerve ending and, through this circuitous route, cathecting the nerve center.

There is no evidence that mental energy is cathected or that cathexis follows the analogy to physical energy. The term "interindividual cathexis" is introduced as a logical construct, a bridge between psychoanalytic studies of personality and experimental research in social psychology. For example, when A loves B, A's libido is object-cathected in B.

In instrumental relationships, the individual's libido is self-cathected, and he expects the libidos of others to be object-cathected into him. In mutual relationships, the individual aims at receiving libido cathexes as well as giving them to those from whom he aims to receive. It is a *give and take* relationship. In vectorial relationships, the individual aims to object-cathect, to give libido to others. Parenthood is a prototype of such a giving without receiving, a one-way object libido cathexis.

A disbalance in interindividual cathexes, caused by interaction be-

---

[87] Benjamin B. Wolman, "Power and Acceptance as Determinants of Social Relations," *International Journal of Group Tensions*, 1974, 4, pp. 151–183.

[88] Harvey London, "Power and Acceptance Theory," in B. B. Wolman (Ed.), *International Encyclopedia of Psychiatry, Psychology, Psychoanalysis and Neurology*, Aesculapius, 1977, Vol. 9, pp. 11–13.

[89] Pavlov, *op. cit.*, p. 121.

tween the individual and his environment, inevitably leads to a disbalance in intraindividual cathexes. In other words, *improper social relations in early childhood must cause personality disorders*. Thus, all sociogenic disorders can be divided into three types: (1) the hypervectorial object-hypercathected, *schizotype* disorders; (2) the hyperinstrumental, self-hypercathected, *sociopathic* type; and (3) the dysmutual, going from one extreme to the other, *cyclic* type.[90]

Developmental Phases

In terms of interactional theory, the *oral* stage is an early form of *instrumentalism*. At this stage, the child's desire is to be helped (to get); deprivation elicits fear and hostility.

The *anal* stage is characterized not only by toilet training but also by walking and talking behavior. The erect position and walking around permit the child manual dexterity and the ability to manipulate objects to a much greater extent than in the oral stage. He (or she) can now explore distant places, disappear from the mother's sight, and reach into areas hitherto forbidden. The beginning of speech is another source of the ever-increasing feeling of power. To be able to comprehend and be comprehended, to call and be called to, to exchange wishes and demands—all this gives the infant a new sense of potency, as does toilet training. At the anal stage, the mother is often at the mercy of the child. She may refuse food to her child, but feces are the child's indisputable possession, the prototype of money and of any future property.

At the *phallic* stage, the child's object love is channeled into genital desires directed toward the parent of the opposite sex and becomes, for the first time, the dominating force, stronger than destrudo, whereas at the oral stage, the cannibalistic object relationship is dominated by destrudo.

Cathexis and conditioning are intertwined in the developmental process. In daily interaction with other children, the child clings to his own possessions while trying to take hold of the attractive toys of his playmates. The playground, the sandbox, the backyard, and the nursery school all serve to teach the child mutuality, for children are born instrumental-minded and selfish. The inevitable frustrating confrontations, as well as parental guidance, will teach them to give in order to receive, and to share in order to enjoy, thus setting them on the path toward *mutualism*.

Freud believed that Thanatos could lead to one's own destruction unless diverted into overt hostility toward the outer world. Part of this hostility, directed against the restricting and prohibiting parents, becomes incorporated in the superego and channeled against one's own ego, that is, against oneself. Wolman contends that the destrudo serves survival and

[90] Herbert H. Krauss and Beatrice J. Krauss, "Nosology: Wolman's System," in B. B. Wolman (Ed.), *International Encyclopedia of Psychiatry, Psychology, Psychoanalysis and Neurology*, Aesculapius, 1977, Vol. 8, pp. 86–88.

that it is initially directed against threats from without and not against one-self.[91]

The fight for survival is better served by a rational, controlled, and goal-directed hostility. The ego, operating on the "reality principle," delays and controls destrudo reactions. The reality principle is not an antipleasure rule; rather, it is a rule aimed at the pursuit of pleasure at minimum risk. Whereas the id is prone to fight at the slightest provocation, the ego fights to win. Thus, discharges of destrudo controlled by the ego are aggressive or defensive or both, and are always aimed at the well-being of the organism.

The superego is formed through the introjection of parental prohibitions and of the idealized parental images. The former carries some elements of destrudo; the latter includes elements of libido. The superego is invested with some of the child's aggressiveness against his parents. This hatred can hardly find satisfactory outlets; normal children do not kill nor do they attack their parents. Thus, the thwarted destrudo turns inward, against the ego, creating feelings of guilt which, in some pathological cases, become quite severe.[92]

In Freud's time, it was believed that during the latency period inhibitory forces acted on the child's libido and destrudo; the child was turning away from the parent of opposite sex and becoming antagonistic to the opposite sex in general. He still loved the parent of the opposite sex, but his love became desexualized and aim-inhibited. At present, Freud's ideas require a cultural–historical adjustment. In early twentieth-century Viennese society, which was based on rather stable interindividual relationships, boys renounced mothers as love objects and girls renounced fathers. Boys played with boys and girls with girls, boys played cops and robbers, girls played house. Boys avoided girls and girls avoided boys.

Today, there is very little inhibition and practically no delay in sexual information. Apparently, the latency period has almost disappeared. The development theories of Freud, Piaget, Gesell, Erikson, and others hold true for those cultural groups in which parental authority, and especially the father's authority, survived two world wars, social upheavals, mass communications, and rapid social mobility. In these more conservative and traditional social groups, latency is still the period of aim-inhibited love for the parent of the opposite sex and aim-inhibited hate for the parent of the same sex.

The biological changes in adolescence seriously affect the balance of the intra- and interindividual cathexes, for it is at this point that the individual becomes capable of reproduction and ultimately attains biological adulthood. In some primitive societies, puberty rites lead to the onset of the three most significant functions of adulthood, namely breadwinning, marriage, and participation in community life. In civilized societies, physical

[91] Wolman, *Call No Man Normal.*
[92] Benjamin B. Wolman, *Children Without Childhood: A Study in Childhood Schizophrenia*, Grune & Stratton, 1970.

maturity antedates psychological and cultural maturity, creating a situation that breeds conflict. When one is physically as tall as one's parents, and physiologically capable of becoming a parent, but is yet unable to assume responsibility in any of the three above-mentioned functions of adulthood, a conflict in one's social role is inevitable.

Personality Structure and Moral Development

Freud's structural theory suggested a tripartite organization of personality comprised of ego, id, and superego. Wolman maintains that the formation of the superego does not necessarily indicate the final phase of personality development, which greatly depends on interaction with one's environment. Wolman suggested the following developmental phases related to social adjustment and moral responsibility: [93]

> (1) morality based on *fear*; (2) morality based on acceptance of authority, parallel to Freud's *superego*; (3) shared morality of social norms based on collective responsibility of the *we-ego*; and finally, (4) mature responsibility, based on one's own moral commitment, the *vector-ego*. The first phase is *anomous*; the second *heteronomous*—the determination by others of our moral behavior. The third phase, the we-ego phase, is *socionomous*—every individual partakes in the social agreement (social contract) and willingly obeys social norms. The highest moral level is attained when the individual becomes *autonomous*—develops a binding moral code even when everyone else is immoral.

At the first and earliest phase of life, which corresponds to Freud's oral stage, the infant is exceedingly narcissistic and selfish. He wants what he wants and does not care about anyone else. Infants and infantile adults refrain from hurting others only when they are restrained from doing so by fear of retaliation and punishment.

The second and higher level of moral development originates in a combination of fear with love. This begins in the anal phase, at the time of toilet training. In essence, the mother requests the child to relinquish the freedom of doing whatever he pleases. When she imposes restraint without undue harshness, and encourages and rewards compliance, she helps the child to accept the limitations of his freedom and develop concern for the rights of others. Parental love and firmness help the child to accept the parents' *do's* and *don't's*. The identification with the parent leads to the formation of the superego. Children of rejecting or overpermissive parents may never reach this second level and act all their lives in a selfish and hostile manner.

Children need strong and friendly parents who set limits, offer consistent guidance and, at the same time, give the child an unswerving vectorial love and protection. Children admire such parents and tend to incorporate the parental image, thus developing an inner moral watchdog—the su-

[93] Benjamin B. Wolman, *Courage to Give* (in press).

perego. They will refrain from violating parental rules because they don't dare to invite disapproval and because they want to please the loving parents. The combination of love and fear is the core of the heteronomous phase.

The next developmental step leads to the willing sharing of social norms of a group and eventually of society at large. The identification with one's social group leads to the formation of the *we-ego*. The growing child identifies with his cultural, religious, ethnic, or sociological group. His moral convictions reflect the norms of the group with which he identifies.

Such a development is a prerequisite for a voluntary sharing of responsibility, for moral do's and don't's. It is a higher level of moral development than the superego identification with the parents; it leads to identification with the society at large and enables the youngster to share the responsibilities of citizens in a free and democratic society.

Identification with a group and sharing of responsibility for mutually agreed on social norms indicates the beginning of a higher phase of moral development. Instead of abiding by heteronomous rules imposed from without, the individual takes part in setting rules for himself and others. This socionomous phase also leads to a higher level of moral development.

Morality starts with the interaction between I and Thou. An isolated individual can be bright or dull, quick or slow, neat or sloppy—all these adjectives have no moral connotation. His behavior is neither moral·nor immoral, and whatever he does cannot be defined as right or wrong.

One can be morally right or wrong only in regard to other people. Concern for the rights of others, and taking an active part in setting rules and norms, indicates the socionomous level of personality development.

There is, however, a higher level of morality which surpasses the rules and norms of a particular group or society, and encompasses the entire human race. At this highest level of personality development, one's moral standards transcend the heteronomous superego and the socionomous we-ego. It is the *vector-ego*, which implies the courage of one's own convictions and moral commitment to all human beings.

The vector-ego is the supreme personality agency of mature, self-confident and self-respecting individuals. A person who has developed a vector-ego assumes moral responsibility for whatever goes on in and around himself.

Moral growth need not be restricted to childhood and adolescence. Human life can be a process of continuous growth. The vectorial-ego may start with parenthood and the assumption of responsibility for one's children, but it can grow and encompass all human children.

Becoming is synonymous with moral development, which proceeds from the irresponsible *anomy*, through the borrowed responsibility of *heteronomy*, toward the shared responsibility of *socionomy*, and finally to the highest level of becoming, the individual's own responsibility, *autonomy*.

6. Psychoanalysis And Experimental Psychology

Methodological Criticism

There is a great deal of difference in the "social climate" of the early splits in the psychoanalytic movement and the later ones. Adler and Jung emphasized the differences between their systems and Freud's. They did their utmost to point to their original contributions to psychology.

This tense atmosphere gradually eased up. Horney, Kardiner, Sullivan, Fromm, and many others readily admit how much they owe to Freud. Perhaps the personal tensions disappeared. However, not only the personal relations but the entire climate of research changed. In times past, almost every year saw a "new" theory thrown into the confused psychological crowd. Today, psychologists are more modest than they used to be and a healthier atmosphere has developed. In view of the continuously growing mass of empirical data and the improving research conditions, no one could dare to claim a monopoly on truth. Psychologists today are less split into "schools" and have learned to adapt various methods and facts endorsed by their opponents. There is a continuous increase in mutual influence and mutual learning between research workers. Instead of barriers between the various schools there is a growing interdependence, interaction, and mutual understanding and learning among them.

Another shift has taken place—the manner of criticism. However psychologists may agree or disagree with Freud, the style of their criticism has changed. The earlier critics attacked psychoanalysis from the viewpoint of true or false. Modern critics evade the question of whether Freud was right or wrong. They ask instead *how* he arrived at his conclusions, what his *empirical data* were, and what *logical inferences* he applied in his system.

This *methodological criticism* does not accept or reject psychoanalysis. Various psychologists point to the obvious weaknesses and deficiencies of clinical studies. The very asset of psychotherapy—transference—is a liability in research. The clinician, especially the analyst, uses in therapy the most precious tool: his own personality. Often the final results of psychoanalytic therapy depend on the personality of the analyst. It is therefore generally accepted that an individual who plans to analyze others should undergo psychoanalysis in order to gain mastery over his own emotional biases. How perfect one can be is a question open to discussion.

But the clinician can hardly claim methodological equality with the experimentalist. Experiments are conducted in such a way as to provide optimum conditions for the isolation or modification of experimental variables. Nothing of that kind is available in the clinical method. Neither Freud nor any other psychologist who studies human nature in clinical situations can modify the conditions of research. He has to study his patients as they come; sampling is not possible in psychoanalytic studies.

Some Experimental Studies

Psychoanalysis cannot become an experimental science since we cannot experiment with human life and destiny and we do not induce experimental upheavals. But to discard psychoanalysis as a science on the ground that it does not admit of experimental proof is as justified "as to discard astronomy. Experimentation with the heavenly bodies is after all exceedingly difficult," remarked Freud.[94] Freud himself, nonetheless, reported several experiments in 1932 that corroborated his hypotheses. Schrotter experimented with sexual symbols. He told a woman to dream about intercourse with her lady friend, and the hypnotized woman dreamt indeed about her friend, who in the dream held a traveling bag with the inscription: "Ladies only." In 1924, Bettelheim and Hartman experimented with patients suffering from Korsakoff's syndrome. The patients were told some sexual stories and then reproduced them with distortions well known in Freud's studies of dream work, dream distortions, and symbols.

Actually, practically all projective techniques are experimental tools which utilize the psychoanalytic frame of reference to a lesser or a greater extent.[95]

Several experimental psychologists have tried to put psychoanalytic findings to experimental test. In an excellent summary of this experimental work, Sears wrote: "The psychoanalytic way of looking at man's motives, defense, and personality structure has been so invigorating to psychological thought that experimentalists have been reluctant to let it remain unincorporated in the general science of psychology." There are two main difficulties in incorporating psychoanalytic findings into the body of experimental psychology. "The subjective character of the [psychoanalytic—B. W.] system has proved a difficulty, however, since it does not permit of conventional scientific tests of proof and disproof. . . ." In addition to this methodological difficulty, "psychoanalysis deals heavily in the more potent emotions and motives, and if society is put hard to it to control sex, aggression, anxiety, pride, idealism, and unreason, it is little wonder the experimentalist shies away from unleashing them in his laboratory."[96]

Among the most significant experimental studies in this area that we shall mention here, were those related to the problems of fixation, frustration, regression, and aggression. Fixation could be partial, that is, fixation of the libido cathexis on a certain object or fixation on a certain developmental stage. Fixations may be caused by insufficient or lacking gratification of the instinctual desire or by an abundant gratification.

No direct experimental confirmation was received, but some experi-

[94] Sigmund Freud, *New Introductory Lectures in Psychoanalysis*, Norton, 1933, p. 36.

[95] Zygmunt Piotrovski, *Perceptoanalysis*, Harper, 1957.

[96] Robert R. Sears, "Experimental Analysis of Psychoanalytic Phenomena," in J. McV. Hunt, *Personality and the Behavior Disorders*, Ronald, 1944, p. 306.

ments seem to offer indirect support to Freud's theory of fixation. Youtz[97] trained rats to press a small brass bar which released a pellet of food. He let one group of rats practice it (with food gratification) ten times and another group forty times. Then he broke the circuit. The group of rats which had forty gratifications was much more resistant to extinction than the group with ten gratifications. Apparently, the more gratification there is, the stronger the tendency to become fixated.

When the individual becomes frustrated, he tends to regress to the point of fixation. He relinquishes the adult pattern of behavior and regresses to childish patterns. Regression can also take place in abundant satiation, when more primitive behavior can become tempting because it resembles the early and more sheltered stages of the individual's life in infancy.

In an experiment by Hamilton and Krechevsky, rats were trained in a T-maze to choose the shorter alley in their run for food. After they had learned it, the sides in the maze were reversed. The rats regressed to original habits.[98]

A similar experiment in instrumental act regression was conducted by O'Kelly, who trained rats in a maze. When the learning pattern was well established, he reversed the direction of running. The rats learned the new way. Then the rats were given plenty of food and they regressed to the former pattern of behavior.[99]

Summarizing the above-mentioned and several other experimental studies Sears concluded that "both data and logic support Freud's statement that regression is a function of fixation—habit strength—but it is a function of frustration in a secondary way only, and what effect frustration has is primarily in the direction of influencing the strength of instrumental act sequences."[100]

Another set of experiments dealt with the problem of aggression resulting from frustration. Dollard and his associates (cf. Chapter 4, Section 6) conducted carefully planned experiments in which frustration led to aggression.

Very often aggression becomes displaced. Whenever the cause of frustration is powerful or inaccessible or invisible, a displaced aggression may take place. N. E. Miller, in experimental studies, exposed rats to electric shocks and taught them to fight each other. Whenever another rat was not available for a fight, the rats attacked another object. In Miller's words,

[97] Richard P. Youtz, "Reinforcement, Extinction, and Spontaneous Recovery in a non-Pavlovian Reaction," *Journal of Experimental Psychology*, 1938, *22*, 305–318.

[98] J. A. Hamilton and I. Krechevsky, "Studies in the Effect of Shock on Behavior Plasticity in the Rat," *Journal of Comparative Psychology*, 1933, *16*, 237–253.

[99] Lawrence I. O'Kelly, "An Experimental Study of Regression: II. Some Motivational Determinants of Regression and Perseveration," *Journal of Comparative Psychology*, 1940, *30*, 55–95.

[100] Sears, *op. cit.*, p. 313.

354   Chapter 8

"When the direct response to the original stimulus is prevented by the absence of that stimulus, displaced responses will occur to other similar stimuli and the strongest displaced response will occur to the most similar stimulus present."[101] As mentioned before (Chapter 4, Section 6) Miller related displacement to stimulus generalization.

In carefully planned experimentation with humans, Doob and Sears studied the relationship between overt aggression and the expected satisfaction in comparison to the expected pain resulting from punishment. The subjects marked on a four-point scale the expected satisfaction and eventual punishment anticipated for their aggressive actions. Whenever the anticipated satisfaction was greater, an overt aggression took place; whenever the expected punishment was greater, the subject preferred a non-overt, inhibited form of aggression.[102]

Sears conducted an ingenious experiment that was related to Freud's theory of repression. He gave his subjects a list of nonsense syllables and asked them to memorize the list. Then a card-sorting test with inevitable failure was administered. Then the subjects were again presented with the task of learning a list of nonsense syllables. This time, as a result of repression caused by failure on the card-sorting test, the subjects failed to learn the syllables. Sears believed that the card-sorting task left uncompleted was a threat to self-esteem and acted as a repressing factor.[103]

Additional, carefully designed experiments in the same area were conducted by Zeller. He used learning of nonsense syllables as the main task, thus following in the footsteps of Sears. The failure experience was provided by an imitative tapping of Knox cubes. In Zeller's experiment the failure was inhibiting, or "repressing," only when it was related to an earlier learned set of syllables. Zeller believes tht his results corroborate Freud's theory of repression, but he does not exclude some other interpretation of the same results.[104]

A few experiments conducted by Kurt Lewin and his associates also seem to corroborate Freud's theory. One is the famous Zeigarnik experiment (cf. Chapter 13). According to Freud, a traumatic experience stimulates the mind to such an extent that no assimilation or discharge is possible. The traumatic situation is kept very much alive in the mind, as though the person had not yet been able to deal adequately with the situation, as though the task were still actually before him, unaccomplished. This unaccomplished task causes lasting disturbances in the distribution of

[101] Neal E. Miller, "Theory and Experiment Relating Psychoanalytic Displacement to Stimulus-Response Generalization," *Journal of Abnormal and Social Psychology,* 1948, *43,* 155–178.
[102] L. W. Doob and Robert R. Sears, "Factors Determining Substitute Behavior and the Overt Expression of Aggression," *Journal of Abnormal and Social Psychology,* 1939, *34,* 293–313.
[103] Robert R. Sears, "Initiation of the Repression Sequence by Experienced Failure," *Journal of Experimental Psychology,* 1937, *20,* 570–580.
[104] Anchard F. Zeller "An Experimental Analogue of Repression: II. The Effect of Individual Failure and Success on Memory Measured by Relearning," *Journal of Experimental Psychology,* 1950, *40,* 411–422, and Part III, *ibid.,* 1951, *42,* 32–38.

the available energy in the mind, Freud said. Lewin's experiments confirmed this idea.

In another experiment, Barker, Dembo, and Lewin observed that children frustrated by the removal of attractive toys regress to a less constructive level of play (cf. Chapter 13). Anna Freud criticized this experiment.[105]
She could not see how the mild frustration caused by the removal of toys
could be compared to the emotional upheavals which S. Freud had in mind.

Observations of Manifest Behavior

In a summary of scientific testings of psychoanalysis, B. A. Farrell concluded that several psychoanalytic propositions had been confirmed to
some extent, strongly or weakly.[106]

1. Infants obtain pleasure from oral stimulation—confirmed by Levy[107]
   and Halverson.[108]
2. Infants obtain pleasure from genital stimulation—confirmed by
   Levy,[109] Halverson,[110] and Sears.[111]
3. Manual masturbation is more frequent among preschool boys than
   girls—confirmed by Koch.[112]
4. Small children exhibit extensive pregenital play—confirmed by
   Isaacs.[113]

All the above-mentioned studies empirically tested psychoanalytic proportions. None of these studies is experimental, but all are careful observations of overt behavior. Although the experimental method offers a definite
advantage in regard to variation and control of data, several empirical
sciences, including biology and astronomy, make wide use of observation.

Furthermore, if an observation failed to corroborate Freud's hypothe-
sis, it could not disprove it for the very simple reason that a great part of
Freud's findings are related to the unconscious and unobservable processes.
Whenever an observation does corroborate the psychoanalytic propositions,

[105] Anna Freud, "The Contribution of Psychoanalysis to Genetic Psychology," American Journal
of Orthopsychiatry, 1951, 21, 476–497.
[106] Brian A. Farrell, "The Scientific Testing of Psychoanalytic Findings and Theory," in H.
Brand, The Study of Personality: A Book of Readings, Wiley, 1954, p. 451.
[107] David M. Levy, "Finger Sucking and Accessory Movements in Early Infancy," American
Journal of Psychiatry, 1928, 7, 881–918.
[108] H. M. Halverson, "Infant Sucking and Tensional Behavior," Journal of Genetic Psychology,
1938, 53, 365–430.
[109] Levy, op. cit.
[110] H. M. Halverson, "Genital and Sphincter Behavior of the Male Infant," Journal of Genetic
Psychology, 1940, 56, 95–136.
[111] Sears, Survey of Objective Studies of Psychoanalytic Concepts, Social Science Research Council, 1943.
[112] H. L. Koch, "An Analysis of Certain Forms of So-Called 'Nervous Habits' in Young Children," Journal of Genetic Psychology, 1935, 46, 139–170.
[113] Suzanne Isaacs, Social Development in Young Children, Routledge, 1933.

it still cannot serve as a final evidence, for it is valid only within the scope of the observation. However, the greater the number of precise, carefully planned, and objectively conducted observations, the stronger is the support lent to the theory. Most of the above-mentioned studies offer such support. But more discussion about observation as a scientific method will be forthcoming in Chapter 15.

Some Sources of Confusion

Additional difficulty has been created by Freud's terminology. Freud's pleasure and reality principles do not refer to pleasure as distinct from displeasure and pain, or reality as distinct from unreality and fantasy. Freud's pleasure principle (*Lustprinzip*) means the principle of immediate, urgent discharge of energy. His reality principle is related to the ability to postpone or modify that urge for immediate discharge of energy. Id operates on the lust principle, ego on the reality principle; both id and ego seek pleasure, but the ego seeks pleasure without unpleasurable aftereffects. The id presses for an immediate discharge of energy which brings relief and pleasure; the ego is more selective (cf. Chapter 6).

O. H. Mowrer was misled by this ambiguity and related simple, classical conditioning to the reality principle. It was Mowrer's belief that simple conditioning is controlled by the autonomic nervous system (cf. Chapter 4, Section 6). Mowrer believed that Pavlov's dogs learned "not what is pleasurable and relieving," but "what is actual, true, real," and related to the reality principle, while the higher type of cognitive learning controlled by the central nervous system is related to the pleasure principle because it is rewarded.[114] This erroneous translation of *lust* is generally accepted and yet quite misleading.

Hilgard disagreed with Mowrer and preferred "to assign reality regulated functions, ego functions, to the cognitive apparatus: to the central nervous system and its related structure." Yet Hilgard also had difficulties with the two Freudian principles.

The probable source of error lies in the confusion of the terms "need," "tension," "pleasure," "reality principle," "reality testing" and "perception of reality." All these terms were used by Freud in a specific connotation which adds difficulties for the experimentalists. In the words of Hilgard, corresponding to Freud's pleasure principle is "the *law of effect* or *reinforcement theory*. The broad conception, common to both psychoanalysis and learning theory, is that a need state is a state of high tension." Hilgard continued:

> Conforming of behavior to reality . . . surely has some resemblance to the earliest ego functions. Learned discrimination always involves conflict, and the conflict is resolved through the weighing of the choices of reward and punishment. . . . Sometimes, when discrimination is difficult, the rat mobilizes his experience

---

[114] O. Hobart Mowrer, *Learning Theory and Personality Dynamics*, Ronald, 1950, pp. 6 ff.

. . . by making short runs first to one side and then to the other before the animal is committed to a choice. This appears to be a kind of symbolic reality-testing, an analogue of ego-type behavior.[115]

Some psychologists did not draw a clear line between the reality principle, reality testing, and reality perception as Freud did (cf. Chapter 6). Actually, the pleasure principle, as said before, is not related to the law of effect. But pleasure is. All behavior, according to Freud, is inspired by avoidance of tension and seeking of pleasurable relief. The reality principle is a modification of the pleasure principle in the direction of avoidance of displeasure. Reality testing is the distinction between inner and outer stimuli; psychotics have lost it. What the rats probably do is perceive reality and avoid pain. How this is related to Freud's theory of personality can not be easily answered by experimentalists using rats for the study of psychoanalytic concepts.

More advanced research in psychoanalysis will be described in the following section.

Further Research in Psychoanalysis

Sarnoff and his co-workers, in an investigation of the usefulness of the psychoanalytic distinction between fear and anxiety with regard to social affiliation, found that as the desire to affiliate increases, fear decreases. Yet as anxiety increases, the desire for affiliation decreases.[116]

Zimbardo and Formica, in a later study of social affiliation, found that fearful subjects are quicker to affiliate than subjects who are not fearful, even when communication is restricted. Moreover, fearful subjects are quicker to affiliate with other subjects who are in a similar emotional state than they are with subjects who may have more relevant information but who are not afraid. Other findings of their study of the determinants of affiliation included the suggestion that ordinal position and self-esteem are joint determinants of affiliation.[117]

In 1967, Bromberg attempted to replicate earlier studies by Sarnoff and Zimbardo. He did indeed find that when anxiety is aroused, subjects prefer social isolation and avoid affiliation, but that fear tends to promote the desire for affiliation. Moreover, when phobic anxiety is aroused, phobic ideation increases. There is, however, no such increase when fear is aroused.[118]

Schlesinger studied the relationship between anal personality traits and

---

[115] Ernest R. Hilgard, *Theories of Learning* (2nd ed.), Appleton-Century-Crofts, 1956, pp. 291–294, and the entire Chapter 9.

[116] I. Sarnoff and P. G. Zimbardo, "Anxiety, Fear and Social Affiliation," *Journal of Abnormal and Social Psychology*, 1961, *62*, pp. 356–363.

[117] P. G. Zimbardo and R. Formica, "Emotional Comparison and Self Esteem as Determinants of Affiliation," *Journal of Personality*, 1963, *31*, pp. 141–162.

[118] P. M. Bromberg, "The Effects of Fear and Two Modes of Anxiety Reduction on Social Affiliation and Phobic Ideation," *Dissertation Abstracts*, 1968, *28* (11-B), pp. 4753–4754.

choice of occupation. He found some evidence of differences among the groups in an examination of the following traits: regularity of routines, responsibility in dealing with others, retentiveness, obstinacy, rigidity, frugality, preoccupation with dirt and contamination, orderliness, self-righteous hostility, anxiety over possible loss of control, sensitivity to smells. Schlesinger believed that psychoanalytic theory might explain some aspects of vocational choice, but further explorations with better controls need to be done.[119]

Based on Freud's hypothesis that there is a relationship between the adult traits of parsimony, obstinacy, and orderliness and the quality of toilet training, Bishop hypothesized that highly anal persons will not conform to predictions based on Festinger's dissonance theory. She found that under conditions of high privation, subjects rated high in anality consistently disliked tasks more than subjects rated low in anality. On the other hand, under conditions of low privation, the opposite results were found, which confirmed Bishop's hypothesis.[120]

Pettit, in a study of anality and time, concluded that there is a relationship between the two which is consonant with psychoanalytic theory.[121]

Ross studied the relationship between separation fear and the fear of death in children. She found that there was such a relationship but that there were several other relevant factors which affected this relationship.[122]

D. Hamburg et al. gathered information from 10,000 initial and 3,000 end-of-treatment questionnaires that they sent to analytic practitioners. They found that 97 percent of all patients were designated as improved by their therapists while 96 percent of the patients felt they had improved. Similar studies at the Columbia Psychoanalytic Clinic found that both patients and therapists felt there had been positive change. Weber et al. found that predictions of outcome by the admitting psychoanalytic candidate in training and his supervisor were related to the kind of treatment offered. O'Connor et al. observed that patients with ulcerative colitis who were treated with a combination of psychotherapy and steroids did better than patients who were treated with steroids alone.[123]

K. Tennes et al. investigated some of the formulations of John Benjamin

[119] V. J. Schlesinger, "Anal Personality Traits and Occupational Choice: A Study of Accountants, Chemical Engineers, and Educational Psychologists," Dissertation Abstracts, 1964, 24 (12), pp. 5551–5552.

[120] F. V. Bishop, "Anality, Privation, and Dissonance," Dissertation Abstracts, 1966, 27 (2-B), p. 596.

[121] T. F. Pettit, "Anality and Time," Journal of Consulting and Clinical Psychology, 1969, 33, pp. 170–174.

[122] R. Ross, "Separation Fear and the Fear of Death," Dissertation Abstract, 1967, 27 (8-B), pp. 2878–2879.

[123] John Weber, "Psychoanalytic Research: Studies of Outcome," in B. B. Wolman (Ed.), International Encyclopedia of Psychiatry, Psychology, Psychoanalysis and Neurology. Aesculapius, 1977, Vol. 9, pp. 211–214.

regarding the concept of the *stimulus barrier* in early infancy. Benjamin had observed that full-term infants show a definite increase in sensitivity to both internal and external stimulation at the age of 3–4 weeks. Benjamin felt that this change in sensitivity was related to the concept of the stimulus barrier, and that this concept described an initial limitation or inability of the nervous system to process a degree of sensory input. Moreover, he felt that, as inhibitory or regulatory mechanisms mature, older infants create a more active barrier through motor activity. Tennes *et al.* designed a short-term longitudinal study in order to observe the relationship between levels of irritability, changes in responsivity to stimuli, and neurophysiological maturation in the first three years of life. They found that their results tended to confirm Benjamin's propositions regarding the first three months of life. They did, however, modify his proposition in that they determined that at three to four weeks there is an increase in the infant's capacity to process stimulus input, even though he still lacks autonomous means of protecting against it. Later changes in responsivity appear to represent a major reorganization in neurofunctioning, but an active stimulus barrier such as the one Benjamin described does not become effective until well into the fourth month instead of earlier, as Benjamin suggested.[124]

Hartvig Dahl has done considerable study of the psychoanalytic process through the use of computers. He has demonstrated that computers can reduce the vast quantity of analytic material into manageable groups of data. They locate and count words, assign them to conceptual categories, and determine the frequency of occurrence of each category. He recommended the establishment of a library of recorded analyses conducted by the most competent analysts. He also suggested the preparation of computer content–analysis dictionaries specifically for psychoanalytic concepts.[125]

7. Critical Analyses of Psychoanalytic Concepts

In addition to experimental studies designed to test the psychoanalytic theory, there have been efforts by Rappaport, Klein, Holt, and others to critically evaluate Freudian theory. Robert R. Holt has written many papers in which he has systematically examined Freudian concepts. According to Holt, Freud's writing is infinitely stimulating, but his theory poses many difficulties and contradictions for the reader. For example, Freud often made points which demand that the reader already be thoroughly familiar with his previous material, even though some of this has never been pub-

[124] Katherine Tennes, Robert Emde, Anthony Kisley, and David Metcalf, "The Stimulus Barrier in Early Infancy: An Exploration of John Benjamin," in R. R. Holt and E. Peterfreund (Eds.), *Psychoanalysis and Contemporary Science*, 1972, Vol. 1, pp. 206–236.

[125] Hartvig Dahl, "A Quantitative Study of a Psychoanalysis," in R. R. Holt and E. Peterfreund (Eds.), *Psychoanalysis and Contemporary Science*, 1972, Vol. 1, pp. 237–257.

lished. Moreover, Holt pointed out certain methodological errors which Freud habitually committed. Some of these include reification and even personification of some theoretical concepts. Furthermore, Freud often failed to clearly distinguish between observations and assumptions, so that conceptual innovations were at times presented as empirical discoveries. These problems seem to arise out of what Holt sees as Freud's cognitive style, a style which can be characterized by considerable inconsistency.[126] Holt pointed out that one source of this inconsistency is the changes that occurred when new facts and ideas arose in the course of Freud's work. Another source of this inconsistency seems to be Freud's aversion to the process of synthesizing. Therefore, it is not unusual to find that Freud revised one of his books by merely adding new material without bothering to omit the old, even when the new contradicts the old. In line with this distaste for synthesis, Freud liked to maintain a certain looseness in his writing and felt that it was a mistake to begin a piece of work by defining concepts too clearly and unambiguously. According to Holt, Freud felt that to do so would render his work barren and speculative, rather than following the spirit of science which struggles with approximations. Despite Freud's desire for this kind of flexibility, he all too often was rigid and even dogmatic in his formulation.

In order to help the reader with these problems, Holt devised ten basic rules for reading Freud: [127]

1. Beware of lifting statements out of context. This practice is particularly tempting to research-minded clinical psychologists, who are generally more eager to get right to the testing of propositions than to undertake the slow study of a large corpus of theory. There is no substitute for reading enough of Freud to get his full meaning, which is almost never fully expressed in a single paragraph, no matter how specific the point.

2. Don't take Freud's extreme formulations literally. Treat them as his way of calling your attention to a point. When he says "never," "invariable," "conclusively" and the like, read on for the qualifying and softening statements.

3. Look out for inconsistencies; don't either trip over them or seize on them with malicious glee, but take them as incomplete dialectic formulations, awaiting the synthesis that Freud's cognitive style made him consistently draw back from.

4. Be on the watch for figurative language, personification in particular. Remember that it is there primarily for color, even though it did at times lead Freud himself astray, and that it is fairest to him to rely primarily on those of his statements of issues that are least poetic and dramatic.

5. Don't expect rigorous definitions; look rather for the meanings of his terms in the ways they are used over a period of time. And don't be dismayed if you find a word being used now in its ordinary, literary mean-

---

[126] Robert R. Holt, "Freud's Cognitive Style," *American Imago*, 1965, 22, pp. 163–179.

[127] Robert R. Holt, "Freud's Mechanistic and Humanistic Images of Man," in R. R. Holt and Emanuel Peterfreund (Eds.), *Psychoanalysis and Contemporary Science*, Macmillan, 1972, pp. 3–24.

ing, now in a special technical sense which changes with the developmental status of the theory.

6. Be benignly skeptical about Freud's assertions of proof, his statements
that something has been established beyond doubt. Remember that he
had different standards of proof from those we have today, that he rejected experiment partly from a too-narrow conception of it and partly
because he had found it stylistically incompatible with his outlook.

7. Freud was overfond of dichotomies, even when his data were better conceptualized as continuous variables; in general, don't assume that the
theory is invalidated by being stated much of the time in this form.

8. Be wary of Freud's persuasiveness. Keep in mind that he was a powerful
rhetorician in areas where his scientific footing was uncertain. Though
he was often right, it was not always for the reasons he gave, which are
almost never truly sufficient to prove it, and not always to the extent that
he hoped.

Finally, be particularly cautious not to gravitate toward either of two extreme
and equally untenable positions: that is,

9. Don't take Freud's every sentence as a profound truth, which may
present difficulties but only because of our own inadequacies. Don't assume that our difficulty is that of a pedestrian plodder trying to keep up
with the soaring mind of a genius who did not always bother to explicate
steps that were obvious to him, but which we must supply by laborious
exegetical scholarship. This is the temptation of the scholars working from
within the psychoanalytic institutes, those earnest Freudians who, to
Freud's annoyance, had begun to emerge already during his lifetime. For
most of us in the universities, the corresponding temptation is the more
dangerous one:

10. Don't let yourself get so offended by Freud's lapses from methodological
purity that you dismiss him altogether. Almost any psychologist can learn
an enormous lot from Freud, if he will listen to him carefully and sympa-
thetically, and not take his pronouncements too seriously!

In addition to considerations of style, Holt felt that there is a pervasive
conflict in Freud's writing which centers around two antithetical images of
man, that is, the mechanistic image and the humanistic image.[128] On the
one hand, Freud was steeped in radical materialism and physicalistic physiology, which promoted the mechanistic image so clearly prevalent in his
metapsychology. Yet in his clinical work and in his broad speculative, qua-
siphilosophical writings in his later years, as well as in his own life and in
his interactions with others, Freud revealed a decided humanistic stance
which acts as a corrective antagonist of his pervasive mechanistic leanings.

[128] Robert R. Holt, "Beyond Vitalism and Mechanism: Freud's Concept of Psychic Energy," in
B. B. Wolman (Ed.), *Historical Roots of Contemporary Psychology*, Harper and Row, 1968, pp.
196–226.

9

Away from Freud: The Sociological School

1. NEW WAYS IN PSYCHOANALYSIS

Culture versus Nature

If someone had asked Freud about the nature of human culture, he would probably have answered as follows: Human nature is the basis of culture. Culture is the product of human nature, and psychology of the individual is the key that opens the door to the study of culture.

If someone should ask Fromm, Horney, or Sullivan what the nature of human nature is, they would probably answer: Culture is the determinant of personality. Human nature is a product of culture, and interpersonal relations are the key to the interpretation of the riddle of human nature.

These imaginary replies point to the far-reaching consequences of one's approach to the problem of personality and culture.

There is a growing mass of data concerning personality and culture, and psychologists, sociologists, and anthropologists are cooperating more and more in cross-disciplinary studies.[1] Yet it seems as though the issue of the causal relationship between personality and culture represents tremendous difficulties. In the previous chapter, we discussed the problem presented in Linton's and Kardiner's studies: Is personality a product of culture or vice versa? Do institutionalized social mores shape one's personality, or do certain types of personality create certain cultures?

Neither Freud nor the neo-psychoanalysts found a final and conclusive solution to this problem. It seems that both orthodox and new psychoanalysis *postulated* a certain type of relationship, and did so in quite opposite directions. To Freud, culture was a result of personality structure. Men are driven by their drives and desires, sometimes sublimated or modified. Their social life is directed by the very same forces; oral or anal problems, for example, may become problems of social behavior.

---

[1] Stansfeld S. Sargent and Marian Smith (Eds.), *Personality and Culture*, Viking Fund, 1949.

Most neo-psychoanalysts (cf. Chapter 8), and especially the sociologically oriented Fromm, Horney, and Sullivan, postulate that society is the first cause in psychology. This assumption carries them beyond the borders of psychoanalysis. According to them, social relations mold personality and there is little, if any, influence of instinctual forces on society and culture.[2] Kardiner, too, is a sociologically oriented psychoanalyst, but he tried to reconcile his findings with Freud's principles. Horney, Fromm, and Sullivan no longer try. They have moved away decisively in the direction of new theoretical systems which have little to do with Freud's concepts. This is why they could not be included in the previous chapter, under "New Theories in Psychoanalysis." They have created new conceptual systems, which, though rooted in Freudianism, can hardly be called Freudian.

The Social Climate

It cannot be a matter of sheer coincidence that sociologically oriented psychoanalysis developed in the United States. Sociological, anthropological, and social-psychological studies in comparative cultures have been appearing in this country on an unprecedented scale. American scientists, whether influenced by Freud or not, have discovered new research possibilities and new techniques for studying cultural patterns and group relations.

Many of these studies, conducted by Benedict, Linton, Kardiner, Mead, Erikson, and others, did away with the narrowness of some earlier theories of culture. A student of comparative sociology cannot assume that his government, his religion, and his country's philosophy are the only possible cultural patterns. His horizons widen and his outlook becomes more relativistic. By virtue of comparison and criticism, psychologists are far more realistic than they were a generation ago.

The United States, as a country of immigration and multiple racial and religious differences, invites that kind of approach and encourages comparative studies. Social psychology has developed here into a scientific system, and there is a tremendous amount of research going on both in the theory and the practical application of social psychology.

Many European scholars came to this country when the centers of free thought had been destroyed in their homelands. They found here an extremely stimulating social climate. Kurt Lewin, Karen Horney, Erich Fromm, and Max Wertheimer, to mention just a few, have developed their best ideas in this country. They have participated in the collective effort of American psychologists and social scientists and have put forward a vigorous empirical study of human relations. Clinical methods have been checked against experimental methods;[3] human groups have been studied

[2] Clara Thompson, *Psychoanalysis: Evolution and Development*, Hermitage, 1950.
[3] Robert R. Sears, *Survey of Objective Studies of Psychoanalytic Concepts*, Social Science Research Council, 1943.

experimentally;[4] individual behavior has been related to social norms and roles.[5]

The merger of the continental and American spirits has proved of great value in furthering scientific research.

The Common Denominator

There are considerable differences between Horney, Fromm, and Sullivan, and even more between the former and the latter two. However, all three have so much in common that it is justifiable to refer to them collectively as the sociological school.

Horney, Fromm, and Sullivan have common roots in Freudianism, but they have even more in common in their deviations from Freud. All of them discard the biological foundations of psychoanalysis: they all deny the Freudian theory of instincts and libido; they all deny the energetic principle of psychoanalysis.

The entire sociological group represents the environmentalist point of view. They minimize the importance of hereditary forces and, therefore, are more optimistic about human nature. Horney and Fromm, and, even more, Sullivan, believe that men can be changed, since man is a product of environmental factors.

The entire sociological school tries to apply only certain concepts of Freud's theory to interpreting human behavior in a changing environment. They often reject very essential principles of Freud and introduce new and challenging hypotheses that need verification. They cannot be called a distinct, settled "school," since for the most part their theories are still being formulated, but they have undoubtedly found new ways in psychoanalysis which lead away from Freud.

2. KAREN HORNEY: PSYCHOANALYSIS WITHOUT LIBIDO

Horney as Freud's Disciple

In 1939, Karen Horney published her book *New Ways in Psychoanalysis.* A practicing psychoanalyst, she had conformed to classic psychoanalysis for many years. Her book was a revelation and a revolution, throwing overboard the most accepted principles of Freudianism. No wonder it caused a storm of protests and violent criticism.

Yet Horney regards herself as a Freudian disciple and accepts unconditionally several principles of classic psychoanalysis. She believes in abso-

[4] Gardner Murphy, Theodore Newcomb, and Lois Murphy, *Experimental Social Psychology,* Harper, 1937.

[5] George Mead, *Mind, Self, and Society,* University of Chicago, 1934.

lute *causality*. There is no room for coincidence in mental life; everything that happens has a cause and, in turn, produces effects. "I regard," says Horney, "as the most fundamental and most significant of Freud's findings his doctrines that psychic processes are strictly determined."[6]

Horney accepts fully the principle of *unconscious motivation*. Unconscious motivation is one of the general postulates of psychoanalysis. It has less to do with the scientific theories of personality; it is rather a general methodological principle. Acceptance of this principle does not prejudge the content of motives, nor does it bring evidence as to the nature of the driving power in man. It is merely a way of interpreting human behavior by assuming that a man's activities may be guided by factors unknown to the man himself.

Horney goes one step farther. She admits that these unconscious factors are emotional. The hypothesis of the unconscious was introduced by Herbart prior to Freud. However, Herbart was an associationist and paid very little attention to emotions (cf. Chapter 1). Horney, following in the footsteps of the Freudian theory, explains the *emotional content* of the unconscious.

In the study of the dynamics of the unconscious, Horney remains faithful to Freud. Unconscious desires may be repressed and they may reappear as wishful content in dreams. The repressed desires are reactivated in the process of analytical therapy; in this process the therapist has to account for resistance and transference phenomena. The neo-analytic therapy also follows Freud's methods of free associations.

Horney is a *non-reductionist* to a much higher degree than was Freud. She praises Freud, for his theory has "encouraged the venture into a psychological understanding of phenomena which hitherto had been ascribed to organic stimuli."[7] But Freud's non-reductionism was methodological only; Freud explained that as things stood, it was safer to develop a non-reductionist type of theory. He did not prejudge the issue, and expressed hope for an eventual final victory of reductionism. Horney holds against Freud "his tendency to regard psychic manifestations as the result of chemical–physiological forces." She seems to be indisputably non-reductionist.

The Challenge to Freud

Horney challenges Freud on several issues. She does not admit that personality development depends on instinctual and unchangeable forces. She denies that sexuality is the omnipotent factor. She challenges the general validity of the Oedipus theory; she doubts whether the troubles of a neurotic result from repetitional patterns formed in childhood. "All these

[6] Karen Horney, *New Ways in Psychoanalysis*, Norton, 1939, p. 18.
[7] *Ibid.*, p. 22.

theories," she says, "are open to criticism and must be regarded rather as an historical burden which psychoanalysis carries than as its pivotal center."[8]

Yet Horney's statement raises very serious doubts, because discarding the libido theory cannot mean anything but a *denial of the very essence of psychoanalysis*. According to Freud, libido is the core of personality, which develops into ego and superego. The libido theory is the frame of reference of the psychoanalytic interpretation of human behavior. Libido is one of the most important logical constructs in psychoanalysis, and most other constructs are derived from it.

It is not easy for Horney to deny libido and still claim to be Freud's disciple. But it would be even more difficult to accept libido and reconcile it with a cultural orientation. This is what Kardiner tried to do. Horney goes one step further: she regards human behavior as a product of cultural influences and not of instinctual forces. Fromm and Sullivan depart even further in a more decisive denial of libido. No wonder orthodox analysts regard the entire "sociological school" as a denial of the first principles of psychoanalysis.

Horney was the first to shift the focal point in psychoanalytic personality study from within the person to without. Constellation is more important than constitution; environment is more relevant than heredity; present conflicts in a personality weigh more than childhood entanglements.

Horney cannot accept Freud's theory regarding developmental stages. She sees in Freud's doctrine that "the libido develops in certain stages presented by heredity, the oral, anal, phallic and genital stages," another sign of Freud's biological orientation, which is "also greatly responsible for the assumption that the Oedipus complex is a regular occurrence."[9]

As a matter of fact, any developmental theory must be based on hereditary principles. This also holds true in regard to Piaget's or Gesell's developmental stages. Environmentalists must reject any theory of fixed stages of development independent from environment. To the environmentalist, child development depends on culture and child-rearing practices, and development cannot be dictated by unchangeable rules. There is good evidence for great differences in child development in various cultures and subcultures, and to this evidence Horney refers.

Environmentalists are skeptical in regard to any instinct theory. Both basic instincts, the love and the death instinct, are denied by the entire sociological school of neo-psychoanalysis. Hatred and aggressiveness are regarded as products of culture and not as innate forces. As a matter of fact, certain societies have more aggressiveness than others.

Eros, as an instinctual and inherited force, is rejected by Horney, but she does not reject love in interhuman relationships: in her writings, love is more than active sexual urge. It is a *nonsexual and passive need to be accepted*.

[8] *Ibid.*, p. 17.
[9] Karen Horney, *The Neurotic Personality of Our Time*, Norton, 1937, p. 39.

This interpretation means a dual shift from Freud's concepts: from sex to *social acceptance*, and from active need to love to *the need to be loved*.

Horney does not deny the pleasure principle, but she objects to regarding it as sexuality. The pleasure principle should be applied to any type of satisfaction, since there is no evidence that all kinds of satisfaction are derived from sex. The pleasure principle should not be identified with sex, and it is not the only principle in human behavior.

Horney does not reject the role of sex as one of the basic and innate needs. She objects to what she calls Freudian "generality" of the sexual drive. "The basic contention implicit in the libido theory though not explicitly stated is that all bodily sensations of a pleasurable nature, or strivings for them, are sexual in nature." [10] This is what she questions, and she regards the libido concept as unproved. Sex is, indeed, one of the basic needs, but not the all-important one. In neurotics, sex is not the cause, but a result and symptom of neurotic maladjustment, says Horney.

All further development of the libido theory meets with Horney's disapproval. She sees no evidence for the theory that character traits are transformations of libido, no evidence that early childhood experiences will reoccur in psychoanalytic treatment; she also doubts whether there is enough proof for the theory of sublimation. Point after point, she discards the principles of psychoanalysis.

Negation does not take one very far, however. Horney had to introduce her own theory of human behavior, and her theory is based on two principles: *safety* and *satisfaction*.

Safety and Satisfaction

"Man is ruled not by the pleasure principle alone but by two guiding principles: safety and satisfaction," says Horney. This statement is the motto of all her writings and the cornerstone of her theories. "People can renounce food, money, attention and affection so long as they are only renouncing satisfaction, but they cannot renounce these things if without them they would be or feel in danger of destitution or starvation or of being helplessly exposed to hostility, in other words, if they would lose their feeling of safety." [11]

This is the core of Horney's theory. Each individual has certain fundamental needs, food, rest, and sex, for example, and these needs must be satisfied. They cannot be combined into one, as Freud combined them into sex. However, all these needs *can* be brought together under the common heading of seeking satisfaction; together they represent the principle of pleasure.

Despite the fact that food and sex are the primary needs, they are not

[10] Horney, *New Ways in Psychoanalysis*, p. 50.
[11] *Ibid.*, p. 73.

the decisive factors in human behavior. "People can renounce these things," Horney states emphatically. They will do so if exposed to danger.

If this is the case, what is the decisive driving power? Horney would say: *the need for safety,* the need to be secure and free from fear.

Fear and safety, these are the two poles of the basic needs. Man needs safety and avoids fear. He cannot enjoy satisfaction of needs unless he feels safe. Fear is the greatest enemy of man's health and happiness, and search for safety is the guiding principle in human behavior.

Horney distinguishes between fear and anxiety. Fear is an emotional reaction to a real dnager, while anxiety is a reaction to a situation perceived subjectively as dangerous. Lack of acceptance in childhood creates the basic anxiety. "According to this concept the child not only fears punishment or desertion because of forbidden drives, but he feels the environment as a menace to his entire development and to his not legitimate wishes and strivings." [12]

Lack of satisfaction produces anxiety, said Freud. Horney says: Lack of acceptance produces *basic anxiety.* Basic anxiety is not innate; it is a result of environmental factors. The rejected or unwanted child, or a child in a broken or hostile home feels that he is "being isolated and helpless in a potentially hostile world. A wide range of adverse factors can produce this insecurity in a child." [13] The driving force in man is postulated by Horney in a non-instinctual manner; fear and anxiety are basic emotions and are the result of life experiences.

Here lies one of the fundamental differences between Freud's system and Horney's. Freud regarded love and hatred as basic emotions while anxiety was a secondary phenomenon produced by a thwarting of the basic desires. Fear is not innate; it develops as a result of coping with reality and must be related to the reality-oriented ego. The counterpart to love is hatred, and fear develops later on.

Horney regards anxiety as a basic feeling and a counterpart to love. People need to be accepted, and basic anxiety is a person's reaction to lack of acceptance.

Theory of Personality

Horney's theory of personality stands somewhere between Freud's, Adler's, and Sullivan's. The first of the two basic factors, satisfaction, falls in line with Freud's theories and represents a new version of the Freudian pleasure principle. The more important factor, safety or security, is close to Adler's self-realization and compensation and is common to Horney and Sullivan.

Horney makes it clear that the need for safety is socially created. She thinks that "particular needs which are relevant to understanding the per-

[12] *Ibid.,* p. 75.
[13] Karen Horney, *Our Inner Conflicts,* Norton, 1945.

sonality and its difficulties are not instinctual in character but are created by
the entirety of conditions under which we live."[14] Since this is the case,
personality traits must be a product of environmental forces.

Horney compares Freud's dynamic concepts of personality to conditioned reflexes and she finds Freud much superior to other students of personality. Especially valuable to Horney is Freud's assumption that human
motivation and driving power is emotional and not rational. But to her,
human emotions themselves are a result of environment, first and foremost
of early childhood experiences.

Horney admits after Freud that character, as well as neurosis, develops
in early childhood, but she rejects the principle of repetition–compulsion.
"We recognize," states Horney, "that the connection between later peculiarities and earlier experiences is more complicated than Freud assumed;
there is no such thing as an isolated experience; but the entirety of infantile
experiences combines to form a certain character structure, and it is this
structure from which later difficulties emanate. . . . Thus the analysis of
the actual character structure moves into the foreground of attention."[15]

Early childhood was regarded by Freud as the most important period in
personality development. In the first five years of life the child passes
through decisive developmental stage which shape his personality.

Horney agrees with Freud as to the importance of early childhood but
disagrees on several fundamental issues. Freud assumed that every child
passes through the oral, anal, and phallic stages. These stages are biogenic
and universal. However, how the child passes through these stages depends on environmental factors and, of course, differs from case to case,
with such various posssibilities and regression.

Horney contends that the development of the child depends upon *how
the child is treated.* There is no such thing as a universal anal stage or a universal Oedipus complex. The child may have an Oedipus complex or may
develop anal inclinations, but this is a result of parental personalities and
behavior. Nothing is universal, Horney would say; everything depends on
culture and environment.

The child's needs can be dealt with in a satisfactory way by the
parents, who thus contribute to his mental health. Or his needs could be
thwarted and frustrated. He might be bullied about, severely punished, or
even entirely rejected by his parents. He could perceive his home environment as "unfair, unjust, begrudging and merciless," and this will influence
his actual behavior and future development as well.

Although Horney agrees with Freud as to the importance of early childhood, she is at variance with him in regard to the impact of unfortunate
events that occur in early childhood. The ways the child reacts to his environment combine and interrelate and form the structure of his personality.
This *character structure* tends to be quite consistent in a person's lifetime

[14] Horney, *New Ways in Psychoanalysis*, p. 78.
[15] *Ibid.*, p. 9.

development, but the isolated experiences themselves are not.[16] This interpretation brings Horney quite close to Alfred Adler.

Horney admits more flexibility in adult personality than Freud did, and she is quite optimistic about the possibility of a change in personality in adult age. Her optimism originates in the denial of instinctual forces and in her belief in the general human tendency toward constructiveness. This optimistic belief in human nature, as compared to Freud's pessimism, is common to her and Fromm and, in a way, to Sullivan too.

Freud postulated, Horney says, that instinct can only be controlled, or at best sublimated. "My own belief," she explains, "is that man has the capacity as well as the desire to develop his potentialities and become a decent human being. I believe that man can change and go on changing as long as he lives."[17]

This is Horney's credo. No "death instinct" and no inherited Eros instinct: man depends on environment. Society can and should be improved, and then men will be happier and healthier.

Once again, Horney comes close to Alfred Alder's optimistic theory of social change and change in human nature.

Theory of Neurosis

Since personality is perceived by Horney in an environmentalist fashion, deviation from normal behavior must be interpreted on similar lines. Normalcy, according to her, is a term related to culture. "With us," she says, "a person would be neurotic or psychotic who talked by the hour with his deceased grandfather, whereas such communication with ancestors is a recognized pattern in some Indian tribes."[18]

The sociological school in psychoanalysis emphasizes that Freud did not pay enough attention to differences in culture. Horney feels strongly that neurosis is a result not of inner conflict between ego, id, and superego, but of conflict between an individual and his environment. She shifts the focal point in a neurosis from within a person to without. However, in her last book she emphasizes the "central inner conflict" between the real potentialities of one's self and the gratification of one's imaginary self.[19]

Horney accuses our society of breeding neurosis. Neurosis is a result of insecurity, and it may develop in childhood as the boy or girl is deprived of acceptance. A society based on competition contributes substantially to development of insecurity and is conducive to neurosis, "carrying the germs of destructive rivalry, disarrangement, suspicion, begrudging, envy into every human relationship."[20]

[16] Horney, *Neurotic Personality*.
[17] Horney, *Our Inner Conflicts*, p. 19.
[18] *Ibid.*, p. 15.
[19] Karen Horney, *Neurosis and Human Growth*, Norton, 1950.
[20] Horney, *Neurotic Personality*, p. 113.

The neurotic person tends to move in one of three possible directions, called by Horney *neurotic trends*. The first is moving toward people, the second against them, the third away from them. Overcompliance is a manifestation of neurotic behavior; a neurotic person cannot risk alienating people and he tries to gain their acceptance by complying with their desires. Another kind of neurotic behavior is hostility and aggressiveness. The third neurotic trend is seclusion and withdrawal; the neurotic person is unable to face people and tries to avoid them. The common denominator of all three "neurotic trends" is obviously social maladjustment.

However, since social maladjustment per se cannot fully explain the nature and origin of neurosis, there must be more specific factors related to it. Horney says that certain personality traits prevent successful adjustment. Neurosis is a "certain rigidity in reaction and discrepancy between potentialities and accomplishments." It is a psychic disturbance "brought about by fears and defenses against these fears, and by attempts to find compromise solutions for conflicting tendencies." [21] This disturbance usually develops in early childhood as a result of child-rearing practices.

The neurotic tries to deny his inner conflicts by creating an artifical and unrealistic image of himself.[22] He believes himself far superior to the man he really is. This "idealized image" has for him the value of reality, thus helping him avoid awareness of his inner conflicts. Instead of using his energies for self-realization he wastes them in "search for glory," that is, in actualization of his idealized self. This is the *central inner conflict*, as presented by Horney in her later writings.

Concluding Remarks

Horney's contribution to psychotherapeutic practice seems greater than her contribution to psychological theory; various psychotherapeutic practices owe much to her daring. However, Horney's contribution to psychological theory is also considerable. Using the frame of reference of the psychoanalytic school, one would say that she has *shifted the focus in the study of personality from id to ego*. Id, the basic part of personality in Freudian theory, has almost disappeared in Horney's studies. This is not merely a cancellation of the term "id"; people may construct scientific models on Freudian lines using different terminology, but this is not the case with Horney. She actually has introduced a new model of personality, leaving very little if anything to innate factors, and has strongly emphasized acquired traits. She regards fear and anxiety as the basic human emotions, while Freud saw love and hatred as basic.

However, this difference is not so great as it appears on the surface.

[21] *Ibid.*, p. 28.

[22] Karen Horney, *Are You Considering Psychoanalysis?* Norton, 1946, p. 21. See also Horney, *Neurosis and Human Growth*.

Both Freud and Horney regard human nature as a product of heredity and environment. Freud never belittled environmental influences; as a matter of fact, the way the child passes from one stage to another, whether the child remains fixated or regresses, sublimates or establishes reaction formation, is a matter of environmental forces. The innate love and hatred are molded into various behavioral patterns by external influences and by an inner balance of forces established under the pressure of these influences. Fear is the guiding factor in ego; fear is "reality oriented" and is a product of coping with external factors. Freud said that fear is acquired through life experiences; Horney, too, emphasizes in a different way that fear is a product of experience; the burned child dreads fire, and a child who has experienced rejection will develop anxieties.

Horney's personality model is far inferior to Freud's in clarity, consistency, and elaboration. Freud's personality model is constructed with the precision of a mathematician and the refinment of a sculptor. It is difficult to reshape it. It is much simpler to reject it or accept it as it is than to remold or restructure it. Most of the efforts to correct Freud bear the stamp of awkwardness and are usually frowned on by orthodox psychoanalysts.

Yet many have accepted or rejected one or another part of Freud's theory, despite the danger that tampering with one of the pillars may damage the entire structure or erect a shaky building. And this is precisely why, without challenging the importance or validity of Horney's findings, one is confronted with so many unanswered questions. The reader of Freud may reject or accept Freud's principles; accepting them, he is compelled to admire the magnificent consistency of the entire structure and the wealth of the empirical material used for it. When reading Horney, one may often admit that she is right but the entire system is often imperfect.

Additional criticism is invited by the combination of Horney's environmentalism with Freud's mechanism. One can readily understand unconsciousness, resistance, repression, and dreams, by applying Freud's libido theory. Rejecting the libido theory, one finds these factors less easily explained.

Both Freud and Horney face complementary difficulties in explaining the nature of emotional disturbances. Horney may ask Freud why it is only in certain cases that libido acts conversely. Freud, in turn, may ask Horney why environment influences only certain individuals and makes them neurotic. Probably a *full* consideration given to both constitution and constellation would be the proper one. Perhaps William Stern's "convergism" would be helpful here (cf. Chapter 11).

Summarizing Horney's contribution to psychological theory, we find that she has paved a new road in psychoanalysis. She called her programmatic book *New Ways in Psychoanalysis,* but her own system is only one of the many possible ways. Her trail is not a well-established highway; too many questions are left open, and too little evidence has been accumulated.

One must, however, admit that Horney has opened new vistas in psychological research. Whether her statements are "true" or "wrong" has yet to be proved, but, with her environmentalist approach, she has shown new horizons in psychoanalysis which invite further research and seem to be promising.

3. ERICH FROMM: HISTORICAL AND ETHICAL PSYCHOANALYSIS

Philosophy of History

It was Sigmund Freud who introduced the laws of evolution of the psyche into contemporary psychology. Freud was convinced that many ancient and archaic patterns are carried over into the personality structure of modern man. This principle has been applied in two ways. First, each individual is supposed to "recapitulate" the development stages of mankind (the biogenetic principle); second, contemporary social institutions such as law, religion, and family have developed from primitive social forms, and they transmit the heritage of the past to the present generation.

Fromm shifted away from Freudian philosophy on several points. He thought less of the biogenetic law and attached more weight to the cultural heritage. In fact, he regards human behavior at *any* historical moment as a product of cultural influences at the given time. His main assumptions are as follows: "Man's nature, his passions and anxieties are a cultural product; as a matter of fact, man himself is the most important creation and achievement of the continuous human effort, the record of which we call history."[23]

This is, indeed, a far-reaching statement. Most psychologists deal with human behavior in terms of individually inherited traits, or of the individual's life experiences, or both. The environmentalists are likely to emphasize one's life history, the field theorists the immediate situation.

Fromm introduced new areas of research into the study of human nature. Human history serves him as a huge laboratory in human nature, where various patterns of behavior are shaped and reshaped. History is both a source of factual data and a major case study which enables us to understand the impact of social factors on human life. Fromm is an environmentalist, but he has found in history a changing scenery of the life of mankind and an important field for psychological study.

Freud's philosophy of history was an addition to his psychological theory; Fromm's philosophy of history was the cornerstone of his psychological theory. The reason is apparent. Freud regarded history as man-made, while Fromm regarded man as history-made. One is tempted, therefore, to say that Fromm has done to Freud what Marx did to Hegel. Both Fromm and Marx applied the principles of their masters in a reverse direction. Marx transferred Hegel's idealism and spiritualism into materialism and

[23] Erich Fromm, *Escape from Freedom*, Rinehart, 1941, p. 13.

economism. Fromm reversed the order of man in society; instead of regarding society as a result of man's instincts, he regarded man as a product of social influences.[24]

The focal point in this shift from orthodox psychoanalysis was described by Fromm as follows:

> The assumption underlying the orthodox Freudian approach was that social phenomena and cultural patterns are to be explained as direct outcomes of certain libidinal trends. Thus, for instance, capitalism was explained as a result of anal eroticism or was the result of the operation of the death instinct. The method used here was the explanation by analogy. One tried to discover analogies between cultural phenomena and neurotic symptoms of a patient and then proceeded to explain the cultural phenomenon as being 'caused' by the same libidinous factors by which the neurotic symptom had been explained.[25]

Culture, according to Fromm, cannot be deduced from and interpreted by a theory of innate instincts, such as love and hate. Societies are not shaped by libidinal forces, as Freud said, but by objective conditions embedded in geography, history, and economics.

> Each society is structuralized and operates in certain ways which are necessitated by a number of objective conditions; such conditions are the methods of production and distribution which in turn depend on new material, industrial techniques, climate, etc., furthermore political and geographical factors and cultural traditions and influences to which society is exposed.[26]

Fromm transferred the focal point from within the individual to the external *objective conditions*. The behavior of individuals is shaped by their society, and the society is molded by "objective conditions."[27]

This is a serious deviation from Freud, and a major step forward in the direction of environmentalism and situationalism. This is what Fromm had in common with Kardiner.

Culture versus Nature

Man is a living organism, and as such he has certain physiological needs. He differs from other organisms in at least two respects. First, he does not satisfy his needs in an animal-like manner, that is, in a uniform, fixed, and unchangeable pattern of behavior called *instinct*.

Fromm accepted the generality of physiological needs. He would not oppose the application of the term "instinct" to these needs. What he could not accept was the idea that all humans follow the same pattern of behavior in pursuing their goals. He rejected instincts as uniform patterns of behav-

[24] Erich Fromm, *The Crisis in Psychoanalysis,* Holt, Rinehart & Winston, 1970.
[25] Erich Fromm, "Psychoanalytic Characterology and Its Application to the Understanding of Culture," in S. S. Sargent and M. Smith (Eds.), *Culutre and Personality,* Viking Fund, 1949, pp. 2–3.
[26] *Ibid.,* pp. 4–5.
[27] *Ibid.,* pp. 4 ff.

ior in man. The higher the species and the more developed the brain of an animal, the less complete and rigid the animal's instincts. The emergence of man occurred when instinctual behavior reached its lowest point. Man does not follow the instinctual pattern; he learns from his environment, and his behavior is conditioned by culture.

Freud regarded id-level behavior as independent of cultural influences, but no adult individual lives on that level. With the exception of severely disturbed individuals, all of us live in some kind of balance between the id, the ego, and the superego, and the two latter are products of cultural influences. Moreover, Freud assumed that instinctual forces can be modified, sublimated, suppressed or repressed, but never annihilated (cf. Chapter 6). Fromm denied their very existence in humans. According to him, only lower animals display full-fledged instinctual behavior, while higher animals use less instinct and more learning. Man learns and reasons and his behavior is flexible and adaptable.

Fromm pointed out the second difference between man and animals. While all men have certain common physiological needs, they differ from each other in their socially created needs.

> Although there are certain needs, such as hunger, thirst, sex, which are common to man, those drives which make for the *difference* in man's character, like love and hatred, lust for power and yearning for submission, enjoyment, of sensuous pleasure and the fear of it, are all products of the social process. The most beautiful as well as the most ugly inclinations of men are not a part of a fixed and biologically given human nature, but result from the social process which creates men. [28]

Is man an exception to the laws of nature? Fromm answered this question paradoxically: yes and no. Man is "a part of nature"; no man can escape the physical laws of the universe and no man can change them. Man can never free himself from the "dichotomies of existence." He lives but he must die; he has many potentialities, but he cannot realize them in his short life; man is a part of society, but he does not live in harmony with it and he is always a separate entity. Man is aware of himself as being a separate entity; he reasons, he may conceive of and understand the order of the universe. Thus he realizes his "powerlessness and the limitations of his existence." He knows that there is no solution to the eternal dichotomies; that he is a part of nature yet "transcends the rest of nature."

Besides these existential dichotomies, man faces historical dichotomies. The contradictions in the life of society and individual are man-made and can be solved by man. The contradiction between the abundance in production and the human inability to enjoy it in peace and welfare is a historical dichotomy. It is not an eternal and insoluble contradiction of mankind; men can solve this problem.

Existential dichotomies cannot be solved. Often people try to deny their existence by development of "ideologies." One of the possible ideolo-

[28] Fromm, *Escape from Freedom*, p. 12.

gies is religion and the belief in an immortal soul. While Freud saw in religion a kind of neurosis, Fromm arrived at the conclusion that "a neurosis is to be explained as a particular form of religion differing mainly by its individual, non-patterned characteristics." [29]

Man can try to escape the dichotomies of his life and appease his mind by a restless activity in business or in an incessant pursuit of pleasure. He may give up his freedom and integrity in order to feel related to others, but he will never find peace and satisfaction in this way.

The only true way to cope with the existential dichotomies is for man to unfold his own powers; they will lead him to achieve happiness. This ability to live a productive life is embedded in human nature.

In contrast to animals, man's most compelling problems are not those of hunger or thirst or sex. Humans strive for power and love, and fight for religious or political ideas; they do not live "by bread alone."

The existential dichotomies compel man to seek to restore the unity between himself and nature. In the search for unity, man needs orientation in and devotion to the world. He can develop various "frames of orientation and devotion," but he must have some aim. These frames of orientation and devotion correspond to what is called *ideals*. Everyone must have some ideal, although the ideals may be different in different persons. Man can choose between being devoted "to reason and love and being devoted to the worship of power and destruction. All men are 'idealists' and are striving for something beyond the attainment of physical satisfaction. They differ in the kind of ideals they believe in." [30] Everyone needs ideals in which to believe, and everyone can make his own life meaningful through devotion to an aim.

Each person can find productive outlets for his energies, "unless he is mentally or emotionally crippled." Man's productiveness creates material things, works of art, and systems of thought, but "by far the most important object of productiveness is man himself."

Man's life is a continuous process of creation. Physical growth proceeds by itself, but "it requires productive activity to give life to the emotional and intellectual potentialities of man, to give birth to his self." [31]

Psyche through the Ages

Animals are a part of and live in accordance with nature. Man's history started with the denial of identity with nature: though he was a part of nature, he was no longer identical with nature. "He changes his role toward nature from that of a purely passive adaptation to an active one: he produces. He invents tools and, while mastering nature, he separates himself— or rather his group—as not being identical with nature." [32]

[29] Erich Fromm, *Man for Himself*, Rinehart, 1947, p. 49.
[30] *Ibid.*
[31] *Ibid.*, p. 91.
[32] Fromm, *Escape from Freedom*, p. 33.

As man moved away from nature, he became more aware of his unchangeable fate. He could not change the laws of nature and he felt helpless and alone. Animals did not face the dichotomies of life; men did. Man realized that his ultimate end was death.

Primitive man tried to escape his fate. He developed myth and religion and identified himself fully with his group or clan. His group-belonging saved him from the feeling of being alone. The group decided how one should live; the group assigned each individual a definite place; the group was the source of security.

The beliefs of the group shared by all its members alleviated man's isolation in nature. Primitive religions tied man to nature; people worshiped sun and moon, land and sea, winds and fire, animals and plants. These *primary ties* served to strengthen man's security feeling and deny, by imaginary and magic devices, that man transcends nature.

This situation could not last forever. Man's critical mind prevented him from remaining subservient to a group. People criticized and revolted, reasoned and developed new concepts. The ties of an individual to his clan, and through it to nature, loosened. In man's primitive stage, "while being aware of himself as a separate entity, he felt also part of the world around him." Later, people revolted against being subjugated to their group and nature. They strove toward independence, toward freedom of reasoning and decision and free use of all their powers. This process "which we may call 'individuation' seems to have reached its peak in modern history in the centuries between the Reformation and the present."[33]

In Western civilization, the Middle Ages represent, in Fromm's view, the era of social security, solidarity, and stability. There was not much personal freedom in that time, since everybody's place in the society was well defined by his class status in the feudal system. However, members of each class enjoyed the feeling of belonging and they felt secure in the frame of their social class.

The Renaissance, the Reformation, and Protestantism destroyed the medieval system. Man gained more freedom, but his position in the new social order was less stable. He could develop more initiative and more criticism but had lost the feeling of solidarity and was more and more alone. The Renaissance encouraged the development of a "passionate egocentricity." Protestantism destroyed the identification with God through belonging to the Church. Man had to pray alone, and alone face his responsibility toward the Lord.

The freedom gained by men in Western civilization is rather a "freedom from" than a "freedom to." Man is free; he is free *from* slavery; he developed his own personality, and his life is more individualized, yet he has less security than in medieval times. Today he does not belong anywhere, and he is often alone and insecure. He is free *from*, but is not free *to* live, to develop, to enjoy life. His happiness is always at stake, always dependent on his being accepted by others.

[33] *Ibid.*, p. 24.

No wonder many individuals are ready to give up their freedom in order to regain security. This is how Fromm explained the rise of totalitarian systems in contemporary society. Quite often, as a result of the lack of "freedom to" live a more happy and secure life, men try to escape their "freedom from." Since this freedom has not brought security and happiness, they readily give it up and escape from it into a totalitarian system.

This is, however, not the only *escape mechanism*. Fromm maintained that there are four mechanisms of escape: sadism, masochism, destructiveness, and automaton conformity. The sado-masochistic mechanisms mean basically the giving up of one's independence. In sadism one can try to "make others dependent on oneself and to have absolute and unrestricted power over them." Another type of sadist trends "to exploit them, to use them, to steal from them, to disembowel them." A third kind of sadistic tendency is the wish "to make others suffer or see them suffer."[34] A masochist feels inferior and tends to submit his own personality to another person. In an extreme case, a masochist is willing to suffer under the control of a strong person in order to escape his feelings of loneliness.

Destructiveness is another escape mechanism. "I can," says Fromm, "escape the feeling of my own powerlessness in comparison with the world outside of myself by destroying it. . . . The destruction of the world is the last, almost desperate attempt to save myself from being crushed by it."[35]

The last escape mechanism is *automaton conformity*. It is a full conformity to social norms, to the point of complete negation of anything that is original and independent. It is a blind acceptance of the social pattern, and a readiness to obey the leader unconditionally.

Childhood

Fromm followed in Freud's footsteps in applying the biogenetic principle. Childhood development presents a pattern similar to that of the history of mankind.

> A child is born when it is no longer one with its mother and becomes a biological entity separate from her. Yet, while this biological separation is the beginning of individual human existence, the child remains functionally one with its mother for a considerable period.[36]

As the child grows, he faces restraints and prohibitions imposed by his parents. Unless parental behavior is exceptionally improper, the child will become more and more independent as he grows. Gradually, the ties connecting him with his parents become weaker as he develops more awareness of his individuality. This process of development brings about dangers similar to those in the history of mankind, for a higher level of individ-

[34] *Ibid.*, p. 144.
[35] *Ibid.*, p. 179.
[36] *Ibid.*, p. 25.

ualization is accompanied by a decline in security feeling. The little child does not have much freedom, but he is happy and secure in his dependence on his parents. Maturity means more independence, but it also means less security. Children who have been reared by hostile or domineering parents will be less prepared to face the problems of maturity; they may feel powerless, forsaken, and isolated.

Many individuals develop *escape mechanisms* similar to those developed by mankind. Thus, they become sadists, masochists, destructionists, or automaton–conformists; the pattern of their defense mechanism is a product not of heredity but of their experiences in childhood.

Not only the defense mechanism, but also the totality of the child's character is molded by his parents. Families usually serve as *psychological agents* of the society and transmit the cultural values of their nation and class to the children. The child's character is formed by social and cultural patterns as represented by the characters of his parents. This is why most members of a group share significant character traits; these common traits were called by Fromm the *social character*. The child's *individual character* is a product of the specific environmental influences exercised by his parents.

Fromm criticized Freud's genetic interpretation of psychological types. Freud saw the origins of the oral or anal type, for example, in fixation on the oral or anal level. Fromm sought the origin of the personality differences between individuals not in the developmental stages of libido, but in their *environmental experiences*. How the parents treat their child—this will determine the child's personality.

If a person develops into the oral-dependent or the anal-obstinate type, it is not because of a fixation, but a result of *child-rearing practices*. Child-rearing practices that influence character formation are not only the feeding of the child and teaching him to control his bowels, but the *total sum* of *social relationships* at home. If the home situation encourages friendliness and acceptance, the child is likely to develop the receptive–dependent personality traits. His childhood experiences will teach him that he got the most out of complying with others in trying to please them. If, however, the child receives everything only after a quarrel, a fight, or a period of stubbornness, he will probably develop the oral-aggressive or, in Fromm's terminology, exploiting-sadistic character. The child who grows up in a home atmosphere of "grab it" will probably follow this pattern of behavior all his life. In a home where scarcity, distrust, and suspicion prevail, the child will learn to keep what he gets and not let people take away anything that belongs to him. This is the typical anal attitude or, in Fromm's division, the hoarding-remote character.

Theory of Personality

Fromm did not deny inherited or constitutional patterns. He called them *temperament*. Temperament is the *mode* of reaction, and is "constitutional and not changeable." Temperament is correlated to somatic processes and is inherited.

Character is formed in life experience through social influences. Character is the relatively permanent "form in which human energy is canalized in the process of assimilation and socialization."[37] Character is determined by the individual's physical constitution and temperament, which are innate, and the totality of social and cultural influences on him. "Character is the specific form in which human energy is shaped by the dynamic adaptation of human needs to the particular mode of existence in a given society. Character in turn determines the thinking, feeling and acting of individuals."[38] Two parts can be distinguished in a person's character. The first is the *individual character*. This part of character indicates the differences among the members of the same cultural group. The individual character carries the innate factors of personality and the specific influences of a given home environment. The other part, the *social character*, is shared by the majority of the members of the same culture. The social character in personality

> has the function of molding human energy for the purpose of the functioning of a given society. The members of the society . . . have to behave in such a way as to be able to function in the sense required by society. It is the function of the social character to shape the energies of the members of society in such a way that their behavior is not left to conscious decisions whether or not to follow the social pattern but that people want to act as they have to act and at the same time find gratification in acting according to the requirements of the culture.[39]

Fromm's "social character," if translated into the terminology of orthodox psychoanalysis, would fit best into superego, as the part of personality that identifies itself with cultural influences. The focal point has been shifted by Fromm from the libido to environment, from the individual person to society. Freud worked from personality to society; Fromm and Sullivan interpreted personality as a product of society.

Another point of difference between Fromm and Freud requires clarification. Freud emphasized the attachment of the fixated libido to the various somatic zones. The anal type, for example, is not only a person who keeps money or hoards other objects; he is stingy in relation to his feces, too. While money or various objects represent the sublimation of his fears, his elimination tract clings to the infantile pattern of behavior in delaying elimination, and in an obvious inclination toward constipation. The same holds true in regard to the oral character, who not only sublimates his oral tendencies but is also an eager drinker and/or eater (cf. Chapter 6).

Fromm did not deny the fact that character traits are somehow related to somatic symptoms. But, he said the causal order has to be reversed. A

[37] Fromm, *Man for Himself*, p. 59.
[38] Fromm, *Escape from Freedom*, p. 278.
[39] Fromm, "Psychoanalytic Characterology," in Sargent and Smith, *op. cit.*, p. 5.

person is not receptive-dependent because he likes to drink or he lacked sucking in his first year of life. His craving for drinking is not the cause but a *symptom*, an expression of his character. His character has little if anything to do with his sucking urge. Character is a result of the total home situation. Friendly, cheerful, and permissive parents might encourage great intakes of food; unfriendly and meticulous ones might be very strict in toilet training. The decisive factor in the child's character development is not the libido experience but the total home atmosphere, which is conducive to the formation of a certain character type. It is proper to mention at this point that this interpretation is similar to Alfred Adler's theory of "style of life" (cf. Chapter 7).

Personality Types

There are, according to Fromm, two kinds of relatedness to the outside world: that of *assimilation* and that of *socialization*. Socialization deals with people, assimilation with things. Socialization can develop into symbiosis, withdrawal-destructiveness, or love.

Symbiotic relatedness is a social relation the basis of which is dependence on others. The person avoids being alone and tries to become a part of another person either by "swallowing" him (*sadism*) or by being "swallowed" (*masochism*).

Withdrawal and *destructiveness* represent the passive and active type of social attitude, respectively. Certain individuals try to gain some sense of security through isolation. They either withdraw from any contact with other individuals or become aggressive and destructive, aiming at the annihilation of others.

The attitude of *love* is the "productive form of relatedness to others and to oneself." Love implies care, respect, and responsibility, and it is the wish for the well-being of the other person.

Assimilation is the way people acquire or assimilate things. Both assimilation and socialization were called by Fromm *orientations*, which form the "core of character." Orientations are not determined by heredity but are shaped by environmental influences.

There are several patterns of assimilation, and all but one of them are nonproductive. The *receptive* orientation in a person is expressed by expectancy of help from the outside. The receptive type is the receiver and not the giver in material processes, in love, or in intellectual functions. The *exploitative* type of person, like the receptive, believes that all good is outside his person. He does not, however, expect to receive from others; he takes by force or cunning.

The *hoarding* orientation leads to negativism, pedantic orderliness, and rigidity. The outside world is perceived by the hoarding type as a threat and he tends to be saving and possessive.

The *marketing* orientation has developed in the modern era, since people's success today depends on a "personal acceptance by those who need their services or who employ them." Success today depends mostly on "how well a person sells himself" and "whether he knows the right people." This situation is not conducive to a feeling of security, since a person's value depends less on his personal qualities, and more on his success in a competitive market. The self-marketing attitude makes a man play the role of: "I am as you desire me."

Fromm's fifth character type is the *productive* one. The productive character is a combination of the previous four characters, but is guided in the direction of love of others and creativity. The main traits of the productive character are devotion to the well-being of his fellow man and productive activity. Even the antisocial traits of the other types, like exploitation, turn into positive traits, such as having initiative or leadership qualities.

Table 1 reflects Fromm's chart in characterology.[40] Fromm offered several other tables of combinations or "blends" of the various orientations and said that the configuration of these elements makes for an endless number of variations in personality.

Society and Ethics

Fromm feels that "the choice between life and death is the basic alternative of the ethics. It is the alternative between productiveness and destructiveness, between potency and impotency, between virtue and vice. For humanistic ethics all evil strivings are directed against life and all good serves the preservation and unfolding of life."[41]

In his studies, Freud carefully avoided value judgments and abstained from introducing moral attitudes in therapy. Fromm criticized him and doubted whether any therapy is possible unless the therapist takes a stand on moral issues. Adjustment is adjustment to a definite society and to definite social modes and ethics. Freud's abstention from taking a stand is a product of a certain era, namely, the era of laissez faire and liberalism.[42] Fromm maintained that the value judgments of a person determine his actions, and neurosis itself is a symptom of moral failure; a neurotic is a person who has failed to achieve maturity and personality intergration; virtue is proportioned to productiveness, and ethics is related to health and confirmation of life.

Fromm said that Freud accepted the "traditional doctrine of the evilness of human nature. Man, to him, is fundamentally antisocial. Society must domesticate him, must allow some direct satisfaction of biologi-

---

[40] Fromm, *Man for Himself,* p. 111.
[41] *Ibid.,* p. 214.
[42] Erich Fromm, "Die gesellschaftliche Bedingtheit der psychoanalytischen Therapie," *Zeitschrift für Sozialforschung,* 1935.

Table 1. Fromm's Chart of Orientations

	Assimilation	Socialization	
I. Nonproductive orientation			
a.	Receiving (accepting)	Masochistic (loyalty)	Symbiosis
b.	Exploiting (taking)	Sadistic (authority)	Symbiosis
c.	Hoarding (preserving)	Destructive (assertiveness)	Withdrawal
d.	Marketing (exchanging)	Indifferent (fairness)	Withdrawal
II. Productive orientation			
	Working	Loving, reasoning	

cal—and hence ineradicable—drives; but for the most part society must refine and adroitly check man's basic impulses."[43]

Fromm was more optimistic. He believed in human "constructiveness" and inherent primary potentialities. He assumed that virtue, courage, honesty, and creativeness are attractive to everyone, and that there is no need for additional incentives for morality since moral behavior is a reward in itself.

The failure of modern culture, said Fromm, lies not in the fact "that people are *too much concerned with their self-interest* but that they are *not concerned enough with the interest of their real self;* not in the fact that they are too selfish, but that they do not love themselves."[44] People too often develop "escape mechanisms" and do not pursue true self-realization.

People are influenced by the authoritarian ethics, which maintains that man is an evil being, and that only by victory over himself can he become moral. The authoritative ethic is based on the patriarchal family. Fromm interpreted the Oedipus complex not as an incestuous conflict, but as "the rebellion of the son against the authority of the father in the patriarchal family."[45] Freud's superego represents the "authoritarian conscience," while Fromm called for a free and harmonious development of all the potentialities latent in an individual.

From made a strong plea for a society in which human problems can be solved. In such a future society "man relates to man lovingly." Fromm suggested the formation of a sane society which gives man "the possibility of transcending nature by creating rather than by conformity, in which a sys-

[43] Fromm, *Escape from Freedom*, p. 10.
[44] Fromm, *Man for Himself*, p. 139.
[45] Quotation from P. Mullahy, *Oedipus—Myth and Complex*, Hermitage, 1948, p. 271.

tem of orientation and devotion exists without man's needing to distort reality and to worship idols."[46]

Concluding Remarks

Fromm's contribution to psychological theory can be summarized in four points:

Use of history as a psychological research area
Theory of character
Ethical interpretation of psychological issues
Sociological orientation in psychological studies

Fromm's analysis of history represents a great challenge both to psychologists and to philosophers of history. He tried to interpret human nature in view of historical events and drew far-reaching conclusions. However, his historical comments do not follow the available data. For example, his story of man's alleged loneliness leading to group formation does not correspond to any data; his picture of medieval life is highly idealized; he omitted all the physical and mental hardships produced by despotism, fanaticism, religious persecutions, witch-hunts, superstitions, plagues, wars, and other disasters. The era of the Renaissance and Reformation is painted black in disregard of the positive and productive aspects of those times. Fromm's story of freedom and escape is an interesting one but contradicts all observable data in the history of the French and American Revolutions. In fact, it does not correspond to any known historical data.

Fromm's characterology invites additional criticism. It reminds one of Spranger's *Lebensformen* (see Chapter 11) or McDougall's emotions (see Chapter 5) with its arbitrarily set classifications. Fromm admits that character is "usually a blend of all of these orientations in which one, however, is dominant."[47] But if each character is a "blend," with no possibility of finding out anything more precise about the composition of the blend, then what scientific purpose is served by the introduction of the "character orientations" hypothesis?

This criticism is aimed at the abundance of types and subtypes, but not against the hypothesis that personality traits are influenced by environmental factors. This hypothesis seems to be a fruitful one.

Fromm's philosophical and ethical system emphasizes an optimistic approach to human nature. Freud's theory of the death instinct and of the conflict between human nature and culture has been regarded by the neo-psychoanalysts as unduly pessimistic. Both Horney and Fromm reject the death-instinct theory and believe in the "productiveness" of human nature. However, Fromm's philosophy of life does not warrant this optimism. Man

[46] Erich Fromm, *The Sane Society*, Rinehart, 1955, p. 362.
[47] Fromm, *Man for Himself*, p. 61.

is doomed to an eternal conflict with nature; since he knows too much, he is unable to accept his fate naïvely. Every historical stage leaves him "discontented and perplexed"; there is never peace of mind, never harmony between man and universe, but only a continuous struggle and search for new solutions, none of them ever a final one. This is, to quote Fromm, man's tragic fate: "to be part of nature, and yet to transcend it."

Yet, and this is worth while mentioning, Fromm calls for creativeness and virtues. Though the discussion of Fromm's philosophy and ethics transcends the borders of a scientific study of true and false statements, it is good to point to this revolt of psychologist against objective truth in favor of moral judgments. Thus, Fromm's writings confront scientific truth-seekers with the human problem of right and wrong.

4. HARRY S. SULLIVAN: A THEORY OF INTERPERSONAL RELATIONS

New Conceptual Tools

Sullivan is perhaps the only neo-psychoanalyst who developed his own conceptual system of psychology. He deviated further from Freud than any other psychoanalyst. He abandoned the Freudian frames of reference and discarded most of the basic concepts of psychoanalysis, such as libido, ego, superego, sex theory, and character formation. He did not even apply Freud's terminology, which is quite an important factor. He borrowed from Freud only some principles in human dynamics, such as unconscious motivation, defense mechanisms, and dream interpretation. Sullivan can hardly be regarded as Freud's disciple. He is rather a fairly independent theoretician of psychology whose thoughts have been considerably influenced by Freud.

One should not study Sullivan with Freud's theories as an introduction. It is much easier to interpret Sullivan's theories using Horney, or even Fromm, as a bridge between Freud and Sullivan.

Sullivan was influenced by both Adolph Meyer's biological method and George Mead's theory of social status and role, and in various points his study shows a considerable similarity to field theory. The most sociological-minded neo-psychoanalyst, Sullivan combined operationism and environmentalism with a certain kind of reductionism. He introduced the term "experience" as Watson would say "behavior," Stern "Erlebnis," or Kurt Lewin "locomotion." He distinguished clearly between "physical" and "cultural" phenomena; he dealt with bodily needs in a fairly consistent reductionist manner. One wonders how much of Descartes's dualism entered into Sullivan's system: Descartes was at a loss to find the necessary bridge between the body perceived as a machine and the psyche perceived as a spirit. Sullivan crossed a similar bridge quite easily; he assumed that the release of energy (energy perceived in physical terms) is always controlled by social relations. This combination of physicalism with sociology is, to say the least, quite interesting and may lead to further fruitful studies.

Sullivan's theories grew out of his psychiatric experience, mostly with psychotics. While Freud introduced into psychology the richness of motivational problems, Sullivan called for more attention to perception and social interrelationships.

Satisfaction

Sullivan accepts the principles of teleology in psychological studies, following Adler and the entire neo-psychoanalytic movement. He postulates two basic purposes in human activities, *satisfaction* and *security*. People pursue the goal of satisfaction by satisfying hunger, thirst, need for sleep and rest, sex, and need for close physical contact with other people. All other activities "which pertain more to the culture which has been imbedded in a particular individual than to organization of his tissues and glands, [are] apt to belong in this classification of the pursuit of security."[48]

Sullivan goes so far as to introduce an almost dualistic approach to psychology. Satisfaction is basically somatic—it is a function of cells and tissues, of muscles and bodily organs—while security is a cultural phenomenon.

Both the striped and the unstriped muscles serve one purpose: satisfaction. What we experience as thirst or hunger, or as a desire for air or sex is a result of muscular contractions. *Physiological tension* "provokes" our pursuit of satisfaction, and satisfaction brings relaxation and relief of tension.

> Tonic changes in the unstriped, involuntary muscles of the viscera—the internal organs of the body—are, from birth onward, intimately related to the experiencing of desires, needs for satisfaction. Heightened tone of the stomach wall is called out by depletion of our chemical supplies. Throughout life the pursuit of satisfaction is physiologically provoked by increased tone in some unstriped muscles; and the securing of the satisfaction is a relaxation of this tone.[49]

The entire process of seeking satisfaction is interpreted in a reductionist manner. The organic state, such as a heightened tone of the stomach wall, causes us to experience a "desire." When satisfaction is secured, the muscles relax and our alertness is reduced. The organism tends to rest or sleep. The highest experience of tension is terror, the most profound satisfaction and relaxation is sleep.

This interpretation of human needs has little in common with Freud. It seems to be closer to some kind of organismic theory (see Kurt Goldstein, Chapter 5). Sullivan's theory invites comparison with Cannon's homeostatic system (*tension* and *relief* follow each other), especially since tension and relief are interpreted by Sullivan in purely physiological terms, as a contraction and relaxation of muscles. This physiological process is later

---

[48] Harry S. Sullivan, *Conceptions of Modern Psychiatry*, W. A. White Foundation, 1947, p. 6.
[49] *Ibid.*, p. 43.

modified by social influences. The child soon learns that on certain occasions, the immediate relaxation of muscles meets with parental disapproval. Parental disapproval causes a feeling of discomfort. This *empathized discomfort* stems not from the organism but from *interpersonal relationships.* The discomfort is so strong that it destroys the original comfort of relaxation. For example, as soon as there is any tension in bladder or bowels, the proper muscles act immediately to bring relief. However, this automatic relaxation may invite parental hostility, which produces in the child a feeling of "empathized discomfort." This feeling will bring the child to learn

> to suffer increasing tension in the bladder and rectum and to resist the automatic relaxation of the sphincter muscles concerned in retaining the urine and feces. Failures in this are often accompanied by empathized discomfort, and success is often the occasion of empathized comfort which is added to the satisfaction from relief of tension.[50]

The child learns how to adjust his behavior to his environment. This process of adjustment is a result of his striving toward security. His activities are influenced by what the environment has to offer him in terms of being accepted and loved by others. The attitude of others toward the child produces in him the feeling of security or insecurity.

Security

Early childhood plays a very important role in the development of a person's feeling of security. The infant feels, by empathy, whether he is accepted or not by the people who take care of him. The accepted and loved child develops a feeling of well-being and happiness. It is the feeling of *euphoria.* The need for satisfaction and the need for security follow the same path. The same mother feeds and cuddles, the same feeding process serves satisfaction and security.

From the very first days of life, "the infant shows a curious relationship or connection with the significant adult, ordinarily the mother. If the mother . . . is seriously disturbed . . . around the time of feeding, then on that occasion there will be feeding difficulty or the infant will have indigestion."[51]

The child somehow "feels" the attitude of people toward himself. This ability to perceive other people's feelings is called *empathy*. Empathy is interpreted by Sullivan as a kind of "emotional contagion or communion" between the child and the adults who take care of him. It is strongest from the age of six months to twenty-five months. The child responds to the emotions of his mother or father or any other parental substitute. All these are *significant* adults in his life, and they produce in him an empathized comfort or discomfort, in accordance with their friendly or unfriendly attitude to him.

[50] *Ibid.*, p. 44.
[51] *Ibid.*, p. 7.

Sooner or later, parents or other significant adults impose rules and restrictions on the child's way of procuring satisfaction. We have already mentioned toilet training; a similar process takes place in telling the child to eat in a civilized manner. Failure to comply with parental requests invites disapproval and destroys the child's feeling of euphoria and security and produces *anxiety*. The patterns of parental behavior are products of the prevailing culture. The child's "euphoria," as said before, results from being accepted by his parents and/or other significant persons in his environment. Since the parents represent the social norms of a certain culture, *the child's adjustment to parental instructions and admonitions is actually adjustment to a certain culture.*

As the child grows, parents, teachers, and other significant persons actively introduce more and more customs and norms of their culture to the child. Acting in accordance with these norms brings the feeling of belonging, of being accepted, of euphoria. Disregard of the social norms causes disapproval, and the child will feel rejected. This is how the inhibitory mechanism is established: the child avoids disapproval and tries to comply with the requirements of his culture by inhibiting his desire for an immediate relief of tensions.

Whenever the biological needs of an individual cannot be satisfied in a socially acceptable way, that is, in the manner in which the individual was trained in childhood, he has a feeling of insecurity and uneasiness, or anxiety. *Anxiety is always connected with an increased muscular tension.* Muscles ready for a socially unacceptable action become inhibited, since their activity is likely to invite disapproval. For instance, the inhibition of crying or screaming stimulates higher tension in throat muscles. Anxiety is a product of a conflict between the need for satisfaction and the need to follow the socially acceptable ways of procuring satisfaction.

Anxiety can be regarded as a socially produced muscular tension. It interferes with "any other tension with which it coincides."[52] Anxiety prevents satisfaction in hunger and sex, interferes with normal mental functioning, and impairs the ability to perceive and understand things. The highest level of anxiety, terror, brings on a breakdown of personality. Avoiding or relieving this socially created anxiety usually brings the pleasant feeling of self-esteem. The ability to attain satisfaction and security means *power*. Self-respect is a result of success in obtaining satisfaction and security.

Tensions and Transformation of Energy

Experience means what is going on within a person. The term *experience* is used by Sullivan in an "energetic" manner. There are two kinds of

[52] Harry S. Sullivan, "The Meaning of Anxiety in Psychiatry and in Life," *Psychiatry*, 1948, *11*, 1–13.

experience. The first type is readiness or "potentiality" for action, which is called by Sullivan "tension." The action itself—the second kind of experience—is called by Sullivan "transformation of energy."

"Tension" and "transformation of energy" sound like physicalism or reductionism, and Sullivan states blatantly: "I use these two terms in exactly the same sense as I would in telling about physics." Sullivan seems to feel pretty strongly about this issue.

Tensions are of two kinds. First, there are tensions of *needs*. Needs are either *general* or *zonal*. The general needs are physiological requirements of man as a living organism—food, water, reproductive activity. The zonal needs develop as a result of interaction between the respective zones of our body and the environment, for example, the oral zone, the genital, the manual, or the visual. "Zonal needs" correspond vaguely to Freud's genetic zones. Although some of the areas pointed out are identical, there is quite a difference in the role attached to them by Freud and Sullivan. Freud perceived the bodily zones as representative of the phylogenetic evolution of mankind and interpreted their ontogenetic role on the lines of the biogenetic theory (cf. Chapter 6). Sullivan perceives the zones as a product of certain life experiences. They are *zones of interaction with the environment* and do not represent phylogenetic developmental stages.

The second kind of tensions are the *anxiety tensions*. As mentioned before, anxiety is first manifested in early infancy.

> Very young infants show grossly identical patterns of behavior when they are subjected to "frightening" situations and when they are in contact with the person who mothers them and *that person* is anxious, angry, or *otherwise disquieted*. Something which develops without a break into the tension state which we have discriminated on the basis of its specific difference from fear can be *induced* in the infant by *interpersonal influence,* in contrast to the evocation of primitive fear by sundry violent influences from "outside" the infant's body. This *interpersonal induction* of anxiety, and the exclusively interpersonal origin of every instance of its manifestations is the unique characteristic of anxiety and of the congeries of more complex tensions in later life to which it contributes.[53]

Modes of Experience

All human experience occurs in three "modes." The first is the *prototaxic*; the earliest experiences in human life are prototaxic. The infant's experiences are undifferentiated, having no division into time units, since he has not yet developed the awareness of being a separate entity. The prototaxic mode is a series of "momentary states," mostly unformulable and therefore incommunicable. Events come and go, and the infant is unable to localize them in time or space. This experience is a sort of mass experience, unorganized, dim, as if made out of one piece. Some such experiences may

[53] *Ibid.*

be mystical and of "cosmic identification." "The one relationship which certainly exists between items of experience in the prototaxic mode is succession, place in organismic or biological time."[54]

As the child grows, he learns "that objects which our distance receptors, our eyes and ears, for example, encounter, are of a quite different order of relationship from things which our tactile or our gustatory receptors encounter."[55] The child is learning to differentiate between respective parts of reality. *Parataxic* experience is prelogical, since the child is unable to relate things and events to each other or to understand the laws of nature. Things are perceived without logical course or order. Experiences "take on personal meaning" and become organized into "personifications of myself." The parataxic mode of experience remains in adult life as dreams, when things come and go without being logically connected. In childhood, most waking experiences are of this kind.[56]

Children's language is "autistic," that is, centered around "myself." Everything is related to personal needs and experiences. Language is a system of symbolic signs, but children's symbols are a product of their personification of themselves and of attaching imaginary traits to other people; children's symbols are therefore subjective, personal, and often imaginary. Step by step the child learns to associate certain signs with the behavior of other people and to pay attention to their experiences too. The child's parataxic mode and autistic talk give way to the *syntaxic* mode and interpersonal language.

The syntaxic mode is related to perceiving other people and validating one's experience against the experience of others. One's observations and judgments are "consensually validated" with the perceptions and conclusions of others. Sullivan is aware of the fact that even checking one's experiences against those of others cannot serve as evidence of absolute truth. It means only some kind of agreement with significant persons and makes possible communication and adjustment in a given social environment and culture. Of course, syntaxic experiences depend on cultural settings. Tensions may occur in either parataxic or syntaxic modes. Any frustration in seeking to satisfy hunger, or sex, or the need for physical proximity may be experienced in the syntaxic mode, or in the unorganized and highly imaginary parataxic mode. *Anxiety is always perceived in the parataxic mode.*

Children, and sometimes adults, develop "parataxic distortions" when they relate to another person on the basis of a distorted identification. They may attach nonexistent traits to certain people or may even invent imaginary characters ("eidetic persons").

---

[54] Harry S. Sullivan, "Multidisciplined Coordination of Interpersonal Data," in Sargent and Smith, *op. cit.*
[55] Sullivan, *Conceptions of Modern Psychiatry*, p. 16.
[56] Harry S. Sullivan, *The Fusion of Psychiatry and Social Science*, Norton, 1964.

Conscious and Unconscious

Although Sullivan refrains from the use of Freudian terminology, he does not disregard the theoretical and clinical importance of the psychological concepts represented by it. A person, Sullivan states, may be "wittingly aware" of certain performances of his own, while other performances remain unnoticed, outside his awareness.

Sullivan offers an interpretation of these facts. In infancy, everything ocurs in the prototaxic mode; through the process of empathy the infant feels the attitude of the significant people toward himself, but all his perceptions are diffuse and vague. Since their approval brings euphoria and their disapproval denies satisfaction and gives anxiety, the child learns to concentrate on the factors pertinent to the significant persons. This is the origin of his "conscious" *self-dynamism*, which is compared by Sullivan to a microscope. Self-dynamism "permits a minute focus on those performances of the child which are the cause of approbation and disapprobation, but very much like a microscope, it interferes with noticing the rest of the world. When you are staring through your microscope, you don't see very much other than that which comes through that channel. So with self-dynamism."[57]

Self-dynamism is conscious, while anything else is not. Everything outside self-dynamism is either *disassociated* or *selectively inattended*. The first term corresponds to Freud's unconscious, while the latter resembles the preconscious (see Chapter 6). Only those processes which are pertinent to relationships with significant people become included in self-dynamism so that the person is "wittingly aware" of them. Tension and energy transformation may be a "felt or wittingly noted state of being" or not. Tension per se is potentiality for action; energy transformations are actions; both tensions and energy transformations may have "felt or representational components" or may "transpire without any witting awareness."[58]

Developmental Stages

Sullivan distinguishes six epochs in personality development. The first developmental stage is *infancy*, which starts at birth and continues until the maturation of the capacity for language. The newborn child strives for unrestricted satisfaction of his needs and unlimited expression of his power. Both tendencies meet with a certain type of response from the mother; she may approve or disapprove of the behavior of the child. Since

---

[57] Sullivan, *Conceptions of Modern Psychiatry*, p. 23.

[58] Sullivan distinguished clearly between potentialities for action and awareness of these potentialities, while Kurt Lewin's "psychological field" represents both the objective potentialities and the situation as perceived by the individual (see Chapter 13).

it is up to her to satisfy him or to deny satisfaction, the infant learns to adjust himself to his mother at an early stage.

This process of adjustment takes place because of the child's ability to feel somehow his mother's state of mind. Empathy is the nonverbal way of communicating emotion. The mother's approval is conducive to a euphoric state in the child, while the mother's disapproval may produce anxiety.

Sooner or later the infant learns to relate his pleasant feeling of euphoria or the annoying feeling of anxiety to his own behavior. Some of his activities are somehow connected with euphoria while others cause anxiety. He learns to perceive the signs of approval or disapproval and to act accordingly. Furthermore, through this compliance he makes considerable progress in the process of acculturation. Cultural influences transmitted through the parents determine the future structure of the self.

The self or self-dynamism develops through the approval and disapproval of others.

> Since the approbation of the important person is very valuable, since disapprobation denies satisfaction and gives anxiety, the self becomes extremely important. . . . It has a tendency to focus attention in performances with the significant other person which got approbation or disfavor. And that peculiarity, closely connected with anxiety, persists thenceforth through life. It comes about that the self, to which we refer when we say "I," is the only thing which has alertness, which notices what goes on, and needless to say, notices what goes on its own field. The rest of the personality gets along outside awareness."[59]

The infant develops three types of personifications of himself. When his behavior is accepted and praised, he develops self-identification of approval: This is the "good-me." Mild anxiety is conducive to a "bad-me" personification of self. Unusual feelings of horror or shock lead to the diffuse and never fully conscious states of "not-me."

In infancy, the child begins to develop personification of other people too. The feeling of euphoria is conducive to a "good-mother" personification, while anxiety states bring "bad-mother" personifications. Out of these personifications of significant people, grow and develope later *eidetic* people, that is, imaginary persons.[60]

The second developmental stage is *childhood*. Sullivan sets the upper limit of this era in the "capacity for living with compeers." The next era, the *juvenile*, will start with school attendance.

Childhood is the era of the most pervasive acculturation process. The child learns toilet habits, eating habits, cleanliness, and most of the habitual ways of behavior regarded as proper by the society and represented by his parents.

---

[59] Sullivan, *Conceptions of Modern Psychiatry*, p. 23.
[60] Sullivan borrowed the term "eidetic" from Jaensch. Sullivan's connotation of eidetic would mean imaginary; eidetic people would mean either invented persons or real persons with imaginary traits.

The child learns how to restrain his drive for *power*. Many of his activities are frustrated or prohibited by his parents. Some of his unacceptable desires are *sublimated*. The anxiety-provoking tendencies are diverted into socially accepted channels; they are partially satisfied by fusion with socially desirable ways of behavior.

The unsatisfied and undischarged parts of the drive or impulse find outlets in dreams, daydreams, or regressions to the pre-sublimation situation. Regression usually represents the unsatisfied part of a drive, but it is also regression in the person's total behavior.

Quite often, the child's efforts to get approval meet with parental lack of patience, fatigue, or some other kind of rejecting behavior. This may lead to distortions of the reality of the child; the child who craves parental love and receives nothing but rejection can develop paranoid distortions. He may regard himself as lonely and rejected in a cold and hostile world.

The child may then try to alleviate his anxiety by producing anger. Outbursts of anger undoubtedly bring relief from frustration, as several studies have proved.[61] A frustrated person may feel better after releasing his anger on an innocent scapegoat.

At this point, Sullivan introduced a theory of emotions which is at great variance with Freud's theory. Freud regarded love and hatred as innate emotions; fear was to come later, as a result of experience. Horney regarded acceptance and the lack of it, anxiety, as the basic emotions. Sullivan saw in anger a substitute for anxiety; most individuals successfully conceal their anxieties even from themselves, and their anger often serves as an outlet and a cover for anxiety.

The *juvenile era* starts in our civilization with school age. "The child manifests a shift from contentment in an environment of totalitarian adults toward an environment of persons significantly *like* him. Along with this budding ability to play with other children, there goes a learning of those performances which we call competition and compromise."[62]

Meeting other children encourages interpersonal validation of perception and leads gradually to the syntaxic mode. The child learns to pay more attention to the opinions of other children; he tries to become *popular* and fears to be alone or, even worse, rejected by his group. The child's process of socialization leads toward the establishment of personal friendship with one or more children.

Preadolescence starts between the ages of eight and a half and twelve. It is characterized by the appearance of the capacity to love. Usually the attachment takes place within the same sex; it is "isophile." Sullivan does not regard this as "homosexuality." Homosexuality comes later, often as a product of failure in heterosexual overtures.

In the preadolescent stage, most people develop "consensual validation" by exchange of words and ideas with their friends. In this exchange,

[61] John Dollard et al., *Frustration and Aggression*, Yale, 1939.
[62] Sullivan, *Conceptions of Modern Psychiatry*, p. 18.

the preadolescent learns to check his perceptions with those of others and yields some of his interests for the sake of his group.

The preadolescent stage plays the decisive role in determining one's future social relationships. Social experiences in this age will determine future social adaptability. In contradistinction to Freudian views, Sullivan asserts that preadolescence determines one's automatic ease or unvarying stress in dealing with any significant number of one's own sex.

Adolescence is an era of *patterning of lustful behavior*. The genital zone comes to the fore. Sex is not the driving power in man, but it is nevertheless a powerful factor in human life. Impulses to genital behavior cannot be easily disassociated, and in some individuals they cannot be disassociated at all. Sex will, "again and again, at whatever great expense to security, whatever suffering from anxiety, manifest itself."[63]

Sex enjoys a privileged position in Sullivan's theory. Sex can defy anxiety or any other tension. However, it cannot be fully satisfied unless intimacy is provided. The heterosexual experiences in this developmental stage determine one's future ease or difficulty in making a satisfactory sexual adjustment in adult life. Thus, Sullivan has shifted the focal point of sexual and other interpersonal adjustment from early childhood to preadolescence and adolescence.

Personality

In discussing personality, Sullivan comes close to field theory psychology (see Chapter 13). Each interpersonal situation influences the personalities of the participating individuals. The total personality includes all possible ways of reaction of a certain individual, but in the presence of different persons, different patterns of behavior come to the fore. Which part of a personality will play the decisive role in a given situation is a product of that situation, that is, of the interpersonal interaction that takes place.

This presentation reflects George Mead's theory of social roles, but even more, it reflects Kurt Lewin's "life space" and field theory. A person may appear in different roles, or a person is a product of social interrelationship.

Sullivan does not believe that personality can be perceived or interpreted outside of the social context of interrelationship. "Personality can never be isolated from the complexity of interpersonal relations in which the person lives and has his being."[64] Personality is a product of interrelationship with other persons; therefore it can hardly be regarded as a separate entity. Moreover, personality per se eludes scientific investigation since it cannot be perceived outside the interpersonal relationship.

[63] *Ibid.*, p. 31.
[64] Harry S. Sullivan, "Sociopsychiatric Research: Its Implications for the Schizophrenia Problem and for Mental Hygiene," *American Journal of Psychiatry*, 1931, *10*, 77–91.

"In the course of psychiatric inquiry one discovers that it is not a person as an *isolated and self-contained entity* that one is studying, or can study, but a situation, an interpersonal situation, composed of two or more people." The traits which characterize the interpersonal situations in which one is integrated describe what one is. "Personality is . . . a function of the kinds of interpersonal situations a person integrates with others, whether real persons or personifications," comments Mullahy on Sullivan's theory of personality.[65]

Sullivan presents personality in two modes: in a "private mode," which is incommunicable, and in which no personality can be studied, and as a "relatively enduring pattern of recurrent interpersonal situations." The latter really deserves the label of personality. This "enduring pattern" is personality as grasped by scientific tools.

The "enduring pattern of behavior" is the way a person uses his energies. Here the conception of *self-dynamism* or *self-system* or *self* enters the picture. Sullivan thinks about energy in physical terms; to him dynamism means a "relatively enduring configuration of energy."

This energy is released in interpersonal relations. Self-dynamism is therefore the only part of personality which is observable and can be scientifically studied.

The directions of use or release of energy are a product of two basic factors. The first is the child's need for satisfaction and security. The second is the influence of the significant persons on the child's behavior. In other words, the child strives to use his energy in order to obtain the satisfaction of his needs and the feeling of euphoria. His activities are determined by the approval or disapproval of significant people. He avoids their disapproval, which brings him anxiety, and tends to seek satisfaction and security in a way which procures social approval.

Actually self-dynamism or the self-system means *how a person behaves.* It is somewhat similar to Adler's "style of life" or Freud's "character." According to Sullivan, energy is universal, but the consistent patterns of use of energy are environmentally conditioned. Self-dynamism, or the self, is a result of "reflected appraisals," since the "child experiences himself and appraises himself in terms of what the parents and others close to him manifest."[66]

As a result of the social pressure exercised by parents and other significant persons, only certain patterns of behavior become disassociated or "selectively inattended." The disassociated processes do not belong to self-dynamism and are excluded from awareness. The person does not recognize them as parts of himself; he will deny their existence and not be able

---

[65] Patrick Mullahy, "A Theory of Interpersonal Relations and the Evolution of Personality," in Sullivan, *Conceptions of Modern Psychiatry*, pp. 122–123. See also Patrick Mullahy, "Non-Freudian Analytic Theories," in B. B. Wolman (ed.), *Handbook of Clinical Psychology*, McGraw-Hill, 1965, pp. 341–380.

[66] Sullivan, *Conceptions of Modern Psychiatry*, p. 27.

to recall them. The disassociated processes may express themselves in dreams, daydreaming, or unintentional activities, and can be recalled in psychoanalytic therapy.

Certain tendencies are not entirely disassociated but are "selectively inattended." Selective inattention applies to activity patterns which are unimportant to the significant person and therefore do not call for his approval or disapproval. The approved tendencies form the self-dynamism; the disapproved ones are rejected. Those tendencies concerning which parents do not express any attitude, will remain unnoticed, dim, and neglected. And as a result of other interpersonal situations, a person can become aware of these tendencies and, eventually, admit them to his self-system.

Interpersonal Relations

Sullivan believes that interpersonal relations are the proper subject matter of the scientific study of personality. The kind of person one is can be inferred from his behavior in relationship to other persons. People cannot be studied *per se*; they can only be studied in a "situation" in which at least one real and one "eidetic" person participate. The eidetic persons are usually people whom one has actually met in the past and personified in an imaginative manner. A man and his real or imaginary partners form the *interpersonal situation*.

This presentation invites comparison with field theory. Sullivan does not subscribe to Kurt Lewin's theory; cultural influences and past experiences as interpreted by Sullivan do not fit into Lewin's "field at a given time." Sullivan gives full consideration to the past, and genetic and developmental factors are of the utmost importance in his theory. But the interpersonal situation as described by him is a "field" (see Chapter 13).

Sullivan's presentation of interpersonal relations also resembles the field theory approach in another aspect. In interpersonal relations as seen by Sullivan, all but one person "may be more or less completely illusory." Social relations develop between an individual and a number of "eidetic" or imaginary persons; even nonexisting persons may influence human behavior, because behavior is oriented toward situations as people perceive them.

Gestalt psychologists would say that reality as perceived by a person is his *psychological field* (Chapter 12). If this "reality" differs considerably from what other people perceive, then, according to Sullivan, the person perceiving unrealistically suffers from parataxic distortions. Mentally sick or disturbed persons distort reality badly and adjust their lives to nonexisting persons, or to persons whom they perceive in an unrealistic manner. Kurt Lewin (see Chapter 13) has distinguished various levels of reality in the psychological field, and Sullivan's modes correspond in a way to Lewin's system.

Sullivan shows a considerable bias against "individuality." "The individuality of a particular electron is of no concern to the physicist; the individuality of the biologist's dog is not apt to confuse his biology of the dog. It is quite otherwise, however, with the traditionally emphasized individuality of each of us, 'myself.' Here we have the very mother of illusions, the ever frequent source of preconceptions that invalidate almost all our efforts to understand other people."[67]

Sullivan's definition of personality as "the relatively enduring pattern of recurring interpersonal situations" must include cultural factors. The child perceives by empathy how his parents feel about his behavior; parental attitudes are a product of culture and reflect the socially accepted pattern; school and society, peers and adults, constantly represent social norms. No person can be fully understood unless the observer relates his behavior to the actual interpersonal situation and to relatively constant social influences.

Concluding Remarks

Watson's theory has been called "a psychology of everybody but me." Sullivan's theory can be defined as "a between-people psychology." While Watson denies the possibility of the psychological study of an individual by himself, Sullivan denies the possibility of the psychological study of an individual not interrelated with other individuals and states that this interrelationships can be studied.

One wonders whether Sullivan's approach represents methodological cautiousness or a statement about matters of fact. Does he propose an epistemological limitation, derived from Kant's idealism, that "things per se" are inaccessible to our cognition? Or does he suggest a temporary methodological restriction, that the best and the safest way to procure truthful information about a person is to see him in interpersonal relations?

Fromm-Reichmann, using Sullivan's frame of reference, says that "emotional difficulties in living are difficulties in interpersonal relationships; and a person is not emotionally hampered, that is, he is mentally healthy to the extent to which he is able to be aware of, and therefore, to handle his interpersonal relationships."[68] One would like to determine whether difficulties in interpersonal relationships are a result of emotional difficulties and a symptom of them, or, as Fromm-Reichmann says, represent the emotional difficulties themselves.

Sullivan answers this question in a quasi-operationist manner. He says: "I can say with Bridgman that I act in two modes—my public mode \in which I feel my inviolable isolation from my fellows. The inimitable private escapes and will always escape the methods of science. The true or absolute individuality of a person is always beyond scientific grasp."[69]

[67] Harry S. Sullivan, "Introduction to the Study of Interpersonal Relations," *Psychiatry*, 1938, *1*, 121–134.

[68] F. Fromm-Reichmann, *Principles of Intense Psychotherapy*, University of Chicago, 1950, p. 14.

[69] Sullivan, *Conceptions of Modern Psychiatry*, Foreword to second printing, p. vii.

This quasi-operationist statement invites clarification. Sullivan can hardly be regarded as a consistent operationist or a faithful student of neo-positivism. Although the "public me" can be subjected to a set of operations, one doubts whether "eidetic persons," "self-dynamism," "not-me," and other Sullivanian constructs fit into any operationism at all (cf. Chapters 1, 3, and 4). Skinner defines operationism as follows: "Operationism may be defined as the practice of talking about (1) one's observations, (2) the manipulative and calculational procedures involved in making them, (3) the logical and mathematical steps which intervene between earlier and later statements, and (4) *nothing else.*" [70]

If this is a correct definition, Sullivan's theory has little in common with operationism, and no operations can be formulated which will prove or disprove most of Sullian's propositions. Still, Sullivan's propositions may be truthful or at least useful tools in scientific research, despite their non-operationist origin.

Another case of lack of clarity is Sullivan's term "tension." "Tensions may be considered to have two important aspects; that of tension as potentiality for action, for the transformation of energy; and that of a *felt* or wittingly noted state of being." [71] Tension *is* potentiality for action, and tension *can* have felt or representational components. The reader may conclude that tensions per se are not identical with tensions as experienced or felt by a person. One cannot help wondering which kind of tension is the subject matter of psychology.

Sullivan's entire system is a *deductive* one. Sullivan *postulates* a dualism of physics (energy) and culture (interpersonal relations) as well as a dualism of heredity (satisfaction) and environment (euphoria), with emphasis on culture and environment. He does not reject innate factors. He admits them into his theory under the heading of "satisfaction." Satisfaction covers all somatic aspects of behavior which are not the product of human experience, or interpersonal relations. Little consideration is given in Sullivan's theory to this factor. One may say that to Sullivan, "given a biological substrate, the human is the product of interaction with other human beings." [72] However, innate factors need not be considered only in the case where all interpersonal differences are a product of social relations. This holds true only in regard to identical twins; any other case represents a combination of innate and acquired factors. No doubt Sullivan, in contradistinction to Freud, puts much more weight on the environmental factors, to the disparagement of innate ones.

Sullivan's self-dynamism or self-system invites comparison with Freud's ego and superego. Self-dynamism or self develops as a result of

[70] B. F. Skinner, "The Operational Analysis of Psychological Terms," *Psychological Review*, 1946, 52, 270–277, 291–294.
[71] Sullivan, "Multidisciplined Coordination of Interpersonal Data," in Sargent and Smith, *op. cit.*, p. 176.
[72] Thompson, *op. cit.*, p. 211.

parental appraisal. The "self" is reality oriented, like the ego, and represents the culture, like the superego. Sullivan denies the instinctual origin of both and, in view of his clinical experience, sees no reason for the Freudian constructs. Instead he introduces his own self-dynamism, which simplifes the relationship between conscious and unconscious.

Sullivan offers an interesting interpretation of the origins of the unconscious: It is the relationship with other significant people that makes the child become aware or unaware of some of his performances. Additional interpretation of this issue is given by inference. Since certain activities of the child may be interrupted by an outburst of hunger or rage, and then picked up and overtly continued, one can infer their *covert*, or unconscious, continuation while they are overtly interrupted.

Summarizing Sullivan's contribution to psychological research and theory, one must admit that Sullivan did develop a full-fledged psychological system. He covered the areas of child psychology and normal and abnormal personality and offered quite important suggestions in social psychology. Man is a combination of nature and culture; he is both nature- and culture-made. The newborn child represents "nature," but as he grows his behavior is more and more shaped by culture. This approach is common to the entire sociological school in psychoanalysis, but only Sullivan offered a highly conceptual system of interpretation of human behavior and development.

Methodologically speaking, Sullivan's theory is a system of postulates that tries to replace the Freudian system. It has apparent advantages in its shift to culture and its vigorous presentation of the social aspects of human life. Many social scientists will be influenced by the analysis of interpersonal situations; Sullivan's method of study in these situations may lead to new and fruitful interpretation of group relations, as it has already brought a considerable change in the clinical patient–doctor setting.

Here, in our opinion, lies Sullivan's greatness. Men become themselves in relation to others. Growth, maturation, adjustment, disturbances, or sickness can be fully understood only in their social interrelationships.

Concluding Remarks on the Sociological School

It is not easy to change the architectonic structure of a castle. Freud was a master in the art of logical thinking and his system is a formidable structure erected by the human mind.

As long as one follows the line of Freud's reasoning and adds an empirical observation here or there or streamlines his conceptual framework, as K. Abraham, E. Jones, O. Fenichel, E. Glover, A. Freud, and scores of others have done, the entire building is well preserved and perhaps improved. But as soon as one rejects any of the fundamental concepts, the entire building crumbles.

Apparently, Freud's theory cannot be edited at will or easily "corrected." Whoever undertakes the daring task of changing the basic structure must be prepared to erect an entirely new structure.

None of the sociologically oriented neo-psychoanalysts was sufficiently equipped to undertake this task. The weakest of all three was, obviously, Fromm, whose theories have the least sufficient empirical background. One can be enchanted by Fromm's ethical zeal, but no one can consider his conclusions part of an empirical system of science.

Horney's studies of the sociological causes of neurosis (*The Neurotic Personality of Our Time*) are an important contribution to the understanding of the etiology of mental disorder. Yet Horney's work cannot, if only by the limitations of its scope, be considered a sufficient substitute for Freud's conceptual system, although Horney was, undoubtedly, a keen observer and a thorough thinker.

The best-developed system was offered by Sullivan. It is a full-fledged psychological system. However, parts of it are a mere translation of Freudian concepts; his field theory concepts are methodologically vulnerable (cf. Chapter 13, "Concluding Remarks"). But his theory of personality and his observations related to perception are thought provoking. Sullian's system is no longer Freudianism; it is, to a great extent, a new psychological theory which stands on its own merits.

In summary, one can say that Freud's theory can be accepted, rejected, or modified, like any other psychological theory. But whoever undertakes the task of remodeling psychoanalysis, must come armed with empirical evidence or a methodological consideration superior to that offered by Freud. Horney and Sullian made important contributions, but their factual or methodological superiority to Freud is in doubt.

5. RECENT DEVELOPMENTS IN HORNEY'S THEORY

In the United States, Karen Horney helped found the American Institute for Psychoanalysis. Analysts who trained and later taught at the Institute went on to expand and develop her ideas. A leading proponent of Horney's school of thought, Harold Kelman, went beyond Horney's teaching and developed a *unitary theory of anxiety*. Kelman hypothesized that tension and oscillation, disintegration, and reintegration are the main and indispensable aspects of an overall process of personality integration. These fluctuations are part of every human system and, as such, must be considered in any attempt to look at the fluctuation of psychological events. As it is natural for all organismic processes to be active and phasic, so it is natural for the organism to be always in tension. Kelman assumed that the mean level of tension oscillates above and below a mean.[73] As the individual actively represses hostility, he necessarily restricts his participation in the process of integration. When he becomes involved in what Horney called

[73] Harold Kelman, *Helping People*, Science House, 1971.

"basic anxiety," his level of tension increases. The variations in his tension level are therefore narrowed. As this occurs, the individual is unable to integrate his feelings and his behavior becomes limited so as to avoid the uncertainty that his hostility represents. Moreover, as the processes of fluctuation are not integrated, the individual is prevented from developing the capacities he needs to deal with future problems. According to Kelman, "When the processes in any experience extend beyond the organismic tolerance and/or capacity for organization, the organism is not adequate to deal with its situation." [74]

In an effort to describe the processes involved in the organizing and integrating of human experience Kelman postulated a metaphorical spiral that "begins in the basic event of being of which there is not awareness."

> *The now moment.* The pure essence of any moment for any person is a silence in which his particular life history is an instantaneous connection to how and what he is in the world. It is an event before words. Then there is immediately a possibility for making forms that express this experience. The number of forms that can emerge are myriad. No single form can ever capture all the possibilities that can come from this pure experience. However, as forms do emerge, they represent the person's attempts to integrate his pure moment.
>
> *The symbolic spiral—lower levels.* The lowest levels of this metaphorical spiral are prerationative, that is, before intellection is possible. Because fluidity is greatest at these levels there is maximum potential for creating many different forms of expressing the possible in the pure experience. At this level we see forms of imagery, metaphor, flash feeling, and the processes of empathy, intuition, and insight. They may be subliminal or subverbal, being forming waves of immediacy. They often penetrate areas of the patient and his reality of which he and his analyst have been unaware in themselves and in each other in the unitary process they are and share. The processes that pertain between mother and infant, namely, of human communing, obtain at these levels. There are no words and no particular structure, but an ongoing process that is undifferentiated, widely connecting, and forming.
>
> *The symbolic spiral—higher levels.* At the higher levels of the metaphorical spiral, we have thoughts, abstract ideas, and dreams. Experience is integrated in forms that have more rigid connections and more relationship to public forms. In compulsive processes of neurosis, we see a tendency to move automatically into these forms and to avoid the more open spontaneous possibilities of the lower levels of the spiral. [75]

Kelman expanded on Horney's notions of the doctor–patient relationship, her revision of Freud's notions of transference and repetition, through his description of communing and relating. [76] He felt that within the analytic relationship there is the possibility of recreating the "mother–child process in which being and becoming emerge prior to and as the ground of relating." [77]

[74] Harold Kelman and David Shainberg, "Karen Horney," in A. M. Freedman, H. I. Kaplan, and B. J. Sadock (Eds.), *Comprehensive Textbook of Psychiatry,* (2nd. ed.), Williams and Wilkins, 1975, p. 586.
[75] *Ibid.*, pp. 593–594.
[76] *Ibid.*, p. 594.
[77] *Ibid.*

David Shainberg, who also studied at Horney's American Institute for Psychoanalysis, developed his own theoretical position. He has studied the schizophrenic process. According to Shainberg, the schizophrenic process is a denial of all self-meaning. The schizophrenic's efforts to assert himself arouse intense anxiety and self-hate. Schizophrenics go through periods of arousal when there is a chance for a breakthrough and sudden improvement. These periods of arousal are marked by four distinct stages:

> (1) *initial alertness* with sensory awareness, (2) *decision and doubt* when there is a fear of moving into engaging tension, but also a direction of possibility, (3) comparing the old neurotic forms with more open forming. Finally, he sees that if the (4) decision is made by a person to explore his own possibilities in tensioning, he moves into the phase of *individuation* where there can be an integration of self and self-in-world.[78]

The work of Kelman, Shainberg, and many others indicates that Horney's theoretical system is far from being narrow and limited. It has proven to be a viable and flexible system open to modification and further development.

[78] *Ibid.*, p. 590.

Summary of Part II

There are three "fathers" of contemporary psychological theory: Pavlov, Freud, and to a certain extent, Dilthey. The second part of this book is devoted to Sigmund Freud and to all those who remained faithful to him or rebelled against him.

Freud was more of a "father" than Pavlov or Dilthey. He created the system; he developed, changed, readjusted, and presented it to the world as one of the most elaborate products of the human mind.

Freud's starting point was the natural sciences. He adhered strictly to the principles of determinism, materialistic monism, conservation of energy, and empiricism. In philosophy, Freud was a positivist, a disciple of J. S. Mill, A. Comte, and H. Spencer, but he did not accept the radical philosophy of the neopositivists. His theory was deeply rooted in the biological sciences and their methods of research.

Yet the biologically oriented Freud, the materialistic positivist Freud, did not hesitate to modify the traditional empiricism and materialism, and developed a most speculative psychological system based on non-reductionism. Freud's point is well taken and well justified. For what is the good of clinging to the naïve empirical observations and stubbornly maintaining that the sun is moving and the earth is not? Or, what is the good of professing that the nervous system offers all the answers to psychological problems while the question is all but solved?

Freud is an example of courage and tenacity in a relentless, unabated search for scientific truth. Whenever a link was missing between observable phenomena, Freud interpolated, always most economically, a speculative hypothesis. This hypothesis could not be directly proved, but its application in the interpretation of observable data and their prediction offered convincing support to Freud's concepts.

On the issue of reductionism Freud offered the best possible solution. While firmly adhering to the idea of a continuum of the organic world, Freud had to postulate that mental energy is a *derivative* of physical energy and that it cannot be perceived and studied in physical terms. It is different, and there is no use in assuming that an encephalogram indicates

403

more than it does, or that the study of glands of inner secretion can help to predict one's behavior.

Scientific honesty and cautiousness forced Freud to accept the principles of methodological non-reductionism, for the only way one can study mental phenomena is to accept them as being different from physical phenomena—different and yet a part of the continuum of living matter, just as flowers are different from roots and yet form a part of the plant in a continuum of growth from root to flower.

Armed with these principles, Freud made the greatest discovery in psychology. He discovered the unconscious processes. He proved their existence through meticulous research of amnestic and hypnotic phenomena, through dream interpretation, through the study of the psychopathology of daily life, and through his work with mentally disturbed individuals.

Then he proceeded to develop his theory in three realms: the realm of the topography of the human mind (conscious, preconscious, and unconscious), the realm of the driving forces (the instinctual drives of life, Eros, and of death, Thanatos), and finally the mental apparatus (id, ego, and superego).

Freud believed that personality is an outcome of (1) the innate, instinctual forces deeply rooted in organic sources, (2) the biologically determined but modifiable-by-environment developmental stages (oral, anal, urethral, phallic, latency, genital), and (3) the interaction between the child and his parents.

Chapter 7 describes the theories of the two first dissidents. Alfred Adler and Carl Gustav Jung. Adler's rebellion against Freud is, primarily, a rebellion against Freud's biological foundations and deterministic philosophy. Adler introduced the humanistic point of view, borrowed from Dilthey and Windelband. In a long evolution of his thinking, he finally arrived at the idea that striving toward superiority and consideration for the fellow man (sociability) are the main driving forces in humans.

Adler's main consideration was the way man relates to man in a conscious way; thus, practically all the neo-psychoanalysts, such as Horney, Sullivan, and Fromm, owe to Adler no less than they owe to Freud.

Jung's theory took an entirely different course of development. Jung's main concern was the unconscious phenomena, divided into the personal and collective unconscious. Jung offered a wealth of research material in the history of culture with special emphasis on religion, symbolic thinking, mysticism, and alchemy.

Chapter 8 is devoted to further studies in psychoanalysis. It starts with the theories of Otto Rank, who, like Adler, believed in the inner creativity of men and developed a highly speculative theory of man's fear of death and fear of life.

Melanie Klein, F. Alexander, S. Ferenczi, W. Reich, and others deviated from Freud to a lesser degree than Rank did. Yet their theories cannot be considered a continuation of Freud's work. They contain more deviation than continuation.

The work of Heinz Hartmann, Anna Freud, Margaret Mahler, and others represent a continuation of Freud's theories with a distinct emphasis on the ego; thus, they are usually called ego psychology. The sociolcultural ideas of Erik Erikson, Abraham Kardiner, and others have greatly widened the scope of psychoanalysis. Wolman's interactional theory represents an effort of relating the tenets of Freud's theory to sociopsychological concepts. Experimental psychologies and criticial analyses of Freud's theories have opened new vistas for future research. Apparently, there has been a good deal of soul searching and experimentation within the framework of Freud's theory, and several new approaches and innovative concepts bear witness to the vitality of psychoanalysis.

Chapter 9 deals with those who definitely broke away from Freud, the sociologically oriented Horney, Fromm, and Sullivan. Horney's starting point was the distinction between the biological need for satisfaction and the social need of humans for safety, for being accepted by others. Man, said Horney, can renounce satisfaction sooner than safety. Thus, the needs for social approval become the central point of Horney's theory. Adler's influence is quite prominent.

Horney's studies of child development led to a series of interesting observations. The rejected child develops "basic anxiety," while the accepted and protected child develops in a satisfactory manner.

E. Fromm's theory starts with a speculative assumption, very similar to Rank's, that there is a dichotomy between nature and culture. Men try to overcome the dichotomy through the security of social groups; when this security was destroyed by contemporary culture, men "escaped from freedom" into dictatorship. Fromm appeals to the "creative forces" in human nature.

The most thorough and scientific among the neo-psychoanalysts is H. S. Sullivan. Sullivan replaced Freud's system by his own, which is only partially a change in terminology. Sullivan's emphasis on field concepts brings him close to K. Lewin. Sullivan's interesting studies on the level of perceptions (prototaxic, parataxic, and syntaxic), derived from his studies of mental disorder, enrich psychological theory and open new research possibilities.

PART III
Understanding, Gestalt, and Field Psychologies

10

Understanding Psychology

1. KANT'S HERITAGE

The Common Problems

For the third and last time in this volume, we have to go back to the "roots" of contemporary psychological theory. This time we must go further back, to the common philosophical foundations of the great variety of theories described in the third part of this volume, including those of Spranger, Stern, Wertheimer, Lewin, and others.

All these systems, which today have very little in common with one another, have their common roots in the German idealistic philosophy of Immanuel Kant and his disciples. Even today, they still struggle with psychological problems as posed by Kant and Wilhelm Dilthey. Neither Kant nor Dilthey is the "father" of this group of psychological theories in the way that Pavlov and Freud are. Although Pavlov continued the works of the early associationists Hartley and Bain and the physiologists Flourens and Sechenov, it was Pavlov who developed the theory of conditioning. And, although Freud was influenced by Darwin, Spencer, Janet, and Charcot, it was Freud who developed the system of unconscious motivation.

Nothing of that kind can be traced in the systems brought together under the names of understanding, gestalt, and field theories. Nor was there here a leader comparable in stature to Pavlov and Freud. However, let us keep in mind that the systems discussed in the first and second parts of this volume often had in common only the topics of controversial issues; they shared the problems but not necessarily the solutions of the problems.

This principle of common problems unites all the theories brought together in Part III. All of them have been influenced by the intellectual heritage left by I. Kant and have faced the psychological problems posed by W. Dilthey.

"Pure" Reason

Kant's main work, *Kritik der Reinen Vernunft* (*Critique of Pure Reason*), appeared in 1781. The second edition of this book (1787) opened with the

409

following sentence: "There can be no doubt that all knowledge begins with experience."[1] But the meaning of this experience, as presented by Kant in the *Kritik* and in several other volumes, became one of the most controversial issues in the intellectual history of mankind.

While scores of disciples and followers believe that Kant opened the way for a truly scientific inquiry, many doubt it. Kant's main idea was that the senualists (Locke, Hume) are right in saying that knowledge comes from sensory perception; but perception gives us knowledge of things not as they really are in themselves (*Ding an sich*), but as they appear to us (phenomena). The things as they are, the *things-in-themselves,* exist, but we perceive them the way our mind is capable of perceiving them. Thus, Kant created a sharp dichotomy between the perceiving or experiencing subject and the perceived object. Therefore, knowledge "starts with experience" but it does "not arise out of experience." Knowledge starts with perception, but we perceive only the perceivable phenomena in a fashion determined by our mind.

The problem of the nature of the world was shifted from the objective facts to the perceiving subject, to the human "transcendental" mind and its boundaries. The content of knowledge necessarily includes sensations coming from the objects—color, weight, sound. But the mind is not a photographic camera; the mind *orders* its perceptions of objects in time and space. Time and space are not found in the objective world; they are not empirical qualities of objects; they are a priori, independent of experience, inherent in the human mind and embedded in its nature. The mind perceives the objects in the dimensions of time and space because this is the only way the subject, the human mind, can perceive the objects. "Take away the thinking subject and the entire corporeal world will vanish, for it is nothing but the appearance in the sensibility of the subject," wrote Kant. The world as perceived is a product of two factors: the sensory perception of the object and the a priori forms of the mind.

Thus, time and space are terms of the mind. They are the a priori, synthetic, general, universal terms of knowledge. They need no proof, for they are the prerequisite of any proof; without them any knowledge would be rendered impossible. They are the way in which the mind perceives the phenomena. In addition to time and space, Kant postulated several rational *categories* inherent in our minds, such as relation (e.g., causation), quantity, quality, and modality. These are not derived from experience; they are pure concepts, a priori forms of perception and reasoning.

Although Kant accepted the fact that part of our knowledge is supplied by sensory perception, it is an information not about the true state of things, but only about their appearance (phenomena) perceived in the framework of the workings of our minds and shaped by our cognitive terms. The only science is mathematics, because it represents a series of synthetic, a priori, absolute, nonempirical judgments which need no fur-

[1] Immanuel Kant, *Critique of Pure Reason* (M. Müller, trans.), Macmillan, 1881.

ther proof. According to Kant, the only true knowledge was the a priori knowledge of pure mathematics or its application in sciences. Any empirical science is a science of phenomena and not of the absolute truth.

Turning to psychology, Kant saw no reason to assume the existence of a soul. The empirical science of man as a part of nature is called *anthropology;* psychology is a part of it.[2] As an empirical or pragmatic science, psychology, deals with the outer manifestations or phenomena of the self. The "self" is the thing-in-itself, but psychology, like any other empirical science, is limited to what is observable in terms of time and space and in the framework of categories.

According to Kant, all psychological phenomena could be reduced to three classes, namely, knowing (the reason), feeling (the emotions), and willing (the will). In the faculty of knowing Kant distinguished the passive *sensation* and the active *understanding.* Sensation is merely a passive receptivity. Mere sensation is not knowledge. Sensory perception is a change in our consciousness caused by external stimuli. The mind receives sensations and intuitively perceives pure time and space independent of phenomena. Then the mind orders the sensory elements within the framework of time, space, and categories.

Kant distinguished between the useful aesthetic feelings and the pain and pleasure feelings which were regarded as obstacles to pure "reason."

Whatever is in human consciousness is a product of a "transcendental synthesis," created by the transcendental self, the mind, and perceived in accordance with the terms of time, space, and categories. Therefore, the subject matter of empirical psychology, the empirical self, is just a phenomenon like all other phenomena. It can be studied by external and internal observations and the statements made about it depend on the perceiving, transcendental mind.

This transcendental mind, which imposes its laws (time, space, etc.) on nature, cannot be a subject matter of empirical studies; it determines the truth of empirical studies by their conformity to the a priori forms of the transcendental mind. The subject matter of psychology is mental phenomena, but not the mind itself.

Kant's Impact on Psychology

The only logical conclusion that could be drawn from Kant's *Kritik* and his treatment of the subject, was that there were two ways in which psychology could develop. The first was the safe way of a priori statements about "spirit" or "transcendental mind," or "subject," counterposed to anything else in the world. The mind is the focal point of the universe. It is the eye which views everything and the center of being. Indeed, this anti-

[2] Immanuel Kant, *Anthropologie in pragmatischen Hinsicht,* 1798. See also B. B. Wolman, "Immanuel Kant and His Impact on Psychology," in B. B. Wolman (Ed.), *Historical Roots of Contemporary Psychology,* Harper & Row, 1968, pp. 229–247.

Copernican revolution brought about by Kant made the cognizant mind and its axioms the only true, safe, absolute, undisputable source of truth. Armed with the forms of space and time and the categories of quantity, quality, relation, and modality, the "mind," or spirit, shapes the image of the world. Arthur Schopenhauer drew the most consistent conclusion and, in 1819, elaborated a theory of *solipsism* which reduced all existence to the will and idea of the perceiving subject.[3]

No empirical scientist could build on such a foundation. But Kant left open another alternative, the so-called empirical or pragmatic psychology which forms a part of anthropology. This empirical psychology has nothing to do with the mind, which, as a thing-in-itself, is inaccessible to empirical studies. Empirical psychology must be confined to observations of phenomena, that is, to what can be observed by the mind and modified by the mind in accordance with its cognitive terms. Accordingly, psychology can be one of two things. It can be an a priori absolute science about something which evades empirical cognition; apparently this something, the "subject," the "mind," is nothing but a cluster of logical concepts produced by Kant with no effort to check them against empirical data. The other alternative, the empirical one, reduces psychology to an observation of real happenings; but it is a peculiar kind of observation dependent on Kant's transcendent's spirit or mind and its a priori set forms. It seems, therefore, that Kant's theory of the absolute mind was saying a lot about nothing, and his empirical psychology was saying nothing about something. In other words, Kant's study of the transcendental self was a system of statements not rlated to reality, and Kant's study of the empirical self said practically nothing about something which was a part of reality.

If Kant were right, no science would be possible, including psychology. The only true science, as perceived by Kant, was mathematics. But Bertrand Russell has shown that mathematics is not a science at all. It does not contain any true or false statements. It is merely a system of symbols. Russell remarked that during the nineteenth century, mathematicians destroyed Kant's theory.[4] Einstein's theory rendered Kant's concepts impossible.

Kant believed that he had put an end to metaphysics. What he actually did was to put an end to empirical and scientific inquiry. According to Kant, the human mind perceived not what is but what the mind itself ascribed to nature. The most consistent of Kant's disciples was undoubtedly Arthur Schopenhauer.

Kant's psychology is one more case in this antiscientific process. The true mind, the perceiving self who operates with time and space and categories, is unknowable. It is the phenomenological part of it, its external appearance, that psychologists are supposed to study.

[3] Arthur Schopenhauer, *The World as Will and Idea* (Haldane and Kemp, trans.), Scribner, 1923.
[4] Bertrand Russell, "Philosophy of the Twentieth Century," in D. D. Runes (Ed.), *Twentieth Century Philosophy*, Philosophical Library, 1947, p. 245.

The great historian of psychology, G. S. Brett, wrote as follows: "Many would regard the legacy of Kant as a disaster for psychology. It perpetuated the rigid distinction between the outer and the inner with its accompanying assumptions both that there is a radical difference between what we know of our own minds and what others know of them, and that overt behavior alone can be scientifically described. . . . It also led people to believe that they were not doing science unless they were using mathematics. We have, therefore, the tendency developing for psychologists to explore all methods of obtaining quantifiable 'data' often without any fruitful assumptions to test."[5]

Freud was never influenced by Kant. Pavlov was opposed to him. But Dilthey, Spranger, Stern, and the gestalt and field theorists never disentangled themselves from Kant's influence.

The Neo-Kantians

In the second part of the nineteenth century, the neo-Kantians modified Kant's theory. Faced with the new experimental psychology and empirical studies of human actions and mental processes, they reconsidered Kant's epistemological apriorism and his theory of the human mind. The revisions of his theory, and the struggle between French and British empiricism against Kantian speculations left its mark on the emerging psychological science.

A contemporary of Kant, and his follower in the Königsberg chair of philosophy, was Johann Friedrich Herbart (cf. Chapter 1, Section 1). Herbart, in opposition to Kant, tried to develop a materialist psychology. He believed that the soul was one of the units or cells (*das Reale*) of which the organism is composed, and hoped to be able to study human mind in a mechanistic manner.

Another solution was proposed by the physicist and philosopher Ernst Mach. Mach rejected the idea of the thing-in-itself. The world is nothing but the sum of our sensations, which form the content of our consciousness. Our sensations are the only source of truth and the task of science is to study these sensations and put them in order. Mach actually "introjected" physics into psychology and made the perceiving mind the center of any scientific inquiry. In his *Analyse der Empfindungen*, published in 1886, he maintained that all that is, the entire world, consists of our sensations.

At the time when Wundt, Ebbinghaus, Meumann, and others were trying to develop an experimental psychology, most neo-Kantians were grouped around the Marburg school led by Hermann Cohen, and later by Paul Natorp and Ernst Cassirer. Kurt Lewin is mostly indebted to Cassirer. The Marburg philosophers went farther than Kant. According to them, science does not discover the truth, but constructs it, and the object is not *gegeben* (given), but *aufgegeben* (assigned as a task), "not presented to us as

[5] G. S. Brett, *History of Psychology* (R. S. Peters, Ed.), Allen & Unwin, 1951, p. 508.

a given fact but set before us as an 'endless task.' In fulfilling this task the mind is governed by formal principles . . . which determine the structure of all possible experience." Thus, "All possible concepts of objects are specifications of these universal *a priori* forms."[6]

The other neo-Kantian group was formed by the Baden school headed by Wilhelm Windelband and Heinrich Rickert. In accordance with the Kantian tradition, they assumed that our cognitive experience (pure reason), practical experience (morality), and aesthetic experience are governed by some a priori abstract principles called by the Baden school *values*.

Windelband and Rickert counterposed the cultural or historical sciences (*Kultur* or *Geschichtswissenschaften*) to the natural sciences. They preferred the name "cultural sciences" to the old usage of "humanities" (*Geisteswissenschaft*), for "humanities" included the eternal values of logic, ethics, and aesthetics, while the *Kulturwissenschaft*, so they believed, dealt with empirical and passing events and values.

Both *Naturwissenschaft* and *Kulturwissenschaft* are empirical sciences. They differ in methods of research. The natural sciences seek the principles and laws that govern the given subject matter. Natural sciences are *nomothetic*, that is, they seek general laws. The natural sciences are not interested in the single case; they are concerned with the necessary occurrences, with the laws that govern the universe.

The historical or cultural sciences deal with the individual, the unrepeatable and unique case; for example, it happened just once that Napoleon retreated from Moscow in 1812. This event was unique and unrepeatable; it was an *idiophenomenon*. Sciences dealing with idiophenomena do not seek general laws; the idiographic sciences are concerned with values and not with natural causes.

According to Windelband, psychology as studied by Wundt, Ebbinghaus, and others was a nomothetic science. Rickert emphasized that the natural sciences deal with cause-and-effect relationships while the historical sciences relate their data to cultural values.

2. Wilhelm Dilthey: The Understanding Psychology

Kant or Empiricism?

Dilthey's role in the history of modern psychological theory is not comparable to that of Ivan P. Pavlov or Sigmund Freud. Dilthey was less productive in the field of psychology proper and less prominent in his own psychological research; thus, his historical role as a "father" of a school is less significant than that played by Pavlov or Freud. However, the theories described in the third part of the present volume start with Kant, Husserl, Dilthey. Some are a direct continuation of Dilthey's ideas; some deviate

[6] H. A. Hodges, *The Philosophy of Wilhelm Dilthey*, Routledge & Kegan Paul, 1952, p. 27.

from him; some oppose him; but all of them discuss the problems posed by him.

Both Pavlov and Freud represent empiricism and materialism in psychology. Both came to psychology from the realm of the natural sciences. Both were influenced by the Anglo-French empiricism, materialism, and sensualism of Hume, Locke, Voltaire, J. S. Mill, A. Comte, Charles Darwin, and H. Spencer. Both were determinists who believed mental processes to be a part of and a derivative of biological processes. Pavlov concentrated on the physiological foundations; Freud dealt with mental processes and applied to them the principles of the methodological non-reductionism. (Cf. Chapter 6, Section 1.) Both were influenced by the associationism of D. Hartley, J. S. Mill, and A. Bain.

Dilthey's approach was different, for his main effort was to bring psychology closer to history, ethics, literature, and the arts.

Kant's transcendentalism influenced Dilthey's reasoning to a great extent. Determinism and causation were reduced by Dilthey to the role of methods of perception. "When we place objects in the relations of cause and effect, the sensory impressions contain only the condition of regular succession, whereas the causal relation itself again arises through a synthesis which springs from within us," wrote Dilthey in 1894.[7]

In contradistinction to Kant, Dilthey believed that the perceiving and the perceived mind are one thing. What we perceive in external perception are mere phenomena and what we ascribe to them. The perception of ourselves is far superior, more objective, and more precise. Dilthey explained: "In contrast to external perception, inner perception rests upon an awareness (*Innewerden*), a lived experience (*Erleben*), it is immediately given. . . . No matter how the sensation of a violet color may have arisen, considered as an inner phenomenon it is something indivisible." The lived experience "has no resemblance to the processes of nature. Here we continually experience combinations and connections in ourselves, while we have to read combination and connection into the sensory stimuli. . . . It is thus that we conceive the ideas of unity in plurality, of parts in a whole, of causal relations, and by means of these understand nature by applying these conceptions to it under definite conditions of regular coexistence or succession."[8] On this point Dilthey deviated from Kant.

Dilthey was opposed to Kant on the issue of epistemology. To Dilthey, psychology, not philosophy, was the fundamental science (*grundlegende Wissenschaft*). Dilthey accepted the viewpoint of the British empiricists D. Hume and J. S. Mill, who believed that a scientific psychology should be the basis of sociology, law, ethics, education, and other human studies, analogous to the way in which mathematics was the basis of the natural sciences.

[7] Quoted from H. A. Hodges, *Wilhelm Dilthey, An Introduction*, Routledge & Kegan Paul, 1949, p. 133.
[8] *Ibid.*, pp. 13–14.

Moreover, Dilthey could not accept the Kantian idea that mind and body are constructs of the perceiving subject and his a priori set rational principles. Kant's psychology dealt with one of the phenomena and its validity depended on epistemology. Dilthey's psychology dealt with the human mind, and to him epistemology depended on psychology in the study of reasoning. Epistemology, or the theory of cognition, wrote Dilthey, is a "psychology in motion, namely a psychology which moves toward a certain goal."[9] Psychology has to be used in human studies as mathematics is used in the study of nature.

Attitude to Husserl and Windelband

The physical world, said Dilthey in opposition to Kant, exists independently of our cognitive processes. The cognitive processes or consciousness can be considered apart from the world they perceive. Their functions, mental acts, cannot be doubted. Whether their content is true or false, there is no doubt that the mind does something, is conscious of something (act), and that it is conscious of some external object (content). Thus, psychology as a study of mental acts, and their content is to be the basis for epistemology, and not vice versa, as Husserl proposed.

Dilthey was even more opposed to the neo-Kantians, both in Marburg and in Baden. He did not accept the idea of a priori values. Values, he said, are merely an expression of emotional attitudes of humans. He rejected the idea of transcendental ethics. Human beings strive to protect and improve their lives.

Dilthey could not accept Windelband's division of the idiographic sciences of history and culture and the nomothetic sciences of nature. As Windelband himself remarked, the same subject matter could be studied from both points of view. Dilthey went farther and said that geography, astronomy, natural history, economics, comparative psychology, philology, and even history have both idiographic and nomothetic aspects. Instead, Dilthey proposed distinguishing between natural sciences and humanities (Geisteswissenschaften). Human studies, which include the mind and its products, have a special interest in the individual case. Whenever we study the individual (psychology), or the arts, or history, it is always the study of our inner processes, while the natural sciences look on their subject matter from without.

Descriptive and Explanatory Psychologies

Dilthey broke away from Kant on many points, but the main difference lies in the realm of psychology. Dilthey agreed with Kant that knowledge of the objective world is not real: it is knowledge of phenomena only. But knowledge of our own mind is a true knowledge of the true mind, the gen-

9 Wilhelm Dilthey, Einleitung in die Geisteswissenschaften, 1883, p. 42.

uine thing in itself. The difference lies in the kind of perception. The external world we observe; our inner mind we experience, we live through (*erlebt*).

Dilthey found good reason to criticize contemporary psychology as being unable to present human experiences in their entirety. Too often it has been said that Shakespeare's *Lear, Hamlet,* and *Macbeth* "contain more psychology than all the psychological textbooks together." Great writers do not deal with "sensory perceptions" or "thresholds," but they do understand man "in his entire reality." Therefore, wrote Dilthey, "one wishes for a psychology which could catch in the net of its descriptions that which these poets and writers contain over and above present-day psychology; a psychology which could take the thoughts which Augustine, Pascal or Lichtenberg make so penetrating by one-sided brilliant illumination, and make them serviceable for human knowledge in a universally valid system." [10]

Nevertheless, Dilthey was not opposed to the experimental psychology of his time. He simply found it inadequate as far as the understanding of man goes.

In 1880, Dilthey was already aware of the limitations of psychology. While British associationist psychology was patterned after contemporary physics, psychology was still far from the precision of the mathematical inferences. Nor could experimental psychology cover the entire area of the human mind. Psychological laws, wrote Dilthey, "are pure laws of form; they deal with the formal side of human actions and dispositions; they do not deal with the content of the human mind." [11] If mathematics is the foundation for all natural sciences, psychology has to play an analogous role in human studies.

A new psychology is required as a foundation for epistemology and other humanistic studies. Dilthey noted the distinction between explanatory and descriptive studies. A descriptive science (*beschreibende*) deals with observable phenomena, classifies and systematizes them. The explanatory science (*erklärende*) goes beyond the observable data and develops a system of hypotheses.

In his *Einleitung in die Geisteswissenschaften* (1883), Dilthey explained that the contemporary experimentally and physiologically oriented psychology applied the wrong method. Even natural scientists have found, under the influence of positivism, that science should be descriptive. Science should not go beyond observable data. Generalization is the only permissible way of conclusion from what was given in the empirical observations. Psychologists too readily assume physiological causes. Dilthey was critical of such an easy reductionism.

Experimental psychology deals with sensations and their associations, and fails to see the man as he sees and feels himself. The higher mental processes are overlooked. Explanatory psychology is unable to see what po-

[10] Hodges, *Wilhelm Dilthey, An Introduction*, p. 132.
[11] Wilhelm Dilthey, *Gesammelte Schriften*, Teubner, 1924. Vol. VI, p. 43.

etry or autobiography or art or religion have seen. Art and literature cannot take the place of a scientific psychology, but explanatory psychology falls short of what it should be. There is no need for explanatory psychology, said Dilthey, and in 1894 he explained his views as follows:

> We know natural objects from without through our senses. However we may break them up or divide them, we never reach their ultimate elements in this way. We supply such elements by an amplification of experience. Again, the senses, regarded from the point of view of their purely physiological function, never give us the unity of the object. This exists for us only through a synthesis of the sense-stimuli which arises from within. . . . How different is the way in which mental life is given to us! In contrast to external perception, inner perception rests upon an awareness (Innewerden), a lived experience (Erleben), it is immediately given. Here, in sensation or in the feeling of pleasure accompanying it, something simple and indivisible is given to us.[12]

The Understanding Psychology

The above quotation was taken from Dilthey's programmatic work, published in 1894. It was after a long period of preparation and hesitation that Dilthey published the *Ideas Concerning a Descriptive and Analytical Psychology* (*Ideen über eine beschreibende und zergliedernde Psychologie*). The main argument was directed against the interpretation of psychology in terms of physics and chemistry as had been introduced by the British associationists. Perhaps the idea of atoms was a useful construct in physics, but the breaking up of our mental life into small units, called sensations, ideas, and feelings, has no justification whatsoever, he said.

Physics is an explanatory science which makes certain a priori assumptions because its elements are not given in empirical observation. The theoretical constructs of physics are a necessary way to introduce a system and unity where unity cannot be found.

There is no need for such an explanatory procedure in psychology. The human mind is a coherent unity and there is no logical reason for splitting it (*zergliedern*) into hypothetical elements. A man is a wholeness, a unit, and not a conglomeration of atoms.

Psychological phenomena are not perceived from without; they are experienced (*erlebt*) from within. They represent not a series of separate phenomena, but a stream of inner processes. "Only by abstraction do we isolate a function or a type of connection from a concrete system." The totality and continuity of the mind is empirically given, and the division of the functions of the mind into elements is a product of logical abstractions, generalizations, and categorizations. "In lived experience the processes of the whole mind work together. . . . The particular process is carried in lived experience by the whole totality of mental life, and the systematic connections within it and between it and the whole life of the mind belong to immediate experience (*Erfahrung*)."[13]

---

[12] Hodges, *Wilhelm Dilthey, An Introduction*, p. 133.
[13] *Ibid.*, p. 135.

In *Ideas*, Dilthey definitely and finally rejected the idea of explanation and introduced the concept of understanding. The main objective of natural sciences is to "explain" (*erklären*) what is going on, while the objective of psychology is to "understand" (*verstehen*). "In understanding we start from the system as a whole, which is given to us as a living reality (*der uns lebendig gegeben ist*), to make the particular intelligible to ourselves in terms of it. . . . The apprehension of the whole makes possible and determines the interpretation of the particular part." [14] Psychological research should not deal with physiological elements, but should be "fruitful for the understanding (*Verständnis*) of life."

The structural unity of the mind should be the main consideration of psychology. The man as a whole is its subject matter. Natural sciences explain nature in terms of causes and effects. Psychology sees the totality of life in the inner experience.

When Dilthey suggested that psychology cease to be an "explanatory" science and confine itself to "descriptive" studies, he expressed an opposition to reductionism and to psychophysical parallelism. Physicists introduce models and theoretical constructs because their observations do not lead to a coherent system. Physicists are forced to go beyond the observed "descriptive" data and form "explanatory" models of atoms, and other scientific hypotheses.

Psychologists, starting with David Hume, developed analogous methods and introduced the idea of mental atoms such as sensations and perceptions, bound together into larger units by association. There is, however, no need to imitate physics. Psychological data, as mentioned before, are given in "inner perception" and form a coherent system. Thus, psychology analyzes life "as it is."

The atomistic, molecular, associationistic psychology failed to perceive man as a whole and to describe the higher mental processes, so well described by poets and writers. The contemporary experimental psychology, said Dilthey, "proved to be the indispensable instrument . . . for the establishment of an accurate description of inner mental processes like the limitation of consciousness, the rapidity of mental processes, the factors involved in memory and in the sense of time. . . . But to knowledge of laws in the inner domain of mind it simply has not led." [15]

The Mental Structure

Psychology should pay more attention to the dynamic unity of the human mind, that is, to its *structure*. This structure is not static, for the human mind grows, undergoes changes, and becomes more coherent. The process of growth is highly individual and unique in each case.

Each man is a separate entity, yet men are similar. Their similarities

[14] *Ibid.*, p. 136.
[15] Quoted after Hodges, *The Philosophy of Wilhelm Dilthey*, p. 203.

should be studied and their common traits and differences described. Each individual is a representative of his time or culture or group.

The methods of psychological research differ greatly from those used in the natural sciences. The natural sciences *explain* by means of purely intellectual processes. Psychological research "grows out of lived experience itself." The psychological understanding "starts from the system as a whole," is given to us "as a living reality." Spontaneous psychological thinking passes over into psychological investigation.

Dilthey further developed Brentano's and Husserl's distinction between mental acts and their contents. Our inner experiences are acts; they are the facts of being aware of objects; the objects of which we are aware are the content. Acts are always a matter of experience (*Erlebnis*); their content is always a matter of presentation (*Vorstellung*). Every lived experience has a content. The act is the fact of being conscious of something; that of which we are conscious is the content.

In accordance with Kant, Dilthey divided all mental acts or attitudes into cognition (perception, memory, judgment), affection (pleasure, pain, fear, love, hate), and volition (wish, decision, obligation). In all three areas, the act and the content should be distinguished. Dilthey explained it as follows: "I perceive a color, pass a judgment of it, feel pleasure, and wish to produce it. The element of the content of perception goes through all the various phases of the act. Yet each phase may relate to different colors and also to other objects."[16]

The unity of life is teleological, wrote Dilthey. "Knowing is in the researcher a teleological system. . . . In this whole teleological system particular functions work together to produce states which somehow have in consciousness the character of values or ends."[17] All the cognitive, emotional, and creative factors combine in the preservation of the teleological unity of life. The purpose is the main factor, and the mind works in the direction of the determinate "mental attitudes" (*Anlagen*).

This new psychology should serve as a foundation for all human studies. Psychological analysis "illuminates" human relations. "Without reference to the mental system on which their relations are grounded, the human studies are an aggregate, a bundle, not a system."

All human studies require psychological knowledge, wrote Dilthey in the *Ideen*.

> Any study of religion leads to the analysis of concepts such as feeling, will, dependence, freedom, motivation; all these concepts must be interpreted in a psychological context. . . . Jurisprudence is based on psychological foundations, to which the concepts of norm, law, and responsibility are related. . . . The political sciences which describe the organization of society find in any social relationship the psychological facts of sociability, social control and subordination. These relationships required a psychological interpretation. . . . All the cultural systems, the economic life, law, religion, art and science, the various forms of

---

[16] *Ibid.*, p. 38.
[17] *Ibid.*, p. 43.

social organization such as the family, community, church and state, are products of the functions of the human mind and, in final analysis, they can be understood only in the terms of the mind.[18]

Concluding Remarks

Kant, Husserl, and Dilthey exposed a new page in the history of psychology. Kant's contribution to psychology was rather negative and may be considered a regression in comparison with the studies of the sensualists and associationists.

However, Kant's impact on psychology has been quite significant, especially in those German psychologists who have been educated in the spirit of his epistemological idealism. Kant introduced a sharp distinction between the perceiving subject and the perceived objective world and put the center of weight into the subject. This is why the author of this book believes that Kant's revolution ran contrary to Copernicus. Copernicus dethroned man and earth; Kant went in the opposite direction.

Dilthey could accept neither Kant's disrespect for empirical studies nor the positivistic approach of experimental psychology. Dilthey did not pave a new road for psychology; he only erected a new sign. Spranger, Stern, and the gestalt and field theories took his sign as their starting point.

Dilthey could never overcome Kant's influence. Being torn between apriorism and empiricism, he accepted empiricism, but not the kind of empiricism practiced in the natural sciences—the empiricism of observation and interpretation. Psychology and other "humanistic" sciences (*Geisteswissenschaften*) were supposed to be empirical up to a certain point. They should describe but not explain.

Dilthey's method may give the impression of being very empirical, but it is not. Science cannot be a catalogue of observations (cf. Chapter 15). However, according to Dilthey, psychological data are so different from the data of any other science that there is no need and no use for interpretation. Kant's anti-Copernican revolution was continued by Dilthey, and the Kantian dichotomy between man and universe occupied a large place in the reasoning of Spranger, Stern, and others.

Dilthey did not solve Kant's problem, for Kant's problem was never a problem that any empirical scientist could solve. Kant's dichotomies do not exist in the realm of empirical studies (cf. Chapter 15). Therefore, Dilthey's solution based on the assumption that we "understand" mental phenomena is merely a game of words.

Moreover, Dilthey preserved for the human mind the central position. Perceptions do not convey the entire truth; there is something coming from within—categories, or, as later postulated by Wertheimer, *Gestalt*. The human mind is goal-directed; hence Ach's *determinierende Tendenz*, in opposition to associationism (cf. Chapter 12). Each human being is unique,

[18] Dilthey, *Gesammelte Schriften*, Vol. V, pp. 147–148.

said Dilthey, and hence Spranger's typology, and Stern's and Allport's *unitas multiplex* (cf. Chapter 11), and Lewin's insistence on the uniqueness of the human situation at a given time (cf. Chapter 13).

No one, with the exception perhaps of E. Spranger, was Dilthey's disciple. But all the psychologists whose theories will be described in Chapters 11, 12, and 13 are indebted to Dilthey and deal with the problems posed by his unsuccessful effort to overcome the Kantian impasse.

11

Personalistic Psychology

1. EDWARD SPRANGER: PSYCHOLOGY OF PERSONALITY

The Mental Structures

The man who implemented Dilthey's ideas of a psychology based on understanding was Edward Spranger. Spranger wholeheartedly accepted Dilthey's distinction between the explanatory, analytic, atomistic psychology related to the sensory elements and their physiological foundations, and the descriptive, understanding, molar psychology whose subject matter is the human mind and its total structure. Leaving the explanatory aspect out, Spranger devoted his studies to the understanding of the individual as a whole, because the study of elements "destroys the meaningful totalities of life." Moreover, Spranger doubted whether an "objective" study was ever possible in psychology. Psychology, as a *Geisteswissenschaft*, depends on the personal philosophies of the psychologists and the cultural influences on their convictions.[1]

Dilthey, Spranger's master, said that psychology should describe rather than analyze; understand rather than interpret; deal with the totality of human actions rather than with their fragments; turn to the humanities rather than to natural science. Spranger unreservedly incorporated Dilthey's theory and combined it with Brentano's influences. Accordingly, his theory was a theory of mental acts, but these mental acts were closed and goal-directed entities.

Spranger utilized Dilthey's concept of mental structures and named his psychology a *Strukturpsychologie* in contradistinction to Wundt's and Ebbinghaus' "atomistic" and reductionistic psychologies. Spranger's emphasis on the molar approach led him to seek total situations to which the total individual would relate himself. These situations were the cultural values found by Spranger in his society.

---

[1] Edward Spranger, "Der Sinn der Voraussetzungslosigkeit in den Geisteswissenschaften," *Preussische Akademie der Wissenschaften*, 1929.

Opposition to Reductionism

Each mental act has a goal and is directed to a certain aspect of cultural life. Culture, whether art or religion or science, is the sum of products of the human mind. The various cultural aspects of mental life represent a choice of goals. The human mind, so Dilthey said, is teleological; the various goals of human life have been developed in the history of mankind and experienced in the life of each individual.

History, and not the laboratory, is the proper place for the study of the human mind. Laboratory studies grasp minute and meaningless details. Experimental psychology is forced to look beyond its empirical data and "interpret them by referring psychological phenomena to physiology." This method, contended Spranger, leads nowhere; human life cannot be understood in physiological terms.

Up to now, wrote Spranger in 1924, "psychologists tried to interpret the mental changes in puberty by relating them to somatic changes. . . . Physiological statements do not help psychology even one step. . . ."[2]

Psychology has to say what man experiences, how he experiences it, and what his former life experiences are. Physiological interpretations lead nowhere.

Explanation is the proper method for the natural sciences. Their subject matter is perceived from without, and they must build a system of hypotheses to link the causes and effects of the observable phenomena.

Psychology, as well as other human sciences, does not need to be explanatory. Its subject matter, human experience, is experienced from within, by the experiencing subject. The proper method for psychology is, therefore, the method of *understanding*.

Understanding means to "grasp in a meaningful way the mental relationships which are perceived in an objectively valid cognition. We understand only meaningful structures. . . . [Understanding] always encompasses the meaning."[3] Meaning is a complexity which represents a total value. Fractions of a mental action as studied by the experimentalists are meaningless. A total act is meaningful and represents a certain value in accordance with the goal toward which it is directed.

A descriptive psychology is based on the reexperiencing of life experiences. The understanding psychology goes deeper; it does not depend on reexperiencing only, but on reexperiencing of the essential elements, the categories, the orders and relationship of the mind. The influence of Kant and of Husserl is quite obvious here. Descriptive psychology, believed Spranger, was the first step; then the understanding grasps the main features of the mental experiences in their relationship to the goal and the values of the individual.

[2] Edward Spranger, *Psychologie des Jugendalters*, Quelle & Meyer. 1925, p. 24.
[3] *Ibid.*, p. 3.

The Six Personality Types

Spranger distinguished six human goal-directed patterns related to six areas of culture, namely, scientific theory, aesthetics, economic life, religion, sociability, and power politics.[4]

No human being is entirely devoted to a single value or a single goal. Spranger was suggesting six "ideal" types. These do not represent any living human personalities; they represent rather six types of philosophies of life. According to Spranger, each individual pursues one of these six philosophies and can be approximately classified as one of the six types. Obviously, no individual can be classified as a "pure" type.

The *theoretical* type is the intellectual who tries to reason out his problems. Whatever he faces in life, his is always an inquisitive approach and a search for the rational and systematic. The theoretical character may be empirical or speculative, a scientist or a philosopher, but he is always concerned with the finding of the truth. He seeks to perceive the world as a systematic, logically ordered unity.

The *economic* type is mostly concerned with the practical aspects of life. His main goal is self-preservation and economic security. He judges everything from the point of view of practicability and usefulness. The economic man looks for material values, and material success is his idol. He considers science a servant and tool to be used toward economic achievements; education, he believes, should be geared toward the goal of a practical adjustment to life.

The *aesthetic* type is individualistic and much impressed by the beauty and harmony of the universe. The aesthetic character is mostly concerned with the diversity of things, with their charm and grace. He is less concerned with the truth than is the theoretical type and with the usefulness of things than is the economic type.

The *sociable* or *social* character is friendly, congenial, considerate, and compassionate. He loves his fellow man and is kind and charitable. Unselfishness characterizes his behavior; the desire to help people is his main goal. The sociable character is less concerned with truth and beauty. His main values are moral good and sympathy.

The *power-politics* character desires to control people. He strives to outdistance people and to subjugate them. His main goal is to gain control over others. He is much concerned with politics and methods of influencing and ruling. He relates to the world in terms of power, of overcoming obstacles, and of domination.

The *religious* type is a mystic who seeks unity between man and the universe. His main consideration is inner truth and harmony. His approach to life is based on contemplation and search for eternal unity with the cosmos.

[4] Edward Spranger, *Types of Men*, Niemyer, 1928, p. 37 ff.

Concluding Remarks

Spranger's radical non-reductionism forced the naïve reductionists to revaluate their statements. Spranger's emphasis on relatedness of personality types to cultural areas has influenced many psychologists, including G. W. Allport, A. Adler, K. Horney, E. Fromm, K. Lewin, and others.

The apparent weakness of Spranger's theory stems from the Kantian dichotomy of man versus nature. Dilthey's solution led psychology into acceptance of a non-objective and non-testable kind of theory construction. "Understanding" cannot be a scientific method if science is a system of propositions open to empirical test (cf. Chapter 15). Spranger's method excludes an objective test.

Spranger's system of values and personality types is arbitrarily set. His use of the term "value" is ambiguous. Value means something leading to a goal, that is, a utilitarian evaluation judgment, describing the usefulness of a certain thing as a means toward a goal. Value can be used as a substitute for cultural achievement.[5] Either way, Spranger's choice of six values is arbitrary, uneconomic, and not representative of the total number of human goals, aims, and achievements.

2. WILLIAM STERN: PERSONS VERSUS THINGS

The Man of Synthesis

No one was better prepared than William Stern to mediate between the experimentalists on one side and the humanists on the other. Stern's broad humanistic education, his philosophical erudition, his talent for keen observation and precise experimentation combined with an inclination to generalization and sophistication, and finally his industrious and indefatigable personality made him the man of synthesis. The synthesis Stern aimed at was not an eclecticism; it was a genuine effort to reconcile opposites and to overcome dichotomies such as body–soul, nature–culture, and associationism–holism.

Stern's contribution to psychology is rich and varied. His role in the history of mental testing in Germany is comparable to Binet's in France, Burt's in England, and Terman's in the United States. Stern's productive work included child psychology, educational and clinical studies, and several other areas.

In the controversy between the naturalist and humanist scientists in German psychology, Stern, being both an experimentalist and a humanist,

---

[5] Benjamin B. Wolman, "Scientific Study of Educational Aims," *Teachers College Record*, 1949, 50, 471–481. See also Wolman, "Does Psychology Need Its Own Philosophy of Science?," *American Psychologist*, 1971, 26, 877–886.

always sought a reasonable compromise. Accordingly, he offered a solution to the distinction between *idiographic* and *nomothetic* sciences and between the descriptive and the understanding psychologies.

According to Stern, science seeks laws. These represent an invariable relationship common to a class or category of objects which have some similarity to one another. Thus, all sciences are nomothetic. However, the "individuality is the asymptote of the science that seeks laws" and could and should be included in scientific research.

The first step in scientific procedure is the acquisition of empirical data. "*Descriptive psychology* is primarily concerned with the *acquisition* of data. Its aim is to represent mental events by succinct statements intelligible to others."[6] Description can deal with single phenomena as they occur or with the essential core of them in the *phenomenological* description, as suggested by Husserl. The described empirical data must be classified. The division of mental phenomena into cognition, emotion, and volition is too rigid. Instead Stern suggested division into perception, memory, thought and imagination, volition, and feeling.

Mental phenomena are complex and should be analyzed. The search for the elements is a legitimate scientific procedure, but it is not true, wrote Stern, that mental phenomena are merely aggregates of elements. The "elementaristic" psychology, starting with Hume, saw in the individual a mechanical sum of elements. This is wrong, wrote Stern,

> for neither simple elements nor purely mechanical structures are immediately given in our experience of mental activity. . . . The fundamental principle opposed to the concept of element throughout this new psychology is that of "Wholeness." . . . Anything mental either is itself a whole (i.e., a unity meaningful in itself that is more or less definitely bounded), or belongs to a whole. Wholeness does not exclude an internal multiplicity of constituent parts and members; these simply lose the character of independent elements capable of existing by and of themselves. Instead they become subordinate "aspects" of the whole and may be understood only in their relation to the "totality." . . . The methodological requirement that *scientific psychology always preserve the correlation* between part and whole, salience and ground, *analysis and totality*, applies without exception.[7]

Being influenced by Dilthey, Stern suggested that psychologists apply both the method of explanation and the method of understanding. Explanation is subordination of concrete data to abstract laws. The three most important categories of psychological explanation are the *causal*, the teleological, and the genetic. These three types of explanation answer respectively the questions Why? What for? and How did it take place?

"It is a fallacy to consider the understanding psychology as being the opposite to and independent of psychology as a natural science. There is but one united psychological discipline; it seeks to know its subject matter

[6] William Stern, *General Psychology from the Personalistic Standpoint*, Macmillan, 1938, p. 10.
[7] *Ibid.*, pp. 14–15.

both in its basic nature and the conceptual laws which explain it, as well as a wholistic value-structures which have a unique significance," wrote Stern in 1924.[8]

Explanation deals with the lawfulness of relationships, and understanding with their meaningfulness. When we comprehend a person as a whole, we understand him.

The distinction between the natural sciences and the humanities (*Geisteswissenschaften*) introduced by Dilthey has become superfluous, wrote Stern. The natural sciences more and more emphasized the "wholeness of the organism and the meaningfulness of all processes of life." On the other hand, the human sciences have started to apply statistics and other techniques borrowed from the natural sciences. The gulf is obviously closing and it is the task of psychology to unite both methods. Stern's method combined explanation and understanding.

Stern advocated a variety of research methods and was critical of any one-sided approach. The behaviorist "shuts himself off" from any introspectionistic data; the psychoanalytic fanatic, from the conscious phenomena; the experimentalist, from all nonexperimental data. An exclusive experimentalism in psychology is a self-defeating device. The more precise is the experiment, wrote Stern, "the more isolated and the more fundamental the observed phenomenon, and the more constant are the experimental conditions, the more it is artificial and remote from the study of the individual."[9] Experimentation as an auxiliary technique can be very useful.

But all other methods can be useful also. Psychological phenomena are "immediately experienced." Accordingly, introspection can be a useful method. Since mental activity includes both the world of nature and the world of culture, the methods of the natural and the cultural sciences should be combined in psychological study.

Mind and Body

Stern faced the problems posed by Kant, but he solved them in a non-Kantian manner. He distinguished between the essence or *substratum* of the mind and the *empirical facts* of the mind. This distinction differs from Kant's thing-in-itself and phenomena.

The substratum of the mind, said Stern, "must be something *that has existence going beyond or prior of the differentiation into the mental and the physical,* thereby certifying the original unity of the individual."[10]

This unity is not found in inorganic nature, which is composed of *things (Sache),* but is typical of a person *(Person).* The person is "a living

[8] William Stern, *Wertphilosophie,* Barth, 1924, p. 380.
[9] William Stern, *Differentielle Psychologie* (3rd ed.), Barth, 1921, p. 34.
[10] Stern, *General Psychology,* p. 69.

whole, individual, unique, striving toward goals, self-contained and yet open to the world around him; he is capable of having experience." [11]

Psychology is "the science of the person having experience or capable of having experience," experience being "identified and interpreted in terms of its matrix, the unitary, goal-directed person." [12] "Personality," said Stern, is a "neutral" term in so far as the body–mind problem is concerned. It incorporates both terms and presents the problem in a new light.

Psychophysics is the science of lawful relations between stimuli and sensations. Physiological psychologists, especially Wundt, enriched psychology by their studies of sensory perception and localization of the functions of the brain. Biological psychology introduced the ideas of evolution, heredity, environment, and adjustment. Dilthey's psychology of history introduced the understanding of the nature of the individual. Spranger's psychology of cultural forms represents six realms of value.

All these diversified areas of psychology should be merged into the study of the individual. "The individual is not partly body and partly mind, but a person with the capacity for experience. He is a portion of a world that, although bounded on the outside, nevertheless continually exchanges substance and function with all other portions of the world; this is his corporeality. And he also has the capacity to reflect himself and the world inwardly; this is his mentality. The life of the person includes *both*; accordingly, there is no experience and no capacity for experience that is not bound up with the physical aspect of life and with bodily functions." [13]

Stern was indebted to Goldstein and Lashley. The nervous system functions both in a specific and localized manner and as a totality; accordingly, psychology deals with both parts and totalities, with the physical and the mental aspects of life.

Three Modalities

Stern distinguished three modalities of life. The first is biological. On this level the individual's *vitality* is dominant. Growth and maturity and reproduction are the vital functions. The vital world of the individual is his *biosphere*.

The second modality is life experience (*Erlebnis*). Experience is "life under cleavage and tension." All experience is either *salient*, standing sharply in focus, or *embedded* within totality, in the background. Each experience contains some salience and some embedding, some focal and some marginal elements, in close analogy to the figure and ground concept (cf. Chapter 12, Section 2).

Experience has objects, stated Stern, accepting Husserl's distinction be-

[11] *Ibid.*, p. 70.
[12] *Ibid.*, pp. vii–viii.
[13] *Ibid.*, p. 84.

tween act and content. The individual experiences himself and others, and there is always cleavage between the person and the world. The mind is "everything about the person that is experience or that is essentially related to experience." [14]

The content of experience is called a mental *phenomenon*. The individual *has* experiences and *acts* through them. Having an experience is a mental state. Acts are produced by contents and processes of thought.

Some experiences are short-lived; some are lasting *dispositions*. Dispositions are the possibilities, abilities for future experiences. Character traits, temperaments, and mnemic abilities are dispositions.

The third level or modality of life is absent in plant and animals. It is purely human and represents cultural, social, moral, and religious values. The individual accepts the social norms and standards, the moral code and cultural values of his social environment. This process is called by Stern *introception*. It resembles Freud's concept of superego formed by introjection and identification.

Experience has an intermediate position between biological vitality and cultural *introception*.

The Main Areas of Psychology

The entire field of psychology has been divided by Stern into (1) sense perception, (2) memory and learning, (3) thought, intelligence, and imagination, (4) drives, instincts, and volition, and (5) affective life. Stern's theory, unlike Pavlov's or Freud's, is a *complete* psychological system. Seemingly no area has been left out.

Stern was opposed to Wundt and the "elementaristic" psychology. Stern remarked that the concept of gestalt was not discovered by the gestalt psychologists, but by Ehrenfels, K. Bühler, Krueger, and himself.

We perceive a gestalt independently of any specific sensory stimulation, wrote Stern. But he did not accept the idea of gestalt as a fundamental phenomenon. It is man who perceives the world in separate wholes. Man can arrange the ticks of his watch in a three-part or four-part rhythm, or combine dots. "No Gestalt without a Gestalter" (the man who forms a gestalt), wrote Stern.

Moreover, the figure–ground distinction of the gestaltists was to Stern a matter of degree of the *salient* and *embedded*. Gestalt is the most salient phenomenon of perception. The ground is the *Ungestalt*, the least clear and least important, the embedded part of perception.

Learning is the acquisition of knowledge through repeated presentations, wrote Stern. *Involuntary* learning can be ascribed to two causes. The first lies in the external stimulus and its constant repetition; the second cause is the susceptivity of the individual. Strong and repeated impres-

[14] *Ibid.*, pp. 78–79.

sions, whether desired or not, conscious or not conscious, become mnemically effective, said Stern. Apparently Stern's point of view is distant from any reward theory (cf. Part I).

A good example of involuntary learning is the acquisition of knowledge by little children. The child, wrote Stern, "asks for little songs not to learn them but to hear them; but all the same, at least he learns them. . . . In his walk he stops at every shop-window and expects all its glories to be pointed out and explained to him, not that he may know them tomorrow or in a year's time, but now, at this moment; but he thus acquires lasting knowledge of the appearance, significance, and use of things. . . ."[15]

While involuntary learning depends on repeated coincidence, voluntary learning depends on the goal, the interest, and the intelligence of the learner.

Stern developed his own theory of thinking. Leaning on Husserl and Külpe, Stern distinguished between the act of thinking and the content of it. In accordance with Brentano and Husserl, Stern described thought as a process that "*intends* something that is not (an object, a class, a relation, a meaning, a solution)."[16]

In the realm of action and striving, Stern proposed several levels. The first is the level of *reflexes* or rigid inherited responses. Reflexes can be acquired or conditioned. However, "it is paradoxical to attempt to make such a *deranged* reflex the prototype of all learning, animal and human alike, and the basis of the science of human nature."[17]

Drives represent a higher level. A drive is an innate disposition toward the implementation of a personal goal. Stern distinguished four classes of drives: (1) *self-preservation*, which includes defense, flight, and nutrition; (2) *self-development*, such as superiority, aggressiveness, and adornment; (3) *social* drives, racial, herd, protective, initiative, and combat drives; (4) *human* drives, such as the craving toward intellectual, ideal, and cultural objectives.

The *needs* represent yet a higher level. Whenever impulse is restrained by inner or outer inhibitions, a need arises. Need is a state of tension. said Stern. Kurt Lewin (cf. Chapter 13) apparently borrowed this concept from Stern.

Drives and needs designate purposive forces. Instinct is a drive "whose direction points not only to the final end, but also the means by which this end is attained."

The highest level of striving is called by Stern *volition*. Volition is a "conscious anticipation of end and means."

Each individual goes through consecutive stages of salience and em-

[15] William Stern, *Psychology of Early Childhood Up to the Sixth Year of Age* (3rd ed.), Holt, 1930, p. 226.
[16] Stern, *General Psychology*, p. 275.
[17] *Ibid.*, p. 379.

bedding. The cognitive and acting functions of the individual tend to become salient; the experiences of embedding are the feelings. Feelings are formless (*Ungestalt*) and in the background.

All feelings can be divided into pleasant and painful. Another polarity has been introduced: the *excitement* of feelings leads to an expansion of energy; and *tranquility* to accumulation.

Character and Personality

In Stern's terminology, character corresponds to personality. "It designates the make up that the person possesses in his *totality*, but considers this totality from one definite standpoint only, that is the predisposition to acts of *will*." [18]

Stern combined the influence of heredity and environment in the theory of *convergence*. Personality is a product of the converging influences of both heredity and environment.

Personality is the meeting ground of physical and mental, heredity and environment, salient and embedded, total and partial. It is a *unitas multiplex*, a unity composed of elements.

Unitas multiplex contains more than mere empirical unity. The fact that the same individual may experience conflicting wishes and still be himself, still be a unity, indicates that unity is the prerequisite of any inner conflict. Personality is the continuum of human life; it is the perpetual and consistent whole which the individual is.

Yet each individual is composed of parts. Stern called the constant and goal-directed parts of the activities of the person *traits*.

> The constancy of a trait is merely an ideal or limiting concept—and for two reasons. One is that man is at no moment of his existence merely an adaptive, self-preserving creature; always there is in his behavior a spark of self-development and growth. For this reason his finished traits are never quite finished. In addition, a trait is never entirely independent of the world outside, but stands in constant active relationship to it. It indicates the way in which the person reacts to the world; but never are the stimuli that provoke the reaction entirely the same, and never therefore are the various expressions of one and the same trait completely in agreement with one another. The trait is each time slightly different because it confronts other determining conditions; and these conditions produce not only a special coloring in each act that a trait arouses, but also can influence the trait itself in a permanent way. [19]

Stern distinguished between the *driving traits*, called *Richtungsdispositionen*, and the *instrumental traits*, called *Rüstungsdispositionen*. "The two factors of *Richtung* and *Rüstung*, however, closely interwoven, have nonetheless a certain independence of one another, and the most varied relations to one another. We are therefore compelled to distinguish beween those dis-

[18] *Ibid.*, p. 436.
[19] Quoted after Gordon W. Allport, *Personality: A Psychological Interpretation*, Holt, 1937, p. 312.

positions that have a prevailingly directional character from those that are principally an implemental character. The former are purposive, they have a 'tendency to,' the latter are capacities, and have a 'potency for.' "[20]

Concluding Remarks

William Stern was a remarkably productive man and his research covered many varied areas. He occupies an important position in contemporary philosophy and psychology as a leading theoretician of personalism. Stern was the Director of the Hamburg Psychological Institute from 1916 to 1933 and was undoubtedly the most influential German psychologist at that time.

Stern's contribution to psychological theory is often underestimated. Stern was the man who pointed to the possibility of reconciliation of opposite viewpoints. Especially significant is his idea of parts and totalities in perception, which may lead to the utilization of both the associationist and the gestalt contributions to psychological theory.

Stern's immediate disciples are G. W. Allport and K. Lewin. Allport took over the personalistic content; Lewin took over the philosophical approach only.

3. GORDON W. ALLPORT: PERSONALITY TRAITS

Idiophenomena

The problem of the nomothetic versus the idiographic approach to research has been analyzed in America by two outstanding psychologists: Gordon W. Allport and Kurt Lewin. Though the answers given respectively by Allport and Lewin to Windelband's question are far apart, a considerable proximity between Allport and Lewin resulted from their dealing with the same problem and facing similar difficulties.

As said before, both Allport and Lewin owe many ideas to William Stern and can be considered the American representatives of the *personalistic* school of thought.

Allport admitted that within a given culture people tend to develop "roughly comparable" ways of behavior or "modes of adjustment." Yet any two indivdiuals never behave the same way. Each represents a unique case and is an idiophenomenon. Human behavior is idiographic and yet lawful.

Behavior is a continuous flow of energy, each successive act representing a convergent mobilization of all energy available at the moment, said Allport. The drives, which use the "plastic and modifiable nervous system," provide energy for action.

[20] *Ibid.*, p. 323.

Motivation

Allport combined the teleological approach with the idea of learning by experience. He defined *drive* as "a vital impulse which leads to the reduction of some segmental organic tension." It has its origin in an internal organic stimulus of peculiar persistence, growing characteristically stronger until the organism acts in such a way as to alleviate the accumulating tension. The tensions within the system are parts of the functioning of the organism.

Allport has been critical of contemporary learning theory (cf. Part I) and yet, he has also been influenced by it. He strongly emphasized learning by experience as opposed to heredity. People develop similar patterns of behavior as a result of certain "constellations of emotion, habit and foresight, better called *sentiments* or *interests,* and regarded as acquired rather than innate." Learning serves as a way not merely of extending and modifying purposes but also of *creating* them. These purposes are shared by numerous individuals, owing to the fact that people who live "in a similar environment, influenced by a similar culture, *would* develop similar goals and employ similar modes of obtaining them." These modes of behavior, though acquired, become *functionally autonomous,* that is, independent of the original instigating drive. Modes of behavior are purposeful. Once established, they persist.

The basic drives can be accounted a cause of an infant's behavior, but not of an adult's. Adult behavior has to be explained as an elaborate process of learning and growth. This process intervenes between the organic wants of infancy and the cultural wants of adulthood, involving all manner of linguistic, imaginal, and rational factors that ultimately transform the segmental cravings of infancy into desires no longer having any functional connection with them, but holding in their own right an autonomous place in personal life. The development of adult goals and aims exemplifies Allport's idea of functional autonomy.

Allport suggested using the term "drive" instead of McDougall's "instinct" or "propensity." Drives are primarily viscerogenic states of excess or deficit stimulation. Besides the pressures that arise in body cavities, the blood stream, and autonomic organs, one may include among drives the irritation of proprioceptors and sensitivity (with customary adient response to external stimulation), wrote Allport.

There is no need to invoke genetic factors to explain human behavior. The functional autonomy of motives and the principle of contemporaneity suffice to explain human motivation.

Personality Traits

Allport accepted Stern's idea that personality was *unitas multiplex* and tried to assess the basic factors of this *unitas.* He emphasized acquired goal-directed factors. Allport calls these acquired determinants of human behavior *traits*. Traits are modes of adjustment noted in one's "neural dispositions of a complex order." They determine the selective perceptions of stimuli and the choice of responses to them; thus they show "motivational, inhibitory and selective effects upon the specific courses of conduct."

A trait is a combination of motives and habits; it is a neuropsychic system that determines to a great extent which stimuli will be perceived (selective perception) and what kind of response will be given (selective action).

> Each individual has a certain number of such mental structures which determine his behavior in a unique way. A trait is a generalized and focalized neuropsychic system (peculiar to the individual) with the capacity to render many stimuli functionally equivalent, and to initiate and guide consistent (equivalent) forms of adaptive and expressive behavior.[21]

Human behavior is determined by several factors. The totality of mutually interdependent traits has to be considered as the main and fairly consistent element in behavior. Traits, sentiments, and attitudes are the "dispositions" to behave in a certain way, dispositions embedded within one's personality. Behavior depends on traits, and on special qualities of stimulus and the temporary distribution of tensions within one's psychophysical system. Motives, says Allport, are

> personalized systems of tensions in which the core of the impulse is not to be divorced from the images, idea of goal, past experience, capacities and style of conduct employed in obtaining the goal. The whole system is integral. If biological drive plays a part (thirst, hunger, sex) it does so, not as *the* motive but merely as an irritable state of bodily tissues set within an intricate and personalized psychophysical system."

Human behavior is determined by a totality of factors acting *at a given time*. Although adult behavior can be traced back to behavior in infancy, the bond between infancy and adulthood is broken. The tie between past and present is "historical," not "functional," says Allport; Lewin made a similar statement.

The motivation for action may come from without (from external stimuli) or from within (from segmental organic tensions or from traits). Traits may act as motives whenever there is a tendency to exhibit a certain type of behavior. Each act of behavior is "a convergent mobilization of energy available at the moment." The best summary of the principle of functional autonomy was given in 1946: This principle means that "(1) motives are contemporary . . . (2) that the character of motives alters so radically from infancy to maturity that we may speak of adult motives as *supplanting* the motives of infancy."[22]

In addition to traits, Allport introduced the concept of attitude. Attitude, as a trait, is a predisposition to act in a certain way, but the attitude

[21] Gordon W. Allport, *Personality: A Psychological Interpretation*, p. 289.

[22] Gordon W. Allport, "Motivation in Personality; Reply to Mr. Bertocci," *Psychological Review*, 1940, 47, 533–554.

reflects the relationship between the person and an object. "Ordinarily *attitude* should be employed when the disposition is bound to an object of value, that is to say, when it is aroused by a well-defined class of stimuli, and when the individual feels toward these stimuli a definite attraction or repulsion."[23] Obviously, the attitudes represent a certain type of trait.

Personality Structure

Psychologically considered, personality is what a man really is and does. It is the dynamic organization, within the individual, of those psychophysical systems that determine his unique adjustments to his environment, wrote Allport. Psychophysical systems mean habits, attitudes, dispositions, "which are neither exclusively mental nor exclusively neural. The organization entails the operation of both body and mind, inextricably fused into a personal unity."[24] Personality indicates the manner in which an individual adjusts to his physical and social environment.

Allport calls the emotional elements in personality which are related to heredity *temperament*. "Temperament refers to the individual's emotional nature including his susceptibility to emotional stimulation, his customary strength and speed of response, the quality of his prevailing mood, and all peculiarities of fluctuation and intensity in mood."[25]

The behavior of a neonate is determined by heredity, innate reflexes, and innate drives. But, in accordance with the law of functional autonomy, the child will become a different person in adulthood.

The uniqueness of the individual, the individual as ididiophenomenon—that is what is meant by the term "personality." Allport (together with P. E. Vernon) elaborated a method of measuring personality, called "Study of Values,"[26] based on Spranger's typology. Thus Allport has shown that the idiographic approach does not prevent one from applying measurements. In later studies, Allport developed additional concepts related to the personality structure.

"An Ego-Structure (Sentiment of Self-Regard) is quite sufficient to keep an individual on the move. It seems to me unnecessary to seek its dynamics as McDougall does it in the twin and abstract properties of self-assertion and submission."[27]

Allport's latest studies introduce the concept of "propriate motives," which keep the personality together. This idea of the integration of personality structure is a necessary supplement to the great variety of motives, traits, and attitudes.

---

[23] Allport, *Personality*, p. 295.
[24] *Ibid.*, p. 48.
[25] *Ibid.*, p. 54.
[26] Gordon W. Allport and P. E. Vernon, *A Study of Values*, Houghton Mifflin, 1931.
[27] Gordon W. Allport, "Geneticism versus Ego-Structure in Theories of Personality," *British Journal of Educational Psychology*, 1946, *16*, 57–68.

Concluding Remarks

Allport's contribution to psychological theory has been criticized chiefly in regard to the concept of functional autonomy. This concept implies discontinuity of development from childhood to adulthood, and between normal and abnormal behavior. It is doubtful whether such a discontinuity can withstand the growing body of contrary interpretations.

Moreover, Allport's fruitful studies seem to be hampered rather than helped by their perpetual reference to the idiographic versus nomothetic dichotomy. One must, however, give well-deserved credit to Allport for his penetrating analysis of problems in the theory of personality, and social and clinical psychology. Allport's latest works[28] represent a further systematization of his position and an elaboration of the idea of internal patterning of personality. Allport has broadened the horizons of psychological inquiry and has also dealt with the philosophical aspects of personality.

[28] Gordon W. Allport, *Personality and Social Encounter*, Beacon, 1960; Gordon W. Allport, *Pattern and Growth in Personality*, Holt, Rinehart, Winston, 1961.

12

Gestalt Psychology

1. Opposition to Associationism

The Associationists

It has often been said that associationism and conditioning developed the theory of learning, psychoanalysis created the theory of motivation, and gestalt and field theories revolutionized the theory of perception and thinking. Undoubtedly, this statement contains a great deal of truth. The origin of the gestalt theory is connected with the difficulties encountered by traditional associationism in regard to perception and thinking. The associationists believed that (1) perception is a copy of objects, or a "mental image" of what has been perceived, and (2) thinking is a mechanical combination of those images.[1] Gestalt psychology challenged both parts of this belief.

In 1829, James Mill formulated the law of association: "Our ideas spring up or exist in the order in which the sensations existed of which they are copies."[2] John Stuart Mill emphasized the analogy between associationism in psychology and the combination of elements in chemistry. He wrote in 1869 as follows: "The laws of the phenomena of mind are sometimes analogous to mechanical, but sometimes also to chemical laws. . . . When impressions have been so often experienced in conjunction that each of them calls up readily and instantaneously the ideas of the whole group, those ideas sometimes *melt and coalesce* into one another, and appear not several ideas but one."[3]

In 1855, Alexander Bain published in England a volume entitled *The Senses and the Intellect*. In this volume, Bain accepted the idea of an inherited, instinctual, "untaught ability," but the emphasis was on association by contiguity, similarity and dissimilarity, causation, and other factors.

---

[1] James Drever, "Some Early Associationists," in B. B. Wolman (Ed.), *Historical Roots of Contemporary Psychology*, Harper and Row, 1968, pp. 11–28.
[2] James Mill, *Analysis of the Phenomena of the Human Mind*, Baldwin, 1829, p. 56.
[3] John S. Mill, *Notes and Annotations on J. Mill, Analysis of the Phenomena of the Human Mind*, Longmans, Green, 1869.

J. Ward and G. F. Stout: British Functionalism

While Wundt, Titchener, and Ebbinghaus, and later Thorndike, Pavlov, and Watson, accepted the associationist tradition with certain modifications, several British, French, and German psychologists rejected it.

In 1886, James Ward started a weighty argument against associationism. His main idea was *continuity*. If associationists or physiologically minded psychologists were right, there would be no continuity in the conscious life of the individual. Continuity of feeling, thinking, memorizing, and acting cannot be understood on the basis of mental atomism and associationism, whether spiritual or material. According to Ward, one must postulate the unity and continuity of self-knowledge, a continuum of being conscious.

This continuity of consciousness cannot be reduced to a spiritual or phenomenological category as in Kant's notion. Nor can it be represented as a series of physiological sensory perceptions. The totality of consciousness is a primary unity; it is the *subject*. The subject is not "a combination or recombination of various elementary units."[4] This totality, the subject, is a non-reductionistic concept.

Ward believed that the subject matter of psychology is the experience (*Erlebnis*) of the subject. All experiences can be divided into (1) *cognition*, which is a "non-voluntary attention" to changes in the sensory continuum, (2) *feeling*, which means being pleased or displeased by these changes, and (3) *conation*, which is a voluntary attention that produces changes in the motor continuum.

The *material* for experience is given from without, but the *synthesis* comes from within. The synthesis, said Ward, comes from the subject, who organizes the material into a certain order. The organizing principles of the mind include time, space, unity, identity, resemblance, difference, substance, and causation. Although these "organizing principles" follow Kant's categories closely, Ward did not accept them as transcendental a priori principles or properties of the subject; they are *modes* of the activity of the human mind which grow and develop in human life.

Ward's idea of a psychology which need be neither physiological nor epistemological, and his theory of the organizing principles of the human mind, and finally his emphasis on continuity and attention, prepared the ground for gestalt psychology.

Ward and George Frederick Stout introduced in Britain a new trend which came close to what has been known in the United States as functionalism. "The presented whole is for them simply the sum of its presented components," said Stout, criticizing the associationists.[5]

Stout aimed at the development of a "pure" psychology, free of physiological explanations and reductionism. Influenced by Brentano, Stout dis-

[4]James Ward, "Psychology," *Encyclopaedia Britannica* (9th ed.), 1886.
[5]George F. Stout, *Analytic Psychology*, 1902, Vol. II, p. 48.

tinguished between mental processes (act) and their content (sensory perception). He divided all mental processes into cognitive and conative and subdivided the conative processes into willing and feeling. Whenever the mental process was related to an object, it was a cognitive process. To have an attitude toward an object is conation, for we either want or don't want it. When our volition is hindered, we experience pain. Unimpeded volition and unhindered action are experienced as pleasure.

Alfred Binet: French Functionalism

Several European psychologists asked the same questions as the American functionalists: What is the *use* of memory, perception, thinking, etc.? Do psychological abilities and action contribute to one's adjustment to life? How, and to what extent do they contribute?

The great enterprise of mental testing, started in France by Binet and Simon, in England by Cyril Burt, in Germany by William Stern, and in the United States by scores of psychologists, served as an example of how psychology could be applied to life. Binet's study of thinking proved that thinking was not a continuation of perception and could not be interpreted in terms of "perceptory elements" as suggested by the associationists.[6] The idea of molar as opposed to molecular concepts was vigorously promoted.

Furthermore, Binet's studies attacked the problem of the "mental images." To the early associationists, the solution was obvious. Human mind perceives the images of objects, and thinking is a combination of these images.

French psychology was relatively free of speculative ideas. The impact of the empiricism of the great Encyclopedists, and later the works of French positivism, had a beneficial influence upon it. French psychologists distinguished themselves in several areas of experimental, clinical, physiological, social, and educational psychology. In 1870, Taine published his famous work on intelligence (*De l'Intelligence*) and Ribot presented British associationist psychology in a volume entitled *La Psychologie Anglaise Contemporaine*. In 1885, Ribot taught the first course in experimental psychology at the Sorbonne, and in 1889, Beaunis and Binet founded there the first psychological laboratory. Ribot himself turned toward abnormal psychology and prepared the ground for the studies of Charcot, Janet, and Freud (cf. Chapter 6).

The cautious empiricism of French psychology, so different from the Germans' speculations, guarded the French psychologists against the eagerness and ease with which the Germans indulged in producing new theories and systems. The empirically minded French-speaking psychologists—Ribot, Binet, Simon, Charcot, Janet, Claparède, Michotte, Pieron, Piaget, and many others—made valuable contributions to the development

[6] Alfred Binet, *L'Étude Expérimentale de l'Intelligence*, Schleicher, 1910.

of psychology. Contemporary psychology is much indebted to Charcot and Janet for their studies in unconscious motivation, to Binet and Simon for mental testing, to Piaget for developmental psychology, and to Claparède, Michotte, Pieron, and others for excellent studies in practically every single area of psychological inquiry. The prevailing climate of French psychology has been the functionalist idea of usefulness and purpose.

From this background came Binet's experimental study on thinking. Binet used his two daughters as subjects and combined experimentation with introspection. He found considerable differences in the way the two girls handled the problems presented to them. These differences could not be interpreted in an associationist manner. Moreover, Binet came to the conclusion that their thinking was done without "images"; it was imageless, just *pensées* (thoughts).

Binet's anti-atomistic and "imageless" interpretation of the thought processes influenced a great many psychologists all over Europe. In Switzerland, the educational psychologist Edouard Claparède developed a utilitarian–functionalist point of view. He considered psychological phenomena from the point of view of "their function in life" or "their use."[7] In his studies on perception, Claparède accepted a point of view similar to gestalt theory, yet eclectic and empirical.

In Belgium, A. Michotte proved that recall of material could not be interpreted by sheer contiguity. The element of organization was emphasized in Michotte's conclusions, which brought him close to the gestalt school. In Germany, the Würzburg school (discussed in the next section), deviated from the Wundt–Titchener method of study and emphasized the mental set and task.[8] All these studies led toward the formation of gestalt theory.

The Würzburg School

Simultaneously with Binet, G. E. Müller in Germany conducted experimental studies in memory which challenged mechanistic associationism from another angle. Müller's subjects, like Michotte's, "organized" the material. Moreover, Müller noticed, memory processes were influenced by what he called the *preparatory set* (*Anlage*). Obviously the set was not given from without.

Müller's idea was utilized by Oswald Külpe and his associates in Würzburg. As early as 1893, Külpe showed that the reactions of subjects to the reaction–time experiments depended on the preparation of the subjects and differed accordingly.[9] The element of motivation was introduced as an experimental variable. Moreover, in a later experiment (1904), Külpe's sub-

---

[7] Edouard Claparède, "Autobiography," in C. Murchison (Ed.), History of Psychology in Autobiography, Clark University, 1930.

[8] A. Michotte, L'Apprentissage du Mouvement et l'Automatisme, Louvain, 1928.

[9] Oswald Külpe, Grundriss der Psychologie, Kirzel, 1893, p. 422.

jects could concentrate on the given task and describe the suggested figure without becoming aware of the other figures. Apparently, these subjects responded to the "figure" and not to the ground.

In 1901, Orth and Mayer published an experimental study on classification. They came to the conclusion that the responses of their subjects depended on a certain set, called by the experimenters *Bewusssteinsanlage* ("sets of the consciousness"), often colored by feelings. In other words, the responses were not mere products of the stimuli, but also depended on some factors within the minds of the subjects, that is, on their mental set.

Along with several other papers by Külpe and his associates, in 1905 the papers by Ach and Watt appeared. Both of them introduced the concept of *task* (*Aufgabe*). The term "task" closely corresponded to motivation as described in Külpe's experimental work.

In Watt's experiment,[10] the task influenced the way his subjects reacted. When the subjects were asked to classify, they had hardly any mental images. When the same subjects were asked to name a part, 50 percent of their responses indicated mental images. The speed and nature of the associative processes could be influenced by the task, concluded Watt.

Ach further developed and elaborated Watt's concepts. The presentation of the aim, the task, obviously influenced the performance of the experimental subjects. The content of the aim-presentation determined the responses of the subjects. The subjects not only saw a colored card (stimulus) but saw it colored in accordance with the instructions. These instructions, which influenced the responses to given stimuli, were called by Ach *determining tendencies*. Experiments with hypnotic suggestions proved that the responses to stimuli could be easily modified in accordance with the determining tendencies.

The study of the determining tendency led Ach to accept the idea of abstract, imageless thinking. He presented his subjects with the letters *C S V S*, but in accordance with the *simultaneous determined abstraction*, they perceived only the letter S. All other letters were left out in the perceptory processes.

The abstraction of one element out of many present elements can be directed toward future reactions also; then it becomes the *successive determined abstraction*. Factors which do not stem from the stimulus and do not participate in association obviously influence the reaction. These factors, presented under the names "set" (*Einstellung*), "task," "aim," or "determining tendency," point to a new factor besides the stimulus–response, that is, the *reproductive tendency*. The subjects showed a productive tendency, and not a mere repetition of acquired images.

Selz continued the work of Ach and Watt on imageless thought and determining tendency. Selz was more radical than Ach and Watt and rejected

---

[10] The English abstract of Watt's experiments was published in 1905: H. J. Watt, "Experimental Contribution to a Theory of Thinking," *Journal of Anatomy and Physiology*, 1905–6, 40, 257–266.

the idea that response was a product of both association (reproductive tendency) and task (determining tendency). He believed that stimulus and task together form a unity, a total *Aufgabe*. Hence, he came to the idea of "productive thinking" in which "the actualization of mental operations or solution methods, that is to say . . . processes of a reproductive nature can give rise to productive mental work."[11] In productive thinking the task with all its determining tendencies initiated the mental operations which served as means toward the problem-solving goal.

Karl Bühler: German Functionalism

Karl Bühler, who was Külpe's disciple and associate, can be classified as a functionalist because of his emphasis on the wholistic processes of adjustment and purposiveness, and his opposition to the molecular–atomistic approach.

In 1907, Bühler published a study with the title "Facts and Problems in Relation to a Psychology of Thought Processes: I. On Thoughts." He was mostly concerned with the question of what is one's actual experience of thinking.

In analyzing the introspective reports of his distinguished subjects (Külpe and Dürr) Bühler concluded that sensory, reproductive elements do not play a significant role in thinking. The most important items of the thought processes are what the subjects describe as "awareness of," "consciousness that," or most frequently "thoughts," in the manner proposed by Binet.

Thought cannot be reduced to sensory processes or mental images. It is a mental process which leads toward the solution of a problem; it is goal directed; it has a task (*Aufgabe*) and it is creative.

Bühler distinguished three types of thought, namely, consciousness of rule, consciousness of relation, and intention. The first type was found mostly in solving mathematical, logical, and grammatical problems. The second type was applied when several parts of thought had to be related as a consequence of each other or in opposition to one another. The intention type of thought occurred when a total problem was reviewed briefly and a solution came as a logical outcome of this review.

More than anyone else in the Würzburg group, Bühler emphasized the goal-directedness of thinking, in opposition to Wundt and associationism. Bühler distinguished between acts and contents of thinking, in accordance with Brentano, to whom all the Würzburg psychologists were indebted.

Bühler wrote about himself as follows: "I came into the field of psychology at the time when all psychological behavior was described in terms of sensory reactions and associations. I never could believe in that 'classical association' theory but felt thinking was more than this. . . .

[11] Quoted after George Humphrey, *Thinking: An Introduction to Its Experimental Psychology*, Methuen, 1951, p. 139.

"As far as *gestalt psychology* is concerned, I was probably the first to enter this field with actual experiments after Ehrenfels and his school developed the new concept theoretically. Recently I have again become interested in the gestalt principle from another angle. The book that I have just finished *'Das Gestalt Prinzip im Leben des Menschen und der Tiere'* (The Principle of Gestalt in the Life of Man and Animals) defends the thesis that only living beings perceive, develop, and create *Gestalten.*" [12] At this point, Bühler came closer to W. Stern than to Wertheimer.

Concluding Remarks

In 1907, W. Wundt published a paper containing a severe criticism of the Würzburg school and related studies. The Würzburg experiments, wrote Wundt, were "experiments without instruments"; their conditions were not varied; the subject, not the experimenter, was the real observer in them; and even the self-observation of the subjects was more of a self-description. Wundt was especially critical of the supposed "creativeness" of thought which was introduced in place of the associationists' reproduction of sensory images.

Associationism rests on the reputable assumption of reproductiveness of mental phenomena. What came from the stimulus can be preserved and reproduced. Any theory of creativeness faces the difficult task of bringing sufficient evidence against the simple and convincing logic of associationism.

Yet it is undeniable that the European functionalists and the Würzburg school had a point in their controversy with associationism. Their emphasis on wholism, purposivism, and meaningful behavior influenced McDougall, Goldstein, and Tolman and prepared the ground for gestalt and field theories. Human behavior cannot be reduced to a chain of consecutive sensory elements, they said. Whether it could be presented as something entirely different—that was the problem to be handled by the gestalt and field theorists.

2. GESTALT: THEORETICAL FOUNDATIONS

Methodological Considerations

The impact of Kant, Mach, and Husserl on the thinking of the gestalt psychologists was considerable. Köhler explained that the naïve experience consists,

> first of all, of objects, their properties and changes, which appear to exist and to happen quite independently of us. So far as they are concerned, it does not seem to matter whether or not we see and feel and hear them. Under these circum-

---

[12] Bühler in a letter to the author of this book.

stances, it was a great step when man began to ask questions about the nature of seeing, feeling and hearing. And it was a revolution when he found that colors, noises and smells, etc., were merely products of influences exerted on him by his surroundings. . . . The form, the weight and the movement of things had to be given the same interpretation as colors and sounds; they, too, depended upon the experiencing organism and were merely end results of complicated processes in its interior.[13]

Gestalt psychologists introduced the concept of *organization* between the "stimulus and response" of the behavioristic theory. The physical environment, believed the behaviorists, is perceived as a series of separate stimuli. Actually, the environment cannot be identified with what the man *experiences* as his environment. Science must, therefore, "construct an objective and independent world of physical things, physical space, physical time and physical movement, and had to maintain that this world appears at no point in direct experience."[14] This applies to the human organism also. The human body is accessible to us only as a part of our sensory experience; but this sensory experience does not reflect several separate sensations. Between the stimulus and the response, processes of organization take place which build the elements into a complex unit.

Köhler admitted the debt to Husserl and phenomenology. Köhler wrote about objects as "objects of experience," as they appear phenomenologically to the perceiving subject. Husserl's idea of fundamental elements appealed to Köhler, who wrote: "The legitimate pursuit of gestalt psychology is the analysis of the essential elements that exist in organization. This analysis is definitely more valuable than the analysis of purely sensory local data. The sensory data do not appear as such to the observer."[15] In other words, the organized totalities, and not the sensory elements, are the truly perceived phenomena.

Opposition to Quantification

Gestalt psychologists were always suspicious of what they considered to be a premature quantitative program of the behaviorist psychologists. "We are still much too easily satisfied by our tests because, as quantitative procedures, they look so pleasantly scientific," remarked Köhler. Actually, I.Q. scores may be a result of various components in varying proportions, such as intelligence, accuracy, ambition, or fatigue. Statistical studies do not measure; they merely count. Without qualitative analysis, behavior psychology "will easily become as sterile as supposedly it is exact."

Gestalt psychologists could not believe in the usefulness of statistical computations for obvious reasons. Measurements are based on the assumption of commeasurability, and such an assumption was feasible only for an atomistic psychology. Gestalt psychologists found that the same number of

[13] Wolfgang Köhler, *Gestalt Psychology*, Liveright, 1947, pp. 5–6.
[14] *Ibid.*, p. 7.
[15] Wolfgang Köhler, *Psychologische Probleme*, Springer, 1933, p. 17.

the same elements could form various configurations and present various experiences. What is the good, for example, of adding the number of dots if the same number of dots can form a circle, a square, a rectangle, or a triangle?

In addition, gestalt psychologists put forward weighty methodological considerations against what they considered to be premature measurements. Köhler wrote:

> If we wish to imitate the physical sciences, we must not imitate them in their highly developed contemporary forms. Rather, we must imitate them in their historical youth, when their state of development was comparable to our own at the present time. Otherwise we should behave like boys who try to copy the imposing manners of full-grown men. . . . If we are to emulate the natural sciences, let us do it intelligently. . . . At present, and in the broader historical perspective, qualitative observation may often be more fruitful than premature measurements. . . . If organisms were more similar to the system which physics investigates, a great many methods of the physicists could be introduced in our science without much change. But in actual fact the similarity is not very great. . . . Actually, however, young psychology could not resist the temptation which arose from the brilliant achievements of contemporary sciences. Every now and then a wave of short-sighted imitation swept it off its feet. Fechner himself was the first to copy adult physics when psychology was hardly born. Apparently he was convinced that measuring as such would make a science out of psychology. . . . Today we can no longer doubt that thousands of quantitative psychophysical experiments were made almost in vain.[16]

Physical Gestalt

The gestaltists were influenced by Brentano, and yet developed a fairly independent point of view. They distinguished between phenomenological and physical realities. Shapes and figures are established by the action of forces which tend toward equilibrium. The perceived figures are "experiences" of the perceiving subject. They are phenomenologically real.

But there is, besides phenomenology, a physical reality. This includes the nervous system and its interaction with the environment. These two parts of reality must be interlocked and ruled by the same set of logical principles, an idea named by the gestaltists the postulate of *isomorphism*. Its content is simple: all phenomenological experiences are a true representation of "a corresponding order" in their "underlying" content of physiological processes.

Order, regularity, gestalt, is the *universal* principle that binds psychology and physiology into one system. Gestalt psychologists had to seek this order, the gestalt, in nature or accept the idea that all gestalts were a priori ideas.

And, indeed, Köhler found gestalt factors in inanimate nature, with all its laws of *Prägnanz*, closure, and others. Electrostatic changes, he wrote,

[16] Köhler, *Gestalt Psychology*, pp. 42–44.

tend toward such a distribution as to produce an equilibrium of forces over the surface of the conducting body. In a drop of oil surrounded by fluids, the inner and external forces interact in such a way as to create a balanced symmetrical, "good" gestalt. Köhler accepted Mach's hypothesis, which implied that macroscopic physical states develop in the direction of equilibrium, stability, regularity, and simplicity. Now psychology could be set on a firm footing. Gestalt existed both in mind and in nature (*Physikalische Gestalten*).

Neurological Theory

The same principles were applied to the study of the nervous system. Gestalt psychologists were critical of the neurological models hitherto developed. Mental events have usually been explained, said Köhler, in terms of either inherited machine or secondary acquired constraints. In the "machine" theory, he wrote, connections between cells in the brain and effector organs are of the same type as the connections between points of sense organs and those cells, in a stimulus–response pattern. Any "local sensory fact" is determined by its stimulus.

Against psychological "atomism," the gestalt psychologists introduced the theory of *functional wholes* based on dynamic distribution and organization, in an analogy with an electric circuit. The theory of electric circuit has been used by the gestalt psychologists in their studies of brain mechanism. Brain activity is guided by the principle of equilibrium, or at least reduced tension. Whenever there is a gap in the current, tensions build on both sides of the gap and the electric current tends to close the gap. Thus, the principle of *closure* is one of the most important principles of both the physical and the phenomenological worlds.

Köhler assumed that in the cerebral cortex a chemical substance is produced that depends on the intensity of stimulation; the figure–ground phenomenon should be interpreted by a high concentration of ions inside the figure and a low concentration in the ground, with a corresponding concentration in the cortex. The cortex is a field, and in it, as in any other dynamic field, the process itself, as well as its conditions, should be considered.

> Two varieties of factors determine the course of physical processes. In the first category are forces at work in the physical process itself; they represent its dynamic aspect. In the second category are those factors of the systems concerned which may be regarded as constant conditions for the particular process taking place. In the case of electric current an example of such a factor would be the spatial arrangement or the topograph of the conducting materials. In physical systems such conditions can sometimes be dominating, sometimes relatively unimportant. The internal dynamics of the process involved in the electric current example would be decisive in determining its course. On the other hand in machines built by human beings the importance of topographical conditions is

almost always so predominant that the role of dynamics is reduced to driving the process along pathways entirely determined by those conditions.[17]

A machine, explained Köhler, is limited in its scope of activity and is determined by its own structure and by external forces. A dynamic field, which is best exemplified by an electric circuit, is regulated by its own forces. Obviously, its activity scope is definitely wider and the freedom of action much greater. The brain functions as a dynamic field, and its forces can be self-distributed and self-regulated, always in the direction of equilibrium.

Köhler and other gestaltists found the machine model for the human nervous system incompatible with experience. Köhler rejected the notion that a local stimulus followed a well-established path toward a definite locus in the brain and that a local reaction was emitted. The sensory and motor systems are not two separate entities connected by the nervous pathways; they are parts of one, total system, contended Köhler. Physiological investigations, he pointed out, "leave no longer any doubt that in ganglionic tissues the functions of individual nerve cells are dynamically related."[18]

Isomorphism

Köhler's theory of isomorphism is based on the assumption of *unity of the universe*. The part–whole relationship, the tendency toward the restoration of equilibrium, the tendency to closure, symmetry, and regularity rule both physical and psychological phenomena. Köhler emphasized that the "specific arrangement" of the psychological experience is "an accurate reproduction" of the dynamic arrangement of "corresponding physiological brain processes."

The principle of isomorphism "covers practically the whole field of psychology," wrote Köhler. It says that the order in which psychological phenomena are experienced is "supposed to be a true representation of a corresponding order in the processes upon which experience depends." In other words, the "experienced order in time is always structurally identical with a functional order in the sequence of correlated brain processes."[19]

Two areas, then, the experiential and the physiological, are ruled by the same set of principles. They are two dynamic fields operated by the same devices and organized in the same way. Gestalt is both physical and mental; the law of *Prägnanz* applies both to the physical world and to how the individual experiences it. The psychological field has often been compared to a geographical map, and its neurological counterpart to a territory represented on the map.

[17] Köhler, *Psychologische Probleme*, p. 84.
[18] Köhler, *Gestalt Psychology*, p. 126.
[19] *Ibid.*, p. 62.

Psychological Field

Since the functions of the brain represent a dynamic field, the overt behavior of humans is a dynamic field as well. This is, as said before, the essence of the principle of isomorphism.

Kurt Koffka was the man who tried to develop a general field theory of behavior. The dynamic field of psychological experience is the individual and his environment, and their interaction within the field forms the content of behavior. This field is a field of forces which tend to establish the best possible balance, the most symmetrical, stable, and simple configuration. The laws of gestalt, and especially of *Prägnanz,* apply to this field.

Human actions are usually related to physical reality not as it is, but as it appears to the perceiving subject. The environment as perceived, together with the perceiving subject, form the *psychological field.* Kurt Lewin (cf. Chapter 13) developed an entirely different concept of the psychological field.

Koffka's psychological field, also called "behavioral environment," corresponds to the phenomenological environment. It can be best exemplified by a story told by Koffka in his main work:

> On a winter evening amidst a driving snowstorm a man on horseback arrived at an inn, happy to have reached a shelter after hours of riding over the wind-swept plain on which the blanket of snow covered all paths and landmarks. The landlord who came to the door viewed the stranger with surprise and asked him whence he came. The man pointed in the direction straight away from the inn, whereupon the landlord, in a tone of awe and wonder, said: "Do you know that you have ridden across the Lake of Constance?" At which the rider dropped stone dead at his feet.
>
> In what environment, then, did the behavior of the stranger take place? The Lake of Constance. . . . And yet . . . there is a second sense to the word environment according to which our horseman did not ride across the lake at all, but across an ordinary snow-swept plain. His behavior was a riding over a plain, but not a riding over a lake.[20]

The idea of a psychological field isomorphic to the physical field enabled the gestalt psychologists to develop a theory of volition and emotions. Disequilibrium between organism and environment causes tensions and activates forces moving in the direction of restoration of balance. A hungry organism seeks food, an angry man starts a fight. Personality is often called *ego* by the gestaltists.

Dembo's studies on anger were generalized by Koffka and developed into a gestaltist theory of emotions.[21] Each psychological field contains an important subfield, the personality or the ego. Emotions will arise, Koffka

[20] Kurt Koffka, *Principles of Gestalt Psychology,* Harcourt, Brace, 1935, pp. 27–28.
[21] Tamara Dembo, "Der Ärger als dynamisches Problem," *Psychologische Forschung,* 1931, 15, 1–144.

says, when an object with powerful positive valence appears in the field but the subject is barred from reaching it. The impenetrable barriers cause strong tension, involving the ego area, and explosive emotional behavior will follow.[22]

This approach to the problem enabled the gestalt psychologists to minimize the anamnestic factors and to emphasize the influence of the present environment. The present environment and the person are the two poles of a dynamic field with forces acting between them. The present action of the forces and their striving toward an equilibrium are the determinants of behavior.

Kurt Lewin went farther and developed a new theory based on the field concept. But let us continue with the analysis of the contribution of gestalt theory to the problems of perception, learning, and thinking.

3. Gestalt: Perception, Learning, and Thinking

The Phi Phenomenon

In 1890, Christian von Ehrenfels introduced the idea of gestalt, or form, shape, and structure. He noticed that the same melody could be played on different notes, and the same notes, differently arranged, gave a different tune. Analogously, the same blocks could be arranged in various ways and create various structures. The blocks and the tones, believed Ehrenfels, were given in perception, while the shape and the total structure came from the mind of the observer. This conclusion was apparently influenced by Kant's distinction between phenomena and the a priori category of quality.

In 1912 in Berlin, Max Wertheimer conducted a series of experiments on perception of motion, with the assistance of Kurt Koffka and Wolfgang Köhler. He started with a vertical line exposed twice, the second time a little to the right or left of the first exposure. When the time interval between the two exposures was one-fifteenth of a second, the experimental subject saw one line moving to the right or the left. The same experiment repeated with several variations always gave the impression of motion. Wertheimer's experiments were carefully planned and they unmistakably led to the following conclusion: If two discrete and stationary lines are exposed a short distance from each other and in close temporal succession, the observer will perceive them as a single line moving from the position of the first line to that of the second. This phenomenon of apparent movement was called by Wertheimer the *phi phenomenon*.[23]

---

[22] Koffka, *op. cit.*, p. 408.

[23] Max Wertheimer, "Experimentelle Studien über das Sehen von Bewegungen," *Zeitschrift für Psychologie*, 1912, *61*, 161–265.

Laws of Gestalt

Wertheimer went one step farther; he concluded that besides the single resting positions of the line, there was an additional factor responsible for the perception of motion. This uniting factor, which combined the separate elements into one whole, he called *Gestalt* (form, shape). This name expressed the anti-atomistic and anti-associationistic convictions of Wertheimer and his emphasis on a molar approach to the problems of perception.

In further studies on perception, Wertheimer analyzed in detail the principle of organization. Suppose we see some dots; the dots can be grouped in several ways, forming a triangle, a square, or a circle. It is the form, the shape, the configuration in which the dots appear that determines our perception.

In less structured situations, the perceiving individual groups the dots in accordance with one or more *principles of organization*. Wertheimer distinguished the principle of (1) *proximity* of the elements to one another, (2) *similarity*, (3) *closure* (if a figure is drawn with incomplete lines, the perceiver completes it in his own mind; a sketch of a house, a person, a tree, a church drawn with a few lines can be easily identified despite its incompleteness). In addition to the aforementioned factors, Wertheimer distinguished the factors of (4) continuity, (5) familiarity, and (6) set; the concept of set was borrowed from the Würzburg studies. Other gestalt psychologists have added scores of principles or laws of organization.

Gestalt psychologists distinguish "good" figures from "poor" figures. A good figure is a figure in which the parts and the whole are well harmonized, and the parts are well subordinated to the figure. Simplicity, clarity, symmetry, and harmony are signs of a "good" figure. The gestalt concept of equilibrium is expressed by the law of *Prägnanz*. The law of *Prägnanz* means that organization tends toward the greatest simplicity, that is, toward the best possible gestalt. This goal-directed tendency (equilibrium being the goal) has often been considered the main law of gestalt.

In 1915, Edgar Rubin, a leading phenomenologist and a disciple of G. E. Müller and D. Katz, introduced the idea of *figure* and *ground*. Perception is selective and not all stimuli are perceived with the same clarity. Perceptory elements organized in a whole catch our attention and are perceived with great clarity; they form the figure, while anything else in our visual field forms the background.

The gestaltists adopted the figure–ground idea. The perceptory elements are organized as a whole, as the gestalt; they form the figure. The remaining elements of perception form the ground. The difference between figure and ground was, as mentioned already, explained in neurological terms by W. Köhler.

The gestalt theory of perception was summarized by Köhler as follows:

Our view will be that, instead of reacting to local stimuli by local and mutually independent events, the organism responds to the *pattern* of stimuli to which it is exposed; and that this answer is a unitary process, a functional whole, which gives in experience, a sensory scene rather than a mosaic of local sensations.[24]

Learning by Insight

Gestalt psychology introduced a new theory of learning associated with the name of Wolfgang Köhler and the term *insight* (*Einsicht*). Köhler's experiment with chimpanzees in the Canary Islands, where he spent several years during the First World War, was a challenge to both the trial-and-error and the conditioning theories of learning.

Köhler's chimpanzees did not try and err in Thorndike's fashion, nor did they become conditioned in Pavlov's style. They grasped the new situation; they displayed orientation in learning and a great deal of intelligence. They did not blindly try all the possible responses; their behavior showed that learning included a considerable amount of goal-directed activity.

Köhler's chimpanzees were put in a cage and a banana was placed at a distance from the cage. Strings, sticks, and boxes were used by the experimental animals to get the banana; apparently, they somehow perceived the situation and displayed *insight* in solving the problems.[25]

Koffka concluded that all learning was perceptual reorganization. "What the animal has developed during its 'latent learning' is a trace of a maze; this trace, being in communication with the present activity, regulates it more or less as the perception of the maze world."[26]

Koffka applied the laws of perception to the learning theory. Instead of reward or reinforcement, he introduced the concept of *goal*. "So long as activity is incomplete, every new situation created by it is still to the animal a transitional situation; whereas when the animal has attained his goal, he has arrived at a situation which is to him an end-situation."[27]

As said before, the main factor in the gestalt theory of learning is *insight*. Since the individual and his environment form a psychological field, perception of the field and gradual restructuring of it is insight. A description of what takes place in insightful learning was given by Yerkes after a series of experiments with primates:

Insight, in different organisms, may reveal common characteristics. (1) Survey, inspection, or persistent examination of problematic situation. (2) Hesitation, pause, attitude of concentrated attention. (3) Trial of more or less adequate mode of response. (4) In case initial mode of response proves inadequate, trial of some other mode of response, the transition from the one method to the other being sharp and often sudden. (5) Persistent or frequently recurrent attention to the objective or goal and motivation thereby. (6) Appearance of critical point at which

---

[24] Köhler, *Gestalt Psychology*, p. 103.
[25] Wolfgang Köhler, *The Mentality of Apes*, Harcourt, Brace, 1925.
[26] Koffka, *op. cit.*, p. 588.
[27] Kurt Koffka, *The Growth of the Mind*, Kegan Paul, 1924, p. 102.

the organism suddenly, directly, and definitely performs the required adaptive act. (7) Ready repetition of adaptive response after once performed. (8) Notable ability to discover and attend to the essential aspect or relation in the problematic situation and to neglect, relatively, variations in non-essentials.[28]

Learning and Perception

Since learning is interrelated with perception, the laws of perception apply to learning. Koffka carefully elaborated this interrelationship.

The most general principle of learning is *Prägnanz,* or the goal-directed tendency to restore the equilibrium. Learning takes place when there is a tension or a disequilibrium of forces in the psychological field; the learning process removes the tension and is, therefore, guided by the principle of *Prägnanz.*

The additional laws of learning are (1) similarity, (2) proximity, (3) closure, and (4) good continuation. When an organism learns a certain material which contains similar and dissimilar elements, the similar ones are learned more readily than the dissimilar ones. This is the *law of similarity.*

The *law of proximity* in perception becomes a law of *temporal contiguity* in the learning theory. Elements are grouped together both by factors of physical proximity (to form a pattern in space) and by proximity in time (to form a temporal configuration such as a tune, a sentence, a story, or any other configuration of elements happening in a temporal proximity).

The *law of closure* reflects the idea of striving for completion. Koffka explained the law of closure as applied to learning as follows: "So long as activity is incomplete, every new situation created by it is still to the animal a transitional situation; whereas when the animal has attained his goal, he has arrived at a situation which is to him an end situation."[29]

The *law of good continuation* implies that we tend to learn better those elements which show consistency in their configurations.

The gestalt psychologists seemed to indicate that learning is improvement in gestalt; the learned figures become more symmetric, better organized, in accordance with the law of *Prägnanz.* Or, in the more general terms of the psychological field, the field is restructured and becomes a better gestalt.

The problems of retention and recall presented considerable difficulties for the gestalt theory. Koffka and Köhler solved this problem of presenting learning processes as *cognitive fields.* Fields can be structured and restructured. Learning processes change the structures of the fields; accordingly, they leave *traces.* In each repetition the former trace system is modified by the new trace system.

In experimental studies by Wulf (1922), Gottschaldt (1926), and others, the importance of memory by association was minimized, and changes in

[28] Robert M. Yerkes, "The Mind of a Gorilla," *Genetic Psychology Monograph,* 1927, 2, 156.
[29] Koffka, *Growth of the Mind,* p. 102.

the structure of the cognitive field were emphasized. In Wulf's experiments, each repetition brought an "improvement" in the perceived figures leading progressively toward a better gestalt. In Gottschaldt's experiment, a picture of the capital letter E was presented a great many times; yet the subjects who saw E only once could distinguish the shape of E in a church window just as well as those who saw E a great many times. Apparently, memory and association did not help learning in this case.

Several gestalt experiments indicated that three processes take place in learning. The first is *leveling* or changing in the direction of symmetry and good distribution. The second, *sharpening*, consists of the accentuation of the essential elements of a figure, which makes it easily distinguishable. The third process is related to the clarity and simplicity of the perceived figure and is called *normalizing*. Apparently all three processes correspond to the general law of *Prägnanz*, or moving toward a "good" gestalt. It is the "productive," goal-directed insight versus the "reproductive" conditioning which has been emphasized in the gestalt theory of learning.

Productive Thinking

The gestalt theory of learning led to studies in "productive thinking." The ground was prepared by the Würzburg school (cf. Section 1 in this chapter). Wertheimer undertook the study of productive thinking and problem solving using a great many subjects, from little children to Albert Einstein.[30]

Wertheimer distinguished three types of processes. Type *a* processes are concerned with decisive issues pertaining to structural problems and include such operations as grouping, reorganization, and discovery of essential features. The best thinking is productive thinking. It relates the means to the tasks and goals, and to the total situation. Whenever an organism faces a problem, the tensions will lead to an activity called problem solving or productive thinking. Productive thinking is assured by type *a* processes and almost eliminated by type *y* processes. Type *y* thought processes are blind and result in premature conclusions, miscentering, or a restless pursuit of a hypothesis without a sense of direction and subject to the influence of external factors. This type corresponds to learning by drill, associations, conditioning, and blind trial and error. Type *b* processes are partially productive and partially mechanized.

Wertheimer implied that analysis is not altogether eliminated by the gestalt theory. Analysis is futile when it is only a mere division into parts. In combination or association, things cannot be thrown together or related at random with utter disregard of structural aspects and interrelations. This does not lead to problem solving.

Wertheimer believed that methods for the description and measure-

[30] Max Wertheimer, *Productive Thinking*, Harper, 1945.

ment of structures and whole-qualities can be developed. Productive thinking deals with whole-qualities and part–whole relationships rather than
with analysis into particles and association of them. Productive thinking
looks for the "structural truth" rather than for a piecemeal truth, said
Wertheimer.

One of the most important ideas of Wertheimer's theory of productive
thinking relates to *centering* and *recentering*. In centering, there is a change
or transition from a subjectively or personally centered view, to a detached
view with an objective grasp of the whole situation and of structural and
functional requirements. This operation makes for the dominance of the objective structural and functional requirements of the situation and for a neutralization of and interference with effects of one's personal experiences and
beliefs. Recentering is the obtaining of a new and penetrating perspective.
It provides a new angle from which to view the question of multiple interests and achievement of creative persons, and the ability of scientists and
engineers trained in certain fields to function, after a brief interval of orientation, in other fields at high levels of productivity.

Wertheimer questioned the usefulness of repetition. He wrote: "Repetition is useful, but continuous use of mechanical repetition also has harm-
ful effects. It is dangerous because it easily induces habits of sheer mechanical action, blindness, tendencies to perform slavishly instead of thinking,
instead of facing a problem freely."[31]

Wertheimer denied any application of trial and error in thinking.
Thinking is goal directed and insightful and creates new gestalts. It changes
the structure of the perceptual field. Several experimental studies, conducted by Duncker, N. R. F. Maier, and others, utilized the gestalt frame of
reference.

Apparently, the gestalt theory of thinking went a long way beyond the
studies of the Würzburg school. The Würzburg school, wrote M. R. Harrower, "brought to light facts for the explanation of which they needed a
concept such as the determining tendency . . . regarded as a force which
could be set against the associative bond and even measured quantitatively.
. . . It was not until the work of Duncker and Maier, following the line of
attack suggested by Wertheimer, that we get a recognition of the determining tendency as the vector or tension produced by the structural properties
of the problem. From this new point of view . . . it is 'needed' by the phenomenal problem situation itself, not merely demanded by the instructions."[32]

The Würzburg school proposed the set and the goal. The gestaltists
ascribed purposeful activity to nature and men, activity leading toward a
perfect gestalt.[33]

[31] *Ibid.*, p. 112.
[32] Quoted after G. Humphrey, *op. cit.*, p. 175.
[33] Mary Henle, "Gestalt Psychology," in B. B. Wolman (Ed.), *International Encyclopedia of Psychiatry, Psychology, Psychoanalysis, and Neurology*, Aesculapius, 1977, Vol. 5, pp. 209–213.

Concluding Remarks

Gestalt was defined by Köhler in two ways. The first connotation is that of a property or quality of things, such as squareness or symmetry of geometric figures, shape or form of objects. The other connotation is that of an individual and characteristic entity existing as something detached and *having* a shape or form as one of its attributes. Gestalt psychologists use the term "gestalt" in this second connotation.

Moreover, they seem to ascribe to the entity peculiar attributes. Obviously, these attributes can never be seen. They can be inferred or introduced as intervening variables for the sake of interpretation of observable facts.

This leads the great question. Gestalt psychology started as a rebellion against the aridity of the molecular studies of Wundt and Titchener. There cannot be any doubt that gestalt psychology stimulated more research work in the field of perception than any other psychological school. There cannot be any doubt that there is, as Tolman said, more than one kind of learning. Or, as Razran suggested, the highest level of learning must be related to perception, understanding, and configuration. There is no doubt that the gestalt studies in neurophysiology, figural aftereffects, and figure–ground are thought provoking. Gestalt psychology has influenced several areas in psychology, including studies in child, social, education, and clinical psychology, and its experimental work stands on its own merits. But, given all this the main concept used by Wertheimer, Koffka, and Köhler seems to be the most vulnerable. Why attach such importance to a whole, a configuration, or a totality? Why ascribe to this concept a central position in psychological theory? To quote Woodworth, "Wertheimer's experiment on visual movement was certainly interesting and important, but we may query why it was regarded as important enough to inaugurate a new school of psychology. Well, it was a clear case of a whole which was not a mere sum of parts."[34]

And this is the problem. Is a whole a new entity, and can a psychological theory be based on such an assumption? An expert on perception, F. H. Allport challenges this assumption.

> We have no objective evidence that a whole is anything other than the parts, provided always that the parts are taken as they *exist and operate together*. A whole that is something more, or other than this, must remain an inference. It is perhaps an "impelling" inference, derived from striking differences in the phenomenology when the parts act together as compared with the phenomenology when they act alone. But it is still an inference. In questioning it, we are in no sense denying that there is a perceived unique "whole character" that appears when the parts exist and operate together. We question only the assumption that this "whole character" comes from something other than, or more than, this set of conditions, or that there is an "independent" whole, or that the whole acts to control the parts.[35]

[34] Robert S. Woodworth, *Contemporary Schools of Psychology* (rev. ed.), Ronald, 1948, p. 124.
[35] Floyd H. Allport, *Theories of Perception and the Concept of Structure*, Wiley, 1955, p. 143.

4. PRESENT STATUS OF GESTALT PSYCHOLOGY

Much of the contribution of the Gestalt psychologists was that they so clearly upset the traditional notions of other theoreticians, forcing many traditionalists to rethink their positions, even if they were not convinced to accept the premises of the Gestaltists.[36] Much of the work started by the original Gestalt psychologists has yet to be adequately explored, and their concepts of space, depth, and distance are still largely unsolved problems. One particularly significant experiment was that of Köhler. Human subjects were given glasses in which the left lens was blue and the right lens was yellow. With these glasses, white objects to the left of center were seen as being blue and objects to the right were seen as yellow. This was predictable, but what was truly startling was that after a period of adaptation the subjects removed the glasses and continued to see the world as blue or yellow when they looked to the left or right. This finding clearly demonstrated that a relational determination of color could be independent of local stimulation.

In 1950, Johansson demonstrated that perceived motion is, in complex ways, dependent on the totality of stimulation. Common motion of parts is often seen as motion of the whole, and the motion of the individual parts is seen as part of the residual motion; these findings supported the Gestalt notions of wholes versus parts. In 1959, Land reported complex experiments which seem to confirm the Gestalt antimosaic hypothesis. He proposed that color perception depends on relationships over the whole retina rather than being dependent on the stimulation of the individual retinal receptors. Land exposed negatives through filters that screen long, or warm, and short, or cool, parts of the light spectrum; thus, the negatives contained information about the color of the objects. The two negatives were then superimposed and projected onto a screen and viewers saw a range of colors even though the film was black and white. Although Land's findings clearly support Gestalt theories of perception, he felt that his results required a reformulation of all present theories of color perception, including that of the Gestaltists.[37]

Stimulated by the work of the original Gestalt psychologists, researchers have continued to work in the field of Gestalt perception. Avant and Helson point out that Shannon developed the informational approach which promoted progress in the study of visual forms. Information theory deals with the extent to which knowledge dispels ignorance and the reduction of possible alternatives through added knowledge. A key concept of information theory is that of redundancy, which represents the amount of surplus information present in any situation. Random patterns are therefore less redundant than structured ones, and meaningless patterns are less re-

[36] Mary Henle, "Gestalt Psychology," in B. B. Wolman (Ed.), *International Encyclopedia of Psychiatry, Psychology, Psychoanalysis, and Neurology*, Aesculapius, 1977, Vol. 5, pp. 209–213.
[37] *Ibid.*, p. 211.

dundant than meaningful ones. Thus, information theory sets up an initial quantitative account of meaning.[38]

Garner and his co-workers demonstrated how the information theory approach to the study of visual forms can become more analytic without affecting their original phenomenological properties. Garner addressed himself to the problem of what constitutes good form or pattern. He maintained that good patterns are redundant ones because, unlike poor patterns, the whole of a good pattern is so easily predicted from any of its parts. The Gestalt theorists have described configurational principles of "good Gestalt" on the basis of single examples. Garner, however, stated that "a stimulus is a member of a set of meaningfully related stimuli, and from any set we can form various meaningful subsets . . . redundancy as a *quantitative* concept is directly related to the size of subsets, not to the individual stimulus itself." With this basic premise, Garner demonstrated that the best figures maintain their properties under rotation and reflection. Moreover, good patterns have fewer alternative patterns than do poor ones.[39]

In the area of perceptual constancy, Gestalt psychologists have suggested that perception is determined by central organizational processes by which sensory stimulation is spontaneously organized within the brain. This premise has stimulated research such as that of Wallach, who determined that neutral color is dependent on the ratio of intensity of neighboring areas, due to an implied interaction in the nervous system between the nerve tissue excited by the various areas. A similar premise, that of *relational determination*, deals with the problem of perceived velocity. Brown found that when all other things are equal, "the smaller the frame of reference, the faster the apparent speed of the object seen within it." Thus, as with neutral color, frame of reference becomes a determining factor in the area of perceptual constancy.[40]

In the area of experimental social psychology, the Gestalt psychologist Asch questioned the associationist position that the prestige of a particular person does not affect the "understanding" of material written by the person, but merely affects a degree of agreement or disagreement. Asch proposed that the prestige of a writer will significantly affect interpretation of his material. For example, when Jefferson's name was substituted for that of Lenin, student evaluation of the material presented changed considerably. Essays by students demonstrated that identification with the presumed author had affected the students' judgment of the material. Ideas judged irresponsible when presented as Lenin's, were seen as praiseworthy when attributed to Jefferson. When Asch's findings are generalized, they can be

[38] Lloyd L. Avant and Harry Helson, "Theories of Perception," in B. B. Wolman (Ed.), *Handbook of General Psychology*, Prentice-Hall, 1973, pp. 422–433.

[39] *Ibid.*

[40] Irvin Rock, "Toward a Cognitive Theory of Perceptual Constancy," in A. R. Gilgen (Ed.), *Contemporary Scientific Psychology*, Academic Press, 1970, pp. 256–259.

seen as a rational attempt at problem solving. In a situation where the individual does not know what response to make, it is quite reasonable to follow the direction of someone else who has been successful in the same situation.[41]

[41] Leonard Berkowitz, "Theoretical and Research Approaches in Experimental Social Psychology," in A. R. Gilgen (Ed.), *Contemporary Scientific Psychology*, Academic Press, 1970, pp. 289–290.

13

Field Theory

1. FIELD THEORY VERSUS CLASS THEORY

"More Physico-Mathematico"

Psychologists have always been enchanted by physics. The exactness and beauty of physical experiments and the resulting mathematical formulas have seemed to psychologists to be the prototype of any scientific research. To be scientific has often been considered synonymous with imitation of the methods and manners of physical research.

It can not be regarded as mere coincidence that Kurt Lewin, the outspoken representative of non-reductionism in psychology, was so much influenced by physical and mathematical concepts. He is, in fact, a radical non-reductionist, and does his best to keep psychological research within the area of psychology. Obviously, this is not a gestalt psychology. Lewin avoids physiology; he never borrows from biology or invites physics or chemistry to solve difficult problems in human behavior. He is painstakingly cautious and consistent, and avoids confusing endocrine glands with behavior, or brain tissues with abilities. His theories are strictly behavioral, and deal only with human beings and their activities.

This stanch non-reductionism notwithstanding, Lewin is more drawn to physics than are many other psychologists. His main efforts seem to be aimed at the establishment of a full-fledged psychological theory with no reference to neurology, physiology, chemistry, or biology, but still on the pattern of the physical sciences—something like the theory of electromagnetism or the theory of light. What he borrows from physics is not its content or laws, but its methodological foundations; he loves the cleanliness of mathematical equations and the beauty of geometrical presentation. This is why one would like to call Lewin's theory *psychologia more physicomathematico*. Lewin's field theory is a product of the prevailing field-theory tendencies in modern physics in modern physics, as associationism in psychology was a product of atomistic theories in physics.

Gardner Murphy regards modern physics as one of the "parents" of gestalt and of field theory. "The era of atomism," he says, "began to come

to an end and particles began to be understood as aspects of field relationships. . . . It is within this frame of reference, notably the developments in physics, that one must understand the development of field theory
in psychology. The movement began when modern physics invaded the
Gestalt psychology."[1]

Modern physics, while being empirical and down to earth, has
achieved astonishing results due to conceptualization. This is the path to be
followed by psychology, says Kurt Lewin.

> Investigators are coming to feel that a mere piling up of facts can only lead to a
> chaotic and unproductive situation. . . . Even from a practical point of view the
> mere gathering of facts has very limited value. It cannot give an answer to the
> question that is most important for practical purposes—namely, what must one
> do to obtain a desired effect in given concrete cases? To answer this question it is
> necessary to have a theory, but a theory which is empirical and not speculative.
> This means that theory and facts must be closely related to each other."[2]

Theory has to "conceptually represent and derive psychological processes." It has to conceptualize the empirical data and go beyond the observed facts.

Theory Construction

How should this theory be constructed?

A theory is a system of concepts related to observable facts in such a
way that the empirical facts may be derived from the concepts. A system of
concepts forms a theory. The concepts fill the gap between one observable
fact and another. Lewin quotes Tolman's statement that "behavior cannot
be derived from behavior." One has to introduce "intervening concepts,"
or as Tolman calls them, "intervening variables."

These concepts should fit the logical structure of psychological phenomena. No science can be purely empirical; empirical laws are functional
relationships of observable data, and they have to be related to dynamic
laws which are functional relationships of concepts. A system of concepts
and dynamic laws forms a theory, and a theory should be constructed in
such a manner that the empirical data are the logical outcome of the concepts and laws.

Any scientific theory, says Lewin, has to apply two types of concepts.
Those of the "first order" are *mathematical*. They must "represent the logical
structure of empirical relationships." Thus, the selection of a proper mathematical system is of greatest importance in theory construction. It is imperative to choose the mathematical concepts that will suit the nature of a
given science and, by "coordinating definitions," to establish the rules of
their application. Lewin believes that psychology should apply geometrical

---

[1] Gardner Murphy, *Historical Introduction to Modern Psychology* (rev. ed.), Harcourt, Brace,
1949, p. 298.
[2] Kurt Lewin, *Principles of Topological Psychology*, McGraw-Hill, 1936, p. 4.

concepts, and he has introduced a topological geometric system into psychology. In fact, his psychological theory has been called "topological psychology."

Lewin realizes that the same mathematical concepts can be used to represent different facts. He suggests, therefore, distinguishing between the formal and mathematical properties of concepts, and their psychological and real content. The mathematical concepts should be accompanied by a set of psychological concepts. These are the *dynamic concepts* of psychological theory. Each of them has to be defined in regard to its conceptual properties, its relation to empirical data, and in relation to the causal laws. Some of these concepts are derived directly from observable data, like behavior and environment. Others cannot be derived from empirical data. They have to be introduced as "intervening variables" which cannot be perceived by observation. These are the *"conditional–genetic concepts"* or *"constructs."* A construct is, by definition, "a dynamic fact which is determined indirectly as 'an intervening variable' by way of 'operational definition.' "[3] Constructs have to be clearly defined such that their existence can be proved or disproved by empirical operations; the definition of conceptual properties of a construct must be coordinated to certain mathematical concepts; then their operational definition indicates the possibility of empirical proof. Lewin's dynamic concepts fill the space of intervening variables wherever behavior takes place. Between the independent variable, which in Lewin's theory is the observable total situation, and the observable behavior, Lewin puts in the logical construct, which explains the relationship between observable facts. This explanation is causal or dynamic. Instinct, libido, drive, association, intelligence, excitatory tendency, tension, force, conditioned reflex—all these terms indicate, not empirical facts, but "dynamic facts the existence of which can be proved only indirectly by means of certain manipulations." They are the *intervening concepts* or *dynamic constructs* that "have been unavoidable in any worth-while psychology. Why not then introduce these concepts in a deliberate and orderly fashion, rather than permit them to slip in secretly and uncontrolled by the back door?"[4] No psychological theory can be developed on a purely empirical level. Theory means interpretation, and interpretation is the derivation of empirical facts from theoretical concepts.

These constructs have been introduced in various ways by the respective psychological theories. Lewin pays more attention than most psychologists to the technique of theory construction. He says: "Logical form and content are closely interwoven in any empirical science. Formalization should include the development of constructs every one of which is considered from the start both as a carrier of formal implication and as an adequate representation of empirical data. This implies that the operational

[3] *Ibid.*, p. 213.
[4] Kurt Lewin, "The Conceptual Representation and the Measurement of Psychological Forces," *Contributions to Psychological Theory*, 1938, 1, 12.

and the conceptual definitions are not arbitrarily related but show an internal coherence (e.g., the possibility of coordinating psychological force operationally to locomotion and conceptually to a vector is mainly based on their common feature of directedness). It further implies that the various constructs should be built up in such a way as to be parts of one logically consistent and empirically adequate system."[5]

The system of constructs as a whole should be empirically testable. Both the conceptual and the coordinating definition of an individual construct is a question of agreement or convenience. *"Laws and definitions are a network of statements which only as a whole can be viewed as right or wrong."*[6] Whether they are right or wrong depends on their relationship to empirically established facts and laws.

Lewin maintains that in modern physics there is considerable liberty concerning a single concept or law, but the system of concepts cannot be established at will. The establishment of a system of concepts represents considerable difficulty. The logical mathematical properties of the concepts and their relation to empirical data cannot be established prior to some knowledge of the empirical data. In Lewin's words, they "should be determined in view of the laws and the empirical data involved." Empirical laws, based on well-proved empirical or experimental data, do not suffice for establishment of the dynamic or conceptual laws. "For, as long as the conceptual properties of the constructs implied in a law are not clearly determined, the law cannot be said to be either right or wrong, because it lacks definite meaning."[7] But the meaning or conceptual properties of the constructs should be determined in view of the laws and the empirical data involved. It is, in a way, a vicious circle.

Lewin was fully aware of these difficulties. He suggested that the first definitions be made in a "tentative manner" and gradually clarified with the inductive method of "abstract classification" or *generalization*. The constructs have to be introduced tentatively and gradually tested and, if necessary, modified. The raison d'être of the constructs depends ultimately on their fruitfulness in research. The conceptual properties of constructs have to be analyzed as to their convenience or necessity in the context of psychological research as a whole. They have to be a priori proposed, and clarified by *gradual approximation* in actual empirical research.

Lewin saw no need to coordinate psychological theory and physiological concepts. H. Feigl quotes Lewin's oral remark that "the time for neurophysiological explanations would not come for a thousand years!"[8]

Lewin was aware of the difficulties faced by the gestalt–field theory. He saw no reason for coordinating physiological systems and psychological

[5] Kurt Lewin, *Field Theory in Social Science*, Harper, 1951, p. 24.
[6] Lewin, "The Conceptual Representation," *Contributions to Psychological Theory*, 1938, 1, 16.
[7] *Ibid.*
[8] Herbert Feigl, "Principles and Problems of Theory Construction in Psychology," in W. Dennis (Ed.), *Current Trends in Psychological Theory*, University of Pittsburgh, 1951, p. 201.

systems; he did not believe that psychology and physiology can be connected by the concept of isomorphism. His dynamic concepts deal with psychological and physiological factors not as two separate systems but as identical ones. They deal with behavior as a whole, as a function of a person and his environment, and thus avoid two terminologies, one of psychology and another of physiology. Lewin sees no methodological advantage in reductionism.

There are four kinds of functional interrelations between constructs (often called dynamic facts) and observable facts, says Lewin: (1) logical interdependence between the constructs, (2) empirical interdependence between the constructs, (3) measurement of the constructs by observable facts, and (4) functional interrelation between observable facts.

Conceptual interdependence operates when one construct can be logically derived from the other by logical inference. There is no need for empirical proof in such a case.

Empirical laws indicate functional interdependence between at least two different constructs established empirically, for example, the empirical relationship between velocity and weight in physics, tension and forces of locomotion in psychology.

The Individual Case

The problem of idiophenomena, which attracted the attention of Windelband and Dilthey (see Chapters 1 and 10), has been attacked again by Lewin. "Laws are nothing more than principles according to which the actual event may be derived from the dynamic factors of the concrete situation"; therefore "the application of the laws presupposes the comprehension of the individual cases."[9]

This is not what Windelband had in mind. He regarded each individual case as a faithful representative of the laws of nature; of course, this statement applies to the natural sciences only. Certain phenomena do not fit into this category, namely, the events of history, psychology, and other *Kulturwissenschaften*. The reason for the distinction between natural and cultural sciences lies in the fact that natural sciences operate with phenomena representative of the general law, whereas cultural sciences deal with unrepeatable, unique, and unpredictable events called *idiophenomena*. No laws can be applied to them.

William Stern (see Chapter 11) tried to solve this problem by ascribing a double role to human beings. The "thing" and the "person" are united in one organism. A "thing" can be interpreted by the laws of nature while a "person" should be interpreted by culture.

Kurt Lewin attacks this problem on a methodological level. "The determination of laws is therefore only one side of the task of explaining mental life. The other side, which is of equal importance and inseparably con-

[9]Lewin, *Principles of Topological Psychology*, p. 11.

nected with the determination of the laws, involves the task of representing concrete situations in such a way that the actual event can be derived from them according to the principles which are given in the general laws." [10]

Lewin regards a law as a principle by which an event can be explained. One has to manipulate the concrete situation so as to be able to derive and single out fact from the total situation in accordance with the principle.

What is derivation or tracing back? It is, Lewin says, the progression from "phenotypical" to "conditional-genetic" or "genotypical" characteristics. Phenotypical characteristics are the observable features of an object or event in a given time and place. Conditional-genetic or genotypical facts are the intrinsic and conceptual properties. If one describes a situation by means of conditional-genetic factors, the flow of observable events can be derived from this description as its logical and unavoidable consequence. If a given empirical situation can be described in a conceptual manner, all the actual events can be derived. Thus "correct representation of what 'is' is at the same an explanation of what happens." [11]

"Galileo's Revolt against Aristotle"

Lewin ascribed the method of testing simultaneously with general laws and specific cases to the great physicist Galileo. Lewin distinguished three epochs in the development of psychology. The first was "speculative" or "Aristotelian." During this stage, psychologists tried to discover the "essence" of things and the cause behind all occurrence. Then came "descriptive" psychology and a reaction against the speculative theories; during this epoch, psychologists tried "to collect as many facts as possible and to describe them exactly." Psychologists were hostile to theories and preferred to classify phenomena by abstraction.

Lewin felt that the time was ripe for the third epoch, the "constructive" or "Galileian," which he introduced. The goal of constructive psychology is "to discover laws" and "to predict individual cases." This constructive psychology aims at elimination of nonpsychological concepts; it is non-reductionist. In contradistinction to speculative psychology, which believed that the causes of human behavior lie in either past or future, "Galileian" psychology believes that facts are the causes of events. Lewin strongly emphasized the *"totality of the contemporary situation"* as the full cause of behavior. [12]

The Aristotelian method in psychology should be discontinued. Psychologists should follow the Galileian methods of research. In a special paper (included in the volume on *Personality*) Lewin discussed the difference between the two types of concept development in physics, and the

[10] *Ibid.*, p. 11.
[11] *Ibid.*, p. 83.
[12] *Ibid.*, pp. 6 ff.

implications for psychology. "For Aristotelian physics the membership of an object in a given class was of critical importance, because for Aristotle the class defined the essence or essential nature of the object and thus determined its behavior in both positive and negative respects." [13] The classes are abstractly defined as the "sum total of those characteristics which a group of objects have in common." Only things which occur always, or at least frequently, are lawful, while other phenomena are not. Galileian physics, said Lewin, introduced the idea that the same law governs the entire physical world. Galileo and his followers shifted the emphasis from the observable traits of a *phenotype* to the conditional–genetic concepts of a genotype.

Relation to the environment has replaced the Aristotelian "nature" of things, and the concrete situation has taken the place of the abstract average. The very same process should take place in psychology. Child psychologists, for example, ask the Aristotelian question: "Do all children do that, or is it at least *common?*" Lewin felt that each individual case is representative of the totality of laws, whether it happens once or every day. There are no exceptions to laws, and the "complete representation of even one given situation would presuppose the solution of all psychological problems and knowledge of all psychological laws. For scientific research the difficulties begin as soon as one tries to represent a 'given' situation. A complete representation of one situation would mean that the whole task of psychology is completed. The representation can be made only step by step and its progress must be parallel to the investigation of the dynamic laws. The representation of a situation implies no less theory than the laws which it presupposes." [14]

Lewin's line of reasoning can be described in a somewhat simplified manner, as follows. The nature of psychological events is idiographic. Each given situation is unique, changing, and dependent on the totality of interrelationships in a given unit of space and time. It is impossible to derive, interpret, or predict the behavior of an individual unless the totality of his interrelationship at a given moment is being considered. Generalizations and classifications are useless, since each person's behavior is not a function of his belonging to a certain category or class, but results from the total situation at a given time.

Each situation can be represented in conceptual terms, that is, in conditional–genetic concepts. A full representation of one situation requires the substitution of the empirical facts by dynamic concepts and laws. That kind of representation of a situation is in fact interpretation, since individual facts "flow" from the situation as its "purely logical consequences." Therefore "a correct representation of what 'is' is at the same time an explanation of what happens."

[13] Kurt Lewin, *A Dynamic Theory of Personality*, McGraw-Hill, 1935, pp. 4 ff.
[14] Lewin, *Principles of Topological Psychology*, p. 82.

2. Lewin's Mathematical Concepts

The Use of Mathematics

It is a legitimate procedure to arrange scientific propositions in mathematical equations. In fact, mathematics is the best way to present empirical data. The ancient Ionian philosophers tried to discover the unity of the universe despite its apparent diversity. They tried to reduce the various and multiple factors to one or a few "elements." Numbers are the unifying element in scientific discovery, and whenever qualities can be perceived as quantities, the process of scientific analysis is greatly advanced.

The discovery of a proper mathematical formula or operation is often a milestone in the progress of scientific research, yet not all empirical data fit into mathematics, perhaps owing to the inadequate development of empirical studies or to the unfortunate choice of a mathematical system to represent these data. Sometimes, empirical research workers wonder whether they can find a mathematical system which will enable them to represent their data.

Mathematics, Russell says, is not a science. It is a system of symbols and nothing else. Whoever introduces or uses a system of symbols has to state clearly how they are to be used in order to represent data typified by them in an unequivocal way. Mathematics is a language, a highly developed and precise means for the representation and communication of truth. Mathematics per se does not discover any truth at all, and mathematical formulas are neither true nor false. They are truthful only in the connotation of the "immanent truth" (cf. Chapters 15 and 16). They can be consistent and exclude self-contradiction but they cannot contribute new information (empirical) or new laws (theoretical). Scientists have to disclose facts and their interrelationships, and can *represent* and *communicate* the discoveries of facts and relationship by using mathematical symbols. Undoubtedly the proper use of mathematics offers tremendous advantages in scientific studies; it adds clarity and consistency, and is far superior to any nonmathematical formulation of scientific data and laws. Lewin feels that empirical facts have to be represented by mathematical concepts in "an absolutely binding way" in order to obtain the benefits of their application. Mathematical concepts are far better than any other concepts, says Lewin. They are "distinguished from other means of representation, such as ordinary speech, in that they belong to a system of concepts which are related to each other in a univocal way."[15] He seems to believe that this univocality can be attained by empirical sciences as a result of the application of mathematical concepts, and he suggests the application of mathematical concepts to empirical research, provided they "represent the logical structure of these empiri-

[15] *Ibid.*, p. 78.

cal relationships adequately."[16] Thus Lewin's question is not "whether mathematics," but "which mathematics" will best suit the nature of psychological data.

Topological Concepts

Lewin feels that geometry offers certain advantages to a psychologist since all psychological schools use terms like approach, withdrawal, social position, change in position, belonging, distance, direction, and area. All these concepts are spatial, that is, geometrical. Geometry can be utilized in any empirical research as long as the kind of geometry chosen fits the dynamic characteristics of the empirical data. Since the basic psychological relationship is that of person and environment, *space* is the proper concept to be applied to psychological data.

Psychological locomotion, like achieving a goal or acquiring a higher status, does not fit the Euclidean geometry which is usually applied by physics. People may "move" toward their goal while moving physically away from it. Therefore psychological processes cannot be "univocally coordinated" to the physical space.

There is one kind of space that does fit psychology, says Lewin. This space, representing the part–whole or point–environment relationship, is the topological space. Topological geometry has been chosen by Lewin to serve psychological theory because he believes that the person–environment relationship can be presented best in topological space.

Topology is defined as "a part of geometry which investigates properties of a figure which remain unchanged under continuous transformation."[17] These properties are non-quantitative. They represent the relationship of parts of a certain area—like part–whole relationship, connection, and position—which are so important in Lewin's psychological theory.

Topological relationships can be illustrated by a bit of elastic rubber. Though the rubber can be stretched out in various directions, the relative position of points on it remains unchanged in the topological frame of reference.[18]

Topological geometry is a nonmetrical field of mathematics. Neither magnitude nor direction is defined; thus distances and sizes are unimportant.

The following topological symbols are used by Lewin:

+ "The topological sum," e.g., $A + B = C$, means region C is the sum of regions A and B.

[16] *Ibid.*, p. 60.
[17] Von B. Kerékjártó, *Vorlesungen über Topologie*, Springer, 1923.
[18] Lewin's theory has often been interpreted from his graphs, but graphs were merely a pedagogical device. Here Lewin's theory is presented without them.

· "Intersection," e.g., $A \cdot B = 0$, means A and B have no common points.
⊃ "Includes," e.g., $A \supset B$, means region A includes region B.
⊂ "Is included," e.g., $K \subset L$, means region K is included in L.

The *sum* of A and B means all points are part of both A and B. If A is a part of B, then $A + B = B$. In this case A is part of B and we use the symbol $A \subset B$. By intersection of A and B is meant the totality of points which are part of both A and B.

A polygon, an ellipse, and a circle represent the same spatial relation in topology: all of them are closed regions. The difference in form, size, or dimension is irrelevant. If all points of a region can be mutually connected by a path, which is entirely included within the region, this region is called a *connected* region. A *closed* region includes its boundary points. The boundary of a closed region is a *Jordan* type of curve. The shape of this curve is of no importance at all, but it has to be a closed curve which does not intersect itself. The Jordan curve which encloses a closed region serves as a boundary between the enclosed and surrounding regions.

A *path* is a part of a Jordan curve; it does not intersect itself; it connects points in a region. Lewin believes that a path can represent *locomotion*, which means psychological activity. A simply connected closed region offers the simplest case for presentation of psychological dynamics: it has a boundary and it permits "locomotion" along the paths connecting the various points within the region.

If two regions have no common points, they are called *foreign*. In such a case, the intersection of these two regions is zero ($A \cdot B = 0$). Boundaries or boundary zones of regions which offer resistance to psychological locomotion are called *barriers*. If the barriers are impenetrable, the space of free movement can be limited. The more *rigid* the barrier, the greater would be the forces necessary to overcome it. The more *permeable* a barrier is, the easier it is to perform locomotion through it.

Some regions are *elastic*, that is, they tend to return to their original state after a change has been induced. The smaller the force needed to produce a certain change, the more *fluid* is the region.

Life Space

Having introduced some topological concepts, Lewin had to prove that these concepts are good for representation and interpretation of empirical data in psychology. In order to do this, he had to manipulate psychological data and transfer them from their phenotypical status (as they are seen by most psychologists) to the genotypical status, which permits topological operations on the empirical data.

The totality of coexisting facts which are mutually interdependent has been defined by physicists as a field. *Psychological field* is a totality of coexisting and mutually interdependent psychological facts, Lewin said; the *life space* is a psychological field which includes the totality of facts determining behavior.

Empirical data prove that the behavior, and even the development, of an individual are functions of his personality and his environment at a given time. Personality and environment in their interrelationship are called *life space* by Lewin. One can state that $B = F (P, E) = F (LSp)$; behavior is a function of personality and environment, or a function of the life space. This function, F, is what is usually called a law. Psychology has to view the life space, including the person and his environment, as one field.

The psychological field has to be represented as it exists for a person, including both his physical setting and his needs, dreams, and desires. The boundaries of the field can be quasi-physical (derived from physics), quasi-social (derived from social science), or quasi-conceptual (derived from logic). When physical obstacles mark the limits of a region, they are called quasi-physical. When social laws, restrictions, or mores prevent the crossing of the boundary of a region, they are called quasi-social barriers. If the barrier is an intellectual one, it is called quasi-conceptual. All these barriers, insofar as they represent a handicap to psychological locomotion, are obviously psychological barriers.

The difference between the physical world and the psychological worlds (life spaces) is that the former is a dynamic closed unity, while the latter are unclosed unities. In physics, all changes are produced within the same physical space, while in psychology changes may come from without, that is from outside the borders of life space. Psychological events are usually determined by the life space, but certain facts coming from physical space outside the life space may influence human behavior. These facts, to speak topologically, come from the "foreign" hull (see Figure 1). These are the limitations to the life space: "If someone saws a board, his behavior is determined not only by his goal but also by the nature of the wood and properties of the saw." Thus Lewin defined the life space as a "dynamically not closed world." [19]

How can one determine which facts ought to be included in the life space? Lewin doubted whether consciousness could be used as the sole criterion for determining whether something belongs to a person's life space. He preferred to include "all real facts," and real to Lewin is "what has effects," whether a person is aware of them or not.

Physical or social facts are included in the life space "only to the extent and in the manner in which they affect the individual in his momentary state." Thus the life space is "the person and the psychological environment as it exists for him. We usually have this field in mind if we refer to needs, moods, goals, anxiety ideals," stated Lewin in a paper published in 1943; he continued: "The principle of representing within the life space all

[19] Lewin, *Principles of Topological Psychology*, pp. 68 ff.

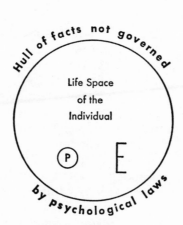

Figure 1

that affects behavior at that time, but nothing else, prevents the inclusion of physical food which is not perceived."[20]

A good definition of life space is offered by Cartwright in the Introduction to a posthumously published volume of Lewin's writings:

> The life space is defined so that at any given time it includes all facts that have existence and excludes those that do not have existence *for the individual or group under study.*
>
> In individual psychology, the environment and the person as consciously perceived by the person are ordinarily included in the life space. But, in addition, unconscious states are also included to the extent that by direct observation or inference the scientist can determine that they leave effects.[21]

Lewin "indicates that it is reasonably easy to decide to include within the life space, many things, such as needs, goals, cognitive structure, and the like and to exclude many others, such as physical and social events occurring at a remote distance and having no direct effect on the individual."[22]

Life Space and Topological Regions

Each part of the life space, said Lewin, has to be presented as a region. The term "region" can be used in two distinct ways, as "(1) Everything in which an object of the life space, for instance a person, has its place; in which it moves; through which it carries out locomotions. (2) Everything in which one can distinguish several positions or parts at the same time, or which is part of a more inclusive whole." The life space itself is a region,

[20] Kurt Lewin, "Defining the 'Field at a Given Time,' " *Psychological Review,* 1943, *50,* 292–310.
[21] Lewin, *Field Theory in Social Science,* Harper, 1951, pp. xi–xii.
[22] Lewin, *Principles of Topological Psychology,* pp. 93 ff.

and a person within the life space is a region too. Obviously, the region of a person is included in the region of the life space. The life space is not indefinitely divisible into smaller parts. The smallest region, which cannot be divided any more, is called a *cell*.

How can the positions of regions be determined? There are two ways. One can determine regions by the *qualitative properties* of a person or group, or by *locomotion or communication*. Lewin preferred the determination of regions by psychological locomotions.

The "space of free movement" includes all the regions to which a person has access from his present situation. The space of free movement is a connected region; there are no barriers within it.

There are two kinds of connection between regions: locomotion and communication. Locomotion must be presented as a path leading from one point to another. The connected region permits locomotion from each point within the region to any other point within it. The *mutual* positions of regions are determined by the paths along which locomotion takes place.

Actions are defined as psychological locomotions and should be presented as paths. Sometimes they can be represented as regions. For instance, a child who is playing with dolls and is called by the mother to go to bed has to change from the region of playing and to enter the region of sleeping. If activity is a region, it is at the same time a *medium*, in contradistinction to a thing. Air is a medium for the flier. A medium is a region in which or through which locomotions can be carried out.

A *psychological goal* is always a region a person would like to enter, or to assume a certain spatial position in relation to. Our activities are usually goal directed; they are paths leading from our present position toward the desired region.

A change in a person's position is represented as a locomotion from one region to another. Lewin reported, as an example, a study carried out in the nursery school of the College of Home Economics of Cornell University. The difficulty in feeding small children is handled by moving the child from unpleasant regions to a pleasant region. Lewin said that the adult tries to bring the child from one region to another. In the first regions the adult meets repulsive force. However, food is in the child's mouth; it will not be ejected. Lewin interpreted this as follows: "As the child enters the region of 'real eating' his position and the direction of the field forces are entirely changed. When the child is in one of the preceding regions, for instance, when he holds the spoon halfway to his mouth, then a region of greater unpleasantness in which the adult tries to push him in, still lies ahead." When the child is once within this region of real eating, the region which lies ahead of him is more pleasant. Thus, Lewin concluded: "The dynamic condition of a person depends in almost every respect directly on his position in a certain region." [23]

[23] *Ibid.*, pp. 97–99.

The Third Dimension

Lewin felt that most of his quasi-social and quasi-physical fields were satisfactorily represented in two dimensions. When he came to represent imagination, hopes, daydreams, and similar phenomena, he felt compelled to introduce the third dimension, which represented "degrees of reality." In order to indicate the level of reality in the life space, one must use the third dimension. The more unreal the level, the greater is its fluidity; that is, its barriers offer less resistance, the boundaries of the part-regions can be easily shifted, and even the boundaries between person and environment are less clear. Usually, perception has the highest degree of reality, thinking has less reality, and daydreaming even less.

3. Lewin's Logical Constructs

Hodological Space

Topology cannot, by itself, represent psychological data, even though the part–whole relations and the concept of paths are of great help in presenting psychological data. Topology does not deal with *direction* and *size*, which are dispensable concepts in psychology. The topological structure of the life space determines which locomotions are possible at a given time, but what actually will happen cannot be predicted with topological concepts only, because change cannot be derived by topology.

Lewin felt compelled to add the concept of "hodological space" to his field theory. Direction in physics can be represented either as the *straight* line (in Euclidean space) or the *straightest* line (in Riemannian space). Lewin thought that psychological direction was neither of these, and therefore he proposed a new type of space to suit the needs of psychological data.

This new space was called by Lewin the *hodological space*. In this space, "the character of the distinguished path varies according to situation and direction in hodological space depends upon the properties of the field at large. . . . Hodological space distinguishes direction toward and direction from." [24]

Lewin was fully aware of the inadequacy of his definition. He said that the purpose of the hodological space "is to find a type of geometry which permits the use of the concept of direction in a manner which will correspond with the meaning that direction has in psychology." [25] Lewin hoped that axiomatization of this new geometry would be done later by "a compe-

[24] Lewin, "The Conceptual Representation and the Measurement of Psychological Forces," *Contributions to Psychological Theory*, 1938, *1*, 22–23.
[25] *Ibid.*, p. 23.

tent mathematician." Lewin did not question whether this new kind of spatial relationship could be constructed, nor did he give any directions as to how to do it. He seemed to believe in the omnipotence of mathematics and sincerely hoped that at some time his *ad hoc* proposed system would be elaborated to form a legitimate branch of mathematics. Meanwhile, he proceeded with utilizing this new tool in the assessment of change, which is one of the most important processes in his psychology.

Psychological change, said Lewin, must have a direction. Behavior is change in a given situation. Behavior is locomotion in a certain direction, either toward an objective or away from it. Lewin assumed that human behavior is goal directed.

Topology does not deal with directions. Psychology does. This difficulty was dealt with by Lewin in a rather unexpected way. He invented a new kind of space, hodological space, in which directions do count. Psychologists may wonder about the ease with which this obstacle was overcome, and this ready solution may be frowned on by mathematicians. However, Lewin felt that he could now go on with his theory construction. He had a new geometry that fit psychological change and enabled him to introduce the concept of direction into a certain kind of space. After solving the problem of direction in human behavior, he was ready to deal with the problem of size and measurement of locomotion.

Force

According to Lewin, all psychological theories can be considered to posit that human behavior is caused by directed entities. Call them propensities or libido, instinct or drive—there is always a directed entity as the cause of behavior.

Mathematicians distinguish between scalars and vectors. Scalars are units of magnitude, while vectors represent both magnitude and direction. Physics operates with both types of unit, but locomotion and change always require vectors.

If anything happens, a change has taken place. Behavior is change. The cause of behavior is, as said before, a directed entity; it is a vector, a directed unit which has a certain magnitude and direction.

Lewin introduced the term "psychological force" as a construct related to what other psychologists called drive, excitatory tendency, or libido. Psychological force is a directed entity which has a certain magnitude analogous to that of physical force.

Galileo and Newton held that each body, if left alone, will move in a straight line with uniform and constant velocity; this is the law of inertia. Any change in the direction or velocity or both is a result of some force. Force is the cause of change.

Lewin considered any activity a change and ascribed it to a "psychological force." The term "force" was obviously borrowed from physics, but it was introduced into psychology and defined by Lewin independently of its physical connotation. Any "tendency to act in a certain direction" or any cause of activity is a force. Force must have *direction*, magnitude, and point of application, and since these properties cannot be represented in the topological geometry, Lewin introduced them in the framework of his own hodological system.

The hodological system allowed the attachment to the construct "force" of the three above-mentioned conceptual properties: direction, magnitude, and point of application. The conceptual property of force is vector; its operational definition links it with psychological locomotion.

What kind of mathematical manipulation can be applied to force? Lewin felt that in some manner forces could be added, but he did not know how. "Can we speak of resultant [of forces—B. W.] if we do not know the laws which determine the direction and the strength of the resultant force of two given forces? Can we assume that the principle of parallelogram of forces which holds in physics holds in psychology too? . . . Everything seems to indicate that this principle does not hold in psychology. . . . Nevertheless, there seems to be a way in psychology to avoid the concept of resultants." [26] However, when several forces act on a certain region, one must assume some kind of combination of them. A combination of forces acting at the same time at the same point is called *resultant force*. Though it is not known how to measure the resultant force, it can be safely assumed that locomotion takes place whenever the resultant force is greater than zero.

Forces can be measured indirectly, said Lewin, by relating them to observable facts. Measurement correlates the observable symptoms to dynamical facts (constructs). Constructs cannot be measured quantitatively because there is no measuring unit, no zero point, nor are equal units determined. But their symptoms satisfy the requirements for non-quantitative measurement. [27] Thus, a rank-order measurement can be applied to measurement of forces. Whenever a person does something, his behavior is an effect of the forces acting on him. Some of these forces are greater, some smaller, and the resultant behavior will indicate the rank-order quantity of forces.

Force Field

Forces act in a field, and a person's behavior in a given life space is a product of the resultant forces. A *force field* "indicates which force would exist at each point in the field if the individual involved were at that point." [28] A *conflict* refers to the overlapping of at least two force fields.

[26] *Ibid.*, pp. 83–84.
[27] *Ibid.*, p. 113.
[28] Kurt Lewin, "Constructs in Psychology and Psychological Ecology," *University of Iowa Studies in Child Welfare*, 1944, *20*, 1–29.

Frustration has the same dimension as conflict. The distribution of forces away from one region is the force field of *aversion*. *Choice* means that a person is located between two positive or two negative, mutually exclusive valences.

Forces acting in one's life space but originating in other persons and their wishes are called *induced* forces. In a group setting, the leader induces forces into the life spaces of the individual members.

How far a force will influence behavior depends on the *potency* of the situation in which a person is involved. Potency of a region within the life space is the relative extent to which one is involved in a given area, when he is involved in more than one area.

A goal has the conceptual dimension of a force field—that is, of a distribution of forces in space. A goal (or, in field theory terminology, a positive valence) is a force field of a special structure, usually a force field where all forces point toward the same region.

Valence

If a region is attractive to a person, it has positive valence. Valence corresponds to a field of force which has the structure of a positive central field, that is, all forces in this field are directed in the direction of valence. If no other valences existed, the person would move in the direction of the positive valence from whatever position he was in.

Lewin defined valence in terms of forces acting on a person: "A region G which has a valence $(Va(G))$ is defined as a region within the life space of an individual P which attracts or repulses this individual." If $Va(G) > 0$, then $[f(P,G)] > 0$. Va is valence, G goal, fPG force from the person to the goal.

Valence is related to force, but is not identical with it. "If the valence of a region decreases or increases because of a change of the intensity of the need the forces corresponding to the valence also will decrease or increase. However, the strength of the force fP,G does not depend only upon the strength of the valence but besides, for instance, upon the relative position of P and G. By P's [person's—B.W.] coming closer to a goal, the force in the direction to the goal might increase."[29]

Forces directed toward a positive valence or away from a negative one are called driving forces; barriers are restraining forces.

Tension

Every construct in psychology needs a definition of its conceptual properties and a coordinating definition. Consider the concept "tension." Its conceptual properties are the following:

[29] *Ibid.*, pp. 88, 89.

It is a state of system S which tries to change itself in such a way that it becomes equal to the state of surrounding systems. It involves forces at the boundary of the system S in tension. . . . The tension in a system S has to be determined always relative to the tension of its neighboring systems.

So much for conceptual properties; the coordinating definition of tension as related to psychology is as follows: "whenever a psychological need exists, a system in a state of tension exists within the individual."[30]

Psychologically speaking, tension is a state of disequilibrium between the individual and his environment. This objective state of disequilibrium or tension is perceived by the individual as a need.

This presentation of the problem of needs, which is actually the problem of motivation in human behavior, requires further consideration. Organisms tend to equilibrium, Lewin said, following Cannon and Goldstein (cf. Chapter 5). The principle of homeostasis was applied by Lewin to forces acting within a system and without it. In Lewin's theory it sounds somewhat behavioristic: whenever the balance is disturbed, the system tends to regain it.

However, Lewin was not satisfied with this objective law of homeostasis. The psychological field of an individual, in which all the forces act, cannot be void of subjective perception. Tension as a lack of balance between force fields is one side of the story, namely, the conceptual one. The other side is psychological reality as experienced by the individual; it is the "operational definition" of the very same process. In this definition, tension is perceived by an individual as his need, like hunger or thirst. Whenever a state of tension exists in the organism, a need is always perceived. Thus, tension and need were not considered by Lewin as cause and effect but as two sides of the same process.

Needs are closely related to valences. Whenever the intensity of a need increases, the valence of objects or activities which may satisfy this need increases too. The hungrier one is, the higher the valence of food. And the hungrier one is, the easier to satisfy his hunger with poor food, because the valence of any kind of food is increased.

Causality

Lewin distinguished two notions of causality. Causality can have a "historical-geographical" meaning in the case where all the relevant antecedent factors are taken into consideration. All the events that happened at a certain time and in a certain place belong to this category of causality. Lewin believed that in developmental psychology and in abnormal psychology the historical concept of causality could be applied.

He felt, however, that the "systematic" concept of causality was far more important. Effects are produced by concrete causes, that is, by other events that *exist* at a certain moment. The question is, what kind of time

[30] *Ibid.*, p. 99.

relationship exists between the event or group of events called "cause" and the event or group of events called "effect"?

Aristotle distinguished between *causa finalis*, the aim or the future as a cause, and *causa efficiens*, the antecedent cause. Lewin felt that both definitions were wrong. Since neither past nor future exists at the present moment, they cannot have effects at the present.

Suppose, said Lewin, the foliage of a tree shelters me from the rain. The "systematic" causal explanation will be based on finding out the direction and velocity of falling drops, the position of leaves, and my own position. "In short," said Lewin, "one can represent the present situation and, by applying the laws of mechanics or other relevant laws, derive what event must occur in such a situation."[31] This systematic causality is in contradistinction to the causality which will tell the history of the tree, and all other events which happened at a given time and in a given space.

Actually both types can be applied in psychology. In psychological dynamics, the systematic causality is far superior, said Lewin, because effects can be produced by contemporary events only. Lewin defined existence by its effects; what exists, he said, has effects, and an effect is an outcome of what exists. Only the present exists, and behavior is an effect of coexisting, simultaneous factors.

"It has been accepted by most psychologists that the teleological derivation of behavior from the future is not permissible. Field theory insists that the derivation of behavior from the past is not less metaphysical, because past events do not exist now and therefore cannot have effect now. The effect of the past on behavior can be only an indirect one, the past psychological field is one of the 'origins' of the present field and this in turn affects behavior."[32]

The study of life space requires "systematic" causation. Behavior of a person is a function of the person and of his environment. Lewin considered causality identical with mathematical function; he believed that behavior and person–environment are simultaneous facts, but he was aware that absolute contemporaneity is almost impossible. He was satisfied with a situation which remained "sufficiently constant" during the interval of time in question.

> Psychology has used diagnosis by *anamneses* rather excessively, particularly in classical psychoanalysis and other clinical approaches of personality. . . . Experimental psychology, on the whole, has shown a progressive trend toward testing the present situation. The method of determining the properties of a situation (S^t) by testing them at that time t avoids the uncertainties of historical conclusions. It does not follow, however, that this method eliminates considerations of time periods altogether. A "situation at a given time" actually does not refer to a moment without time extension, but to a certain time-period.
>
> Field theory states that the change dx/dt at the time t depends only on the sit-

---

[31] Lewin, *Principles of Topological Psychology*, p. 31.

[32] Kurt Lewin, "Field Theory of Learning," *Forty-First Yearbook of the National Society for the Study of Education*, 1942, 41 (Part II), 215–242.

uation S^t at that time t. The field-theoretical principle of contemporaneity in psychology then means that the behavior B at the time t is a function of the situation S at the time t only (S is meant to include both the person and his psychological environment), $B^t = F(S^t)$ and not, in addition, a function of past or future situations S^{t-n} or $S^t + n$.[33]

4. LOCOMOTION: THEORY OF BEHAVIOR

Equilibrium

Behavior is change, says Lewin. What are the reasons for change? Lewin assumes a state of equilibrium between person and environment. Should this equilibrium be disturbed, a *tension* arises which leads to locomotion that brings relief (restores the equilibrium).

Human behavior is a sequence of tensions, locomotions, and reliefs. Tension is "a state of a system of an individual" in relation to the tension of neighboring systems. Whenever there is a lack of equilibrium between two systems, a state of tension arises. A system in tension tends to change to become equal to the state of surrounding systems. The activity directed toward removal of tension and establishment of equilibrium is *locomotion*. Locomotion is a directed activity which aims at restoration of the equilibrium.

The sequence tension–locomotion–equilibrium is equivalent to the sequence need–activity–relief. Whenever a psychological need is felt, there is a state of tension, and the individual acts in order to achieve relief. Failure or frustration causes additional tension; discharge of a system under tension corresponds to what other psychologists call satisfaction of a drive or a motive. The satisfaction of the need corresponds to a release of the tension within the system.

An individual's behavior is a product of the situation, said Lewin. This statement qualifies as a definite sort of environmentalism. Lewin has in mind the environment "at a given time" in contradistinction to other environmentalists, who are mainly concerned with the past influences of the environment on a person's behavior.

Since Lewin cares little about past influences and is concerned with the environment as it is in the present, his system should be called *situationism* rather than environmentalism. Behavior depends on the state of equilibrium or disequilibrium between the forces acting in the field. The kind of behavior one can expect from an individual depends mainly on the individual's situation. In different situations he will behave differently, responding to the structure of environment, to forces, and to valences.

According to Lewin, there are two ways to explain behavior. Theories of the first type locate the forces for locomotion within a person; they correlate needs to tensions within his inner–personal regions. Freud's theory of

[33] Kurt Lewin, "Defining the 'Field at a Given Time,' " *Psychological Review*, 1943, 50, 292–310.

libido falls into this category since it emphasizes the inner and instinctual forces.

Lewin considers this kind of theory fallacious, since forces for locomotion cannot be derived logically from tensions within the person. Wherever a positive or negative valence exists in the environment, there is a state of tension within the organism. Valence is only partially dependent on the state of the organism; for example, the valence of food is related both to the degree of hunger and to the extent of its availability, which is independent of psychological factors. When food appears in the psychological field of a person whose system is in tension (of hunger), the food is a positive valence because it can reduce the tension. Thus, the entire issue of motivation, and the problems of inner drives and outer incentives (cf. Chapter 2, 3, and 4), has been restructured by Lewin. In his theory, behavior is a movement or locomotion which has a definite direction. This direction is either toward objects and persons having positive valence or away from objects and persons having negative valence. Things have positive valence if they can remove a tension. Tension is a state of disequilibrium. Tensions arise within the organism; valences are in the environment.

Both, however, are included in a dynamic field within which forces are acting on a person in the direction of the positive valence or away from the negative valence. As a result of the action of forces (which results from tensions and valences), a locomotion takes place. This locomotion reduces tension and brings relief. Locomotion is, topologically speaking, movement from one region to another in a given space. Psychologically speaking it is goal-directed behavior which results, according to Lewin, from the "totality of coexisting facts." J. F. Brown summarizes Lewin's theory of locomotion as follows: "Psychological activities may be ordered to *locomotions*. One individual in this sense has the character of a *thing*. The space through which the locomotion occurs has the properties of a *medium*. . . . Media have dynamic properties such as fluidity, permeability, cohesiveness and the like." All these terms can be operationally defined, says Brown.

> *Fluidity* is defined as the ease of locomotion in the medium. *Degree of freedom* of social locomotion is the comparative number of directions in which social locomotion is possible. *Permeability* means the ease with which locomotions are executed through the barrier. And the forces activating all locomotions in the psychological field are to be ordered to the concept of vector. These vectors represent forces causing psychological locomotion.[34]

One can readily conclude that Lewin has shifted the force point of human dynamics from inner drives, impulses, and libido, toward the external factors of stimulation, incentive, and situation. Even tension within the organism cannot arise independently from environment. Man cannot be considered, according to Lewin, a separate entity; he is part of a dynamic

[34] J. F. Brown, "On the Use of Mathematics in Psychological Theory," *Psychometrika*, 1936, 1, 7–15, 77–90.

field. Person and environment are bound together in a field and cannot be separated.

Tension Systems

An experimental study of the behavior of individuals in a state of tension was conducted by Lewin's pupil, Bluma Zeigarnik.[35] Zeigarnik found that uncompleted tasks are much better retained in the memory than are completed ones. Her findings support Lewin's hypothesis that attainment of a goal or successful locomotion in the direction of positive valence relieves tension, while an uncompleted task preserves the existing tension. Once a tension has been created by a task or goal, the organism is inclined to act in order to remove the tension by a locomotion in the direction of the goal. As long as the goal is not attained, and the need is not satisfied, a force corresponding to the valence of the goal region exists and leads the individual to an action in that direction. And this is precisely why uncompleted tasks are kept very much alive in the individual's memory.

Zeigarnik's experiment was based on the following assumptions. First, the intention to reach a goal G corresponds to a tension t in a certain system S^c within the person, so that t $(S^c) > 0$. Then, if the goal is achieved the tension is released: t $(S^G) = 0$, if $P \subset G$. An additional assumption was made, namely, that a need leads not only to an overt activity of locomotion toward the goal, but to thinking about the activity too. Using the topological presentation one may say that the force causing the tendency to locomotion in the direction of the goal $f_{P,G}$ acts both on the reality level of doing and on the unreality level of thinking.

Zeigarnik gave 18 to 22 tasks to 138 subjects. The subjects were permitted to complete some of the tasks and were prevented from completing others. If memory was correlated to satisfaction, the completed tasks should be retained longer. However, the experiment brings evidence to the contrary and challenges the Freudian assumption of forgetting of unpleasant experiences. Zeigarnik's subjects recalled much better the unfinished tasks, as compared to the satisfactorily completed tasks. The ratio of recalled unfinished tasks (RU) to recalled completed tasks (RC) was approximately 1.9:1. Obviously, says Lewin, the force acting on a person who has not completed the task is greater than the force acting on a person who has completed it. Thus, f $(PU) > f$ (PC).

A similar experiment was conducted by Ovsiankina.[36] She studied the frequency of resumption of interrupted activities. Her hypothesis was that once a quasi-need is induced, it tends toward discharge by activity. Ov-

[35] Bluma Zeigarnik, "Über das Behalten erledigter und unerledigter Handlungen," *Psychologische Forschung*, 1927, 9, 1–85.

[36] Maria Ovsiankina, "Die Wiederaufnahme unterbrochener Handlungen," *Psychologische Forschung*, 1928, 11, 302–379.

siankina gave her subjects various tasks to perform. Then she interrupted them and watched through a one-way screen what they were doing. About 80 percent of the subjects resumed the task. The frequency of resumption indicated the existence of a system of tension which caused activity directed toward completion of the tasks.

Lissner gave his subjects a puzzle, a riddle, and a translation, then interrupted them at a certain point and gave some substitute activities. Some of the substitute activities were easier and some more difficult than the original tasks. The difficulty of a task was measured by the amount of time needed for its completion. After completion of the substitute activities, some subjects tended to resume the interrupted activity. The ratio of resumption was adversely proportional to the difficulty of the substitute task. Apparently, the more difficult the substitute task, the greater was its substitute value and the less the subjects felt the need to resume the original activity. The conclusion is that the difficult substitute task was better able to relieve the tension.[37]

Karsten's studies tested the hypothesis that repetition may reduce the positive valence of certain activities and even change it to a negative one.[38] These experiments are of considerable importance to the theory of learning and challenge the law of frequency (cf. Chapters 2, 3, and 4). Karsten ordered her subjects to make strokes in a certain rhythm until they refused to continue, even if the experimenter urged them to do so. As the subjects showed that they had had enough, they were asked to make strokes in another rhythm until spontaneous cessation. Then the subjects were asked to continue to make strokes in another rhythm; this was continued until the subjects refused to make any strokes whatsoever. Each sort of rhythm was regarded by Karsten as a separate region. At the beginning, the subjects were willing to enter the new region, which meant that the region had positive valence, but repetition changed the positive valence into a negative one. The "satiated" subjects refused to remain in that region. Thus, concludes Lewin, satiation leads to change of the positive valence into a negative one, and repetition can be of no help in learning, or even give adverse results.

Barriers, Distances, and Valences

Dembo studied the problem of frustration and anger.[39] When a goal is unobtainable, a *barrier* is said to prevent the person from locomotion in the direction of the desired region. Dembo asked her subjects to throw rings over a bottle. The experimenter increased the difficulties by such actions as

[37] K. Lissner, "Die Enspannung von Bedürfnissen durch Ersatzhandlungen," *Psychologische Forschung*, 1933, *18*, 218–250.

[38] Anitra Karsten, "Psychische Sättigung," *Psychologische Forschung*, 1928, *10*, 142–254.

[39] Tamara Dembo, "Der Ärger als dynamisches Problem," *Psychologische Forschung*, 1931, *15*, 1–144.

catching the rings and moving the bottles. The subjects started to rethrow the rings and, when severely frustrated, placed the rings on the stick. Frustrated adults behaved "childishly," shifting from a realistic field to a nonrealistic one.

Usually, barriers increase the valence of an object. However, whenever the barriers are very difficult, they produce frustration, anger, and regression to a less realistic type of behavior.

As the distance between an object of a certain valence and a person increases, the force of the valence usually decreases. As the child comes closer to a toy, its valence increases. Fajans studied one- to six-year-old children. She put objects of great positive valence before them in distances varying from 8 to 100 centimeters. With increasing distance, the positive valence of the objects tended to decrease, as witnessed by the decrease of emotional tension in the infants. In older children, responses were more complicated, probably because they viewed the obstacle as dependent on the will of the examiner.[40]

Level of Aspiration

A person's evaluation of success and failure depends on previous experience and standards based on it. Hoppe [41] administered a certain task to 124 subjects. The task was performed in 88 seconds on the average. When Hoppe set the goal of performing the task at 120 seconds or more, his subjects refused to accept their achievements as success. Similarly, when he set the goal at 60 seconds or less and most of his subjects failed, the failure did not produce in them a feeling of having failed. Apparently, they evaluated their own performance on a certain level of expected achievement. This expected level of future performance has been named by T. Dembo *level of aspiration*. Hoppe's subjects experienced feelings of success and failure when the goals ranged from 65 to 110 seconds. Obviously, this was the range of their level of aspiration.

In Lewin's theory, the level of aspiration is related to the problem of real or unreal psychological fields. The degree of reality of a goal influences an individual's evaluation of his own achievement.

Most of the recent experiments on level of aspiration utilize the following technique. The subject is required to state quantitatively his expected achievement, mark on examination, adding, or scoring. Then the task is administered. The difference between the actual level of performance and the expected one is the "difference score." Gould [42] used six measures: synonyms, substitution of digits, speed in addition, steadiness, cancellation of

---

[40] Sara Fajans, "Erfolg, Ausdauer und Aktivität beim Säugling und Kleinkind," *Psychologische Forschung*, 1933, *17*, 268–305.

[41] F. Hoppe, "Erfolg und Misserfolg," *Psychologische Forschung*, 1930, *14*, 1–62.

[42] R. Gould, "An Experimental Analysis of "Level of Aspiration,' " *Genetic Psychology Monographs*, 1939, *21*, 1–115.

letters, and sliding metal disks into a bull's eye. The "scores of difference" between expected and actual behavior (which also indicate that the level of aspiration varied) and their intercorrelations ranged from .04 to .44.

Frank[43] found that there are at least three factors involved in setting the level of aspiration: first, the need to keep the level of aspiration as high as possible; second, the need not to fail; third, the need to be realistic.

Several studies on the level of aspiration have indicated that the level depends on the potentialities of the individual (as perceived by him) and on environmental influences.

Perception and Memory

Perception and learning are as closely interrelated in Lewin's system as they are in the gestalt theory (see Chapter 12). Lewin, however, elaborated the issues less than the gestalt psychologists did.

Perception cannot be regarded as a source of energy, nor can perception serve as the driving power in human behavior, said Lewin. Perception of an object may *influence* behavior in the following manner. A newly perceived object may elicit a certain tension within the organism, either of attraction or of repulsion, depending on whether the object represents a positive or a negative valence to the person. Consequently, he may start locomotion toward the perceived object or away from it. Behavior is not dynamically produced by perception (perception does not supply the energy), but nevertheless the direction of behavior is related to and guided by perception.

Perception plays a prominent role in one's psychological field. Whatever is perceived by an individual belongs to his psychological field. Lewin made hardly any specific statement about memory, though Zeigarnik's experiment deals with this problem. As stated above, Zeigarnik's subjects had to perform some tasks, half of which they were permitted to complete and half of which were interrupted by the experimenter. Then the subjects were asked to recall their tasks. The ratio of recalled completed tasks to recalled incompleted tasks was 1:1.9. This was explained as an indication of better memorizing of an interrupted task. The plausible interpretation offered by Lewin relates memory to a state of tension in the organism. Whatever has been completed does not give rise to tension and tends to be forgotten. Uncompleted tasks are related to tension (need to complete) and, therefore, are kept alive in the subjects' memory.

A critic of Lewin[44] has raised the question of why the completed tasks

[43] J. D. Frank, "Recent Studies of the Level of Aspiration," *Psychological Bulletin*, 1941, *38*, 218–226.

[44] Sylvia H. MacCall, "A Comparative Study of the Systems of Lewin and Koffka with Special Reference to Memory Phenomena," *Contributions to Psychological Theory*, Duke University, 1939, *2*, No. 1.

were recalled at all. If memory is related to tension, what kind of tension accompanies the completed tasks? An additional difficulty arises from Lewin's insistence on contemporary causation. How can past events influence one's behavior if they do not exist any more? Or, perhaps, should our memories be included in the field-at-a-given-time? Apparently Lewin did not elaborate sufficiently his point of view on the problem of memory, which poses considerable difficulties to a field theorist.

Learning

Lewin's theory of learning is at variance with associationist and conditioning theories of learning. Lewin does not see learning as a stimulus–response process, but as a process of *perceptual organization* or *reorganization*. Learning always involves insight, he says, and insight is a perceptual process. Thus, Lewin, together with the gestalt psychologists, represents what Spence[45] calls the sign–significate theories of learning in contradistinction to the stimulus–response theories (cf. Chapter 16).

Lewin shares with the gestalt psychologists the idea that learning is basically perception, and insight is a process of structuring or restructuring the perceived area. The structure of a region as perceived by an individual is the *cognitive structure*. Learning is behavior, that is, a locomotion from one region to another. When a person changes his position from one region to another, the structure of his life space undergoes a change. The same holds true of locomotion of learning. Learning and insight "can always be viewed as a change in the cognitive structure of the situation. It frequently includes differentiating and restructuring in the sense of separating certain regions which have been connected and connecting regions which have been separated."[46]

Thus, perception is the main issue in Lewin's theory. One has to admit that gestalt and field theories have raised an important issue which has been either overlooked or at least insufficiently clarified by other theories of learning. What is the relation of learning to perception? Is any perception learning or any learning perception, as Lewin suggests? Obviously these problems are far from being solved (cf. Chapter 16).

Lewin distinguishes four types of learning: (1) learning as a change in knowledge, that is, in the cognitive structure; (2) learning as a change in motivation, that is, in valences and values; (3) learning as acquisition of skills by voluntary control of the body musculature; and (4) learning as a

[45] Kenneth W. Spence, "Theoretical Interpretations of Learning," in S. S. Stevens (ed.), *Handbook of Experimental Psychology*, Wiley, 1951.

[46] Kurt Lewin, "Behavior and Development as a Function of Total Situation," in L. Carmichael (Ed.), *Manual of Child Psychology*, Wiley, 1946, p. 804.

change in group belonging or ideology, that is, learning as a process of acculturation.[47]

Learning as a change in knowledge is basically a process of differentiation of a formerly unstructured area. What has been unclear, diffuse, and unstructured becomes differentiated, specific, divided into subregions, and connected by paths.

Learning may involve another type of change in the cognitive structure, not necessarily the "subdividing of regions into smaller units." Learning may take place through *any* change in the cognitive structure of the psychological field, such as connections and disconnections, differentiations and dedifferentiations. Any change in the meaning of a word or of a situation means learning; thus, any perception or any change in perception is learning. During childhood, time perspective undergoes considerable change and becomes enlarged. The child learns to distinguish between reality and unreality levels of the life space (whereas the little child does not discern between daydreams and reality).

Lewin criticizes the use of repetition in learning. As Karsten proved, too many repetitions may lead to satiation, which may result in dedifferentiation of the field and unlearning. All changes in the cognitive structure are produced by forces, either acting in the field itself or resulting from the needs, valences, and hopes of the individual. All intellectual processes are influenced by the goals of a person; therefore, repetition without a goal may lead to unlearning. Change in valences and attitudes is another kind of learning. The valence of an activity, says Lewin, depends partly on its meaning, and therefore, on the cognitive structure of the psychological field. Studies on food preferences have shown that dislike for a food can easily be changed by attaching a new meaning to it, for example, by telling a story in which the disliked food is much liked by the hero of the story. Any change of motivation is a change either in the needs of a person or in the means of their satisfaction; obviously it is some sort of learning too.

Level of aspiration is an important factor in learning. Level of aspiration depends both on the potentialities of an individual and on the influences of the group to which he belongs. Too high or too low a level of aspiration discourages learning, but one can learn to set his level of aspiration properly.

Lewin distinguishes between "learning by force" and "learning democracy." Sometimes an individual is forced into a given situation, and then he may adjust himself. Learning by punishment is an enforced learning that narrows the space of free movement and produces a sort of prison-like situation. In reward, the individual is permitted more freedom than in punishment, but all the ways to reward are blocked "save the disliked but requested activity." Learning by punishment always involves enforcement

[47] Kurt Lewin, "Field Theory of Learning," *Forty-First Yearbook of the National Society for the Study of Education*, 1942, 41 (Part II), 215–242.

and "policing" to prevent the individual from avoiding punishment and to preclude his escape from the field.

5. Theory of Personality

Personality as a System of Regions

Personality can be represented as a region or a group of regions. It cannot be represented in the same way as the environment, because the environment is a medium through which locomotion takes place, while a person cannot serve as a medium through which or within which locomotion is carried out.

The various regions and boundaries within a person are *dynamically interdependent*. This interdependence of regions means that the state of one region is influenced by the state of another. Speaking topologically, they are "connected" regions. However, there is no "locomotion" within a person, only communication, says Lewin.

In Lewin's theory, personality plays the role of a part of a field. Person and environment together form a field. What is the person? The person is one part of this field, perhaps the central part of it, which does not serve for locomotion but may change its place as a whole.

Does this presentation satisfy the psychologist's need for explanation? Lewin believes so. He maintains that from this conceptualization or representation of personality as a region or a system of regions within a field, relevant acts can be predicted. Consider the difference between the outer, inner, and innermost regions within the personality; the Freudian problem of regression can be interpreted as dedifferentiation of the regions of personality. Though this method of interpretation ignores many problems, it can be considered an earnest effort by Lewin to escape Stern's dualism of "person" and "thing" (cf. Chapter 11). Lewin's theory permits one to interpret personality as *"unitas multiplex,"* since personality can be represented either as one region or as a system of regions.

Lewin says that

> It is always necessary to represent both person and environment in the life space. We also have mentioned that one has to distinguish within the person certain strata and regions. For certain problems, however, one can represent the person in a first approximation as a point, for the following reason: The person is a strongly unified whole. When we are not dealing with the dynamic differentiation of the person into past regions, we can consider the person as a single system and can represent it as an undifferentiated region or as a point in the sense explained above. One can use such a representation especially in cases that concern the locomotion of a person as a whole. For more exact representation one will always have to show the person as a differentiated region.[48]

---

[48] Lewin, *Principles of Topological Psychology*, p. 113.

Inner and Outer Regions

In the analysis of personality structure, Lewin follows the gestalt pattern. The person is represented as a "connected region" (or system of regions) divided into part-regions and separated from the environment by a Jordan curve. Some of the regions are inner, some are outer; the outer regions are motor-perceptual, analogous to the division suggested by Koffka (Chapter 12).

There are difficulties in distinguishing between the inner-personal system of regions and the motor-perceptual system; for example, the understanding of speech may be considered as taking place in either zone. Additional difficulties are encountered in distinguishing between the perceptual regions and the motor regions within the boundary zone, since, for example, the eye serves both as a perception and as a motor (expression) region.

In the motor-perceptual boundary zone the more peripheral regions should be distinguished from the central ones. The motor system, says Lewin, can be "dynamically connected" to one inner zone only, serve only one inner region at a time. In other words, when a personality is involved in a given activity, other activities are excluded. When one fights, for example, his entire personality is directed toward his motor activities, and any other motor activity must stop.[49]

The inner regions of personality can be divided into peripheral and central regions. The central regions have less communication with the environment. This distinction seems to result from Karsten's and Dembo's studies on satiation and anger. Karsten[50] proved that the more central the involved regions are, the more quickly they are satiated. Dembo[51] showed that the peripheral zones of personality respond more easily to anger-provoking stimuli because they are closer to the motor zone and the overt expression of anger comes readily. When the inner strata are touched, they seldom respond with overt anger, since there is no direct connection between them and the motor zone.

In emotional tension, people tend to impose on themselves more self-control, that is, to strengthen the boundaries between the peripheral and motor regions in order to avoid an immediate outburst of emotions. The central regions tend to unite under emotional strain, which compresses the entire inner region and makes it less differentiated so that the individual behaves in a less mature manner. People under great emotional tension regress and become more primitive. When the tension within the inner regions becomes unbearable, emotions may break through the barriers,

---

[49] Cf. B. B. Wolman, "Violent Behavior," *International Journal of Group Tensions,* 1973, 3, 127–141.
[50] Karsten, *op. cit.*
[51] Dembo, *op. cit.*

sweep the motor regions, and cause overt and sometimes violent physical motion, says Lewin.

Lewin believes that his theory of emotion, within the framework of topology, enables one to solve most empirical problems. Emotions are tensions within the inner regions; control of emotions depends on the strength of interregional walls. All emotions are expressed by locomotion but not all emotions act in the same way. Joy, for instance, weakens the boundaries between the inner and the motor regions, thus facilitating an overt expression. Sorrow acts in the opposite direction. Powerful emotions destroy the inner boundaries, reduce the number of regions, and lead to dedifferentiation of the total personality system.

Personality Types

There are considerable differences in the personality structures of different persons. A child's personality is less differentiated and less integrated than that of an adult.

Lewin does not advise comparison of the number of regions, because what may give the impression of being one homogeneous region may turn out, on closer analysis, to be more than one. The dynamic unity of a region does not prejudge the degree of differentiation.

The degree of *wholeness* in the child is greater than that in the adult. "A change of one part of the system in the child usually influences all other parts to a much greater extent than in the adult," says Lewin,[52] and the relative separateness of the regions is smaller in the child than in the adult. A person is *harmonious* if the various part-regions are balanced. If some regions are poorly connected or isolated, a person is mentally disturbed.

"The degree of primitiveness of behavior," says Lewin, "seems to be a good symptom of the degree of differentiation of a person. Also the achievement of a person in an intelligence test seems to depend above all on the degree of differentiation of the person, or at least on the differentiation of certain part regions."[53] Stress may bring dedifferentiation of the whole personality, thus lowering the mental level of behavior.

Certain regions within a person may play more important roles than others. These may shift in accordance with the pressure of environmental forces. Usually, new (young) regions are more flexible than old ones and are less resistant to change. Consistency in behavior depends on the older regions and their relative strength. Lewin distinguishes various types of personality which develop as a result of environmental influences, for example, the German personality type is a "closed" type as compared to the American "open" type (see Section 6 of this chapter).

[52] Lewin, *Principles of Topological Psychology*, p. 183.
[53] Lewin, *Dynamic Theory of Personality*, p. 207.

Differentiation and Dedifferentiation

The life space of the neonate is an undifferentiated field. As the child grows, his life space becomes more and more differentiated since perception and learning areas hitherto inaccessible or unshaped become structuralized and differentiated. There is a differentiation of needs which can be represented as an increase in differentiation of inner regions. Development is differentiation of both inner and outer regions of personality, and of the total life space as well.

The child's life space contains many inaccessible regions and the space of free movement is rather limited. As the child grows, more areas become accessible (e.g., play forbidden to little children is now permitted), but certain areas close down.

Lewin has proved experimentally that frustration leads to regression. A group of five children were carefully observed in order to determine their level of constructive playing with toys. The average mental age of the children was fifty-five months. Lewin, Barker, and Dembo let the children play with some toys and rated the level of constructiveness.[54] The use of a toy telephone for conversation apparently indicated a considerable degree of constructiveness. The children were then shown very interesting new toys and were permitted to play with them for a brief time. After a few minutes the new toys were taken away. Undoubtedly the children felt badly frustrated. When brought back to the old toys, the children did not continue to play in a constructive manner in accordance with their mental age, but regressed seventeen months, on the average, and struck the telephone or scribbled with pencils. Frustration, Lewin concluded, leads to regression. The differentiated regions of personality become dedifferentiated and less mature.

Personality and Environment

No student of personality has ever denied the importance of environment and the impact of changing situations. Surely personality undergoes changes, and various devices have been invented in order to account for both the continuity and the changeability of human nature. However, Lewin seems to deal with changeability only. "If the life space is a totality of possible events, then 'things' that enter the situation, especially the person himself and psychological 'objects,' have to be characterized by their relationship to possible events."[55]

Sociologically minded psychologists would say: a person is the product of environmental influences and of some hereditary factors. After environmental forces have been active for a time, they have some influence on the

---

[54] Roger Barker, Tamara Dembo, and Kurt Lewin, "Frustration and Regression: an Experiment with Young Children," *University of Iowa Studies in Child Welfare*, 1941, *18*, 1–314.

[55] Lewin, *Principles of Topological Psychology*, p. 16.

individual. When the individual comes to face a new situation, this new situation probably modifies, to a certain extent at least, his way of behaving. But there are already some established ways of behavior which might or might not be modified by the new situation. In Lewin's terminology, this would mean that a "thing" entering the situation will behave in accordance with its own nature. Obviously, this is a "class theory" statement which cannot be accepted by field theorists.

In Lewin's description, the personality per se seems almost to disappear. The behavior of an individual is a product of interrelationships. Various objects in one's psychological field invite him to do or not to do certain things. However, these valences and their strength and distribution are "properties of the environment" and not of the person. A person's needs are "tensions," or disequilibrium between him and his environment.

Only overt and manifest behavior like locomotion or communication caused by attraction or repulsion seems to be considered by Lewin. The interplay between person and environment is the only way to study personality. The functions of the inner and outer layers of personality cannot be dealt with outside the context of the personality–environment field.[56]

6. GROUP DYNAMICS

Principle of Transfiguration

Lewin's studies in social psychology are usually referred to as *group dynamics*. In this area, Lewin has achieved his greatest success and prominence. The outstanding feature of his social psychology is the application to group behavior of concepts borrowed from the psychology of the individual. Apparently, Lewin does not subscribe to the concept of group mind, but he does strive to introduce a substitute term for it. He feels pretty strongly that a group is a unit which has to be analyzed as a whole rather than as an aggregate of individuals.

Lewin applies the gestalt principle of transfiguration to the study of small groups.

> To the psychologist who has observed the historical development of the concept of "whole" or Gestalt in psychology, most of the argumentation about the group mind sounds strangely familiar. It took psychology many steps before it discovered that a dynamic whole has properties which are different from the properties of their parts or from the sum of their parts. [Therefore,] whatever has been of scientific value in the concept of group mind resolves itself into the concrete and familiar problems of dynamic wholes in sociology and social psychology.[57]

---

[56]It is worthwhile to compare Sullivan's theory (Chapter 9) to Lewin's. Sullivan seems to have been influenced by Lewin.

[57]Lewin, *Field Theory in Social Science*, p. 146.

The individual and his environment form a psychological field. Similarly, the group and the environment of the group form a *social field*. Lewin explained this as follows: "A basic tool for the analysis of group life is the representation of the group and its setting as 'a social field.' This means that the social happening is viewed as occurring in, and being the result of, the totality of coexisting social entities, such as groups, subgroups, members, barriers, channels of communication, etc. One of the fundamental characteristics of this field is the relative position of the entities, which are parts of the field."[58] The structure, the possible locomotions, and the distribution of forces within the field are the decisive factors in group behavior.

This analogy between group psychology and individual psychology is the first principle of Lewin's group dynamics. The mutual position of regions within a person's field and the forces acting there are the decisive factors in a person's behavior. The very same statement applies to group behavior, provided the term "person" is replaced by the term "group."

The second outstanding feature of Lewin's approach to the study of groups is the issue of *causation*. Most psychologists trace behavior to factors in time and seek the causal antecedents to a given situation. What happened before is usually the cause of what happens afterwards. Lewin sticks consistently to his "systematic causation" in regard to group behavior. He considers group behavior as a function of the total situation. The social-field-at-a-given-time offers the entire interpretation of group behavior. Simultaneous interrelationships are causal relationships, and group behavior can be causally derived from the totality of coexisting factors.

The third principle in Lewin's theory of group behavior lies in the application of topological and vector concepts to the group, in close analogy to the topological and vector psychology of the individual. Regions, boundaries, barriers, forces, and valences are applied to groups with no reservation whatsoever.

Forces within the Group

There has been some confusion in the definition of group. Group has been defined as a number of individuals who share some common traits, or have some common norms, or other similarities.

Lewin distinguishes between class and group. People who have the same or similar traits can be said to belong to the same category or class. Similarity in traits, or even goals, is not a prerequisite of a group.

Groups are characterized by the *dynamic interdependence* of their members. This means that the state and actions of each member depend on the state and actions of other members. A group can be represented best as a system of connected regions or as a differentiated region. A person's status within the group can be topologically represented as the position of his

[58] Ibid., p. 200.

region as related to other regions (members) of the group. This dynamic interdependence of regions (members) within a group resembles the dynamic interdependence of the respective regions within a person.

Any group is exposed to cohesive and disruptive forces. The disruptive forces may result from (1) too strong barriers between the members of the group that hamper communication within the group, or (2) conflict of the individual's goals with those of the group.[59]

Each group is a field of forces. Individuals are attracted to or repelled from a group depending on the kind of valence the group represents to them. Interaction and communication within a group depend on the mutual position of its regions, which represent the respective group members, the barriers between the members, and other factors. The "we-feeling" of a group is represented as a force corresponding to the needs of the group as a whole. Cohesiveness of a group depends on the relationship between the forces that attract the members and the forces that repel or disrupt. If a group is in a position to satisfy the needs of its members, it has a positive valence, the term "valence" being used in the same connotation as in the psychology of an individual.

Morale of an individual and of a group depends on "time perspective." It is related to the hope that "sometime in the future the real situation will be changed so that it will equal my wishes." Hope means similarity between the level of expectation and the unreality level of wishes. "Tenacity in the face of adversity is the most unequivocal index of high morale. Group morale depends on 'time perspective,' " said Lewin.[60]

Social Climate, Leadership, and Group Decision

Lewin, Lippitt, and White[61] conducted experiments in "social climate." They established two children's clubs and induced in them a "social climate" of democracy and autocracy respectively. Later, they developed three "climates," namely, democracy, autocracy, and laissez-faireism.

Each group was composed of five children equated in regard to age, intelligence, and physical and socioeconomic status, with proper consideration given to balanced social relations within the groups. The behavior of each group was determined by specially trained leaders. The "democratic" leader cooperated with group members and encouraged group discussion and decision. The "autocratic" leader made all decisions himself and gave orders to group members. The laissez-faire leader remained passive, allowing the children to do whatever they pleased. The "social climate" of each

[59] John R. P. French, "The Disruption and Cohesion of Groups," *Journal of Abnormal and Social Psychology*, 1941, *36*, 361–377.

[60] Kurt Lewin, *Resolving Social Conflicts* (G. W. Lewin, Ed.), Harper, 1948, p. 105.

[61] Ronald Lippitt, "An Experimental Study of the Effect of Democratic and Authoritarian Group Atmospheres," *Iowa University Studies in Child Welfare*, 1940, *16*, 44–195; Benjamin B. Wolman, "Education and Leadership," *Teachers College Record*, 1958, *59*, 475–473.

group was actually created by its leader. In the democratic group children were friendly to one another. The feeling of group belongingness was stronger in the democratic than in the autocratic club. The democratic group as a whole had greater potency, and children in that group were less aggressive toward each other. In the authoritarian group the children were rather aggressive; they attacked one child and this "scapegoat" had to leave the group. The laissez-faire social climate was introduced by a leader who let the children do whatever they pleased, himself offering very little encouragement and guidance. The cohesiveness of this group was quite low and its efficiency limited.

The main idea of the experiment was that group behavior depends on a social climate which can be artificially induced by the leader. The same idea has been applied by Lewin and his associates in several other settings.

Lewin also conducted experiments in group decision.[62] In one of them he tried to change deeply established food habits. Two methods were used: lecturing and group discussion. A follow-up study showed that only 3 percent of the housewives participating in the lecture group shifted to the new kind of food as compared to 32 percent who changed food habits as a result of group discussion.

Similar results have been obtained with rural mothers in a maternity hospital. Twenty percent of the mothers who were approached individually by the nutritionist about the value of feeding their infants cod-liver oil followed the instruction, as a follow-up study two weeks later proved. The mothers who received the same information in a group, discussed it, and decided to follow it, gave better results; 45 percent of them were feeding the infants cod-liver oil.

Lewin interpreted his findings with the help of two factors. First, group pressures do not permit easy change in habits. It is much easier to change a habit if the entire group participates. Second, group discussion activates the group members and more forces are made available for a change in behavior.

Intergroup Relations

Lewin also applied topology to studies of intergroup relations and ethnic tensions, representing each group as a region. A minority group in a given country may live as a closed group or it may be scattered all over the country. In the first case, minority group A corresponds to a connected limited region within enclosing region B. In the second case, the scattered group is topologically a nonconnected region.[63]

Lewin exemplified his theory using the history of Jews. The ghettos formed a connected limited region within the enclosing region of the Gen-

[62] Kurt Lewin, "Group Decision and Social Change," in T. Newcomb and E. Hartley (Eds.), *Readings in Social Psychology*, Holt, 1947.
[63] Kurt Lewin, "Psycho-Social Problems of a Minority Group," *Character and Personality*, 1935, 3, 175–187.

tile world. Jews came in contact with one another, without having "much contact with the rest of the population." The abolishment of ghettos necessarily changed the topological structure of the Jewish minority, making them a scattered group and a nonconnected region. Quite a bit of Jewish security feeling and cohesiveness was lost in the new situation.

Lewin distinguishes communication from locomotion. Locomotion must be represented as a path, while communication is considered a region or a part of it. Though communication between the various parts of the Jewish population was not impaired much, locomotion and interaction were hampered.

Minority groups enjoy less freedom of movement than the majority group. Regions or areas of activity are restricted and barriers of prejudice and discrimination prevent free movement. Thus, minority groups suffering from restriction of their "space of free movement" may become aggressive. This also applies to children or adolescents whose space of free movement has been restricted by powerful adults.

Social relations are not stationary; Lewin calls them *quasi-stationary* processes. For example, a degree of discrimination against a minority group indicates the interaction between two parts of a population. Certain social forces move toward more discrimination, while other forces may oppose it. A change in the quasi-stationary equilibrium may mean a change from the present level to the desired one, and this is how research and action can be combined. Lewin has always stressed that action requires a sound theory for action, and that theory should be applicable to action. Once the social psychologist understands the forces which cause intergroup tensions, he can, by manipulating them, alleviate the tension or even remove it. Lewin was very optimistic concerning the role social psychology might play in human relations.

Human attitudes and beliefs are a product of belonging to a group and sharing its social norms. These beliefs, once established, are quite consistent and it is almost impossible to influence an individual's mind unless a proper change in the social climate of his group takes place.

Therefore, the reeducation of a nation (Lewin referred to the de-Nazification of Germany) requires deep changes in the social norms of the entire nation. "It is obviously hopeless to change the cultural patterns of millions of people by treating them individually," said Lewin. "Fortunately, the methods generally called 'group work' permit reaching whole groups of individuals at once and, at the same time, seem actually to be more efficient in bringing about deep changes than the individual approach is." [64] An individual is more likely to accept new norms and patterns of behavior if this change encompasses his group as a whole and the new values and patterns do not jeopardize his group belongingness. The experiments on group decision mentioned above fully corroborate this hypothesis of a change in beliefs produced by influencing an entire group, according to Lewin.

[64] Lewin, *Resolving Social Conflicts*, pp. 40–41.

Personality and Culture

Personality changes with the change of the position of regions and other interrelations within the life space. Life space includes person and environment, and social factors form a substantial part of the environment and of the total life space of a person.

The individual is exposed to pressures of external forces and inner tensions resulting from a disequilibrium between himself and his environment. The kind of tensions produced by forces stemming from the social environment are of utmost importance for the development of the personality. Pressures that are too strong, as stated above, may compress the regions of personality and reduce their number. The structure of one's life space is highly dependent on these social forces, and since different cultures activate different kinds of pressures, one should conclude that personality type depends on culture.

Child-rearing practices represent social forces that mold personality. Each stage in child development represents a restructuring of the life space. "The change from the group of children to that of the adults is a shift to a more or less unknown position. Psychologically, it is equivalent to entering an unknown region, comparable to coming into a new town," said Lewin.[65] The child's "space of free movement" can be represented as a topological region surrounded by inaccessible regions. The barriers are either the child's inability to enter these regions or the prohibitions on entering them imposed by parents.

Adolescents belong to an overlapping region of children and adults. They do not wish to belong to the children group, but they are not yet accepted in the adult group. They are "marginal men" and, like all marginal men, are insecure, unstable, and hypersensitive.

The space of free movement allowed to a child varies from one culture to another. In pre-Nazi Germany this space was much narrower than it is in the United States. Differences in child-rearing methods have necessarily produced considerable differences in national characteristics. The German type of personality is more closed, less sociable, less inclined to informal and casual human relations than is the American personality type.

7. FIELD THEORY AS AN EXPERIMENT IN THEORY CONSTRUCTION

The Issue of Conceptualization

Lewin's field theory requires additional study from the angle of theory construction. His theory is undoubtedly a major contribution to psychological thought and especially to its top-level theory construction. Lewin never tried to cover the entire field of psychological research, nor did he develop a full-fledged "system" like Freud's. What he had in mind was a sys-

---

[65] Lewin, *Field Theory in Social Science*, p. 137.

tem of very general concepts from which psychological empirical data could be derived by means of logical manipulation.

This is undoubtedly a legitimate procedure, and Lewin's theory offers a challenging example of theory construction. His method is hypothetico-deductive, like Hull's (cf. Chapter 4), but it is different from Hull's in its fundamental principles of theory construction.

Lewin's method of theory construction can be summarized briefly as follows: Theory is a system of concepts. These concepts are not classificatory but constructive and represent psychological reality as it is, including each individual and specific case. Representation of reality is the task of scientific theory in psychology. Lewin did not escape the pitfalls of this reasoning. He was not aware of the fact that conceptualization means classification; any time Lewin or his disciples talk about regions or boundaries, they do not talk about a given field but apply to a given situation some general concepts or categories. Lewin included a given situation in a *class* or category of similar situations to which it belongs. This procedure is contradictory to Lewin's bias against class theory, but any conceptualized system such as mathematics or syntax does operate with generalized terms or concepts; mathematics and syntax are class theories. Conceptualization means classification, since any concept is a logical procedure of giving a common *name* to one or more bodies, events, or symbols, by which any other body or symbol called by the same name is a member in the same class. Any object "belongs" to *several* classes owing to certain similarities or identical elements; classification may be more or less conducive to developing knowledge, but any system of knowledge starts with grouping similar objects into classes and creating general concepts.

This is the *nominalist* notion of concept. Surely Lewin and other contemporary psychologists would not subscribe to the *realist* notion of concepts, which attaches separate and independent existence to general concepts like the idea of speed or the idea of warmth—independent, that is, of all given and empirically perceived speeds or temperatures. Speed and warmth are general concepts derived from phenomena grouped together under a common name. Obviously, psychologists operate with concepts derived from empirical observations by means of abstraction, generalization, and formation of *classes*. These concepts serve as the common names for all objects included in the class, and the various objects are *designates* of the common name or concept.

Lewin's conceptualization is self-contradictory. To be consistent, he should have denied the existence of any psychological laws at all, since each situation contains everything. Actually he generalizes, and puts similar situations like "punishment," "regression," and "tension" under a common heading, whereas he should have discussed the punishment of a certain child, regression in a given personality, or tension in a particular organism.

Conceptualization is abstraction, generalization, and classification and nothing else. In the early stages of scientific development, this was regarded as the scientific procedure. Surely it is one of the first steps of scientific inquiry, because scientific research tries to see the general despite the particular and to grasp the general law despite the unique cases (see Chapter 15).

Lewin opposed the Aristotelian notion of classification based on external appearance. In his paper on Aristotle, Lewin stated that "these classifications lose their importance" and today we seek "to classify the whole field on the basis of other, essentially functional differences." [66] This is exactly what is taking place in all sciences, and Lewin was aware of it. Unfortunately, in his later writings Lewin seems to have lost this conception and to have given up the idea of any classification at all.

The "revolt" against Aristotle is oversimplified by Lewin. Aristotle's concept formation was corrected by Galileo but not rejected. In the course of scientific inquiry, more economic and more valuable classifications have been introduced. In botany, for example, instead of division of plants into trees, bushes, and flowers, a division has been introduced based on genetic laws. The new division is not a denial of classification, nor is it field theory. It is simply more convenient methodologically because it enables us to discover some valid relationships between the objects of study and facilitates new and promising abstractions, generalizations, and classifications. No one can say that Aristotelian division was "false"; it was uneconomical because it left some gaps and overlaps and it was rather futile because it did not help to discover relevant causal factors. This is why Aristotelian classifications have been abandoned and replaced by more scientific classifications. However, the most important Aristotelian contention, which says that no single object has any meaning whatsoever unless referred to "an abstract term applicable to other individuals," is still valid. [67]

The other pitfall in Lewin's method of theory construction is his belief that presentation equals interpretation. Lewin was probably misled by the shift in physics from the search for the "nature" of things to a more functional approach. Instead of seeking in vain for the "true nature" of fire, scientists now know fairly well the processes that take place within the observable phenomenon of fire.

Lewin interpreted this shift as if representation meant interpretation. Representation, like the shift from the phenotypes to the genotypes, may be a useful step in theory construction and sometimes it offers a better and more convenient setup for derivation of the causal relationship. However, presentation per se is never a theory; it is, if properly done, a step leading toward the theory, but it is not the theory itself.

Field as a Construct in Psychology

"The psychological field," explained J. F. Brown, [68] "is a *space* construct to which descriptions of psychological behavior may be ordered. Space is a

[66] Lewin, *Dynamic Theory of Personality*, p. 5.

[67] Cf. Morris R. Cohen, *Reason and Nature*, Harcourt, Brace, 1931, p. 13.

[68] Brown, "On the Use of Mathematics in Psychological Theory," *Psychometrika*, 1936, *1*, 7–15, 77–90.

manifold in which *positional relationships* may be expressed. In general the manifold may be *continuous* or *discrete,* and position may be defined in terms of *distance* and *direction* as in *Euclidean* space or only in terms of relation as in *topological* space." "In the language of constructs, there is a vector in the psychological field, activating the rat (man) towards the goal (cheese or the solution of the problem). Both the organism and goal are to be ordered to positions in the psychological field. . . . The value of this vector depends on its position in the field. . . . But the magnitude which must be assigned to position within the psychological field is non-metricized. *Point values in the psychological field are not yet metricized in character while those in physical fields are metricized."*

"Not yet," said Brown. "Certainly at the present time," said Lewin, "there are no metrical determinations available concerning psychological life space. . . . not only the concept of distance but also that of direction goes beyond purely topological determinations. As a matter of fact the determination of directions in the psychological life space is as difficult as that of distance."

Is *field* a convenient construct in psychology? Lewin answered that psychological theory is a system of concepts which determine causal relationships. Causal relationships in human behavior must include both general laws and individual cases, and encompass both person and environment. Field theory and no other theory can meet these requirements.

Two problems are brought together here. Lewin could never rid himself of the dichotomy postulated by Windelband. Lewin never realized that all phenomena are idiophenomena and that, in spite of this, science deals with abstraction and generalization; there is no need for special techniques to deal with special cases.

The second problem is personality versus environment. Undoubtedly one cannot give a full account of a person's behavior without considering environment. However, Lewin never brought any evidence to deny the fact that each individual has certain abilities and personality traits due to heredity and not to environment; and there is no reason not to deal with human behavior as the result of interaction between heredity and environment.

Lewin felt that the use of the field theory in psychology was justified by the nature of psychological phenomena and field phenomena. But how did Lewin know that this is precisely the nature of psychological happenings? His theory is a logical conclusion drawn from this assumption. Yet he never brought any evidence to that effect and actually, he begged the principle. Surely he could have made any hypothetical assumption, but this should have been made explicit. He could have said, for example, that psychological phenomena are idiophenomena. That kind of statement in an empirical science requires either empirical proof or methodological approval. Empirical proof could follow a pattern such as this: Suppose such-and-such is the nature of psychological phenomena; then comes a series of observations, experimentations, or other truth-discovering procedures; finally comes the conclusion that our hypothetical statement has been verified or at least strongly supported by our investigation and can, therefore, be accepted in our system. Unfortunately, Lewin assumed that, on the basis of language usages like "approaching" and "striving," psychological phenomena are field-theoretical, and he concluded that field theory is best suited to deal with these phenomena.

Psychological field already has two connotations in gestalt theory. One is reality as perceived by the individual; the other is the brain and the environment, called sometimes the dynamic field and other times a psychological field. The first connotation is *perceptual* only, while the latter forms a part of the reductionist notion of mind (mind as a field) introduced by gestalt psychologists (see Chapter 12).

Kurt Lewin added his own interpretation. Psychological field means "a totality of coexisting facts." This is usually identified with life space, which means the total sum of possible activities of an individual. The two notions, though similar, are by no means identical. If psychological field is defined as a field which includes all facts that have an effect on an individual, there should be no objection to having such a term, but this term may prove of little use, for it may include practically everything.

The conception of a "psychological field at a given time" may lead to some difficulties, because a given time may be a small fraction of time. Lewin is aware of this danger of breaking behavior into microcosmic units, and he sets arbitrarily "sufficient units of time"; which is not a very precise statement. The criticism of Lewin's "historical approach" was raised by Gardner Murphy.

> Let the time on the chronoscope gradually reduce to zero and try to imagine just what is "going on" in the organism in zero duration. Indeed, the typical Lewinian experiments, . . . deal with transformations in time, as must all experiments on the functions of living individuals. Moreover, the difference between short time and long time durations can scarcely be elevated to a position of such tremendous importance.[69]

Lewin said that the level of aspiration is "influenced by the ability of the individual." But what exists before: abilities or the level of aspiration? Obviously, the level of aspiration is a result in the measuring of "historical causality" so much disliked by Lewin. However, how can Lewin admit the term "ability"? How can ability be squeezed into life space or field-at-a-given-time?

At best, field theory can operate with momentary and overt actions in an ultra-behaviorist manner. Innate capacities or acquired abilities, drives and motivational patterns, all of which exist persistently and evidence themselves in the constancies of human behavior, cannot be reached by a field theory.

[69] Gardner Murphy, *Historical Introduction to Modern Psychology* (rev. ed.), Harcourt, Brace, 1949, p. 305.

Lewin's Mathematics

Lewin tried to fit psychology into geometry. It was a difficult and unrewarding task. Human behavior does not fit into either Euclidean geometry or the Riemannian system, so Lewin tried topology. He did not know much about it and was aware that he was using a not very convenient tool, as he wrote: "The mathematical concepts allow us to distinguish only connected and nonconnected regions. In terms of topology there are no transitional cases. Dynamically, however, there are doubtless transitions between completely dependent and completely independent regions."[70] The main difficulties arose out of the difference between mathematical "boundary" and psychological "barrier." The issue of personality represented as a system of regions creates additional difficulties in using topology. Are the various regions that form personality independent regions or are they subparts of one region?

Lewin knew very well that often one had to make arbitrary decisions while trying to adjust psychological (dynamic) facts to topological concepts. Moreover, one of the most important features in Lewin's psychology, the concept of direction, is left out by topology. "Although topological principles are necessary, in themselves, they are not sufficient to determine directions," Lewin wrote, and so he felt compelled to introduce a new mathematical system, "hodology." Lewin admitted that he was not a mathematician and did not "axiomatize" his geometry. He hoped, however, that this "could well be done later on by a more competent mathematician."

But this has not been done and perhaps cannot be done. At any rate, how can one "explain" psychological data by a vague and not elaborated proposal for a mathematical system? "The purpose of hodological space is to find," says Lewin, "a type of geometry which permits us to use the concept of direction in a manner which will correspond essentially with the meaning that direction has in psychology."

But the concept of "direction" in psychology has to be interpreted or derived from mathematical constructs. These mathematical constructs have to be introduced as part of a mathematical system. They cannot be found in any of the existing mathematical systems. Lewin knew that they had to be defined and axiomatized by a competent mathematician, and all this has not been done. In the meantime he has developed a psychological system based on these as yet nonexisting mathematical foundations.

Lewin may be considered a victim of his love for mathematics. His was a creative mind, unusually productive, ingenious, alert, and stimulating. His works contain virtually hundreds of daring and challenging ideas about such relations as those between perception and motivation, regression and dedifferentiation, level of aspiration and satisfaction, group decision and change of social norms. His experimental techniques are ingenious, thought provoking, and realistic, and pave the road for new research.

[70] Lewin, *Principles of Topological Psychology*, p. 173.

Yet one is tempted to raise the question: What is the relationship between the tremendous experimental work done by Lewin and his disciples
and Lewin's theory? Most of Lewin's findings about level of aspiration,
group dynamics, regression, recall in tension, satiation, and other topics,
could be interpreted easily without topology.

In fact, topology has imposed heavy and unnecessary restrictions on
Lewin's studies. Wherever he tried to force his findings into the narrow
frames of topology, he did injustice to himself and impaired his own work.
Neither Lewin nor his associates ever made any mathematical operations
using the topological or hodological systems. At best, topological and vector
symbols were used as a *means* of communication, and even this in a kind of
private language which shortened good English words and made them understandable to a limited number of interested followers. Lewin's mathematics is merely a system of symbols, not real mathematics, since there are
no rules as to how these symbols can be manipulated in any arithmetic or
algebraic operations. Lewin did not go beyond the stage of definitions and
graphic presentation of his system and did not establish rules for mathematical operations with his symbols. Therefore, his mathematics can hardly
be called mathematics at all.

At any rate, even the best-elaborated system of symbols, such as a language or mathematics, serves only for the presentation and communication
of truth; it does not discover any truth and cannot be regarded as scientific
theory.

Systematic Causality

Lewin suggested the distinction between two types of causality, neither being causality in any of the accepted terms. Any definition of causality includes at least two phenomena, sequence in time, called by John
Stuart Mill "the unconditional, unvariable antecedent," and result, the "invariable, certain and unconditional sequence." Spinoza defined causality as
follows: "*Ex data causa determinata necessario sequitur effectus, et contra si
nulla detur determinata causa, impossible est, ut effectus sequetur.*"[71] ("Effect
follows a given determined cause; it is impossible for an effect to follow if
there is no such a determined cause.")

In the long and eventful history of the concept of causality, it has been
generally agreed that causality is some kind of temporal sequence. The controversial issue was whether causality involves anything besides this
sequence, and if it does, what does that additional factor involve? David
Hume fought against causality because he felt that all we know is the temporal sequence, and there is no reason or evidence to assume anything besides this sequence in time (*post hoc* but not *propter hoc*).

In modern physics, the usability of causality has been challenged. In
microcosmic physics the issue has been raised as to whether causality re-

[71] Benedictus Spinoza, *Ethica*, I, axiom 3.

tains its usefulness in view of the quantum theory. In all the discussions centering around causality, causation is considered a peculiar type of sequence in time which may or may not enable us to make predictions.[72]

Lewin believed that representation of a given situation plus application of proper laws is *systematic causation* "which permits the derivation of the next phenomena, while the historical causality gives an account of what happened but once."

No causal studies fit into Lewin's second category of just telling about the past, nor in the first category, which "refers to types and to laws in which there are no dates."

All causal studies deal with phenomena which have place and date, insofar as they deal with *individual causation*, which happened once, or *types* or classes of objects or events if they deal with general laws of causation. For example, Mr. A, had a breakdown because his life history was such and such, and he suffered from too great a conflict; this is individual causation. Many people have a breakdown when their life history is a given kind and the stress is too great; this is a law of general causation which deals with a class or type of people. What Lewin suggested as a "systematic" causality is not causation but interpretation, which may or may not be causal.

Explanation or derivation is not necessarily equivalent to causality. One can use a reverse causal relation as explanation; for example, there were clouds because later there was rain. Raining is not the cause of the clouds, but it is a good logical explanation by *implication*. Explanation is not necessarily related to time, while causality is. Explanation can be teleological, based on classification.

Similarly, one has to reject the identification of mathematical function with causality. Function indicates that whenever *a* changes, *b* changes and vice versa. Obviously it holds true in causality, because any causal system can be represented as a mathematical function. But the reverse is not true. There are many mathematical functions which are not causal—for example, two effects from the same cause, or two factors which stand in no time relation to each other.

Lewin insisted that past events cannot be a cause of present ones because the past does not exist any more, and only what exists has effects. If Lewin is right, psychological life space may be a cause of behavior of an individual, but it cannot be a result of anything else, because the life space is the totality of present factors (personality and environment). Lewin did not go to this extreme. He did acknowledge historical causality. "Past events can only have a position in the historical causal chains whose interweavings create the present situation."[73] And yet (on the same page) Lewin said: "Past events cannot influence present events." The difference is in approach: in "historical" causation they can influence events, in the sys-

[72] Cf. Benjamin B. Wolman, "Chance: A Philosophical Study," *Tarbitz, Hebrew University Quarterly* (Hebrew), 1938, *10*, 56–80.
[73] Lewin, *Principles of Topological Psychology*, p. 35.

tematic they cannot. One wonders why two contradictory notions of the same term were used, one of them generally accepted (historical causation) and the other contradicting the general notion as well as the first one used in the same theory. Lewin defined existence by causality and causality by existence, which sounds tautological.

Lewin used the following example: He would like to know whether the floor of his attic is strong enough to support a certain weight. He may, in this case, follow two procedures. The first would be an anamnesis, or a life history. This anamnesis has to test the properties of the attic in the past and, which is more difficult, to prove that nothing unknown happened to the attic. If he has done both, and, in the case of changes, if he knows the nature of the changes, he may get a satisfactory test. But a much better method of testing the strength of the floor would be to test its present situation.

This example indicates a confusion between interpretation and causation. Causation can be used as interpretation, but there are other methods of interpretation besides causality. What Lewin had in mind is a diagnosis without causal studies, which is often undertaken. A Rorschach or Stanford–Binet tests the present situation and is a quite reliable diagnostic tool. However, successful therapy requires more than an analysis of the "situation-at-a-given-time." The genetic and causal factors that lie in the past are needed for understanding of the situation-at-a-given-time and, needless to say, are extremely important for the proper therapeutic procedure. In fact, without full understanding of the *etiology*, any treatment is more guesswork than scientific procedure. Scientific inquiry is not only the description or analysis of the situation-at-a-given-time, as Lewin suggested, but the assessment of the *dynamic, causal* factors that precede and cause the given situation.

Here we come to the source of the main weakness of Lewin's theory. Lewin painstakingly developed a system of concepts and constructs and initiated a series of most ingenious and important experiments. Yet his theory falls short of being a dynamic interpretation of behavior inasmuch as it is a field theory. Why, for example, do groups behave differently? Why do people have different potentialities? Lewin's answer, the total situation, merely repeats the questions but offers no answer. Lewin's "situation" or "field" includes cause and effect together and does not permit causal studies that distinguish clearly between cause and effect.

Concluding Remarks

The ingenious experiments of Lewin and his pupils and associates are an important contribution to psychological research. Studies of interrupted tasks, substitution, level of aspiration, regression as a result of frustration, and group dynamics represent a weighty addition to psychological data and thought. One may ask whether these and other findings could not be established without field theory or topological and hodological systems. Certainly one can accept the validity of the experiments and utilize their findings without accepting Lewin's mathematics. It is not too difficult to incorporate Lewin's experimental heritage into the great treasury of psychological research, without considering it the logical result of or derivation from Lewin's field theory. The findings stand on their own merits, and, as many friendly critics have pointed out, Lewin's experiments may outlive his general theory.

However, Lewin's theoretical work should not be underestimated. The idea of field theory can be utilized in furthering psychological research. Several psychologists have faced the difficulty of the cause-goal dichotomy, for example, Freud and Adler, Watson and McDougall. Freud and Watson postulated deterministic causality, while Adler and McDougall sought the purpose of human behavior.

Kurt Lewin's solution to the problem is remarkable. In fact, this problem is already solved by Lewin's definition of behavior as locomotion caused by forces. Psychological forces could be either scalars or vectors. Obviously they are vectors; they are directed entities. Thus, Lewin combines in vector psychology both causal and purposive interpretation.

Lewin's emphasis on the interrelationship between intellectual processes and goals has opened new vistas in psychological research. Lewin tied cognitive structure to valences, or perception to motivation. All intellectual processes are determined by purposes, said Lewin, and no research in perception can overlook this point (see Chapter 16).

The theory of learning is much indebted to Lewin. His incorporation of perceptual factors in learning and his explanation of the organization factor in perception seem to have permanent value in the theory of learning.

In group dynamics Lewin was a pioneer and inventor of new and realistic research techniques. His experiments with groups in action suggested new possibilities for experimental work in social psychology. His slogan of uniting research and action has been extremely rewarding. Actually, Lewin has contributed most in spotting new areas of research and new possibilities. Perhaps this contribution is more important and more valid than his efforts to create a system of psychological laws. Some critics doubt whether Lewin defined any laws or developed a full-fledged theory. "Laws," said Spence, "are statements of relations between *independently defined variables*." Lewin's formula $B = f(P, E)$, meaning behavior is a function of person and environment, seems to overlook the problems involved in the usual formula $R = f(S)$.

Spence concluded: "That this field approach to the problems of psychology has been fruitful and valuable is amply supported by the experimental contributions it has made, although in the writer's opinion, the theoretical superstructure has played a much less significant role than is sometimes credited to it."[74]

One is tempted to compare the role of Lewin in the history of modern psychology not to that of Galileo, but to that of Heraclitus in ancient philosophy. The Ionian philosophers were concerned with the nature of things, while Heraclitus maintained that the only continuum is change. This is what Lewin tried to introduce into psychology: "The center of interest shifts from *objects to processes*, from state to change of state."

[74] K. W. Spence, "The Nature of Theory Construction in Contemporary Psychology," *Psychological Review*, 1944, *51*, 47–68.

14

Humanistic Psychology

1. THE HUMANISTIC MOVEMENT

The humanistic movement in psychology represents an attempt by a diverse group of theorists to extend the scope of psychology and personality theory beyond the areas of behaviorism and psychoanalysis. In its efforts to provide alternatives to these two long-standing areas of psychological thinking, the humanistic movement has come to be known as a "third force" in psychology. This term was introduced by Abraham Maslow, a major proponent of this movement. Theorists such as Erich Fromm, Gordon W. Allport, Henry A. Murray, Kurt Goldstein, Andras Angyal, Abraham Maslow, Gardner Murphy, and Carl Rogers, to name a few, are highly individual in their own work, and their theories have little in common. However, all these psychological thinkers have stressed the uniqueness of the individual and believe that the improvement of the human condition is at least theoretically possible. Indeed, all of them hold a fundamentally optimistic view of human potentialities and maintain that traditional scientific approaches with their limited and fragmented view of the individual have obscured the actual range of human capacities. Many of these theorists agree that man is living a constricted and unsatisfying life, particularly because he is not in touch with areas of his awareness which are vital aspects of his humanity. Therefore, Eastern philosophy, with its emphasis on higher states of consciousness and other aspects of creativity and self-actualization, has become a legitimate area of psychological investigation. Moreover, greater self-awareness and fulfillment have been suggested as the foremost goals in psychotherapy, education, and day-to-day living.[1]

Kurt Goldstein, who was the most influential proponent of the organismic approach, can also be considered one of the forerunners of the humanistic movement because of his emphasis on the individual as an integrated, holistic unit. Goldstein, along with Angyal, Maslow, Murray, and Rogers,

---

[1] William Thetford and Helen Schucman, "Other Psychological Personality Theories," in A. N. Freedman, H. I. Kaplan, B. J. Sadock (Eds.), *Comprehensive Textbook of Psychiatry* (2nd ed.), Williams and Wilkins, 1975, pp. 687–688.

was among the founders of the Association for Humanistic Psychology.[2] At its founding in 1962, A. J. Sutich made the following statement:

> Humanistic psychology may be defined as the third branch of the general field of psychology (the two already in existence being the psychoanalytic and the behaviorist) and as such is primarily concerned with those human capacities and potentialities that have little or no systematic place, either in positivist or behaviorist theory or in classical psychoanalytic theory; e.g., love, creativity, self, growth, organism, basic need-gratification, self-actualization, higher values, being, becoming, spontaneity, play, humor, affection, naturalness, warmth, ego-transcendence, objectivity, autonomy, responsibility, meaning, fair-play, transcendental experience, psychological health, and related concepts. This approach can also be characterized by the writings of Allport, Angyal, Asch, Bühler, Fromm, Goldstein, Horney, Maslow, May, Moustakas, Rogers, Wertheimer, etc., as well as by certain aspects of the writings of Jung, Adler, and the psychoanalytic ego-psychologists, existential and phenomenological psychologists.[3]

Another major influence on the development of humanistic psychology is existential philosophy and the psychotherapy derived from it. Existentialism stems from the work of Kierkegaard and Nietzsche and stresses the significance of values and meaning in personality. Rollo May stated that "Existentialism is the endeavor to understand man by cutting below the cleavage between subject and object which has bedeviled Western thought and science since shortly after the Renaissance."[4] May believes that modern man's problem is his resistance to, avoidance of, and repression of concern with *being*. Moreover, this lack of concern threatens him with a loss of the sense of being, a situation which is fostered by collectivist and conformist trends in our culture. According to May, a partial solution to this problem is *intentionality* and *will*, which lead an individual toward experiencing his identity. Victor Frankl maintains that the modern individual suffers from "existential neurosis," stemming from the inability to find meaning in life. Frankl's therapeutic method, called *logotherapy*, is designed to help the individual to develop a more authentic system of values and to accept the responsibility to make choices.[5]

Under the influence of Goldstein's holistic theories, the philosophical concepts of the existentialists,[6] and some borrowing from the non-Freudian theories of Adler, Jung, Horney, and Fromm, who stressed the spiritual and social aspects of personality formation, humanistic psychologists have developed a variety of theories which express their particular view of man.

[2] *Ibid.*

[3] A. J. Sutich, American Association for Humanistic Psychology: Progress Report, 1962 (mimeo). (Reprinted in part in *Journal of Humanistic Psychology*, 1964, 4, 22.)

[4] Rollo May, Ernest Angel, and Henri Ellenberger (Eds.), *Existence: A New Dimension in Psychiatry and Psychology*, Basic Books, 1958, p. 11.

[5] S. Stansfeld Sargent, "The Humanistic Approach to Personality," in B. B. Wolman (Ed.) *Handbook of General Psychology*, Prentice-Hall, 1973, p. 818.

[6] Medard Boss and Gion Condrau, "Existential Psychoanalysis," in B. B. Wolman (Ed.), *Psychoanalytic Techniques*, Basic Books, 1967, pp. 443–470.

2. Andras Angyal

Angyal developed his holistic approach around the cental concept of the *biosphere*.[7] He defined the notion of biosphere as an actual realm of life which encompasses both the person and the environment, not as separate entities but as two aspects of the same reality. These aspects cannot be understood separately, nor does the concept of interaction adequately describe their interrelationship. In conscious experience, the individual distinguishes between these two aspects as the "I" and the "not I." The tension that arises between the two aspects provides the energy required for the necessary biospheric functions. Indeed, life itself is determined by the two components of self-regulation and external regulation. Personality represents a series of systems or holistic units of the biosphere. Any particular system represents a functional organization, shifting in order to meet the changing requirement of the changing biospheric organization. When a particular need arises, a part of the larger system differentiates out of the whole in order to meet the particular need. The very fluidity of biospheric systems represents the ongoing processes which allow for adaptive and integrated behavior.[8]

Angyal viewed life as a constant process of self-expansion, a sort of biospheric process of flow between the individual and the environment. The individual both gives and takes from the environment, and mental health is a result of a balance of autonomy and homonomy, that is, the processes of assimilation (taking) from and giving to the environment.

Angyal described personality organization in terms of his concepts of *universal ambiguity*. Every human being has traumatic and fortutious experiences in life which lead to the development of two different personality patterns, one representing personal adequacy and the other personal inadequacy. Ultimately, the individual's mental health, or lack of it, depends on which the two systems is predominant in the individual. Angyal seemed to believe that at any moment, the individual is either totally healthy or totally disturbed. Shifts between these two states do occur but they always remain separate, total entities. Anxiety is the individual's response to the nondominant pattern in his dual personality organization. For example, when the neurotic organization predominates, the individual is threatened by movements toward health and therefore develops defenses against health. However, Angyal believed that the healthy core of the individual can never be completely extinguished; it is "present potentially in its full power in the most destructive, most baneful, most shameful behavior."[9]

[7] Thetford and Schucman, *op. cit.*, pp. 697–699.
[8] *Ibid.*
[9] *Ibid.*

3. ABRAHAM MASLOW

Abraham Maslow was originally interested in animal behavior, but later in his life he began to question the adequacy of scientific psychology to describe human behavior and experience. He is considered the spokesman of the "third force" in psychology and was the leading exponent of humanistic psychology.[10]

Maslow, who was influenced by the self-actualization theory of Kurt Goldstein, did not intend to discard traditional methods of studying human behavior. Rather, he saw humanistic concepts as complementary methods, rather than as alternatives. Many important aspects of human function and levels of awareness have been neglected by traditional approaches because of the research difficulties they presented. These omissions might have resulted in the overlooking of certain relevant aspects of the individual. Maslow sought to remedy this situation by maintaining that individuality, consciousness, purpose, ethics, morality, goodness, beauty, authenticity, and identity, are scientifically respectable issues. Although it is difficult to approach these areas with precise research techniques, psychologists must not overlook their significance. Maslow believed that there had been an overemphasis on pathology in contemporary psychology. He suggested that much more could be learned from the study of healthy individuals who have overcome deficiencies and attained high levels of creativity and self-actualization.[11]

Maslow proposed that the *impulse to actualize* one's potential is an innate one. Every individual has two kinds of inherent needs. The first kind are the *D* or *deficiency needs* such as hunger and thirst, which must be met before they can be transcended. Maslow called the second kind of needs *B* or *being* needs, such as the needs for wholeness, uniqueness, and self-fulfillment. Basic needs must be met if the individual is to grow. A negative and frustrating environment, poor habits, or destructive attitudes can overcome the innate pressure to actualize one's inner potential. In some ways, D-needs and B-needs are in conflict, for D-needs require dependency on others, while B-needs require a certain independence and self-reliance.[12]

Maslow's main concern was the study of individuals who exemplified the ultimate in creativity and self-development. This did not necessarily mean that they were unusually gifted, but that they had developed their own capacities to the fullest. The study of these individuals enabled Maslow to develop a list of shared characteristics. The self-fulfilling individuals were usually realistically oriented, problem centered, accepting of themselves and others, spontaneous, independent, and creative. They identified with mankind and were able to transcend their environments. They all appeared to have had one or more mystical or ego-transcending experiences

---

[10] *Ibid.*, pp. 699–701.
[11] *Ibid.*
[12] *Ibid.*

which Maslow later termed *peak experiences*. He defined these experiences as episodic, brief occurrences in which the individuals experience themselves as suddenly transformed into full and transcending humanness. This kind of experience became a focal point for Maslow's work, for in such a state the individual achieves an "unmotivated, nonstriving, nonself-centered, purposeless, self-validating" orientation. In this peak experience, the individual realizes the ultimate of his humanness. While the experience is usually a brief one, it facilitates the individual's achievement of a sustained and lofty sense of living which transcends the ordinary ways of living. Maslow became convinced that he could demonstrate the positive view of man's inherent nature, and that faith in mankind is the crucial aspect of the "third-force" movement in psychology.

4. HENRY A. MURRAY

Murray introduced the term *personology*, which he defined as "the branch of psychology which principally concerns itself with the study of human lives and the factors that influence their course."[13] Since Murray defined personology as the science of man, he felt it to be the most inclusive area of psychology; other branches were, essentially, special areas within it. Moreover, the personologist must construct a theory of personality and devise special techniques for studying it.[14] Owing to his involvement in psychoanalysis, Murray sought to develop a health-oriented continuum of the "illness-oriented Freudian system."[15]

Murray defined personality as "the hypothetical structure of the mind, the consistent establishments and processes of which are manifested over and over again . . . in the internal and external proceedings which constitutes [sic] a person's life."[16] Murray saw personality as an ever-changing process, a sort of continual compromise between the person's own desires and impulses and those of others. Personality represented the integrated and independent processes operating as a whole, a unity made possible because the processes of personality represent organizations in the brain. This emphasis on the centrality of the brain/personality relationship represented Murray's belief that personality cannot be separated from its biological roots.[17]

For the most part, Murray subscribed to a Freudian view of personality development. But he differed from this view in his belief that there are positive constructive aspects of the id, and that the ego has its own source of energy, a position held by ego psychologists such as Hartmann, among

[13] *Ibid.*, pp. 693–695.
[14] *Ibid.*
[15] *Ibid.*
[16] *Ibid.*
[17] *Ibid.*

others. Murray maintained that the *process* of tension reduction is basically more satisfying to the individual than its outcome, that is, than the actual reduction of tension.[18]

Murray is particularly known for his development of the Thematic Apperception Test, or TAT, an extremely valuable projective device which is presently included in almost every battery of psychological tests. Through the use of the TAT, Murray delineated the *thema* of a particular force coming from the outside and the *form* in which this force is interpreted by the individual. Murray felt that adult behavior can be represented by thema linked to early childhood. These thema represented to Murray the proper unit of study of the personality.[19]

5. J. F. T. BUGENTAL

Bugental proposed five basic tenets of humanistic psychology:

> *Man, as man, supercedes the sum of his parts.* He must be recognized as something other than an additive product of various part functions.
> *Man has his being in a human context.* The unique nature of man is expressed through his always being in relationship with his fellows.
> *Man is aware.* All aspects of his experience are not equally available to man, but awareness is an essential part of man's being.
> *Man has choice.* When man is aware, he is aware that his choices make a difference and that he is not a bystander but a participant in experience.
> *Man is intentional.* Man intends through having purpose, through valuing, and through creating and recognizing meaning. Man's intentionality is the basis on which he builds his identity, and it distinguishes him from other species.[20]

Bugental maintains that humanistic psychology stresses the value of man, puts meaning ahead of procedure, seeks human validation as opposed to nonhuman validation, and sees all knowledge as relative. He stresses his indebtedness to existential philosophy by calling himself an existential analytical psychotherapist.

Bugental feels that all human beings should strive toward authenticity or "a way of being in the world in which one's being is a harmony with the being of the world itself." Only by achieving authenticity can man hope to resolve the subject/object split which pervades twentieth century life.[21]

6. GARDNER MURPHY

Gardner Murphy is, probably, the most open-minded, diversified and eclectic theoretician in the humanistic movement. He stressed the need for

[18] *Ibid.*
[19] *Ibid.*
[20] Sargent, *op. cit.*, pp. 819–822.
[21] *Ibid.*

integration of all relevant approaches in the investigation of man, including the psychology of the Far East.[22] Among his major contributions is the *biosocial theory of personality*. Murphy sees the individual as "an inner–outer structure which is the product of a particular organism–culture interaction . . . [and] part of a still larger context, as an aspect not only of a community but of a cosmos."[23] He feels that the concept of a separate person is largely mythical, that personality represents an organism–environment field. In this aspect, his theory resembles Kurt Lewin's field theory concepts.

Murphy distinguishes three basic stages of development. At the beginning of life, the individual is in a state of *undifferentiated wholeness*. He proceeds from this state to the stage of *differentiation of function*, and then on to the stage of *integration*. The movement from stage to stage can be an uneven process, and regression is as possible as progression. The many individual personality differences are a result of the particular developmental patterns. Within each stage, particular functions peculiar to that stage are involved, which explains why the adult personality is not a mere extension of earlier stages. Adult personality is a product of the increasing complexity which comes with development. The various individual preferences, attitudes, and interests come out of the various ways in which the person has gratified his sensory and motor needs. Small wonder that human diversity is practically unlimited.[24]

Murphy considers the psychological dispositions or *organic traits* as the basic structural units. The personality characteristics which develop out of these organic traits are either channeled into specific forms of behavior or are redirected through conditioning. Murphy believes that learning is a fundamental aspect of personality development, but considers it to be the end-point of the organism–environment interactions. Motivated by four basic needs, namely, visceral, motor, sensory, and emergency, human personality undergoes a series of *canalizations*, Murphy's term for the process by which connections are made between a need and a specific way of satisfying it. Canalization thus represents the discharging of the energy of a need. Early canalizations, which are the bases for later ones, represent the kind of regressive behavior seen in adults during stressful experiences. Early bodily canalizations form what Murphy calls the *self*, or the unifying aspect of the personality. The self enables the individual to cope with disunities and disharmonies in interaction with the environment. Murphy distinguishes canalizations from conditioning by defining conditioning as a preparatory process that readies the person for change, while canalization actually causes changes in tension levels. Moreover, conditioned responses can easily be generalized, shifted, and extinguished, while canalizations are

[22] Thetford and Schucman, *op. cit.*, pp. 704–705.
[23] *Ibid.*
[24] *Ibid.*

much more permanent in nature. Together, these two processes account for both perceptual and behavioral learning.[25]

7. CARL ROGERS

Rogers' theory represents a synthesis of phenomenological, holistic, organismic, interpersonal, and self theories. The concept of *self* is the key element in Rogers' theory. As viewed by him, the self originates in the organism's interactions with the environment. It can be influenced by values borrowed from other people, but basically it represents the individual's striving for consistency. Every individual perceives experiences not consistent with the self as threats. However, the self is not a closed entity; it is capable of change through maturation and learning.[26]

In addition to the concept of self, Rogers' theory includes the idea of *organism*, which represents the totality of experience. The organism reacts to the phenomenological field as an organized whole. The basic motive of the organism is to actualize, maintain, and enhance itself. The organism is capable of either symbolizing experiences so that they remain conscious or denying them symbolization so that they remain unconscious. The phenomenological field may or may not be conscious, depending on the experiences which make up the field, whether they are symbolized or their symbolization is denied.

Rogers described the following concepts and their interrelationships in a series of nineteen propositions in his book *Client Centered Therapy*:[27]

1. Every individual exists in a continually changing world of experience of which he is the center.
2. The organism reacts to the field as it is experienced and perceived.
3. The organism reacts as an organized whole to this phenomenological field.
4. The organism has one basic tendency and striving: to actualize, maintain and enchance the experiencing organism.
5. Behavior is a basically goal-directed attempt of the organism to satisfy its needs as experienced, in the field as perceived.
6. Emotion accompanies and in general facilitates such goal-directed behavior; the kind of emotion being related to the seeking versus the consummatory aspects of the emotion, being related to the perceived significance of the behavior for the maintenance and enhancement of the organism.
7. The best vantage point for understanding behavior is from the internal frame of reference of the individual himself.
8. A portion of the total perceptual field gradually becomes differentiated as the self.
9. As result of interaction with the environment, and particularly as a result of evaluation interactions with others, the structure of self is formed— an organized, fluid, but consistent conceptual pattern of perceptions of

[25] *Ibid.*
[26] Carl Rogers, *On Becoming a Person*, Houghton Mifflin, 1961.
[27] Carl Rogers, *Client Centered Therapy*, Houghton Mifflin, 1951.

characteristics and relationships of the 'I' or the 'me' together with values attached to these concepts.

10. The values attached to experiences and the values which are a part of the self-structure, in some instances are values experienced directly by the organism, and in some instances are values introjected or taken over from others, but perceived in a distorted fashion, as if they had been experienced directly.

11. As experiences occur in the life of the individual, they are either (a) symbolized, perceived and organized into some relationship to the self, (b) ignored because there is no perceived relationship to the self-structure, (c) denied symbolization or given a distorted symbolization because the experience is inconsistent with the structure of the self.

12. Most of the ways of behaving which are adopted by the organism are those which are consistent with the concept of the self.

13. Behavior may, in some instances, be brought about by organic experiences and needs which have not been symbolized. Such behavior may be inconsistent with the structure of the self, but in such instances the behavior is not 'owned' by the individual.

14. Psychological maladjustment exists when the organism denies to awareness significant sensory and visceral experiences, which consequently are not symbolized and organized into the gestalt of the self-structure.

15. Psychological adjustment exists when the concept of self is such that all the sensory and visceral experiences of the organism are, or may be, assimilated on a symbolic level into a consistent relationship with the concept of the self.

16. Any experience which is inconsistent with the organization or structure of the self may be perceived as a threat, and the more of these perceptions there are, the more rigidly the self-structure is organized to maintain itself.

17. Under certain conditions, involving primarily complete absence of any threat to the self-structure, experiences which are inconsistent with it may be perceived and examined and the structure of self revised to assimilate and include such experiences.

18. When the individual perceives and accepts into one consistent and integrated system all his sensory and visceral experiences, then he is necessarily more understanding of others and is more accepting of others as separate individuals.

19. As the individual perceives and accepts into his self-structure more of his organic experiences, he finds that he is replacing his present value system—based so largely upon introjections which have been distortedly symbolized—with a continuing valuing process.

Rogers feels that his theory can be unified around three basic concepts: the need for positive regard; the need for self-regard; and conditions of worth.[28]

---

[28] Carl Rogers, "A Theory of Therapy, Personality and Interpersonal Relationships as Developed in a Client-Centered Framework," in S. Koch (Ed.), *Psychology: A Study of Science*, McGraw-Hill, 1959, Volume 3.

Summary of Part III

All the psychological systems described in the third part of the present volume faced the problems posed by Kant, Husserl, and Dilthey.

Thing versus person was the main problem discussed by W. Stern. Content versus act was the problem of Brentano and of Husserl. Sensory atomism versus organization was the problem of gestalt theory. Idiophenomena versus generalizations intrigued Lewin.

Chapter 10 deals mainly with Kant and Dilthey. Immanuel Kant's transcendental idealism created a grave problem for any future scientific inquiry. Psychology had to become either an "empirical" description of "mental phenomena" whose true existence could not be proved or an a priori epistemology dealing with the "transcendental subject" whose existence could be doubted.

The neo-Kantians struggled with the problems created by Kant. But obviously there is no solution to nonexisting problems. The cleavage between the "perceiving subject" and everything else created insurmountable difficulties for those psychologists who were influenced by Kant's heritage.

Dilthey's contribution has been more of a roadsign than a paving stone. His psychology is more of a hint than a statement, more an indication of scientific needs than their satisfaction. Dilthey suggested a way out. The natural sciences have to *explain* their phenomena using hypotheses; this does not apply to psychology, which has direct access to the mental process which are experienced (*erlebt*). The proper method of psychology is to *describe* mental life in its totality and to *understand* its aim and meaning.

Spranger's theory of personality types, which was actually a theory of types of culture (*Lebensformen*), implemented Dilthey's program. Spranger did not seek causes and effects or build a scientific system of hypotheses. Instead he suggested dividing humans into six types according to their preference for abstract truth (theoretical), material achievements (economic), mysticism (religious), beauty (aesthetic), sympathy for human beings (sociable), and power (political).

Chapter 11 describes the personalistic theories of E. Spranger, W. Stern, and G. W. Allport. As said before, Spranger was the only psycholo-

gist who fully implemented Dilthey's ideas of a descriptive and understanding psychology.

Stern's work was thorough and encompassing. Stern is one of the few
psychologists who developed an all-embracing system. He hoped to reconcile the two methods distinguished by Dilthey. According to Stern, personality is *unitas multiplex*. As long as we deal with the elements of this unity,
we may apply the explanatory method; wherever we deal with personality
as a whole, we must describe and understand.

Allport continued Stern's work with the main emphasis on *unity in
complexity*. He develped an original theory of "mental traits" and the idea
of "functional autonomy."

The first section of Chapter 12 describes several theories opposed to associationism. Some of them, especially those of Ward, Binet, and Bühler,
have often been called "the European functionalism." Their functionalism
resembles the American functionalism in its criticism of the atomistic molecular approach and of associationism.

The opponents of the simulus–response theories introduced the idea of
task, imageless thought, and preparatory set. A group of experimental psychologists led by Külpe and the so-called Würzburg school went even farther in the rejection of the notion that mental life is a series of reactions to
series of stimuli. Thought was the main area of interest in Würzburg, and
according to their school of thought, thinking was guided by a "task" and
"determining tendencies."

The main part of Chapter 12 is devoted to gestalt psychology and its
three great creators, Wertheimer, Köhler, and Koffka. Gestalt psychology
started as an opposition to atomism and associationism. The famous experiments on motion proved beyond a doubt that a series of still positions
could be perceived as one continuous motion.

Additional experimental studies led to the development of a new
theory of perception and learning. The organism does not react with isolated responses to isolated stimuli, but it responds as a whole to complex
patterns of stimulation. These patterns organize the parts into a whole,
shape, a figure, in German, a *Gestalt*.

Accordingly, learning cannot be a process of association or conditioning. It is a perceptual process of orientation in the patterns of environment.
Insight was the new term coined by the gestaltists, and it means grasping of
the gestalt of the situation, orientation in the totality of relationship, and
ability to act accordingly.

While Köhler studied learning, Wertheimer devoted a great deal of
time to the problems of thinking. Again, the organization, the grasp of the
structure of the situation, the gestalt was found to be the main factor in creative thinking.

Where does the gestalt come from? Gestalt psychologists faced an alternative: either to accept Kant's categories or Dilthey's synthetic ability of the
mind and ascribe the gestalt to the perceiving mind, or to ascribe the gestalt

to nature. They took an anti-Kantian stand and looked for "physical gestalts" everywhere, in inanimate and living nature.

The best model for a physical gestalt was the electromagnetic field. The human brain is not a machine but is such a field, concluded the gestaltists. Thus the organism responds with a total organized pattern of reactions to the pattern of stimuli with which it is exposed.

The next step the gestaltist took was to coordinate the mental and the neurological processes. The concept of *isomorphism* was the solution. Brain and behavior are two dynamic fields; the psychological field represents the neurological field in the same way as a geographic map represents a region.

Chapter 13 analyzes field theory. Kurt Lewin took over, almost literally, the idea of the psychological field, in which the individual and his present environment are the two poles. Being well educated in philosophy and always method-conscious, he proceeded to develop a system of hypothetical constructs. His studies represent a case in sophisticated theory construction, daring and ingenious, yet very open to empirical criticism.

Lewin was more influenced by the neo-Kantians Windelband and Cassirer than by any of the gestalt theorists. He looked for a scientific method capable of dealing with idiophenomena, and his solution was highly original.

Lewin invoked Galileo versus Aristotle, Windelband versus Comte, non-metricized topology versus any other mathematics, contemporaneity versus causation, and physical models of vectors versus biological motivation. His system was never completed, his mathematics never put to a test; his ingenious experiments discovered many significant solutions, but never offered a complete picture of his theory.

Lewin's main contribution seems to lie rather in posing penetrating questions than in offering satisfactory solutions. But his philosophical analysis of psychology as a science, his belief that to describe means to interpret, is undoubtedly a great challenge to the methodology of scientific inquiry in psychology. Thus, in the present volume, which emphasizes the theoretical and systematic approach to psychology, the chapter devoted to Lewin is one of the largest.

The problems raised by Kant, Windelband, and Dilthey have been answered in various ways. Spranger, Stern, the gestalt psychologists, and the field theory accepted the challenge of Dilthey, and the discussion of Dilthey's ideas and postulates forms the bulk of the above-mentioned theories. All of these dealt with problems posed by Dilthey, but each solved them in a different way. All have common roots and similar topics of discussion, but they differ in the answers they offer to the problems of *Kultur*, *Geist*, and *Naturwissenschaften*.

Chapter 14 describes humanistic psychology. It traces the humanistic origins to existentialism and Goldstein's holistic ideas, and describes the theories of Angyal, Maslow, Murray, Bugental, Murphy, and Rogers.

PART IV
Psychology and the Scientific Method

15

The Scientific Method

1. First Principles

Definition of Science

The term "science" denotes both a certain type of activity and the results of it. Often a distinction is made, and rightly so, between the *research* activity and the resulting *system*, both legitimately described as "scientific."

Scientific research is a human activity aimed at the discovery of truth. A scientific system is a system of propositions, statements, or sentences representing this truth.

Men can seek truth in various ways, but not all of them are scientific. If someone inquires about the price of a given car, he is obviously in search of the truth, yet neither the buyer nor the seller is a scientist. However, someone investigating the relationship between national income and the prices of cars is probably engaged in a scientific research which may lead toward a series of statements which form a scientific system or a part of it.

The scientific search for truth, the research, and the resulting scientific system evidently deal with a certain kind of truth and seek it in a certain manner. Science has no monopoly on truth; most of the statements we make in our daily life are truthful, but only a few of them are scientific. Research does not deal with the obvious.

The following criteria for a definition of science, derived from what sciences are like, are empirical, not a priori; they seek the common elements in research and systems of physics, astronomy, biology, and other sciences.

1. Scientific statements express a *discovery of truth*. They contain the best available information about things and about what happens to them. They express the results of the search for truth. Obviously, the definition of truth requires further clarification, which will be offered later on.

2. There is an *objective proof* or *evidence* for each scientific statement. Evidence is the mark that distinguishes between scientific and nonscientific statements. Scientific research is, to a great extent, an effort to bring evidence for the scientific statements or propositions. This evidence is *objec-*

tive, that is, independent of a given researcher; any other researcher should be able to verify, refute, or corroborate the statements. Scientific systems are not dogmatic; they change with the progress of research.

3. Scientific statements are *general,* or as general as the research in a given field warrants. The general concepts are a product of abstraction and classification; science groups things and events, classifies them, and seeks the most general truthful information concerning them. The more advanced sciences operate with highly generalized and abstract statements.

4. Scientific statements are *systematic.* They are put in a certain order depending on the objectives of the researchers, the nature of the subject matter, or the method of research. A mere collection of true statements does not form a science; a scientific system requires a certain order—premises, theorems, proof, or independent, dependent, intervening variables, or any other systematic arrangement.

5. Scientific statements go beyond the empirical data. They *interpret* the data and *infer* relationships between the observable things and events. They seek the *relationships,* whether causal, teleological, formal-logical (implication, inference), mathematical (e.g., functions), or any other.

6. These relationships are presented as a system of *hypotheses,* which express the *laws of nature* or a part thereof in a given area of research. The laws of nature, such as gravitation, evolution, osmosis, indicate the regularities of all happenings in the universe.

7. Scientific statements concerning present or past events lead to a correct *prediction* of future developments. The aim of scientific research is to discover the truth in order to predict future happenings. *"Savoir pour prévoir,"* said Auguste Comte, the father of positivism. Predictability is often used as a method of verification; when the scientist, knowing the present, correctly predicts the future, his knowledge of the present is confirmed.

8. Scientific statements are *applicable* to future research and to practical life. Applied sciences, technologies, and techniques rely on scientific inquiry and its results. Success in applied sciences, such as agriculture, medicine, and education, depends largely on their scientific foundations.

9. All sciences deal with things and with what happens to them (events). Thus all sciences are *empirical.* Nonempirical systems, such as mathematics and logic are not sciences. They are methods of research or methods of presentation (languages).

Sciences can be divided at will (depending on the purpose of those who divide them) into physics, chemistry, biology, sociology and history, or into social and biological or into sciences dealing with inanimate and animate nature.[1] Like any other classification (cf. this chapter, Section 2), the classification of sciences should be useful (serving some purpose) and economical (able to find a place for each item without unnecessary over-

[1] Carl G. Hempel, "The Logical Analysis of Psychology," in H. Feigl and W. Sellars, *Readings in Philosophical Analysis,* Appleton-Century-Crofts, 1949, p. 382.

lapping). Some classifications are better than others. Comte suggested the classification of sciences in the order of decreasing abstraction; psychology was not included in his system.[2] Windelband and Dilthey (cf. Chapter 10) excluded cultural sciences and humanities from the realm of the natural sciences, which was neither useful nor economical (cf. Section 2 of this chapter).

It has been proposed to include *all* sciences under the name of natural sciences, and to divide them into *descriptive* and *praxiologic* sciences.[3] The descriptive sciences would present their statements as true or false propositions; the praxiological sciences would deal with statements related to what and how to do. Obviously, the applied sciences are praxiologies; politics and ethics should be included among them.

Psychology is an empirical, descriptive science belonging to the group of biological sciences, since it deals with living organisms. It deals with them from a very peculiar and highly *controversial* point of view. Obviously, psychology has overlapping areas with physiology and sociology; its subject matter is behavior, or overt and covert behavior, or experiences of organisms. Whatever its limits, it seeks the truth in accordance with the nine principles stated above.

Epistemological Problems

There are various methods of ascertaining the truth, starting with naïve realism and ending with critical idealism, or even solipsism, and including various other methods such as critical realism and pragmatism. Naïve realism assumes that our senses never err; Kant's critical idealism assumed that they never tell the truth.

Some philosophers believe that they can determine the criteria of truth. Kant's critical idealism and James' pragmatism have been discussed in the present volume.

An assumption is made here that the world exists independently of the "perceiving subject" or of anyone who "thinks," "doubts," or "experiments." It does not seem too reasonable to assume that philosophers know more about the nature of the physical world than did Newton, Einstein, or Darwin.[4] Unless it is assumed that the world exists and man is a part of it, any further reasoning seems illogical. Any discussion of one biological species outside the context of nature is self-contradictory.

Whoever studies the nature of things and events must start with the assumption that he studies something; otherwise he is wasting his time. This assumption of the existence of the world, independent of man's knowledge of it, is the assumption of *radical realism*, which believes that the world does

[2] Auguste Comte, *Cours de Philosophie Positive*, (2nd ed.), Bailière et Fils, 1864.
[3] Benjamin B. Wolman, "Scientific Study of Educational Aims," *Teachers College Record*, 1949, 50, 471–481.
[4] Benjamin B. Wolman, "Theory of History," *Philosophical Review*, 1949, 46, 342–351.

not start or end with one of its species, called *Homo sapiens* or subject or mind or any other name. For if one doubts the existence of the world, there cannot be any reason to assume the existence of one species.

Man, like many other biological species, lives and acts or behaves. One of his actions is directed to the search for truth or the knowledge of things and events. James emphasized the usefulness of this action. Suffice it to say that "scientific research" is part of this action, guided by the principles described above. It is immaterial for our purposes to discuss the usefulness of research; even useless research is research.

Once we assume that man is a part of an existing world, we may ask *how correct his perception is,* and to what extent his propositions concerning the world or a part of it (even be it himself) correspond to what the world is.

Modern students of cognition theory, the epistemologists, distinguish two basic types of truth: *immanent* and *transcendent* truth. Immanent truth is assured whenever a system of propositions is free from inner contradictions. The geometrical system of Euclid represents such a system of statements based on immanent truth.

Some of the neo-positivists of the Viennese circle (*Wiener Kreis*) suggested relating any scientific inquiry to a system of logical propositions independent of empirical proof. Others, among them M. Schlick, in addition to immanent truth, introduced the principle of transcendent truth, that is, truth free from any contradiction with empirical data obtained by observation. The Warsaw logicians (*Szkola Warszawska*) insisted on transcendent truth as the criterion for scientific inquiry.

Mathematicians may be satisfied with immanent truth. Any other branch of human inquiry which deals with any part of reality, be it physics or astronomy, history or psychology, must insist on checking its statements against reality as empirically perceived by our sensory apparatus.

Obviously, an empirical science must accept the demands of epistemologic maximalism, as represented by Moritz Schlick and the Warsaw School. The maximalists are not satisfied with the "inner consistency" of a system of propositions interpreted as a "lack of inner contradictions." The world is a world of things, and science is the cognition of them.

T. Kotarbinski, in his classic work on logic,[5] has coined the term *reism*, understood as a conviction that only physical bodies actually exist. No one should attach the same type of existence to relationships, generalizations, and logical constructs. Logical constructs should be introduced as methodological help in the interpretation of what happens to the bodies.

Let us follow in the footsteps of Bertrand Russell. There are two types of propositions, the analytic and the synthetic or descriptive. *Analytic* statements are definitions. Definitions are arbitrary logical constructions that can be set at will. A definition is absolute or necessary only inasmuch as

[5] Tadeusz Kotarbinski, *Elementy Logiki, Teorji Poznania i Metodolgii Nauk,* (Polish), Warszawa, 1929.

those who apply it like to have it so. All mathematical propositions are actually symbolic definitions, freely constructed and operated according to the rules set by those who like to have those rules set. Euclidean geometry is a system of symbolic operations based on a set of arbitrarily set axiomatic statements. Once we accept some proposition, we may derive other propositions from it by manipulations performed according to arbitrarily set mathematical or logical rules. Having accepted a definition and determined the rules of the game, we may arrive at absolutely certain conclusions, such as, for instance, the formula that $(a + b)^2 = a^2 + 2ab + b^2$ or the Pythagorean law of a triangle, $a^2 = b^2 + c^2$.

Synthetic or *descriptive* propositions are statements about things and what is going on with them. These propositions result from our perception of nature and the interpretation of our perception. Obviously, they are neither "necessary" nor certain nor absolute. Only formal–logical and mathematical statements, based on arbitrary definitions and rules, are absolutely proved. No descriptive proposition has ever been absolutely proved. All descriptive and empirical sciences operate with synthetic propositions that are subject to change with the improvement of our perceptive tools and method and better understanding of the nature of things.[6]

Accepting Russell's explanations, one may say that the progress of scientific research depends on (1) improvement of our perceptual tools, by which we perceive things and events, and (2) improvement of our theoretical interpretation of the things and events.

Facts and Theories

Empirical sciences deal with their subject matter on two levels. First come the *data,* as perceived by our senses with the help of the tools that make perception more testable, more accurate, and more precise. Then science has to *interpret* the data and, going beyond empirical studies, to formulate a *theory.* A theory without facts is a useless speculation, said D. Hume. But data without a theory is not a science either, said Poincaré; they are merely catalogues or inventories of facts, not scientific systems.

A theory is a result of carefully amassed, scrutinized, and analyzed empirical data. A theory that contradicts these data is meaningless, say the epistemological maximalists, who require that theory be free from both inner contradictions (immanent truth) and contradictions with reality (transcendent truth).

Since the time of the Ionian philosophers, human minds have tried to penetrate the variety and diversity of observable facts and disclose the unifying factor or factors behind what happens in nature. The Ionian philosophers believed that there were only a few "elements," which appeared in the empirical world as a variety of objects and bodies.

Modern scientists use better tools and are more critical, but the aim of

[6] Bertrand Russell, *Principles of Mathematics* (2nd ed.), Norton, 1938.

scientific inquiry has not changed much. Facts today are better perceived and carefully measured by more precise tools, but the purpose of any scientific inquiry is to go beyond the observable data and to discover the *laws of nature*. A theory in present-day science tries to uncover and to present as precisely as possible the *regularities of the universe* in such a manner that each single body or event can be related, interpreted, and predicted by these laws of nature.

The same holds true for the science of human nature, psychology. Plato and Aristotle tried to interpret human behavior by postulating an immortal soul. In present-day psychological language, the soul is a hypothetical construct that was once used to interpret human behavior. Plato tried to go beyond the diversity of human types and to disclose the underlying and unifying factors. He believed that the human soul is composed of three strata: the vegetative, the appetitive, and the rational. Kant distinguished reason, emotions, and will. In judging the need for hypothetical constructs, the question is whether these or any other interpretations help to interpret, relate, and predict the facts.

Present-day psychology does the same thing, though in a highly skilled manner. Mere cognition of facts is of little scientific value. Scientific inquiry in psychology endeavors to discover the laws that govern its area of research.

As long as psychology belonged to the realm of speculation, it was easy to form a system of arbitrarily set statements and call them a psychological theory. In the first two or three decades of our century, it was comparatively easy to bring together a cluster of facts and to write down a great many far-fetched statements. Owing to the lack of factual data it was possible, and perhaps even advisable, to fill the empirical gap with a sophisticated "system." Step by step, the hypothetical systems were confronted with the growing body of empirical data accumulated by scores of empirically minded workers. Today we sometimes hear voices warning against the overdoing of empirical research together with insufficient work in theory construction. Obviously, psychology needs a balanced production in both the collection of data and their interpretation.

2. COLLECTION OF DATA

Observation

A systematic, planned activity of perceiving things and events is called observation. What does a psychologist do? He observes bodies and events. If his subject matter is human psychology, he observes human organisms and what those organisms do.

Science may discover unity where simple, crude perception reports variety, and disclose differences in complex things that seem to be uniform. Psychologists, like all other scientists, gradually improve their tools, techniques, and methods and gain more precise knowledge of mental processes.

The body–soul, physical-mental, organic-psychological issue does not belong to methodology. In what way psychological processes differ from other physical processes is not a question that can be answered in a chapter on methodology. It is one of the issues that all psychological theories struggle with (cf. Chapter 16). One thing is obvious: psychological processes are processes of living matter.

Obviously, there is a great deal of overlap between psychological and physiological research. It is sufficient to look into the studies of Weber, Fechner, Wundt, Pavlov, Köhler, Lashley, Goldstein, Hebb, and others; the overlap is obvious since both psychology and physiology deal with the functions of organisms.

Several psychological processes—pain and pleasure, for instance—can be directly observed only by the individual in whom they take place. Obviously, the truthfulness (validity) of results obtained by *introspection* as a method of observation must be verified by other methods, because introspection cannot be as objective as any other observational methods. Yet introspection produces a wealth of information about psychological processes, and in some cases it is the main source of information. Introspection seems, therefore, to be inevitable in psychology. To give it up would be throwing away a precious tool because it is not precise enough.

Psychologists cannot afford to reject any method that brings factual information. The studies of Suzanne Isaacs and W. Stern on child psychology, of Charlotte Bühler and Stanley Hall on adolescence, of Ebbinghaus and K. Lewin on retention, and of Piaget and Gesell on development, represent a great variety of research methods. All these studies, whether based on biography, systematic observations, questionnaires, interviews, or experimentation, exemplify the various approaches within the empirical method.

Some psychologists, in their effort to adhere to strict empiricism, seem to be more severe than physicists. The natural sciences go beyond observable data to develop hypotheses and theorems which contradict our daily observations. Not everyone has "seen" that our earth is round and that it is rotating. Everyone can easily "see" the sun rising at dawn and setting at dusk. Several chemical elements have been discovered before they have been empirically observed. Einstein's theory of the fourth dimension contradicts our empirical sensory experiences.

But some psychologists insist on a radical version of empiricism. The early behaviorists insisted on the study only of overt, manifest, observable phenomena.

Even today, some psychologists suggest staying away from unobservable phenomena; B. F. Skinner represents this point of view. Guthrie insists that "the laws of nature describe the *observable* conditions under which certain classes of events take place."[7]

No wonder several psychologists opposed Freud's theories and accused him of being nonempirical. But obviously a certain class of psychological facts is unobservable. Consider amnesia. When an individual forgets something and, influenced by hypnosis or psychoanalysis, recalls what he has forgotten, the entire process is inaccessible to any observation, from within or from without. Yet the process of amnesia undoubtedly took place, for its end products were observable. The *inference* of their existence is a legitimate procedure of empirical sciences, which will be discussed in Section 3 of the present chapter.

Operationism

One of the most radical methods of observation is called *operationism*. Operationism was defined by E. C. Tolman as a science which "seeks to define its concepts in such a manner that they can be stated and tested in terms of concrete repeatable operations by independent observers."[8] In other words, operationism observes not only the object to be observed but also the operations performed by the observers in the process of observing objects.

P. W. Bridgman, the creator of operationism, stated that "the original impetus toward the operational analysis in physics came from a consideration of Einstein's procedure in the theory of relativity. Einstein had realized that certain terms, like 'absolute length,' 'absolute duration,' 'absolute simultaneity' were devoid of empirical meaning because no observational or experimental procedures were or could be specified for their application. The operational criterion here serves to distinguish physics from metaphysics."[9]

As long as operationism points to the need for careful definitions and critical observation of the tools and operations performed by the observing scientist, it can be considered a useful brand of empiricism. However, there is nothing new in it. F. Bacon, D. Hume, J. S. Mill, C. S. Peirce, and others carefully elaborated the methodology of empirical studies and the principles of the inductive method.

But according to operationism, if a question is to have a meaning it must be possible to find operations by which an answer may be given to it. And this is no longer empiricism. It is, once more, a return to the "perceiving subject."

[7] Edwin R. Guthrie, *The Psychology of Learning*, Harper, 1935, p. 187.
[8] Edward C. Tolman, "Operational Behaviorism and Current Trends in Psychology," *Proceedings of the Twenty-fifth Anniversary Celebration of Inauguration of Graduate Studies*, University of Southern California, 1936.
[9] Herbert Feigl, "Operationism and Scientific Method," *Psychological Review*, 1945, 52, 250–259.

The man who overemphasized the observation of the observer was I. Kant. Kant "psychologized" the universe, so to say, and made man the center of the world. Kant's "perceiving subject" is not a real man, who is, indeed, but a speck of dust in the gigantic world. Kant's "subject" is a giant viewing the empirical world through the glasses of his a priori set categories. As mentioned in Chapter 10, A. Schopenhauer went one step farther and concluded that the subject creates the world at will.

When Bridgman focussed on the operations performed by scientists, he could not predict that he would land on Schopenhauer's barren island of solipsism. But nothing else could have been expected. Once the center of scientific inquiry was moved from the objects of inquiry to the operations, machinations, speculations, and/or imaginations of the inquiring subject, all roads led to solipsism. This is the inevitable outcome of Kantianism, Machism, and operationism. P. W. Bridgman, being a consistent and daring thinker, stated bluntly what others had hidden under various excuses. If scientific inquiry depends on the "operations" conducted by the researcher, the conclusion reached by Bridgman is perfectly logical: "In the last analysis science is only my private science,"[10] defined in terms of operations performed by "me." If all knowledge has to be presented in terms of the perceiving subject and his "operations," the perceiver and not the perceived objects becomes the center of the universe.

Psychologists were shocked by this development. A leading exponent of psychological theory, S. S. Stevens, tried to save operationism by introducing the concept of social agreement. It resembles Sullivan's consensual validation. But does it save operationism?

The defense of operationism by Stevens is an honest effort to preserve the objectivity of scientific inquiry. Stevens suggested following operational principles; he believed that they were "induced generalizations" and "verifiable."

1. Science, as we find it, is a set of empirical propositions agreed upon by members of society. This agreement may be always in a state of flux, but persistent disagreement leads eventually to rejection. . . .
2. Only those propositions based upon operations which are public and repeatable are admitted to the body of science.[11]

Stevens's rejection of solipsism was well made, for science cannot be developed as the private world of a scientist. Thus, Stevens saved the public character and objectivity of science. But he did not save operationism; operationism as a method which insists on defining scientific statements in terms of the operations performed by scientists leads either to solipsism or to solipsism-in-groups, that is, group folly. The fact that many people participate in the operations does not make them scientific or truthful. Con-

[10] Peter W. Bridgman, *The Nature of Physical Theory*, Princeton University, 1936.
[11] S. S. Stevens, "Psychology and the Science of Science," *Psychological Bulletin*, 1939, *36*, 221–263.

sider witchcraft or superstitions, both "public and repeatable" and both unscientific and untrue.

Stevens believed that operationism discovers pseudo-problems, and a pseudo-problem is a proposition which cannot be put to experimental test.[12] When no operation can be formulated which either proves or disproves a proposition, the proposition represents a pseudo-problem. In Stevens's words, "A term or proposition has meaning (denotes something) if, and only if, the criteria of its applicability or truth consist of concrete operations which can be performed."[13]

Now operationism becomes an epistemological theory which, as will be shown, can be easily refuted. The naïve realist says: "If I see it, it is. What cannot be seen does not exist and is therefore a pseudo-problem." The operationist says: "If I can do something with it, it is. I prove things by doing, by performing operations. If I cannot do anything with them, they are pseudo-problems." For example, a mute catatonic may have delusions. If they cannot be "operationally defined," they represent a pseudo-problem. Circulation of blood prior to the discovery of methods by which it could be observed was a pseudo-problem. Copernicus, Kepler, Newton, and Laplace are guilty of dealing with problems not necessarily operationally defined. The same holds true for Pavlov, Freud, Goldstein, Piaget, Rorschach, Binet, and many other great scientists and psychologists.

Furthermore, a question can be raised as to the validity of the operational method. What is the proof that the observations of the operationist made on his own concrete observations are more valid than any other nonoperational observations? How can such a statement be verified, operationally or otherwise? In what way can one "operationally" disprove superstition and witchcraft? Definite "concrete" operations have been performed and "proved." Moreover, if intelligence is what intelligence tests measure, no objective truth will ever be discovered. The Russian psychologists, for example, prefer not to use intelligence tests, yet they seem to make quite intelligent statements about intelligence. Since the producers of tests of intelligence may have their disagreements, a uniform definition of intelligence in terms of operations may be impossible. Thus, operationism without Stevens's correction is a solipsistic denial of science, and even with Stevens's social correction it does not offer any protection against "group solipsism" or errors committed by a group of research workers.

What is good in operationism has been said and practiced by all empiricists. But empiricists do not insist on narrowing their propositions to terms of the operations performed by them. One must conclude, therefore, that the operationists overdid themselves in psychology. Even in physics a strict operational theory is practically impossible. An analysis of Divac's quantum theory has proved that even this theory "presupposes a particle

[12] Ibid.
[13] S. S. Stevens, "The Operational Definition of Psychological Concepts," Psychological Review, 1935, 42, 517–527.

analogy which is not directly given in experimental data" and therefore does not meet the rigorous requirements of operationism.[14]

Kant told philosophers to look at the looking eye. Bridgman called scientists to look at their hands and tools. Kant should be given credit for his criticism of naïve realism in epistemology and Bridgman should be given credit for his criticism of naïve realism in the methodology of sciences. But both Kant and Bridgman overdid their observations of the observer and attached too much importance to him, in view of the proportion between man and the entire universe; and they both rather naïvely believed that observations of the actions of the observer are more truthful than observations of all other things.

Classification

When the scientist perceives objects and events, he compares them, seeking similarities and differences. Trees growing in a park show similarities and differences; some of them have similar bark, leaves and fruit, and the botanist groups them together as a *class* of, for example, oak trees.

No two oak trees are identical; they differ in size, shape, number of branches and leaves. The scientist *abstracts* or overlooks the differences and groups objects together on the basis of at least one similarity. For example, all objects made for sitting, whether they are made of wood, aluminum, iron, or any other material, whether they are tall or short, old or new, are called chairs. One common denominator suffices for classification.

Objects can be classified in more than one way. The objects in a room can be divided on the basis of their shape, use, material, color, size, weight, age, price, or human attachment to them.

Classification can be done at will, but scientists usually abide by two rules. First, any classification must serve some *useful* purpose as far as scientific inquiry is concerned. The botanist sees no point in classifying trees into short, medium, and tall ones, but he finds it scientifically useful to distinguish oaks, pines, or birches. The reason for his preference is obvious and simple and has nothing to do with the "essential" elements of the phenomenologists. A classification of trees according to height does not help in the discovery of the biological processes in trees, while the classification along genetic lines does. For a lumber-trade economic researcher the size of the trees may be important. In abnormal psychology, the problem of classification of mental disorder is highly controversial and quite important, because it determines diagnosis and prognosis.[15]

The second rule of classification is *economy*. A certain object should not

---

[14] Mary Hesse, "Operational Definition and Analogy in Physical Theories," *British Journal of Philosophy of Science*, 1952, 2, 282–294.

[15] Otto Fenichel, *The Psychoanalytic Theory of Neurosis*, Norton, 1945; Harry S. Sullivan, *The Interpersonal Theory of Psychiatry*, Norton, 1953; Benjamin B. Wolman, *Call No Man Normal*, International Universities Press, 1973.

belong to two classes within the same system of classification or the classification is self-contradictory. If we classify as young anyone below fifty, and as old anyone above forty, all people between forty and fifty belong to both classes.

Practically all typological efforts in psychology violate the principles of classification to a lesser or greater extent. On the Allport–Vernon scale, everyone belongs to more than one Sprangerian type. There is no way of distinguishing between the introverts and extroverts of Jung; Kretschmer's and Sheldon's types badly overlap; in clinical experience, individuals usually show Freudian fixations on more than one level; other typologies seem to be even less economic, and to promote science even less.

Classification leads toward the formation of *abstract concepts*. The formation of classes and the formation of class concepts, or conceptualization, are functions of the human mind; there is nothing absolute or external about concepts. To quote William James, paper can be conceived as a "thin thing," or a "hydrocarbonaceous thing," or a surface for writing, and "whichever one of these aspects of its being I temporarily class it under, makes me unjust to the other aspects. But as I always am classing it under one aspect or another, I am always unjust, always partial, always exclusive. My excuse is necessity—the necessity which my finite and practical nature lays upon me. My thinking is first and last and always for the sake of my doing, and I can only do one thing at a time." [16]

Nothing is truly essential. Essential to what? It depends on the purposes and ends of man; obviously, the phenomenological distinction of essentials is arbitrarily set.

Generalization and the Problem of Idiophenomena

Once objects are classified on the basis of one common denominator, true statements can be made regarding a certain class of objects. Such a statement concerning a class is called a *generalization*. It expresses a truth concerning a class, or group, or category of objects. It can be phrased: "some" members of a certain class or "all" members of a certain class are so and so. Sometimes psychologists do not pay enough attention to this distinction and confuse "some" with "all." In the "Conclusion" about each system discussed in the present book, the generality of the propositions of a given system has often been discussed. McDougall's pairing of instincts and emotions led to a question as to whether the respective feelings did always accompany a certain propensity. Many psychoanalytic and related propositions represent the type "often," instead of "always" it is so and so. The principle of reward in learning should, as Razran pointed out, be stated as a generalization applicable to a certain class of learning situations, but not to all of them.

A considerable methodological difficulty was created by Windelband's

16 William James, *The Principles of Psychology*, Holt, 1890, Vol. II, p. 333.

distinction between the nomothetic and the idiographic sciences. The unrepeatable, individual, unique phenomena evade generalization and are not subject to the laws of nature. Therefore, concluded Windelband, the individual and unrepeatable events are not the subject matter of natural sciences. Natural science deals with *generalia* such as water, rain, air, waves, or iron, but cannot deal with, for example, the fact that Napoleon lost the battle of Waterloo or that John lost his memory as result of a shell shock.

The medieval discussion between "realism" and "nominalism" has been revived in thinking about idiophenomena. The "realists" ascribed existence to water in general, iron in general, love in general, while the "nominalists" dealt with drops of water, pieces of iron, and men in love and believed that water, iron, and love in general are merely *names of classes* of objects and events.

The nominalist point of view, to which this writer subscribes, ascribes existence to things and events and to nothing else. It can be shown that each thing or event is an idiophenomenon. Not only the lost battle of Waterloo is a unique and unrepeatable phenomenon, but even the sunrise of that day, and the death of so many men, and the water that flowed that day in the rivers of France, and the rain that fell on the plains, and the amount of electricity in the air at that time—all these were also unrepeatable events. There is no such thing as water, iron, or love in general. The subject matter of all sciences is idiophenomena.[17]

Yet sciences strive toward the most general truth. Science, explained H. Poincaré, does not pile up facts like bricks, but connects them and builds houses on the basis of generalizations.[18] The scientist isolates elements (abstracts) and groups the idiophenomena on the basis of common elements. Each lion, each eucalyptus tree, each piece of iron, each somatic cell, each case of gravitation, each case of love, each mental breakdown is an idiophenomenon, and yet they can be put together with other idiophenomena on the basis of at least one common trait. The scientific statements about each class can be worded in such a way as to express a general truth. Accordingly, each schizophrenic patient is definitely an idiophenomenon, for no other human being has suffered from exactly the same disorder in exactly the same way. Yet all schizophrenic patients can be grouped together and valid statements can be made about their common hardships.[19]

In this discussion of idiophenomena, it is worthwhile to quote the philosopher Morris Cohen: "That all existing beings, animate or inanimate, are individuals, no rationalists needs to deny. But that is in no way inconsistent with the fact pointed out by Aristotle that there is no knowledge or significant assertion with reference to any individual, except in terms of uni-

---

[17] Benjamin B. Wolman, "Concerning Psychology and the Philosophy of Science," in B. B. Wolman (Ed.), *Handbook of General Psychology*, Prentice-Hall, 1973, pp. 22–48.

[18] Henri Poincaré, *La Science et l'Hypothèse*, Flammarion, 1903.

[19] Benjamin B. Wolman, "Explorations in Latent Schizophrenia," *American Journal of Psychotherapy*, 1957, *11*, 560–588.

versals or abstractions. I may in a dumb way point to a single object or I may grasp it with my hand, but I cannot mean anything and I cannot even say 'this' about it without using an abstract term applicable to other individuals. If I use a proper name, it has the meaning only by convention which ultimately involves abstract terms."[20] Our language uses generalia, but generalia are mere names and nothing else.

All general concepts of psychology stem from classification and generalization. Each individual case can be fully interpreted only by relating it to all the possible classes to which it belongs. The movement of a speck of dust cannot be described in terms of gravitation only; it proceeds according to the laws of nature, which include in this case gravitation, friction, movements of air, and many more. A scientist who took into consideration *all* the relevant laws could predict all the movements of the speck of dust flying in the air. For there cannot be any violation of the laws of nature.

Such knowledge of a single fact, however, is practically impossible. Usually scientists try to study their problems by reducing the number of variables and simplifying the process under consideration. This is a standard laboratory procedure—to look for "typical," "normal," "usual," "average" examples in which the individual peculiarities are kept at a minimum. Statistical methods are geared to this goal.

However, the higher and more complex the processes, the more dissimilarities are found. Two drops of water are not identical, but even less identical are two plants belonging to the same species, and even less so are two humans. And that is one of the sources of objection to generalizations in psychology.

But dissimilarities do not prevent generalization. A combination of similar elements may lead to different total structures, and similar structures may be composed of different elements. In the pursuit of truth, psychologists seek the different and the common, the individual and the general, the molecular and the molar. Each of them contains some truth: the case study and the statistical survey, the life history of an individual and the results of a nation-wide study of intelligence.

Quantification in Psychology

Quantification is indicative of a higher level of comparison, abstraction, and generalization. Counting indicates the degree of similarity between two aggregates such as the number of books on a shelf and the number of students in a class. Two aggregates may have one identical element, their number.

Counting is an abstraction, and a precise one. Quantification in the form of counting and, even more, measurement are very exact methods of comparison, abstraction, classification, and generalization. The use of quantification increases the precision of research methods and makes them more scientific.

[20] Morris R. Cohen, *Reason and Nature*, Harcourt, Brace, 1931, p. 13.

Mathematics can be used in psychology in three ways: first, as counting and measurement on the level of collecting empirical data; second, as a method of testing hypotheses in experimental and statistical studies (e.g., the hypotheses of Hull have been laboratory-tested in a quantitative manner and discussion of the etiology of mental disorder often utilizes statistical data as one of the best methods of evidence); third, as offering unusual advantage in precision of statements.

The syntactic (mathematical) statements, theorems, and equations "are absolutely true or absolutely false. They are true if they are consistent with the rules laid down for playing the game, they are false if they break the law. But these absolutely true statements say nothing at all, unfortunately, about objects or events, and they reveal no secrets of nature. It is by way of semantical rules that we tie the mathematical model to the empirical world," but it often fits as poorly "as a borrowed hat."[21]

These sound words of warning were said in a time when some psychologists tend to overdo measurements and others endeavor to introduce into psychology the methods of non-metricized mathematics.

J. F. Brown wrote that at the present time fundamental measurement is impossible in psychology and in social science: "Where fundamental measurement is not possible, simple assignation of number to the qualities of nature has advantages, but such assignations ought not to be honored with the title of measurement. For psychology such a service is performed by rating scales, Intelligence Quotients, and the common psychophysical methods. In general, sciences start with such numerical assignations and through a very complicated process reduce these to measurements."[22]

But it is practically obvious that there are several kinds of measurement possible in all sciences of behavior: How many are unemployed? How many marry, divorce, migrate? How often are crime, theft, violence, and suicide committed? How many vote? All this is measurement, namely, measurement by enumeration.

To quote Stevens again, any new number is admitted to the union of numbers "provided it obeys the old rules. It is analogous to the admission of a state to the union: the new state must agree to obey the federal laws. The laws of the number union have to do with addition, multiplication, subtraction, and division, and the new numbers must behave themselves when these operations are applied."

How do Kurt Lewin's numbers "behave?" They do not behave at all, because Lewin did not operate with them. He was a brilliant psychologist and an ingenious experimenter. He introduced a set of signs, calling them topology, hodology, field theory, and vector psychology. All these were signs, and signs invite the formal discipline of syntactics. Mathematics is one of these formal disciplines and, like any other formal discipline, it sets rigorous rules. Kurt Lewin did not violate these rules, but he has not added or developed any mathematical rules at all.

[21] Stevens (Ed.), *Handbook of Experimental Psychology*, Wiley, 1951, p. 3.
[22] J. F. Brown, *Psychology and the Social Order*, McGraw-Hill, 1936, p. 470.

The Experimental Method

The most precise, planned, and controlled observation is experiment. Experiment is the most scientific research method. Only experiments make possible controlled observation, variation of factors, perfect quantifications, and rigorous, objective checking of hypotheses.[23]

The advantages offered by the experimental method should not, however, prevent us from looking into its shortcomings. The main weakness of experimentation as far as behavior of the organism is concerned, lies in the fact that an experiment is an observation of an artificially determined pattern of behavior. Thorndike's experimental animals had virtually no choice but trial and error. Imagine an organism enclosed in a maze with high walls which would prevent any insight or oversight; he would be *forced* to try and to err. But give him low or transparent walls and he would probably find the solution with one glance as Köhler's chimpanzees did. A great part of the difference between classic and operant conditioning stems from the differences in the tools used, in the nature of the equipment, and in the experimental design.

The experimental method sets its own limits by establishing the experimental situation. The greatness of experimentalism lies in its precision and control of variables, but the experimental set itself creates a new pattern of behavior. No biologist would limit his studies of animals to observations in a circus with specially trained animals; some psychologists would. Biologists prefer the *ecological* method, which is the study of the animal in its natural environment. One wonders how albino rats, pigeons, or cats would learn in situations which are different from a puzzle box, maze, or Skinner apparatus.

Even more spectacular are the differences between the experiments of Thorndike and Guthrie. Both used a cat in a problem box with a release mechanism inside the box and food as incentive outside. Despite similar settings, they arrived at different results. Thorndike's cat struggled against odds for quite a while, and only after a long series of trials and errors, learned to open the box. Thorndike explained the behavior of his cat as typical for all cats and perhaps all mammals, and saw in this behavior the clue to a general learning theory based on trial and error, illustrated by the learning curve and the law of effect.

On the other hand, Guthrie's cat seemed to be bound to defeat all the opponents of the learning theories of his master. Guthrie's cat found the solution almost immediately. Then there was quite a lot of consistency and stereotypy in the following trials, with a minimum of deviations from the established pattern.

Behavior is, for all practical purposes, in interaction between the organism and its environment. Obviously there is more than one way for such interaction to take place. And this is probably why experimental data have

[23] Cf. Oscar Kempthorne, *The Design and Analysis of Experiments*, Wiley, 1952.

to be presented not as the total truth, but as a limited truth. One may say that if a certain organism is enclosed in such and such an apparatus (a definite type of environment) and exposed to such and such a stimulus, this will be the reaction. If the statement is backed up by a vigorous experimentation, it is a true statement insofar as it reports the behavior of a *certain* organism in a *certain* setting. It does not, however, cover what was not covered in the experiment, namely, any other situation in which the organism may respond to a given stimulus in a slightly, or substantially, different way. Especially in experiments with the highest biological organisms, capable of a great variety of responses, caution should be advised.

Once we are reconciled to these limitations, we can and should admit that the experimental method is the most reliable method. Some suggestions, however, should be offered at this point. First, conclusions derived from experiments must be limited to what has actually been done in the experimental situation. Experiments should be designed to be as close as possible to realistic situations in which subjects face their usual environments. For example, formal intelligence testing of small children seems so remote from the child's usual interactions that one cannot be surprised at the unreliability of test results. And, as far as learning theory is concerned, there must be more than one kind of learning for the various species and more than one way of learning for each organism. Accordingly, a realistic setting for experimentation can offer certain advantages.

However, even a so-called realistic setting can be misleading. A remarkable case is the experiment in "social climate" conducted by Lewin, Lippitt, and White (cf. Chapter 13). In this experiment, three social climates were supposedly established by the experimenters, the autocratic, the democratic, and the laissez-faire, and far-reaching conclusions were drawn by the experimenters.

Actually, leadership in all of the groups was autocratic, because all the leaders were appointed by the experimenter and not chosen by the children. In the so-called democratic group the leader was benevolent and, like a sort of liberal-minded despot, permitted the children to participate in group decisions. The children knew very well that he was their leader and that they had no power to overthrow him. The true choice of a leader is the outstanding feature of democracy. Benevolent tyrants who listen to the needs and voices of their subjects are *not* representatives of a democratic system.

The second leader was a cold, ineffectual autocrat. Autocrats are not necessarily cold or unfriendly. At any rate, this was a poor type of leadership; in the assignment of duties and division of labor the leader overlooked the interests and inclinations of the group members. Not all autocratic leaders are poor judges of human nature.

The laissez-faire leader was not a leader at all. The children expected him to be one, that is, to take initiative and to offer guidance. His passivity was a denial of leadership. Were he absent, the children would probably have organized themselves better. In his presence they did not dare to do so, for they probably knew that he had the power of leadership even if he did not exercise it.[24]

A criticism of the use of the experimental method in psychology was offered by G. S. Klein.[25] Klein remarked that the appearance of *significant relations* was often prevented by the rigorous experimental procedure of keeping variables constant. Instead of grasping the process as a whole, experimentalists often omit important factors by their tendency to eliminate and isolate experimental variables or to keep them constant.

However, this criticism cannot undermine the validity or reliability of experimental procedure. The criticism should be directed against oversimplification of mental processes and overgeneralization of conclusions. The experimental method is undoubtedly the most valid and reliable method in psychology.

Additional limitations of the experimental method in psychology stem from the fact that experiments cannot handle the patterns of covert behavior very well; nor do overt, violent types of action fit into a laboratory setting. Experimenters cannot test the entire gamut of human drives and feelings.

This part of psychology is handled daily by clinical psychologists. The clinicians deal with *all* phenomena of human nature, normal and abnormal, overt and covert, rational and irrational. The wealth of clinical material is overwhelming; child growth, perception and reasoning, learning and forgetting, love and hate, happiness and misery, physiology and psychosomatics are seen day by day in a great variety of situations.

The clinician sees his subjects in homes and schools, in hospitals and clinics. He interviews them and their families and reports on all that is going on in their minds and actions. Clinical studies broaden our knowledge of psychology; experimental studies make it more reliable.

The experimentalist studies only a part of human behavior, but he studies it with great precision. The clinician studies the totality of human behavior. It is no wonder this wealth of clinical material is not very conducive to precision and can be easily misinterpreted. The scientifically minded clinician cannot help envying the experimentalist's precision. When the experimentalist says that three plus five equal eight, it is so. When the clinician says 3000 plus 5000 equals 8000, he is not sure he counted carefully; some errors are almost inevitable.

Thus, observational and experimental studies aimed at the verification of clinical findings are exceedingly important for the future development of psychological theory. The results obtained by the two methods independently of each other cannot be identical, but they should not be mutually exclusive.

[24] Benjamin B. Wolman, "Education and Leadership," *Teachers College Record*, 1958, 59, 465–473.
[25] George S. Klein, "A Clinical Perspective for Personality Research," *Journal of Abnormal and Social Psychology*, 1949, 44, 42–50.

3. Interpretation of Data and Theory Construction

Induction and Deduction

Science is not a collection of facts, just as a house is not a pile of bricks, said the great French mathematician and philosopher H. Poincaré. How is this house built? Let us listen to a great American philosopher, E. Nagel: "While every experiment requires the use of principles of interpretation, the evidence for the truth of these principles comes ultimately through observation and experiment. . . . The propositions which science at any time certifies are either confirmed in all possible experiments, or are modified in accordance with the best available evidence. There is thus a continual appeal from facts to principles, and from principles to facts. . . . *In the order of the development of our knowledge,* therefore, theory and observation are of equal rank." [26]

Which should come first, observation of facts or their interpretation? The answer is obvious, and in the empirical sciences the method of choice is the *inductive* method. However, a *deductive* method can be used just as well in empirical sciences. Science can proceed from fact to interpretation, or a tentative interpretation can be tested by facts. Any scientific system must be composed of empirical data and their interpretation.

Edna Heidbreder wrote in 1933: "The simple truth is that psychology does not at present possess enough facts with which to test its systems. Its need of facts makes it disparage speculation, its lack of facts makes it resort to practice, and it does so at times with a bad conscience. . . ." But "scientific knowledge does not merely accumulate. . . ." Frequently "guesses on the basis of inadequate evidence have proved to be powerful and, in actual practice, indispensable tools, which science regularly employs." [27]

The tendency to develop deductive systems in psychology became prominent with C. L. Hull and K. Lewin. Many scholars seem to believe that this is the only or the best road for psychological theory. Feigl suggested defining "theory" as "a set of assumptions from which can be derived by purely logico-mathematical procedures, a larger set of empirical laws." The theory "furnishes an explanation of these empirical laws and unifies the originally heterogeneous areas of subject matter characterized by those empirical laws." [28]

But the most important problem is whether the statements called by Feigl "empirical laws" can pass the test of observation and experiment. If they do, their theoretical assumptions are still not proved, but they are not rejected, which is a satisfactory situation for any theory.

Moreover, it seems that Feigl's "levels" correspond specifically to a

[26] Ernest Nagel, *Logic Without Metaphysics,* Free Press, 1956, p. 152.

[27] Edna Heidbreder, *Seven Psychologies,* Appleton-Century, 1933, p. 15.

[28] Herbert Feigl, "Principles and Problems of Theory Construction in Psychology," in W. Dennis (Ed.), *Current Trends in Psychological Theory,* University of Pittsburgh, 1951, p. 182.

Hull type of theory. From a more general point of view, it seems advisable to distinguish between a hypothesis or hypothetical interpretation and a system of hypotheses, that is, a theory.

Hypothesis

A hypothesis is a statement which is not yet proved to be true. The statement "two and two is four" is not a hypothesis. Nor is it a hypothesis that birds have two legs or that all humans are mortals. These are observed, well-known facts.

Hypothetical statements are used for information which we believe to be true. Scientists use hypotheses whenever they deal with unobservable bodies and events or unobservable relationships. Phlogiston was such a hypothesis; it proved to be wrong. The theories of airplanes, television, and submarines used to be hypothetical hopes; now they are facts.

Some hypothetical statements have been proved. The prevention of poliomyelitis by the use of the Salk vaccine proved that the hypothesis concerning the nature of poliomyelitis was true. Empirical studies have shown that the hypothesis which related schizophrenia to tuberculosis was untrue. Watson's hypothesis of subvocal speech was never proved; nor was the "drive reduction" hypothesis. Goldstein's theory of compensation and Freud's hypothesis of the unconscious have a great body of supportive evidence.

The aim of scientific inquiry is to discover the truth. Sometimes it is useful to state the truth tentatively, as a hypothesis, even before all the evidence, or even a part of it, has been produced. Let us call such a hypothesis a *postulate*. In the inductive method it is legitimate to draw a tentative conclusion from insufficient empirical data and then to test it against further data. In the deductive method it is legitimate to start from any tentative assumption and then put it to an empirical test.

Hypotheses should be formed in such a way that they are a help and not a hindrance in the search for truth. Accordingly, the formation of hypotheses must follow certain rules.

1. *Immanent truth.* Hypotheses may be true or false as their future testing will prove. They must, however, be free of inner contradiction; each hypothesis or each system of hypotheses should be developed in accordance with the principles of logical implication and inference. Obviously, the use of hypotheses must be persistent. Once a hypothesis has been stated, it must be applied until further empirical research or other methodological considerations suggest its modification or abandonment. Careless use of hypotheses and their modification at will (cf. Jung, Rank, and others) is self-defeating.

2. *Testability.* A hypothesis should be open to proof or refutation by empirical test. The best test is a controlled experiment.

3. *Usefulness and parsimony.* New hypotheses have to be introduced only when old ones fail to account for empirical data or some other method-

ological considerations. Hypotheses should be as sparse as possible, and as simple as possible.

4. *Anticipation*. Hypotheses should be geared to the goal of anticipation of future events. *"Savoir pour prévoir."*

5. *Wording*. The wording of a hypothesis must not be ambiguous.

Hypotheses, Constructs, and Intervening Variables

Some students of the scientific method in psychology seem to believe that there is only one way to form hypotheses, briefly explained as follows: Psychology as an empirical science must start from the observable interaction between the organism and its environment. This interaction is called behavior and is sometimes misrepresented as an equivalent of the subject matter of psychology, although even J. B. Watson had to admit that psychology must deal with phenomena which do not belong to the category of this overt interaction; thus Watson included *implicit* behavior in his studies.

This is not the end, but only the beginning of the difficulties. Behavior can be conveniently presented as a *stimulus–response continuum*, the stimulus standing for the totality of actions done by the environment and the response standing for whatever happened with the organism as a result of the stimulation. However, even a superficial observation shows that the response of the organism is *more* than a response to the stimulation: a hungry rat and a satiated one will respond differently to the sight of food. Credit has to be given to R. S. Woodworth for modifying the S-R formula into S-O-R, in which O stands for the organism, and it is understood that R is a result of what was produced by S and O together. Undoubtedly, it was a substantial improvement in the presentation of psychological events.

Tolman refined Woodworth's proposition and presented the S-O-R formula in a continuum of experimental variables in which S is the independent, R the dependent, and O the intervening variable.

It must be said that this way of treating psychological data is by no means the only one. Lewin, Sullivan, and others would not distinguish between S and P. McDougall's propensity does not fit well either. Wertheimer's gestalt is not an intervening variable. Tolman's intervening variable stands for a partial cause of the dependent variable; the other partial cause is the independent variable.

There are obviously many types of hypothetical statements and not all of them can be presented as variables intervening between the independent and dependent variables. Consider Allport's trait, Freud's ego, Hull's drive, gestalt insight, Pavlov's irradiation, and Lewin's field. All these are *logical constructs*. MacCorquodale and Meehl suggested that the logical constructs are better elaborated, more meaningful elements than the intervening variables.[29]

This distinction between intervening variables and hypothetical con-

[29] K. MacCorquodale and Paul E. Meehl, "On a Distinction Between Hypothetical Constructs and Intervening Variables," *Psychological Review*, 1948, 55, 95–107.

structs introduced by MacCorquodale and Meehl has been further elaborated by Feigl, who preferred to call the constructs *existential hypotheses.* These "fill out" the space assigned to intervening variables, as, for example, the hypothetical constructs of the theory of genes "fill out" Mendel's conceptions of heredity, or the intervening variable of temperature is identified with the existential hypothesis of micro-states of molecules. The existential hypotheses are introduced "on the basis of some new and heterogeneous area of evidence." "At the price of existential hypotheses we achieve a reduction (often a very considerable one) of the hitherto unreduced dispositional concepts or intervening variables."[30]

A scientific theory can introduce logical constructs at any level of explanation, provided they are clearly defined and serve a useful purpose. Logical constructs fill a gap in observation. Watson's subvocal speech, Allport's trait, and Freud's unconscious are intended to report facts which cannot be directly observed. They cannot be presented as intervening variables.

"*Unconscious* has more and more been made to mean a mental province rather than a quality which mental things have," said Freud.[31] The unconscious as a "mental province" is a logical construct of mind. Most logical constructs are "methodological bridges" used for interpretation of behavior. Freud's model of personality is composed of several constructs: id, ego, and superego. These constructs are more complex. So is reinforcement, intelligence, Oedipus complex, adjustment, and learning. All are logical constructs, or concepts useful in the search for truth.

As said before, in certain situations the experimental variables can be grouped as independent, dependent, and intervening variables. Logical constructs are often used as intervening variables.

Molar and Molecular Hypotheses

Psychologists have expressed their preference for the use of either molar or molecular hypotheses for the explanation of behavior. Associationists presumably preferred molecular hypotheses; contemporary psychologists seem to prefer molar ones.

Psychologists' molar concepts, according to Feigl, are "close-to-life" empirical laws. By analogy with physics, Feigl suggested switching from macro- to micro-explanations in psychology, because the molar type of analysis "yields at best a set of empirical laws, always of statistical character, often with only rather low degrees of correlation." Feigl thinks "that physics as well as psychology cannot get away from the mediaeval ideas of powers, capacities, or faculties as long as they remain on macro-level."

For instance, said Feigl, the "soporific power of opium" does not explain the empirical regularity, but it does tell about each individual case. This type of explanation is a "low level explanation." A higher level expla-

---

[30] Feigl, "Principles and Problems," in Dennis, *op. cit., pp.* 194–195.
[31] Sigmund Freud, *New Introductory Lectures in Psychoanalysis*, Norton, 1933, p. 102.

nation "would have to enter into the physiological-chemical effects of alkaloids upon the nervous system."[32]

The same can be said about psychology. There is an interesting parallel between the opposition of Mach and Ostwald to the atomic theory in chemistry and physics and of gestalt and field psychologists to "atomistic" explanations of behavior.

To Feigl, all molar theories represent a rather low level of interpretation. A higher level will be approached with the introduction of microtheories. Freud's or Lewin's models should be "appraised in terms of the isomorphism they attain with the corresponding structures and processes certified by the physiological approach."

Feigl seems to identify micro-theories with neurophysiology. The history of psychological thought offers no proof for his standpoint. A vitalist may be molar and neurophysiologically minded. Kurt Goldstein is a neurosurgeon and holistic and molar; gestalt has introduced the molar concept of magnetic field, which is based on neurophysiology.

Reductionism

It is a legitimate scientific procedure to relate less-known facts to better-known facts. This is the origin of reductionism in psychology.

One of the leading representatives of reductionism in psychology, Carroll Pratt, would like psychology to "resolve itself" in a "basic" discipline like physiology. Only then will psychology become a truly scientific system.[33]

Pratt's idea is tempting, but let us consider it in a broader context and learn by comparison. Can biology resolve itself in physics? All living organisms are physical bodies. When a hungry animal goes hunting, the laws of gravitation, acceleration, and thermodynamics are still binding, but they are not sufficient for the interpretation of animal behavior—or even of the behavior of a simple cell. For, although biology is rooted in physics and chemistry, it cannot be reduced to or interpreted by them.

It seems that there is some confusion in the discussion of reductionism. Reductionism in *methods* should not be confused with reductionism in *theory*. Methods of research can follow the paths established in other, let us say more "basic," sciences, but the results of research formulated as psychological law may defy the laws of other sciences. Or, notwithstanding a non-reductionist method of research, psychologists may arrive at the formulation of psychological laws identical with the laws discovered in other sciences.

For example, Köhler's reductionism in psychological theory is not a product of a methodological reductionism. Gestalt psychologists have always been opposed to quantification or any other emulation of the

[32]Feigl, "Principles and Problems," in Dennis, *op. cit.*, p. 191.
[33]Carroll C. Pratt, *The Logic of Modern Psychology*, Macmillan, 1948.

methods of physics, but they have presented the results of their research in the terms of the physical sciences—such as forces, fields, and isomorphism. Freud developed his theory in psychogenic terms, but he believed that mental processes are derivatives of physical processes. Not Köhler, nor Pavlov, nor Freud, nor Goldstein believed that *anger* is a secretion or a contraction of muscles.

Let us use the following example for a better explanation of the problem. One may push a stone in anger or grief, knowingly or unknowingly, in a dream or in a waking state. All these are irrelevant factors for the interpretation of the stone's movements and the prediction of its behavior; the relevant factors are the amount of energy, the direction of the movement, the weight of the stone and friction.

However, when one individual pushes another individual, all the aforementioned factors become secondary. Of course they do exist, but it is far more important to know the motives and perceptions of the pushing individual and the motives and perceptions of the pushed one. In order to interpret what happened and to predict what will happen next, an analysis of motivations and perceptions of the two persons is necessary. Men are not stones, and no behaviorist theories borrowed from physics would enable us to predict human behavior. A heartbeat is not fear, a swollen jaw is not toothache, birthgiving cramps are not labor pains, alcohol in the stomach is not identical with a gay mood. It is important to see and to seek to interpret these relationships; the psychophysical parallelism, Pavlov's methodological dualism, Köhlers' isomorphism, Lashley's brain mechanisms, Goldstein's theory of organism, Freud's cautious restraint from physiology—all these are legitimate efforts to face the problem.

The problem remains unsolved. Psychology cannot be dissolved in physics or reduced to physiology because psychological phenomena deal with problems that do not exist in the other sciences. The two outstanding psychological issues, perception and motivation, do not exist in inanimate nature. Awareness of pain and pleasure, striving toward goals, and all conscious and unconscious activities are the subject matter of psychology only.

This is precisely why all efforts toward reductionism are doomed to fail, and methodological reductionism has even less chance than theoretical reductionism. Theoretical reductionism, which tries to derive psychological phenomena from physics, chemistry, and physiology, has at least good backing in empirical facts. Perhaps there is some kind of isotropism, or parallelism, or energetism; at any rate human beings are living organisms. Unfortunately, we do not know today much more about it than was known at the time of Descartes. Naïve statements and sweeping generalizations were made then and are made today.

Methodological reductionism forces the issue. The presentation of human behavior as a series of physicochemical changes, tensions, reactions, or tropisms is rather inadequate and does not help much in the understanding and prediction of the higher mental processes. Nor does any kind of field theory operating with forces or vectors.

We know today the weaknesses and shortcomings of the solutions proposed by Dilthey or Titchener, and we have made considerable progress, thanks to Pavlov, Freud, and Hull, but the main issues are far from being solved. Psychological issues and problems can and should be attacked from various angles, but there is no escaping the fact that these problems are not found in physics, and that no solution borrowed from that science can solve them.

Psychologists have to learn to face reality, psychological reality. Physicists too do not know the answers to some of their basic problems, but they do not try to borrow dubious answers from other sciences.

As said before, it is a legitimate procedure to relate less-known facts to better-known facts. If physiology, biology and neurology can help, let us make use of them. But to invite neurological speculations is even less justified than to use psychological ones. Speculations in psychology can perhaps be forgiven because so many psychological symptoms are unobservable. Neurology should be called in to increase the number of observed data and to reduce the area of speculative interpolations. But there is no reason to increase the vagueness of psychological theory or to add neurological speculations to psychological speculations. Physiological and neurological elements introduced into a psychological theory must belong to the category of observed phenomena; otherwise psychological theory does not need them. We already have too many constructs and inferential statements, and there is no need to add new ones borrowed from an area where external observation is the only legitimate scientific procedure.

The conclusion is that psychologists, like all other scientists, are entitled to and should be encouraged to borrow from other sciences, especially from the more "basic" sciences such as biology, physiology, and neurology. They should borrow the best-proved statements for support of their own findings and hypotheses. But, since these statements cannot take the place of psychological inquiry, the best policy is to be found in *methodological non-reductionism*. (For more about this issue, see Chapter 16, Section 1.)

Causation

After a painstaking search for facts and grouping them together in classes, the research worker is tempted to seek the interrelationships between the various factors. These interrelationships disclose *how* and *why* things happen; they are the milestones in scientific inquiry.

The relationships can be logical (inferences), mathematical (functions and correlations), teleological, and causal. It is our belief that only causation offers interpretation and makes possible prediction.

Let us start with discussion of the other types of relations. Logical inferences are made irrespective of physical reality; mathematicians operate very well with $\sqrt{-1}$ or i, which is obviously an unreal number. Inference is a formal logical procedure which is independent of the content of the propositions. This is obviously not what is sought by empirical scientists, including psychologists.

Mathematical functions and correlations are often used in empirical studies. They may be related to causal relations in one of three ways: (1) the causal relations do not exist, and the only factual relationship between bodies and events is the mathematical function; (2) the functional and the causal relationships are one and the same thing; (3) the only relationship is the causal one, which can be expressed in terms of a mathematical function.

The second alternative can be easily discarded. Consider the functional (but not causal!) relationship between the sine of one angle in a triangle and the sines of the other angles. The last alternative seems to be acceptable. The first requires further clarification of the concept of causation.

The issue of teleology should be divided into two. As long as teleology is presented as the striving of the organism toward a goal (cf. K. Goldstein), it does not contradict causation, nor does it contradict empirical observation. The idea of a universal goal has practically no supportive evidence.

Actually, no scientific research is possible without some sort of causality. Scientific inquiry usually seeks the unknown factor x, as follows:

$$a + b = x, \qquad \text{ergo } x = a + b$$

or

$$a + x = b, \qquad \text{ergo } x = b - a.$$

In empirical sciences we may proceed from the known causes to the known laws toward unknown results. Very often we proceed from the known causes to the known results toward the discovery of unknown laws.

Even if one substitutes probability[34] for strict causality, probability in the natural sciences represents causal relations, although inexactly defined. Without causation no statistical probability could exist beyond the point of sheer chance.

The opposition to the causal principle started with D. Hume, who wrote as follows: "We have no other notion of cause and effect, but that of certain objects, which have been always *conjoined* together, and which in all past instances have been found inseparable. We cannot penetrate into the reason of the conjunction. We only observe the thing itself, and always find that from constant conjunction the objects acquire an union in the imagination."[35]

Kelson thinks that the inclination to consider experience as a two-

[34] Hans Reichenbach, *The Theory of Probability* (2nd ed.), University of California, 1949.
[35] David Hume, *A Treatise of Human Nature* (T. H. Green and T. H. Grose, Eds.), Longmans, Green, 1874, Part III, Volume VI, p. 394.

element process, one of which is the cause and the other the effect, can be derived from the primitive tendency to consider all experience as an expression of divine laws in which offense and retribution are interpreted as cause and effect.[36]

Even if this were true, it would only point to the historical roots of the concept of causality and would not help in resolving the question of causal relationship in present-day science.

Auguste Comte went farther. *"Tous les bons esprits reconnaissent aujourd'hui que nos études réelles sont strictement circonscrites à l'analyse des phénomènes pour découvrir leurs lois effectives, c'est à dire leurs relations constantes de succession ou de similitude, et ne peuve nullement concerner leur nature intime, ni leur cause, ou première ou finale, ni leur mode essentiel de production. . . . Ainsi toute hypothèse qui franchit les limites de cete sphère positive ne peut aboutir qu'à engendrer des discussions interminables, en prétendant prononcer sur des questions nécessairement insoluble pour notre intelligence."* (In short, our real studies are confined to the analysis of phenomena in order to discover their laws, that is, their constant relationships of sequence or similarity, and we should not be concerned with their nature or cause.)[37]

Similar reservations concerning causation have been presented by W. Dingle:

> All that observation tells us on this matter is that certain states of a physical system invariably succeed other states. We go beyond this at our peril. We have no right to say that there is some hidden element, some "cause" in the first state which fashions the second; or, if we do say it, we must perpetually remind ourselves that it is merely a mode of expressing invariable sequence and nothing more. "Cause" is like Newton's "force," a term used as a conventional means of describing phenomena, and if we give it a significance beyond that we will sooner or later meet our Einstein who will take it from us.[38]

In two studies devoted to the methodology of natural[39] and behavioral[40] sciences, the following proposals have been made. The proposals represent *one* principle, for the behavioral sciences are a special case within the realm of the natural sciences. Causation is a *genetic sequence which comes with an ontological necessity*. The case of an event is given by the answer to the question: *Why* did it happen? The cause of a body is given by the answer to the question: *What* did it come from? The effect *results* from the cause; it is its inevitable product. Why did this house fall? The *total cause* must include material, construction, erosion, climate, and wear and tear.

Causation is a peculiar type of necessary sequence. That $\sqrt{4}$ is$\pm$ 2 is a

[36] H. Kelson, "Causality and Retribution," *Philosophy of Science*, 1941, *8*, 553–556.

[37] Comte, *op. cit.*, p. 229.

[38] William Dingle, *Science and Human Experience*, Williams & Norgate, 1931, p. 88.

[39] Benjamin B. Wolman, "Chance: A Philosophical Study," *Tarbitz, Hebrew University Quarterly* (Hebrew), 1938, *10*, 56–80.

[40] Wolman, "Concerning Psychology and the Philosophy of Science," in B. B. Wolman (Ed.), *Handbook of General Psychology*, Prentice-Hall, 1973, pp. 22–48.

logical necessity, a sequence related to agreed on laws in mathematics. That days follow nights is an *ontological* necessity, a sequence related to the laws of nature. But nights do not result in days; therefore this is not a causal sequence. Fertilization *results* in birth; a bullet in the head *results* in death; here the sequence is *genetic* and ontologically necessary and, according to our definition, *causal*. The striking of a match lights a fire; the ingestion of medicine kills germs; traumatic experiences lead to neurosis. All these cases are cases of partial causation. Complete causation, as pointed out before, must include the totality of causation factors.

It is proposed here to postulate that all that happens is a chain of causes and effects. This postulate of *determinism*, accepted by Pavlov, Freud, Goldstein, Lashley, and many others, cannot be directly proved. But it is being proved daily by all our observations, and to doubt it would mean to doubt any regularity in the universe.

Contemporary physics has certain difficulties with causation in one area. This is the quantum theory, in which the deterministic principle is not applicable. Yet physicists have not given up determinism in any other area of research. A leading physicist, M. Planck, stated that "physical science together with astronomy and chemistry and mineralogy are all based on the strict and universal validity of the principle of causality."[41]

Such a difficulty does not exist in psychology. A deviation from determinism in psychology would make things unexplainable.

Laws of Nature in Psychology

Laws of nature represent the permanent patterns of happenings. They express the regularity of the world. Sun and stars, plants and animals move in a certain and definite manner. Gravitation, electrolysis, splitting of atoms, growth of plants and animals—these are the eternal regularities, the laws of nature. One who knows the present facts and the laws of nature can predict the future facts. The ultimate goal of theory is that knowledge.

"A theory in present-day physics," wrote Spence, "is a system of highly abstract constructs used to integrate sets of empirical laws that without the theory would appear to be quite unrelated. Examples of such integrating devices are the electromagnetic theory of radiation and the kinetic theory of gases. In contrast, what passes for theory in the behavior sciences serves primarily as a device to aid in the formulation of descriptive laws. Theory in psychology, then, consists primarily in the introduction or postulation of hypothetical constructs to represent tht unknown or uncontrolled factors in a situation under observation."[42]

Spence's judgment may sound a bit harsh. Psychology deals with more

[41] Hugo Bergmann, *Der Kampf um das Kausalitätsprinzip in der jüngsten Physik*, Barth, 1929; Max Planck, *Where Science Is Going*, Norton, 1932, p. 147.
[42] Kenneth Spence, "Theoretical Interpretations of Learning," in S. S. Stevens (Ed.), *Handbook of Experimental Psychology*, Wiley, 1951, p. 690.

complex problems and has had less time to study them; undoubtedly, psychology is methodologically less advanced than physics. However, psychology and physics and all other sciences introduce constructs in the process of theory formation. But ultimately any scientific system is a system of laws of nature. Their degree of abstraction must vary from science to science.

There is still a great deal of controversy among psychologists (cf. Chapter 16, Section 5), but the growing body of empirical data leads inevitably to an ever increasing agreement in conclusions. Cannon, Pavlov, Köhler, Freud, and Goldstein talk about the same principle of equilibrium even when they use different terms. There is general agreement that the laws of preservation of energy apply to mental processes. S. Freud, J. Piaget, and A. Gesell introduced the laws of development.

The laws of nature in psychology are part of the general laws of nature. They express the regularity of happenings in the area of nature studied by psychologists. Psychologists deal with highly complex processes, and the discovery of laws of nature in that area is not an easy task. No wonder there is still so much controversy.

Laws of nature in psychology either exist or do not exist. They cannot be invented. They must be discovered, proved, and put in words. Some philosophers seem to believe that the logic of science is merely the logical syntax of the language of science.[43] Obviously this is not true. The problem of language is legitimate, but it is not the only or even the main methodological problem.

4. THE LANGUAGE OF SCIENCES

The Problem of Communication

All scientific data have to be recorded and communicated. Science is a system of *statements*—a definite kind of statements (true, proved, systematic general, etc.) made or *expressed* by a scientist and *communicated* to others. Scientific discoveries are not included in the body of science unless they are properly stated and communicated.

Scientists today do a painstaking job in presentation and communication. They like to say what they have to say in a clear, unambiguous manner. A special science of communication, a science of language, has been developed, mostly in two forms: the first is *syntax*, which deals with the conventional language and its proper use; the other is *mathematics* or the language of abstract symbols.

The tremendous growth of the *science of signs* may lead sometimes to an overenthusiastic distortion of the goals of scientific inquiry. The only goal of scientific inquiry is the search for truth: everything else is a means toward this goal.

[43] Rudolf Carnap, *Philosophy and Logical Syntax*, Kegan Paul, 1935.

One of these means is presentation and communication. Syntax and mathematics are indispensable tools of scientific research, but they are not the only ones, nor can they take the place of empirical research.

Some philosophers seem to believe that these tools are the science proper.[44] They regard scientific systems as systems of signs, whereas scientific systems are systems of true statements about things. These systems can be ordered by or expressed in systems of signs. While the formal study of signs plays an important role in scientific theory, it is nothing more than a study of the tools of presentation and communication. Poor systems of signs may unfavorably present scientific systems; a good, convenient, consistent system of signs may enhance the clarity and communicability of a scientific system. However, even the most formalized system of signs does not make a scientific system more scientific and more truthful.

The problems of presentation and communication of scientific data are more modest than the neo-positivists believe. Still, they are of considerable importance for the development of scientific theories.

Systems of Signs

The choice of a system of signs in which to put the results of empirical research is a matter of methodological convenience, but it is not an entirely free choice. Deciding on a definite system of signs requires a thorough examination of the facts concerned, the character of the scientific data, and the nature of a given system of signs. The character of the scientific data cannot be manipulated; nature does not try to please the scientist. Obviously, the system of signs must be adjusted to a given research area and branch of science, but there are definite limitations to the manipulation of signs. No system of signs which is self-contradictory can be used for scientific inquiry. This basic law of immanent truth does not prescribe how a system of signs is composed or constructed, how flexible it is, or how useful it must be for future studies.

Careful studies are required in order to state the degree of adaptability of a certain system of signs to a certain area of scientific investigation. Quite often new systems of signs are invented and after careful scrutiny applied to a certain area of research.

Mathematicians do not care whether their statements do or do not represent any portion of reality. The role played by the sign i, which is $\sqrt{-1}$, is well known in the history of electricity. It is the task of the empirical scientist to find or to invent a system of signs in which scientific data can be presented.

Any system, even a system of signs, has its own logic. Without this, it would be not a system but an aggregate. An empirical research worker must be aware of the rules underlying a given system of signs *before* he

44 *Ibid.*

utilizes it for presentation and communication of his findings. Unless a given system of signs fully corresponds to the empirical data and enables free transition in both directions—from the observed facts to the conceptualized signs and vice versa—this system should not be accepted as the tool for presentation and communication. Sometimes a system of signs is unable to carry and transmit the content it is supposed to carry. Composers know that not every system of notes can transmit faithfully the content of their compositions, nor is every instrument capable of reproducing each musical composition. One cannot translate the works of masters like Dostoevski or Romain Rolland or Shakespeare into the language of a primitive tribe. But literary Russian, French, English, and many other languages can do a perfect job.

Language Problems in Psychology

The "linguistic" decision of an empirical research worker can be quite important for the presentation of his findings; it can do justice or injustice to his entire work. Many research works suffer from unclear presentation. The terms used are often ambiguous or not well defined; the reasoning may not be rigorous enough; the terms may be used loosely. Especially in psychology, the dangers are great because the conventional languages are permeated with pictorial and nonprecise statements.

The history of human knowledge includes many never ending arguments that result from verbal confusion and lack of clarity in the definitions of terms applied. The use of mathematical symbols instead of conventional language has often resulted in greater clarity and avoidance of pseudo-problems.

Psychologists today successfully apply a great variety of mathematical devices, especially in the field of mental measurements.[45] It seems that the usual statistical methods are very well suited to handling most of the problems presented by laboratory work in perception, learning, and related areas.

Sometimes, however, difficulties arise from an improper choice of the system of signs. Herbart, for example, tried to order his metaphysical ideas to concepts of numbers. Obviously, his data could not be measured, and Herbart's mathematics was neither mathematics nor psychology.[46]

Kurt Lewin was much more cautious. Most of his definitions are clear and logical, his statements precise and well elaborated. Yet one cannot help feeling that Lewin was, in a way, a victim of his mathematical system. Once he decided to order psychology to the language of topological geometry, he had to adjust his empirical findings to such rules and laws of topol-

[45] Herold Gulliksen, *The Theory of Mental Testing*, Wiley, 1950.
[46] Benjamin B. Wolman, "The Historical Rule of Johann Friedrich Herbart," in B. B. Wolman, (Ed.), *Historical Roots of Contemporary Psychology*, Harper and Row, 1968, pp. 29–46.

ogy as barriers and regions. After Lewin's untimely death, his work in group dynamics was continued by his disciples, but there has been very little continuity in the use of his mathematical concepts and language.

Apparently, topology imposed on Lewin additional difficulties in communicating his findings. Either topology is not suited to the presentation of psychological data or Lewin failed to make proper use of it. In either case, he was compelled to construct a kind of "one-man language," and this is exactly the opposite of what scientific language is meant for.

5. SOME CURRENT METHODOLOGICAL PROBLEMS

As psychology continues to develop and mature, methodological issues become sharper and more focused. Two diverse issues will be discussed here: one theoretical and the other moral.

Scientific Paradigms

Thomas Kuhn[47] outlined a history of scientific development which is characterized by a preparadigmatic stage in which many rival schools exist. At that stage, there is little or no agreement as to fundamental issues or methodologies, and investigations focus on obvious and easily observed phenomena. Research is random; there is no clear overall organization in any particular field. A science is said to become paradigmatic when a discovery or achievement is significant enough to engage the various members of the scientific community and facilitates their organization around this discovery. Thus, it becomes an integrative schema and serves as a guide for further research. In the history of natural sciences, Benjamin Franklin's theory of electricity is an example of such an organizing system, or what Kuhn calls a true paradigm. As this paradigm becomes widely adopted, the previously rival schools either fade away or become isolated. Serious members of the scientific community take up the issues suggested by the paradigm. Controversy over fundamentals dwindles as the focus is shifted to the development of sophisticated hardware and the momentum of more precise hypotheses and telling observations becomes possible. There is an air of excitement and optimism throughout the scientific community and a reluctance to acknowledge the growing number of discrepancies between expected versus observed results as research becomes more and more precise. Gradually, the weaknesses of the paradigm become more and more obvious, and there is a fragmentation within the community until such time as a new discovery or achievement takes place.[48]

---

[47] Thomas S. Kuhn, *The Structures of Scientific Revolutions* (2nd ed.), Chicago University, Press, 1970.
[48] Albert Gilgen, "Introduction: Progress, a Paradigm, and Problems in Scientific Psychology," in A. R. Gilgen (Ed.), *Contemporary Scientific Psychology*, Academic Press, 1970, pp. 412.

Albert Gilgen asserts that despite the importance of research of the learning processes and conditioning, this research does not constitute a universal paradigm for scientific psychology. Gilgen questions the practice of calling psychology the *scientific* study of behavior. He asserts that psychology is still in the preparadigmatic stage, for the observation of behavior is a source of data, but not an end in itself. Psychologists are still arguing over such fundamental issues as: "What is the nature of psychology?" and "What should research in psychology entail?" Gilgen proposes that a truly paradigmatic stage would have to include more than just a study of behavior. It should focus on all the crucial processes in organism–environment interactions, such as perceiving, thinking, emoting, feeling, sensing, and so on. These processes do not correlate highly with gross behavior changes and therefore require investigation through other data sources such as biochemical, physiological, and introspective ones. Gilgen notes that physiological psychology has almost approximated a multileveled approach which he feels is necessary for a paradigmatic psychology. Yet, even in this area, too little data is available regarding the functional organization of the nervous system to enable psychologists to identify the underlying experiential states and transformations. Given the advances made during the last fifteen years, however, this area has indeed provided psychology with its first working paradigm. Gilgen feels that psychology underwent a period of premature mentalism in the years 1860–1915, before it entered the productive but limited period of behaviorism between 1915–1970. In the late 1970's, however, the foundation has been laid for entering a period of what could be called "mature mentalism," which will be supported by reliable procedures for studying both the behavioristic and the mentalistic functioning of the organism. The paradigmatic discipline, envisioned by Gilgen, would be a cognitive psychology developed through reliable multilevel data-gathering techniques.

In a discussion of significant contributions to the problems of development of a paradigmatic psychology, Gilgen quotes Karl Pribram as saying that both psychology and neurophysiology have tended to be technique oriented rather than problem oriented. But the imbalance that this tendency has created could be corrected if researchers in the two areas would work more closely together, thus avoiding duplication and enabling theorists to build on each others' work. Pribram himself is a prime example of the effectiveness of this approach: in his research, he has derived a model of brain functioning through the use of concepts and methods from psychology, neurophysiology, biochemistry, physics, linguistics, the computer sciences, and mathematics.[49]

D. D. Thiessen has proposed a new focus in behavior genetics, representing a shift from the repetition of well-established studies of the relationship between genetic factors and behavior to an emphasis on delinea-

[49] Karl H. Pribram, *Languages of the Brain: Experimental Paradoxes and Principles in Neuropsychology*, Prentice-Hall, 1971.

tion of the mechanisms developed by organisms to enable them to cope with environmental demands.

In the area of comparative psychology, Stanley Ratner has proposed an approach to comparative research which appreciates evolutionary theory in such a way as to use those animals which most appropriately demonstrate the studied behavioral patterns.

Lewis Lipsitt has suggested that it is time to move from observing and making inventories of infant and child behavior to controlled laboratory studies of the sensory, perceptual and behavioral capacities of neonates and infants.

Arthur Staats believes that in the areas of classical and operant conditioning, there is a need for a symbol system which will integrate these two aspects of learning theory. Such a system could serve as a framework for investigation and understanding of the more complex processes, such as, for example, the structure of language.[50]

Experimenting with Human Subjects

In recent years, psychologists have begun to concern themselves not only with the theoretical aspects of methodology, but also with the moral aspects of psychological research. In 1973 the *American Psychologist* published a report outlining the principles which the American Psychological Association deemed necessary to prevent what it considered to be abuses perpetrated by overzealous or sloppy experimenters. The Association's aim is to set standards which preserve the welfare and dignity of human subjects and maintain reasonable confidentiality of data at all times. The principles that were developed are as follows:

1. In planning a study the investigator has the personal responsibility to make a careful evaluation of its ethical acceptability, taking into account these Principles for research with human beings. To the extent that this appraisal, weighing scientific and humane values, suggests a deviation from any Principle, the investigator incurs an increasingly serious obligation to seek ethical advice and to observe more stringent safeguards to protect the rights of the human research participant.
2. Responsibility for the establishment and maintenance of acceptable ethical practice in research always remains with the individual investigator. The investigator is also responsible for the ethical treatment of research participants by collaborators, assistants, students and employees, all of whom, however, incur parallel obligations.
3. Ethical practice requires the investigator to inform the participant of all features of the research that reasonably might be expected to influence willingness to participate, and to explain all other aspects of the research about which the participant inquires. Failure to make full disclosure increases the investigator's responsibility to maintain confidentiality, and to protect the welfare and dignity of the research participant.
4. Openness and honesty are essential characteristics of the relationship be-

---

[50] Gilgen, *op. cit.*

tween investigator and research participant. When the methodological requirements of a study necessitate concealment or deception, the investigator is required to ensure the participant's understanding of the reasons for this action and to restore the quality of the relationship with the investigator.

5. Ethical research practice requires the investigator to respect the individual's freedom to decline to participate in research or to discontinue participation at any time. The obligation to protect this freedom requires special vigilance when the investigator is in a position of power over the participant. The decision to limit this freedom increases the investigator's responsibility to protect the participant's dignity and welfare.

6. Ethically acceptable research begins with the establishment of a clear and fair agreement between the investigator and the research participant that clarifies the responsibilities of each. The investigator has the obligation to honor all promises and commitments included in that agreement.

7. The ethical investigator protects participants from physical and mental discomfort, harm and danger. If the risk of such consequences exists, the investigator is required to inform the participant of that fact, to secure consent before proceeding, and to take all possible measures to minimize distress. A research procedure may not be used if it is likely to cause serious and lasting harm to participants.

8. After the data are collected, ethical practice requires the investigator to provide the participant with a full clarification of the nature of the study and to remove any misconceptions that may have arisen. Where scientific or humane values justify delaying or withholding information, the investigator acquires a special responsibility to assure that there are no damaging consequences for the participant.

9. Where research procedures may result in undesirable consequences for the participant, the investigator has the responsibility to detect and remove or correct these consequences, including, where relevant, long-term aftereffects.

10. Information obtained about the research participants during the course of an investigation is confidential. When the possibility exists that others may obtain access to such information, ethical research practice requires that this possiblity, together with the plans for protecting confidentiality be explained to the participants as a part of the procedure for obtaining informed consent.[51]

In a recent article on research with the mentally ill, the *APA Monitor* reported that the National Commission for the Protection of Human Subjects recommended the use of institutionalized "mentally ill" persons in research, despite the absence of consent by the subject. The issue of informed consent has been a major problem with research subjects who are often unable to give informed consent due to diminished capacity. Therefore, the Commission has tried to set a balance between the right of self-determination and the ethical obligation of the state to protect individuals from being victimized. Through the use of review boards and a "consent auditor" it is hoped that research projects will be developed which represent a minimal risk, that privacy and confidentiality will be maintained, and that subjects

[51] "Ethical Principles in the Conduct of Research with Human Participants," *American Psychologist*, 1973, *28*, (1), pp. 79–80.

will be protected from being forced to participate in studies against their will. Under the law, in the United States the subject's assent is not required in a mimimal risk study, as long as the subject does not actively object to participating in the study. But in studies in which there is more than minimal risk, albeit possible benefit, it is required that either the subject or a guardian give a formal consent.[52]

[52] Herbert Wray, "Panel Gives Approval to Research on Mentally Ill," *APA Monitor*, 1978, *9*, (4), p. 11.

16

Selected Issues

1. The Mind–Body Dichotomy

The Dichotomy

Psychologists have tried to escape the dualistic conflict inherited from traditional philosophy. Dualism has split the world into bodies and souls, leaving bodies to scientific study and assigning souls to psychologists.

Several attempts have been made to revise this division of the subject matter of research. Dilthey and all who followed in his footsteps assigned to psychology all the *products* of human mind, the culture. They made psychology the queen of the humanities, which do not deal with objects or bodies but study the immense area of human culture.

The structuralists entrenched themselves in *consciousness*. They recognized the supremacy of physiology and leaned heavily on studies of the nervous system in a perpetual search for a neurological interpretation for psychology. They discarded the immortal soul with its faculties and borrowed the empirical and experimental methods from the natural scientists. Psychology, they said, deals with phenomena which cannot be seen from the outside; hence introspection is the perfect and the only possible substitute for extrospection. Rigorous methods, resembling those of physical and physiological laboratories, were developed. Psychologists did not define their topic as nonmaterial. They drew a thin line between themselves and other natural scientists out of sheer necessity, because the phenomena they had to cover could be seen by inner observation only. No one could blame Titchener or Wundt for being a priori mentalistic. Even less blame could be put on the phenomenological school or the functionalists. The phenomenologists studied what was going on inasmuch as it was observable. James rejected the concept of soul and sought an integrating force instead.

The functionalists took an additional step in the direction of the natural sciences, especially biology. They refused to deal with consciousness or with phenomena given by introspection outside the context of biological processes. Psychological capacities whether conscious or not, are regarded by functionalists as important functions in the adjustment to the environment; they are no less needed, no less vital than the legs which carry the organism or the stomach which digests the food. Psychological capacities are, in Dewey's way of thinking, an *instrument* in adjustment, and one of the most necessary functions of the organism.

The "objective" psychologists rejected mentalism and studied the *behavior* of men. Behavior does not prejudge the issue. Methodologically speaking, behaviorism is a naïve empiricism: you can easily see, compare, predict, and verify. No wonder behaviorism was received with so much enthusiasm and hope.

But too many problems remained unsolved. The so-called higher mental processes resisted the efforts of simple explanations. Is thinking really nothing but prevocal talking? Cannot deaf-mutes solve problems and reason without any talk whatsoever?

The neo-behaviorists could not avoid the soma–psyche issue. Tolman, Hull, Skinner, and others contributed immensely both to the methodology and to factual data of psychology, but they could not solve this problem.

Some solutions were offered by Lashley, Kantor, Hebb, and the gestaltists. Each of the proposed solutions has been discussed in the present volume. Each increased our knowledge of factual data, but none could find the bridge between the somatic and the psychic.

The cautious Pavlov avoided psychological terms but left the door open for a "methodological dualism" in the spirit of a bridge-building philosophy. The Soviet psychologists kept working on various problems in neurology and psychology on the assumption that the psychological reflects the physical. This methodological dualism enabled Soviet psychology to overcome the arid and naïve reductionism of Bekhterev, but it does not solve the problem under consideration.

Freud was fully aware of this problem. When he started his work at the turn of the century, the general atmosphere in psychiatry was unfavorable to a nonorganic theory of mental disturbances. Freud was accused of mentalism, but it was he who said: "The future may teach us how to exercise a direct influence, by means of particular chemical substances, upon the amounts of energy and their distribution in the apparatus of mind."[1]

Reductionism

As mentioned in Chapter 15, one must distinguish between *theoretical* and *methodological* reductionism. The first attempts to reduce the theoretical body of the to-be-reduced science to the terms of the reducing science which is believed to encompass the data of the reduced-to-be-science, for example, some philosophers of science believe that biology could be reduced to chemistry.

Methodological reductionism advocates the application of research methods of one science to another, such as, for example, the application of

[1] Sigmund Freud, *Outline of Psychoanalysis*, Norton, 1949, p. 79.

statistical methods developed in agriculture to economics, or the application of physical methods of measurement and other quantitative techniques to the study of human behavior.

One can distinguish three types of theoretical reductionism. Theoretical reductionism in the realm of psychology is belief

1. That the subject matter of psychology can presently be stated in terms of the subject matter of another science, for example, neurophysiology
2. That future research may discover such a reduction is feasible
3. That the scientific propositions and theories derived from empirical studies in psychology could and should be presented as logical consequences of the scientific propositions of other sciences

The subject matter of psychology—the human personality—is reduced to biochemical and neurological processes.

Not all psychologists share the belief that such a reduction is possible and they oppose *radical reductionism*. They feel that presently radical reductionism is an untenable hypothesis, yet they share the belief that such a reduction may become possible in the future. This belief, which we shall call *hoped-for reductionism*, is widely accepted in psychology.

A third alternative, *logical reductionism*, tries to reduce the formal logical propositions derived from empirical studies and conceptualization of psychological theory to scientific propositions of other sciences.

Radical reductionism insists that events described by the "science-to-be-reduced" are mere appearances or illusions. Actually, these events are more truthfully explained in terms of the other "reducing science." The facts as described by the science-to-be-reduced are believed to be unreal and have to be replaced by scientific data described by the reducing science. The reducing science must "take over" the science-to-be-reduced.

The history of philosophy and science offers several instances of such developments. The pre-Socratic philosophers introduced the concept of four elements in an effort to reduce the variety of phenomena perceived in the universe to the four elements of the "true" world. Plato believed the material world to be a mere reflection of the world of ideas. It was the same in Hegel's philosophical system. Galileo's theory of falling bodies was "reduced" by Newton's theory of gravitation and mechanics. In our times, metabolic processes are being reduced to chemistry.

Although the efforts to solve the psyche–soma dichotomy can develop in either direction, by reducing body to mind or mind to body, the latter has been more common. Karl Vogt in *Vorlesungen über den Menschen* (1863) defended the idea that consciousness should be regarded as one of the many brain functions. Vogt asserted that human thought is related to the brain just as gall is related to the liver. Similar ideas were expressed by H. Moleschott: "No thought without phosphorus." Moleschott, in his *Krieslauf des Lebens* (1852), made an effort to re-establish the unity of the universe in the place of the "hopeless" division of the world into material and spiritual which, he believed, was a division between the real and the imaginary. Herbart also advocated radical reductionism and presented mental life as a function of material units.[2]

The difference between psychology and physiology as Watson saw it, is that physiology studies separate physiological functions, whereas psychology deals with the functions of the organism as a whole. The findings of psychology become the functional correlates of structure and lend themselves to explanation in physico-chemical terms, Watson wrote.[3] Bekhterev believed that consciousness is a state of physical energy related to central inhibition and resistance in cortical processes.[4] Hebb wrote about "the kind of activity *throughout the cerebrum* which we call consciousness." He also believed that "interest or motivation" can be "provisionally translated into the stability and persistence of the phase sequence" in nerve cells.[5]

Some psychologists vigorously rejected any sort of theoretical reductionism. According to Skinner, "modern science has attempted to put forth an ordered and integrated conception of nature. . . . The picture which emerges is almost always dualistic. The scientist humbly admits that he is describing only half of the universe, and he defers to another world—a world of mind or consciousness—for which another mode of inquiry is assumed to be required."[6] According to Skinner, there is no valid reason to reduce psychology, physiology, physics, chemistry, or any other science. Kurt Lewin (1951) also saw no advantage in reducing psychology to physiology, and objected to the Gestaltists' isomorphic theory of mind and body.[7]

Most psychological theorists have neither accepted nor rejected reductionism, but profess a hoped-for-reductionism. For instance, C. L. Hull (1943) maintained that there is no adequate neuropsychology to which psychology could be reduced at the present time. Freud also believed that the future might teach us how to exercise a direct influence, by means of particular chemical substances, on the amount of energy and its distribution in the apparatus of mind.

Another solution was suggested by *logical reductionists*. According to Nagel:[8]

> The objective of the reduction is to show that the laws or general principles of the secondary science are simply logical consequences of the assumptions of the primary science (the reducing science). However, if these laws contain expressions that do not occur in the assumptions of the primary science, a logical deri-

---

[2] B. B. Wolman, "Johann Friedrich Herbart," in B. B. Wolman (Ed.), *Historical Roots of Contemporary Psychology*, Harper & Row, 1968, pp. 29–46.

[3] J. B. Watson, *Psychology from the Standpoint of a Behaviorist*, Lippincott, 1919, p. 20.

[4] V. M. Bekhterev, *Objektive Psychologie–Reflexologie*, Teubner, 1913, pp. 45 ff.

[5] D. O. Hebb, *The Organization of Behavior*, Wiley, 1949, pp. 219, 223.

[6] B. F. Skinner, *Science and Human Behavior*, MacMillan, 1953, p. 276.

[7] Kurt Lewin, *Field Theory in Social Science*, Harper & Row, 1951.

[8] Ernst Nagel, *The Structure of Science*, Harcourt, Brace, Jovanovich, 1953, p. 541.

vation is clearly impossible. Accordingly, a necessary condition for the derivation
is the explicit formulation of suitable relations between such expressions in the
secondary science and the expressions occurring in the premises of the primary
discipline.

However, logical reductionism does not prove either that mental and
somatic processes are the same or that they are different. Experts in brain
science find little help in logical reductionism and, as Sherrington put it,
mind and brain, "for all I can tell, they remain refractory apart."[9]

The Concept of Identity

Apparently, the problem of mind and body cannot be resolved within
the framework of reductionism. One should, perhaps, embark on the road
of logical analysis. Are mind and body two different things or can they be
perceived as one and the same thing?[10]

In order to tackle this question, one must start by clarifying the terms
"the same," "identical," and so on. Let us start with the mathematical sign
= (equals). Consider the equation

$$a + b = 0 \tag{1}$$

This equation does not imply identity. In the above equation, the sign a
and the sign b have the same numerical value, one of them positive, the
other negative. The sign symbol "zero" is not necessarily identical with the
composite sign "$a + b$." The above equation merely represents a mathematical operation, but not an identity relationship. Translated into simple English, it reads as follows: a added to b *equals* 0, but they are a and b, and
they are *not* a zero.

The philosophy of science is full of concepts uncritically borrowed from
mathematics. Such a state of affairs was perhaps jusified in the times of
Spinoza or Kant, when philosophers believed in the alleged superiority and
self-evidence of mathematical propositions. However, the development of
newer mathematical systems, such as, for example, Riemann's and Lobachevki's geometry, Boyle's system, matrix algebra, and topology have challenged the axiomatic nature of the mathematical systems and made mathematics into a systematic aggregate of symbolic signs and operations, a sort
of language or game.

This change in the role of mathematics permits a far-reaching revision
of several concepts. Consider the equation

$$a = a \tag{2}$$

[9] C. S. Sherrington, *Man On His Nature*, MacMillan, 1941, p. 212.
[10] B. B. Wolman, "Does Psychology Need Its Own Philosophy of Science?" *American Psychologist*, 1971, 26, 877–886.

This equation seems to be self-evident, but this alleged self-evidence can be questioned. For instance, in traditional algebra:

$$a + b = b + a \qquad (3)$$

but in matrix algebra

$$\{a + b\} \neq \{b + a\} \qquad (4)$$

In topological mathematics, the equation $a + b = b + a$ can become meaningless since the relative position of the elements in regard to each other is the relevant issue in topology.

Furthermore, consider the chemical equation

$$C + C + O = C_2O \qquad (5)$$

Is C_2O identical with $C + C + O$? The empirical evidence militates against such an assumption, for the *quality* of C_2O is different from two unbound C's and an O. Thus, Equation (5) does not represent an identity, but merely describes a complex process by which C and C and O can become C_2O. Moreover, this description is far from being accurate, which may undermine one's belief in the applicability of simple mathematical signs to the description of complex phenomena. One is tempted to remark at this point that the irrational mathematical sign i in the equation

$$i = \sqrt{-1} \qquad (6)$$

has played a constructive role in the history of electricity.

The development of thermodynamics should have aroused serious doubts concerning the possibility of anything ever being identical with anything, including itself. In thermodynamics, heat *changes* into kinetic energy; does this mean that heat *is* kinetic energy? Is fuel identical with energy? Is water identical with vapor and ice? Empirically speaking, ice $\neq$ water $\neq$ vapor. Are they, therefore, the same? Or are they not?

Heraclitus said that no one can bathe twice in *the same* river. It also seems obvious, however, that no one could ever remain the same person. A person P at time t and environment e, is not exactly the same as the "same" person a while later at time t_2 and in an environment e_2. Thus,

$$P_{t_1e_1} \neq P_{t_2e_2} \qquad (7)$$

K. Lewin, H. S. Sullivan, B. B. Wolman, and several others have pointed to the *field-theoretical* nature of human personality. Prognosis of mental or physical diseases can be, at best, a statistical approximation. In order to predict an individual case, a clinican must possess a complete knowledge of *all* relevant factors affecting his patient, and the prediction, if any, must be field-theoretical. "The same" patient reacts differently to "the same" disease in different environment and under different type of treatment.

Continuity in Change

Apparently no one is, nor can ever be, identical with oneself, and the term "identical" should be put in the vocabulary of archaic terms together with witchcraft, phlogiston, ether, and so on. The fact that heat may *turn* into motion, electric current into light, and an egg into a chicken, does not mean that, in any of these cases, the antecedent is identical with that which follows. Complex processes of change take place in every one of the three above-mentioned instances, and each process of change is different.

Change does not imply discontinuity. A fertilized egg becomes a zygote, and the zygote becomes an embryo, fetus, neonate, infant, toddler, little child, adolescent, college student, and eventually, perhaps, a famous pediatrician. Is the pediatrician "the same" as or "identical" with the nursery child he or she was 40 or 50 years ago? The answer is yes, in the sense of continuity, but not in the sense of identity.

It is an undeniable fact that, under certain conditions, certain bodies change, merge, split, grow, shrink, move, stop, fall apart, and so on. Indians in Montana used to squeeze the skulls of their newborn infants to make them look prettier by the standards of the prevailing fashion. Contemporary women starve themselves to meet the standards set by the Garment Center's fashion designers. When a woman has lost twenty pounds, is she still the same woman or not? When a child has grown up, when an attic has been added to a house, when a man has shaved his beard: are these all still the same?

Obviously, there are degrees of change. When a pot of water is put on a stove, the temperature of the water changes. When the water reaches the boiling point, further changes take place. Logically speaking, as long as at least one element A_1 persists in A_2, we speak of *continuity*.

There are a great many types and degrees of change and, as mentioned before, there is no reason to ascribe to them one path and one pattern. The fact of continuity in change is evident in many, if not all, phenomena and events in the universe. As observed by Greek philosophers and by the Hebrew Ecclesiastes, rivers evaporate and turn into clouds, and clouds give rain and fill rivers with water. Lava erupts and turns into fertile soil, and some fertile soil is eroded or covered by dunes. Species develop and perish, and new worlds develop out of old ones.

This continuous change is expressed in a universal theory, the theory of *monistic transitionism*.[11] Monistic transitionism (1) takes into account the

[11] B. B. Wolman, "Principles of Monistic Transitionism," in B. B. Wolman and E. Nagel (Ed.), *Scientific Psychology: Principles and Approaches*, Basic Books, 1965, pp. 563–585.

diversity and *variability* of nature, (2) unites this empirical diversity into an over-all continuous *unity*, and (3) introduces the general idea of *continuous changeability* of things. Transitionism does not assume uniformity of the universe; it assumes only its continuity.

Monistic transitionism is neither reductionism of any type nor an emergence theory. It simply states that, empirically speaking, heat is not motion; heat and motion are measured by different units and have different impacts. They act differently; they are different.

Yet, heat and motion can be, under certain conditions, transformed into one another. Thus, transitionism at the empirical level states that although things are different, some things have many similarities, and certain things can be transformed into other things.

Obviously, certain phenomena, although empirically different, can be partially reduced to each other. This rule does not apply to all phenomena, for unity does not mean uniformity. Certain sciences can be reduced in a radical sense, while other sciences can be reduced only in the sense of logical reductionism, that is, merely interpreted in terms of the laws of other sciences. Perhaps chemistry will be formally reduced to quantum mechanics. Certain areas, however, are not reducible. But even those areas that are not reducible can be presented in a continuum of changes. The issue is not an issue of faith, but of empirical evidence and logical inference.

Transitionism

Transitionism aims at the development of a set of theoretical constructs applicable to living organisms. These theoretical constructs would permit the presentation of mental phenomena as a continuum of all other organic processes. Organic processes, called O, under certain conditions, called k_1, are transformed ($\Rightarrow$) into mental processes, called M. Thus,

$$O_{k_1} \Rightarrow M \tag{8}$$

which means O_{k_1} is transformed into M. A reverse process of transformation of mental processes (M) into organic ones (O) is also feasible under the condition k_2. Thus,

$$M_{k_2} \Rightarrow O \tag{9}$$

which means M_{k_2} is transformed into O.

Transitionism is a general theory which views the universe as a system of continuous transitions from one form into another. It is a theory of unity and continuity. Transitionism encompasses Einstein's principle of transformation of energy into matter; then it presents the evolution of matter in three recognizable phases: (1) The inanimate or inorganic matter at a certain point of evolution undergoes changes and becomes (2) organic, as described in the experimental studies of Oparin,[12] then, at a certain phase in evolution, becomes (3) psychological processes (which can also be called behavior). Transitionism links all three phases into one process of change and continuity. This process is also reversible, for, as inorganic matter may become organic and organic matter may become psychological, the psychological elements can turn organic and organic elements may turn inorganic. For example, under the impact of alcohol, human feelings can change, and under the impact of human feelings, body chemistry can change. Nature crosses this bridge from mind to body and from body to mind every day in a series of psychosomatic and somatopsychic phenomena. Extrasensory perception and psychokinesis are but particular cases of the universal process of transition.

The principles of *monistic transitionism* can be summarized as follows:

1. Change does not disrupt continuity of the universe.
2. The unity of the universe remains always the same in a continuous process of change.
3. Einstein's formula $E = mc^2$ is a particular case of the more general principle of continuous transition.
4. Biological evolution is a particular case of the universal process of change which may go in any direction, from energy to matter, from mind to body, from past to future, or the reverse of each.
5. Mind and body are two levels of transition, the mind being merely a higher level of evolution.
6. Higher evolutionary levels incorporate the lower ones, but not vice versa. Thus, both theoretical and methodological reductionism must be limited to clearly reducible issues.
7. Causal thinking is, in a sense, anthropomorphic, for it ascribes human features to the universe. However, causality, as a biological phenomenon, applies to human behavior and partly to all life processes.
8. Parapsychological phenomena are the area where mind and body are transformed into each other; these phenomena do not occur everywhere, but are determined by complex factors, just as are other psychosomatic and somatopsychic processes.

Transitionism in Neuropsychology

Soviet experiments in interoceptive conditioning by Ayrapetyants,[13] and Bykov,[14] prove that the viscera are closer to the unconscious than to the conscious. The inner organs can be conditioned without the subject being

---

[12] A. I. Oparin, *The Origins of Life on Earth*, Academic Press, 1957.
[13] E. S. Ayrapetyants, *Higher Nervous Functions and the Receptors of Internal Organs*, U.S.S.R. Academy of Science, 1952.
[14] K. M. Bykov, *The Cerebral Cortex and the Inner Organs*, Chemical Publishing, 1957.

aware of it. For example, in an experiment performed by Balakshina in denervated kidneys with a destroyed hypophysis, the physiological processes in the kidneys could be interpreted in terms of physics. In experiments on pain reception, where speech signals were used, the role of the cerebral cortex was established. Stimulation of exteroceptors has usually been accompanied by a "subjectively perceived sensation." In Russian psychology, this term denotes mental processes. Stimulation of interoceptors was either not perceived subjectively at all, or at least not accompanied by any definite, localized perception. Soviet research has contributed to the differentiation of what might be called "levels" in the transition from organic to mental. Interoceptive conditioning in man was proven to be unconscious.

Empathy

Dreams and hypnosis are certainly unconscious phenomena, but empathy can be viewed neither as an entirely unconscious, nor as a purely mental process. Empathy has been defined by Wolman's *Dictionary of Behavioral Science* [15] as the ability to perceive the mood and feelings of another person, that is, the understanding of the feelings, sufferings, and situation of another person without these feelings being communicated by words.

Moreover, empathy encompasses communication across large distances; thus, it borders on and often transgresses the borders of ESP. The ability to perceive communication not expressed in words is a prerequisite of a successful patient–therapist relationship in practically every type of psychotherapy, but this is a one-to-one proximity relationship.

Sullivan interpreted empathy in organismic terms. Sullivan's theory invites comparison with Cannon's homeostatic system. *Tension* and *relief* follow each other, especially since they are interpreted by Sullivan in purely physiological terms, as a contraction and relaxation of muscles. This physiological process is later modified by social influences. The child soon learns that on certain occasions the immediate relaxation of bowel muscles meets with parental disapproval. Parental disapproval causes a feeling of discomfort. This *empathized discomfort* stems not from the organism but from *interpersonal relationships*. This discomfort is so strong that it destroys the original comfort of relaxation. For example, as soon as there is any tension in the bladder or bowels, the proper muscles act immediately to bring relief. However, this automatic relaxation may invite parental hostility, which produces in the child a feeling of empathized discomfort. This feeling will bring the child to learn "to suffer increasing tension in the bladder and rectum and to resist the automatic relaxation of the sphincter muscles concerned in retaining the urine and feces. Failures in this are often accompanied by emphathized discomfort, and success is often the occasion of

[15] B. B. Wolman, *Dictionary of Behavioral Science*, Van Nostrand Reinhold, 1973, p. 119.

empathized comfort which is added to the satisfaction from relief of tension."[16]

Transitionism includes hypnosis, dreams, empathy, the unconscious, cathexis, and a host of other psychosomatic and somatopsychic phenomena. It includes the infant and "the same" infant who grew up and became an adult, the seed and and the tree, the mind and the body. It does not stand alone; modern physics has accepted the dual nature of light, and Firsoff's theory of *neutrino* offers an important addition to Einstein's theory of transformation of energy into matter.

2. Beyond Pleasure and Pain

The Problem of Pleasure

Pleasure and reduction of tension are not identical terms. Pleasure can increase glandular or muscular tension, as it does in sexual foreplay or in the sight of food to a hungry man. Goldstein was critical for Fechner's and Freud's systems of pleasure–relief versus displeasure–tension. He suggested instead the pleasurable tension on an optimal level of fuctioning.

In our discussion of learning processes (cf Chapter 2, 3, and 4) the distinction between reward and reinforcement has been clarified. Reward is the concomitant of pleasure; reinforcement, as used by Pavlov, is not. Nor is it in Hull's theory.

The only solution is to assume that there are at least two different types of learning, one not related to pleasure and the other more or less related to pleasure. Skinner believed that Pavlov's classic conditioning depended on the autonomic responses and not on Thorndike's law of effect with its satisfiers and annoyers. Operant conditioning is a function of the skeletal muscles and depends on the law of effect.

It can be hypothesized that in phylogenetic evolution the prehedonic stage antecedes the hedonic. Probably, lower organisms are incapable of pleasure–displeasure, yet they function, and even learn. No one can ascribe pleasure to plants or to their vital functions of osmosis, assimilation of carbon, or tropism.

Many of the functions of higher mammals, on the other hand, are accompanied by pain or pleasure. Undoubtedly, the greatest part of human functioning is performed on the pleasure level, and Thorndike's annoyers and satisfiers stem from empirical observations of animals and human beings.

One must distinguish between meeting one's needs and the feeling of pleasure. Such words as satisfaction, gratification, and relief serve both purposes. We often say, "The meal was satisfying," without making it clear whether it provided a reduction of organic need or a feeling of pleasure.

[16] H. S. Sullivan, *Conceptions of Modern Psychology*, 1947, p. 44.

The same lack of clarity applies to pain. To be hurt means to suffer damage, whether painful or not, and at the same to be hurt means to experience pain, whether a damage was caused to the organism or not.

The Pre-Hedonic Level

Not all organic diseases cause pain. Sometimes an insignificant damage to the organism causes severe pain, for example, pain perceived from a nonexistent limb after amputation or from harmless electric shock. On the other hand, a severe disease such as cancer may play havoc with an organism without causing pain until the later stages. Carmichael[17] has noticed that "picking a guinea pig fetus with a needle so as to bring a drop of blood may not be so effective in eliciting a response as would be a fine hair applied to a corresponding point." Obviously, certain parts of the body respond to tactile stimuli but do not respond to pain–pleasure stimuli. Hence, damage can be caused without eliciting pain.

According to Bykov, "it has now been definitely proven that some organs (the visceral peritoneum, the surface of the cerebral cortex, and perhaps some parts of the intestine) are devoid of pain sensibility." However, "the absence of pain receptors does not necessarily mean the absence of other interoceptors."[18]

It has been observed on several occasions that individuals with a lethal disease may experience a kind of premonition. A patient of Wolman's, diagnosed as having a hysterical character disorder, began to complain about fatigue, occasional nausea, and loss of weight. His family physician dismissed him as a hypochondriac. Wolman insisted that he consult another physician. The second physician did not find anything wrong, but gave him some medication and the patient did not complain any more. Several weeks later, the patient told the following dream: "My brother is in war. The Germans throw bombs and hit my brother in the underbelly; the young man is in a mortal danger and must be immediately hospitalized." Free associations revealed that Germans represented germs or disease, and that the patient identified himself with his younger brother. Wolman took the patient's unconscious communication seriously and insisted on an immediate and thorough checkup by a fist-rate internist. The internist reported that the patient suffered from cancer.[19]

Razran pointed to the fact that in the simplest, lowest-level conditioning there is no reward or pleasure.[20] Simple classic conditioning based on

[17] Carmichael, "Ontogenetic Development," in S. S. Stevens (Ed.), *Handbook of Experimental Psychology*, Wiley, 1951, p. 297.

[18] Bykov, *op. cit.*, p. 279.

[19] B. B. Wolman, *Success and Failure in Psychoanalysis and Psychotherapy*, Macmillan, 1972, pp. 232–252.

[20] G. Razran, "Evolutionary Psychology," in B. B. Wolman and E. Nagel (Eds.), *Scientific Psychology*, Basic Books, 1965, pp. 207–252.

dominance can be found in invertebrates, decorticated animals, earliest infancy, and visceral organs.

Several studies confirm this point of view. Apparently, a great part of human activities is conducted outside the pain–pleasure continuum. This is the *pre-hedonic* level of functioning. A great many other human activities, motivated by pain and pleasure feelings, are conducted on the hedonic level.

The Hedonic Level

Freud perceived mental life as taking place in the pleasure–displeasure continuum. This continuum was related by Freud to an increase and decrease (relief) in the amount of excitation. The demand for immediate relief, notwithstanding possible consequences, was called the *pleasure principle*, and the postponement of gratification dictated by self-preservation was called the *reality principle*.

"We have decided," wrote Freud in 1920, "to relate pleasure and unpleasure to the quantity of excitation that is present in the mind but is not in any way 'bound'; and to relate them in such a manner that unpleasure corresponds to an *increase* in the quantity of excitation and pleasure to a diminution." At this point, Freud quoted G. T. Fechner's hypothesis that reads, "Every psychophysical movement crossing the threshold of consciousness is attended by pleasure in proportion as, beyond a certain limit, it approximates to complete stability, and is attended by unpleasure in proportion as, beyond a certain limit, it deviates from complete stability." Freud continued, "If the work of the mental apparatus is directed toward keeping the quantity of excitation low, then anything that is calculated to increase that quantity is bound to be felt as adverse to the functioning of the apparatus, that is, unpleasurable."[21]

Alcoholism, drug addiction, and overeating prove beyond doubt that people can indulge in pleasurable activities even when these activities bring harm. Pleasure and pain can be more powerful motives than protection of life. Hyperalgesic individuals may refuse treatment if it causes too much pain.

It can be hypothesized that in the phylogenetic evolution, the pre-hedonic stage antecedes the hedonic one. Most probably, lower organisms are incapable of pleasure–displeasure sensations, and yet they function and even learn.

A crucial place in this controversy has to be assigned to the experimentation in viseral conditioning conducted by Bykov and his associates.[22] These studies prove beyond doubt that some inner organs are responsive to sensory stimuli but do not react with pain or pleasure. The pain–pleasure

[21] S. Freud, *Beyond the Pleasure Principle*, Perma, 1950.
[22] Bykov, *op. cit.*

reactions are not universal and probably start on a certain evolutionary level.

It seems, therefore, worthwhile to introduce three main levels in mental processes: the *pre-hedonic, hedonic,* and *post-hedonic.* This does not mean that classic conditioning is pre-hedonic and operant conditioning is hedonic. The prehedonic level corresponds to Ukhtomski's prepotence or sheer-force conditioning; conditioning on the hedonic level is related to reward and punishment. Certain functions of the human body are not accompanied by the feeling of pleasure. For instance, the functions of division, growth, and decline of cells, the secretion of thyroxine, the growth of hair and nails, the growth of bones and muscles, and the growth of tumors in their initial stages are usually not accompanied by pleasure or pain. They are pre-hedonic On the other hand, the secretion of semen, sucking, eating and drinking, rhythmical movements, overcoming of obstacles, singing, and hugging and kissing are usually accompanied by pleasure. Deprivation of food is painful; deprivation of certain nutritional values can ultimately be dangerous for the organism, yet it is not painful, at least in its beginning. Thus, pleasure applies to a certain part of human actions; other actions are guided by prepleasure or postpleasure factors that will be explained below.

The Post-Hedonic Level

There are many instances when men and women acted in disregard of pain and pleasure. When a tired mother gets up in the middle of the night to take care of an infant, she certainly does not follow her wishes for comfort and pleasure. Restful sleep is definitely more enjoyable than sleepless nights spent at the crib of a sick child. When hungry parents give away the last piece of bread to their infant, they renounce pleasure and accept pangs of hunger. Many parents will go into fire to save the lives of their children. Some people will do it for their friends; some will do it for strangers or for any human being in distress, as the history of the Danish resistance to the Nazis has proven.

History is full of examples of men and women who acted in an apparent renunciation of pleasure and disregard of pain. Consider the early Christians, who did not seek escape from Roman persecution and sang "Hallelujah" while being burned alive or thrown into cages of wild beasts. If avoidance of pain and pursuit of pleasure were the only motives of human actions, there would be no Christianity today, or Judaism either. In the wars of Judea against the Roman Emperors, the Jewish people displayed utter disregard for pain and death. In medieval and contemporary times, Jewish people have been exposed to discrimination, hate, and persecution. The persecutors, whether the Crusaders, the flagellants, the Christian kings, or the Holy Inquisition, gave the Jews the choice of conversion to Christianity with all its privileges and joys, or terrible persecution and torture for those who remained faithful to the religion of their fathers. Some

Jews could not reject pleasure and withstand pain. Most of them, however, made the choice and proudly refused to surrender. The heroic story of the Warsaw Ghetto's fight in 1943 against the Nazis is symbolic of the history of mankind; the history of religious, national, and social movements knows many cases of self-sacrifice, courage, willing martyrdom, and heroism. Some men and women have been willing to accept deprivation and pain and refused to renounce or betray their friends, families, country, and ideals. An unconditional avoidance of pain and unswerving search for pleasure would render loyalty, honor, heroism, and morality impossible.

Apparently, pain may be decreased and even become completely inhibited by psychological procedures, such as hypnosis, suggestion, and distraction.[23] The most convincing cases are those in which major operations and obstetrical deliveries have been performed under hypnosis. Some patients have had amputations performed while praying to religious images, and have said they felt no pain. Personality traits and sociocultural factors can affect the sensitivity to pain to a remarkable degree.[24]

Bykov reported a series of experiments conducted by A. T. Pshonik.[25] These experiments were devoted to the study of "the cortical dependence of pain reception." Pain was caused by the pricks of a needle and by the application of heat (63°C) to the skin. In preliminary experiments, the pain lasted for ten seconds and resulted in vascular constriction and, consequently, a fall of the plethysmogram. The plethysmogram has been used by research workers as an objective yardstick of pain.

Pshonik's experiments threw light on what Bykov called *psychogenic pain*. Pshonik applied twenty different combinations of the bell and temperature below that of the pain stimulation and elicited in his subjects "the same vaso-constriction (a fall of the plethysmogram) and the same subjective pain sensations as the usual pain combinations of the bell and 63°." The conditioned stimulus, the bell, "transforms a subdolorific stimulation into a pain stimulation."

In some experiments, the unconditioned stimulus gave zero on the plethysmogram, but the conditioned stimulus (a combination of a tactile stimulus with the bell) changed the effect of the unconditioned stimulus and evoked a constriction of the vessels and, when applied with light, evoked dilation. Even words or speech signals of the second order evoked more intense pain or pain inhibition reactions than unconditioned stimuli.

Antigone Principle

There are apparently, human actions in which the pain–pleasure consideration seems to disappear, or at least becomes weaker. Bykov reported cases of wounded men who controlled their own pain. Apparently, certain

[23] E. R. Hilgard and J. R. Hilgard, *Hypnosis in the Relief of Pain*, Kaufmann, 1975.
[24] R. A. Sternbach, *Pain Patients: Traits and Treatment*, Academic Press, 1974.
[25] Bykov, *op. cit.*, pp. 339 ff.

individuals are capable of suffering for the sake of others and sacrifice themselves to make others happy. The prototype of this attitude is parenthood. Wolman named this attitude the *Antigone Principle,* after Antigone, the daughter of King Oedipus.[26] When Oedipus left Thebes, his two sons fought and one was killed. The new king forbade the burial of the fractricidal brother. According to Greek religion, the refusal to bury meant eternal suffering of the soul. Antigone decided to save her brother's soul and to bury him, knowing very well that the king imposed capital punishment.

History bears witness not only to human actions guided by pleasure and pain, but also to the actions of men and women who relentlessly pursued truth, such as Galileo, or social justice, such as Johann Huss. Thousands of fighters for freedom of conscience, whether persecuted by religious or secular authorities, whether tortured in dungeons or burned alive, defended their convictions in utter disregard of pain or pleasure.

The commitment toward one's friends or children, one's country or religion, one's moral and political convictions, *reflect vectorial* attitude, attitude of unconditional *giving without asking anything in return.* Its prototype is parental love and devotion. A loving parent may not be aware of his own pain while he tries to alleviate that of his suffering child. A loving person willingly renounces his own pleasures when the happiness of the beloved one is at stake, and can function on a post-hedonic level, that is, their actions are guided by the Antigone Principle.

3. PERCEPTION

Theories and research in perception underlie much of the entire field of psychology. Indeed, most systems of psychology incorporate theories of perception. Historically, perception was an aspect of behavior that was most amenable to experimental and quantitative treatment, and there is, therefore, a rich fund of experimental data available.[27]

The earliest formal studies of perception were made by Wundt, Müller and Titchener who, using introspective analysis, developed an approach called structuralism. In reaction to this approach, other researchers began to develop their own theories of perception. Critical of the structuralists' concept of perception as a sum of visual sensations, Gestalt psychologists began to assert that perception is always of wholes, forms and configurations. For a number of years, structuralism and Gestalt theory dominated the field of perceptual psychology, but by the late 1970's, a variety of new theoretical approaches began to supplant these two schools of psychological thought.

[26] B. B. Wolman, "The Antigone Principle," *American Imago*, 1965, *22*, 186–201.
[27] Lloyd L. Avant and Harry Helson, "Theories of Perception," in B. B. Wolman (Ed.), *Handbook of General Psychology*, Prentice-Hall, 1973, pp. 422–448.

The "New Look" in Perception

One of the theories that challenged both the structuralists and Gestaltists was called the *New Look* by D. Krech. Proponents of the *New Look* have taken issue with the treatment of perception as a self-sufficient process which does not take into consideration the perceiver, his needs, motives, predispositions, and past learning. Several researchers, among them Bruner and Postman, have emphasized the perceiver's current state, biological and emotional, as a determinant of perception. This part of the behavioral analysis of perception was called a "hypothesis, which 'denotes the attempt to perceive a stimulus configuration in a certain way, for a given purpose, or with a given meaning,' "[28] The main determinants of the hypothesis are:

1. *Frequency of past confirmation*—the frequency with which a hypothesis has been confirmed in the past lessens the amount of information which is required for subsequent accurate perception.
2. *Number of alternative hypotheses*—the smaller the number of possible hypotheses, the less appropriate stimulus information is required for confirmation of perception.
3. *Motivational support*—instrumental hypotheses are stronger than noninstrumental ones. Hypotheses connected with means such as, for example, fork, may become stronger than ones related to ends, such as food, especially when hunger passes the peak of the hunger cycle.
4. *Cognitive support*—the more a hypothesis is an integral part of a larger cognitive organization of hypotheses, the smaller is the amount of appropriate information required for confirmation. For example, the reversal of a letter in an otherwise normal word is less noticeable in a tachistoscopic presentation than in a nonsense word.
5. *Consensual validation*—that social process whereby the child builds within a "system of hypotheses which will prepare him to perceive and know his environment in ways which his culture favors."[29]

The research on which the *New Look* was built falls into six categories: (1) biological needs, (2) positive and negative reinforcements, (3) stress, (4) emotionality, (5) set or expectancy, and (6) needs and values.[30]

It has been repeatedly demonstrated that when subjects are hungry, they will show an increase in food responses to ambiguous stimuli. Researchers such as Sanford,[31,32] Levine, Chein and Murphy,[33] McClelland

---

[28] L. Postman and J. S. Bruner, "Perception Under Stress," *Psychological Review*, 1948, 55, 314–323.

[29] Avant and Helson, *op. cit.*, pp. 423–425.

[30] *Ibid.*, p. 425.

[31] R. N. Sanford, "The Effects of Abstinence from Food Upon Imaginal Processes," *Journal of Psychology*, 1936, 2, pp. 129–136.

[32] R. N. Sanford, "The Effects of Abstinence from Food Upon Imaginal Processes: A Further Experience," *Journal of Psychology*, 1937, 3, pp. 145–159.

[33] R. Levine, I. Chein, and G. Murphy, "The Relation of the Intensity of a Need to an Amount of Perceptual Distortion: A Preliminary Report," *Journal of Psychology*, 1942, 13, pp. 283–293.

and Atkinson,[34] and Bruner and Postman[35] have shown in a variety of experiments the effects of need (hunger) on perception.[36]

Other researchers have demonstrated the effects of reinforcement on perception. Proshansky and Murphy[37] found that subjects who are positively reinforced for correct perceptions of length of lines showed greater improvement than unreinforced subjects. Shafer[38] found that when he rewarded one profile of a reversible figure, the subjects gave an overwhelmingly significant number of responses to that profile. Postman and Bruner[39] showed that when children were shown toys and blocks of the same size, they perceived the toys as larger than the blocks.

McGinnies[40] demonstrated that emotionally loaded stimuli, such as words with sexual connotations, took longer to be perceived tachitoscopically than neutral ones. Finally, Bruner and Goodman[41] demonstrated the influence of needs and values on perception by showing that very poor children consistently overestimated the size of various coins far more often than less poor children.

Perception as Continuous Transaction

The transactional point of view of perception is similar in many ways to other popular theories of perception. Areas of probable overlap include Helmholtz's unconscious inferences, *New Look* hypotheses, and so on. The unique thrust of this point of view lies in its concept of perception as a continuous transaction between the individual and all aspects of his environment.[42] Kilpatrick describes transactional theory in the following manner:

> By perception, then, is meant that part of the transactional process which is an implicit awareness of the probable significance for action of present impingements from the environment, based on assumptions related to the same or similar impingements from the environment.[43]

---

[34] D. C. McClelland and J. W. Atkinson, "The Projection of Expression of Need. I. The Effects of Different Intensities of the Hunger Drive," *Journal of Psychology*, 1949, 62, pp. 205–222.

[35] J. S. Bruner and L. Postman, "An Approach to Social Perception," in W. Dennis (Ed.), *Current Trends in Social Psychology*, University of Pittsburgh Press, 1948, pp. 71–118.

[36] Avant and Helson, *op. cit.*, p. 425.

[37] H. Proshansky and G. Murphy, "The Effects of Rewards and Punishment on Perception," *Journal of Psychology*, 1942, 13, pp. 294–305.

[38] R. Shafer and G. Murphy, "The Role of Autism in Figure-Ground Relationships," *Journal of Experimental Psychology*, 1943, 32, pp. 335–343.

[39] J. S. Bruner and L. Postman, "On Perception of Incongruity: A Paradigm," *Journal of Personality*, 1949, 18, pp. 206–223.

[40] E. McGinnies, "Emotionality and Perceptual Defense," *Psychological Review*, 1949, 56, pp. 244–251.

[41] J. S. Bruner and C. C. Goodman, "Value and Need as Organizing Factors in Perception," *Journal of Abnormal and Social Psychology*, 1947, 42, pp. 33–44.

[42] Avant and Helson, *op. cit.*, p. 431.

[43] F. P. Kilpatrick, "Statement of Theory," in F. P. Kilpatrick (Ed.), *Human Behavior from the Transactional Point of View*, Institute for Associated Research, 1952, p. 89.

Kilpatrick defines the assumptions as basically unconscious aspects of the transactional process representing a weighted average of past experiences. They function as probabilities which are developed, checked, and/or modified by action. It is our assumptions that we bring to every situation and on which we base our perceptions. Kilpatrick maintains that the world as we know it is determined by such assumptions, and that constancy in the environment and continuity of experience is a representation of these internal assumptions.[44]

Ittelson[45] defines four major characteristics of the perceptual process: (1) the transaction which must be seen in the total situation of the transaction; (2) the experience of inner and outer events; (3) the process of weighing various assumptions; and (4) perceptions become guidelines for actions which define and modify the subjective probability which has been assigned to various assumptions.[46]

Ames[47] conducted highly relevant research that supports the transactional point of view. In one of his experiments, the floors and ceilings of a specially constructed room are distorted in such a way that the room appears to be cubical. When the subject is asked to place a stick on a particular spot on the far wall, it befomes readily apparent that the room is far from the usual. As the experimental subject gradually modifies his actions, his perceptions of the room change and the distortions become clear. Thus, Ames concluded, without overwhelming evidence to the contrary, subjects tend to make judgements based on assumptions they believe to be true. When the subject is unconsciously forced to choose between seeing the distortions of the room or distorting persons moving about in the room, he will invariably distort the perception of the person.[48]

Other studies, including Engel's investigation of binocular resolution of structurally dissimilar figures presented independently to the subject's two eyes,[49] demonstrate the gradualness with which assumptions are modified.

Transactional theory has generated considerable interest and its influence has not only affected theories of perception, but has also influenced theories of personality.[50]

[44] Ibid.

[45] W. H. Ittelson, "Perception and Transactional Psychology," in S. Koch (Ed.), Psychology: A Study of Science, McGraw-Hill, 1962, 4, pp. 660–704.

[46] Avant and Helson, op. cit., pp. 431, ff.

[47] A. Ames, "Visual Perception and the Rotating Trapezoidal Window," Psychological Monographs, 1951, No. 14, p. 65.

[48] W. H. Ittelson and F. P. Kilpatrick, "The Monocular and Binocular Distorted Rooms," in F. P. Kilpatrick (Ed.), Explorations in Transactional Psychology, New York University Press, 1961, Chapter 8.

[49] E. Engel, "The Role of Content in Binocular Resolution," American Journal of Psychology, 1956, 69, pp. 87–91.

[50] D. L. Wolitzky and P. L. Wachtel, "Personality and Perception," in B. B. Wolman (Ed.) Handbook of General Psychology, Prentice-Hall, 1973, pp. 826–860.

The Sensory–Tonic Field Theory of Perception

Werner and Wapner have defined perception as a sensory–tonic process.[51] The tonic factors, represented by the state of organismic tension (evidenced by visceral and somatic activity), together with the sensory data, contribute to the total process of perception. According to Werner and Wapner, perception is not a mere combination of these factors, but a complex process of interaction between them.[52]

Perhaps the best known studies formulated in sensory–tonic theory terms were studies of the impact of body tilt on perception of the visual vertical. In these studies, subjects adjusted a luminous rod attached to a rotating chair in a dark room while the rods were being accelerated or decelerated in a clockwise or counterclockwise direction. In these studies, Werner and Wapner demonstrated the power of extraneous stimulation on perception, which is one of the basic tenets of sensory–tonic theory. Moreover, their study lent support to the idea of the functional equivalence of different sensory systems. One particular study, that of Wapner and Witkin,[53] sparked the interest of many personality theorists who saw it as a demonstration of the effects of personality factors on perception. In this study, Wapner and Witkin found that maintenance of body balance on an unstable platform grew increasingly difficult for subjects as the visual field was first reduced and then obliterated by blindfold. A further finding of this study was particularly significant: women were found to be more dependent on the visual field than men. This dependence was evidenced by their poor balance as the field became unstable; there were marked perceptual differences between men and women throughout the study.[54]

Hebb's Neuropsychological Approach to Perception

According to Hebb, a theory of perception must deal with the problem of how behavior relates to the activity of individual neurons. Hebb sought to develop a "comparatively simple formula of cortical transmission . . . a conceptual system . . . which relates the individual nerve cell to psychological phenomena, a bridge . . . across the great gap between the details of neurophysiology and the molar conceptions of psychology."[55]

Hebb views psychological processes as comprised of a central semiautonomous process made up of cell assemblies and phase sequences. All sensory and motor events are recorded centrally as cell assemblies and the associations occurring between assemblies create the structure within which

---

[51] H. Werner and S. Wapner, "Sensory–Tonic Field Theory of Perception," *Journal of Personality*, 1949, *18*, pp. 88–107.

[52] Avant and Helson, *op. cit.*, p. 433.

[53] S. Wapner and H. A. Witkin, "The Role of Visual Factors in the Maintenance of Body-Balance," *The American Journal of Psychology*, 1950, *63*, pp. 385–408.

[54] Wolitzky and Wachtel, *op. cit.*

[55] D. O. Hebb, *The Organization of Behavior*, Wiley, 1949, p. 101.

sensory input initiates motor activity. Phase sequences are then consolidated briefly into a series of cell assemblies which correspond to events in perception and thought. Hebb[56] described the development of cell assemblies through the use of four basic assumptions:

1. Cell assemblies develop gradually in infancy in response to a repeated particular kind of sensory event.
2. Many assemblies which are repeatedly active at the same time will come to form a single assembly. For example, the several assemblies and their related motor components which correspond to the various sides and angles of a triangle, combine to form a single assembly which corresponds to the perception of the triangle as a whole.
3. Most assemblies have motor components, e.g., visual assemblies produce eye movements.
4. Each assembly seems to correspond to a rather simple sensory input, such as a particular vowel sound.[57]

While Hebb intended to develop a general theory of behavior, studies of perception have constituted the strongest evidence supporting his system. For example, Senden's[58] studies of adults whose congenital blindness was corrected by cataract removal in adulthood and Riesen's[59] work with dark-reared chimpanzees, have offered significant support for Hebb's theory. Based on Senden's report on the first vision of the newly-sighted adult, Hebb noted distinctions among (1) primitive unity, (2) nonsensory figure–ground organization, and (3) figural identity in perception. He maintains that these distinctions were not made in Gestalt theory. Moreover, the theory appeared to negate learning in basic perceptual organization. Hebb asserts that the primitive unit of a figure is "that unity and segregation from the background which seems to be a direct product of the pattern of sensory excitation and the inherited characteristics of the nervous system on which it acts."[60] According to Hebb, the primitive separation between figure and ground appears to be a native capacity of the organism as evidenced by the first vision of the newly-sighted adult.

Gibson's Psychophysical Approach to Perception

J. J. Gibson's main focus is on the process through which the organism maintains "contact" with the environment. According to Gibson, perception is a function of stimulation and stimulation is a function of the environment; hence, perception is a function of the environment. Moreover, "for every aspect of property of the phenomenal world of an individual in contact with his environment, however subtle, there is a variable in the

[56] D. O. Hebb, *A Textbook of Psychology,* Saunders, 1958, p. 105.
[57] Avant and Helson, *op. cit.,* pp. 434–435.
[58] M. V. Senden, *Space and Sight,* Free Press, 1960.
[59] A. H. Riesen, "The Development of Visual Perception in Man and Chimpanzee," *Science,* 1947, *106,* pp. 107–108.
[60] D. O. Hebb, *The Organization of Behavior,* p. 19.

energy flux at his receptors, however complex, with which the phenomenal property would correspond if a psychophysical experiment could be performed."[61] Gibson maintained that potential information about objects and events in the world rests in the mass of energy at the organism's receptive surface. The perceptual mechanisms function in such a way as to gain that information which creates contact with the environment. Stimulation represents energy for all perceptual systems which is separate from the stimulation's source in the environment. Perceptual learning represents a growing awareness of the details of stimulation. Perception is not innate, nor is it a mental act; rather, it is the result of attention to stimulation coming from the environment.

Apparently, there are two theories of space perception: the cue theory, which has its origins in the work of John Locke and Bishop Berkeley and has been more recently treated by Ames[62] and Ittelson,[63] and the psychophysical theory of Gibson.[64,65] Both theories are based on research in the area of visual perception. According to the cue theory, the three-dimensional visual world is translated into a flat, two-dimensional, retinal picture, and the third dimension must be inferred through the use of picture cues. These cues are part of the retinal picture which one puts together through the knowledge of the three-dimensional scene. For example, although the retinal picture of the average door is trapezoidal, one consistently sees doors as rectangular because one knows this to be factually so.[66]

Gibson's psychophysical theory is a seemingly simpler one. He maintains that the succession of retinal images, which are discrete when separated by saccadic eye movements and continuous when produced by bodily motion or pursuit movement, contains all the information necessary for a proper construction of a three-dimensional representation of the visual world. By looking at retinal images as patterns of optical information instead of as two-dimensional pictures, Gibson opened up a new area of research. He demonstrated that the perceiver need not infer a third dimension, for he has all the information that he needs in the perceived image.[67]

Cue theorists based their contentions on the easily demonstrable fact that that which is perceived can be manipulated under impoverished stimulus conditions by the presence or absence of one or more picture cues. Yet Gibson has shown through the analysis of the correspondence of information in the retinal images to the pattern of light reflected from the three-

[61] J. J. Gibson, "Perception as a Function of Stimulation," in S. Koch (Ed.), *Psychology: A Study of Science*, Volume 1, McGraw-Hill, 1959, p. 465.

[62] A. Ames, "Visual Perception and the Rotating Window," *Psychological Monographs*, 1951, *65*, No. 14.

[63] W. H. Ittelson, *Visual Space Perception*, Springer-Verlag, 1960.

[64] J. J. Gibson, *The Perception of the Visual World*, Houghton Mifflin, 1950.

[65] J. J. Gibson, *The Senses Considered as Perceptual Systems*, Houghton Mifflin, 1966.

[66] Ralph Norman Haber, "Visual Perception," *Annual Review of Psychology*, 1978, *29*, pp. 31–32.

[67] *Ibid.*, p. 32.

dimensional scene, that these two are isometric. Thus, there is nothing to be inferred because nothing has been left out or compressed. Because Gibson's theory abrogates the prevailing metaphor that the eye is like a camera, with the retinal image being the photograph, it has been difficult for psychologists to accept it. But the researcher who no longer expects the retinal image to replicate the scene it reflects, becomes free to study the retinal image for other forms of information which define the objects seen.

4. PERSONALITY

General Issues

Attempts to achieve the highest standards in scientific rigor during the late 1960's, and an overemphasis on refinements in measurement, have served to diminish interest in personality research. In an effort to reverse this trend and to keep from losing the person in personality research, Craik[68] emphasized the need for the *personality paradigm* approach. This paradigm places the emphasis on the person as the basic unit of study. It is a person-centered approach that attempts to study the relationships between dimensions of personality and the social and behavioral outcomes.[69]

Other authors have written about new approaches to the study of personality which place less emphasis on experimentation and strict empiricism. Hogan[70] discussed the root ideas of various personality theories and pointed out that in contrast to learning theorists, personality theorists are less concerned with observable behavior, but tend to seek causal explanations.

Maddi[71] suggested that rather than looking at specific acts, or what is usually called behavior, one must look at the complexity, individuality, and functions related to major goals and directions in a person's life.

Lifton[72] sees the process of symbolism as central to the person; the lack of symbolic processes causes psychic numbing. He believes that understanding is based on metaphors and, therefore, postulates the paradigm of the metaphors of life, death, and continuity or immortality. Lifton suggests a study of the "life of the self," based on processes related to the above-mentioned metaphors.

These writers have brought new ideas and directions to personality research and have pointed out the subjectivity of theory in psychology.

[68] K. H. Craik, "The Personality Research Paradigm in Environmental Psychology," in S. Wapner, S. B. Cohen, and B. Kaplan (Eds.), *Experiencing the Environment*, Plenum, 1976, pp. 55–79.

[69] R. Helson and V. Mitchel, "Personality," *Annual Review of Psychology*, 1978, 29, pp. 556–557.

[70] R. Hogan, *Personality Theory: The Personological Tradition*, Prentice-Hall, 1975.

[71] S. R. Maddi, *Personality Theories: A Comparative Analysis*, Dorsey, 1976.

[72] R. J. Lifton, *The Life of the Self: Toward a New Psychology*, Simon & Schuster, 1976.

Atwood and Tomkins[73] made the point that the field of personality is a collection of schools of thought which, for the most part, conduct their research independently of each other. They lack a common focus because of the subjectivity of personality theory. Each theorist formulates his theory out of his own life experience, and the followers of a particular theory are equally affected by subjective ideological factors. Atwood and Tomkins suggested that a psychobiographical approach which would interpret theoretical ideas in terms of the theorists' formative experiences could eventually lessen the effects of subjectivity.

Stolorow and Atwood[74] demonstrated this approach by constructing psychobiographies of Freud, Jung, Rank, and Reich. By doing so, they hoped to develop a means of integrating the contributions of the various theorists.

Not unlike psychobiography, psychohistory has also become a significant area in the psychology of personality. Psychohistory represents a study of patterns of historical motivations; it includes the psychobiography and psychohistory of group behavior as well as the role of individuals in group processes and historical events. Often, history is examined from a particular point of a view such as, for example, that presented in Wolman's *The Psychoanalytic Interpretation of History.*[75]

Cross-cultural studies represent an attempt to overcome the tendency to indulge in ethnocentrism and to determine the extent to which personality characteristics transcend culture. For example, Butcher and Pancheri[76] determined that the MMPI factor structures occurring in samples from seven different countries were quite similar. Other researchers have shown how greatly a culture shapes its individuals.[77] Lesser states that "people who share a common cultural background will also share . . . common patterns of intellectual abilities, thinking styles, and interests." In his reviews of his own and other studies of mental ability patterns of ethnic groups, he found, for example, that Chinese children are particularly skilled in spatial conceptualization and relatively weak in verbal ability. For Jewish children, the pattern is just the opposite.[78]

Some personologists have attempted to enrich studies of personality by sharpening their focus on ideographic phenomena. Pervin[79] did an open-ended study in which he tried to look at the affective linkages between situ-

[73] G. E. Atwood and S. S. Tomkins, "On the Subjectivity of Personality Theory," *Journal of History of Behavioral Science*, 1976, 12, pp. 166–177.

[74] R. D. Stolorow and G. E. Atwood, *Faces in a Cloud: The Subjective World in Personality Theory*, Aronson, 1978.

[75] B. B. Wolman (Ed.), *The Psychoanalytic Interpretation of History*, Harper, 1973.

[76] J. N. Butcher and P. Pancheri, *A Handbook of Cross-National MMPI Research*, University of Minnesota Press, 1976.

[77] S. Messick, *Individuality in Learning*, Jossey-Bass, 1976.

[78] Helson and Mitchel, *op. cit.*, p. 561.

[79] L. A. Pervin, "A Free-Response Description Approach to the Analysis of Person–Situation Interaction," *Journal of Personality and Social Psychology*, 1976, 34, pp. 465–474.

ations and the behavior they engendered. He asked his subjects to describe various situations both objectively and subjectively and then to quantify these situations on a set of dimensions that the subjects had previously generated. His results show that this technique not only provides for ideographic mapping, but can also develop new areas for interindividual comparisons. Pervin states that "a priori taxonomies based on laboratory research will not be useful in advancing understanding and prediction; rather, observations related to individuals in situations in the natural setting are needed."

Language and verbal structure are coming to be viewed as valuable sources of information about both the content and organization of psychic systems. Studies of language represent a link between sociology and psychology in that there is an attempt to study the interface between the structure of intrapsychic thought and the rules of social communications.[80] This ethogenic approach is grounded in the writings of Mead and Goffman who are among the most significant writers to describe "each person's movement through a web of subjective meanings (intrapsychic content) toward a network of shared meanings which underlie interpersonal life, and back again to a reformulated subjective."[81]

The controversy of trait versus situational perspective has occupied a considerable amount of the literature in personality psychology. The critics of the trait approach claim that support for the notion of traits in predicted behavior is largely insubstantial, that the observer ratings are riddled with bias, and that the same traits in different inventory measures do not have the same correlates. Epstein,[82] who described traits as relatively stable dispositions manifested by individuals, stated that single behavior criterion is an inadequate test of the predictive power of trait measures. Therefore, when trait measures are tested across many events, their reliability is markedly increased.[83]

Block[84] pointed out that many criticisms of trait theory have been leveled on the basis of methodologically insufficient studies. His own longitudinal studies, which utilized observation and self-report data, have yielded correlations of .4–.9 between a variety of trait measures from periods ranging from one to ten years. Finally, Huba and Hamilton,[85] in

---

[80] Albert E. Goss, "Speech and Language," in B. B. Wolman (Ed.), *Handbook of General Psychology*, Prentice-Hall, 1973, pp. 568–629.

[81] Helson and Mitchel, *op. cit.*

[82] C. F. Epstein, "Traits are Alive and Well," in D. Magnusson and N. S. Endler (Eds.), *Personality at the Crossroads*, Wiley-Earlbaum, 1977.

[83] John D. Hundleby, "Traits: Measurement," in B. B. Wolman (Ed.), *International Encyclopedia of Psychiatry, Psychology, Psychoanalysis and Neurology*, Aesculapius, 1977, Vol. 11, pp. 213–215. Hundleby, "Traits: Their Scientific Status," *ibid.*, pp. 215–219.

[84] J. Block, "Advancing the Psychology of Personality," in D. Magnusson and N. S. Endler (Eds.), *Personality at the Crossroads*, Wiley-Earlbaum, pp. 37–63.

[85] G. J. Huba and D. L. Hamilton, "On the Generality of Trait Relationships: Some Analyses Based on Fiske's Paper," *Psychological Bulletin*, 1976, 83, pp. 868–876.

reviewing the different measures of Murray's "need" construct, found substantial evidence of intertrait relationships and underlying structural dimensions.

K. Lewin, H. Murray, M. Mead, H. S. Sullivan, E. Brunswik and B. B. Wolman have presented the notion of *interaction* in personality theory. Currently, there is an effort to systematize the components of interaction, and the interactionist position is now appearing in the literature as an articulated model with implications for both theory and research. For example, studies reported in Stockholm have demonstrated that the interactionist design can explain short and episodic behaviors. Taylor and Koivumaki[86] demonstrated in a study conducted among married students that there was a significant tendency for subjects to attribute "good actions" to people and "bad actions" to situations. Coyne, in a study of depression, found that depressed persons evoke feelings of depression, hostility, anxiety, and rejection in nondepressed controls during telephone conversations. Coyne concluded that depressed persons create an environment which maintains their depressed views and behavior.[87]

As neurologists gather more and more data about right versus left brain functioning, psychologists are beginning to use this data to augment their concepts of personality. Paredes and Hepburn,[88] in reviewing anthropological literature, feel that the differences between primitive and civilized thought correspond to what is being described as right and left hemisphere thought. Ten Houten[89] has proposed a relationship between social subordination and the predominance of right-hemisphere thought processes. Roland Fischer[90] has developed a different model, which he feels represents a "cartography of the transformations of consciousness." He stated that ordinary thought is related to medium levels of overall brain activation, while other kinds of consciousness, such as ecstatic or meditative, accompany very high or very low levels of arousal. He further stated that different rules for processing information operate at different levels of arousal.

While studies of creativity and personality became fewer and fewer during the 1960's and early 1970's, an increased interest in this area has developed in the late 1970's. Getzels and Csikszentmihalyi[91] studied various aspects of the artistic behavior of students at the Chicago Art Institute. Each student made a painting in an experimental situation; the paintings were

[86] S. E. Taylor and J. H. Koivumaki, "The Perception of Self and Others: Acquaintanceship, Affect, and Actor–Observer Differences," *Journal of Personality and Social Psychology*, 1976, *33*, pp. 403–408.

[87] Helson and Mitchel, *op. cit.*, pp. 564–565.

[88] J. A. Paredes and M. J. Hepburn, "The Split Brain and the Culture-and-Cognition Paradox," *Current Anthropology*, 1976, *17*, pp. 121–127.

[89] W. Ten Houten, "More on Split-Brain Research, Culture, and Cognition," *Current Anthropology*, 1976, *17*, pp. 503–511.

[90] Roland Fischer, "Transformations of Consciousness: a Cartography. I. The Perception–Meditation Continuum," *Contemporary Psychiatry*, 1976, *19*, pp. 1–23.

[91] J. W. Getzels and M. Csikszentmihalyi, *The Creative Vision: A Longitudinal Study of Problem Finding in Art*, Wiley, 1976.

then rated as to originality. Those rated highest were done by artists who did not rush into their work, but who spent a great deal of time contemplating and planning before they embarked on their creative task.[92]

Helson did a Q-sort of items describing the work style of fifty-seven authors. He found that the creativity of the books and their stylistic–motive pattern were related to the authors' descriptions of their work styles and also to assessed personality characteristics. Since interest in creativity predictably leads to an exploration of intrapsychic processes, the symbolic, irrational, and individual creativity research is valuable to personality theory.

Trends Representing an Effort toward Broader Syntheses

Loevinger,[93] a developmental psychologist, has been working toward integrating ego psychology and types and patterns such as those studied by trait psychologists. Loevinger described her holistic construct of the ego as a "master trait" on which the overall personality is developed. In order to empirically evaluate her theory, Loevinger developed her own Sentence Completion Test, which was used by Frank and Quinlan[94] to study the ego levels of delinquent and nondelinquent girls. They found the use of this measure did enable them to distinguish between delinquents and nondelinquents.

O'Connell,[95] working within the developmental framework created by Erikson, focused on the hypothesis that a woman's identity is not resolved in adolescence. O'Connell found that female identity tends to vary in relation to a woman's career commitment and the age of her children. He further observed that tradition-minded women lose interest in a sense of personal identity from the time of their adolescence until they are through with child rearing. Nontraditional women, on the other hand, see their identity as strong and individual throughout the life cycle.

In light of the feminist analyses of sex-role assumptions, there has been a considerable amount of work on redefining the meaning, measurement, and relationships among traits which have traditionally been considered masculine or feminine. This research has been motivated by a growing awareness that sex roles are becoming more and more obsolete.

Pleck[96] enumerated the difficulties inherent in the masculine role. He pointed out that the multiple changes in role expectations are due to cultural changes as well as to the inherent strain in the masculine role and the

---

[92] R. Helson, "The Creative Spectrum of Authors of Fantasy," *Journal of Personality*, 1977, 45, pp. 310–336.

[93] J. Loevinger, *Ego Development*, Jossey-Bass, 1976.

[94] S. Frank and D. M. Quinlan, "Ego Development and Female Delinquency: A Cognitive–Developmental Approach," *Journal of Abnormal Psychology*, 1976, 86, pp. 505–510.

[95] A. N. O'Connell, "The Relationship Between Life Style and Identity Synthesis and Resynthesis in Traditional, Neo-traditional and Nontraditional Women," *Journal of Personality*, 1976, 44, pp. 675–688.

[96] J. H. Pleck, "The Male Sex Role: Definitions, Problems and Sources of Change," *Journal of Social Issues*, 1976, 32, pp. 155–163.

overdependence on work for self-esteem. Hyde and Rosenberg[97] proposed a multidimensional model which would allow for the diverse ways in which masculinity and femininity may be manifested. Moreover, studies of subjects compared on scales of masculinity and femininity have generally shown that those subjects who score high on both scales (indicating an androgynous organization) seem to fare best in our society. Heilbrun,[98] for example, has shown that these individuals have the most stable identities and are less likely to suffer from emotional problems. Kelly and Worrell[99] reported that this type of individual received emotional support and intellectual encouragement and stimulation from both parents. Although the subjects in the various studies were of many different ages, and almost every study used different measures, these and several other findings clearly indicate that the traditional sex-roles concepts are totally inadequate.[100]

Research in vocational psychology has become increasingly consonant with trends in personality research. Marcia[101] has developed an interview technique which assesses vocation with respect to four likely positions on Erikson's identity–diffusion continuum. Various researchers have used this technique to study identity concepts and the problems of adult men. Heath,[102] using a multidimensional model of maturity which includes an increasing capacity for symbolization, greater allocentricity, increased respect for multiple perspectives, and greater stability, conducted a longitudinal study of sixty-eight professional and managerial men. He found that vocational adaptation was closely related to work satisfaction as well as competence in other areas. Other studies have demonstrated that vocational satisfaction is strongly related to the feeling of having lived up to one's potential. Although, traditionally, vocational studies have dealt with the problems of men, there has recently been a focus on the vocational adjustment of women. Laws,[103] Hennig and Jardim,[104] Douvan,[105] and others have

[97] J. S. Hyde and B. G. Rosenberg, *Half the Human Experience*, Heath, 1975.

[98] A. B. Heilbrun, "Measurement of Masculine and Feminine Sex Role Identities as Independent Dimension," *Journal of Consulting and Clinical Psychology*, 1976, 44, pp. 183–190.

[99] J. A. Kelly and L. Worell, "Parent Behaviors Related to Masculine, Feminine and Androgynous Sex Role Orientation," *Journal of Consulting and Clinical Psychology*, 1976, 44, pp. 843–851.

[100] B. B. Wolman, "Psychology of Women," in B. B. Wolman (Ed.), *Psychological Aspects of Gynecology and Obstetrics*, Medical Economics, 1978.

[101] J. E. Marcia, "Ego-identity Status: Relationship to Change in Self-Esteem, in 'General Maladjustment' and Authoritarianism," *Journal of Personality*, 1967, 35, pp. 118–123.

[102] D. H. Heath, "Adolescent and Adult Predictor of Vocational Adaptation," *Journal of Vocational Behavior*, 1976, 9, pp. 1–19.

[103] J. L. Laws, "Work Motivation and Work Behavior of Women: New Perspectives," in J. Sherman and F. Denmark (Eds.), *The Psychology of Woman: Future Directions in Research*, Psychological Dimensions, 1978.

[104] M. Hennig and A. Jardim, "Women Executives in the Old-Boy Network," *Psychology Today*, 1977, 10, pp. 76–81.

[105] E. Douvan, "The Role of Models in Women's Professional Development," *Psychology of Women Quarterly*, 1976, 1, pp. 5–20.

pointed out that the vocational psychology of women is significantly different from that of men for a variety of reasons including social influences and educational bias.

Finally, there has been a tendency toward merger of the normal and the pathological in personality research. Klein and Seligman[106] have shown similarities between a learned helplessness that can be induced in normals when the connection between response and reinforcement is cut, and the observed depression of hospitalized mental patients. The stressful effects of such seemingly mundane events as traveling on a crowded commuter train or working at a machine-determined pace as opposed to an employee-determined pace, have been documented as being correlated with changes in the brain chemistry. Changes in social attitudes are reflected in studies of male and female homosexuals which suggest that it might be erroneous to conceive of homosexuality as a neurosis. Stringer and Gryier[107] found little overlap between the distinctive profiles of homosexuals and neurotics. Wolman[108] examining the concepts of masculinity and femininity, found a much more complex patterning of sex-role dimensions than the traditional ideas.

[106] D. C. Klein and E. P. Seligman, "Reversal of Performance Deficits in Learned Helplessness and Depression," *Journal of Abnormal Psychology*, 1976, *85*, pp. 11–26.

[107] P. Stringer and T. G. Gryier, "Male Homosexuality, Psychiatric Patient Status and Psychological Masculinity and Femininity," *Archives of Sexual Behavior*, 1976, *5*, (1), pp. 15–28.

[108] B. B. Wolman, "Between Men and Women," in R. K. Unger and F. Denmark (Eds.), *Woman: Dependent or Independent Variable?* Psychological Dimensions, 1975, pp. 177–194.

Summary of Part IV

Chapters 15 and 16 form the last part of this book. Chapter 15 analyzes some problems related to the application of the scientific method in psychology, but it does not describe the research methods of psychology in detail.

The chapter starts with the distinction between research and the resulting system of propositions or statements. Nine principles are suggested, among them verifiability, generality, and objectivity. The position of maximalism in epistemology is suggested.

Scientific statements are statements about something which is a part of nature. Accordingly, all sciences, including psychology, are natural sciences, and their propositions are a result of (1) perception of things and what is happening to them, and (2) interpretation of these perceptions.

A systematic and planned perception of things and events is called observation. All scientists, psychologists included, observe their subject matter. However, certain parts of human behavior, for example, pain and pleasure, are directly perceivable to the organism in which they take place; some are not observable at all. This fact gave rise to the introspective method in psychology. Introspection is the least objective, but still an indispensable method in psychology.

The usual principles of empiricism are applicable to psychology. Psychological theory has been influenced lately by operationism. Operationism can be interpreted as a radical empiricism which applies the rules and canons of F. Bacon, J. S. Mill, and others. Taken literally, as it was by its creator, P. W. Bridgman, operationism leads to an overemphasis on the operations performed by the scientist himself and ultimately ends in an arid solipsism. S. S. Stevens tried to save operationism by the legitimate demand for "public" versus "private" operations. Even the improved version of operationism is still open to criticism directed against the assumption that the perception of activities (operations) of the research worker is superior to observations of things and events.

The most precise research method in psychology is experimentation. Some caution is required in regard to the influence of the experimental design and apparatus on the results. In addition, the unobservable parts of behavior, as well as the more emotional expressions of overt behavior, do not fit into a laboratory. The experimentalist deals with a part of behavior in a precise manner; the scope of clinical research is broad, but its methods are not always exact. The application of both research methods for a mutual checking of results seems to be promising.

The third section of the chapter is devoted to the interpretation of data by formation of hypotheses and theory construction. Both inductive and deductive methods are legitimate ways of empirical research.

Some rules for hypothesis formation have been suggested; the most important are immanent truth and testability. Hypothetical statements can be made in a great variety of forms; some of them can be simply postulated as guiding principles which can never be fully proved but are accepted as long as they are not refuted by empirical data or modified by methodological convenience. Hypothetical statements can be introduced in the form of definitions, logical constructs, and intervening variables. Experimental psychologists favor intervening variables because this is the most convenient way of presenting their data.

Psychological hypotheses use constructs such as "instinct," "drive," "need," and "ego"; interpretation in psychology can be psychogenic or it can be reduced to any other source, preferably physics, chemistry, biology, or physiology.

A system of hypotheses forms a theory. Theories deal with the relationship between bodies and events, and seek to discover "laws of nature." The relationship between bodies and events in psychology is permeated with causation. Determinism in psychology must be postulated as the first principle for interpretation of scientific data.

Laws of nature express the regularity of everything that happens in nature. Laws of nature have been discovered in all other natural sciences; they must be discovered in psychology too. Some of them, such as homeostasis or constancy, adjustment, and learning by experience, are generally recognized. Some, such as molar versus molecular or gestalt versus association, are highly controversial. Laws of nature in the realm of psychology must be formulated in such a way as to make possible the prediction of behavior.

The fourth section of the chapter is devoted to some problems related to the use of language, both conventional and symbolic, in psychology.

The last section of Chapter 15 deals with some current methodological problems, such as Kuhn's theory of scientific paradigms, and experimentation with human subjects.

Chapter 16 is divided into four sections, describing (1) the mind–body dichotomy, (2) the question of pain and pleasure, (3) theories of perception, and (4) personality theory. The chapter introduces a theory of universal *transition* from energy to matter, from inorganic matter to organic, and finally, from body to mind, thus suggesting a solution to the mind–body gulf. The traditional pain and pleasure continuum is expanded to include

prehedonic and predolorific phenomena as well as posthedonic and postdo-
lorific ones. Several theories of perception are described, among them the
"new look" and transactional theories. A review of current personality
theories concludes the chapter.

Bibliography

General

Boring, E. G. *A history of experimental psychology*. (2nd ed.) New York: Appleton-Century-Crofts, 1950.

Brett, G. S. *History of psychology*. London: Allen & Unwin, 1912–1921, 3 vols.

Dennis, W. *Readings in the history of psychology*. New York: Appleton-Century-Crofts, 1948.

Dessoir, M. *Outlines of the history of psychology*. New York: Macmillan, 1912.

Döring, W. *Die Haupströmungen in der neueren Psychologie*. Leipzig: Engelmann, 1932.

Erdmann, J. E. *History of philosophy*. London: Allen & Unwin, 3 vols.

Flugel, J. C. *A hundred years of psychology*. (2nd ed.) London: Duckworth, 1951.

Garrett, H. E. *Great experiments in psychology*. (3rd ed.) New York: Appleton-Century-Crofts, 1951.

Heidbreder, E. *Seven psychologies*. New York: Century, 1933.

Helson, H. (Ed.) *Theoretical foundations of psychology*. New York: Van Nostrand, 1950.

Hilgard, E. R., & Bower, G. H. *Theories of learning*. New York: Appleton-Century-Crofts, 1966.

Koch, S. (Ed.) *Psychology: A study of science*. New York: McGraw-Hill, 1959–1963, 6 vols.

Murchison, C. (Ed.) *History of psychology in autobiography*. Worcester, Mass.: Clark University Press, 1930–1936, 3 vols.

Murphy, G. *Historical introduction to modern psychology*. (Rev. ed.) New York: Harcourt, Brace, 1949.

Peters, R. S. (Ed.) *Brett's history of psychology*. London: Allen & Unwin, 1953.

Wolman, B. B. (Ed.) *International encyclopedia of psychiatry, psychology, psychoanalysis and neurology*. New York: Aesculapius, 1977, 12 vols.

Wolman, B. B. (Ed.) *Historical roots of contemporary psychology*. New York: Harper & Row, 1968.

Wolman, B. B. (Ed.) *Handbook of general psychology*. Englewood, N.J.: Prentice-Hall, 1973.

Woodworth, R. S. *Contemporary schools of psychology*. (Rev. ed.) New York: Ronald, 1948.

Zilboorg, G., & Henry, G. W. *A history of medical psychology*. New York: Norton, 1941.

Chapter 1. The Great Beginnings

1. Psychophysical Parallelism and Introspectionism

Bain, A. *Mental science: A compendium of psychology and the history of philosophy*. New York: Appleton, 1868.

Baldwin, J. M. *History of psychology: A sketch and an interpretation*. New York: Putnam, 1913.

Boring, E. G. *Sensation and perception in the history of experimental psychology*. New York: Appleton-Century, 1942.

Boring, E. G. A history of introspection. *Psychol. Bull.*, 1953, *50*, 169–189.

Ebbinghaus, H. *Memory*. New York: Teachers College, Columbia University, 1913.

Hall, G. St. *Founders of modern psychology*. New York: Appleton, 1912.

Helmholtz, H. L. F. *On the sensation of tone*. (4th ed.) New York: Longmans, Green, 1912.

Herbart, J. F. *Sämtliche Werke*. Langesalza: Kehrbach, 1891, 12 vols.

Ladd, G. T., & Woodworth, R. S. *Elements of physiological psychology*. New York: Scribner, 1911.

Locke, J. *An essay concerning human understanding*. London: Basset, 1690.

Müller, G. E. Experimentelle Beiträge zur Untersuchung des Gedächtnisses. *Z. Psychol.*, 1894, *6*, 81–190, 250–339.

Randall, J. H. *The making of the modern mind*. (Rev. ed.) Boston: Houghton Mifflin, 1940.

Ribot, T. A. *German psychology of today*. New York: Scribner, 1886.

Titchener, E. B. The postulates of a structural psychology. *Phil. Rev.*, 1898, *7*, 449–465.

Titchener, E. B. Structural and functional psychology. *Phil. Rev.*, 1899, *8*, 290–299.

Titchener, E. B. *Experimental psychology, a manual of laboratory practice*. New York: Macmillan, 1901–1905, 2 vols.

Titchener, E. B. *Lectures on the experimental psychology of the thought processes*. New York: Macmillan, 1909.

Titchener, E. B. *A textbook of psychology*. New York: Macmillan, 1909–1910.

Titchener, E. B. *Systematic psychology: Prolegomena*. New York: Macmillan, 1929.

Warren, H. C. *A history of the association psychology from Hartley to Lewes*. New York: Scribner, 1921.

Woodworth, R. S. *Experimental psychology*. New York: Holt, 1938.

Wundt, W. *Principles of physiological psychology*. London: Macmillan, 1874, 2 vols.

Wundt, W. *Lectures on human and animal psychology*. London: Allen, 1894.

Wundt, W. *Outlines of psychology*. New York: Stechert, 1907.

Wundt, W. *Elements of folk-psychology*. London: Macmillan, 1916.

2. Functionalism

Angell, J. R. *Psychology, an introductory study of the structure and function of human consciousness*. New York: Holt, 1904.

Angell, J. R. The province of functional psychology. *Psychol. Rev.*, 1907, *14*, 61–91.

Angell, J. R. *An introduction to psychology*. New York: Holt, 1918.

Carr, H. A. *Psychology, a study of mental activity*. New York: Longmans, Green, 1925.

Carr, H. A. The laws of association. *Psychol. Rev.*, 1931, *38*, 212–228.

Carr, H. A. *An introduction to space perception*. New York: Longmans, Green, 1935.

Darwin, C. R. *The origin of species*. London: 1859.

Darwin, C. R. *The expression of the emotions in man and animals*. London: 1872.

Dewey, J. The reflex arc concept in psychology. *Psychol. Rev.*, 1896, *3*, 357–370.

Dewey, J. *How we think*. Boston: Heath, 1910.

Dewey, J. *Influence of Darwin on philosophy*. New York: Holt, 1920.

Dewey, J. *Human nature and conduct*. New York: Holt, 1922.

Dewey, J. *Logic, the theory of inquiry*. New York: Holt, 1938.

Dewey, J., & Bentley, A. F. *Knowing and the known*. Boston: Beacon, 1949.

Henderson, L. J. *The fitness of the environment*. New York: Macmillan, 1913.

Hobhouse, L. R. *Mind in evolution*. New York: Macmillan, 1901.

Hobhouse, L. R. *Development and purpose*. New York: Macmillan, 1913.

Hunter, W. S. *Human behavior*. Chicago: University of Chicago Press, 1928.

Huxley, J. *The living thoughts of Darwin*. New York: Longmans, Green, 1939.

Huxley, J. *Evolution, the modern synthesis*. New York: Harper, 1942.

James, W. *Principles of psychology*. New York: Holt, 1890, 2 vols.

James, W. *Pragmatism*. New York: Longmans, Green, 1907.

James, W. *A pluralistic universe*. New York: Longmans, Green, 1909.

James, W. *Essays in radical empiricism*. New York: Longmans, Green, 1912.

Luh, C. W. The conditions of retention. *Psychol. Monogr.*, 1922, *31*, No. 142.

McGeoch, J. A. Forgetting and the law of disuse. *Psychol. Rev.*, 1932, *39*, 352–370.

McGeoch, J. A., & Irion, A. L. *The psychology of human learning.* (Rev. ed.) New York: Longmans, Green, 1942.

Mayhew, K. C., & Edwards, A. C. *The Dewey School: The laboratory school at the University of Chicago, 1896–1903.* New York: Appleton-Century, 1936.

Melton, A. W. Learning. In W. S. Monroe (Ed.), *Encyclopedia of educational research.* New York: Macmillan, 1941.

Ratner, J. *Intelligence in the modern world: John Dewey's philosophy.* New York: Modern Library, 1939.

Robinson, E. S. *Association theory today.* New York: Appleton-Century, 1932.

Robinson, E. S. *Man as psychology sees him.* New York: Macmillan, 1932.

Spencer, H. *Principles of psychology.* London: 1855.

Washburn, M. F. *The animal mind.* New York: Macmillan, 1908.

Weiss, A. P. *A theoretical basis of human behavior.* (2nd ed.) Columbus, Ohio: Adams, 1929.

Woodworth, R. S. *Dynamic psychology.* New York: Columbia University Press, 1918.

Woodworth, R. S. Situation- and goal-set. *Amer. J. Psychol.*, 1937, *50*, 130–140.

3. Edward L. Thorndike: Connectionism

Gates, A. I. Connectionism: Present concepts and interpretations. In *41st Yearb. nat. Soc. Stud. Educ.*, 1942, Part 2.

Lorge, I. Irrelevant rewards in animal learning. *J. comp. Psychol.*, 1936, *21*, 105–128.

Meehl, P. E. On the circularity of the law of effect. *Psychol. Bull.*, 1950, *47*, 52–75.

Postman, L. The history and present status of the Law of Effect. *Psychol. Bull.*, 1947, *44*, 489–563.

Rock, R. T., Jr. The influence upon learning of the quantitative variation of after-effects. *Teach. Coll. Contr. Educ.*, 1935, No. 650.

Thorndike, E. L. Animal intelligence: an experimental study of the associative processes in animals. *Psychol. Rev. Monogr. Suppl.*, 1898, *2*, No. 8.

Thorndike, E. L. *Educational psychology.* New York: Lemcke & Buechner, 1903.

Thorndike, E. L. The effect of practice in the case of a purely intellectual function. *Amer. J. Psychol.*, 1908, *19*, 374–384.

Thorndike, E. L. *Animal intelligence.* New York: Macmillan, 1911.

Thorndike, E. L. *Educational psychology.* New York: Teachers College, 1913, 2 vols.

Thorndike, E. L. The influence of primacy. *J. exp. Psychol.*, 1927, *10*, 18–29.

Thorndike, E. L. *The fundamentals of learning.* New York: Teachers College, 1932.

Thorndike, E. L. Reward and punishment in animal learning. *Comp. Psychol. Monogr.*, 1932, *8*, No. 39.

Thorndike, E. L. A proof of the law of effect. *Science*, 1933, *77*, 173–175.

Thorndike, E. L. An experimental study of rewards. *Teach. Col. Contr. Educ.*, 1933, No. 580.

Thorndike, E. L. *The psychology of wants, interests, and attitudes.* New York: Appleton-Century, 1935.

Thorndike, E. L. *Human nature and the social order.* New York: Macmillan, 1940.

Thorndike, E. L. *Selected writings from a connectionist's psychology.* New York: Appleton-Century-Crofts, 1949.

Thorndike, E. L., & Lorge, I. The influence of relevance and belonging. *J. exp. Psychol.*, 1935, *18*, 574–584.

Tilton, J. W. Gradients of effect. *J. genet. Psychol.*, 1945, *66*, 3–19.

4. *The Origins of the New Systems**

Allport, F. H. *Theories of perception and the concept of structure.* New York: Wiley, 1955.

Dashiell, J. F. Some rapprochements in contemporary psychology. *Psychol. Bull.,* 1939, *36,* 1–24.

Dennis, W. (Ed.) *Current trends in psychological theory.* Pittsburgh: University of Pittsburgh Press, 1951.

Hilgard, E. R., & Marquis, D. G. *Conditioning and learning.* New York: Appleton-Century, 1940.

Klüver, H. Contemporary German psychology as a "cultural science." In G. Murphy (Ed.), *An historical introduction to modern psychology.* New York: Harcourt, Brace, 1929.

Miller, H. *An historical introduction to modern philosophy.* New York: Macmillan, 1947.

Morgan, C. L. *An introduction to comparative psychology.* London: Scott, 1894.

Sachs, H. *Freud, master and friend.* Cambridge, Mass.: Harvard University Press, 1944.

Wolman, B. B.(Ed.) *Historical roots of contemporary psychology.* New York: Harper & Row, 1968.

CHAPTER 2. CONDITIONED REFLEXES

Anan'yev, B. G., et al. (Eds.) *Materials of the conference on psychology* (Russian). Moscow: Acad. Pedag. Nauk SSSR, 1957.

Anrep, G. V. The irradiation of conditioned reflexes. *Proc. Royal Soc.,* 1923, *94B,* 404–426.

Asratian, E. A. *I. P. Pavlov: His life and work.* Moscow: Foreign Lang, Publ. House, 1953.

Ayrapetyants, E. Sh. *Higher nervous activity and the receptors of internal organs* (Russian). Moscow: Acad. Nauk SSSR, 1952.

Babkin, B. P. *Pavlov, a biography.* Chicago: University of Chicago Press, 1949.

Bauer, R. *The new man in Soviet psychology.* Cambridge, Mass.: Harvard University Press, 1952.

Bekhterev, V. M. *Objective psychology* (Russian). St. Petersburg: Soikin, 1907.

Bekhterev, V. M. *Psychology, reflexology, and Marxism* (Russian). Leningrad: Giz, 1925.

Bekhterev, V. M. *General principles of human reflexology.* New York: International Publishers, 1932.

Burns, E. (Ed.) *A handbook of Marxism.* New York: International Publishers, 1935.

Bykov, K. M. *The cerebral cortex and the internal organs.* New York: Chemical Publishing, 1957.

Delgado, J. M. R., Roberts, W. W., & Miller, N. E. Learning motivated by electrical stimulation of the brain. *Amer. J. Physiol.,* 1954, *179,* 587–593.

Engels, F. *Ludwig Feuerbach and the outcome of German classical philosophy.* New York: International Publishers, 1927.

Frolov, I. P. *Pavlov and his school.* New York: Oxford University Press, 1937.

Gantt, W. H. An experimental approach to psychiatry. *Amer. J. Psychiat.,* 1936, *92,* 1007–1021.

Gantt, W. H. Pavlov's system. In B. B. Wolman & E. Nagel (Eds.), *Scientific psychology: Principles and approqches.* New York: Basic Books, 1965, pp. 127–149.

Haldane, J. B. S. *The Marxist philosophy and the sciences.* New York: Random House, 1939.

Hilgard, E., & Marquis, D. G. *Conditioning and learning.* New York: Appleton-Century-Crofts, 1940.

Hook, S. *From Hegel to Marx.* New York: Reynal, 1936.

Kornilov, K. M., Smirnov, A. A., & Teplov, M. (Eds.) *Psychology* (Russian). Moscow: Uchpedgiz, 1948.

Lenin, N. *Materialism and empirico-criticism.* New York: International Publishers, 1934.

London, I. D. Research on sensory interaction in the Soviet Union. *Psychol. Bull.,* 1954, *51,* 531–563.

Loucks, R. B. An appraisal of Pavlov's systematization of behavior from the experimental standpoint. *J. comp. Psychol.,* 1933, *15,* 1–47.

*A part of Section 1, Chapter 1.

Luria, A. R. *The nature of human conflict*. New York: Liveright, 1932.

Marx, K. *Capital*. New York: Scribner, 1925.

Pavlov, I. P. *Conditioned reflexes*. London: Oxford University Press, 1927.

Pavlov, I. P. *Lectures on conditioned reflexes*. New York: International Publishers, 1928.

Pavlov, I. P. *Pavlov's Wednesday seminars* (Russian). Moscow: Acad. Nauk SSSR, 1949, 3 vols.

Pavlov, I. P. *Complete works* (Russian). (2nd ed.) Moscow: Acad. Nauk SSSR, 1951, 5 vols.

Pavlov, I. P. *Selected Works*. Moscow: Foreign Lang. Publ. House, 1955.

Pavlov, I. P. *Experimental psychology and other essays*. New York: Philosophical Library, 1957.

Razran, G. Theory of conditioning and related phenomena. *Psychol. Rev.*, 1930, *37*, 25–43.

Razran, G. Conditioned responses: A classified bibliography. *Psychol. Bull.*, 1937, *34*, 191–256.

Razran, G. The nature of the extinctive process. *Psychol. Rev.*, 1939, *46*, 264–297.

Razran, G. The dominance-contiguity theory of the acquisition of classical conditioning. *Psychol. Bull.*, 1957, *54*, 1–46.

Razran, G. Soviet psychology since 1950. *Science*, 1957, *126*, 1100–1107.

Razran, G. Soviet psychology and psychophysiology. *Science*, 1958, *128*, 1187–1194.

Schlossberg, H. The relationship between success and the laws of conditioning. *Psychol. Rev.*, 1937, *44*, 379–394.

Scientific Session on the Physiological Teachings of I. P. Pavlov. Moscow: Foreign Language Publishing House, 1951.

Sechenov, I. M. *Reflexes of the brain*. Moscow: Uchpedgiz, 1942.

Simon, B. (Ed.) *Psychology in the Soviet Union*. Stanford, California: Stanford University Press, 1957.

Smirnov, A. A., Leont'yev, A. N., Rubinstein, S. L., & Teplov, B. M. (Eds.) *Psychology* (Russian). Moscow: Uchpedgiz, 1956.

Stagner, R. Conditioned reflex theories of learning. *Psychol. Rev.*, 1931, *38*, 42–59.

Wortis, J. *Soviet psychiatry*. Baltimore, Md.: Williams & Wilkins, 1950.

Yaroshevski, M. G. I. M. Sechenov—The founder of objective psychology. In B. B. Wolman (Ed.), *Historical roots of contemporary psychology*. New York: Harper & Row, 1968, pp. 77–110.

7. Current Soviet Psychology

Anokhin, S. K. Ivan P. Pavlov and psychology. In B. B. Wolman (Ed.), *Historical roots of contemporary psychology*. New York: Harper & Row, 1963, pp. 131–159.

Brožek, J. Soviet writings of the 1960's on the history of psychology and the physiology of behavior. *History of Science*, 1972, *10*, 56–87.

Brožek, J. History of Soviet psychology: Recent source of information in English (1965–1975). In S. A. Corson & E. D. Corson (Eds.), *Psychiatry and Psychology in the U.S.S.R.* New York: Plenum, 1976, pp. 59–82.

Brožek, J. U.S.S.R. Psychology. In B. B. Wolman (Ed.), *International Encyclopedia of Psychiatry, Psychology, Psychoanalysis and Neurology*. New York: Aesculapius, 1977, Vol. 11, pp. 328–331.

Cole, M., & Maltzman, I. (Eds.) *A handbook of contemporary Soviet psychology*. New York: Basic Books, 1969.

Leontyev, A. K., & Luria, A. R. The psychological ideas of L. G. Vigotski. In B. B. Wolman (Ed.), *Historical roots of contemporary psychology*. New York: Harper & Row, 1968, pp. 338–367.

O'Connor, N. (Ed.) *Present-day Russian psychology*. Oxford: Pergamon Press, 1966.

Wolman, B. B. (Ed.) *Historical roots of contemporary psychology*. New York: Harper & Row, 1968.

Yaroshevski, M. G. I. M. Sechenov, the founder of objective psychology. In B. B. Wolman (Ed.), *Historical roots of contemporary psychology*. New York: Harper & Row, pp. 77–110.

CHAPTER 3. BEHAVIORISM AND REDUCTIONISM

Beach, F. A., Hebb, D. O., Morgan, C. T., & Nissen, H. W. (Eds.) *The neuropsychology of Lashley: Selected papers of K. S. Lashley.* New York: McGraw-Hill, 1960.

Cannon, W. B. *Bodily changes in pain, hunger, fear, and rage.* (2nd ed.) New York: Appleton, 1929.

Cannon, W. B. *The wisdom of the body.* New York: Norton, 1932.

Carmichael, L. Some historical roots of contemporary animal psychology. In B. B. Wolman (Ed.), *Historical roots of contemporary psychology.* New York: Harper & Row, 1968, pp. 47–76.

Coghill, G. E. *Anatomy and the problem of behavior.* London: Cambridge University Press, 1929.

Darwin, C. *Expression of emotions in man and animals.* (2nd ed.) London: Murray, 1872.

Diserens, C. M. Psychological objectivism. *Psychol. Rev.,* 1925, *32,* 121–152.

Franz, S. I. On the functions of the cerebrum: The frontal lobes. *Arch. Psychol.,* 1907, No. 2.

Franz, S. I. *Nervous and mental re-education.* New York: Macmillan, 1923.

Franz, S. I., & Lashley, K. S. The effects of cerebral destruction upon habit formation and retention in the albino rat. *Psychobiol.,* 1917, *1,* 71–139.

Hebb, D. O. Studies of the organization of behavior: I. Behavior of the rat in a field orientation. *J. comp. Psychol.,* 1938, *25,* 333–352.

Hebb, D. O. Studies of the organization of behavior: II. Changes in the field orientation of the rat after cortical destruction. *J. comp. Psychol.,* 1938, *26,* 427–444.

Hebb, D. O. *The organization of behavior: a neuropsychological theory.* New York: Wiley, 1949.

Hebb, D. O. *A textbook of psychology.* Philadelphia: Saunders, 1958.

Hebb, D. O., & Foord, E. N. Errors of visual recognition and the nature of the trace. *J. exp. Psychol.,* 1945, *35,* 335–348.

Holt, E. B. *The concept of consciousness.* New York: Macmillan, 1914.

Holt, E. B. *The Freudian wish and its place in ethics.* New York: Holt, 1915.

Holt, E. B. *Animal drives and the learning process.* New York: Holt, 1931.

Hunter, W. S. *Human behavior.* Chicago: University of Chicago Press, 1928.

Hunter, W. S. The psychological study of behavior. *Psychol. Rev.,* 1932, *39,* 1–24.

Hunter, W. S. Basic phenomena in learning. *J. gen. Psychol.,* 1933, *8,* 299–317.

Hunter, W. S. Conditioning and extinction in the rat. *Brit. J. Psychol.,* 1935, *26,* 135–148.

Hunter, W. S. Conditioning and maze learning in the rat. *J. comp. Psychol.,* 1935, *19,* 417–424.

Hunter, W. S. Learning curves for conditioning and maze learning. *J. exp. Psychol.,* 1936, *19,* 121–128.

Lashley, K. S. The human salivary reflex and its use in psychology. *Psychol. Rev.,* 1916, *23,* 446–464.

Lashley, K. S. Reflex secretion of the human parotid gland. *J. exp. Psychol.,* 1916, *1,* 461–493.

Lashley, K. S. The behavioristic interpretation of consciousness. *Psychol. Rev.,* 1923, *30,* 237–272.

Lashley, K. S. *Brain mechanisms and intelligence.* Chicago: University of Chicago Press, 1929.

Lashley, K. S. Basic neural mechanisms in behavior. *Psychol. Rev.,* 1930, *37,* 1–24.

Lashley, K. S. Cerebral control versus reflexology: A reply to Professor Hunter. *J. gen. Psychol.,* 1931, *5,* 3–20.

Lashley, K. S. Nervous mechanisms in learning. In C. Murchison (Ed.), *A handbook of general experimental psychology.* Worcester, Mass.: Clark University Press, 1934.

Lashley, K. S. Experimental analysis of instinctive behavior. *Psychol. Rev.,* 1938, *45,* 445–472.

Lashley, K. S. Coalescence of neurology and psychology. *Proc. Amer. philos. Soc.,* 1941, *84,* 461–470.

Lashley, K. S. Structural variation in the nervous system in relation to behavior. *Psychol. Rev.,* 1947, *54,* 325–334.

Lashley, K. S., & Wade, M. The Pavlovian theory of generalization. *Psychol. Rev.,* 1946, *53,* 72–87.

Liddell, H. S. The conditioned reflex. In F. A. Moss (Ed.), *Comparative psychology*. New York: Prentice-Hall, 1934.

Mateer, F. *Child behavior, a critical and experimental study of young children by the method of conditioned reflexes*. Boston: Badger, 1918.

Sherrington, C. S. *Man on his nature*. New York: Macmillan, 1941.

Sherrington, C. S. *The integrative action of the nervous system*. (New ed.) New Haven: Yale University Press, 1947.

Smith, S., & Guthrie, E. R. *General psychology in terms of behavior*. New York: Appleton, 1921.

Washburn, M. F. *The animal mind*. New York: Macmillan, 1908.

Watson, J. B. Kinesthetic and organic sensations: Their role in the reaction of the white rat to the maze. *Psychol. Monogr.*, 1907, *8*, No. 33.

Watson, J. B. Psychology as a behaviorist views it. *Psychol. Rev.*, 1913, *20*, 158–177.

Watson, J. B. *Behavior: An introduction to comparative psychology*. New York: Holt, 1914.

Watson, J. B. The place of the conditioned reflex in psychology. *Psychol. Rev.*, 1916, *23*, 89–117.

Watson, J. B. The effect of delayed feeding upon learning. *Psychobiol.*, 1917, *1*, 51–60.

Watson, J. B. *Psychology from the standpoint of a behaviorist*. Philadelphia: Lippincott, 1919.

Watson, J. B. Behaviorism: a psychology based on reflexes. *Arch. Neurol. Psychiat.*, 1926, *15*, 185–204.

Watson, J. B. *Behaviorism*. (Rev. ed.) New York: Norton, 1930.

Watson, J. B., & Morgan. J. J. B. Emotional reactions and psychological experimentation. *Amer. J. Psychol.*, 1917, *28*, 163–174.

Watson, J. B., & Raynor, R. Conditioned emotional reactions. *J. exp. Psychol.*, 1920, *3*, 1–14.

Weiss, A. P. *A theoretical basis of human behavior*. (2nd ed.) Columbus, Ohio: Adams, 1929.

Weiss, A. P. Feeling and emotion as forms of behavior. In M. L. Reymert (Ed.), *Feeling and emotions: The Wittenberg symposium*. Worcester, Mass.: Clark University Press, 1930.

Wolman, B. B. *Dictionary of behavioral science*. New York: Van Nostrand Reinhold, 1973.

CHAPTER 4. NEO-BEHAVIORISM AND LEARNING THEORY

1, 2, 3, 4, 5. Guthrie, Hull, Skinner, Tolman, Razran

Adams, O. K. Experimental studies of adaptive behavior in cats. *Comp. Psychol. Monogr.*, 1929, *6*, No. 27.

Arnold, W. J. Simple reaction chains and their integration. I. Homogeneous chaining with terminal reinforcement. *J. comp. physiol. Psychol.*, 1947, *40*, 349–363.

Baernstein, H. D., & Hull, C. L. A mechanical model of the conditioned reflex. *J. gen. Psychol.*, 1931, *5*, 99–106.

Bass, M. J., & Hull, C. L. The irradiation of a tactile conditioned reflex in man. *J. comp. Psychol.*, 1934, *17*, 46–65.

Bendig, A. W. Latent learning in a water maze. *J. exp. Psychol.*, 1953, *43*, 134–137.

Bergmann, G., & Spence, K. W. The logic of psychological measurement. *Psychol. Rev.*, 1944, *51*, 1–24.

Birch, H. G., & Bittermann, M. E. Reinforcement and learning: The process of sensory integration. *Psychol. Rev.*, 1949, *56*, 292–308.

Blodgett, H. C. The effect of the introduction of reward upon the maze performance of rats. *Univer. Calif. Publ. Psychol.*, 1929, *4*, 113–134.

Brown, J. S., & Farber, I. E. Emotions conceptualized as intervening variables—with suggestions toward a theory of frustration. *Psychol. Bull.*, 1951, *48*, 465–495.

Buxton, C. E. Latent learning and the goal gradient hypothesis. *Contr. psychol. Theor.*, 1940, *2*, No. 2.

Chisholm, R. M. Intentionality and the theory of signs. *Philos. Stud.*, 1952, *3*, 56–63.

Christie, R. The role of drive discrimination in learning under irrelevant motivation. *J. exp. Psychol.*, 1951, *42*, 13–19.

Christie, R. The effect of some early experiences in the latent learning of adult rats. *J. comp. physiol. Psychol.*, 1952, *43*, 281–288.

Cook, S. W., & Skinner, B. F. Some factors influencing the distribution of associated words. *Psychol. Rec.*, 1939, *3*, 178–184.

Crespi, L. P. Quantitative variation of incentive and performance in the white rat. *Amer. J. Psychol.*, 1942, *55*, 467–517.

Crespi, L. P. Amount of reinforcement and level of reinforcement. *Psychol. Rev.*, 1944, *51*, 341–357.

Daub, C. T. The effect of doors on latent learning. *J. comp. Psychol.*, 1933, *15*, 49–58.

Denny, M. R. The role of secondary reinforcement in a partial reinforcement learning situation. *J. exp. Psychol.*, 1946, *36*, 373–389.

Denny, M. R., & David, R. H. A test of latent learning for a non-goal significate. *J. comp. physiol. Psychol.*, 1951, *44*, 590–595.

Elliott, M. H. The effect of appropriateness of rewards and of complex incentives on maze performance. *Univer. Calif. Publ. Psychol.*, 1929, *4*, 91–98.

Ellson, D. G. Quantitative studies of the interaction of simple habits. I. Recovery from specific and generalized effects of extinction. *J. exp. Psychol.*, 1938, *23*, 339–358.

Estes, W. K. An experimental study of punishment. *Psychol. Monogr.*, 1944, *57*, No. 3.

Estes, W. K. Effects of competing reactions on the conditioning curve for bar-pressing. *J. exp. Psychol.*, 1950, *40*, 200–205.

Estes, W. K. Learning theory and the new "mental chemistry." *Psychol. Rev.*, 1960, *67*, 207–223.

Estes, W. K., Koch, S., MacCorquodale, K., Meehl, P. E., Mueller, C. G., Jr., Schoenfeld, W. N., & Verplanck, W. S. *Modern Learning Theory*. New York: Appleton-Century-Crofts, 1954.

Estes, W. K., & Skinner, B. F. Some quantitative properties of anxiety. *J. exp. Psychol.*, 1941, *29*, 390–400.

Felsinger, J. M., Gladstone, A. I., Yamaguchi, H. G., & Hull, C. L. Reaction latency ($_s t_R$) as a function of the number of reinforcements (N). *J. exp. Psychol.*, 1947, *37*, 214–228.

Finan, J. L. Quantitative studies in motivation. I. Strength of conditioning in rats under varying degrees of hunger. *J. comp. Psychol.*, 1940, *29*, 119–134.

Gibson, E. J. A systematic application of the concepts of generalization and differentiation to verbal learning. *Psychol. Rev.*, 1940, *47*, 196–229.

Gilchrist, J. C. Characteristics of latent and reinforcement learning as a function of time. *J. comp. physiol. Psychol.*, 1952, *45*, 198–203.

Gladstone, A. I., Yamaguchi, H. G., Hull, C. L., & Felsinger, J. M. Some functional relationships of reaction potential (sEr) and related phenomena. *J. exp. Psychol.*, 1947, *37*, 510–526.

Gleitman, H. Studies in motivation and learning: II. Thirsty rats trained in maze with food but not water; then run hungry. *J. exp. Psychol.*, 1950, *40*, 169–174.

Graham, C. H., & Gagné, R. M. The acquisition, extinction, and spontaneous recovery of a conditioned operant response. *J. exp. Psychol.*, 1940, *26*, 251–280.

Grice, G. R. An experimental test of the expectation theory of learning. *J. comp. physiol. Psychol.*, 1940, *41*, 137–143.

Grindley, G. C. Experiments on the influence of the amount of reward on learning in young chickens. *Brit. J. Psychol.*, 1929, *20*, 173–180.

Guthrie, E. R. Purpose and mechanism in psychology. *J. Phil.*, 1924, *21*, 673–682.

Guthrie, E. R. Conditioning as a principle of learning. *Psychol. Rev.*, 1930, *37*, 412–428.

Guthrie, E. R. On the nature of psychological explanations. *Psychol. Rev.*, 1933, *40*, 124–137.

Guthrie, E. R. Association as a function of time interval. *Psychol. Rev.*, 1933, *40*, 355–367.

Guthrie, E. R. Reward and punishment. *Psychol. Rev.*, 1934, *41*, 450–460.

Guthrie, E. R. *The psychology of learning*. New York: Harper, 1935.

Guthrie, E. R. Psychological principles and scientific truth. *Proc. 25th Anniv. Celeb. Inaugur. grad. Stud.*, University of Southern California, 1936.

Guthrie, E. R. *The psychology of human conflict.* New York: Harper, 1938.

Guthrie, E. R. The effect of outcome on learning. *Psychol. Rev.*, 1939, *46*, 480–485.

Guthrie, E. R. Association and the law of effect. *Psychol. Rev.*, 1940, *47*, 127–148.

Guthrie, E. R. Conditioning: a theory of learning in terms of stimulus, response and association. *Yearb. nat. Soc. Stud. Educ.*, 1942, *41*, 17–60.

Guthrie, E. R. The principle of associative learning. In F. P. Clarke, & M. C. Nahm (Eds.), *Philosophical essays in honor of Edgar Arthur Singer, Jr.* Philadelphia: University of Pennsylvania Press, 1942.

Guthrie, E. R. Psychological facts and psychological theory. *Psychol. Bull.*, 1946, *43*, 1–20.

Guthrie, E. R. The status of systematic psychology. *Amer. Psychologist*, 1950, *5*, 97–101.

Guthrie, E. R. *The psychology of learning.* (Rev. ed.) New York: Harper, 1952.

Guthrie, E. R., & Horton, G. P. *Cats in a puzzle box.* New York: Rinehart, 1946.

Guthrie, E. R. & Powers, F. F. *Educational psychology.* New York: Ronald, 1950.

Haney, G. W. The effect of familiarity on maze performance of albino rats. *Univer. Calif. Publ. Psychol.*, 1931, *4*, 319–333.

Hempel, C. G. The logical analysis of psychology. In H. Feigl & W. Sellars (Eds.), *Readings in philosophical analysis.* New York: Appleton-Century-Crofts, 1949, pp. 373–384.

Herb, F. H. Latent learning—non-reward followed by food in blinds. *J. comp. Psychol.*, 1940, *29*, 247–255.

Heron, W. T. The rate of extinction in maze-bright and maze-dull rats. *Psychol. Rev.*, 1940, *4*, 11–18.

Heron, W. T. Internal stimuli and learning. *J. comp. physiol. Psychol.*, 1949, *42*, 486–492.

Heron, W. T., & Skinner, B. F. Changes in hunger during starvation. *Psychol. Rev.*, 1947, *1*, 51–60.

Hilgard, E. R. & Bower, G. H. *Theories of learning.* New York: Appleton-Century-Crofts, 1966.

Hill, C. H. Goal gradient, anticipation, and perseveration in compound trial-and-error learning. *J. exp. Psychol.*, 1930, *25*, 566–585.

Hovland, C. I. The generalization of conditioned responses: I. The sensory generalization of conditioned responses with varying frequencies of tone. *J. gen. Psychol.*, 1937, *17*, 125–148.

Hovland, C. I. The generalization of conditioned responses: II. The sensory generalization of conditioned responses with varying intensities of tone. *J. genet. Psychol.*, 1937, *51*, 279–291.

Hovland, C. I. The generalization of conditioned responses. IV. The effects of varying amounts of reinforcement upon the degree of generalization of conditional responses. *J. exp. Psychol.*, 1937, *21*, 261–276.

Hull, C. L. A functional interpretation of the conditioned relfex. *Psychol. Rev.*, 1929, *36*, 498–511.

Hull, C. L. Simple trial-and-error learning: A study in psychological theory. *Psychol. Rev.*, 1930, *37*, 241–256.

Hull, C. L. Knowledge and purpose as habit mechanisms. *Psychol. Rev.*, 1930, *37*, 511–525.

Hull, C. L. Goal attraction and directing ideas conceived as habit phenomena. *Psychol. Rev.*, 1931, *38*, 487–506.

Hull, C. L. The goal gradient hypothesis and maze learning. *Psychol. Rev.*, 1932, *39*, 25–43.

Hull, C. L. Differential habituation to internal stimuli in the albino rat. *J. comp. Psychol.*, 1933, *16*, 255–274.

Hull, C. L. The concept of the habit-family hierarchy, and maze learning. Part I. *Psychol. Rev.*, 1934, *41*, 33–54.

Hull, C. L. The concept of the habit-family hierarchy, and maze learning. Part II. *Psychol. Rev.*, 1934, *41*, 134–152.

Hull, C. L. Learning: II. The factor of the conditioned reflex. In C. Murchison (Ed.), *A handbook of general experimental psychology.* Worcester, Mass.: Clark University Press, 1934.

Hull, C. L. The rat's speed of locomotion gradient in the approach to food. *J. comp. Psychol.*, 1934, *17*, 393–422.

Hull, C. L. The mechanism of the assembly of behavior segments in novel combinations suitable for problem solution. *Psychol. Rev.*, 1935, *42*, 219–245.

Hull, C. L. The conflicting psychologies of learning—a way out. *Psychol. Rev.*, 1935, *42*, 491–516.

Hull, C. L. The influence of caffeine and other factors on certain phenomena of rote learning. *J. gen. Psychol.*, 1935, *13*, 249–274.

Hull, C. L. Special review: Thorndike's *Fundamentals of learning. Psychol. Bull.*, 1935, *32*, 807–823.

Hull, C. L. Mind, mechanism and adaptive behavior. *Psychol. Rev.*, 1937, *44*, 1–32.

Hull, C. L. The goal-gradient hypothesis applied to some "field-force" problems in the behavior of young children. *Psychol. Rev.*, 1938, *45*, 271–300.

Hull, C. L. The problem of stimulus equivalence in behavior theory. *Psychol. Rev.*, 1939, *46*, 9–30.

Hull, C. L. Modern behaviorism and psychoanalysis. *Trans. N.Y. Acad. Sci.*, 1939, *1*, Ser. II, 78–82.

Hull, C. L. Simple trial-and-error learning—an empirical investigation. *J. comp. Psychol.*, 1939, *27*, 233–258.

Hull, C. L. Explorations in the patterning of stimuli conditioned to the G.S.R. *J. exp. Psychol.*, 1940, *27*, 95–110.

Hull, C. L. *Psychological seminar memoranda, 1939–1940.* Bound mimeographed manuscript on file in the libraries of Yale University, University of Iowa, & Oberlin College.

Hull, C. L. Conditioning: Outline of a systematic theory of learning. *Yearb. nat. Soc. Stud. Educ.*, 1942, *41*, Part 2, 61–95.

Hull, C. L. *Principles of behavior: An introduction to behavior theory.* New York: Appleton-Century-Crofts, 1943.

Hull, C. L. The problem of intervening variables in molar behavior theory. *Psychol. Rev.*, 1943, *50*, 273–291.

Hull, C. L. A postscript concerning intervening variables. *Psychol. Rev.*, 1943, *50*, 540.

Hull, C. L. *Psychological memoranda, 1940–1944.* Bound mimeographed manuscript on file in the libraries of Yale University, University of Iowa, & University of North Carolina.

Hull, C. L. The place of innate individual and species differences in a natural-science theory of behavior. *Psychol. Rev.*, 1945, *52*, 55–60.

Hull, C. L. The discrimination of stimulus configurations and the hypothesis of afferent neural interaction. *Psychol. Rev.*, 1945, *52*, 133–142.

Hull, C. L. Research memorandum concerning the quantitative empirical determination of certain basic behavioral constants and their functional relationships. May 20, 1945. (Mimeographed manuscript on file in Yale Library.)

Hull, C. L. The problem of primary stimulus generalization. *Psychol. Rev.*, 1947, *54*, 120–134.

Hull, C. L. Reactively heterogeneous compound trial-and-error learning with distributed trials and terminal reinforcement. *J. exp. Psychol.*, 1947, *37*, 118–135.

Hull, C. L. Reactively heterogeneous compound trial-and-error learning with distributed trials and serial reinforcement. *J. exp. Psychol.*, 1948, *38*, 17–28.

Hull, C. L. Memorandum on behavior theory. Oct. 4, 1949. (Mimeographed manuscript on file in Yale Library).

Hull, C. L. Stimulus intensity dynamism (V) and stimulus generalization. *Psychol. Rev.*, 1949, *56*, 67–76.

Hull, C. L. Behavior postulates and corollaries—1949. *Psychol. Rev.*, 1950, *57*, 173–180.

Hull, C. L. Simple qualitative discrimination learning. *Psychol. Rev.*, 1950, *57*, 303–313.

Hull, C. L. A primary social science law. *Sci. Mon., N.Y.* 1950, *71*, 221–228.

Hull, C. L. Memorandum concerning behavior theory. Feb. 7, 1950. (Mimeographed manuscript on file in Yale Library.)

Hull, C. L. Memorandum concerning behavior theory. Mar. 6, 1950. (Mimeographed manuscript on file in Yale Library.)

Hull, C. L. *Essentials of behavior.* New Haven: Yale University Press, 1951.

Hull, C. L. *A Behavior System.* New Haven: Yale University Press, 1952.

Hull, C. L. Clark L. Hull. In E. G. Boring, H. S. Langfeld, H. Werner, & R. M. Yerkes (Eds.), *A history of psychology in autobiography—Volume IV.* Worcester, Mass.: Clark University Press, 1952.

Hull, C. L., & Baernstein, H. D. A mechanical parallel to the conditioned reflex. *Science,* 1929, *70,* 14–15.

Hull, C. L., Felsinger, J. M. Gladstone, A. I., and Yamaguchi, H. G. A proposed quantification of habit strength. *Psychol. Rev.,* 1947, *54,* 237–254.

Hull, C. L., Hovland, C. I., Ross, R. T., Hall, M., Perkins, D. T., & Fitch, F. B. *Mathematicodeductive theory of rote learning: A study in scientific methodology.* New Haven: Yale University Press, 1940.

Hull, C. L., Johnston, R. L., Rouse, R. O., & Barker, A. H. True, sham, and esophageal feeding as reinforcements. *J. comp. physiol. Psychol.,* 1951, *44,* 236–245.

Hull, C. L., & Krueger, R. C. An electro-chemical parallel to the conditioned reflex. *J. gen. Psychol.,* 1931, *5,* 262–269.

Hull, C. L., & Mowrer, O. H. *Hull's psychological seminars, 1936–38. Notices and abstracts of proceedings.* Bound mimeographed material on file in the libraries of the University of Chicago, University of North Carolina, & Yale University.

Hull, C. L. & Spence, K. W. "Correction" vs. "non-correction" method of trial-and-error learning in rats. *J. comp. Psychol.,* 1938, *25,* 127–145.

Humphreys, L. G. The effect of random alteration of reinforcement on the acquisition and extinction of conditioned eyelid reactions. *J. esp. Psychol.,* 1939, *25,* 141–158.

Humphreys, L. G. Generalization as a function of method of reinforcement. *J. exp. Psychol.,* 1939, *25,* 361–372.

Jenkins, W. O., & Stanley, J. C. Partial reinforcement: A review and critique. *Psychol. Bull,* 1950, *47,* 193–234.

Kappauf, W. E., & Schlosberg, H. Conditioned responses in the white rat. III. Conditioning as a function of the length of the period of delay. *J. genet. Psychol.,* 1937, *50,* 27–45.

Karn, H. W., & Porter, H. M., Jr. The effects of certain pre-training procedures upon maze performance and their significance for the concept of latent learning. *J. exp. Psychol.,* 1946, *36,* 461–469.

Kendler, H. H. Drive interaction: II. Experimental analysis of the role of drive in learning theory. *J. exp. Psychol.,* 1945, *35,* 188–198.

Kendler, H. H. A comparison of learning under motivated and satiated conditions in the white rat. *J. exp. Psychol.,* 1947, *37,* 545–549.

Kendler, H. H. An investigation of latent learning in a T-maze. *J. comp. Psychol.,* 1947, *40,* 265–270.

Kendler, H. H. "What is learned?"—a theoretical blind alley. *Psychol. Rev.,* 1952, *59,* 269–277.

Kendler, H. H., & Ianner, J. H. A further test of the ability of rats to learn the location of food when motivated by thirst. *J. exp. Psychol.,* 1950, *40,* 762–765.

Kimble, G. A. Conditioning as a function of the time between conditioned and unconditioned stimuli. *J. exp. Psychol.,* 1947, *37,* 1–15.

Kimble, G. A. An experimental test of a two-factor theory of inhibition. *J. exp. Psychol.,* 1949, *39,* 15–23.

Kimble, G. A. *Foundations of conditioning and learning.* New York. Appleton-Century-Crofts, 1967.

Koch, S. The logical character of the motivation concept. I. *Psychol. Rev.,* 1941, *48,* 15–38.

Koch, S. Review of Hull's Principles of Behavior. *Psychol. Bull.,* 1944, *41,* 269–286.

Koch, S. Form and content in hypothetico-deductive systems: A reply to Woodbury. *J. Psychol.,* 1947, *24,* 237–246.

Koch, S. & Hull C. L. In W. K. Estes & others. (Eds.), *Modern learning theory*. New York: Appleton-Century-Crofts, 1954.

Koch, S., & Daniel, W. J. The effect of satiation on the behavior mediated by a habit of maximum strength. *J. exp. Psychol.*, 1945, *35*, 167–187.

Konorski, J. *Conditioned reflexes and neuron organization*. New York. Oxford, 1948.

Krechevsky, I. "Hypotheses" versus "chance" in the presolution period in sensory discrimination-learning. *Univer. Calif. Publ. Psychol.*, 1932, *6*, 27–44.

Leeper, R. The role of motivation in learning: A study of the phenomenon of differential motivational control of the utilization of habits. *J. genet. Psychol.*, 1935, *46*, 3–40.

Leeper, R. Dr. Hull's Principles of Behavior. *J. genet. Psychol.*, 1944, *65*, 3–52.

Leeper, R. The experiments by Spence and Lippitt and by Kendler on the sign-gestalt theory of learning. *J. exp. Psychol.*, 1948, *38*, 102–106.

Littman, R. A. Latent learning in a T-maze after two degrees of training. *J. comp. physiol. Psychol.*, 1950, *43*,135–147.

Littman, R. A., & Rosen, E. Molar and molecular. *Psychol. Rev.*, 1950, *57*, 58–65.

MacCorquodale, K. Preliminary suggestions as to a formalization of expectancy theory. *Psychol. Rev.*, 1953, *60*, 55–63.

MacCorquodale, K., & Meehl, P. E. "Cognitive" learning in the absence of competition of incentives. *J. comp. physiol. Psychol.*, 1949, *42*, 383–390.

Meehl, P. E. An examination of the treatment of stimulus patterning in Professor Hull's Principles of Behavior. *Psychol. Rev.*, 1945, *52*, 324–332.

Meehl, P. E. On the circularity of the law of effect. *Psychol. Bull.*, 1950, *47*, 52–75.

Meehl, P. E. A failure to find the Blodgett effect, and some secondary observations on drive conditioning. *J. comp physiol. Psychol.*, 1951, *44*, 178–183.

Meehl, P. E. Some methological comments concerning expectancy theory, *Psychol. Rev.*, 1951, *58*, 230–233.

Meehl, P. E. Drive conditioning as a factor in latent learning. *J. exp. Psychol.*, 1953, *43*, 20–24.

Meehl, P. E., & MacCorquodale, K. A. A further study of latent learning in the T-maze, *J. comp. physiol. Psychol.*, 1948, *41*, 372–396.

Miller, N. E. Studies of fear as an acquirable drive: I. Fear as motivation and fear-reduction as reinforcement in the learning of new responses. *J. exp. Psychol.*, 1948, *38*, 89–101.

Miller, N. E. Learnable drives and rewards. In S. S. Stevens (Ed.), *Handbook of experimental psychology*. New York: Wiley, 1951.

Miller, N. E. Learning of visceral and glandular responses. *Science*, 1969, *163*, 434–445.

Montgomery, K. C. "Spontaneous alternation" as a function of time between trials and amount of work. *J. exp. Psychol.*, 1951, *42*, 82–93.

Montgomery, K. C. Exploratory behavior and its relation to spontaneous alternation in a series of maze exposures. *J. comp. physiol. Psychol.*, 1952, *45*, 50–57.

Mowrer, O. H. Two factor learning theory reconsidered with special reference to secondary reinforcement and the concept of habit. *Psychol. Rev.*, 1956, *63*, 114–128.

Mowrer, O. H., & Jones, H. M. Extinction and behavior variability as functions of effortfulness of task. *J. exp. Psychol.*, 1943, *33*, 369–386.

Muenzinger, K. F., Koerner, L., & Irey, E. Variability of an habitual movement in guinea pigs. *J. comp. Psychol.*, 1929, *9*, 425–436.

Nissen, H. W. Description of the learned response in discrimination behavior. *Psychol. Rev.*, 1950, *57*, 121–131.

Notterman, J. M. A study of some relations among aperiodic reinforcement, discrimination training, and secondary reinforcement. *J. exp. Psychol.*, 1951, *41*, 161–169.

Perin, C. T. Behavior potentiality as a joint function of the amount of training and the degree of hunger at the time of extinction. *J. exp. Psychol.*, 1942, *30*, 93–113.

Perin, C. T. A quantitative investigation of the delay-of-reinforcement gradient. *J. exp. Psychol.*, 1943, *32*, 37–51.

Postman, L. The history and present status of the law of effect. *Psychol. Bull.*, 1947, *44*, 489–563.

Prentice, W. C. H. Continuity in human learning. *J. exp. Psychol.*, 1949, 39, 187–194.

Razran, G. Sensory capacities of the dog as studied by the conditioned reflex method (with C. J. Warden). *Psychol. Bull.*, 1929, 26, 202–222.

Razran, G. Theory of conditioning and of related phenomena. *Psychol. Rev.*, 1930, 37, 225–243.

Razran, G. Conditioned responses in animals other than dogs. *Psychol. Bull.*, 1933, 30, 261–324.

Razran, G. Conditioned withdrawal responses in adult human subjects. *Psychol. Bull.*, 1934, 31, 111–143.

Razran, G. Salivary conditioning in adult human subjects, *Psychol. Bull.*, 1934, 31, 634–635.

Razran, G. Conditioned responses: An experimental study and a theoretical analysis. *Arch. Psychol.*, 1935, 28, No. 191.

Razran, G. Psychology in the U.S.S.R. *J. Phil.*, 1935, 32, 19–25.

Razran, G. Salivary conditioning in adult human subjects. *Psychol. Bull.*, 1935, 32, 561–562.

Razran, G. The conditioning of voluntary reactions. *J. exp. Psychol.*, 1936, 19, 653–655.

Razran, G. Attitudinal control of human conditioning. *J. Psychol.*, 1936, 2, 327–337.

Razran, G. Conditioned responses: A classified bibliography. *Psychol. Bull.*, 1937, 34, 191–256.

Razran, G. Configural and colligated conditioning. *Psychol. Bull.*, 1937, 34, 515–516.

Razran, G. Semantic and phonetographic generalizations of salivary conditioning to verbal stimuli. *J. exp. Psychol.*, 1949, 39, 642–652.

Razran, G. Attitudinal determinants of conditioning and of generalization of conditioning. *J. exp. Psychol.*, 1949, 39, 820–829.

Razran, G. Some psychological factors in the generalization of salivary conditioning to verbal stimuli. *Amer. J. Psychol.*, 1949, 62, 247–256.

Razran, G. Stimulus generalization of conditioned responses. *Psychol. Bull.*, 1949, 46, 337–365.

Razran, G. The conditioned evocation of attitudes (cognitive conditioning). *J. exp. Psychol.*, 1954, 48, 278–282.

Razran, G. Conditioning and perception. *Psychol. Rev.*, 1955, 62, 83–95.

Razran, G. Backward conditioning. *Psychol. Bull.*, 1956, 53, 55–69.

Razran, G. Extinction re-examined and re-analyzed: A new theory. *Psychol. Rev.*, 1956, 63, 39–52.

Razran, G. The dominance-contiguity theory of the acquisition of classical conditioning. *Psychol. Bull.*, 1957, 54, 1–46.

Razran, G. Pavlov and Lamarck. *Science*, 1958, 128, 758–760.

Reynolds, B. A. The acquisition of a trace conditioned response as a function of the magnitude of the stimulus trace. *J. exp. Psychol.*, 1945, 35, 15–30.

Reynolds, B. A. The relationship between the strength of a habit and the degree of drive present during acquisition. *J. exp. Psychol.*, 1949 39, 296–305.

Ritchie, B. F. Hull's treatment of learning. *Psychol. Bull.*, 1944, 41, 640–652.

Ritchie, B. F. Studies in spatial learning. III. Two paths to the same location and two paths to two different locations. *J. exp. Psychol.*, 1947, 37, 25–38.

Ritchie, B. F. Studies in spatial learning. VI. Place orientation and direction orientation. *J. exp. Psychol.*, 1948, 38, 659–669.

Ritchie, B. F. Theories of learning: A consumer report. In B. B. Wolman (Ed.), *Handbook of general psychology.* Englewood Cliffs, N.J.: Prentice-Hall, 1973, pp. 451–460.

Schiller, P. S. Analysis of detour behavior. I. Learning of round-about pathways in fish. *J. comp. physiol. Psychol.*, 1949, 42, 463–475.

Schoenfeld, W. N. An experimental approach to anxiety, escape and avoidance behavior. Chapter 5 in P. Hoch & J. Zubin (Eds.), *Anxiety.* New York: Grune & Stratton, 1950.

Sellars, W. S. Concepts as involving laws and inconceivable without them *Phil. Sci.*, 1948, 15, 287–315.

Sellars, W. Mind, meaning, and behavior. *Philos. Stud.*, 1952, 3, 83–95.

Seward, J. P. A theoretical derivation of latent learning. *Psychol. Rev.*, 1947, 54, 83–98.

Seward, J. P. An experimental analysis of latent learning. *J. exp. Psychol.*, 1949, 39, 177–186.

Seward, J. P. Secondary reinforcement as tertiary motivation: A revision of Hull's revision. *Psychol. Rev.*, 1950, 57, 362–374.

Seward, J. P., Levy, N., & Handlon, J. P., Jr. Incidental learning in the rat. *J. comp. physiol. Psychol.*, 1950, *43*, 240–251.

Shaw, M. E., & Waters, R. H. An experimental test of latent learning in a relatively free-choice situation. *J. genet. Psychol.*, 1950, *77*, 283–292.

Sheffield, F. D. Avoidance training and the contiguity principle. *J. comp. physiol. Psychol.*, 1948, *41*, 165–177.

Sheffield, F. D., & Roby, T. B. Reward value of a non-nutritive sweet taste. *J. comp. physiol. Psychol.*, 1950, *43*, 471–481.

Simmons, Rietta. The relative effectiveness of certain incentives in animal learning. *Comp. psychol. Monogr.*, 1924, *2*, 1–79.

Skinner, B. F. On the conditions of elicitation of certain eating reflexes. *Proc. nat. Acad. Sci.*, 1930, *16*, 433–438.

Skinner, B. F. The concept of the reflex in the description of behavior. *J. gen. Psychol.*, 1931, *5*, 427–458.

Skinner, B. F. Drive and reflex strength. *J. gen. Psychol.*, 1932, *6*, 22–37.

Skinner, B. F. Drive and reflex strength: II. *J. gen. Psychol.*, 1932, *6*, 38–48.

Skinner, B. F. On the rate of formation of a conditioned reflex. *J. gen. Psychol.*, 1932, *7*, 274–286.

Skinner, B. F. On the rate of extinction of a conditioned reflex. *J. gen. Psychol.*, 1933, *8*, 114–129.

Skinner, B. F. The measurement of "spontaneous activity." *J. gen. Psychol.*, 1933,*9*, 3–23.

Skinner, B. F. The rate of establishment of a discrimination. *J. gen. Psychol.*, 1933, *9*, 302–350.

Skinner, B. F. "Resistance to extinction" in the process of conditioning, *J. gen. Psychol.*, 1933, *9*, 420–429.

Skinner, B. F. The abolishment of a discrimination. *Proc. nat. Acad. Sci.*, 1933, *19*, 825–828.

Skinner, B. F. The extinction of chained reflexes. *Proc. nat. Acad. Sci.*, 1934, *20*, 234–237.

Skinner, B. F. A discrimination without previous conditioning. *Proc. nat. Acad. Sci.*, 1934, *20*, 532–536.

Skinner, B. F. The generic nature of the concepts of stimulus and response. *J. gen. Psychol.*, 1935, *12*, 40–65.

Skinner, B. F. Two types of conditioned reflex and a pseudotype. *J. gen. Psychol.*, 1935, *12*, 66–77.

Skinner, B. F. A discrimination based upon a change in the properties of a stimulus. *J. gen. Psychol.*, 1935, *12*, 313–336.

Skinner, B. F. The extinction ratio and its modification by a temporal discrimination. *Psychol. Bull.*, 1936, *33*, 784. (Abstr.)

Skinner, B. F. A failure to obtain "disinhibition." *J. gen. Psychol.*, 1936, *14*, 127–135.

Skinner, B. F. The reinforcing effect of a differentiating stimulus. *J. gen. Psychol.*, 1936 *14*, 263–278.

Skinner, B. F. The effect of the amount of conditioning of an interval of time before reinforcement. *J. gen. Psychol.*, 1936, *14*, 279–295.

Skinner, B. F. Conditioning and extinction and their relation to drive. *J. gen. Psychol.*, 1936, *14*, 296–317.

Skinner, B. F. Thirst as an arbitrary drive. *J. gen. Psychol.*, 1936, *15*, 205–210.

Skinner, B. F. The verbal summator and a method for the study of latent speech. *J. Psychol.*, 1936 *2*, 71–107.

Skinner, B. F. The distribution of associated words. *Psychol. Rec.*, 1937, *1*, 71–76.

Skinner, B. F. Two types of conditioned reflex: A reply to Konorski and Miller. *J. gen. Psychol.*, 1937, *16*, 272–279.

Skinner, B. F. *The behavior of organisms: An experimental analysis.* New York: Appleton-Century-Crofts, 1938.

Skinner, B. F. The alliteration in Shakespeare's sonnets: A study of literary behavior. *Psychol. Rec.*, 1939, *3*, 186–192.

Skinner, B. F. A method of maintaining an arbitrary degree of hunger. *J. comp. Psychol.*, 1940, *30*, 139–145.

Skinner, B. F. A quantitative estimate of certain types of sound patterning in poetry. *Amer. J. Psychol.*, 1941, *54*, 64–79.

Skinner, B. F. The processes involved in the repeated guessing of alternatives. *J. exp. Psychol.*, 1942, *30*, 495–503.

Skinner, B. F. Reply to Dr. Yacorzynsky. *J. exp. Psychol.*, 1943, *32*, 93–94.

Skinner, B. F. Review of Hull's Principles of Behavior. *Amer. J. Psychol.*, 1944, *57*, 276–281.

Skinner, B. F. The operational analysis of psychological terms. *Psychol. Rev.*, 1945, *52*, 270–277.

Skinner, B. F. Experimental psychology. In W. Dennis (Ed.), *Current trends in psychology*. Pittsburgh: University of Pittsburgh Press, 1947.

Skinner, B. F. "Superstition" in the pigeon. *J. exp. Psychol.*, 1948, *38*, 168–172.

Skinner, B. F. Are theories of learning necessary? *Psychol. Rev.*, 1950, *57*, 193–216.

Skinner, B. F. *Cumulative record*. New York: Appleton-Century-Crofts, 1959.

Skinner, B. F. *Contingencies of reinforcement: A theoretical analysis*. New York: Appleton-Century-Crofts, 1969.

Skinner, B. F., & Heron, W. T. Effects of caffeine and benzedrine upon conditioning and extinction. *Psychol. Rec.*, 1937, *1*, 340–346.

Spence, K. W. The nature of discrimination learning in animals. *Psychol. Rev.*, 1936, *43*, 427–449.

Spence, K. W. Analysis of the formation of visual discrimination habits in the chimpanzee. *J. comp. Psychol.*, 1937, *23*, 77–100.

Spence, K. W. The differential response in animals to stimuli varying within a single dimension. *Psychol. Rev.*, 1937, *44*, 430–444.

Spence, K. W. Continuous versus non-continuous interpretations of discrimination learning. *Psychol. Rev.*, 1940, *47*, 271–288.

Spence, K. W. Failure of transposition in size discrimination of chimpanzees. *Amer. J. Psychol.*, 1941, *54*, 223–229.

Spence, K. W. The basis of solution by chimpanzees of the intermediate size problem. *J. exp. Psychol.*, 1942, *31*, 257–271.

Spence, K. W. Theories of learning. In F. A. Moss (Ed.), *Comparative psychology*. (Rev. ed.) New York: Prentice-Hall, 1942.

Spence, K. W. An experimental test of the continuity and non-continuity theories of discrimination learning. *J. esp. Psychol.*, 1945, *35*, 253–266.

Spence, K. W. The role of secondary reinforcement in delayed reward learning. *Psychol. Rev.*, 1947, *54*, 1–8.

Spence, K. W. The postulates and methods of "behaviorism." *Psychol. Rev.*, 1948, *55*, 67–78.

Spence, K. W. Cognitive versus stimulus-response theories of learning. *Psychol. Rev.*, 1950, *57*, 159–172.

Spence, K. W. Theoretical interpretations of learning. In C. P. Stone (Ed.), *Comparative psychology*. (3rd ed.) New York: Prentice-Hall, 1951.

Spence, K. W. Theoretical interpretations of learning. In S. S. Stevens (Ed.), *Handbook of experimental psychology*. New York: Wiley, 1951.

Spence, K. W., Bergmann, G., & Lippitt, R. O. A study of simple learning under irrelevant motivational-reward conditions. *J. exp. Psychol.*, 1950, *40*, 539–551.

Spence, K. W., & Lippitt, R. O. "Latent" learning of a simple maze problem with relevant needs satiated. *Psychol. Bull.*, 1940, *37*, 429.

Spence, K. W., & Lippitt, R. O. An experimental test of the sign-gestalt theory of trial and error learning. *J. exp. Psychol.*, 1946, *36*, 491–502.

Sprow, A. J. Reactively homogenous compound trial-and-error learning with distributed trials and terminal reinforcement. *J. exp. Psychol.*, 1947, *37*, 197–213.

Strange, J. R. Latent learning under conditions of high motivation. *J. comp. physiol. Psychol.*, 1950, *43*, 194–197.

Thistlethwaite, D. L. A critical review of latent learning and related experiments. *Psychol. Bull.*, 1951, *48*, 97–129.

Thistlethwaite, D. L. An experimental test of a reinforcement interpretation of latent learning. *J. comp. physiol. Psychol.*, 1951, *44*, 431–441.

Thistlethwaite, D. L. Conditions of irrelevant incentive learning. *J. comp, physiol. Psychol.*, 1952, *45*, 517–525.

Tinbergen, N. The hierarchical organization of nervous mechanisms underlying instinctive behavior. In *Physiological mechanisms in animal behavior*. New York: Academic Press, 1950.

Tinklepaugh, O. L. An experimental study of representative factors in monkeys. *J. comp. Psychol.*, 1928, *8*, 197–236.

Tolman, E. C. More concerning the temporal relations of meaning and imagery. *Psychol. Rev.*, 1917, *24*, 114–138.

Tolman, E. C. Nerve process and cognition. *Psychol. Rev.*, 1918, *25*, 423–442.

Tolman, E. C. Retroactive inhibition as affected by conditions of learning. *Psychol. Monogr.*, 1918, *25*, No. 107.

Tolman, E. C. Instinct and purpose. *Psychol. Rev.*, 1920, *27*, 217–233.

Tolman, E. C. Can instincts be given up in psychology? *J. abnorm. soc. Psychol.*, 1922, *17*, 139–152.

Tolman, E. C. A new formula for behaviorism. *Psychol. Rev.*, 1922, *29*, 44–53.

Tolman, E. C. A behavioristic account of the emotions. *Psychol. Rev.*, 1923, *30*, 217–227.

Tolman, E. C. The effects of underlearning upon long- and short-time retentions. *J. exp. Psychol.*, 1923, *6*, 466–474.

Tolman, E. C. The nature of instinct. *Psychol. Bull.*, 1923, *20*, 200–216.

Tolman, E. C. The inheritance of maze-learning ability in rats. *J. comp. Psychol.*, 1924, *4*, 1–18.

Tolman, E. C. Behaviorism and purpose. *J. Phil.*, 1925, *22*, 36–41.

Tolman, E. C. Purpose and cognition: The determiners of animal learning. *Psychol. Rev.*, 1925, *32*, 285–297.

Tolman, E. C. A behavioristic theory of ideas. *Psychol. Rev.*, 1926, *33*, 352–369.

Tolman, E. C. The nature of the fundamental drives. *J. abnorm. soc. Psychol.*, 1926, *20*, 349–358.

Tolman, E. C. A behaviorist's definition of consciousness. *Psychol. Rev.*, 1927, *34*, 433–439.

Tolman, E. C. Habit formation and higher mental processes in animals. Psychol. Bull., 1927, *24*, 1–35; 1928, *25*, 24–53.

Tolman, E. C. Purposive behavior. *Psychol. Rev.*, 1928, *35*, 524–530.

Tolman, E. C. "Insight" in rats. *Univer. Calif. Publ. Psychol.*, 1930, *4*, 215–232.

Tolman, E. C. Maze performance a function of motivation and of reward as well as of knowledge of the maze paths. *J. gen. Psychol.*, 1930, *4*, 338–342.

Tolman, E. C. *Purposive Behavior in animals and men*. New York: Appleton-Century, 1932.

Tolman, E. C. The law of effect. A reply to Dr. Goodenough. *J. exp. Psychol.*, 1933, *16*, 463–470.

Tolman, E. C. Sign-gestalt or conditioned reflex? *Psychol. Rev.*, 1933, *40*, 246–255.

Tolman, E. C. Backward elimination of errors in two successive discrimination habits. *Univer. Calif. Publ. Psychol.*, 1934, *5*, 145–152.

Tolman, E. C. Theories of learning. In F. A. Moss (Ed.), *Comparative psychology*. New York: Prentice-Hall, 1934, pp. 367–408.

Tolman, E. C. Psychology versus immediate experience. *Philos. Sci.*, 1935, *2*, 356–380.

Tolman, E. C. Operational behaviorism and current trends in psychology. *Proc. 25th Anniv. Celeb. Inaugur. grad. Stud.* Los Angeles: University of Southern California Press, 1936.

Tolman, E. C. The perception of spatial relations by the rat: A type of response not easily explained by conditioning. *J. comp. Psychol.*, 1936, *22*, 287–318.

Tolman, E. C. Demands and conflicts. *Psychol. Rev.*, 1937, *44*, 158–169.

Tolman, E. C. The acquisition of string-pulling by rats—conditioned response—or sign-gestalt? *Psychol. Rev.*, 1937, *44*, 195–211.

Tolman, E. C. An operational analysis of "demands." *Erkenntnis*, 1937, *6*, 383–392.

Tolman, E. C. The action of punishment in acceleration learning. *J. comp. Psychol.*, 1938, *26*, 187–200.

Tolman, E. C. The determiners of behavior at a choice point. *Psychol. Rev.*, 1938, *45*, 1–41.

Tolman, E. C. A reply to Professor Guthrie. *Psychol. Rev.*, 1938, *45*, 163–164.

Tolman, E. C. The law of effect. *Psychol. Rev.*, 1938, *45*, 200–203.

Tolman, E. C. Prediction of vicarious trial and error by means of the schematic sowbug. *Psychol. Rev.*, 1939, *46*, 318–336.

Tolman, E. C. Spatial angle and vicarious trial and error. *J. comp. Psychol.*, 1940, *30*, 129–135.

Tolman, E. C. Discrimination vs. learning and the schematic sowbug. *Psychol. Rev.*, 1941, *48*, 367–382.

Tolman, E. C. Motivation, learning and adjustment. *Proc. Amer. philos. soc.*, 1941, *84*, 543–563.

Tolman, E. C. A drive-conversion diagram. *Psychol. Rev.*, 1943, *50*, 503–513.

Tolman, E. C. A stimulus-expectancy need-cathexis psychology. *Science*, 1945, *101*, 160–166.

Tolman, E. C. Studies in spatial learning. II. Place learning vs. response learning. *J. exp. Psychol.*, 1946, *36*, 221–229.

Tolman, E. C. Studies in spatial learning. IV. The transfer of place learning to other starting paths. *J. exp. Psychol.*, 1947, *37*, 39–47.

Tolman, E. C. Studies in spatial learning: VII. Place and response learning under different degrees of motivation. *J. exp. Psychol.*, 1949, *39*, 653–659.

Tolman, E. C. Discussion: Interrelationships between perception and personality. *J. Pers.*, 1949, *18*, 48–50.

Tolman, E. C. The nature and functioning of wants. *Psychol. Rev.*, 1949, *56*, 357–369.

Tolman, E. C. The psychology of social learning. J. soc. Issues, 1949, *5*, Suppl. No. 3, 5–18.

Tolman, E. C., & Brunswik, E. The organism and the causal texture of the environment. *Psychol. Rev.*, 1935, *42*, 43–77.

Tolman, E. C., & Davis, F. C. A note on the correlations between two mazes. *J. comp. Psychol.*, 1924, *4*, 125–135.

Tolman, E. C., & Geier, F. M. Goal distance and restless activity. I. The goal gradient of restless activity. *J. comp. Psychol.*, 1943, *35*, 197–204.

Tolman, E. C., & Gleitman, H. Studies in learning and motivation: I. Equal reinforcements in both end-boxes, followed by shock in one end-box. *J. exp. Psychol.*, 1949, *39*, 810–819.

Tolman, E. C., Hall, C. S., & Bretnall, E. P. A disproof of the law of effect and a substitution of the laws of emphasis, motivation, and disruption. *J. exp. Psychol.*, 1932, *15*, 601–614.

Tolman, E. C., & Honzik, C. H. Degrees of hunger, reward and non-reward, and maze learning in rats. *Univer. Calif. Publ. Psychol.*, 1930, *4*, 241–257.

Tolman, E. C., & Honzik, C. H. Introduction and removal of reward and maze performance of rats. *Univer. Calif. Publ. Psychol.*, 1930, *4*, 257–275.

Tolman, E. C., & Horowitz, J. A. A reply to Mr. Koffka. *Psychol. Bull.*, 1933, *30*, 459–465.

Tolman, E. C. & Kalish, D. Studies in spatial learning. I. Orientation and the short-cut. *J. exp. Psychol.*, 1946, *36*, 13–24.

Tolman, E. C., & Krechevsky, I. Means-end-readiness and hypothesis. A contribution to comparative psychology. *Psychol. Rev.*, 1933, *40*, 60–70.

Tolman, E. C., & Levin, M. Individual differences in emotionality, hypothesis formation, vicarious trial and error, and visual discrimination learning in rats. *Comp. Psychol. Monogr.*, 1941, *17*, No. 3.

Tolman, E. C., & Minium, E. VTE in rats: Overlearning and difficulty of discrimination. *J. comp. Psychol.*, 1942, *34*, 301–306.

Tolman, E. C., & Ritchie, B. F. Correlation between VTE's on a maze and on a visual discrimination apparatus. *J. comp. Psychol.*, 1943, *36*, 91–98.

Tolman, E. C., Ritchie, B. F., & Kalish, D. Studies in spatial learning. V. Response learning vs. place learning by the non-correction method. *J. exp. Psychol.*, 1947, *37*, 285–292.

Tolman, E. C., & Robinson, E. W. The effect of degrees of hunger upon the order of elimination of long and short blinds. *Univer. Calif. Publ. Psychol.*, 1930, *4*, 189–202.

Tolman, E. C., & Sams, C. F. Time discrimination in white rats. *J. comp. Psychol.*, 1925, *5*, 255–263.

Tolman, E. C., & White, A. E. A note on the elimination of short and long blind alleys. *J. comp. Psychol.*, 1923, *3*, 327–332.

Voeks, V. W. Formalization and clarification of a theory of learning. *J. Psychol.*, 1950, *30*, 341–362.

Walker, E. L. The acquisition of a response to food under conditions of food satiation. *Amer. Psychologist*, 1948, *3*, 239. (Reported by title only).

Walker, E. L. Drive specificity and learning. *J. exp. Psychol.*, 1948, *38*, 39–49.

Walker, E. L. Drive specificity and learning: Demonstration of a response tendency acquired under a strong irrelevant drive. *J. comp. physiol. Psychol.*, 1951, *44*, 596–603.

Walker, E. L., Knotter, M. C., & DeValois, R. L. Drive specificity and learning: The acquisition of a spatial response to food under conditions of water deprivation and food satiation. *J. exp. Psychol., 1950, 40*, 161–168.

Webb, W. B., & Nolan, C. Y. Cues for discrimination as secondary reinforcing agents: A confirmation. *J. comp. physiol. Psychol.*, 1953, *46*, 180–181.

White, R. K. The case for the Tolman-Lewin interpretation of learning. *Psychol. Rev.*, 1943, *50*, 157–186.

Wilcoxen, H. C., Hays, R., & Jull, C. L. A preliminary determination of the functional relationship of effective reaction potential (sEr) to the ordinal number of Vincentized extinction reactions (n). *J. exp. Psychol.*, 1950, *40*, 194–199.

Williams, K. A. The reward value of a conditioned stimulus. *Univer. Calif. Publ. Psychol.*, 1929, *4*, 31–55.

Williams, S. B. Resistance to extinction as a function of the number of reinforcements. *J. exp. Psychol.*, 1938, *23*, 506–522.

Wingfield, R. C., & Dennis, W. The dependence of the white rat's choice of pathways upon the length of the daily trial series. *J. comp. Psychol.*, 1934, *18*, 135–148.

Wolfle, H. M. Time factors in conditioning finger-withdrawal. *J. gen. Psychol.*, 1930, *4*, 372–378.

Woodbury, C. B. The learning of stimulus patterns by dogs. *J. comp. Psychol.*, 1943, *35*, 29–40.

Yamaguchi, H. G. Superthreshold reaction potential (sEr) as a function of experimental extinction (n). *J. exp. Psychol.*, 1951, *41*, 391–400.

Yamaguchi, H. G. Drive (D) as a function of hours of hunger (h). *J. exp. Psychol.*, 1951, *42*, 108–117.

Yamaguchi, H. G., Hull, C. L., Felsinger, J. M., & Gladstone, A. I. Characteristics of dispersons based on the pooled momentary reaction potentials (sEr) of a group. *Psychol. Rev.*, 1948, *55*, 216–238.

Youtz, R. E. P. The weakening of one Thorndikian response following the extinction of another. *J. exp. Psychol.*, 1939, *24*, 294–304.

6. *Learning Theory Influenced by Psychoanalysis*

Dollard, J., Doob, L. W., Miller, N. E., Mowrer, O. H., Sears, R. R., Ford, C. S., Hovland, C. I., & Sollenberger, R. T. *Frustration and aggression.* New Haven: Yale University Press, 1939.

Dollard, J., & Miller, N. E. *Personality and psychotherapy.* New York: McGraw-Hill, 1950.

Eriksen, C. W. Defense against ego-threat in memory and perception. *J. abnorm. soc. Psychol.*, 1942, *47*, 230–235.

Friedman, S. M. An empirical study of the castration and oedipus complexes. *Genet. Psychol. Monogr.*, 1952, *46*, 61–130.

Hilgard, E. R. *Theories of learning.* (Rev. ed.) New York: Appleton-Century-Crofts, 1956.

Hilgard, E. R., Kubie, L. S., & Pumpian-Mindlin, E. *Psychoanalysis and science.* Stanford, Calif.: Stanford University Press, 1952.

Hull, C. L. Modern behaviorism and psychoanalysis. *Trans. N.Y. Acad. Sci.*, 1939, *1*, 78–82.

Maier, N. R. F. *Frustration, the study of behavior without a goal.* New York: McGraw-Hill, 1949.

Miller, N. E. Experiments relating Freudian displacement to generalization of conditioning. *Psychol. Bull.*, 1939, *36*, 516–517.

Miller, N. E. The frustration-aggression hypothesis. *Psychol. Rev.*, 1941, *48*, 337–342.

Miller, N. E. Experimental studies in conflict. In J. McV. Hunt (Ed.), *Personality and the behavior disorders.* New York: Ronald, 1944.

Miller, N. E. Theory and experiment relating psychoanalytic displacement to stimulus-response generalization. *J. abnorm. soc. Psych.*, 1948, *43*, 155–178.

Miller, N. E., & Dollard, J. *Social learning and imitation.* New Haven: Yale University Press, 1941.

Misbach, L. Psychoanalysis and theories of learning. *Psychol. Rev.*, 1948, 55, 143–156.

Mowrer, O. H. Anxiety reduction and learning. *J. exp. Psychol.*, 1940, 27, 497–516.

Mowrer, O. H. An experimental analogue of "repression" with incidental observations on "re-action formation." *J. abnorm. soc. Psychol.*, 1940, 35, 56–87.

Mowrer, O. H. On the dual nature of learning: a re-interpretation of "conditioning" and "problem-solving." *Harvard educ. Rev.*, 1947, 17, 102–148.

Mowrer, O. H. Learning theory and the neurotic paradox. *Amer. J. Orthopsychiat.*, 1948, 18, 577–610.

Mowrer, O. H. *Learning theory and personality dynamics.* New York: Ronald, 1950.

Mowrer, O. H. Two-factor learning theory: Summary and comment. *Psychol. Rev.*, 1951, 58, 350–354.

Mowrer, O. H. *Psychotherapy: Theory and research.* New York: Ronald, 1953.

Mowrer, O. H. Learning theory: historical review and re-interpretation. *Harvard educ. Rev.*, 1954, 24, 37–58.

Murray, E. J., & Berkum, M. M. Displacement as a function of conflict. *J. abnorm. soc. Psychol.*, 1955, 51, 47–56.

Sarbin, T. R. Mental age changes in experimental regression. *J. Pers.*, 1950, 19, 221–228.

Sears, R. R. Experimental studies of projection: I. Attribution of traits. *J. soc. Psychol.*, 1936, 7, 151–163.

Sears, R. R. Experimental studies of projection: II. Ideas of reference. *J. soc. Psychol.*, 1937, 8, 389–400.

Sears, R. R. *Survey of objective studies of psychoanalytic concepts.* Soc. Sci. Res. Counc., 1943.

Sears, R. R. Effects of frustration and anxiety on fantasy aggression. *Amer. J. Orthopsychiat.*, 1951, 21, 498–505.

Sears, R. R. Social behavior and personality development. In T. Parsons & E. A. Shils (Eds.), *Toward a general theory of action.* Cambridge, Mass.: Harvard University Press, 1951.

Sears, R. R. A theoretical framework for personality and social behavior. *Amer. Psychologist*, 1951, 6, 476–482.

Sears, R. R., & Wise, G. W. The relation of cup feeding in infancy to thumb-sucking and the oral drive. *Amer. J. Orthopsychiat.*, 1950, 20, 123–138.

7. Some Problems in the Theory of Learning

Estes, W. K., Koch, S., MacCorquodale, K., Meehl, P. E., Mueller, C. G., Jr., Schoenfeld, W. N., & Verplanck, W. S. *Modern learning theory.* New York: Appleton-Century-Crofts, 1954.

Hilgard, E. R. *Theories of learning.* (2nd ed.) New York: Appleton-Century-Crofts, 1956.

Kentucky Symposium. *Learning theory, personality theory, and clinical research.* New York: Wiley, 1954.

Melton, A. W. Learning. In W. S. Monroe (Ed.), *Encyclopedia of educational research.* (Rev. ed.) New York: Macmillan, 1950.

Newman, E. B. Learning. In H. Helson (Ed.), *Theoretical foundations of psychology.* New York: Van Nostrand, 1951.

Spence, K. W. Theoretical interpretations of learning. In S. S. Stevens (Ed.), *Handbook of experimental psychology.* New York: Wiley, 1951.

Spence, K. W. *Behavior theory and conditioning* (Silliman Lectures). New Haven: Yale University Press, 1956.

8. The Current Status of Learning Theory

Bower, G. H. (Ed.) *Psychology of Learning and Motivation.* London: Academic, 1972.

Dickinson, A., & Mackintosh, A. J. Classical conditioning in animals. *Ann. Rev. Psychol.* 1978, 29, 587–612.

Estes, W. K. (Ed.) *Handbook of learning and cognitive processes.* New York: Earlbaum, 1975.
Honig, W. K., & Staddon, J. E. R. (Eds.) *Handbook of operant behavior.* Englewood Cliffs, N.J.: Prentice-Hall, 1977.
Kimble, G. A. *Foundations of conditioning and learning.* New York: Appleton-Century-Crofts, 1967.
Konorski, J. *Integrative activity of the brain.* Chicago: University of Chicago Press, 1967.
Miles, R. C. Animal learning: An overview. In B. B. Wolman (Ed.), *Handbook of general psychology.* Englewood Cliffs, N.J.: Prentice-Hall, 1973, pp. 461–482.
Prokasy, W. F. (Ed.) *Classical conditioning: A Symposium.* New York: Appleton-Century-Crofts, 1965.
Ritchie, B. F. Theories of learning: A consumer report. In B. B. Wolman (Ed.), *Handbook of general psychology.* Englewood Cliffs, N.J.: Prentice-Hall, 1973, pp. 451–460.
Skinner, B. F. *About behaviorism.* New York: Knopf, 1974.
Wolman, B. B. (Ed.) *International encyclopedia of psychiatry, psychology, psychoanalysis and neurology.* New York: Aesculapius, 1977, 12 vols.

CHAPTER 5. HORMIC AND HOLISTIC THEORIES

Bernard, L. L. *Instinct, a study of social psychology.* New York: Holt, 1924.
Bugnion, E. The origins of instinct. *Psyche,* 1925, *5,* 6–41.
Dunlap, K. Are there any instincts? *J. abnorm. Psychol.,* 1919, *14,* 307–311.
Freiman, J. S. Kurt Goldstein—an appreciation. *Amer. J. Psychother.,* 1954, *8,* 1–10.
Goldstein, K. Das Wesen der amnestischen Aphasie. *Dtsch. Ztschr. Nervenheilkunde,* 1924, *82,* 324–339.
Goldstein, K. Das psychophysische Problem in seiner Bedeutung für ärztliches Handeln. *Therapie der Gegenwart,* 1931, *72,* 1–11.
Goldstein, K. Clinical and theoretical aspects of lesions of the frontal lobes. *Arch. Neurol. Psychiat.* 1939, *41, 856–867.*
Goldstein, K. *The organism, a holistic approach to biology derived from pathological data in man.* New York: American Book, 1939.
Goldstein, K. *Human nature in the light of psychopathology.* Cambridge, Mass.: Harvard University Press, 1940.
Goldstein, K. Organismic approach to the problem of motivation. *Trans. N.Y. Acad. Sci.,* 1947, *9,* 218–230.
Goldstein, K. *Language and language disturbances.* New York: Grune & Stratton, 1948.
Goldstein, K. Frontal lobotomy and impairment of abstraction. *J. nerv. ment. Dis.,* 1949, *110,* No. 2.
Goldstein, K. On emotions: considerations from the organismic point of view. *J. Psychol.,* 1951, *31,* 37–49.
Goldstein, K. The effect of brain damage on personality. *Psychiatry,* 1952, *15,* 245–260.
Goldstein, K. New ideas on mental health. In J. Fairchild (Ed.), *Personal problems and psychological frontiers.* New York: Sheridan, 1957.
Goldstein, K., & Scherer, M. Abstract and concrete behavior: An experimental study with special tests. *Psychol. Monogr.,* 1941, *53,* No. 2.
Journal of individual Psychology. Kurt Goldstein 80th Anniversary Issue, 1959, 15.
Kantor, J. R. *Principles of psychology.* New York: Knopf, 1924–1926, 2 vols.
Kantor, J. R. *An outline of social psychology.* Chicago: Follett, 1929.
Kantor, J. R. *A survey of the science of psychology.* Bloomington, Ind.: Principia Press, 1933.
Kantor, J. R. *Problems of physiological psychology.* Bloomington, Ind.: Principia Press, 1947.
Kuo, Z. Y. The fundamental error of the concept of purpose and the trial and error fallacy. *Psychol. Rev.,* 1928, *35,* 414–433.

McCurdy, H. G. William McDougall. In B. B. Wolman (Ed.), *Historical roots of contemporary psychology*. New York: Harper & Row, 1968, pp. 111–130.

McDougall, W. *Physiological psychology*. London: Dent, 1905.

McDougall, W. *Introduction to social psychology*. London: Methuen, 1908.

McDougall, W. *Psychology, the study of behavior*. London: Williams & Norgate, 1912.

McDougall, W. *Outline of psychology*. New York: Scribner, 1923.

McDougall, W. Fundamentals of psychology. *Psyche*, 1924, *5*, 13–32.

McDougall, W. *Outline of abnormal psychology*. New York: Scribner, 1926.

McDougall, W. An experiment for the testing of the hypothesis of Lamarck. *Brit. J. Psychol.*, 1927, *17*, 267–304.

McDougall, W. *Modern materialism and emergent evolution*. London: Methuen, 1929.

McDougall, W. *The energies of men, a study of the fundamentals of dynamic psychology*. London: Methuen, 1932.

McDougall, W. Experimental psychology and psychological experiment. *Charact. & Pers.*, 1932–1933, *1*, 195–213.

McDougall, W. *Psychoanalysis and social psychology*. London: Methuen, 1936.

Meiers, J., & Mintz, N. L. Kurt Goldstein bibliography: 1936–1959. *J. indiv. Psychol.*, 1959, *15*, 15–19.

Meyer, A. The role of the mental factors in psychiatry. *Amer. J. Insan.*, 1908, *65*, 39–56.

Meyer, A. *Common sense psychiatry*. (New ed.) New York: McGraw-Hill, 1948.

Morgan, C. T., & Stellar, E. *Physiological psychology*. (2nd ed.) New York: McGraw-Hill, 1950.

Pratt, K. C., Nelson, A. K., & Sun, K. H. The behavior of the newborn infant. *Iowa Univer. Contrib. Psychol.*, 1934, No. 10.

Richards, E. L. *Introduction to psychobiology and psychiatry*. St. Louis: Mosby, 1941.

Robinson, A. L. *William McDougall, a bibliography together with a brief outline of his life*. Durham, N.C.: Duke University Press, 1943.

Rosenblueth, A., Wiener, N., & Bigelow, J. Behavior, purpose, and teleology. *Phil. Sci.*, 1943, *10*, 18–24.

Smuts, J. C. *Holism and evolution*. New York: Macmillan, 1926.

Swindle, P. F. An analysis of nesting activities. *Amer. J. Psychol.*, 1919, *30*, 173–186.

Tead, O. *Instincts in industry*. Boston: Houghton Mifflin, 1918.

Tolman, E. C. Instinct and purpose. *Psychol. Rev.*, 1920, *27*, 217–233.

Werner, H. *Comparative study of mental development*. (Rev. ed.) Chicago: Follett, 1948.

Wolman, B. B. & Nagel, E. (Eds.), *Scientific psychology: Principles and approaches*. New York: Basic Books, 1965.

Chapter 6. Psychoanalysis

Abraham, K. *Selected papers on psychoanalysis*. London: Hogarth, 1927.

Alexander, F., Freud, A., Levine, M., & De Saussure., M. *Evolution et tendence actuelle de la psychanalyse*. Paris: Hermann, 1950.

Bernfeld, S. *The psychology of the infant*. New York: Brentano, 1929.

Blum, G. *Psychoanalytic theories of personality*. New York: McGraw-Hill, 1953.

Brill, A. A. *Fundamental conceptions of psychoanalysis*. New York: Harcourt, Brace, 1921.

Charcot, J. M. *Lectures on the diseases of the nervous system*. London: New Sydenham Soc., 1877.

Ey, H. Pierre Janet: The man and the work. In B. B. Wolman (Ed.) *Historical roots of contemporary psychology*. New York: Harper & Row, 1968.

Fenichel, O. *The psychoanalytic theory of neurosis*. New York: Norton, 1945.

Freud, Anna. *The ego and the mechanisms of defense*. New York: International Universities Press, 1946.

Freud, S. *Gesammelte Werke chronologisch geordnet*. London: Imago, 1940–48, 17 vols.

Freud, S. *Collected papers*. London: Hogarth, 1924–1950, 5 vols.

Freud, S. *General selection from his works.* (New ed.) London: Hogarth, 1953.

Freud, S. *The standard edition of the complete work of Sigmund Freud.* London: Hogarth, 1953.

Freud, S. *The origins of psychoanalysis, letters to Wilhelm Fliess, drafts and notes. 1887–1902.* New York: Basic Books, 1954.

Frosch, J., & Ross, N. (Eds.) *The annual survey of psychoanalysis.* New York: International Universities Press, 1950–1969, 15 vols.

Galdston, I. (Ed.) *Freud and contemporary culture.* New York: International Universities Press, 1956.

Glover, E. *Psychoanalysis.* London: Bole Medical Publishers, 1939.

Grinstein, A. *The index of psychoanalytic writings.* New York: International Universities Press, 1952–1959, 5 vols.

Groddeck, G. *The book of It.* Washington: Nervous & Mental Disease Publishing Co., 1928.

Greenfield, N. S. & Lewis, W. C. *Psychoanalysis and Current Biological thought.* Madison: University of Wisconsin Press, 1965.

Hartmann, H. *Ego psychology and the problem of adaptation.* New York: International Universities Press, 1958.

Hook, S. (Ed.) *Psychoanalysis, scientific method and philosophy.* New York: New York University Press, 1959.

Janet, P. *L'automatisme psychologique.* Paris: Alcan, 1889.

Jekels, L. *Selected papers.* New York: International Universities Press, 1952.

Jones, E. *Papers on psychoanalysis.* New York: Wood, 1913.

Jones, E. *The life and work of Sigmund Freud.* New York: Basic Books, 1953–1957, 3 vols.

Kubie, L. S. *Practical and theoretical aspects of psychoanalysis.* New York: International Universities Press, 1950.

Lorand, S. (Ed.) *Psychoanalysis today, its scope and function.* New York: International Universities Press, 1944.

Lorand, S. (Ed.) *The yearbook of psychoanalysis.* New York: International Universities Press, 1945–1959, 10 vols.

Munroe, Ruth L. *Schools of psychoanalytic thought.* New York: Dryden, 1955.

Münsterberg, W., & Axelrod, S. *Psychoanalysis and the Social Sciences.* New York: International Universities Press, 1949–1959, 5 vols.

Murphy, G. The current impact of Freud upon psychology. *Amer. Psychologist,* 1956, *11,* 663–672.

Nunberg, H. *Principles of psychoanalysis.* (Rev. ed.) New York: International Universities Press, 1955.

Pumpian-Mindlin, E. (Ed.) *Psychoanalysis as science.* Stanford, California: Stanford University Press, 1952.

Puner, H. W. *Freud, his life and his mind.* New York: Howell, Soskin, 1947.

Rapaport, D. *Emotions and memory.* (2nd ed.) New York: International Universities Press, 1950.

Rapaport, D. On the psychoanalytic theory of thinking. *Int. J. Psychoanal.,* 1950, *31,* 1–10.

Rapaport, D. The conceptual model of psychoanalysis. *J. Pers.,* 1951, *20,* 56–81.

Rapaport, D. (Ed.) *Organization and pathology of thought.* New York: Columbia University Press, 1951.

Reik, T. *From thirty years with Freud.* New York: Farrar & Rinehart, 1940.

Sachs, H. *Freud, master and friend.* Cambridge, Mass.: Harvard University Press, 1944.

Sears, R. R. *Survey of objective studies of psychoanalytic concepts.* New York: Soc. Sci. Res. Counc., 1943.

Sterba, R. *Introduction to the psychoanalytic theory of the libido.* Nerv. & ment. Dis. Monogr., No. 68, 1947.

Symonds, P. M. *The dynamics of human adjustment.* New York: Appleton-Century-Crofts, 1946.

Thompson, Clara. *Psychoanalysis: Evolution and development.* New York: Hermitage, 1950.

Zilboorg, G. *Sigmund Freud, his exploration of the mind of man.* New York: Norton, 1941.

Zilboorg, G., & Henry, G. W. *A history of medical psychology.* New York: Norton, 1941.

CHAPTER 7. INDIVIDUAL AND ANALYTIC PSYCHOLOGIES

1. Alfred Adler: Individual Psychology

Adler, A. *The neurotic constitution*. New York: Moffat, 1917.
Adler, A. *A study of organ inferiority and its psychical compensation*. Nerv. & ment. Dis. Monogr., No. 24, 1917.
Adler, A. *The practice and theory of individual psychology*. New York: Harcourt, Brace, 1927.
Adler, A. *Understanding human nature*. New York: Greenberg, 1927.
Adler, A. *The science of living*. New York: Greenberg, 1929.
Adler, A. *The pattern of life*. New York: Rinehart, 1930.
Adler, A. *What life should mean to you*. Boston: Little, Brown, 1931.
Adler, A. Persönlichkeit als geschlossene Einheit. *Int. Z. indiv. Psychol.*, 1932, *10*, 81–89.
Adler, A. *Social interest: a challenge to mankind*. London: Faber, 1938.
Adler, A. Physical manifestations of psychic disturbances. *Ind. Psychol. Bull.*, 1944, *4*, 3–8.
Adler, A., & Furtmüller, C. (Eds.) *Heilen und Bilden*. Münich: Reinhardt, 1914.
Ansbacher, H. L. Causality and indeterminism according to Alfred Adler and some current American personality theories. *Ind. Psychol. Bull.*, 1951, *9*, 96–107.
Ansbacher, H. L., & Ansbacher, R. R. *The individual psychology of Alfred Adler*. New York: Basic Books, 1956.
Bottome, Phyllis. *Alfred Adler, a biography*. New York: Putnam, 1939.
Colby, K. M. On the disagreement between Freud and Adler. *Amer. Images*, 1951, *8*, 229–238.
Dreikurs, R. *Fundamentals of Adlerian psychology*. New York: Greenberg, 1950.
Ganz, Madeleine. *La psychologie d'Alfred Adler et le développement de l'enfant*. Geneva, 1935.
Orgler, Hertha. *Alfred Adler, the man and his work*. London: Daniel, 1939.
Sperber, M. *Alfred Adler: der Mensch und Seine Lehre*. Münich: Bergmann, 1926.
Vaihinger, H. *The philosophy of "as if"; a system of the theoretical, practical and religious fictions of mankind*. New York: Harcourt, Brace, 1925.
Way, L. *Adler's place in psychology*. New York: Macmillan, 1950.
Wexberg, E. *Individual psychology*. New York: Cosmopolitan Book, 1929.

2. Carl Gustav Jung: Analytic Psychology

Adler, G. *Studies in analytical psychology*. New York: Norton, 1948.
Campbell, J. *The hero with a thousand faces*. New York: Pantheon, 1949.
Fordham, Frieda. *An introduction to Jung's psychology*. London: Penguin, 1953.
Fordham, M. Professor C. G. Jung. *Brit. J. med. Psychol.*, 1945, *20*, 221–235.
Glover, E. *Freud or Jung*. New York: Norton, 1950.
Gray, H. Freud and Jung: Their contrasting psychological types. *Psychoanal. Rev.*, 1949, *36*, 22–44.
Harding, Mary E. *Psychic energy, its course and goal*. New York: Pantheon, 1947.
Jacobi, J. *The psychology of Jung*. (Rev. ed.) New Haven: Yale University Press, 1951.
Jung, C. G. *Collected papers on analytical psychology*. New York: Moffat, 1917.
Jung, C. G. *Contributions to analytical psychology*. New York: Harcourt, Brace, 1928.
Jung, C. G. *Psychological types*. New York: Harcourt, Brace, 1933.
Jung, C. G. *The integration of personality*. New York: Farrar and Rinehart, 1939.
Jung, C. G. *Über psychische Energetik und des Wesen der Träume*. Zürich: Rascher, 1948.
Jung, C. G. *Collected works*. New York: Pantheon, Bollingen Series, 1953–. 18 vols.
Jung, C. G. *Psychological reflections, anthology of writings*. Ed. by J. Jacobi. New York: Pantheon, 1953.
Jung, C. G. *Von den Wurzeln des Bewusstseins*. Zürich: Rascher, 1954.

Jung, C. G. *The undiscovered self.* Boston: Little, Brown, 1959.
Jung, C. G., & Kerenyi, C. *Essays on a science of mythology.* New York: Pantheon, 1949.
Jung, C. G., & Pauli, W. *The interpretation of nature and the psyche.* New York: Pantheon, 1955.
Neumann, E. *The origins and history of consciousness.* New York: Pantheon, 1954.
Neumann, E. *The great mother.* London: Routledge & Kegan Paul, 1955.
Progoff, I. *Jung's psychology and its social meaning.* New York: Julian, 1953.
Thompson, Clara. *Psychoanalysis: Evolution and development.* New York: Hermitage, 1950.
Wickes, Frances G. *The inner world of man.* New York: Holt, 1948.
Wilhelm, R., & Jung, C. G. *The secret of the golden flower.* New York: Harcourt, Brace, 1931.

Chapter 8. New Theories in Psychoanalysis

Alexander, F. *Fundamentals of psychoanalysis.* New York: Norton, 1949.
Alexander, F. *Psychosomatic medicine: Its principles and applications.* New York: Norton, 1950.
Alexander, F. *Our age of unreason.* Philadelphia: Lippincott, 1951.
Alexander, F., & Ross, H. (Eds.) *Twenty years of psychoanalysis.* New York: Norton, 1953.
Bergler, E. *Superego, unconscious, conscience.* New York: Grune & Stratton, 1952.
Bergmann, G. Psychoanalysis and experimental psychology: A review from the standpoint of scientific empiricism. *Mind,* 1943, *52,* 122–140.
Blanck, G., & Blanck, R. *Ego psychology: Theory and practice.* New York: Columbia University Press, 1974.
Brierley, M. *Trends in psychoanalysis.* London: Hogarth, 1951.
Coles, R. Erikson, Erik Homburger (b. 1902) In B. B. Wolman (Ed.), *International encyclopedia of psychiatry, psychology, psychoanalysis and neurology.* New York: Aesculapius, 1977, Vol. 4, pp. 370 ff.
Dahl, H. A quantitative study of a psychoanalysis. In R. R. Holt & E. Peterfreund (Eds.) *Psychoanalysis and contemporary science: An annual of integrative and interdisciplinary studies.* New York: Macmillan, 1972, pp. 237–257.
Daim, W. *Umwertung der Psychoanalyse.* Wien: Herold, 1951.
Deutsch, F. *On the mysterious leap from the mind to the body.* New York: International Universities Press, 1959.
Erikson, E. K. *Childhood and society.* New York: Norton, 1950.
Fairbairn, W. R. D. *Psychoanalytic studies of personality.* London: Routledge, 1952.
Fairbairn, W. R. D. *An object-relations theory of personality.* New York: Basic Books, 1954.
Federn, P. *Ego psychology and the psychoses.* New York: Basic Books, 1953.
Fenichel, O. *Collected papers.* New York: Norton, 1953–1954, 2 vols.
Ferenczi, S. *Contributions to psychoanalysis.* Boston: Badger, 1916.
Ferenczi, S. *Further contributions to the theory and technique of psychoanalysis.* London: Hogarth, 1926.
Ferenczi, S. *Sex in psychoanalysis.* New York: Basic Books, 1950.
Ferenczi, S. *First contributions to psychoanalysis.* London: Hogarth, 1953.
Freud, A. *The ego and the mechanisms of defense.* International Universities Press, 1946.
French, T. M. *The integration of behavior. Vol. I. Basic postulates.* Chicago: University of Chicago Press, 1952.
Gill, M. Topography and systems in psychoanalytic theory. *Psychological Issues,* 1963, *10.*
Glover, E. Examination of the Klein system of child psychology. *Psychoanal. Study of the Child,* 1945, *1.*
Goodman, S. (Ed.) *Psychoanalytic education and research.* New York: International Universities Press, 1976.
Hanly, C., & Lazerowitz, M. *Psychoanalysis and philosophy.* New York: International Universities Press, 1970.

Hartmann, H. Comments on the psychoanalytic theory of the ego. *Psychoanal. Study of the Child*, 1950, 5.

Hartmann, H. *Ego psychology and the problem of adaptation.* New York: International Universities Press, 1959.

Hartmann, H., Kris, E., & Loewenstein, R. M. Comments on the formation of psychic structure. *Psychoanal. Study of the Child*, 1947, 2.

Holt, R. R. Motives and thought. *Psychological Issues*, 1967, 18–19.

Holt, R. R. Beyond vitalism and mechanism: Freud's concept of psychic energy. In B. B. Wolman (Ed.), *Historical roots of contemporary psychology.* New York: Harper & Row, 1968, pp. 196–226.

Holt, R. R. Freud's mechanistic and humanistic images of man. In R. R. Holt & E. Peterfreund (Eds.), *Psychoanalysis and contemporary science: An annual of integrative and interdisciplinary studies.* New York: Macmillan, 1972, pp. 3–24.

Jacobson, E. *The self and the object world.* International Universities Press, 1964.

Kahn, M. Winnicott, Donald W. (1896–1971). In B. B. Wolman (Ed.), *International encyclopedia of psychiatry, psychology, psychoanalysis, and neurology.* New York: Aesculapius, 1977, Vol. 11, pp. 424–425.

Kanzer, M., and Blum, H. Classical Psychoanalysis since 1939. In B. B. Wolman (Ed.), *Psychoanalytic techniques.* New York: Basic Books, 1967, pp. 93–147.

Kaplan, H. I., Sardock, B. J., & Freedman, A. M. Erik Erikson, In A. M. Freedman, H. I. Kaplan, & B. J. Sardick (Eds.), *Comprehensive textbook of psychiatry.* (2nd ed.) Baltimore: Williams & Wilkins, 1975, pp. 566–573.

Kardiner, A. *The individual and his society.* New York: Columbia University Press, 1939.

Kardiner, A. *The psychological frontiers of society.* New York: Columbia University Press, 1945.

Karpf, M. *Psychology and psychotherapy of Otto Rank.* New York: Philosophical Library, 1953.

Klein, G. S. (Ed.) *Psychological issues.* New York: International Universities Press, 1959, Vol. 1.

Klein, G. S. *Psychoanalytic theory: An examination of essentials.* New York: International Universities Press, 1973.

Klein, M. *The psychoanalysis of children.* London: Hogarth, 1932.

Klein, M. *Contributions of psychoanalysis, 1921–1948.* London: Hogarth, 1948.

Klein, M., Heimann, P., Isaacs, S., & Riviere, J. *Developments in psychoanalysis.* London: Hogarth, 1952.

Klein, M., & Riviere, J. *Love, hate and separation.* London: Hogarth, 1938.

Kohut, H. *The analysis of the self.* New York: International Universities Press, 1971.

Kris, E. The nature of psychoanalytic propositions and their validation. In S. Hook & R. Konvitz (Eds.), *Freedom and experience.* Ithaca: Cornell University Press, 1947.

Kris, E. *Psychoanalytic explorations in art.* New York: International Universities Press, 1952.

Kubie, L. S. Psychoanalysis and scientific method. *J. nerv. ment. Dis.*, 1960, *131*, 495–512.

Lifton, R. J. The protean man. In B. B. Wolman (Ed.), *The psychoanalytic interpretation of history.* New York: Harper Torchbook, 1973.

Lowenstein, R. M. (Ed.) *Drives, affects, behavior: Contributions to the theory and practice of psychoanalysis and its applications.* New York: International Universities Press, 1953.

Mahler, M. *On human symbiosis and the vicissitudes of individuation.* New York: International Universities Press, 1968.

Marcus, I. M. (Ed.) *Currents in psychoanalysis.* New York: International Universities Press, 1971.

Marmor, J. *Psychiatry in transition.* New York: Bruner/Mazel, 1974.

Mayman, M. Psychoanalytic research. *Psychological Issues*, 1973, 30.

Meissner, W. W., Mack, J. E., & Semrad, E. V. Classical psychoanalysis. In A. M. Freedman, H. I. Kaplan, & B. J. Sadock (Eds.), *Comprehensive textbook of psychiatry.* (2nd ed.) Baltimore: Williams & Wilkins, 1975, pp. 482–566.

Miller, N. E., & Dollard, J. *Social learning and imitation.* New Haven: Yale University Press, 1941.

Mowrer, O. H. *Learning theory and personality dynamics.* New York: Ronald, 1950.

Mullahy, P. *Oedipus myth and complex.* New York: Hermitage, 1948.

Nuttin, J. *Psychoanalysis and personality.* New York: Sheed & Ward, 1953.

Oberndorf, C. P. *History of psychoanalysis in America.* New York: Grune & Stratton, 1953.

Peterfreund, E. Information, systems, and psychoanalysis. *Psychological Issues,* 1971, 25–26.

Pettit, T. F. Anality and time. *J. Consult. Clin. Psychol.* 1969, *33,* 170–174.

Pumpian-Mindlin, E. (Ed.) *Psychoanalysis as science.* New York: Basic Books, 1952.

Rank, O. *Art and artist.* New York: Knopf, 1932.

Rank, O. *Modern education.* New York: Knopf, 1932.

Rank, O. *Beyond psychology.* New York: Haddon, 1941.

Rank, O. *Will therapy and truth and reality.* New York: Knopf, 1945.

Rank, O. *Psychology and the soul.* Philadelphia: University of Pennsylvania Press, 1950.

Rank, O. *The myth of the birth of the hero.* New York: Brunner, 1952.

Rank, O. *Trauma of birth.* New York: Brunner, 1952.

Rank, O., & Ferenczi, S. *The development of psychoanalysis.* New York: Nervous & Mental Disease Publishing Co., 1925.

Rapaport, D. On the psychoanalytic theory of thinking. *Int. J. Psychoanal.,* 1950, *31,* 1–10.

Rapaport, D. On the psychoanalytic theory of affects. *Int. J. Psychoanal.,* 1953, *34,* 177–198.

Rapaport, D., & Gill, M. The points of view and assumptions of metapsychology. *Int. J. Psychoanal.* 1959, *40,* 153–162.

Reich, W. *Character analysis.* New York: Orgone Institute, 1945.

Reik, T. *Listening with the third ear.* New York: Harcourt, Brace, 1949.

Roheim, G. *Psychoanalysis and anthropology; culture, personality, and the unconscious.* New York: International Universities Press, 1950.

Roheim, G. *The gates of the dream.* New York: International Universities Press, 1952.

Sachs, H. *The creative unconscious: Studies in the psychoanalysis of art.* (2nd ed.) Boston: Sci-Art, 1951.

Sarnoff, I. *Testing Freudian concepts.* New York: Springer, 1971.

Sarnoff, I., & Zimbardo, P. G. Anxiety, fear and social affiliation. *J. abnorm. soc. Psychol.,* 1961, *62,* 356–363.

Sartre, J. P. *Existential psychoanalysis.* New York: Philosophical Library, 1953.

Schafer, R. An overview of Heinz Hartmann's contributions to psychoanalysis. *Int. J. Psychoanal.,* 1970, *51,* 425–446.

Spitz, R. A. *The first year of life.* New York: International Universities Press, 1965.

Sutherland, J. D. Fairbairn, W. Ronald D. (1890–1964). In B. B. Wolman (Ed.), *International encyclopedia of psychiatry, psychology, psychoanalysis and neurology.* New York: Aesculapius, 1977, Vol. 4, pp. 449–450.

Tennes, K., Emde, R., Kisley, A., & Metcalf, D. The stimulus barrier in early infancy: An exploration of John Benjamin. In R. R. Holt & E. Peterfreund (Eds.), *Psychoanalysis and contemporary science.* New York: Macmillan, 1972, Vol. 1, pp. 206–236.

Watkins, J. G. Psychotherapeutic methods. In B. B. Wolman (Ed.), *Handbook of clinical psychology.* New York: McGraw-Hill, 1965, pp. 1143–1168.

Weber, J. Psychoanalytic research: Studies of outcome. In B. B. Wolman (Ed.), *International encyclopedia of psychiatry, psychology, psychoanalysis and neurology.* New York: Aesculapius, 1977, Vol. 9, pp. 211–212.

Wolman, B. B. Schizophrenia and related disorders. In B. B. Wolman (Ed.), *Handbook of clinical psychology.* New York: McGraw-Hill, 1965, pp. 976–1030.

Wolman, B. B. (Ed.) *The psychoanalytic interpretation of history.* New York: Basic Books, 1971.

Wolman, B. B. (Ed.) *Dictionary of behavioral science.* New York: Van Nostrand Reinhold, 1973.

Wolman, B. B. *Call no man normal.* New York: International Universities Press, 1973.

Wolman, B. B. Power and acceptance as determinants of social relations. *Int. J. Group Tensions,* 1974, *4,* 151–182.

Wolman, B. B. Principles of interactional psychotherapy. *Psychotherapy: Theory, Research, and Practice,* 1975, *12,* 149–159.

Wolman, B. B. New ideas on mental disorders. *Am. J. Psychotherapy,* 1977, *31,* 546–560.

Wolman, B. B. Interactional psychoanalytic theory. In B. B. Wolman (Ed.), *International encyclopedia of psychiatry, psychology, psychoanalysis and neurology*. New York: Aesculapius, 1977, Vol. 6, pp. 122–125.

Wolman, B. B. Psychoanalysis as science. In B. B. Wolman (Ed.), *International encyclopedia of psychiatry, psychology, psychoanalysis and neurology*. New York: Aesculapius, 1977, Vol. 9, pp. 149–157.

Zimbardo, P. G., & Formica, R. Emotional comparison and self esteem as determinants of affiliation. *J. Pers.*, 1963, *31*, 141–162.

Chapter 9. Away from Freud: The Sociological School

Beaglehole, E. Notes on interpersonal theory. *Psychiatry*, 1940, *3*, 511–526.

Fromm, E. *Die Entstehung des Christusdogma*. Vienna: Psychoanal. Verlag, 1930.

Fromm, E. *Escape from freedom*. New York: Farrar & Rinehart, 1941.

Fromm, E. *Man for himself*. New York: Rinehart, 1947.

Fromm, E. The Oedipus complex and the Oedipus myth. In Ruth N. Anshen (Ed.), *The family: its function and destiny*. New York: Harper, 1948.

Fromm, E. *Psychoanalysis and religion*. New Haven: Yale University Press, 1950.

Fromm, E. *The forgotten language: An introduction to the understanding of dreams, fairy tales, and myths*. New York: Rinehart, 1951.

Fromm, E. *Sane society*. New York: Rinehart, 1955.

Horney, K. *The neurotic personality of our time*. New York: Norton, 1937.

Horney, K. *New ways in psychoanalysis*. New York: Norton, 1939.

Horney, K. *Our inner conflicts*. New York: Norton, 1945.

Horney, K. *Neurosis and human growth*. New York: Norton, 1950.

James, W. T. Karen Horney and Erich Fromm in relation to Alfred Adler. *Indiv. Psychol. Bull.*, 1947, *6*, 105–116.

Kelman, H. *Helping people*. New York: Science House, 1971.

Kelman, H., & Shainberg, D., "Karen Horney." In A. M. Freedman, H. I. Kaplan, & B. J. Sadock (Eds.), *Comprehensive Textbook of Psychiatry*, (2nd ed.), New York: Williams and Wilkins, 1975.

Mullahy, P. A theory of interpersonal relations and the evolution of personality. *Psychiatry*, 1945, *8*, 177–206.

Mullahy, P. *Oedipus—myth and complex*. New York: Hermitage, 1948.

Mullahy, P. (Ed.) *A study of interpersonal relations*. New York: Hermitage, 1949.

Mullahy, P. (Ed.) *The contributions of Harry Stack Sullivan*. New York: Hermitage, 1952.

Slater, R., & Kelman, H. Horney's theory. In B. B. Wolman (Ed.), *International encyclopedia of psychiatry, psychology, psychoanalysis and neurology*. New York: Aesculapius, 1977. Vol. 5, pp. 414–420.

Sullivan, H. S. Introduction to the study of interpersonal relations. *Psychiatry*, 1938, *1*, 121–134.

Sullivan, H. S. *Conceptions of modern psychiatry*. Washington: W. A. White Foundation, 1947.

Sullivan, H. S. *The interpersonal theory of psychiatry*. New York: Norton, 1953.

Sullivan, H. S. *Psychiatric interview*. New York: Norton, 1954.

Thompson, Clara. *Psychoanalysis: Evolution and development*. New York: Hermitage, 1950.

Witenberg, E. (Ed.) *Interpersonal explorations in psychoanalysis*. New York: Basic Books, 1973.

Wolman, B. B. Psychoanalysis without libido: K. Horney's contribution to psychological theory. *Amer. J. Psychother.*, 1954, *8*, 21–31.

Chapter 10. Understanding Psychology

Brett, G. S. *History of psychology* (Ed., R. S. Peters). London: Allen & Unwin, 1951.

Dilthey, W. *Gesammelte Schriften*. Leipzig: Teubner, 1924.

Ebbinghaus, H. *Memory*. New York: Teachers College, Columbia University, 1913.

Hodges, H. A. *Wilhelm Dilthey, an introduction.* London: Routledge & Kegan Paul, 1949.

Hodges, H. A. *The philosophy of Wilhelm Dilthey.* London: Routledge & Kegan Paul, 1952.

Husserl, E. Phenomenology. In *Encyclopaedia Britannica* (14th ed.) New York: 1929.

Husserl, E. *Ideas: General introduction to pure phenomenology* (Trans., W. R. Boyce Gibson). London: Allen & Unwin, 1931.

Kant, I. *Prolegomena to metaphysics* (Ed., P. Cerus). La Salle, Ill.: Open Court, 1902.

Kant, I. *The critique of pure reason.* New York: Macmillan, 1914.

Kaufmann, F. In memoriam Edmund Husserl. *Soc. Res.,* 1940, 61–91.

Kaufmann, F. Cassirer, neo-Kantianism, and phenomenology. In P. A. Schilpp (Ed.), *The philosophy of Ernst Cassirer.* Evanston, Ill.: Living Philosophies, 1949.

Klüver, H. Contemporary German psychology as a "cultural science." In G. Murphy (Ed.) *An historical introduction to modern psychology.* New York: Harcourt, Brace, 1929.

Laird, J. *Recent philosophy.* London: Butterworth, 1936.

Mach, E. *The analysis of sensation.* La Salle, Ill.: Open Court, 1914.

MacLeod, R. B. The phenomenological approach to social psychology. *Psychol. Rev.,* 1947, *54,* 193–210.

Mead, G. H. *Movements of thought in the nineteenth century.* Chicago: University of Chicago Press, 1936.

Miller, H. *An historical introduction to modern philosophy.* New York: Macmillan, 1947.

Puglisi, M. Franz Brentano: A biographical sketch. *Amer. J. Psychol.,* 1924, *35,* 414–419.

Randall, J. H. *The making of the modern mind.* Boston: Houghton Mifflin, 1926.

Russell, B. *The history of Western philosophy.* New York: Simon & Schuster, 1945.

Soucek, R. Alfred Binet et l'école de Brentano. *J. Psychol. norm. path.,* 1924, *21,* 883–888.

Windelband, W. *An introduction to philosophy.* London: Allen & Unwin, 1921.

CHAPTER 11. PERSONALISTIC PSYCHOLOGY

Allport, G. W. The functional autonomy of motives. *Amer. J. Psychol.,* 1937, *50,* 141–156.

Allport, G. W. The personalistic psychology of William Stern. *Charact. and Pers.,* 1937, *5,* 231–246.

Allport, G. W. *Personality: A psychological interpretation.* New York: Holt, 1937.

Allport, G. W. Effect: A secondary principle of learning. *Psychol. Rev.,* 1946, *53,* 335–347.

Allport, G. W. *The individual and his religion.* New York: Macmillan, 1950.

Allport, G. W. *The nature of personality: Selected papers.* Cambridge, Mass.: Addison-Wesley, 1950.

Allport, G. W. The psychological nature of personality. *Personalist,* 1953, *34,* 347–357.

Allport, G. W. *The nature of prejudice.* Cambridge, Mass.: Addison-Wesley, 1954.

Allport, G. W. *Becoming: Basic considerations for a psychology of personality.* New Haven: Yale University Press, 1955.

Allport, G. W., & Vernon, P. E. *A study of values.* Boston: Houghton Mifflin, 1931.

Allport, G. W., & Vernon, P. E. *Studies in expressive movement.* New York: Macmillan, 1933.

Bertocci, P. A. A critique of G. W. Allport's theory of motivation. *Psychol. Rev.,* 1940, *47,* 501–532.

Casper, S. *Die personalistische Weltanschauung W. Stern's.* Leipzig: Barth, 1933.

Coutu, W. *Emergent human nature.* New York: Knopf, 1949.

Spranger, E. *Psychologie des Jugendalters.* Leipzig: Quelle & Meyer, 1925.

Spranger, E. *Types of men* (Trans., P. J. W. Pigors). Halle: Niemyer, 1928.

Spranger, E. Der Sinn der Voraussetzungslosigkeit in den Geisteswissenschaften. *Preuss. Akad. d. Wissenschaften,* 1929.

Stern, W. *Über Psychologie der individuellen Differenzen.* Leipzig: Barth, 1900.

Stern, W. *Person and Sache: System der philosophischen Weltanschauung.* Leipzig: Barth, 1906–24.

Stern, W. *Psychology of early childhood up to the sixth year of age.* (3rd ed.) New York: Holt, 1930.

Stern, W. *Studien zur Personwissenschaft.* Leipzig: Barth, 1930.

Stern, W. *General psychology from the personalistic standpoint* (Trans., H. D. Spoerl). New York: Macmillan, 1938.

CHAPTER 12. GESTALT PSYCHOLOGY

1. Opposition to Associationism

Ach, N. *Über den Willensakt und das Temperament: Eine experimentelle Untersuchung.* Leipzig: Quelle & Meyer, 1910.

Binet, A. Étude expérimentale de l'intelligence. Paris: Schleicher, 1910.

Boring, E. G. *A history of experimental psychology.* (2nd ed.) New York: Appleton-Century-Crofts, 1950.

Bühler, K. Tatsachen und probleme zu einer Psychologie der Denkvorgänge. I. Über Gedanken. II. Über Gedanken Zusammenhänge. III. Über Gedanken erinnerungen. *Arch. Psychol.*, 1907, *9*, 297–305; 1908, *12*, 1–23; 1908, *12*, 24–92.

Bühler, K. *Gestalt Perzeption.* Stuttgart: Speeman, 1913.

Bühler, K. *Die Theorie der Perzeption.* Jena: Fischer, 1922.

Claparède, E. La genése de l'hypothèse, étude expérimentale. *Arch. Psychol.*, 1933, *24*, 1–154.

Humphrey, G. *Thinking: An introduction to its experimental psychology.* London: Methuen, 1951.

Janet, P. *L'automatisme psychologique.* Paris: Alcan, 1889.

Külpe, O. Aussichten der experimentellen Psychologie. *Philos. Monatshefte*, 1894, *30*, 281–294.

Külpe, O. Über die Objektivierung und Subjektivierung von Sinnesausdrücken. *Philos. Stud.*, 1902, *19*, 508–556.

Külpe, O. Pour la psychologie du sentiment. *J. Psychol. norm. path.*, 1910, *7*, 1–13.

Külpe, O. *Vorlesungen über die Psychologie.* (2nd ed., Ed., K. Bühler.) Leipzig: Hirzel, 1922.

Messer, A. Experimentell-psychologische Untersuchungen über das Denken. *Arch. gen. Psychol.*, 1906, *8*, 1–224.

Michotte, A. *La perception de la causalité.* Louvain: Inst. Supérieur Philos., 1946.

Müller, G. E. Experimentelle Beiträge zur Untersuchung des Gedächtnisses. *Z. Psychol.*, 1894, *6*, 81–190, 257–339.

Müller, G. E. *Komplextheorie und Gestalttheorie.* Göttingen: Vanderhoeck, 1923.

Murphy, G. *Historical introduction to modern psychology.* (Rev. ed.) New York: Harcourt, Brace, 1949.

Stout, G. F. *Analytic psychology.* London: Allen & Unwin, 1902, 2 vols.

Ward, J. Psychology. In *Encyclopaedia Britannica.* (9th ed.) London: 1886.

Watt, H. J. Experimentelle Beiträge zu einer Theorie des Denkeus. *Arch ges. Psychol.*, 1905, *4*, 289–436.

2, 3. Gestalt

Adamson, R. E., & Taylor, D. W. Functional fixedness as related to elapsed time and set. *J. exp. Psychol.*, 1954, *47*, 122–126.

Allport, H. *Theories of perception and the concept of structure.* New York: Wiley, 1955.

Asch, S. Max Wertheimer's contribution to modern psychology. *Soc. Res.*, 1946, *13*, 81–102.

Birth, H. G. The role of motivational factors in insightful problem-solving. *J. comp. Psychol.*, 1945, *38*, 295–317.

Boring, E. G. The gestalt psychology and the gestalt movement. *Amer. J. Psychol.*, 1930, *42*, 308–315.

Duncker, K. On problem solving. *Psychol. Monogr.*, 1945, *58*, No. 270.

Ehrenfels, C. V. On gestalt qualities. *Psychol. Rev.*, 1937, *44*, 521–524.

Ellis, W. D. *A source book of gestalt psychology.* New York: Harcourt, Brace, 1938.

Hartmann, G. W. *Gestalt psychology, a survey of facts and principles.* New York: Ronald, 1935.

Helson, H. The fundamental propositions of gestalt psychology. *Psychol. Rev.*, 1933, *40*, 13–32.

Henle, M. An experimental investigation of past experience as a determiant of visual form of perception. *J. exp. Psychol.*, 1942, *30*, 1–22.

Henle, M. (Ed.) *Documents of Gestalt psychology.* Berkeley: University of California Press, 1961.

Humphrey, G. *Thinking.* London: Methuen, 1951.

Katona, G. *Organizing and memorizing: Studies in the psychology of learning and teaching.* New York: Columbia University Press, 1940.

Katz, G. *Gestalt psychology, its nature and significance.* New York: Ronald, 1950.

Koffka, K. *The growth of the mind.* London: Kegan Paul, 1924.

Koffka, K. *Principles of gestalt psychology.* New York: Harcourt, Brace, 1935.

Köhler, W. *Die physikalischen Gestalten in Ruhe und in stationären Zustand.* Erlangen: Weltkreis, 1920.

Köhler, W. *The mentality of apes.* New York: Harcourt, Brace, 1925.

Köhler, W. *Psychologische Probleme.* Berlin: Springer, 1933.

Köhler, W. Zur Psychophysik des Vergleichs und des Raumes. *Psychol. Forsch.*, 1933, *18*, 343–360.

Köhler, W. *The place of value in a world of facts.* New York: Liveright, 1938.

Köhler, W. *Dynamics in psychology.* New York: Liveright, 1940.

Köhler, W. On the nature of associations. *Proc. Amer. Philos. Soc.*, 1941, *84*, 489–502.

Köhler, W. *Gestalt psychology.* New York: Liveright, 1947.

Köhler, W., & Restorff, H. Analyse von Vorgängen im Spurenfeld. *Psychol. Forsch.*, 1935, *21*, 56–112.

Köhler, W., & Wallach, H. Figural after-effects: an investigation of visual processes. *Proc. Amer. Philos. Soc.*, 1944, *88*, 269–357.

Kruger, F. E. Über psychische Ganzheit. *Neue psychol. Stud.*, 1926, *1*, 1–123.

Newman, E. B. Forgetting of meaningful material during sleep and waking. *Amer. J. Psychol.*, 1939, *52*, 65–71.

Pechstein, L. A., & Brown, F. D. An experimental analysis of the alleged criteria of insight learning. *J. educ. Psychol.*, 1939, *30*, 38–52.

Petermann, B. *The gestalt theory and the problem of configuration.* New York: Harcourt, Brace, 1932.

Spence, K. W. Cognitive versus stimulus-response theories of learning. *Psychol. Rev.*, 1950, *57*, 159–172.

Spitz, H. The present status of the Köhler-Wallach theory of satiation. *Psychol. Bull.*, 1958, *55*, 1–28.

Stolurov, L. M. (Ed.) *Readings in learning.* New York: Prentice-Hall, 1953.

Wertheimer, M. Experimentelle Studien über das Sehen von Bewegung. Z. *Psychol.*, 1912, *61*, 161–265.

Wertheimer, M. Untersuchung zur Lehre von der Gestalt. *Psychol. Forsch.*, 1922, *1*, 47–65; 1923, *4*, 301–350.

Wertheimer, M. *Drei Abhandlungen zur Gestalttheorie.* Berlin: Erlangen, 1935.

Wertheimer, M. *Productive thinking.* New York: Harper, 1945.

Yerkes, R. M. The mind of a gorilla. *Genet. Psychol. Monogr.*, 1927, *2*.

CHAPTER 13. FIELD THEORY

Barker, R. G., Dembo, T., & Lewin, K. Frustration and regression: An experiment with young children. *Univer. Iowa Stud. Child Welf.*, 1941, *18*, 1–314.

Brown, J. F. On the use of mathematics in psychological theory. *Psychometrika*, 1936, *1*, 7–15, 77–90.

Cassirer, E. *Substanzbegriff und Funktionsbegriff.* Berlin: Cassirer, 1910.

Cohen, M. R. *Reason and nature.* New York: Harcourt, Brace, 1931.

Dembo, T. Der Ärger als dynamisches Problem. *Psychol. Forsch.,* 1931, *15*, 1–144.

Deutsch, M. Field theory in social psychology. In G. Lindzey (Ed.), *Handbook of social psychology.* Cambridge, Mass.: Addison-Wesley, 1954.

Estes, W. K., & others. *Modern learning theory.* New York: Appleton-Century-Crofts, 1954.

Fajans, S. Erfolg, Ausdauer und Aktivität beim Säugling und Kleinkind. *Psychol. Forsch.,* 1933, *17*, 268–305.

Feigl, H. Principles and problems of theory construction in psychology. In W. Dennis (Ed.), *Current trends in psychological theory.* Pittsburgh: University of Pittsburgh Press, 1951.

Garrett, H. E. Lewin's "topological" psychology: An evaluation. *Psychol. Rev.,* 1939, *46*, 517–524.

Hilgard, E. R. *Theories of learning.* (2nd ed.) New York: Appleton-Century-Crofts, 1956.

Hodges, H. A. *Wilhelm Dilthey: An introduction.* London: Routledge and Kegan Paul, 1949.

Hoppe, F. Erfolg und Misserfolg. *Psychol. Forsch.,* 1930, *14*, 1–62.

Keredjarto, von B. *Vorlesungen über Topologie.* Berlin: Springer, 1923.

Leeper, R. W. *Lewin's topological and vector psychology.* Eugene, Ore.: University of Oregon Press, 1943.

Lewin, K. Die psychische Tätigkeit bei der Hemmung von Willensvorgängen und das Grundgesetz der Assoziation. *Z. Psychol.,* 1917, *77*, 212–247.

Lewin, K. Das Problem der Willensmessung und das Grundgesetz der Assoziation. *Psychol. Forsch.,* 1921, *1*, 191–302; 1922, *2*, 65–140.

Lewin, K. *Der Begriff der Genese in Physik, Biologie, und Entwicklungsgeschichte.* Berlin: Bornträger, 1922.

Lewin, K. *Forsatz, Wille, und Bedürfnis.* Berlin: Springer, 1926.

Lewin, K. Gesetz und Experiment in der Psychologie. *Symposium,* 1927, *1*, 375–421.

Lewin, K. *Die Entwicklung der experimentellen Willenspsychologie und die Psychotherapie.* Leipzig: Hirzel, 1929.

Lewin, K. Vectors, cognitive processes, and Mr. Tolman's criticism. *J. gen. Psychol.,* 1933, *8*, 318–345.

Lewin, K. Environmental forces. In C. Murchison (Ed.), *Handbook of child psychology.* Worcester, Mass.: Clark University Press, 1934.

Lewin, K. *A dynamic theory of personality.* New York: McGraw-Hill, 1935.

Lewin, K. *Principles of topological psychology.* New York: McGraw-Hill, 1936.

Lewin, K. The conceptual representation and measurement of psychological forces. *Univer. Iowa Contr. psychol. Theory,* 1938, *1*, No. 4, 1–247.

Lewin, K. Formalization and progress in psychology. *Univer. Iowa Contr. psychol. Theory,* 1940, *3*, 7–42.

Lewin, K. Field theory of learning. *Yearb. nat. Soc. Stud. Educ.,* 1942, *41*, Part II, 215–242.

Lewin, K. Defining the "field at a given time." *Psychol. Rev.,* 1943, *50*, 292–310.

Lewin, K. Constructs in psychology and psychological ecology. *Univer. Iowa Stud. Child Welf.,* 1944, *20*, 1–29.

Lewin, K. Behavior and development as a function of the total situation. In L. Carmichael (Ed.), *Manual of child psychology.* New York: Wiley, 1946.

Lewin, K. Cassirer's philosophy of science and the social sciences. In P. A. Schilpp (Ed.), *The philosophy of Ernst Cassirer.* Evanston, Ill.: Living Philosophies, 1949.

Lewin, K. *Field theory in social science.* New York: Harper, 1951.

Lippitt, R. An experimental study of the effect of democratic and authoritarian group atmospheres. *Univer. Iowa Stud. Child Welf.,* 1940, *16*, 3, 44–195.

London, I. O. Psychologists' misuse of the auxiliary concepts of physics and mathematics. *Psychol. Rev.,* 1944, *51*, 266–291.

MacCall, S. H. A comparative study of the systems of Lewin and Koffka with specific reference to memory phenomena. *Contr. psychol. Theory, Duke University Press,* 1939, *2*, No. 1.

Marrow, A. J. Goal tension and recall. *J. gen. Psychol.,* 1938, *19*, 3–35, 37–64.

Ovsiankina, M. Die Wiederaufnahme von unterbrochener Handlungen. *Psychol. Forsch.*, 1928, 11, 302–389.

Sierpinski, W. *Introduction to general topology*. Toronto: University of Toronto Press, 1934.

Spence, K. W. The nature of theory construction in contemporary psychology. *Psychol. Rev.*, 1944, 51, 47–68.

Spence, K. W. Theoretical interpretations of learning. In S. S. Stevens (Ed.), *Handbook of experimental psychology*. New York: Wiley, 1951.

White, R. K. The case for the Tolman-Lewin interpretation of learning. *Psychol. Rev.*, 1943, 50, 157–186.

Wolman, B. Chance: A philosophical study. *Tarbitz, Hebrew Univer. Quart.* (Hebrew), 1938, 10, 56–80.

Wolman, B. Historical laws—do they exist: *Proceedings of the Tenth International Congress of Philosophy*, Amsterdam, 1948. (Abstr.)

Zeigarnik, B. Über das Behalten erledigter und unerledigter Handlungen. *Psychol. Forsch.*, 1927, 9, 1–85.

CHAPTER 14. HUMANISTIC PSYCHOLOGY

Allport, G. W. *Becoming*. New Haven: Yale University Press, 1955.

Allport, G. W. *Pattern and growth in personality*. New York: Holt, Rinehart & Winston, 1961.

Bischof, L. J. *Interpreting personality theories*. New York: Harper & Row, 1964. (2nd ed.), 1970.

Bonner, H. *On being mindful of man*. Boston: Houghton Mifflin, 1965.

Bonner H. The proactive personality. In J. F. T. Bugental (Ed.), *Challenges of humanistic psychology*. New York: McGraw-Hill, 1967.

Bugental, J. F. T. The third force in psychology. *J. humanist. Psych.*, 1964, 4, 19–26.

Bugental, J. F. T. *The search for authenticity*. New York: Holt, Rinehart & Winston, 1965.

Bugental, J. F. T. (Ed.) *Challenges of humanistic psychology*. New York: McGraw-Hill, 1967.

Buhler, C. *Values in psychotherapy*. New York: Free Press, 1962.

Buhler, C. Human life as a whole as a central subject of humanistic psychology. In J. F. T. Bugental (Ed.), *Challenges of humanistic psychology*, New York: McGraw-Hill, 1967.

Fingarette, H. A fresh perspective on a familiar landscape. *J. humanist. Psych.*, 1962, 2, 75–89.

Fingarette, H. *The self in transformation*. New York: Basic Books, 1963.

Frankl, V. *The doctor and the soul*. New York: Knopf, 1957.

Frankl, V. Self-transcendence as a human phenomenon. *J. humanist. Psych.*, 1966, 6, 97–106.

Fromm, E. *Escape from freedom*. New York: Holt, Rinehart & Winston, 1941.

Fromm, E. *The sane society*. New York: Holt, Rinehart & Winston, 1955.

Fromm, E. *The art of loving*. New York: Harper & Row, 1956.

Goldstein, K. *The organism*. New York: American Book, 1939.

Hall, C. S., and Lindzey, G. Psychoanalytic theory and its applications to the social sciences. In G. Lindzey (Ed.), *Handbook of social psychology*. Reading, Mass.: Addison-Wesley, 1954.

Hall, M. H. The psychology of personality—a conversation with Henry A. Murray, *Psychology Today*, 1968, 2 (4), 56–63.

Jourard, S. M. *The transparent self*. New York: Van Nostrand Reinhold, 1964.

Jourard, S. M. Experimenter-subject dialogue: A paradigm for a humanistic science of psychology. In J. F. T. Bugental (Ed.), *Challenges of humanistic psychology*. New York: McGraw-Hill, 1967.

Jourard, S. M. *Disclosing man to himself*. New York: Van Nostrand Reinhold, 1968.

Jourard, S. M., & Overlade, D. C. (Eds.) *Reconciliation: A theory of man transcending*. New York: Van Nostrand Reinhold, 1966.

Jung, C. G. *Modern man in search of a soul*. New York: McGraw-Hill, 1935.

Lewin, K. *Dynamic theory of personality*. New York: McGraw-Hill, 1935.

Maddi, S. R. Humanistic psychology: Allport and Murray. In J. M. Wepman & R. W. Heine (Eds.), *Concepts of personality*. Chicago: Aldine, 1963.

Maslow, A. H. *Motivation and personality*. New York: Harper & Row, 1954.

Maslow, A. H. *Toward a psychology of being*. New York: Van Nostrand Reinhold, 1962. (2nd ed.), 1968.

Maslow, A. H. Self-actualization and beyond. In J. F. T. Bugental (Ed.), *Challenges of humanistic psychology*. New York: McGraw-Hill, 1967.

May, R. Intentionality, the heart of human will. *J. humanist. Psychol.*, 1965, 5, 202–209.

May, R., Engel, E., and Ellenberger, H. F. (Eds.) *Existence-A new dimension in psychiatry and psychology*. New York: Basic Books, 1958.

Moustakas, C. *Loneliness*. Englewood Cliffs, N.J.: Prentice-Hall, 1961.

Moustakas, C. Heuristic research. In J. F. T. Bugental (Ed.), *Challenges of humanistic psychology*. New York: McGraw-Hill, 1967.

Murphy, G. *Personality: A biosocial approach to origins and structure*. New York: Harper & Row, 1947.

Murphy, G. *Human potentialities*. New York: Baisc Books, 1958.

Murray, H. A., and others. *Explorations in personality*. New York: Oxford University Press, 1938.

Rogers, C. R. Some observations on the organization of personality. *Am. Psychol.*, 1947, 2, 358–68.

Rogers, C. R. *Client-centered therapy*. Boston: Houghton Mifflin, 1951.

Rogers, C. R. The necessary and sufficient conditions of therapeutic personality change. *J. consulting Psychol.*, 1957, 21, 95–103.

Rogers, C. R. A theory of therapy, personality, and interpersonal relationships as developed in a client-centered framework. In S. Koch (Ed.), *Psychology: A study of a science*, Vol. 3. New York: McGraw-Hill, 1959.

Sargent, S. S. Humanistic methodology in personality and social psychology. In J. F. T. Bugental (Ed.), *Challenges of humanistic psychology*. New York: McGraw-Hill, 1967.

Sargent, S. S. The humanistic approach to personality. In B. B. Wolman (Ed.), *Handbook of general psychology*. Englewood Cliffs, N.J.: Prentice-Hall, 1973, pp. 817–825.

Severin, F. T. (Ed.) *Humanistic viewpoints in psychology*. New York: McGraw-Hill, 1965.

Shaw, F. J. The problem of acting and the problem of becoming. *J. humanist. Psychol.*, 1961, 1, 64–69.

Sutich, A. J. The growth experience and the growth-centered attitude. *J. Humanist. Psychol.*, 1949, 28, 293–301. (Reprinted in *J. humanist. Psychol.*, 1967, 7, 155–62.)

Sutich, A. J. American Association for Humanistic Psychology: Progress Report, 1962 (mimeo). Reprinted in part in *J. humanist. Psychol.*, 1964, 4, 22.)

Sutich, A. J. Transpersonal psychology. *J. humanist. Psychol.*, 1968, 8, 77–78.

Thetford, W., & Schucman, H. Other psychological personality theories. In A. M. Freedman, H. I. Kaplan, & B. J. Sadock (Eds.), *Comprehensive textbook of psychiatry*. (2nd ed.) Baltimore: Williams and Wilkins, 1975.

Watts, A. W. Oriental and occidental approaches to the nature of man. *Journal of Humanistic Psychology*, 1962, 2, 107–109.

Chapter 15. The Scientific Method

Bergmann, G., & Spence, K. Operationism and theory in psychology. *Psychol. Rev.*, 1941, 48, 1–14.

Bertalanffy, L. von. Theoretical models in biology and psychology. *J. Pers.*, 1951, 20, 24–38.

Boring, E. The role of theory in experimental psychology. *Amer. J. Psychol.*, 1953, 66, 169–184.

Bridgman, P. W. *The logic of modern physics*. New York: Macmillan, 1927.

Bridgman, P. Some general principles of operational analysis. *Psychol. Rev.*, 1945, *52*, 246–249.

Brunswik, E. *The conceptual framework of psychology.* Chicago: University of Chicago Press, 1952.

Cohen, M. *Reason and nature.* New York: Harcourt, Brace, 1931.

Cohen, M. R., & Nagel, E. *An introduction to logic and scientific method.* New York: Harcourt, Brace, 1934.

Dallenbach, K. M. The place of theory in science. *Psychol. Rev.*, 1953, *60*, 33–39.

Einstein, A., & Infeld, L. *The evolution of physics.* New York: Simon & Schuster, 1942.

Feigl, H., & Scriven, M. *Minnesota studies in the philosophy of science.* Minneapolis: University of Minnesota Press, 1956–1958, 2 vols.

Gilgen, A. R. (Ed.) *Contemporary scientific psychology.* New York: Academic Press, 1970.

Höffding, H. *Modern philosophers.* New York: Macmillan, 1915.

Kotarbinski, T. *Elements of logic, epistemology, and methodology of science.* (Polish) Warsaw: Atlas, 1929.

Laird, J. *Recent philosophy.* London: Methuen, 1936.

MacCorquodale, K., & Meehl, P. E. On a distinction between hypothetical constructs and intervening variables. *Psychol. Rev.*, 1948, *55*, 95–107.

Marx, M. (Ed.) *Psychological theory.* New York: Macmillan, 1951.

Nagel, E. *Logic without metaphysics.* Glencoe, Ill.: Free Press, 1956.

Peters, R. S. (Ed.) *Brett's history of psychology.* London: Allen & Unwin, 1951.

Poincaré, H. *The foundations of science.*sNew York: Science Press, 1913.

Pratt, C. C. *The logic of modern psychology.* New York: Macmillan, 1939.

Reichenbach, H. *Experience and prediction.* Chicago: University of Chicago Press, 1938.

Russell, B. *Human knowledge, its scope and limits.* New York: Norton, 1948.

Russell, B., & Whitehead, A. N. *Principia Mathematica.* (2nd ed.) Cambridge: Oxford University Press, 1925–1927, 2 vols.

Spence, K. W. The nature of theory construction in contemporary psychology. *Psychol. Rev.*, 1944, *51*, 47–68.

Stevens, S. S. Psychology and the science. *Psychol. Bull.*, 1939, *36*, 221–263.

Tarski, A. *Introduction to logic.* New York: Oxford University Press, 1941.

Tolman, E. C. Operational behaviorism and current trends in psychology. *Proc. 25th Anniv. Celeb. Inaug. grad. Stud.* Los Angeles: University of Southern California Press, 1936.

Whitehead, A. N. *Science and the modern world.* New York: Macmillan, 1925.

Wolman, B. B. Chance, a philosophical study. *Tarbitz, Hebrew Univer. Quart.* (Hebrew), 1938, *10*, 56–80.

Wolman, B. B. Toward a science of psychological science. In B. B. Wolman & G. Nagel (Eds.), *Scientific psychology: Principles and approaches.* New York: Basic Books, 1965, pp. 3–23.

Wolman, B. B. Concerning psychology and the philosophy of science. In B. B. Wolman (Ed.), *Handbook of general psychology.* Englewood Cliff, N.J.: Prentice-Hall, 1973, pp. 22–48.

CHAPTER 16. SELECTED ISSUES

1. The Mind–Body Dichotomy

Ayrapetyants, E. S. *Higher nervous function and the receptors of internal organs.* Moscow: U.S.S.R. Academy of Science, 1952.

Barber, T. X. Experimental hypnosis. In B. B. Wolman (Ed.), *Handbook of general psychology,* Englewood Cliffs, N.J.: Prentice-Hall, 1973, pp. 942–963.

Bechterev, V. M. *Objective psychologie-reflexologie.* Leipzig: Teubner, 1913.

Bykov, W. H. *The cerebral cortex and the internal organs.* New York: Chemical Publishing, 1957.

Eccles, J. C. *The neurophysiological basis of mind.* Oxford: Clarendon Press, 1953.

Feynman, R. P. *Quantum electrodynamics.* New York: Benjamin, 1961.

Firsoff, V. A. *Life, mind and galaxies.* Edinburgh and London: Oliver & Boyd, 1967.

Freud, S. *Outline of psychoanalysis*. New York: Norton, 1949.

Freud, S. *New introductory lectures on psychoanalysis*. Vol. 22, Standard Edition. London: Hogarth Press, 1964.

Hebb, D. O. *The organization of behavior*. New York: Wiley, 1949.

Hull, C. L. The problem of intervening variables in molar behavior theory. *Psychol. Rev.*, 1943, *50*, 273–291.

Jeans, J. *The mysterious universe*. New York: Dutton, 1958.

Koestler, A. *The roots of coincidence*. New York: Random House, 1972.

Köhler, W. *Gestalt psychology*. New York: Liveright, 1947.

Lewin, K. *Field theory in social science*. New York: Harper, 1951.

Nagel, E. *The structure of science*. New York: Harcourt, Brace, 1953.

Oparin, A. I. *The origins of life on earth*. New York: Academic Press, 1957.

Pavlov, I. P. *Lectures on conditioned reflexes*. New York: Liveright, 1928.

Rhine, J. B., and Pratt, J. G. *Parapsychology: Frontier science of the mind*. Springfield, Ill.: Charles C Thomas, 1957.

Rubinstein, S. L. Questions of psychological theory. In B. Simon (Ed.), *Psychology in the Soviet Union*. Stanford, Cal.: Stanford University Press, 1957, pp. 264–278.

Scriven, M. The frontiers of psychology: Psychoanalysis and parapsychology. In R. G. Colodny (Ed.), *Frontiers of science and philosophy*. Pittsburgh: University of Pittsburgh Press, 1962, pp. 79–129.

Sherrington, C. S. *Man on his nature*. New York: Macmillan, 1941.

Skinner, B. F. Are theories of learning necessary? *Psychol. Rev.*, 1950, *57*, 193–216.

Skinner, B. F. *Science and human behavior*. New York: Macmillan, 1953.

Sullivan, H. S. *Conceptions of modern psychiatry*. Washington, D.C.: White Foundation, 1947.

Vasiliev, L. L. *Experiments in mental suggestion*. Church Crookham, England: Institute for the Study of Mental Images, 1963.

Watson, J. B. Psychology as the behaviorist sees it. *Psychol. Rev.*, 1913, *20*, 158–177.

Watson, J. B. *Psychology from the standpoint of a behaviorist*. Philadelphia: Lippincott, 1919.

Webb, W. B. Sleep and dreams. In B. B. Wolman (Ed.), *Handbook of general psychology*. Englewood Cliffs, N.J.: Prentice-Hall, 1973, pp. 734–748.

Whitehead, A. N. *Nature and life*. Cambridge: Cambridge University Press, 1934.

Wolberg, L. *The technique of psychotherapy*. New York: Grune & Stratton, 1967.

Wolman, B. B. (Ed.) *Historical roots of contemporary psychology*. New York: Harper & Row, 1968.

Wolman, B. B. Principles of monistic transitionism. In B. B. Wolman & E. Nagel (Eds.), *Scientific psychology: Principles and approaches*. New York: Basic Books, 1965, pp. 563–585.

Wolman, B. B. Johann Friedrich Herbart. In B. B. Wolman (Ed.), *Historical roots of contemporary psychology*. New York: Harper & Row, 1968, pp. 29–46.

Wolman, B. B. (Ed.) *Success and failure in psychoanalysis and psychotherapy*. New York: Macmillan, 1972.

Wolman, B. B. Concerning psychology and the philosophy of science. In B. B. Wolman (Ed.), *Handbook of general psychology*. Englewood Cliffs, N.J.: Prentice-Hall, 1973, pp. 22–48.

Wolman, B. B. *Dictionary of behavioral science*. New York: Van Nostrand Reinhold, 1973.

Wolman, B. B. (Ed.) *Handbook of parapsychology*. New York: Van Nostrand Reinhold, 1977.

2. Beyond Pleasure and Pain

Bykov, K. M. *The cerebral cortex and the inner organs*. New York: Chemical Publishing, 1957.

Hilgard, E. R., and Hilgard, J. R. *Hypnosis in the relief of pain*. San Francisco: Kaufman, 1975.

Razran, G. Evolutionary psychology. In B. B. Wolman & E. Nagel (Eds.), *Scientific psychology: Principles and approaches*. New York: Basic Books, 1965.

Sternbach, R. A. *Pain patients: Traits and treatment*. New York: Academic Press, 1974.

Wolman, B. B. The Antigone principle. *American Imago*, 1965, *22*, 186–201.

Wolman, B. B. *Vectoriasis praecox or the group of schizophrenias.* Springfield, Ill., Charles C Thomas, 1966.
Wolman, B. B. (Ed.) *Success and failure in psychoanalysis and psychotherapy.* New York: Macmillan, 1972.

3. Perception

Ames, A. Visual perception and the rotating window. *Psychol. Monogr.,* 1951, *65,* 7–63.
Avant, L. L., & Helson, H. Theories of perception. In B. B. Wolman (Ed.), *Handbook of general psychology.* Englewood Cliffs, N.J.: Prentice-Hall, 1973, pp. 423–448.
Bevan, W. Perception: Evolution of a concept. *Psychol. Rev.,* 1958, *65,* 34–55.
Bruner, J. S. On perceptural readiness. *Psychol. Rev.,* 1957, *64,* 123–152.
Bruner, J. S., & Goodman, C. C. Value and need as organizing factors in perception. *J. Abnorm. Soc. Psychol.,* 1947, *42,* 33–44.
Bruner, J. S., & Postman, L. On perception of incongruity: A paradigm. *J. Pers.,* 1949, *18,* 206–223.
Engel, E. The role of content in binocular resolution. *Amer. J. Psychol.,* 1956, *69,* 87–91.
Gibson, E. J. *Principles of perceptual learning and development.* New York: Appleton-Century-Crofts, 1969.
Gibson, J. J. *The perception of the visual world.* Boston: Houghton Mifflin, 1950.
Gibson, J. J. Perception as a function of stimulation. In S. Koch (Ed.), *Psychology: A study of science,* Vol. 1. New York: McGraw-Hill, 1959.
Gibson, J. J. *The senses considered as perceptual systems.* Boston: Houghton Mifflin, 1966.
Haber, R. N. Visual perception. *Ann. Rev. Psychol.,* 1978, *29,* 31–59.
Hebb, D. O. *The organization of behavior.* New York: John Wiley, 1949.
Helson, M. *Adaptation-level theory: An experimental and systematic approach to behavior.* New York: Harper & Row, 1964.
Ittelson, W. H. *Visual space perception.* New York: Springer-Verlag, 1960.
Ittelson, W. H., & Kilpatrick, F. P. The monocular and binocular distorted rooms. In F. P. Kilpatrick (Ed.), *Explorations in transactional psychology.* New York: New York University Press, 1961, Chapter 8.
Mach, E. *Analysis of sensation* (1886). Chicago: Open Court, 1914.
Proshanky, H., & Murphy, G. The effects of rewards and punishment on perception. *J. Psychol.,* 1942, *13,* 294–305.
Riesen, A. H. The development of visual perception in man and chimpanzee. *Science,* 1947, *106,* 107–108.
Senden, M. V. *Space and sight.* New York: Free Press, 1960.
Wapner, S., & Witkin, H. A. The role of visual factors in the maintenance of body-balance. *Amer. J. Psychol.,* 1950, *63,* 385–408.
Werner, H., & Wapner, S. Sensory-tonic field theory of perception. *J. Pers.,* 1949, *18,* 88–107.

4. Personality

Allport, G. W. *Pattern and growth in personality.* New York: Holt, Rinehart & Winston, 1961.
Atwood, G. E., & Tomkins, S. S. On the subjectivity of personality theory. *J. Hist. behav. Sci.,* 1976, *12,* 166–177.
Berg, I. A. *Response set in personality.* Chicago: Aldine, 1967.
Block, J. Advancing the psychology of personality. In D. Magnusson & N. S. Endler (Eds.), *Personality at the crossroads.* New York: Wiley-Earlbaum, 1977, pp. 37–63.
Butcher, J. N., & Pancheri, P. *A handbook of cross-national MMPI research.* Minneapolis: University of Minnesota Press, 1976.

Craik, K. H. The personality research paradign in environmental psychology. In S. Wapner, S. B. Cohen, & B. Kaplan (Eds.), *Experiencing the environment.* New York: Plenum, 1976.

Epstein, C. F. Traits are alive and well. In D. Magnusson & N. S. Endler, (Eds.), *Personality at the crossroads.* New York: Wiley-Earlbaum, 1977.

Eysenck, H. J. *Dimensions in personality.* London: Kegan Paul, 1947.

Helson, R., and Mitchell, V. Personality. *Ann. Rev. Psychol.,* 1978, *29,* 555–586.

Hogan, R. *Personality theory: The personological tradition.* New York: Prentice-Hall, 1975.

Huba, G. J., & Hamilton, D. L. On the generality of trait relationships: Some analyses based on Fiske's paper. *Psychol. Bull.,* 1976, *83,* 868–876.

Jackson, D. N., & Messick, S. J. (Eds.) *Problems in human assessment.* New York: McGraw-Hill, 1967.

Kelly, J. A., & Worell, L. Parent behaviors related to masculine, feminine and androgynous sex role orientation. *J. clin. Psychol.,* 1976, *44,* 843–51.

Lifton, R. J. *The life of the self: Toward a new psychology.* New York: Simon & Schuster, 1976.

Loevinger, J. *Ego development.* San Francisco: Jossey-Bass, 1976.

Maddi, S. R. *Personality theories: A comparative analysis.* Homeward, Ill.: Dorsey, 1976.

Magnusson, D., and Endler, N. S. (Eds.) *Personality at the crossroads.* New York: Wiley-Earlbaum, 1977.

Messick, S. *Individuality in learning.* San Francisco: Jossey-Bass, 1976.

Murphy, G. *Personality.* New York: Harper & Row, 1947.

Murray, H. A., and others. *Explorations in personality.* New York: Oxford, 1938.

Rogers, C. R. *On becoming a person.* Boston: Houghton Mifflin, 1961.

Rychlak, J. F. Personality theories: An overview. In B. B. Wolman (Ed.), *International encyclopedia of psychiatry, psychology, psychoanalysis and neurology.* New York: Aesculapius, 1977, Vol. 8, pp. 314 ff.

Stolorow, R. D., & Atwood, G. E. *Faces in a Cloud: The Subjective World in Personality Theory.* New York: Aronson, 1978.

Tomkins, S. S., & Messick, S. (Eds.) *Computer simulation of personality.* New York: Wiley, 1963.

Wolman, B. B. (Ed.) *Clinical diagnosis of mental disorders.* New York: Plenum, 1978.

Wolman, B. B. (Ed.) *The psychoanalytic interpretation of history.* New York: Harper Torchbooks, 1973.

Author Index

Abraham, K., 235, 236, 237,
  265, 267, 322, 332, 399
Ach, N., 442, 617
Adams, K. D., 96, 138
Adams, R. G., 84
Adler, A., 3, 19, 61, 81,
  283–297, 298, 316, 321,
  368, 381, 386, 404, 426,
  505, 508
Aichorn, A., 338
Alexander, F., 320, 321, 404
Allport, F. H., 456, 592
Allport, G. W., 187, 422, 426,
  432, 433–437, 456, 507,
  508, 516, 517, 532, 541, 542
Ames, A., 575, 578
Amsel, A., 177
Angell, J. R., 27–29, 31, 197,
  590
Angyal, A., 507, 508, 509, 518
Ansbacher, R. R., 284, 286,
  297
Arieti, S., 191
Aristotle, 465, 466, 498, 518
Arnold, W. J., 120
Asch, S. 458, 508
Atkinson, J. W., 574
Atwood, G. W., 580
Avant, L. L., 457, 458, 572,
  573, 575, 576, 577
Ayrapetyants, E. S., 565

Bacon, F., 124, 205, 528, 586
Bain, A., 6, 31, 32, 33, 409, 415,
  438
Balint, M., 324
Balakschina, V. L., 70
Barker, R. G., 355, 490
Barnett, S. A., 174

Bateson, G., 332, 333
Beaunis, H., 440
Bekhterev, V. M., 61, 62–65,
  66, 67, 76, 78, 82, 84, 88,
  171, 193, 560
Bell, C., 8
Benedict, R., 341, 363
Benjamin, J., 359
Bergmann, H., 548
Bergson, H., 299
Berkeley, B., 578
Berkowitz, L., 459
Bernheim, H., 217
Bertocci, P., 435
Bettelheim, B., 352
Bibring, E., 338
Binet, A., 16, 38, 426, 440–441,
  443, 517, 530
Bishop, F. V., 358
Blanck, R., 317, 324, 325, 327,
  329, 330, 331
Blanck, G., 317, 324, 325, 327,
  329, 330, 331
Block, J., 581
Blodgett, H. C., 145
Blum, H., 317, 318
Boring, E. C., 4
Boss, M., 508
Boyle, R., 561
Braid, J., 216
Brand, H., 355
Brentano, F., 11, 423, 439, 443,
  446, 516
Brett, G. S., 66, 413
Breuer, J., 17, 205, 217, 218
Brian, S., 72
Bridgman, P. W., 397, 528,
  531, 586
Brill, A. A., 225
Broadbent, D. E., 174

Bromberg, P. M., 357
Brown, J. F., 480, 498, 499, 535
Brown, J. S., 123, 150, 458
Brozek, J., 73, 75
Bruner, J. S., 573, 574
Brunswik, E., 151, 582
Büchner, L., 63, 67
Bugelski, B. P., 179
Bugental, J. F. T., 512, 518
Bühler, C., 162, 280, 527
Bühler, K., 430, 443, 444, 508,
  517
Burns, E., 67
Burt, C., 16, 426, 440
Butcher, J. N., 580
Bykov, K. M., 70, 71, 72, 88,
  102, 154, 172, 198, 565,
  568, 569, 571

Cannon, W. B., 42, 175, 188,
  386, 477, 549, 566
Carmichael, L., 568
Carnap, R., 104, 549
Carr, H. A., 27–29
Cartwright, D., 471
Cassirer, E., 413, 518
Charcot, J. M., 17, 205, 209,
  217, 409, 440, 441
Chein, I., 573
Chernakov, E. T., 68, 70
Claparède, E., 440, 441
Cohen, H., 413
Cohen, M. R., 498, 533, 534
Cohen, S. B., 579
Cole, M., 63
Coles, R., 338
Comte, A., 206, 403, 415, 518,
  522, 523, 547
Condrau, G., 508

Copernicus, N., 421, 530
Corson, E. O., 74
Corson, S. A., 58, 61, 74
Cowles, J. T., 150
Craig, W., 142
Craik, K. H., 579
Csikszentmihalyi, M., 582
Culler, E., 49

Dahl, H., 359
Darwin, C., 7, 16, 20, 21, 22,
    31, 62, 181, 204, 242, 268,
    284, 289, 341, 401, 415, 523
Day, W., 196
de Lamarck, J. B. P. A., 20, 21,
    182
de Laplace, P. S., 530
Dembo, T., 355, 449, 482, 483,
    488, 490
Denmark, F., 584
Dennis, W., 463, 539, 574
Derner, G. F., 191
Descartes, R., 15, 16, 63, 82,
    171, 385, 544
Deutsch, H., 338
Dewey, J., 24–27, 29, 32, 33,
    76, 197, 199, 558
d'Holbach, P., 62
Dickinson, A., 177
Diderot, D., 62
Dilthey, W., 19, 20, 41, 68,
    171, 263, 403, 404, 409,
    413, 414–422, 423, 424,
    426, 427, 428, 429, 464,
    516, 517, 523, 545, 557
Dingle, W., 547
Dollard, J., 123, 138, 163–167,
    169, 170, 175, 344, 353, 393
Doob, L. W., 166, 344, 354
Douvan, E., 584
Drever, J., 438
Driesch, H., 180
Dunker, K., 455
Dunlap, K., 143
Durkheim, E., 306
Dürr, E., 443

Ebbinghaus, H., 32, 413, 414,
    423, 527
Einstein, A., 7, 136, 454, 523,
    527, 567
Endler, N. S., 581
Engel, E., 575
Engels, F., 65, 67

Epstein, C. F., 581
Erikson, E. H., 338–341, 344,
    348, 363, 403, 583
Estes, W. K., 122, 135, 138,
    174, 178

Faibairn, W. R., 323
Fajans, S., 483
Farrell, B. A., 355
Fechner, G. T., 9, 10, 215, 446,
    527, 569
Federn, P., 230, 319
Feigl, H., 463, 522, 528, 539,
    542, 543
Fenichel, O., 204, 211, 247,
    263, 317, 399, 531
Ferenczi, S., 320–321, 404
Festinger, L., 358
Fischer, R., 582
Flourens, P., 9, 409
Flugel, J. C., 41
Ford, C. S., 166
Formica, R., 357
Frank, T. D., 484
Franks, V., 508
Franz, S. I., 88, 89
Freedman, A. M., 324, 401,
    507
French, J. R. P., 493
French, T., 320
Freud, A., 292, 317, 322, 355
Freud, S., 3, 4, 18, 19, 21, 26,
    32, 41, 42, 60, 61, 83, 135,
    137, 138, 143, 153, 154,
    162, 163, 164, 166, 168,
    169, 171, 175, 184, 188,
    192, 193, 203, 204, 205,
    206, 207, 208, 209, 210,
    211, 213, 214, 215, 217,
    218, 219, 220, 221, 222,
    223, 224, 225, 226, 227,
    228, 229, 230, 231, 232,
    233, 234, 235, 236, 238,
    239, 240, 241, 242, 243,
    244, 245, 246, 248, 250,
    251, 252, 253, 254, 255,
    258, 259, 260, 261, 262,
    263, 265, 267, 268, 269,
    270, 271, 272, 273, 274,
    275, 276, 277, 280, 281,
    282, 283, 284, 286, 287,
    288, 289, 290, 291, 293,
    295, 298, 303, 304, 315,
    316, 317, 318, 319, 320,

Freud (cont.)
    321, 322, 323, 325, 326,
    331, 332, 333, 334, 335,
    338, 340, 341, 343, 345,
    347, 348, 349, 351, 352,
    353, 354, 355, 356, 357,
    358, 359, 360, 361, 362,
    363, 364, 365, 366, 367,
    368, 369, 372, 373, 375,
    378, 379, 380, 382, 383,
    384, 385, 386, 389, 391,
    393, 394, 395, 398, 399,
    400, 401, 403, 404, 405,
    409, 414, 415, 430, 440,
    496, 505, 511, 528, 530,
    540, 541, 542, 543, 544,
    545, 548, 549, 558, 560,
    567, 569, 580
Fritsch, G., 50
Fromm, E., 297, 319, 321, 333,
    351, 362, 363, 364,
    373–385, 404, 405, 426,
    507, 508
Fromm-Reichmann, F., 397

Galileo, G., 465, 474, 498, 506,
    518, 559, 572
Galton, F., 21, 22, 181
Gantt, W. H., 70
Garner, 458
Gesell, A., 242, 348, 366, 549
Getzels, J. N., 582
Gibson, J. J., 577, 579
Gilgen, A. R., 458, 459, 552,
    553, 554
Girden, E., 61, 154
Glover, E., 317, 399
Goldstein, K., 3, 92, 94, 180,
    187–193, 195, 199, 200,
    203, 279, 285, 386, 429,
    444, 477, 507, 508, 510,
    518, 527, 530, 540, 543,
    544, 546, 548, 549
Goodman, C. C., 574
Goffman, E., 581
Gould, R., 483
Gottschaldt, K., 453, 454
Green, T. H., 546
Grose, T. H., 546
Gryier, T. G., 585
Gulliksen, H., 551
Guthrie, E. R., 18, 33, 60,
    97–103, 111, 138, 158, 168,
    172, 198, 280, 527, 528, 536

Haber, R. N., 578
Haeckel, E., 228, 242, 284
Hall, S., 527
Halverson, H. M., 355
Hamburg, D. A., 358
Hamilton, D. C., 581
Hamilton, J. A., 353
Harrower, M. R., 455
Hartley, D., 6, 409, 415
Hartley, E. L., 494
Hartmann, H., 317, 324–327, 330, 338, 344, 352, 405, 511
Heath, D. H., 584
Hebb, D. O., 92–96, 172, 193, 198, 527, 558, 560, 576, 577
Hegel, G. W. F., 275, 373, 559
Heidbreder, E., 3, 539
Heilbrun, A. B., 584
Heinz, L., 284
Helson, H., 61, 457, 458, 572, 573, 577
Helson, R., 579
Helveticus, C. A., 62
Hempel, C. G., 522
Henle, M., 455, 457
Henning, M., 584
Henry, G. W., 216
Heraclitus, 300, 562
Herbart, J. F., 6–7, 11, 31, 63, 365, 413, 551, 560
Hesse, M., 531
Hilgard, E. R., 90, 102, 138, 163, 356, 357, 571
Hilgard, J. R., 571
Hippocrates, 59, 295
Hitzig, E., 50
Hodges, H. A., 414, 415, 417, 418
Hogan, R., 579
Holt, E. B., 85–96, 198
Holt, R. R., 359, 360, 361
Honzik, C. M., 151
Hook, S., 66
Hoppe, F., 483
Horney, Karen, 4, 19, 60, 279, 293, 297, 321, 333, 351, 362, 363, 364–373, 384, 393, 400, 401, 402, 404, 405, 426, 508
Horton, G. P., 99
Hovland, C. I., 121, 123, 166
Huba, G. J., 581
Hull, C. L., 3, 18, 32, 52, 53, 60, 86, 90, 103–124, 130, 138,

Hull (cont.)
151, 152, 155, 158, 163, 164, 165, 169, 170, 172, 173, 175, 176, 177, 178, 187, 193, 199, 279, 280, 497, 535, 539, 541, 545, 558, 560, 567
Hume, D., 6, 82, 103, 104, 410, 415, 419, 525, 528, 546
Humphrey, G., 443, 455
Hundleby, J. D., 581
Hunt, J. McV., 99
Hunter, W. S., 87, 198
Husserl, E., 19, 414, 416, 420, 421, 424, 429, 431, 444, 445, 516
Huxley, T., 21
Hyde, J. S., 584

Isaacs, S., 527
Ittelson, W. H., 575, 578

Jackson, E., 329
Jaensch, E. R., 392
James, W., 10, 22–24, 29, 32, 76, 197, 199, 305, 523, 532
Janet, P., 17, 86, 217, 409, 440
Jardim, A., 584
Jones, E., 204, 317, 399
Jung, C. G., 3, 19, 297–315, 316, 321, 404, 508, 532, 540, 580

Kahn, M., 324
Kant, I., 11, 19, 86, 206, 275, 397, 409, 410, 411, 412, 413, 414, 415, 416, 420, 421, 428, 437, 444, 450, 516, 517, 518, 523, 526, 529, 531, 561
Kantor, J. R., 193–195, 200, 558
Kanzer, M., 317, 318
Kaplan, B., 579
Kaplan, H. I., 324, 401, 507
Kardiner, A., 19, 333–338, 344, 351, 362, 363, 366, 374, 405
Karsten, A., 482, 486, 488
Katz, D., 451
Kelly, J. A., 584
Kelman, H., 400, 401, 402
Kelson, H., 546, 547
Kempf, E. J., 143
Kempthorne, O., 536
Kepler, J., 530

Kerenyi, K., 307, 308
Kernberg, O., 330, 331
Kessen, M. L., 165, 173
Kierkegaard, S., 508
Kilpatrick, F. P., 574, 575
Kimble, G. A., 111, 123, 174, 176
Klein, D. C., 585
Klein, G. S., 321, 359, 538
Klein, M., 321–322, 323, 404
Klüver, H., 90
Koch, S., 122, 138, 515, 575, 578
Koffka, K., 138, 449, 450, 452, 453, 456, 484, 488, 517
Köhler, W., 3, 90, 92, 93, 138, 444, 445, 446, 447, 448, 450, 451, 452, 453, 456, 457, 517, 527, 536, 543, 544, 549
Kohut, H., 331
Koivumaki, J. H., 582
Konorski, J., 177
Konradi, G. P., 71
Kornilov, K. N., 65, 66
Korsakoff, S. S., 352
Kotarbinski, T., 524
Krasnogorski, N. I., 78
Krauss, B. J., 347
Krauss, H. H., 347
Krauss, R. M., 374
Krech, D., 573
Krechevsky, I., 90, 353
Kreinheder, A., 315
Kertschmer, E., 532
Kris, E., 317, 325, 338
Kroeber, A., 338
Krueger, F. E., 430
Kuhlmann, F., 16
Kuhn, T. S., 552, 586
Külpe, O., 20, 431, 441, 442, 444, 517
Kuo, Z. Y., 77, 183

la Mettrie, J. O., 62, 83
Land, 457
Lange, C. G., 24
Lange, S. A., 63
Lashley, K. S., 88–92, 198, 429, 527, 548, 558
Laws, J. L., 584
Lawson, R., 341
Le Bon, G., 270
Leeper, R. W., 152

Lenin, W. I., 42, 65, 67, 73
Leontyev, A. N., 68, 73, 74
Levine, R., 573
Levy, D. M., 355
Lévy-Bruhl, L., 306
Lewin, K., 3, 4, 20, 57, 96, 103,
    122, 138, 141, 151, 153,
    195, 279, 293, 296, 354,
    355, 363, 385, 391, 394,
    396, 405, 409, 413, 426,
    431, 433, 435, 449, 450,
    460–505, 513, 516, 518,
    527, 535, 537, 539, 541,
    543, 551, 552, 560, 562, 582
Liebault, A., 17
Lifton, R. J., 341, 579
Linton, R., 333–338, 362, 363
Lippitt, R., 493, 537
Lipsitt, A., 554
Lissner, K., 482
Lobachevki, N. I., 561
Locke, J., 6, 410, 415, 578
Loeb, J., 17
Loevinger, J., 583
Loewenstein, R., 317, 326, 327
London, H., 346
London, I. D., 65
Luria, A. R., 68, 72, 73, 74, 75,
    198

MacCall, S. H., 484
MacCorquodale, K., 122, 541,
    542
MacKintosh, N. J., 177
McClelland, D. C., 573, 574
McDougall, W., 4, 18, 30, 31,
    33, 116, 138, 142, 152,
    180–187, 189, 199, 285,
    384, 433, 436, 444, 505,
    532, 541
McGeoch, J. A., 28
McGinnies, E., 574
McReynolds, P., 195
Mach, E., 125, 155, 413, 444,
    447, 543
Mack, J. E., 324
Maddi, S. R., 579
Magendie, F., 8
Magnusson, D., 581
Mahler, M., 328–329, 405
Maier, N. R. F., 455
Malinowski, B., 332
Maltzman, I., 63

Marcia, J. E., 584
Marx, K., 42, 65, 66, 67, 70, 72,
    73, 198, 373
Marx, M., 139, 194
Maslow, A., 507, 508, 510–511,
    518
Mateer, F., 78
May, R., 508
Mayer, A., 442
Mead, G. H., 305, 364, 385, 394
Mead, M., 332, 333, 341, 363,
    581, 582
Mednick, S. A., 174
Meehl, P. E., 122, 138, 541, 542
Meissner, W. W., 324
Mekeel, S., 338
Melton, A. W., 28
Mendel, G., 542
Mendeleyev, D. I., 136
Mesmer, A., 216
Messick, S., 580
Metcalf, D., 359
Mettler, F. A., 49
Meumann, E., 16, 413
Meyer, A., 193, 383
Michotte, A., 440, 441
Miles, R. C., 176
Mill, J., 6, 438
Mill, J. S., 6, 124, 205, 403, 415,
    438, 502, 528, 586
Miller, N. E., 124, 138,
    163–167, 169, 170, 173,
    175, 199, 344, 353, 354
Mitchell, V., 579, 580, 582
Moleschott, J., 63, 67, 559
Moloney, J. C., 335
Moreno, J. L., 305
Morgan, C. L., 17, 175
Moustakas, 508
Mowrer, O. H., 124, 163, 166,
    167–170, 199, 344, 356
Mueller, C. G., Jr., 122, 138
Mullahy, P., 383, 395
Müller, G. E., 441, 451
Müller, J., 8, 9, 10, 572
Murchison, C., 3, 65, 242, 441
Murdock, B. B., 179
Murphy, G., 4, 86, 216, 297,
    316, 317, 365, 460, 461,
    500, 507, 512–513, 518,
    573, 574
Murphy, L. B., 364
Murray, H. A., 507, 511–512,
    518, 582

Nagel, E., 177, 539, 560, 563
Natorp, P., 413
Newcomb, T., 364, 494
Newton, I., 6, 474, 523, 530,
    559
Nietzsche, F., 508
Nissen, H. W., 150

O'Connell, A. N., 583
O'Connor, 358
O'Kelly, L. I., 353
Olds, J., 174
Oparin, A. I., 565
Orth, J., 442
Ostwald, W., 543
Ovsiankina, M., 481

Paredes, J. A., 582
Parsons, T., 169
Pauli, W., 299
Pavlov, I. P., 3, 4, 18, 32, 33,
    35, 41, 42–62, 63, 64, 67,
    68, 69, 70, 71, 72, 73, 76,
    78, 86, 88, 90, 91, 92, 93,
    98, 100, 102, 107, 171, 172,
    179, 188, 192, 197, 198,
    199, 203, 279, 280, 344,
    346, 356, 403, 409, 413,
    414, 415, 430, 437, 452,
    527, 530, 541, 544, 545,
    548, 549, 558, 567
Pervin, L. A., 580, 581
Peterfreunds, E., 359
Peters, R. S., 66
Pettit, T. F., 358
Piaget, J., 74, 242, 250, 348,
    366, 440, 441, 530, 549
Pierce, C. S., 528
Pieri, M., 122
Pieron, H., 440, 441
Piotrowski, A., 191, 353
Planck, M., 548
Plato, 213, 526
Pleck, J. H., 583
Poincaré, H., 104, 525, 533,
    539
Postman, L., 573, 574
Pratt, C., 543
Pribram, K., 553
Proshansky, H., 574
Pshonik, A. T., 71, 571

Quinlan, D. M., 583

Rank, O., 317, 318, 320, 404, 405, 540, 580
Rapaport, D., 204, 359
Ratner, S., 554
Razran, G., 18, 60, 65, 70, 90, 154–164, 168, 172, 173, 199, 456, 532, 568
Reich, W., 265, 317, 333, 404, 580
Reichenbach, H., 546
Rescorla, R. A., 178
Ribot, T., 440
Richert, H., 414
Riemann, G. F. B., 561
Riesen, A. H., 577
Riesman, D. W., 341
Ritchie, B. F., 173, 174, 175
Roback, A. A., 294
Robinson, E. S., 27–29
Roby, T. B., 102, 173
Rock, I., 179, 458
Rogers, C., 507, 508, 514–515, 518
Rogers, J. P., 179
Roheim, G., 335
Rorschach, H., 530
Rosenberg, B. G., 584
Ross, R., 358
Rowland, J., 27
Rubin, E., 451
Rubinstein, S. L., 69–70, 198
Rudy, J. W., 177
Runes, D. D., 412
Russell, B., 412, 467, 524, 525

Sadock, B. J., 324, 401, 507
Sanford, R. N., 573
Sargent, S. S., 362, 374, 390, 508, 512
Sarnoff, I., 357
Schlessinger, V. J., 358
Schlick, M., 104, 524
Schoenfeld, W. N., 138
Schopenhauer, A., 13, 232, 412, 529
Schröter, K., 532
Schucman, H., 507, 509, 513
Scriven, M., 138
Sears, R. R., 166, 169–170, 199, 344, 355, 363
Sechenov, I. M., 69, 197, 409
Seligman, E. P., 585
Sellars, W., 522

Selz, 442
Semrad, E. V., 324
Senden, M. V., 577
Seward, J. P., 39, 102, 163
Shafer, R., 574
Shainberg, D., 401, 402
Sheffield, F. D., 102, 163, 173
Sheldon, W. H., 532
Sherrington, C. S., 89, 91, 101, 561
Shills, E. A., 169
Sidman, M., 174
Simon, T., 16, 440, 441
Skinner, B. F., 3, 4, 18, 22, 53, 90, 116, 124, 137, 141, 153, 155, 172, 173, 175, 199, 203, 280, 398, 527, 536, 558, 560, 567
Smirnov, K. M., 198
Smith F. V., 31, 183, 186
Smith, M., 362, 374, 390
Sollenberger, R. T., 166
Spearman, C. E., 16, 38
Spence, K. W., 124, 138, 154, 163, 174, 176, 177, 485, 505, 506
Spencer, H., 21, 31, 33, 204, 232, 403, 409, 415
Spinoza, B., 193, 502, 561
Spitz, R., 327–328
Spranger, E., 20, 68, 171, 198, 263, 293, 296, 384, 413, 421, 422, 423–426, 429, 436, 516, 618
Staats, A., 554
Stalin, J., 70
Stern, W., 4, 16, 20, 38, 69, 175, 280, 372, 385, 409, 413, 421, 422, 426–433, 440, 444, 464, 516, 518
Sternbach, R. A., 571
Stevens, S. S., 138, 154, 529, 530, 535, 548, 568, 586
Stolurow, R. D., 580
Stout, G. F., 439
Strachey, J., 227
Stringer, P., 585
Sullivan, H. S., 4, 19, 169, 279, 291, 292, 297, 305, 321, 351, 362, 363, 364, 368, 380, 385–400, 404, 405, 529, 531, 541, 562, 566, 567, 582
Sully, J., 15

Sutherland, J. D., 323
Sutich, A. J., 508

Taine, H., 440
Tarchanoff, 119
Taylor, C., 196
Taylor, S. E., 582
Tchakotine, S., 154
Teitelbaum, P., 176
Ten Houten, W., 582
Tennes, K., 358, 359
Terman, L. M., 16, 426
Thetford, W., 507, 508, 513
Thiessen, D. D., 553
Thompson, C., 278, 297, 313, 363, 398
Thorndike, E. L., 4, 16, 20, 25, 31–40, 51, 52, 53, 62, 78, 83, 98, 99, 100, 102, 107, 111, 117, 121, 130, 138, 145, 153, 154, 155, 159, 165, 171, 172, 173, 179, 197, 280, 437, 536, 567
Titchener, E. B., 13–16, 17, 19, 23, 29, 30, 197, 437, 456, 545, 557, 572
Tolman, E. C., 3, 18, 30, 32, 38, 53, 90, 122, 138–154, 155, 172, 178, 187, 195, 199, 279, 280, 285, 444, 456, 461, 528, 541, 558
Tomkins, S. S., 580
Tschernigowski, W. N., 71

Ukhtomski, A. A., 157, 172, 570

Vaihinger, H., 286
Vernon, P. E., 436, 532
Verplanck, W. S., 122, 138
Voeks, V. W., 103
Vogt, K. C., 62, 67, 559
Voltaire, F., 415
von Ehrenfels, C., 430, 444, 450
von Helmholtz, H., 10, 574
von Kerékjarto, B., 468
Voskresensky, L. N., 55
Vygotskii, L. S., 68, 73, 74

Wade, M., 88
Wagner, A. R., 177
Wallace, A. R., 181
Wapner, S., 576
Warden, C. J., 139, 176

Watchel, P. L., 575, 576
Watkins, J. G., 319
Watson, J. B., 17, 25, 30, 31,
  32, 33, 60, 61, 63, 76–84,
  85, 86, 90, 91, 92, 93, 95,
  96, 133, 138, 170, 171, 181,
  193, 198, 199, 203, 280,
  385, 439, 505, 540, 541,
  542, 560
Watt, H. J., 442
Webb, W. W., 175
Weber, H. J., 442
Weber, J., 358
Weiss, A. P., 84–85, 92, 198
Weissmann, A., 21
Werner, H., 576
Wertheimer, M., 4, 363, 409,
  421, 444, 450, 451, 454,
  455, 456, 508, 517, 541
White, R. K., 493
Whitlow, J. W., 177
Whitmont, E. C., 314

Whittell, 150
Windelband, W., 19, 20, 284,
  404, 414, 416, 464, 499,
  518, 522
Winnicott, D., 324
Witkin, H. A., 576
Wittgenstein, R., 104
Wolitzky, D. L., 575, 576
Wolman, B. B., 4, 6, 60, 74,
  111, 173, 175, 176, 177,
  179, 186, 191, 204, 206,
  209, 275, 281, 315, 317,
  319, 323, 324, 338,
  341–350, 361, 395, 405,
  411, 426, 455, 457, 488,
  493, 503, 508, 522, 531,
  533, 538, 547, 551, 560,
  561, 562, 563, 568, 572,
  575, 581, 582
Woodworth, R. S., 3, 29–30,
  51, 52, 138, 176, 197, 204,
  456, 541

Worrell, L., 584
Wortis, J., 68
Wozniak, R. H., 74
Wray, H., 556
Wulf, F., 453, 454
Wundt, W., 11, 12, 13, 14, 15,
  16, 17, 19, 20, 23, 197, 413,
  414, 423, 439, 444, 456,
  527, 557, 572

Yamaguchi, H. G., 124
Yenchman, 65, 82
Yerkes, R. M., 16, 76, 452, 453
Young, P. T., 176
Youtz, R. P., 353

Zeigarnik, B., 75, 354, 481, 484
Zeller, A. F., 354
Zener, K. E., 138
Zilboorg, G., 216
Zimbardo, P. G., 357

Subject Index

Abstract and concrete behavior (Goldstein), 190, 191
Act and content in psychology, 438–444
Adjustment
  Angell on, 27
  Carr on, 28
  Darwin on, 21, 22
  Dewey on, 25, 26
  James on, 23, 24
  Spencer on, 21
Affect, affection. see Emotion
Aggression
  Adler on, 286, 287
  Dollard and Miller on, 166
  Doob and Sears on, 340
  Freud on, 229–232, 272, 276, 277, 342
  Pavlov on, 56, 57
Analytic psychology, 297–315
  archetypes, 304–308
  complexes, 304–306
  and conscious, unconscious, 302–304
  and dream interpretation, 302–304
  and libido, 299–301
  and method of research, 297–299
  and personality types, 309–312
  and religion, 315
  self, 308–309
  symbols, 301–302
Analyzers (Pavlov), 43–44
Anthroponomy (Hunter), 87
Antigone principle (Wolman), 571, 572
Anxiety
  Freud on, 253–255
  Horney on, 368, 400–402
  Sullivan on, 387–390
Apperception
  Herbart on, 7
  Titchener on, 14
  Wundt on, 13

Archetypes and complexes (Jung), 306–309
Assembly of neurons (Hebb), 93, 94
Associationism, 438–440
  of Bain, 6, 33
  of Guthrie, 97
  of Hartley, 6, 33
  of Herbart, 6, 7, 33
  of James, 24
  of Mill, J. S., 6
  of Spencer, 21
  of Wundt, 13
Attention (Titchener), 14

Behaviorism
  background of, 18
  criticism of, 83–85
  Holt and, 85–87
  Hunter and, 87
  Lashley and, 88–92
  methodological, 84
  principles of, 76–77
  Skinner and, 124–138
  Tolman and, 138–154
  Watson and, 76–84
  Weiss and, 84–85
Birth trauma (Rank), 319
Body–soul dichotomy. See Soma-psyche
Brain, 74, 75, 88–91

Catharsis, 217, 218
Causation
  Adler on, 285, 286
  Freud on, 208, 209
  Jung on, 297–300
  Lewin on, 477–479
  Skinner on, 125
  Wolman on, 545–548
Character types. See Typology

Child development
    Adler on, 289–291
    Freud on, 232–243
    Fromm on, 378, 379
    Horney on, 364–368
    Klein on, 321–323
    Sullivan on, 391–394
Classification of sciences, 411–419
Classification as a scientific method (Wolman), 531–534
Conditioning. *See* also Learning theory; Reflex
    association, 55
    background of, 18
    Bekhterev on, 62–65
    Bykov on, 70–72
    concentration and, 44, 45
    and conditioned reflex, definition of, 50
    and connectionism, 45, 64
    conduction and connection in, 45–47
    contiguity in, 97–103
    configural, 163, 164
    and decortication, 49
    delayed, 51, 101, 105
    and discrimination, 52, 65, 89
    excitation and, 44, 45, 47, 53,·54, 65
    extinction, 58, 101, 105, 120
    evolutionary levels of, 154–163
    generalization in, 50, 65, 89, 117, 118, 168
    Guthrie on, 97–103
    higher-order, 50
    Hull on, 109–124, 175–177
    induction, 45, 54
    inhibition, 53–55, 65, 101, 113, 116, 118
    irradiation, 45
    Lashley on, 89, 92
    one-trial learning and, 179
    Pavlov on, 41–62
    principles of, 41–43
    Razran on, 154–163
    and reinforcement, 51–53, 101–104,
        109–124, 130–132, 162, 168, 173–175
    and reward, 53, 102, 103, 162
    Skinner on, 124–138
    Tolman, 138–154, 178
    and unconditioned reflexes, 47–48
    Watson on, 78, 79
Connectionism (Thorndike), 31–40
Consciousness (conscious)
    Adler on, 291–292, 298
    Bekhterev on, 64
    Freud on, 216–225
    Jung on, 302–315
    James on, 23, 24

Consciousness (*cont.*)
    Marx and Engels on, 68, 69
    Sullivan on, 394–396
    Titchener on, 15
    Watson on, 76, 77
    Wundt on, 12
Contiguity
    Guthrie on, 97–103
Criticism of object relations theories
        323–324. *See also* Ego psychology;
        Psychoanalysis and studies of culture;
        Interactional psychoanalysis
Cultural sciences
    Adler on, 283, 284
    Dilthey on, 414–420
    Freud on, 267–277
    Fromm on, 373
    Jung on, 312–315
    Kardiner and Linton on, 333–338
    Marxism on, 68–70
    Spranger on, 20
    Stern on, 20
    Windelband on, 20, 404, 414, 416, 518, 522
    Wundt on, 12

Death instinct, Freud on, 231–232, 271. *See*
        also Aggression
Deductive method
    Hull and, 109, 110
    Razran and, 154
    Wolman and, 539, 543
Descriptive method
    Dilthey and, 414–423
    Skinner and, 126
    Wolman and, 539–543
Dream interpretation
    Freudian, 220–224
    Jungian, 302–304
Drives
    Freud and (instinctual drives), 225–232
    Hull and, 113, 114, 175–177
    Skinner and, 132, 133
    Stern and, 432, 433
    Watson and, 78
    Wolman and (instinctual drives), 343–345
Dynamic psychology (Woodworth), 29, 30

Ego
    Freud and, 246–259
    Jung and, 304, 311
Ego psychology
    of Hartmann, Heinz, 324–327
    of Jacobson, Edith, 329–330
    of Kernberg, Otto, 330–331

Ego psychology (*cont.*)
  of Kohut, Heinz, 331
  of Mahler, Margaret, 328–329
  of Spitz, René, 327–328
Emotion
  Adler on, 287–291
  Darwin on, 17, 23
  Hebb on, 96
  James–Lange on, 25
  McDougall on, 185, 186
  Skinner on, 133–135
  Stern on, 432–433
  Titchener on, 14
  Watson on, 80, 81
  Wundt on, 12
Empathy, 386, 387, 566, 567
Empiricism
  Freud and, 204, 205
  Hull and, 103–105
  James and, 23
  Skinner and, 125, 126, 137
  Wolman and, 526–528
Energy (energetism)
  Bekhterev and, 62–65
  Freud and, 211–212
  Jung and, 299–301
Entropy (Jung), 300
Epistemology
  Dilthey and, 414–416
  Kant and, 409–414
  Wolman and, 523–525
Equilibrium, theories of,
  constancy (Freud), 209, 210
  equilibration (Goldstein), 188, 189
  equilibrium (Lewin), 479–483
  homeostasis (Cannon), 42
Equipotentiality (Lashley), 89, 90
Equivalence (Jung), 299
Ethics
  Dewey and, 26
  Freud and, 259, 260, 273, 274, 276
  Fromm and, 382–384
Evolution theory, 8, 21, 22, 24, 28
Experience as subject matter of psychology
  Dilthey on, 416–422
  Husserl on, 429, 431, 516
  Stern on, 426–432
  Titchener on, 14
  Ward on, 439
  Wundt on, 12
Experimental method
  Dilthey and, 416–419
  Hull and, 122, 123
  with human subjects, 554–556

Experimental method (*cont.*)
  and psychoanalysis, 531–359
  Skinner and, 128–129
  Titchener and, 13–16
  Wolman on, 536–538
  Wundt and, 11–16, 20
Experimental neurosis, 57, 58
Explanation and explanatory method
  Dilthey on, 414–422
  Skinner on, 126
  Titchener on, 13

Fear, 56, 57
Feeling. *See* Emotion
Field theory, 460–506
  and causation, 477–479, 502–504
  and force, 474–477
  and hodological space, 473, 474
  idiophenomena of, 464–466
  learning and, 468–470, 484–487
  and level of aspiration, 483–484
  mathematics of, 467–473
  and personality, 487–491
  and psychological field, 469–477
  and social psychology, 491–496
  and theory construction, 460–464, 496–506
  topology of, 468–473
Figure and ground
  Gestalt, 451
  Goldstein on, 191
Force
  Herbart on, 7
  Lewin on, 474–477
Functionalism
  Angell and, 27–28
  background of, 20–22
  Binet and, 440–441
  Bühler and, 443–444
  Carr and, 28–29
  Dewey and, 24–27
  James and, 22–24
  Robinson and, 28, 29
  Stout and, 439–440
  Ward and, 439–440

Gestalt vs. associationism, 438, 444–446
  field concept, 449, 450
  isomorphism of, 448–449
  laws of, 451, 452
  and learning, 452–454
  mathematics of, 445
  and perception, 450–454, 457
  and thinking, 454–459

Group dynamics
  Lewin and, 491–496
  Wolman and, 345–347

History and psychology
  Dilthey on, 400, 401, 405
  Freud on, 267–277
  Fromm on, 373–378
  Jung on, 312–315
  Wundt on, 13, 20
Holistic psychology, 187–193
Hormic psychology, 180–187
Humanistic psychology, 507–515
  Angyal and, 509
  background of, 507–508
  Bugental and, 512
  impact of existentialism on, 508
  Maslow and, 510–511
  Murphy and, 512–514
  Murray and, 511–512
  Rogers and, 514–515
Hypnotism, 18, 216, 217
Hypothetico-deductive method (Hull),
      103–106

Identity, concept of, 561–564
Idiophenomena, 433, 434, 464–466
Individual differences
  Hull on, 121
  Stern on, 412, 416
Individual psychology, 283–299
  and aggression, 286, 287
  and causation, 285, 286
  and inferiority, 287–289
  and purposivism, 285, 286
  and sociability, 289–291
  and style of life, 292–294
  and typology, 294–295
Inductive method
  Pavlov on, 45, 46
  Razran on, 155, 156
  Skinner on, 124
  Wolman on, 539–543
Instincts
  Dewey on, 26
  Freud on, 225–232
  James on, 25
  McDougall on, 183–187
  Pavlov on, 48, 49, 57, 58
  Wolman on, 343–345
Instrumental, mutual and vectorial groups
      (Wolman), 345–347
Instrumentalism (Dewey), 26
Interactional psychoanalysis, 341–350
  developmental phases of, 347–350

Interactional psychoanalysis (cont.)
  and love, sex, and power, 344–345
  and self-preservation, 343–345
  and social relations, 345–347
Interpersonal theory (Sullivan), 385–398
Introspection
  criticism of, 16–18
  Titchener on, 14, 15
  Wundt on, 12, 15
Introversion and extraversion (Jung),
      310–312
Irrationality as a method, 297–299, 313–315

Kant's influence upon psychology, 409–414

Laws of nature, Windelband on, 447
  Wolman on, 548–549
Learning theory,
  criticism of, 170–173
  current status of, 173–179
  Dewey on, 26
  Dollard and Miller on, 163–167
  Gestalt, 452–454
  Guthrie on, 99–102
  Hebb on, 94
  Hull on, 108–125
  Lashley on, 90–91
  Lewin on, 484–487
  Mowrer on, 167–169
  Pavlov on, 41–61
  Razran on, 154–163
  Skinner on, 131–137
  Thorndike on, 31–40
  Tolman on, 144–152
  Watson on, 78, 79
Libido
  Freud on, 207, 208, 224–228
  Jung on, 299–301
Life instinct
  Goldstein on, 187–193
  Pavlov on, 55, 56, 63, 64
  Wolman on, 344, 345

Marxism, 66–72
Mass action (Lashley), 89, 90
Materialism
  dialectic, 66–68
  metaphysical, 6
  naïve, 65
  Pavlov and, 42, 43
Mathematics
  Gestalt, 445–446
  Hull on, 104–106
  Kant on, 409–414
  Lewin on, 467–473

Mathematics (*cont.*)
  Wolman on, 534, 535
Metaphysics, 5, 6, 7, 11
Molar vs. molecular
  Binet on, 440, 441
  Dewey on, 27
  Hull on, 107–109
  Spranger on, 423, 424
  Stern on, 432–433
  Tolman on, 142
  Watson on, 83
Motivation
  Allport on, 433–435
  Carr on, 29
  Hebb on, 94–95
  Hull on, 112–118
  Tolman on, 142–144
  Woodworth on, 29, 30

Narcissism, 230–231
Nature vs. nurture, 47–48
Neo-Kantians, 409–414
Nervous system
  analyzers of, 44, 45
  Gestalt theory on, 452–454
  Hebb and, 94, 95
  Hull and, 109, 111
  Lashley and, 88–92
  Pavlov and, 43, 47
  Thorndike and, 32
  Watson and, 78, 79
Neurosis, 57, 58, 370, 371

Oedipus complex, 237–240
Operant and respondent behavior, 129–130
Operationism
  Bridgman on, 528
  Dewey on, 28
  Skinner on, 124–126
  Stevens on, 529, 530
  Tolman on, 138–142
  Wolman on, 528–531
Organismic psychology (Kantor), 193–195

Parapsychology, 261–263
Parsimony, principle of, 16
Perception
  Dilthey on, 416–419
  Gestalt, 450–454, 457
Watson, 78, 79
Personality theories, 423–437, 572–589
  of Adler, 284–297
  of Allport, 434–437
  of Freud, 266

Personality theories (*cont.*)
  of Fromm, 379–385
  of Horney, 368–373
  of James, 24, 25
  of Jung, 308–312
  of Lewin, 487–491
  of Murphy, 512–514
  of Pavlov, 55–59
  of Spranger, 423–426
  of Stern, 432–433
  of Sullivan, 394–396
  of Watson, 81, 82
Phenomenology, 423, 439, 444, 445, 516
Physiology in relation to psychology,
  McDougall on, 181–182
  Pavlov on, 42–44, 62–64
  Titchener on, 14
  Watson on, 82–84
  Wundt on, 11
Pleasure and pain, 215, 567–572
  Hebb on, 96
  Horney on, 367, 368
  James on, 25
  Mowrer on, 169
  Pshonik on, 72
  Thorndike on, 35
  Wolman on, 567–572
Pleasure principle, 168, 245, 246
Postulates
  of Freud, 203–210
  of Hull, 109–120
Pragmatism, 22–24
Psychoanalysis, 203–282
  and anxiety, 253–255
  and catharsis, 217, 218
  and causation, 208, 209
  conscious, preconscious, unconscious,
    216–225
  and constancy principle, 212–214
  critical analysis of, 359–361
  and defense mechanisms, 255–258
  and dream interpretation, 220–224
  and education, 277
  and experimental studies, 351–359
  fixation and regression in, 242–243
  and instincts, 225–232
    of death, 231–232, 268–271, 277, 281
    of life, 227, 228
    of self-preservation, 229, 230
    sexual, 227–229
  and interpretation of history and culture,
    267–277
  and methods of research, 203, 275, 281, 282
  and narcissism, 230–231

Psychoanalysis (cont.)
  overview of, 18, 19
  and personality, 243–261
    ego, 246–259
    id, 244–246
    superego, 259–261
  and pleasure principle, 245, 246
  and reality principle, 249
  and religion, 271–273
  and stages of development, 232–243
    anal, 235–237
    latency, 240
    neonate, 230
    oral, 233–235
    phallic and Oedipus complex, 237–240
    puberty, 241, 242
    urethral, 237
Psychoanalysis and studies of culture,
  by Erikson, Erik H., 238–341
  by Kardiner and Linton, 333–338
  by Lifton, Robert J., 341
  by Reich, Wilhelm, 333
  Polyculturalism, 331–333
Psychoanalysis, new theories in
  Fairbairn, W. R., 323
  Federn, Paul, 319, 320
  Ferenczi, Sandor, 320, 321
  Freud, Anna, 317, 318
  Klein, Melanie, 321–323
  Rank, Otto, 318, 319
Psychological field
  Koffka on, 449, 450
  Lewin on, 469–477
Psychophysical parallelism, 9–11, 14
Purposivism
  Adler on, 286, 287
  Goldstein on, 187–193
  McDougall on, 180–181
  new ideas on, 195–196

Reactology (Kornilov), 68
Reale, das (Herbart), 6
Reality principle (Freud), 248–250
Reductionism
  Bekhterev and, 62–65
  Freud and, 209–211
  Gestalt and, 448, 449
  Guthrie and, 99
  Hebb and, 97
  Herbart and, 7
  Hull and, 110, 124, 125
  Lashley, and, 91
  and Marxism, 66–68
  Morgan and, 18

Reductionism (cont.)
  Pavlov and, 62, 63
  Skinner and, 125–127
  Thorndike and, 33
  Titchener and, 15
  Watson and, 80, 82, 83
  Weiss and, 85
  Wolman on, 543–545, 558–561
Reflex
  arc (Dewey), 8
  Bell on, 8
  Skinner on, 127–129
  unconditioned (Pavlov), 47, 48, 50
Religion
  Freud on, 267–277
  Fromm on, 382
  Jung on, 312, 313
  Rank on, 323, 324

Safety and satisfaction (Horney), 367, 368
Satisfaction and security (Sullivan), 386–390
Schizophrenia, 61, 259
Science and scientific method (Wolman),
  521–556
  causation in, 545–548
  classification in, 531–534
  deductive and inductive method of,
    539–543
  definition of, 521–523
  empiricism, observation, and
    operationism, 526–528
  hypotheses, constructs, and variables,
    539–543
  language of, 549–552
  and laws of nature, 548, 549
  mathematics, 534, 535
  methodological problems in, 552–556
  and reductionism, 543–545, 558–561
  and truth, scientific, 523–525
Self
  James on, 24
  Jung on, 308–309
  Skinner on, 135
  Sullivan on, 378, 379
Self-actualization (Goldstein), 189
Self-observation. See Introspection
Sign-gestalt (Tolman), 142–147, 149–155
Sleep
  Freud on, 217, 218, 230
  Pavlov on, 53–55
Social psychology
  Adler and, 285–291
  Dollard and Miller and, 163–167
  Freud and, 267–272

Social psychology (*cont.*)
  Fromm and, 373–384
  Gestalt, 458, 459
  Jung and, 308–309, 312–314
  Kardiner and Linton and, 333–338
  Lewin and, 491–496
  Sullivan and, 396–399
  Wolman and, 541–542
Sociological school of psychoanalysis,
    362–402
Soma-psyche dichotomy
  Bekhterev on, 62–65
  Descartes on, 16
  James on, 23
  Lashley on, 92, 93
  Marxism on, 65–75
  Pavlov on, 42, 43, 63, 64
  Stern on, 428–429
  Wolman on, 557–567
Soviet psychology, 65–75
Structuralism, 13, 14

Temperaments, 294–295
  Hippocrates on, 59, 295
  Pavlov on, 58, 59
Theory formation
  Dilthey and, 416–422
  Freud and, 206–208, 274, 275, 281, 282
  Hull and, 103–106
  Jung and, 309–312
  Lewin and, 460–464, 496–506
  Wolman on, 525–526

Transitionism (Wolman), 557–566
Tropism, 17
Truth, 523–525
  Kant and, 409–411
Typology (types of personality)
  of Adler, 294, 295
  of Allport, 433–437
  of Freud, 263–266
  of Fromm, 381–384
  of Jung, 312
  of Lewin, 489–491
  of Pavlov, 58–59
  of Spranger, 425–428
  of Stern, 429–430

Unconditioned reflex. *See* Reflex; Condition-
    ing
Unconscious and preconscious,
  Adler on, 291, 292
  Freud on, 216
  Jung on, 302–315
  Sullivan on, 391, 396
Understanding psychology, 19, 20, 409–422

Variables
  dependent, 139–142
  independent, 139–142, 519
  intervening, 139–142
Vitalism, 21, 22, 180

Würzburg School, 441–443